A PEOPLE'S HISTORY OF AMERICAN EMPIRE

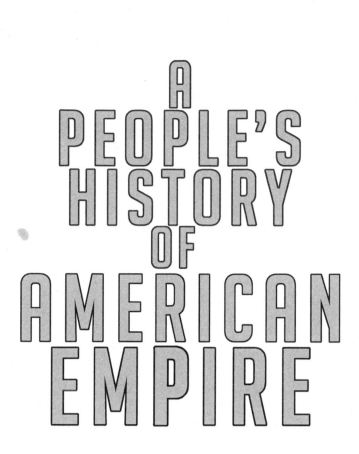

A PEOPLE'S HISTORY OF AMERICAN EMPIRE

A GRAPHIC ADAPTATION

Howard Zinn

Mike Konopacki

Paul Buhle

METROPOLITAN BOOKS
HENRY HOLT AND COMPANY
NEW YORK

Metropolitan Books
Henry Holt and Company, LLC
Publishers since 1866
175 Fifth Avenue
New York, New York 10010
www.henryholt.com

Metropolitan Books® and ® are registered trademarks of Henry Holt and Company, LLC.

Library of Congress Cataloging-in-Publication Data

Zinn, Howard, 1922–
  A people's history of American empire / Howard Zinn, Mike Konopacki, Paul Buhle.—1st ed.
      p. cm.
  Includes bibliographical references and index.
  ISBN-13: 978-0-8050-7779-7 (hardcover)
  ISBN-10: 0-8050-7779-0 (hardcover)
  ISBN-13: 978-0-8050-8744-4 (pbk.)
  ISBN-10: 0-8050-8744-3 (pbk.)
 1. United States—Foreign relations—Comic books, strips, etc. 2. United States—
Territorial expansion—Comic books, strips, etc. 3. Imperialism—History—Comic books,
strips, etc. 4. United States—Social conditions—Comic books, strips, etc. 5. Social
movements—United States—History—Comic books, strips, etc. 6. Zinn, Howard, 1922– —
Comic books, strips, etc. 7. Historians—United States—Biography—Comic books, strips,
etc. I. Konopacki, Mike. II. Buhle, Paul, 1944– III. Title.
E183.7.Z56 2008
741.5'6973—dc22   2007031150

Henry Holt books are available for special promotions and premiums. For details contact: Director, Special Markets.

First Edition 2008
Designed by Mike Konopacki
Printed in the United States of America
10 9 8 7 6 5 4 3 2 1

Contents

Foreword

The history of the United States was written for many generations as a heroic conquest of the land and its original inhabitants, and as the steady spread of democracy from border to border and sea to sea. It culminated in the current nation being uniquely suited by history, perhaps by divine destiny, to make the rules for the planet and carry them out when necessary. Every sacrifice made, by Americans and others, was justified by that end. Even when, by 1950, atomic and finally thermonuclear war threatened to wipe out civilization, the sense of rectitude remained firmly in place. Americans had sought to make the world a better place, a nearly perfect place, even if they had been thwarted in the task.

The Vietnam War changed the perceptions of a generation. Some few earlier dissenting historians, such as W.E.B. DuBois, had pointed toward a markedly darker national saga, but they had been not much heard. Then, an evident crisis in empire brought into view past crises of empire, internal as well as external, and the high price that had been paid for those crises. Another story began to be told, not of America as a wicked place or Americans as wicked people but of the trouble in the soul of an imperial nation.

Beginning in the 1960s, scholars of various kinds started to write widely about Indians, African Americans, working people, and women, of struggles for reform won and lost, of wealth gained at vast public expense in squandered dollars and lives. This was the saga of the internal empire, precursor in many ways to the transcontinental empire to follow. None of the scholars charting this empire epitomized the truth teller and political visionary better than the then young professor Howard Zinn. None reached as many readers, a decade after the decline of the social movements of the 1960s, as an older Zinn. *A People's History of the United States* (first published in 1980), its pages afire with lucidity, set a new standard for the retelling of the nation's story, this time linked closely to other peoples everywhere, and likewise to a distant human past and a hoped for future.

A People's History of American Empire is not intended to displace *A People's History*, something that would be impossible in any case. It is intended to present the key insights in Howard Zinn's marvelous volume in the light of another art form, with artist Mike Konopacki working from a script developed chiefly by Dave Wagner. The pages that follow are narrated largely by Zinn himself, or rather by a character based as closely as possible upon Zinn's own words. Herein, we find the story of the narrator as an inescapable part of the history he wrote.

Comics, sequential art forms, are as old as cave drawings. They precede written history and, like oral history, lend themselves best to storytelling. Perhaps for that reason, comics flow almost naturally from the writings of the superb storyteller. The editor and the writer-artist have taken some liberties with the original, mainly for reasons of dramatic presentation, but with no essential shift from the original ground. Also, the autobiographical Howard Zinn of *You Can't Be Neutral on a Moving Train* here becomes part of the story, of the twentieth century—and beyond.

By this means, and armed with an artistic technique that brings together visual documents of various kinds with original art, we hope to say that we have brought something original into the world.

PAUL BUHLE

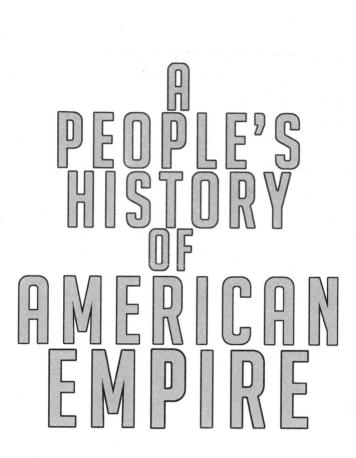

A PEOPLE'S HISTORY OF AMERICAN EMPIRE

PROLOGUE

"We can all feel a terrible anger at whoever, in their insane idea that this would help their cause, killed thousands of innocent people. But what do we do with that anger? Do we react with panic, strike out violently and blindly just to show how tough we are?"

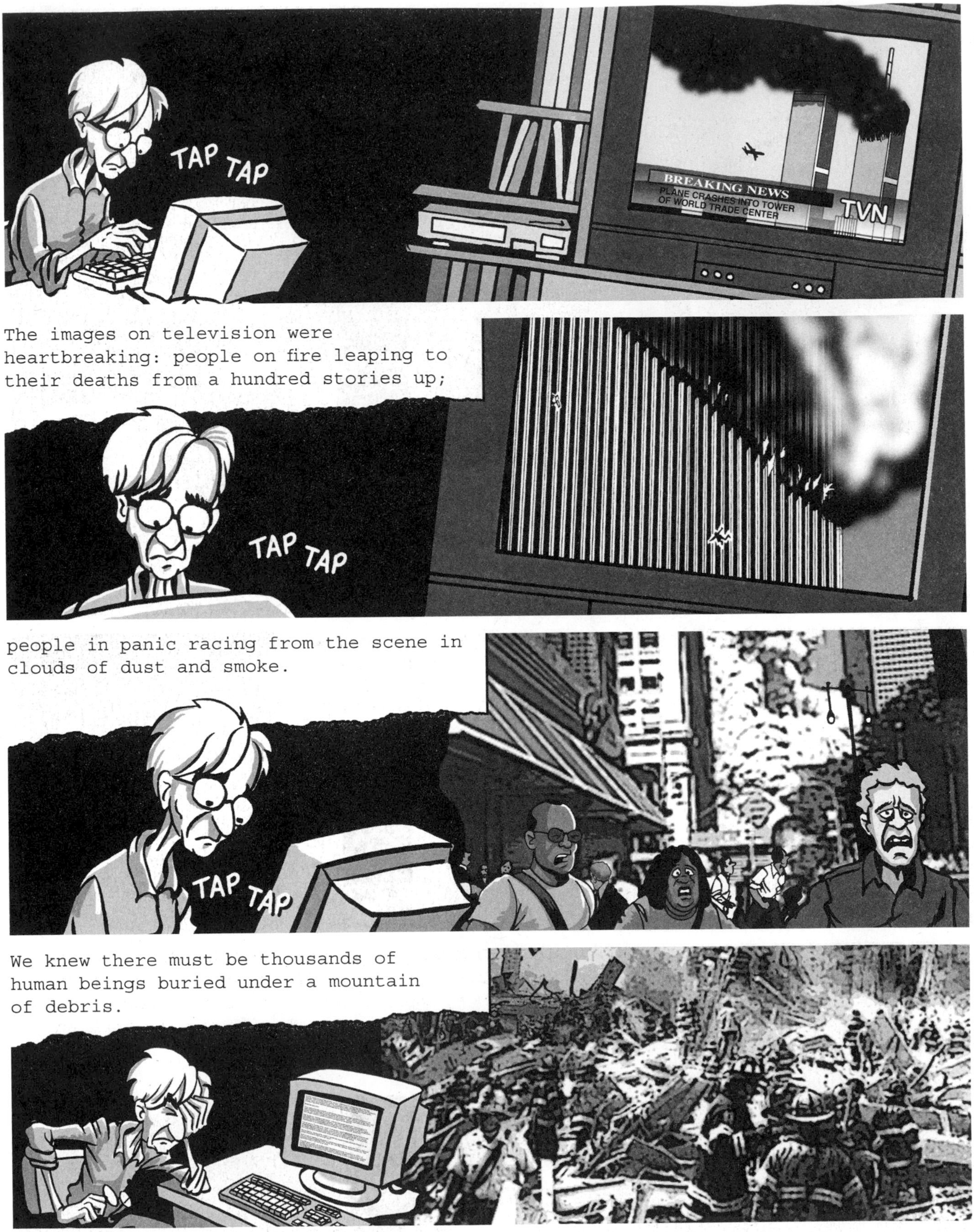
TAP TAP
BREAKING NEWS
PLANE CRASHES INTO TOWER
OF WORLD TRADE CENTER
TVN
The images on television were heartbreaking: people on fire leaping to their deaths from a hundred stories up;
TAP TAP
people in panic racing from the scene in clouds of dust and smoke.
TAP TAP
We knew there must be thousands of human beings buried under a mountain of debris.

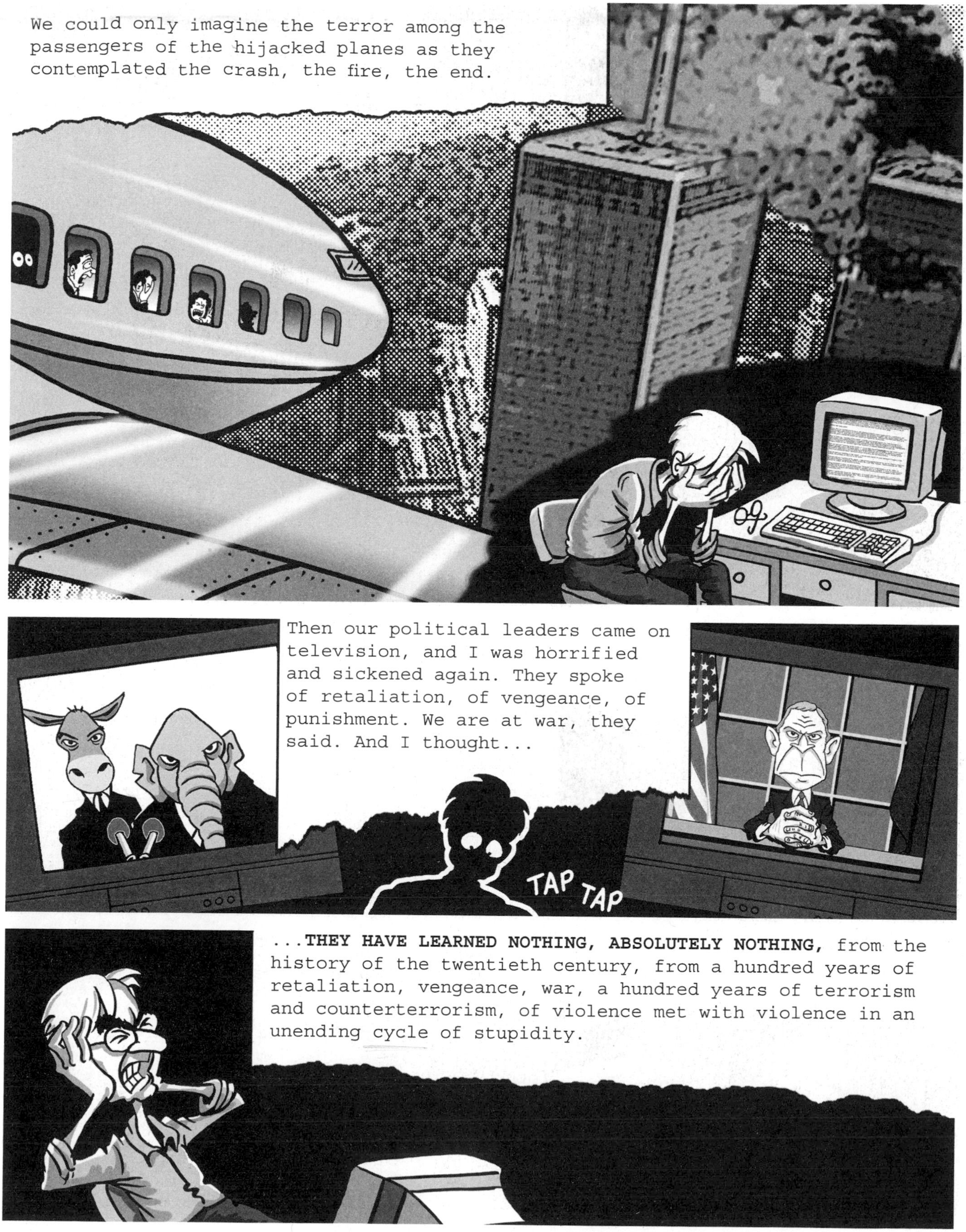

We could only imagine the terror among the passengers of the hijacked planes as they contemplated the crash, the fire, the end.
Then our political leaders came on television, and I was horrified and sickened again. They spoke of retaliation, of vengeance, of punishment. We are at war, they said. And I thought...
TAP TAP
...**THEY HAVE LEARNED NOTHING, ABSOLUTELY NOTHING,** from the history of the twentieth century, from a hundred years of retaliation, vengeance, war, a hundred years of terrorism and counterterrorism, of violence met with violence in an unending cycle of stupidity.

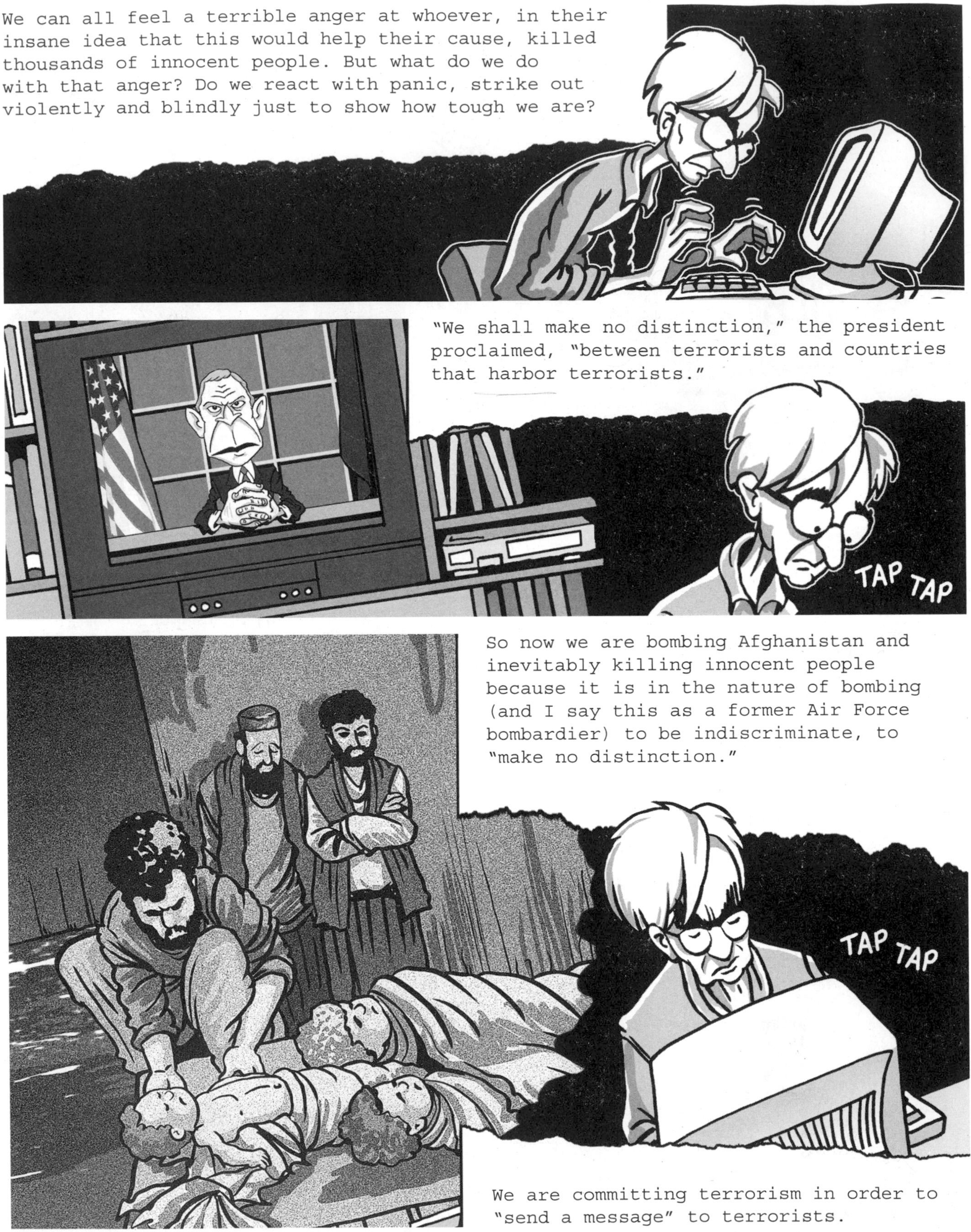
We can all feel a terrible anger at whoever, in their insane idea that this would help their cause, killed thousands of innocent people. But what do we do with that anger? Do we react with panic, strike out violently and blindly just to show how tough we are?
"We shall make no distinction," the president proclaimed, "between terrorists and countries that harbor terrorists."
TAP TAP
So now we are bombing Afghanistan and inevitably killing innocent people because it is in the nature of bombing (and I say this as a former Air Force bombardier) to be indiscriminate, to "make no distinction."
TAP TAP
We are committing terrorism in order to "send a message" to terrorists.

The Old Way of Thinking

We have done that before. It is the old way of thinking, the old way of acting. It has never worked.

Progressive Magazine
Column
The Old Way of Thinking
by
Howard Zinn

The images on television were heartbreaking: people on fire leaping to their deaths from a hundred stories up; people in panic racing from the scene in clouds of dust and smoke.

We knew there must be thousands of human

In Vietnam, we terrorized peasant villages with bombing attacks, using napalm and cluster bombs. We supported dictators and death squads in Chile and El Salvador, Guatemala, and Haiti. In Iraq, more than 500,000 children died as a result of economic sanctions the United States insisted on.

We need new ways of thinking. We need to think about the resentment felt by people all over the world who have been victims of American military action.

We need to decide that we will not go to war regardless of the reasons conjured up by the politicians and the news media.

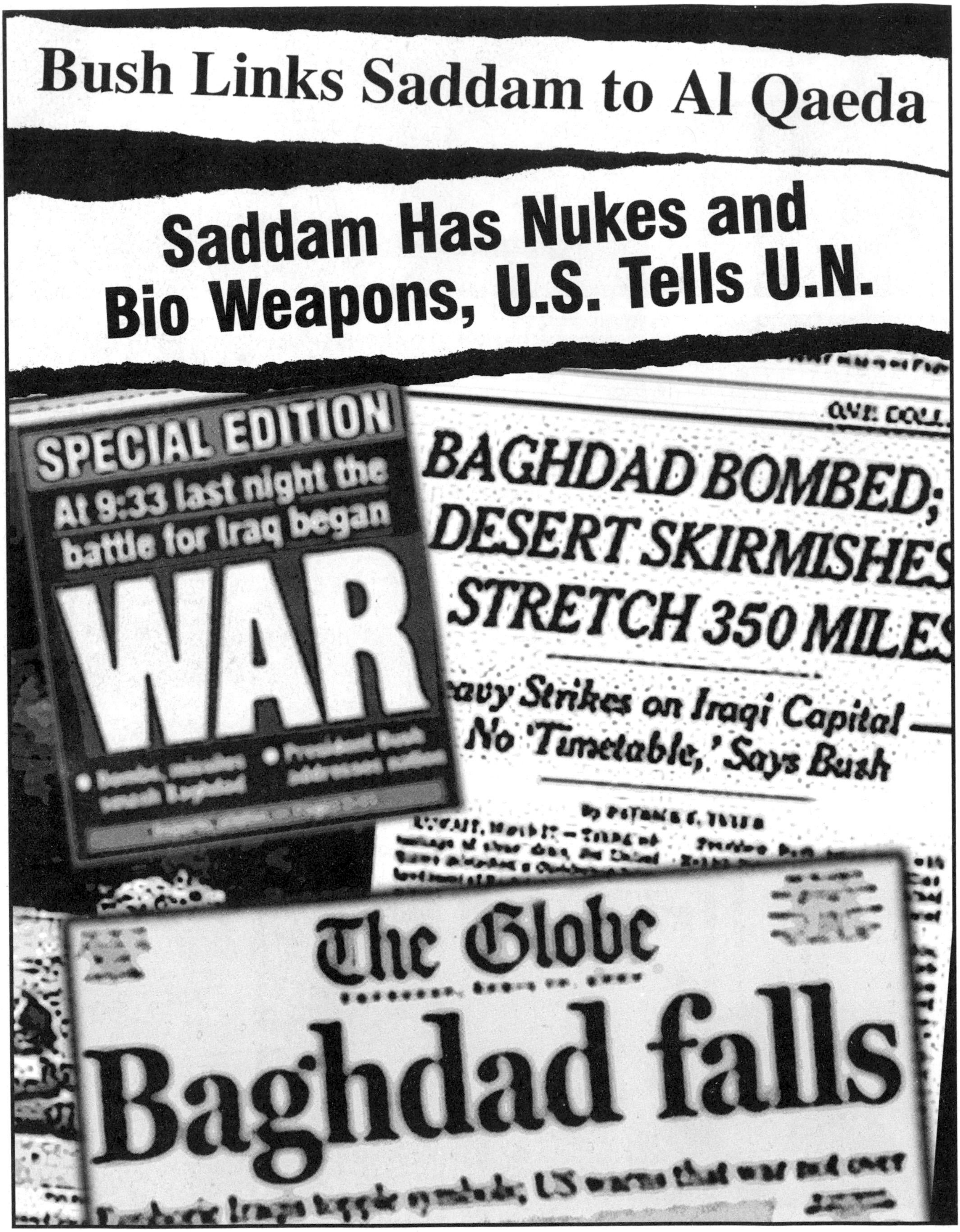

Bush Links Saddam to Al Qaeda
Saddam Has Nukes and Bio Weapons, U.S. Tells U.N.
SPECIAL EDITION
At 9:33 last night the battle for Iraq began
WAR
BAGHDAD BOMBED; DESERT SKIRMISHES STRETCH 350 MILES
eavy Strikes on Iraqi Capital— No 'Timetable,' Says Bush
The Globe
Baghdad falls

INSTEAD OF CREATING A NEW WAY OF THINKING, OUR GOVERNMENT USED 9/11 AS AN EXCUSE FOR ANOTHER *RAMPAGE OF EMPIRE!*

IT'S IMPORTANT TO REMEMBER THAT OUR INVASIONS OF AFGHANISTAN AND IRAQ ARE NOT UNIQUE EVENTS. THEY ARE PART OF A CONTINUING PATTERN OF AMERICAN BEHAVIOR.

DEFEND YOUR CIVIL LIBERTIES

MONEY FOR SCHOOLS NOT WAR

NO IRAQ WAR!!

TEACH IN

NO TO WAR NO TO RACISM

TRUE, WE LIBERATED AFGHANISTAN FROM TALIBAN RULE *BUT NOT FROM US!* WE LIBERATED IRAQ FROM SADDAM HUSSEIN *BUT NOT FROM US!*

JUST AS IN 1898, WE LIBERATED CUBA FROM SPANISH TYRANNY *BUT NOT FROM US.*

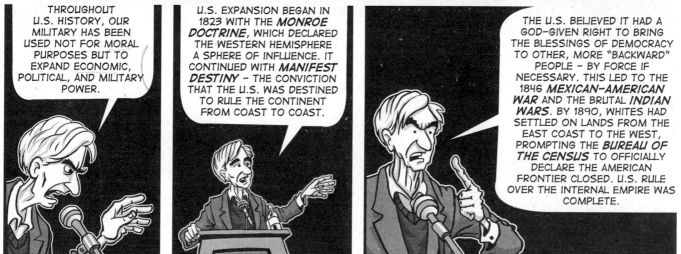

THROUGHOUT U.S. HISTORY, OUR MILITARY HAS BEEN USED NOT FOR MORAL PURPOSES BUT TO EXPAND ECONOMIC, POLITICAL, AND MILITARY POWER.

U.S. EXPANSION BEGAN IN 1823 WITH THE *MONROE DOCTRINE*, WHICH DECLARED THE WESTERN HEMISPHERE A SPHERE OF INFLUENCE. IT CONTINUED WITH *MANIFEST DESTINY* – THE CONVICTION THAT THE U.S. WAS DESTINED TO RULE THE CONTINENT FROM COAST TO COAST.

THE U.S. BELIEVED IT HAD A GOD-GIVEN RIGHT TO BRING THE BLESSINGS OF DEMOCRACY TO OTHER, MORE "BACKWARD" PEOPLE – BY FORCE IF NECESSARY. THIS LED TO THE 1846 *MEXICAN-AMERICAN WAR* AND THE BRUTAL *INDIAN WARS*. BY 1890, WHITES HAD SETTLED ON LANDS FROM THE EAST COAST TO THE WEST, PROMPTING THE *BUREAU OF THE CENSUS* TO OFFICIALLY DECLARE THE AMERICAN FRONTIER CLOSED. U.S. RULE OVER THE INTERNAL EMPIRE WAS COMPLETE.

Chapter I

THE INTERNAL EMPIRE

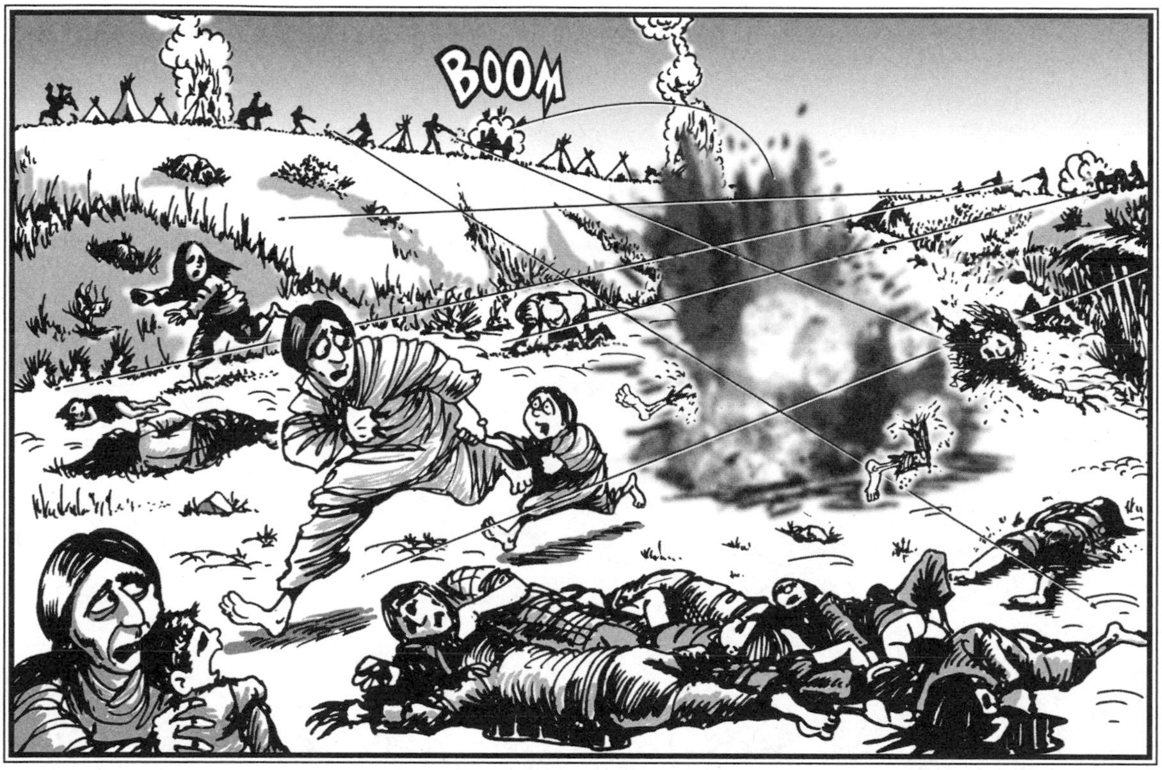
BOOM

"The massacre at Wounded Knee marked the domination of the continent by white men...but only certain white men."

The Massacre at Wounded Knee

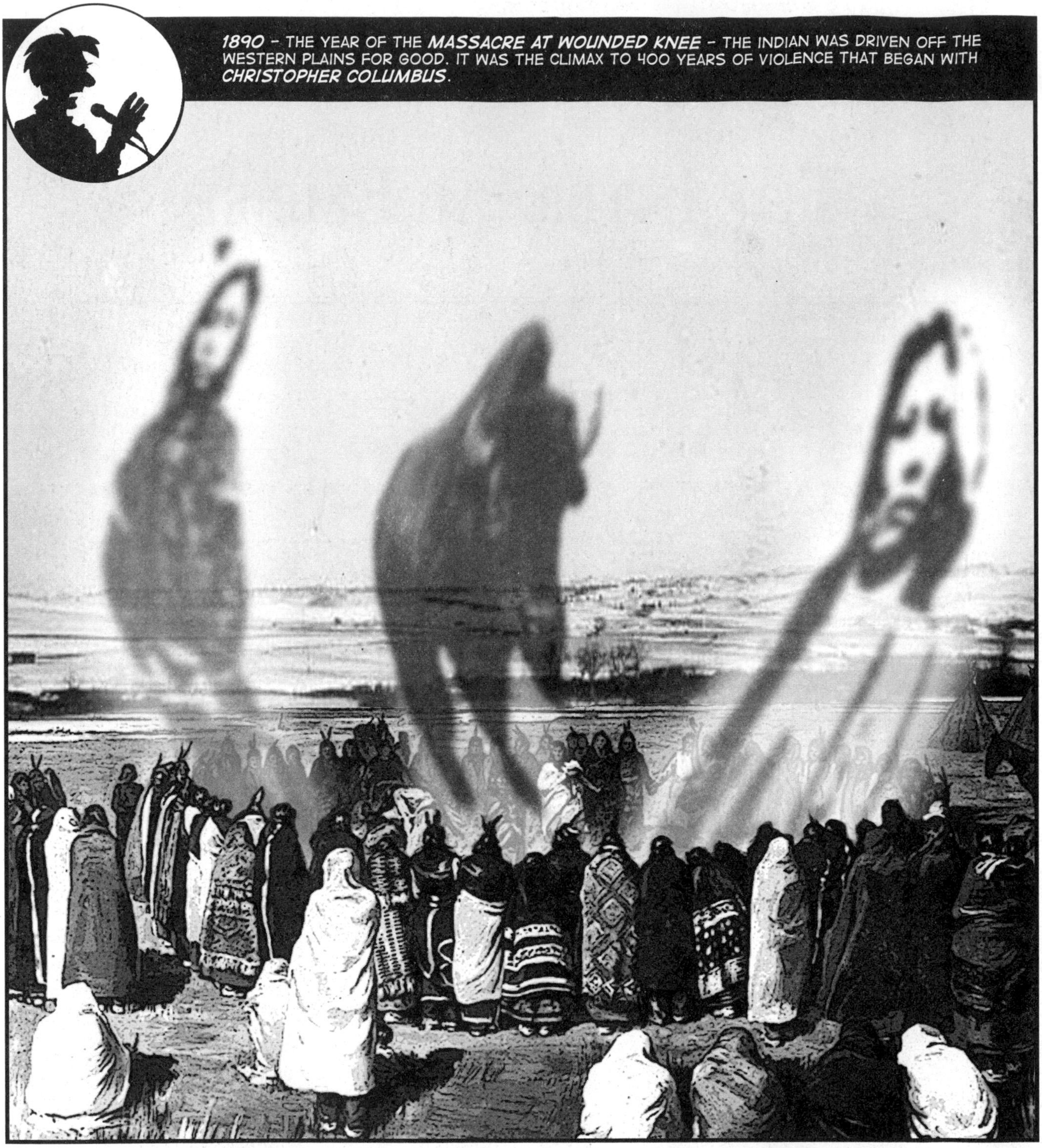
1890 – THE YEAR OF THE ***MASSACRE AT WOUNDED KNEE*** – THE INDIAN WAS DRIVEN OFF THE WESTERN PLAINS FOR GOOD. IT WAS THE CLIMAX TO 400 YEARS OF VIOLENCE THAT BEGAN WITH ***CHRISTOPHER COLUMBUS***.

YEARS OF WAR AND GOVERNMENT SUPPRESSION DECIMATED THE REMAINING INDIANS OF THE WEST. THE BUFFALO, ON WHICH THEIR FOOD, SHELTER, AND EVEN RELIGION DEPENDED, SUFFERED THE SAME FATE, DECLINING FROM 60 MILLION TO FEWER THAN 100 BY 1889. MOURNING THE DEMISE OF THEIR PEOPLE, THE THEFT OF THEIR LANDS, AND THE DESTRUCTION OF THEIR WAY OF LIFE, THE INDIANS TURNED TO A NEW SPIRITUAL MOVEMENT: THE ***GHOST DANCE***, A BLEND OF INDIAN MYSTICISM AND CHRISTIANITY TAUGHT BY THE PAIUTE HOLY MAN ***WOVOKA***. THE SIOUX ADOPTED THE RITUAL, WHICH PROMISED TO RESURRECT ALL THE INDIANS AND BUFFALO SLAIN BY THE WHITE INVADER. THE EARTH, THEY BELIEVED, WOULD BE DESTROYED AND RE-CREATED, THE WHITE MAN WOULD BE NO MORE, AND THE INDIANS WOULD REIGN ONCE AGAIN.

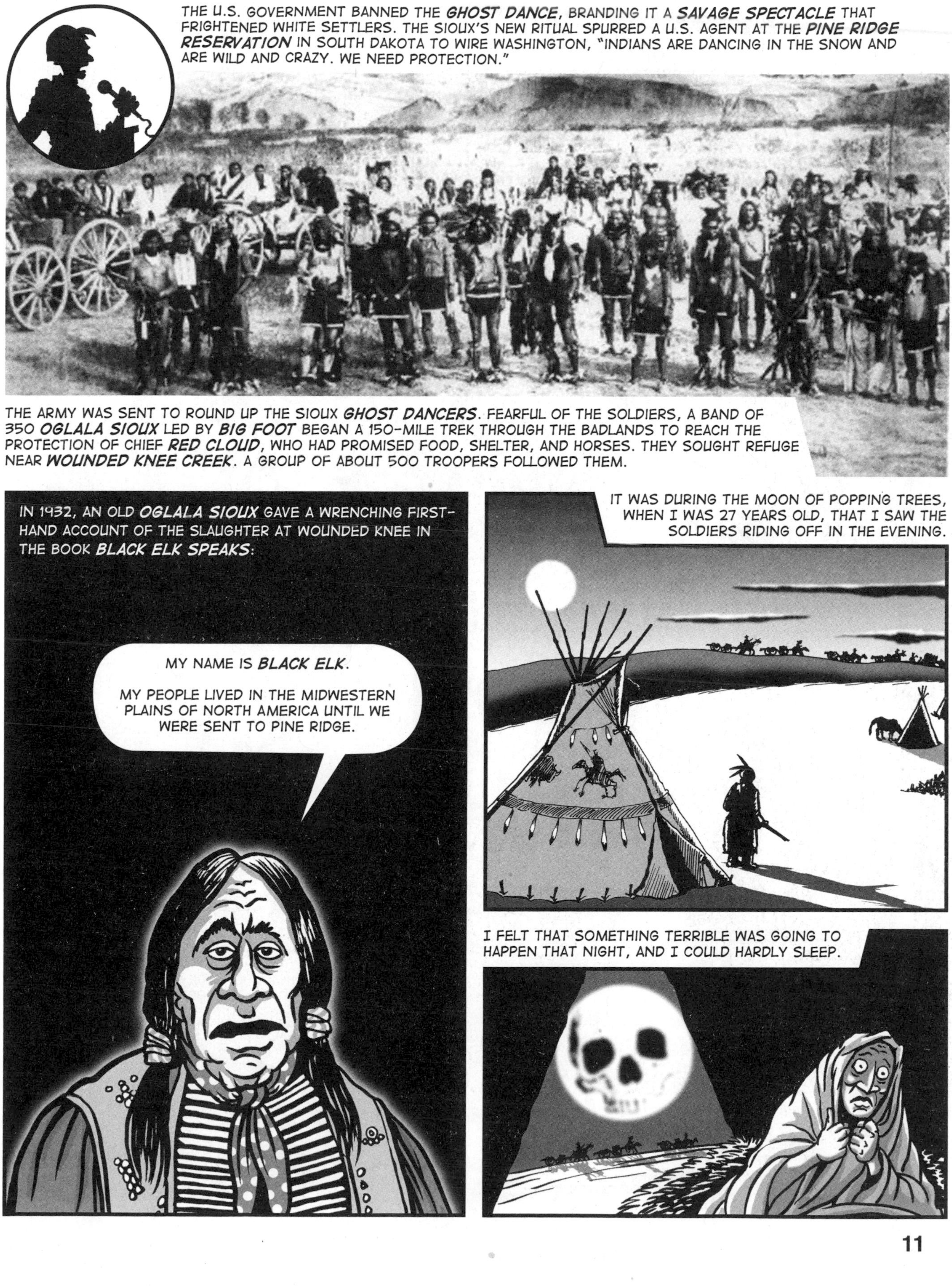
THE U.S. GOVERNMENT BANNED THE GHOST DANCE, BRANDING IT A SAVAGE SPECTACLE THAT FRIGHTENED WHITE SETTLERS. THE SIOUX'S NEW RITUAL SPURRED A U.S. AGENT AT THE PINE RIDGE RESERVATION IN SOUTH DAKOTA TO WIRE WASHINGTON, "INDIANS ARE DANCING IN THE SNOW AND ARE WILD AND CRAZY. WE NEED PROTECTION."
THE ARMY WAS SENT TO ROUND UP THE SIOUX GHOST DANCERS. FEARFUL OF THE SOLDIERS, A BAND OF 350 OGLALA SIOUX LED BY BIG FOOT BEGAN A 150-MILE TREK THROUGH THE BADLANDS TO REACH THE PROTECTION OF CHIEF RED CLOUD, WHO HAD PROMISED FOOD, SHELTER, AND HORSES. THEY SOUGHT REFUGE NEAR WOUNDED KNEE CREEK. A GROUP OF ABOUT 500 TROOPERS FOLLOWED THEM.
IN 1932, AN OLD OGLALA SIOUX GAVE A WRENCHING FIRST-HAND ACCOUNT OF THE SLAUGHTER AT WOUNDED KNEE IN THE BOOK BLACK ELK SPEAKS:
MY NAME IS BLACK ELK.
MY PEOPLE LIVED IN THE MIDWESTERN PLAINS OF NORTH AMERICA UNTIL WE WERE SENT TO PINE RIDGE.
IT WAS DURING THE MOON OF POPPING TREES, WHEN I WAS 27 YEARS OLD, THAT I SAW THE SOLDIERS RIDING OFF IN THE EVENING.
I FELT THAT SOMETHING TERRIBLE WAS GOING TO HAPPEN THAT NIGHT, AND I COULD HARDLY SLEEP.

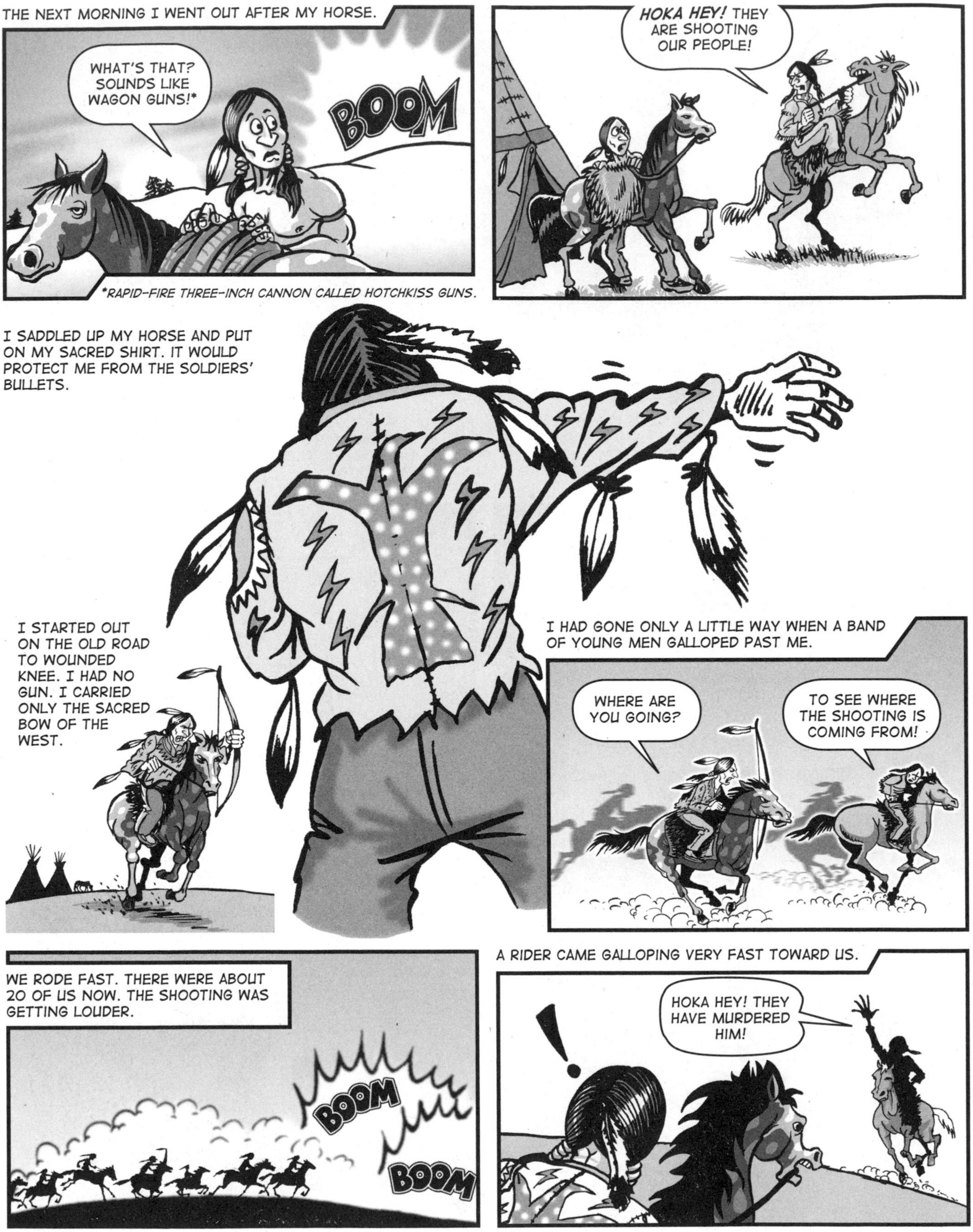
THE NEXT MORNING I WENT OUT AFTER MY HORSE.
WHAT'S THAT? SOUNDS LIKE WAGON GUNS!*
BOOM
*RAPID-FIRE THREE-INCH CANNON CALLED HOTCHKISS GUNS.
HOKA HEY! THEY ARE SHOOTING OUR PEOPLE!
I SADDLED UP MY HORSE AND PUT ON MY SACRED SHIRT. IT WOULD PROTECT ME FROM THE SOLDIERS' BULLETS.
I STARTED OUT ON THE OLD ROAD TO WOUNDED KNEE. I HAD NO GUN. I CARRIED ONLY THE SACRED BOW OF THE WEST.
I HAD GONE ONLY A LITTLE WAY WHEN A BAND OF YOUNG MEN GALLOPED PAST ME.
WHERE ARE YOU GOING?
TO SEE WHERE THE SHOOTING IS COMING FROM!
WE RODE FAST. THERE WERE ABOUT 20 OF US NOW. THE SHOOTING WAS GETTING LOUDER.
BOOM
BOOM
A RIDER CAME GALLOPING VERY FAST TOWARD US.
!
HOKA HEY! THEY HAVE MURDERED HIM!

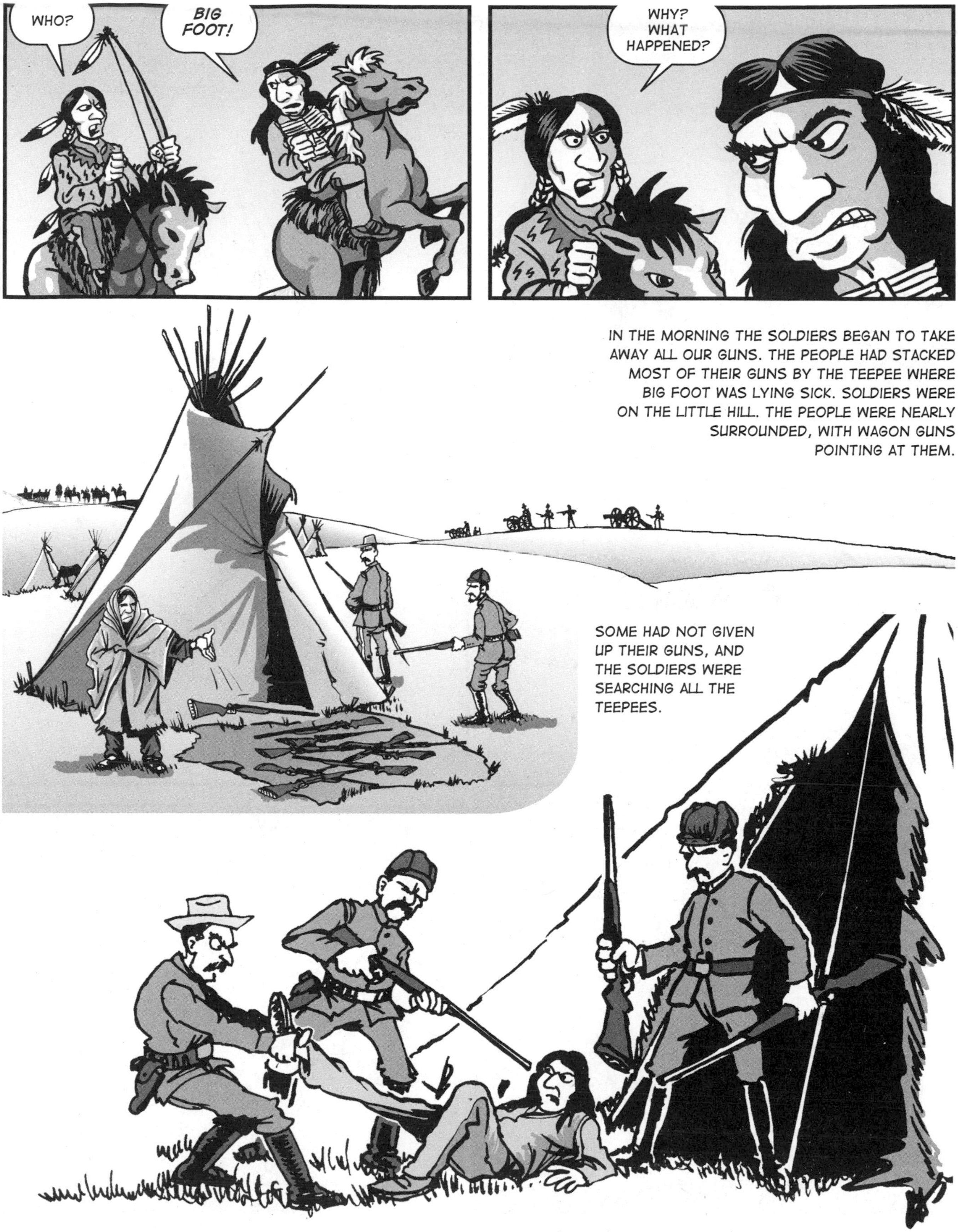
WHO?
BIG FOOT!
WHY? WHAT HAPPENED?
IN THE MORNING THE SOLDIERS BEGAN TO TAKE AWAY ALL OUR GUNS. THE PEOPLE HAD STACKED MOST OF THEIR GUNS BY THE TEEPEE WHERE BIG FOOT WAS LYING SICK. SOLDIERS WERE ON THE LITTLE HILL. THE PEOPLE WERE NEARLY SURROUNDED, WITH WAGON GUNS POINTING AT THEM.
SOME HAD NOT GIVEN UP THEIR GUNS, AND THE SOLDIERS WERE SEARCHING ALL THE TEEPEES.

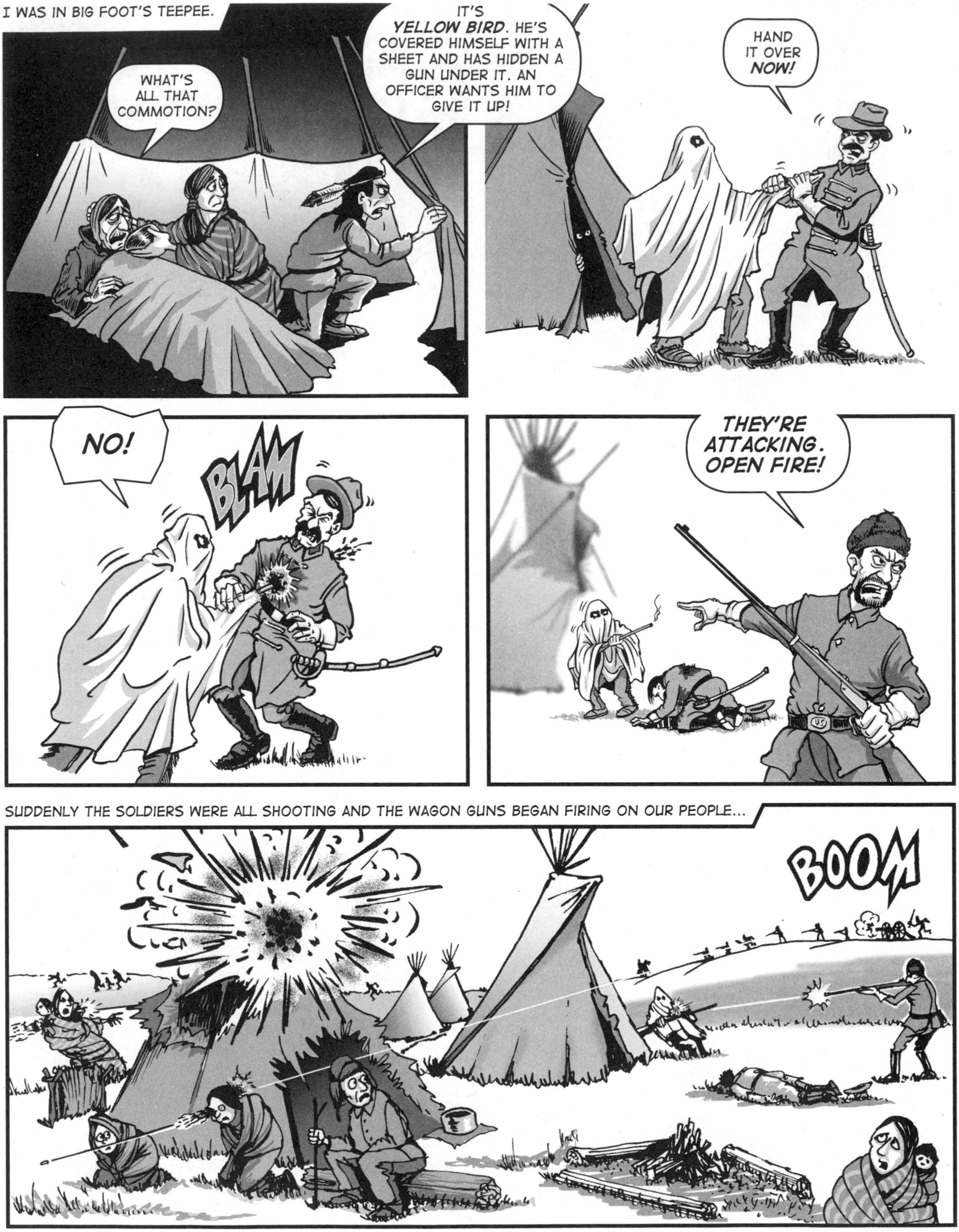
I WAS IN BIG FOOT'S TEEPEE.
WHAT'S ALL THAT COMMOTION?
IT'S YELLOW BIRD. HE'S COVERED HIMSELF WITH A SHEET AND HAS HIDDEN A GUN UNDER IT. AN OFFICER WANTS HIM TO GIVE IT UP!
HAND IT OVER NOW!
NO!
BLAM
THEY'RE ATTACKING. OPEN FIRE!
SUDDENLY THE SOLDIERS WERE ALL SHOOTING AND THE WAGON GUNS BEGAN FIRING ON OUR PEOPLE...
BOOM

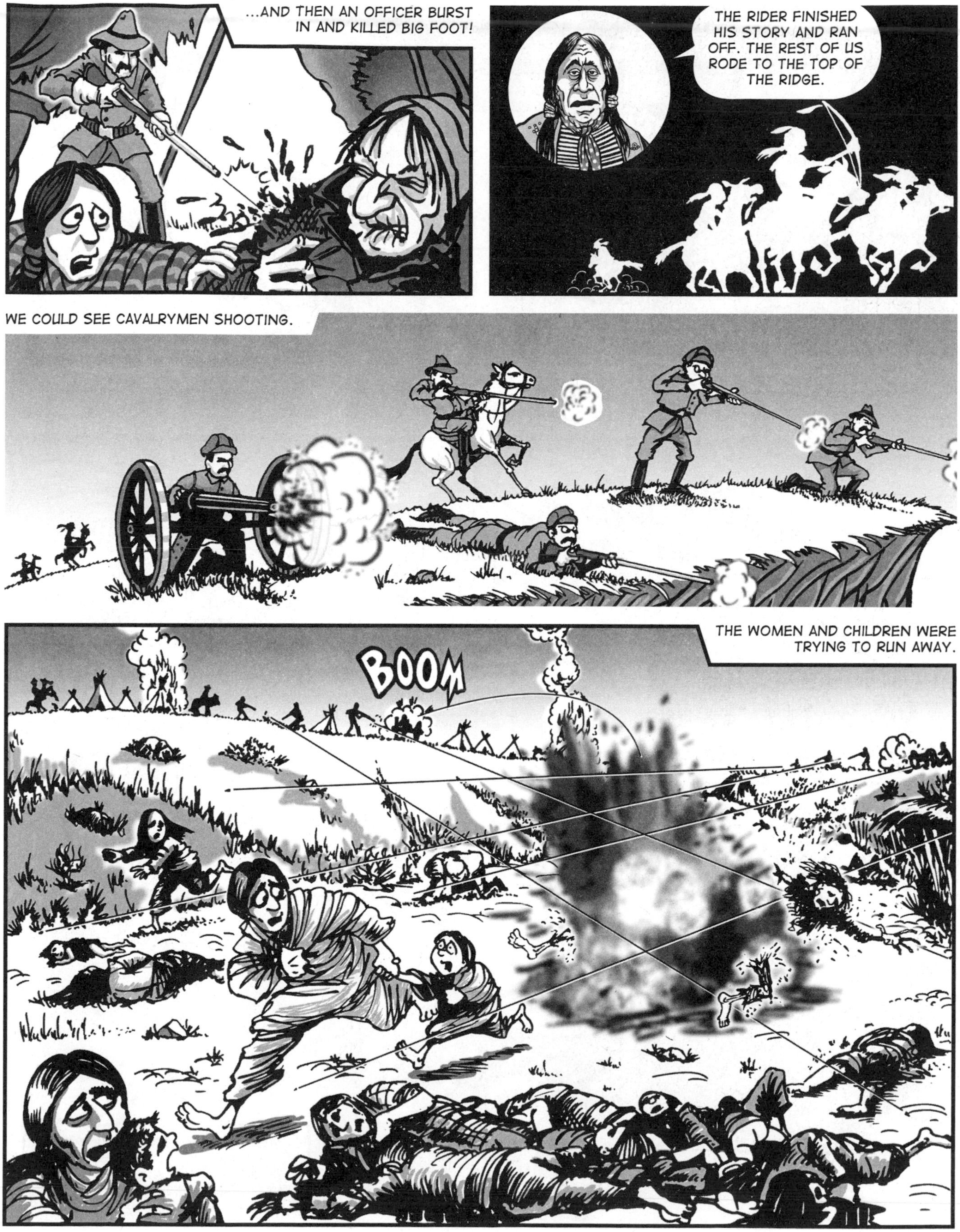
...AND THEN AN OFFICER BURST IN AND KILLED BIG FOOT!
THE RIDER FINISHED HIS STORY AND RAN OFF. THE REST OF US RODE TO THE TOP OF THE RIDGE.
WE COULD SEE CAVALRYMEN SHOOTING.
THE WOMEN AND CHILDREN WERE TRYING TO RUN AWAY.
BOOM

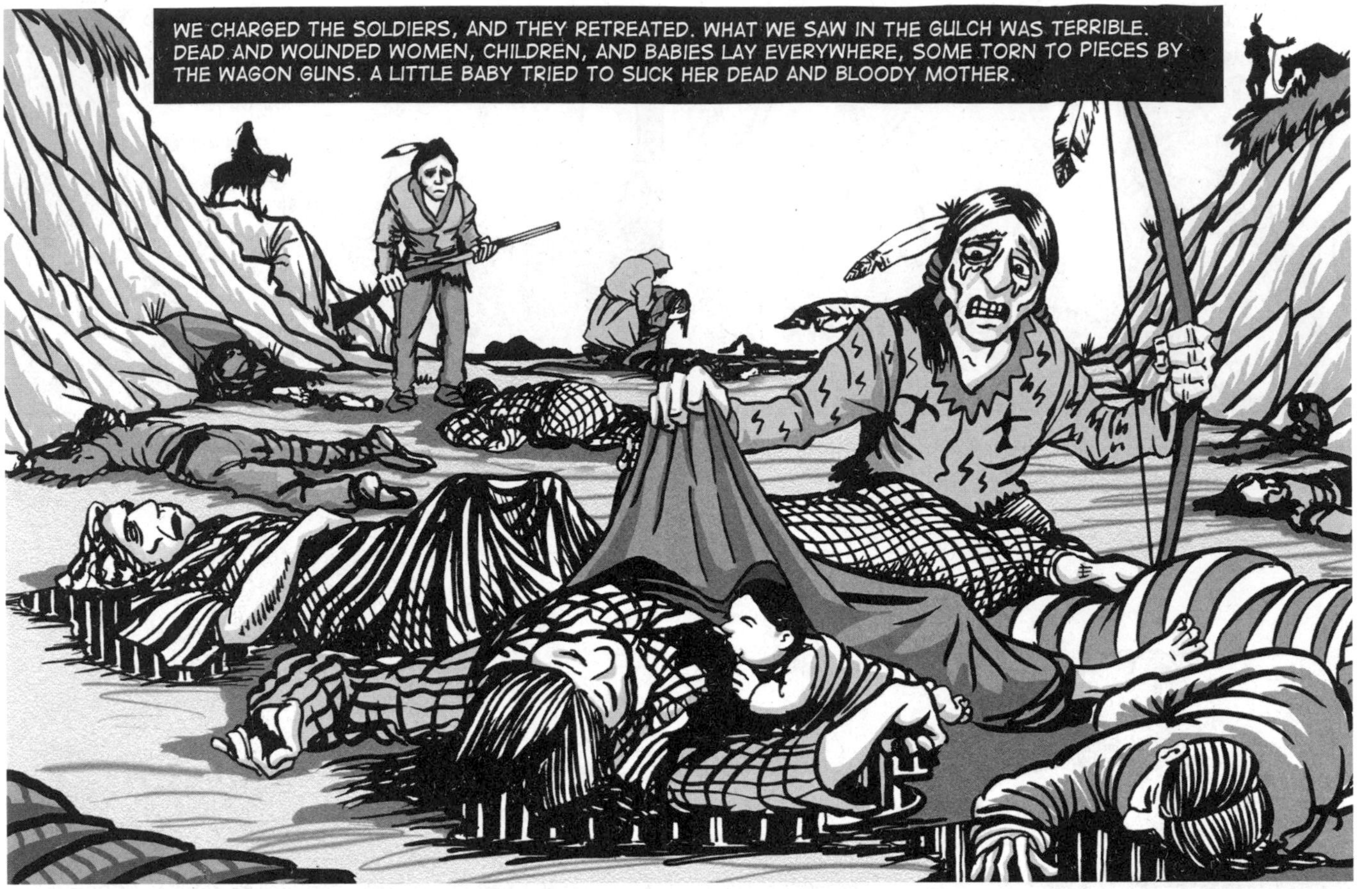
WE CHARGED THE SOLDIERS, AND THEY RETREATED. WHAT WE SAW IN THE GULCH WAS TERRIBLE. DEAD AND WOUNDED WOMEN, CHILDREN, AND BABIES LAY EVERYWHERE, SOME TORN TO PIECES BY THE WAGON GUNS. A LITTLE BABY TRIED TO SUCK HER DEAD AND BLOODY MOTHER.

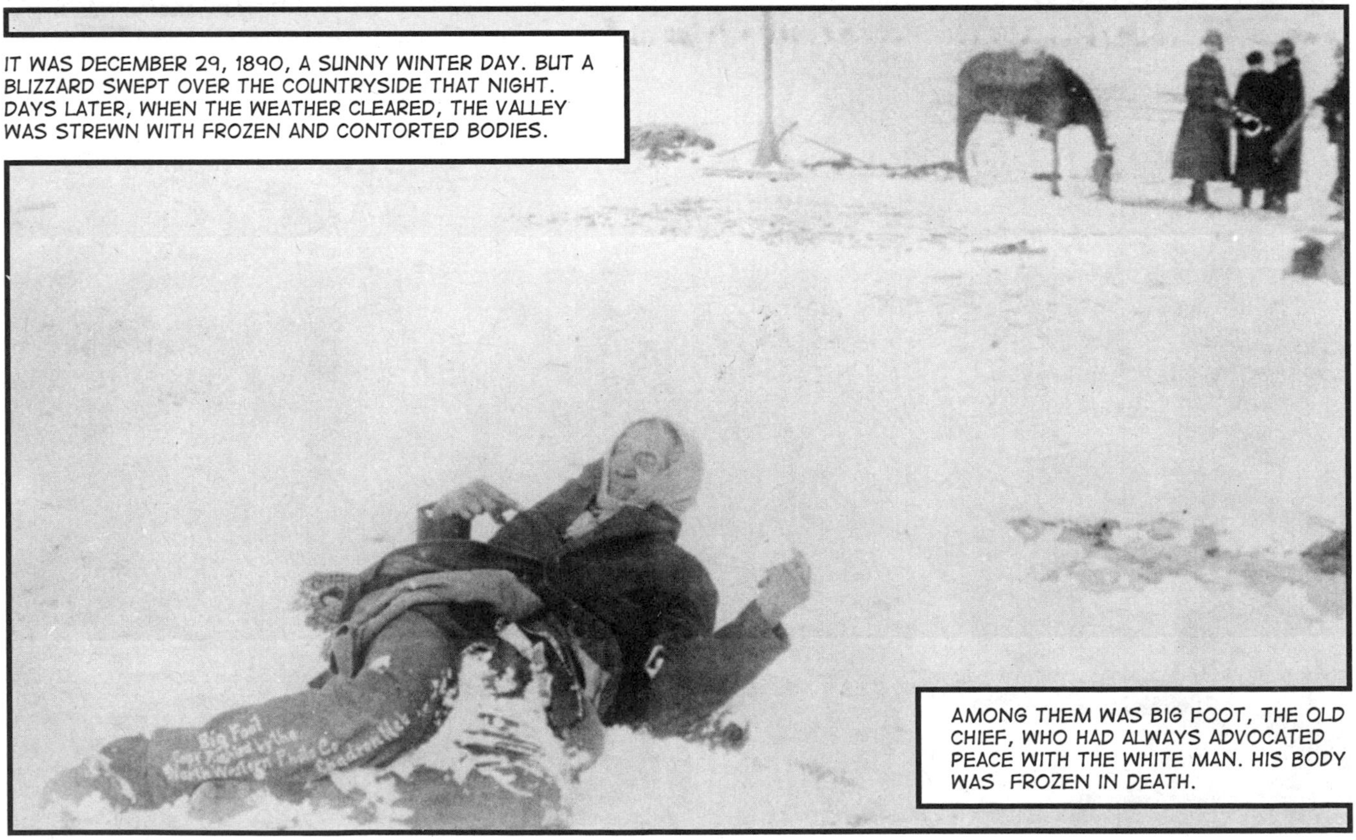
IT WAS DECEMBER 29, 1890, A SUNNY WINTER DAY. BUT A BLIZZARD SWEPT OVER THE COUNTRYSIDE THAT NIGHT. DAYS LATER, WHEN THE WEATHER CLEARED, THE VALLEY WAS STREWN WITH FROZEN AND CONTORTED BODIES.
AMONG THEM WAS BIG FOOT, THE OLD CHIEF, WHO HAD ALWAYS ADVOCATED PEACE WITH THE WHITE MAN. HIS BODY WAS FROZEN IN DEATH.

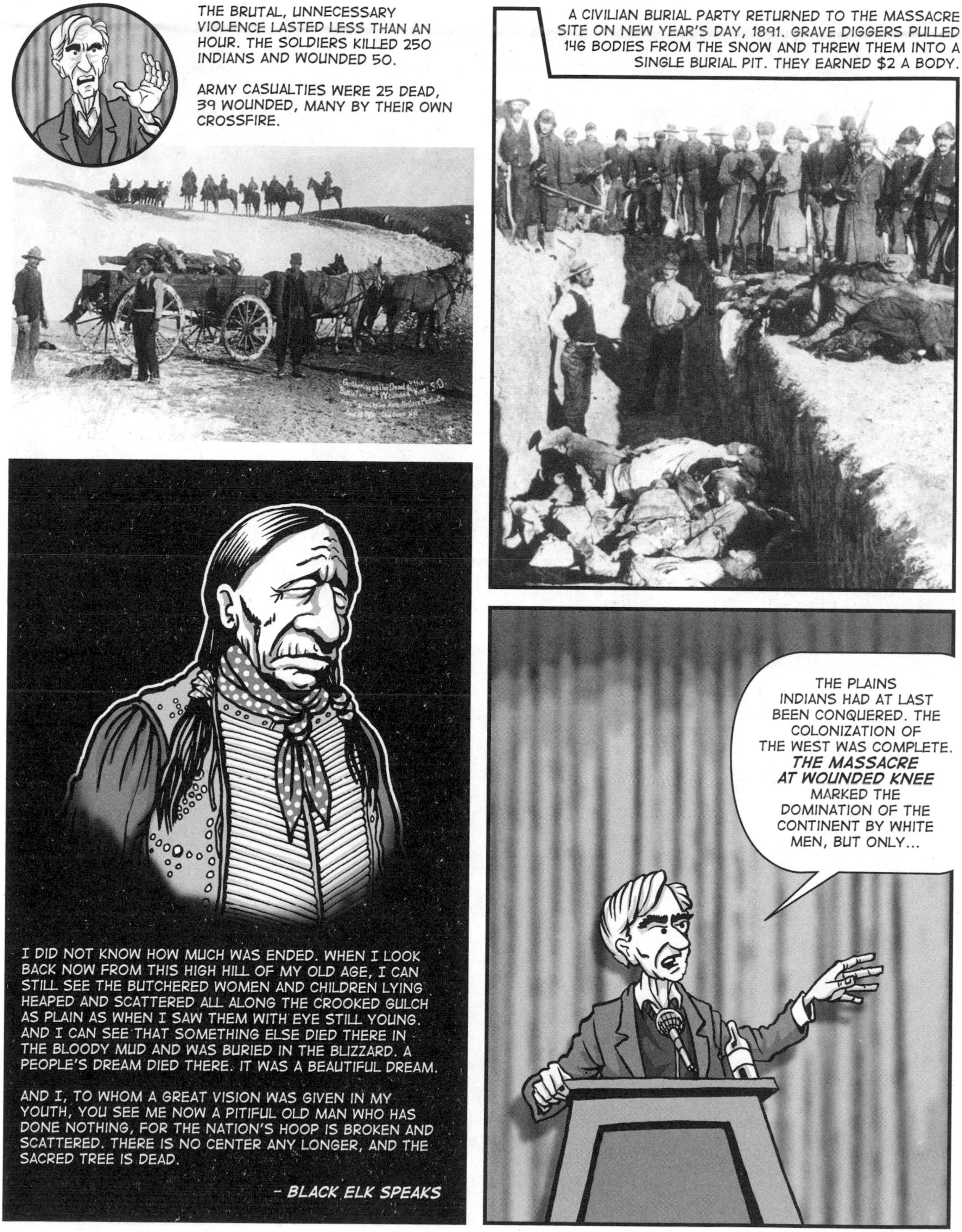
THE BRUTAL, UNNECESSARY VIOLENCE LASTED LESS THAN AN HOUR. THE SOLDIERS KILLED 250 INDIANS AND WOUNDED 50.
ARMY CASUALTIES WERE 25 DEAD, 39 WOUNDED, MANY BY THEIR OWN CROSSFIRE.
A CIVILIAN BURIAL PARTY RETURNED TO THE MASSACRE SITE ON NEW YEAR'S DAY, 1891. GRAVE DIGGERS PULLED 146 BODIES FROM THE SNOW AND THREW THEM INTO A SINGLE BURIAL PIT. THEY EARNED $2 A BODY.
I DID NOT KNOW HOW MUCH WAS ENDED. WHEN I LOOK BACK NOW FROM THIS HIGH HILL OF MY OLD AGE, I CAN STILL SEE THE BUTCHERED WOMEN AND CHILDREN LYING HEAPED AND SCATTERED ALL ALONG THE CROOKED GULCH AS PLAIN AS WHEN I SAW THEM WITH EYE STILL YOUNG. AND I CAN SEE THAT SOMETHING ELSE DIED THERE IN THE BLOODY MUD AND WAS BURIED IN THE BLIZZARD. A PEOPLE'S DREAM DIED THERE. IT WAS A BEAUTIFUL DREAM.
AND I, TO WHOM A GREAT VISION WAS GIVEN IN MY YOUTH, YOU SEE ME NOW A PITIFUL OLD MAN WHO HAS DONE NOTHING, FOR THE NATION'S HOOP IS BROKEN AND SCATTERED. THERE IS NO CENTER ANY LONGER, AND THE SACRED TREE IS DEAD.
– *BLACK ELK SPEAKS*
THE PLAINS INDIANS HAD AT LAST BEEN CONQUERED. THE COLONIZATION OF THE WEST WAS COMPLETE. ***THE MASSACRE AT WOUNDED KNEE*** MARKED THE DOMINATION OF THE CONTINENT BY WHITE MEN, BUT ONLY...

Certain White Men

EMULATING AND CONTENDING WITH EUROPEAN IMPERIALISM, AMERICA'S EARLY ***ROBBER BARONS*** SET OUT TO BUILD VAST EMPIRES OF WEALTH FOR THEMSELVES. FIRST, HOWEVER, THEY WOULD HAVE TO CRUSH RESISTANCE TO THEIR POWER.

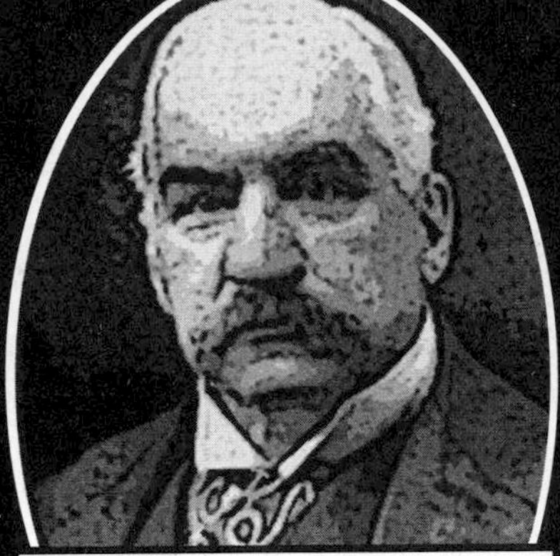

J. P. MORGAN

...THE SON OF A BANKER, SOLD RAILROAD STOCKS FOR GOOD COMMISSIONS. DURING THE ***CIVIL WAR*** HE BOUGHT 5,000 RIFLES FOR $3.50 EACH FROM AN ARMY ARSENAL, THEN SOLD THEM TO A GENERAL IN THE FIELD FOR $22 EACH. BY 1900, J. P. MORGAN CONTROLLED 100,000 MILES OF RAILROAD, ***HALF THE TRACK IN THE COUNTRY***.

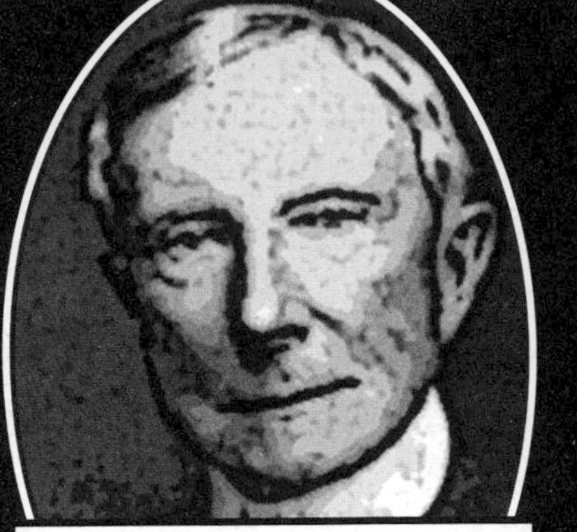

JOHN D. ROCKEFELLER

...STARTED AS A BOOKKEEPER IN CLEVELAND AND BOUGHT HIS FIRST OIL REFINERY IN 1862. BY 1870, HE SET UP ***STANDARD OIL OF OHIO*** AND MADE SECRET DEALS TO SHIP HIS OIL ON RAILROADS THAT GAVE HIM DISCOUNTS. IT DROVE HIS COMPETITORS OUT OF BUSINESS. BY 1899, HIS FORTUNE WAS ESTIMATED AT $200 MILLION.

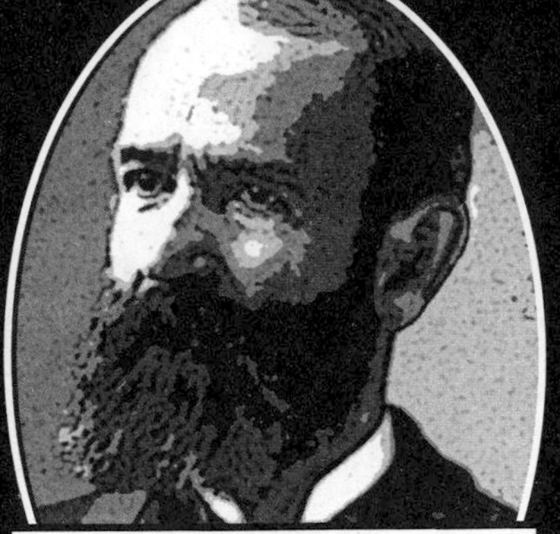

JAY GOULD

...BORN POOR, BECAME ONE OF THE RICHEST AND MOST HATED MEN IN AMERICA THROUGH STOCK MANIPULATION, SPECULATION, BRIBERY, AND A STRANGLEHOLD ON SOUTHWESTERN RAILROADS. HIS STRIKEBREAKING LED TO THE 1886 DEMISE OF THE ***KNIGHTS OF LABOR***. HE BOASTED: "I CAN HIRE ONE-HALF OF THE WORKING CLASS TO KILL THE OTHER HALF."

WHILE THE ROBBER BARONS ENJOYED THEIR FABULOUS RICHES, WORKERS PAID THE PRICE: DEATH AND MUTILATION FROM MINE CAVE-INS, FIRES, AND EXPLOSIONS. IN STEEL AND TEXTILE MILLS, THOUSANDS DIED OR WERE CRIPPLED.

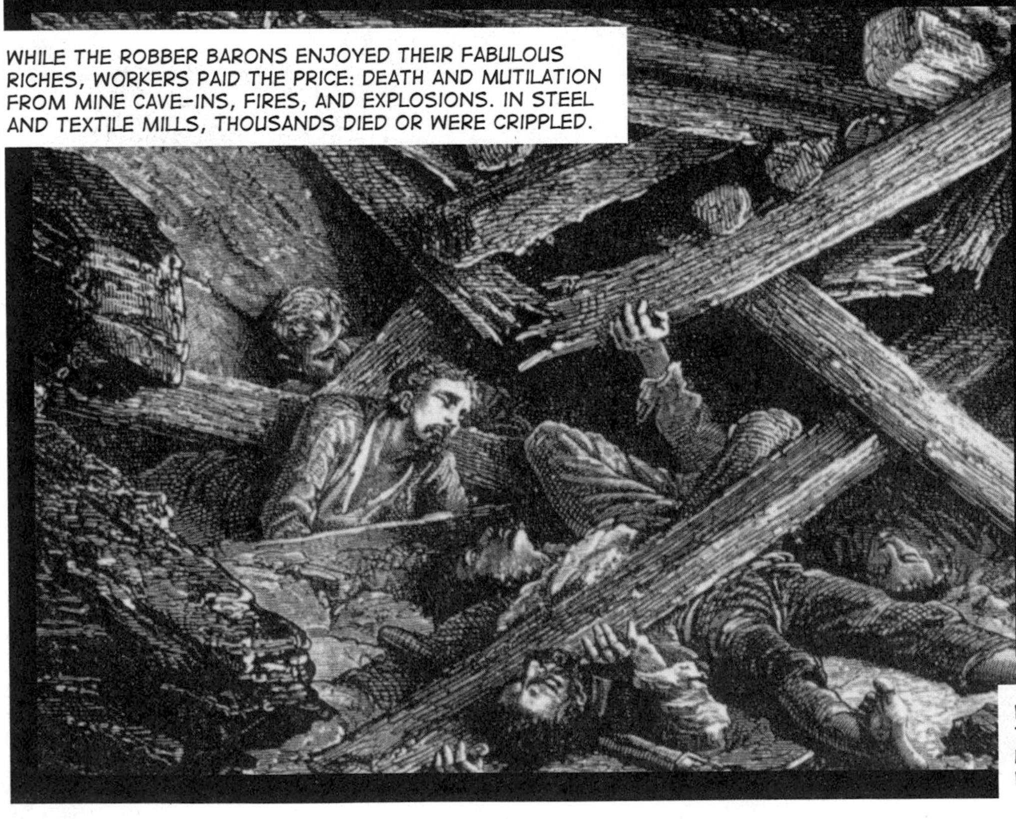

IN 1889, MORE THAN 22,000 RAILROAD WORKERS WERE KILLED OR INJURED.

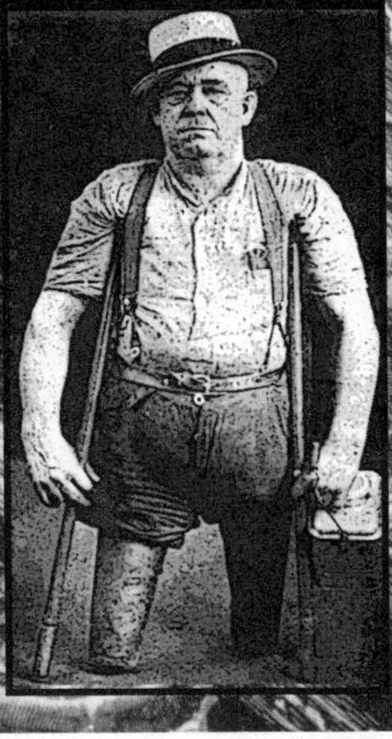

WHOLE FAMILIES WERE FORCED TO WORK IN MINES AND MILLS FOR LONG HOURS AND PUNY WAGES. THE PEOPLE REBELLED.

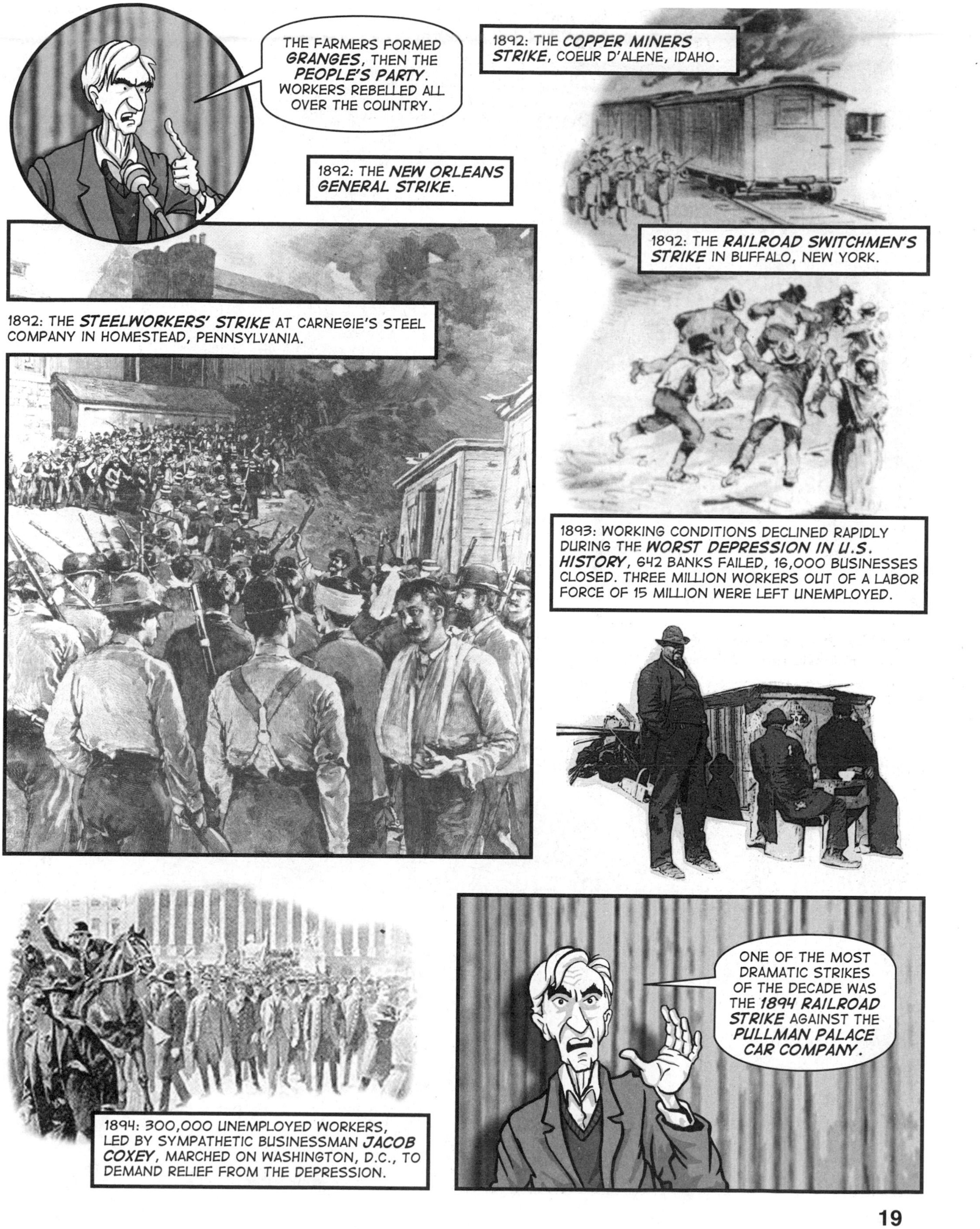
THE FARMERS FORMED GRANGES, THEN THE PEOPLE'S PARTY. WORKERS REBELLED ALL OVER THE COUNTRY.
1892: THE COPPER MINERS STRIKE, COEUR D'ALENE, IDAHO.
1892: THE NEW ORLEANS GENERAL STRIKE.
1892: THE RAILROAD SWITCHMEN'S STRIKE IN BUFFALO, NEW YORK.
1892: THE STEELWORKERS' STRIKE AT CARNEGIE'S STEEL COMPANY IN HOMESTEAD, PENNSYLVANIA.
1893: WORKING CONDITIONS DECLINED RAPIDLY DURING THE WORST DEPRESSION IN U.S. HISTORY, 642 BANKS FAILED, 16,000 BUSINESSES CLOSED. THREE MILLION WORKERS OUT OF A LABOR FORCE OF 15 MILLION WERE LEFT UNEMPLOYED.
1894: 300,000 UNEMPLOYED WORKERS, LED BY SYMPATHETIC BUSINESSMAN JACOB COXEY, MARCHED ON WASHINGTON, D.C., TO DEMAND RELIEF FROM THE DEPRESSION.
ONE OF THE MOST DRAMATIC STRIKES OF THE DECADE WAS THE 1894 RAILROAD STRIKE AGAINST THE PULLMAN PALACE CAR COMPANY.

The Pullman Strike

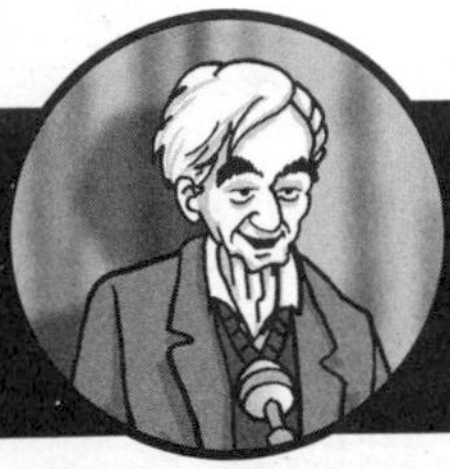

GEORGE PULLMAN TRIED TO SOLVE HIS LABOR PROBLEMS BY BUILDING A COMPANY TOWN OUTSIDE CHICAGO THAT HE NAMED AFTER HIMSELF. HE CHARGED HIGH RENTS AND CONTROLLED EVERY ASPECT OF HIS WORKERS' LIVES. HE CALLED THEM "MY CHILDREN." IT WAS A VERSION OF THE INDIAN RESERVATION SYSTEM. ON MAY 11, 1894, CHICAGO WORKERS OF THE ***PULLMAN PALACE CAR COMPANY*** STRUCK TO PROTEST WAGE CUTS AND THE FIRING OF UNION REPRESENTATIVES.

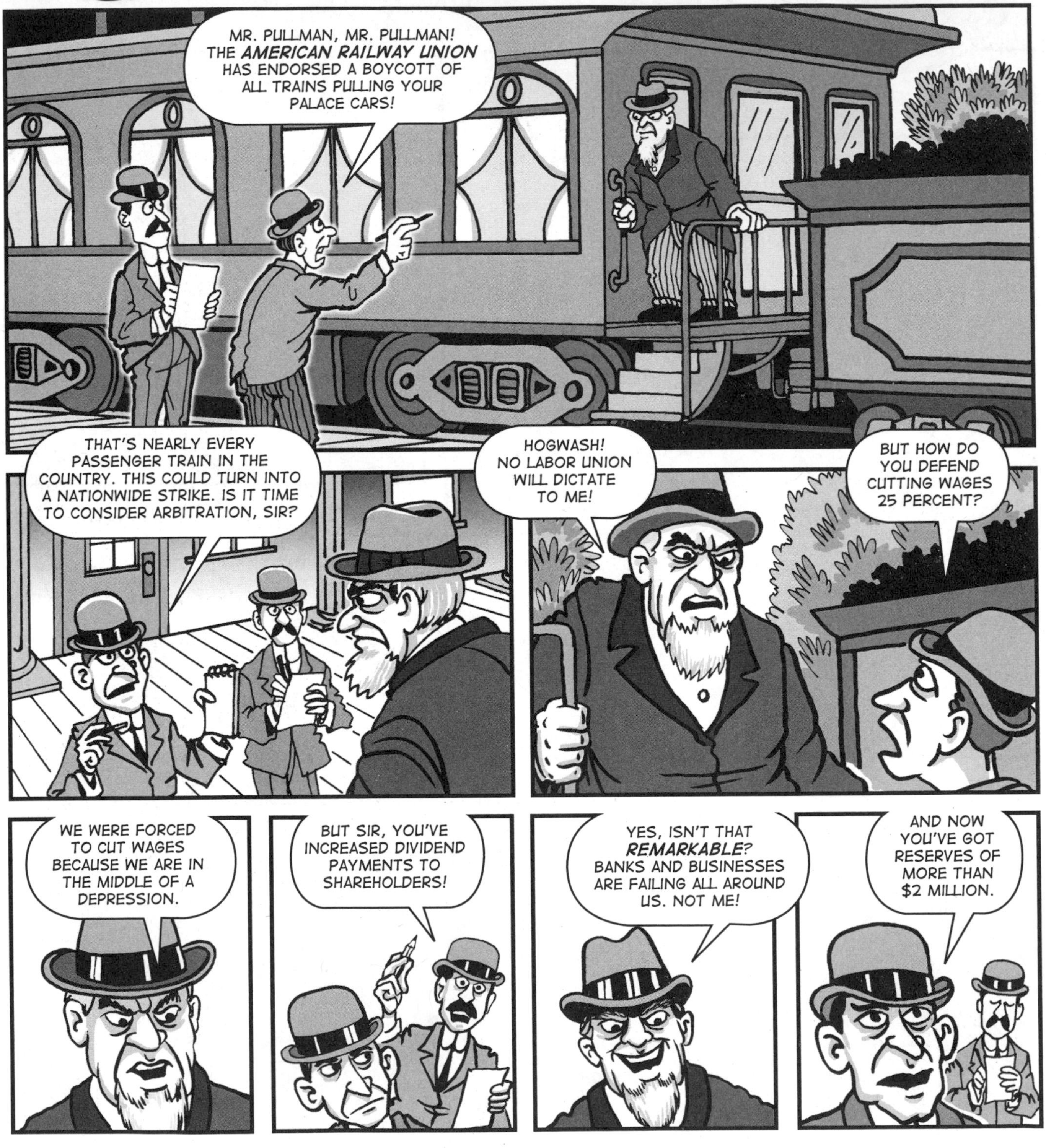
MR. PULLMAN, MR. PULLMAN! THE AMERICAN RAILWAY UNION HAS ENDORSED A BOYCOTT OF ALL TRAINS PULLING YOUR PALACE CARS!
THAT'S NEARLY EVERY PASSENGER TRAIN IN THE COUNTRY. THIS COULD TURN INTO A NATIONWIDE STRIKE. IS IT TIME TO CONSIDER ARBITRATION, SIR?
HOGWASH! NO LABOR UNION WILL DICTATE TO ME!
BUT HOW DO YOU DEFEND CUTTING WAGES 25 PERCENT?
WE WERE FORCED TO CUT WAGES BECAUSE WE ARE IN THE MIDDLE OF A DEPRESSION.
BUT SIR, YOU'VE INCREASED DIVIDEND PAYMENTS TO SHAREHOLDERS!
YES, ISN'T THAT REMARKABLE? BANKS AND BUSINESSES ARE FAILING ALL AROUND US. NOT ME!
AND NOW YOU'VE GOT RESERVES OF MORE THAN $2 MILLION.

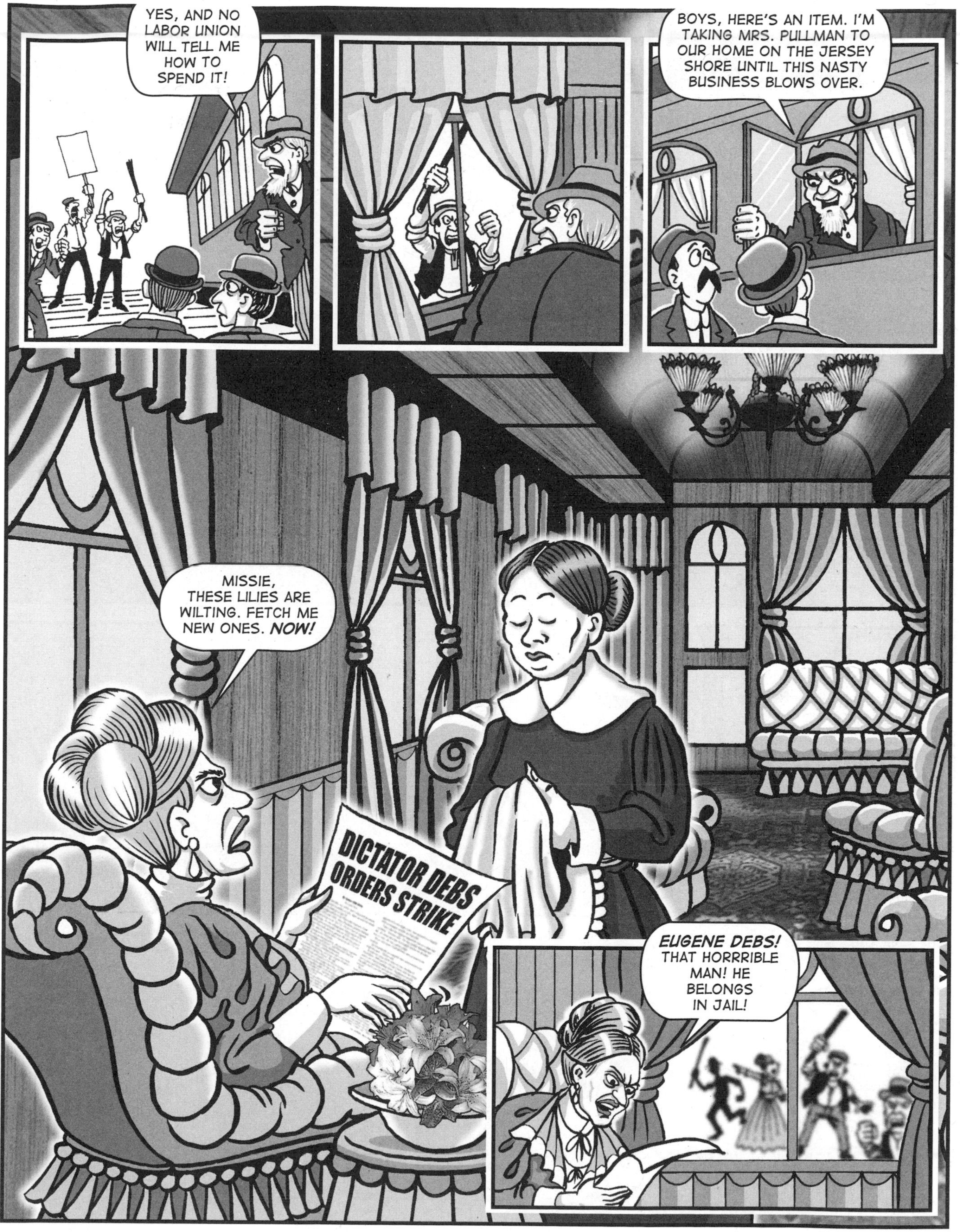
YES, AND NO LABOR UNION WILL TELL ME HOW TO SPEND IT!
BOYS, HERE'S AN ITEM. I'M TAKING MRS. PULLMAN TO OUR HOME ON THE JERSEY SHORE UNTIL THIS NASTY BUSINESS BLOWS OVER.
MISSIE, THESE LILIES ARE WILTING. FETCH ME NEW ONES. **NOW!**
DICTATOR DEBS ORDERS STRIKE
EUGENE DEBS! THAT HORRRIBLE MAN! HE BELONGS IN JAIL!

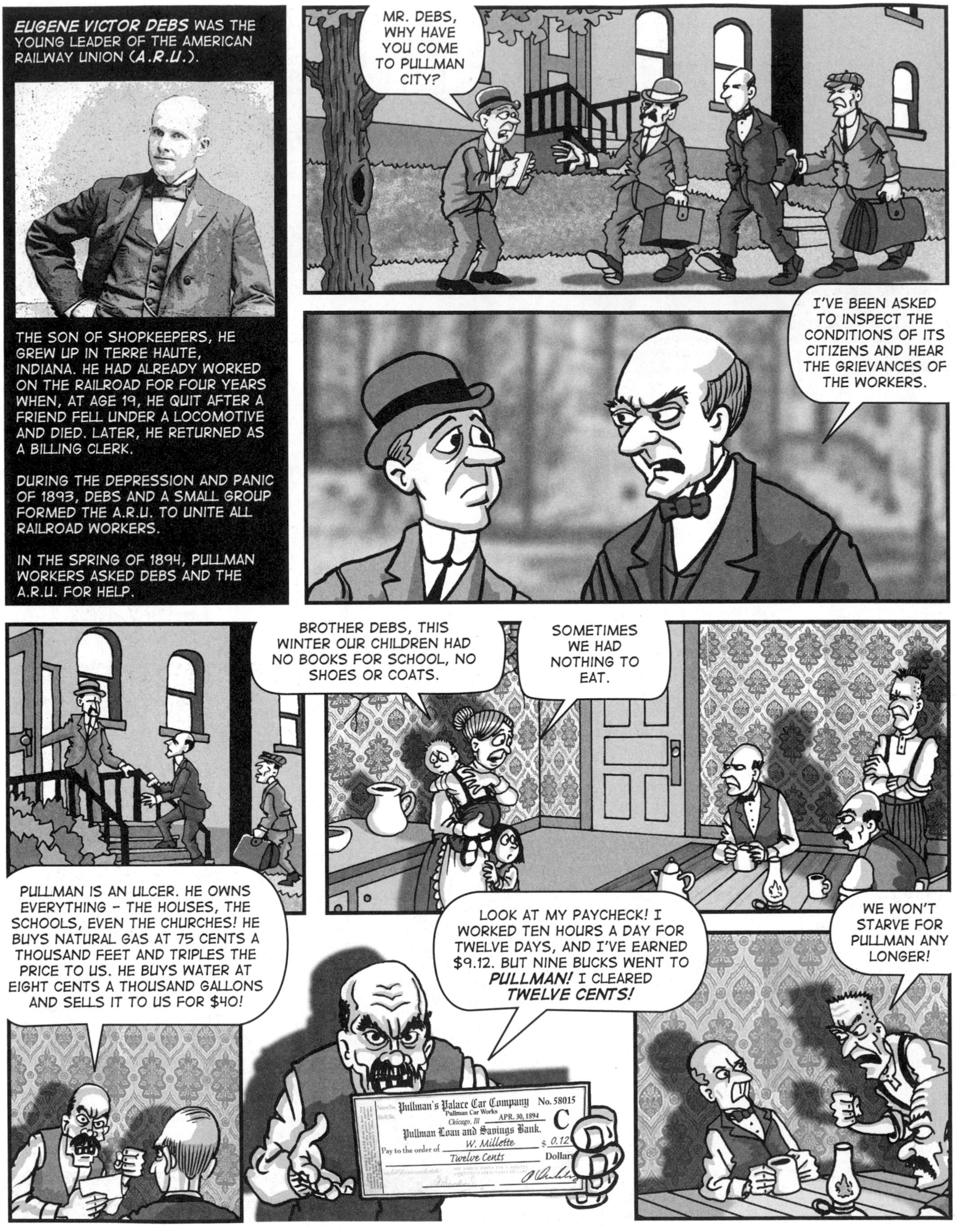
EUGENE VICTOR DEBS WAS THE YOUNG LEADER OF THE AMERICAN RAILWAY UNION (A.R.U.).
THE SON OF SHOPKEEPERS, HE GREW UP IN TERRE HAUTE, INDIANA. HE HAD ALREADY WORKED ON THE RAILROAD FOR FOUR YEARS WHEN, AT AGE 19, HE QUIT AFTER A FRIEND FELL UNDER A LOCOMOTIVE AND DIED. LATER, HE RETURNED AS A BILLING CLERK.
DURING THE DEPRESSION AND PANIC OF 1893, DEBS AND A SMALL GROUP FORMED THE A.R.U. TO UNITE ALL RAILROAD WORKERS.
IN THE SPRING OF 1894, PULLMAN WORKERS ASKED DEBS AND THE A.R.U. FOR HELP.
MR. DEBS, WHY HAVE YOU COME TO PULLMAN CITY?
I'VE BEEN ASKED TO INSPECT THE CONDITIONS OF ITS CITIZENS AND HEAR THE GRIEVANCES OF THE WORKERS.
BROTHER DEBS, THIS WINTER OUR CHILDREN HAD NO BOOKS FOR SCHOOL, NO SHOES OR COATS.
SOMETIMES WE HAD NOTHING TO EAT.
PULLMAN IS AN ULCER. HE OWNS EVERYTHING – THE HOUSES, THE SCHOOLS, EVEN THE CHURCHES! HE BUYS NATURAL GAS AT 75 CENTS A THOUSAND FEET AND TRIPLES THE PRICE TO US. HE BUYS WATER AT EIGHT CENTS A THOUSAND GALLONS AND SELLS IT TO US FOR $40!
LOOK AT MY PAYCHECK! I WORKED TEN HOURS A DAY FOR TWELVE DAYS, AND I'VE EARNED $9.12. BUT NINE BUCKS WENT TO PULLMAN! I CLEARED TWELVE CENTS!
Pullman's Palace Car Company No. 58015
Pullman Car Works
Chicago, Ill APR. 30, 1894
C
Pullman Loan and Savings Bank.
Pay to the order of W. Millette $ 0.12
Twelve Cents Dollars
WE WON'T STARVE FOR PULLMAN ANY LONGER!

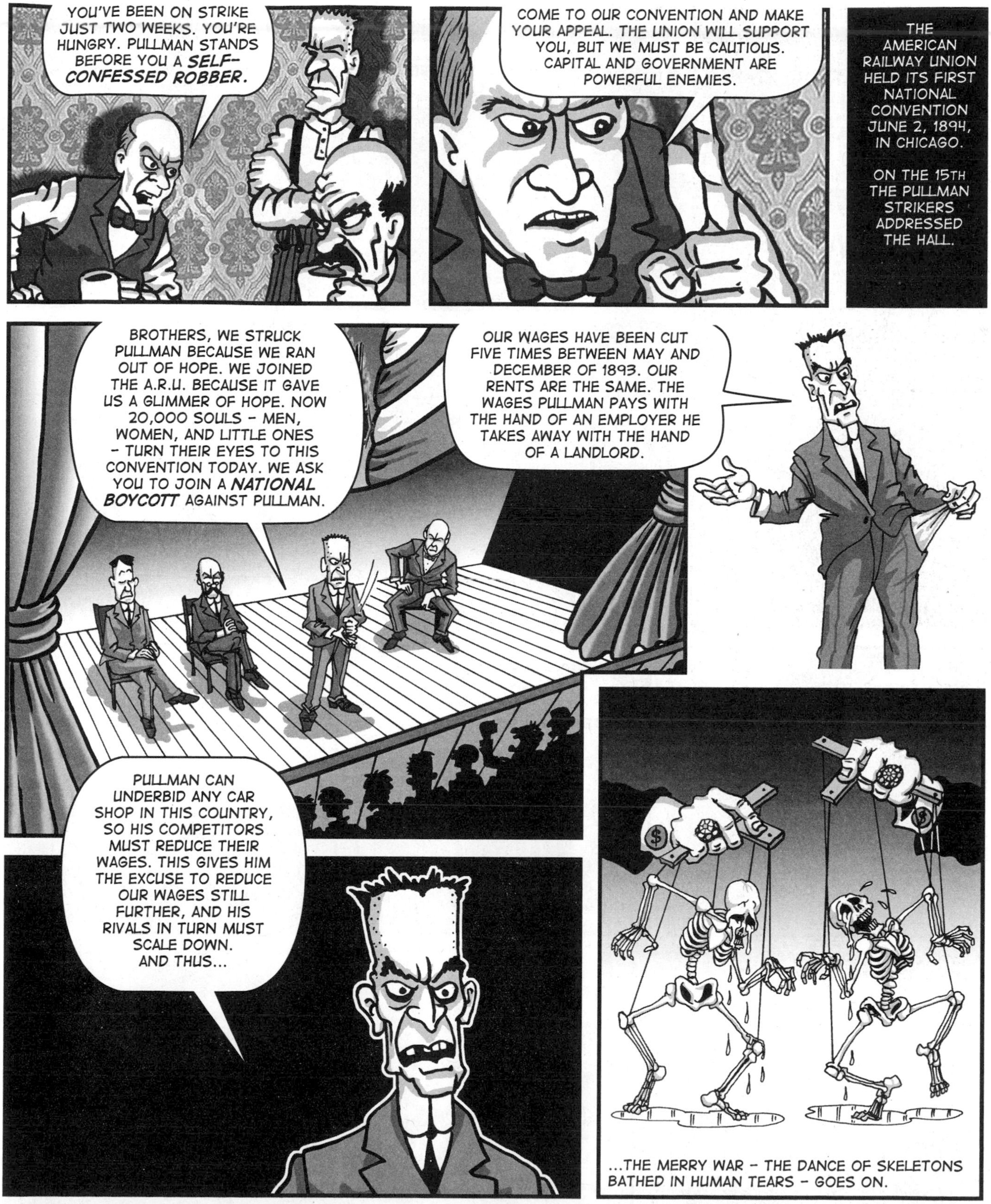
YOU'VE BEEN ON STRIKE JUST TWO WEEKS. YOU'RE HUNGRY. PULLMAN STANDS BEFORE YOU A SELF-CONFESSED ROBBER.
COME TO OUR CONVENTION AND MAKE YOUR APPEAL. THE UNION WILL SUPPORT YOU, BUT WE MUST BE CAUTIOUS. CAPITAL AND GOVERNMENT ARE POWERFUL ENEMIES.
THE AMERICAN RAILWAY UNION HELD ITS FIRST NATIONAL CONVENTION JUNE 2, 1894, IN CHICAGO.
ON THE 15TH THE PULLMAN STRIKERS ADDRESSED THE HALL.
BROTHERS, WE STRUCK PULLMAN BECAUSE WE RAN OUT OF HOPE. WE JOINED THE A.R.U. BECAUSE IT GAVE US A GLIMMER OF HOPE. NOW 20,000 SOULS - MEN, WOMEN, AND LITTLE ONES - TURN THEIR EYES TO THIS CONVENTION TODAY. WE ASK YOU TO JOIN A NATIONAL BOYCOTT AGAINST PULLMAN.
OUR WAGES HAVE BEEN CUT FIVE TIMES BETWEEN MAY AND DECEMBER OF 1893. OUR RENTS ARE THE SAME. THE WAGES PULLMAN PAYS WITH THE HAND OF AN EMPLOYER HE TAKES AWAY WITH THE HAND OF A LANDLORD.
PULLMAN CAN UNDERBID ANY CAR SHOP IN THIS COUNTRY, SO HIS COMPETITORS MUST REDUCE THEIR WAGES. THIS GIVES HIM THE EXCUSE TO REDUCE OUR WAGES STILL FURTHER, AND HIS RIVALS IN TURN MUST SCALE DOWN. AND THUS...
...THE MERRY WAR - THE DANCE OF SKELETONS BATHED IN HUMAN TEARS - GOES ON.

ZINNFORMATION *A CENTURY LATER THIS WOULD BE CALLED* ***THE RACE TO THE BOTTOM****. IT WOULD ALSO BECOME THE BUSINESS MODEL FOR* ***WAL-MART****.*

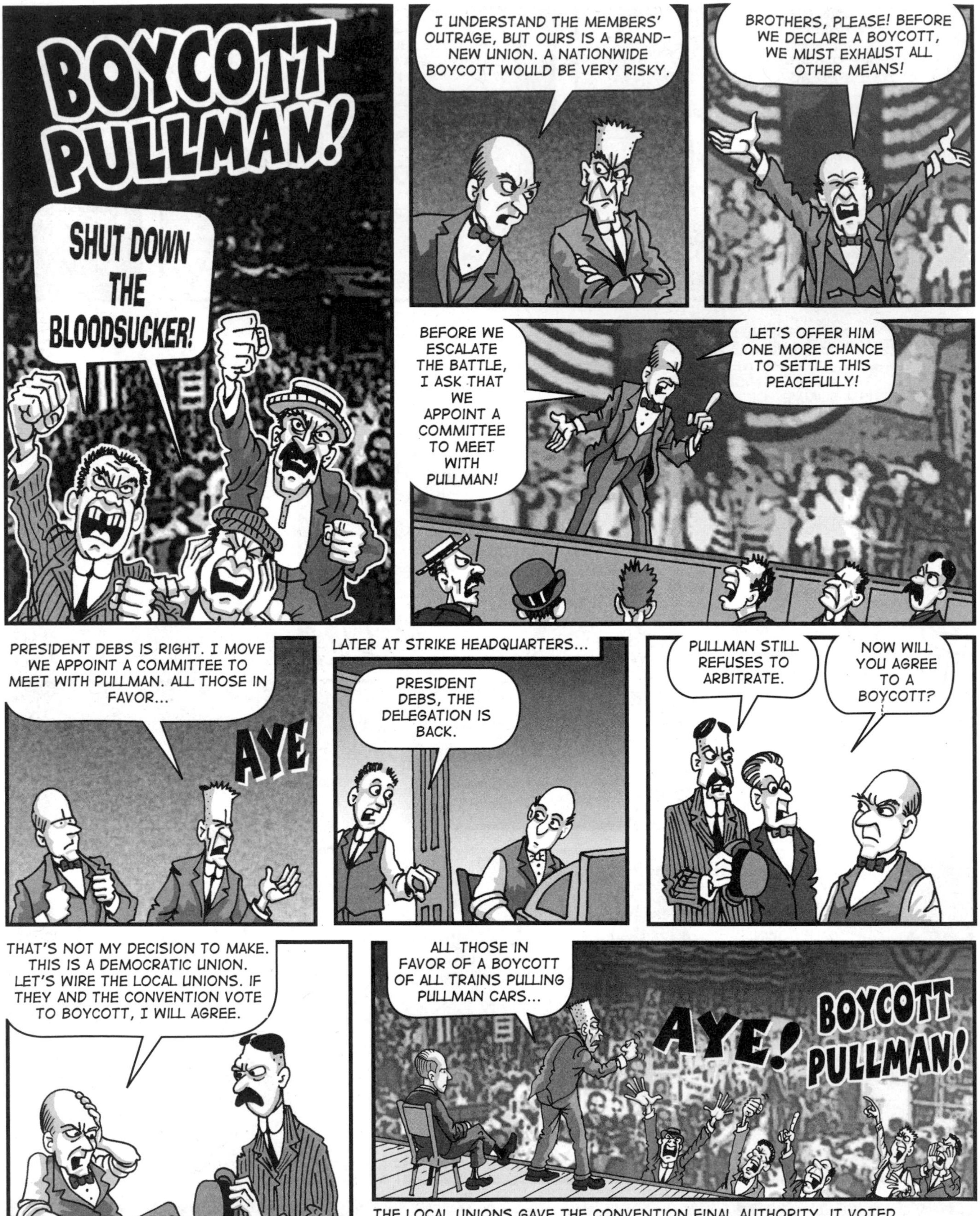
BOYCOTT PULLMAN!
SHUT DOWN THE BLOODSUCKER!
I UNDERSTAND THE MEMBERS' OUTRAGE, BUT OURS IS A BRAND-NEW UNION. A NATIONWIDE BOYCOTT WOULD BE VERY RISKY.
BROTHERS, PLEASE! BEFORE WE DECLARE A BOYCOTT, WE MUST EXHAUST ALL OTHER MEANS!
BEFORE WE ESCALATE THE BATTLE, I ASK THAT WE APPOINT A COMMITTEE TO MEET WITH PULLMAN!
LET'S OFFER HIM ONE MORE CHANCE TO SETTLE THIS PEACEFULLY!
PRESIDENT DEBS IS RIGHT. I MOVE WE APPOINT A COMMITTEE TO MEET WITH PULLMAN. ALL THOSE IN FAVOR...
AYE
LATER AT STRIKE HEADQUARTERS...
PRESIDENT DEBS, THE DELEGATION IS BACK.
PULLMAN STILL REFUSES TO ARBITRATE.
NOW WILL YOU AGREE TO A BOYCOTT?
THAT'S NOT MY DECISION TO MAKE. THIS IS A DEMOCRATIC UNION. LET'S WIRE THE LOCAL UNIONS. IF THEY AND THE CONVENTION VOTE TO BOYCOTT, I WILL AGREE.
ALL THOSE IN FAVOR OF A BOYCOTT OF ALL TRAINS PULLING PULLMAN CARS...
AYE!
BOYCOTT PULLMAN!
THE LOCAL UNIONS GAVE THE CONVENTION FINAL AUTHORITY. IT VOTED UNANIMOUSLY TO BOYCOTT ALL PULLMAN CARS NATIONWIDE AS OF JUNE 26. WITHIN DAYS, ALL 24 RAIL LINES LEADING OUT OF CHICAGO WERE SHUT DOWN.

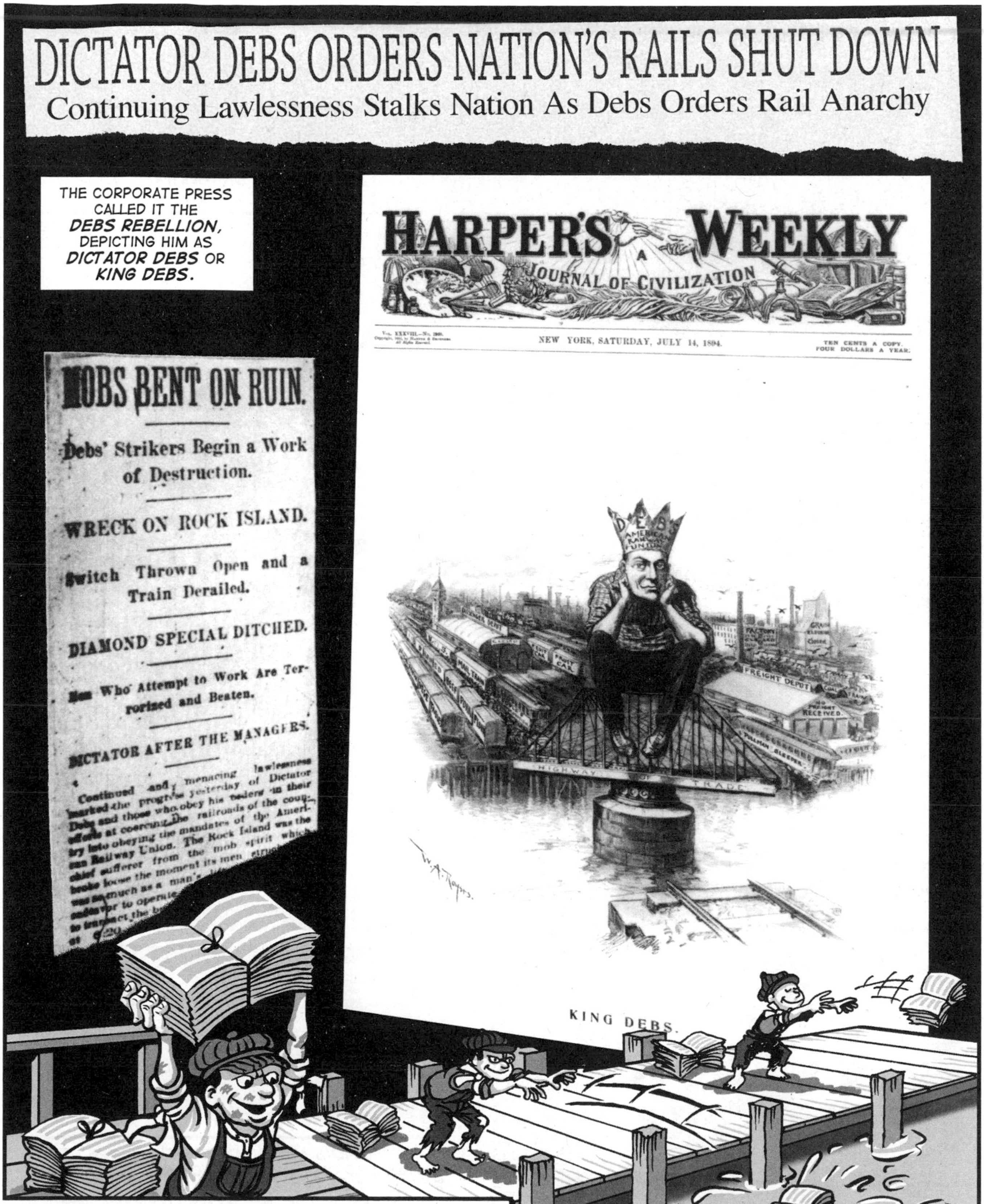
DICTATOR DEBS ORDERS NATION'S RAILS SHUT DOWN
Continuing Lawlessness Stalks Nation As Debs Orders Rail Anarchy
THE CORPORATE PRESS CALLED IT THE *DEBS REBELLION,* DEPICTING HIM AS *DICTATOR DEBS* OR *KING DEBS*.
HARPER'S WEEKLY
A JOURNAL OF CIVILIZATION
Vol. XXXVIII.—No. 1960. Copyright, 1894, by Harper & Brothers. All Rights Reserved.
NEW YORK, SATURDAY, JULY 14, 1894.
TEN CENTS A COPY. FOUR DOLLARS A YEAR.
MOBS BENT ON RUIN.
Debs' Strikers Begin a Work of Destruction.
WRECK ON ROCK ISLAND.
Switch Thrown Open and a Train Derailed.
DIAMOND SPECIAL DITCHED.
Men Who Attempt to Work Are Terrorized and Beaten.
DICTATOR AFTER THE MANAGERS.
DEBS
AMERICAN RAILWAY UNION
FREIGHT DEPOT
HIGHWAY OF TRADE
KING DEBS.
BUT THE STRIKERS HAD SOME ALLIES IN THE PRESS. THE *CHICAGO NEWSBOYS* WORE THE STRIKERS' SYMBOL, A WHITE RIBBON, AND OFTEN DUMPED ANTISTRIKE NEWSPAPERS.

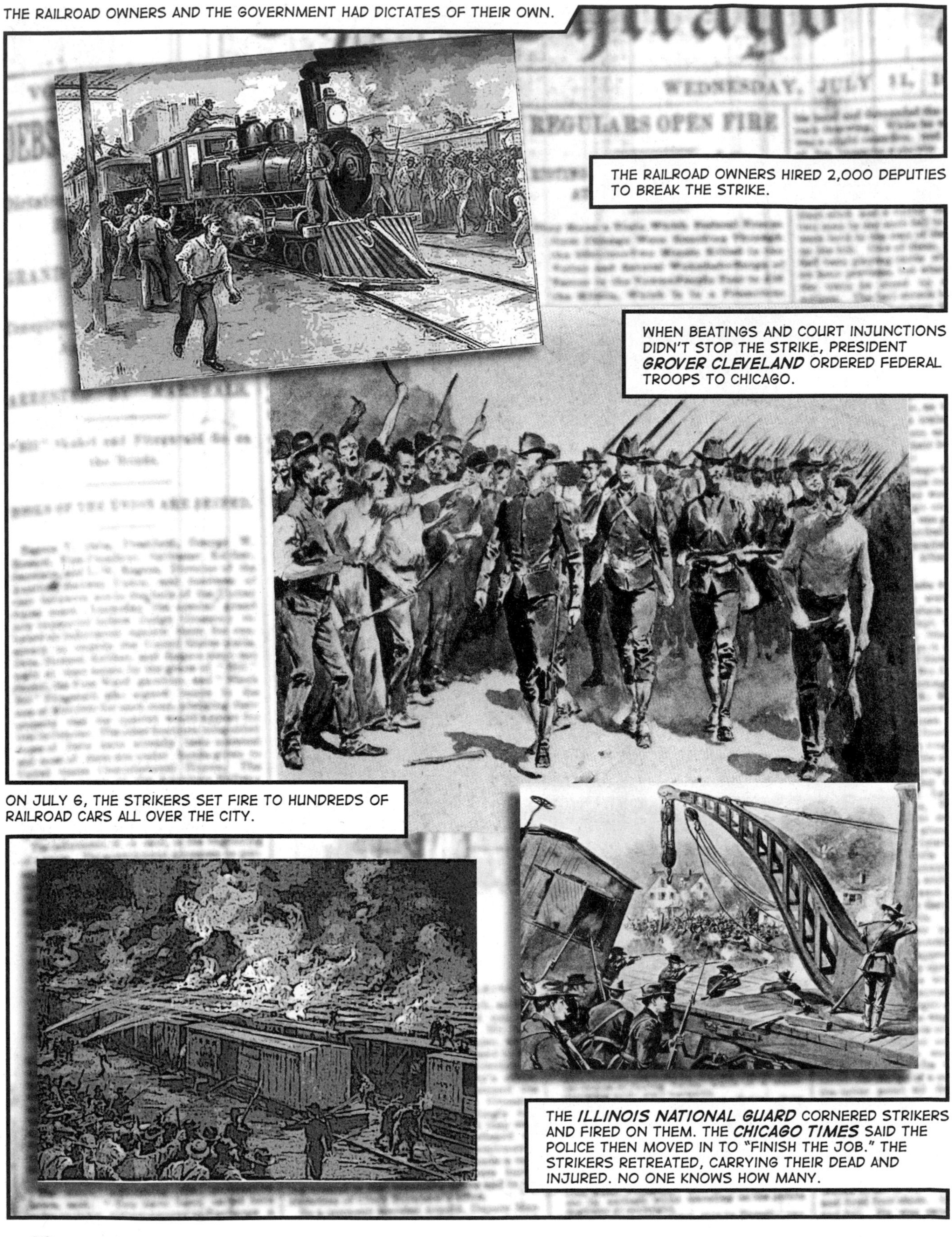
THE RAILROAD OWNERS AND THE GOVERNMENT HAD DICTATES OF THEIR OWN.
THE RAILROAD OWNERS HIRED 2,000 DEPUTIES TO BREAK THE STRIKE.
WHEN BEATINGS AND COURT INJUNCTIONS DIDN'T STOP THE STRIKE, PRESIDENT ***GROVER CLEVELAND*** ORDERED FEDERAL TROOPS TO CHICAGO.
ON JULY 6, THE STRIKERS SET FIRE TO HUNDREDS OF RAILROAD CARS ALL OVER THE CITY.
THE ***ILLINOIS NATIONAL GUARD*** CORNERED STRIKERS AND FIRED ON THEM. THE ***CHICAGO TIMES*** SAID THE POLICE THEN MOVED IN TO "FINISH THE JOB." THE STRIKERS RETREATED, CARRYING THEIR DEAD AND INJURED. NO ONE KNOWS HOW MANY.

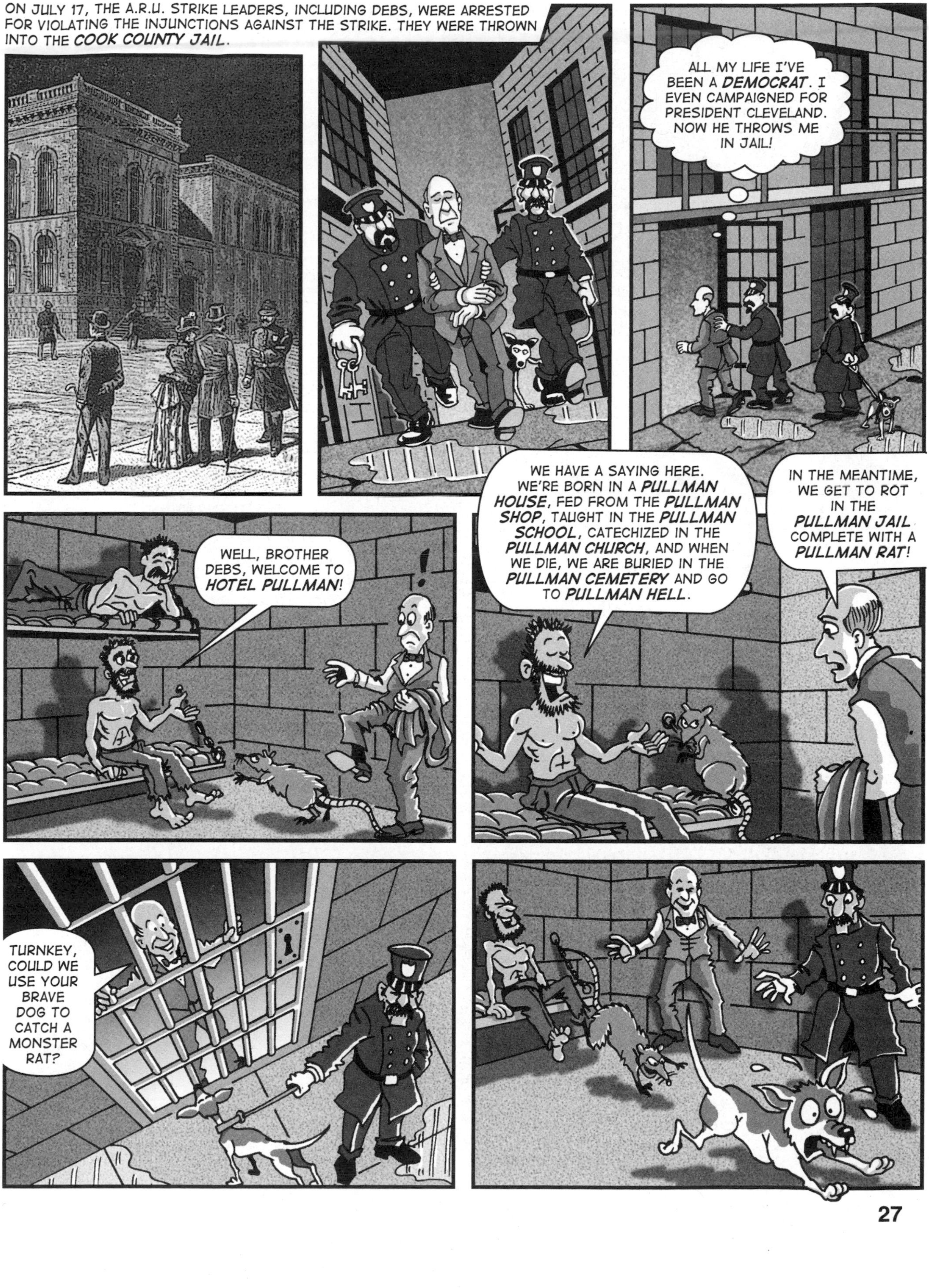
ON JULY 17, THE A.R.U. STRIKE LEADERS, INCLUDING DEBS, WERE ARRESTED FOR VIOLATING THE INJUNCTIONS AGAINST THE STRIKE. THEY WERE THROWN INTO THE COOK COUNTY JAIL.
ALL MY LIFE I'VE BEEN A DEMOCRAT. I EVEN CAMPAIGNED FOR PRESIDENT CLEVELAND. NOW HE THROWS ME IN JAIL!
WELL, BROTHER DEBS, WELCOME TO HOTEL PULLMAN!
WE HAVE A SAYING HERE. WE'RE BORN IN A PULLMAN HOUSE, FED FROM THE PULLMAN SHOP, TAUGHT IN THE PULLMAN SCHOOL, CATECHIZED IN THE PULLMAN CHURCH, AND WHEN WE DIE, WE ARE BURIED IN THE PULLMAN CEMETERY AND GO TO PULLMAN HELL.
IN THE MEANTIME, WE GET TO ROT IN THE PULLMAN JAIL COMPLETE WITH A PULLMAN RAT!
TURNKEY, COULD WE USE YOUR BRAVE DOG TO CATCH A MONSTER RAT?

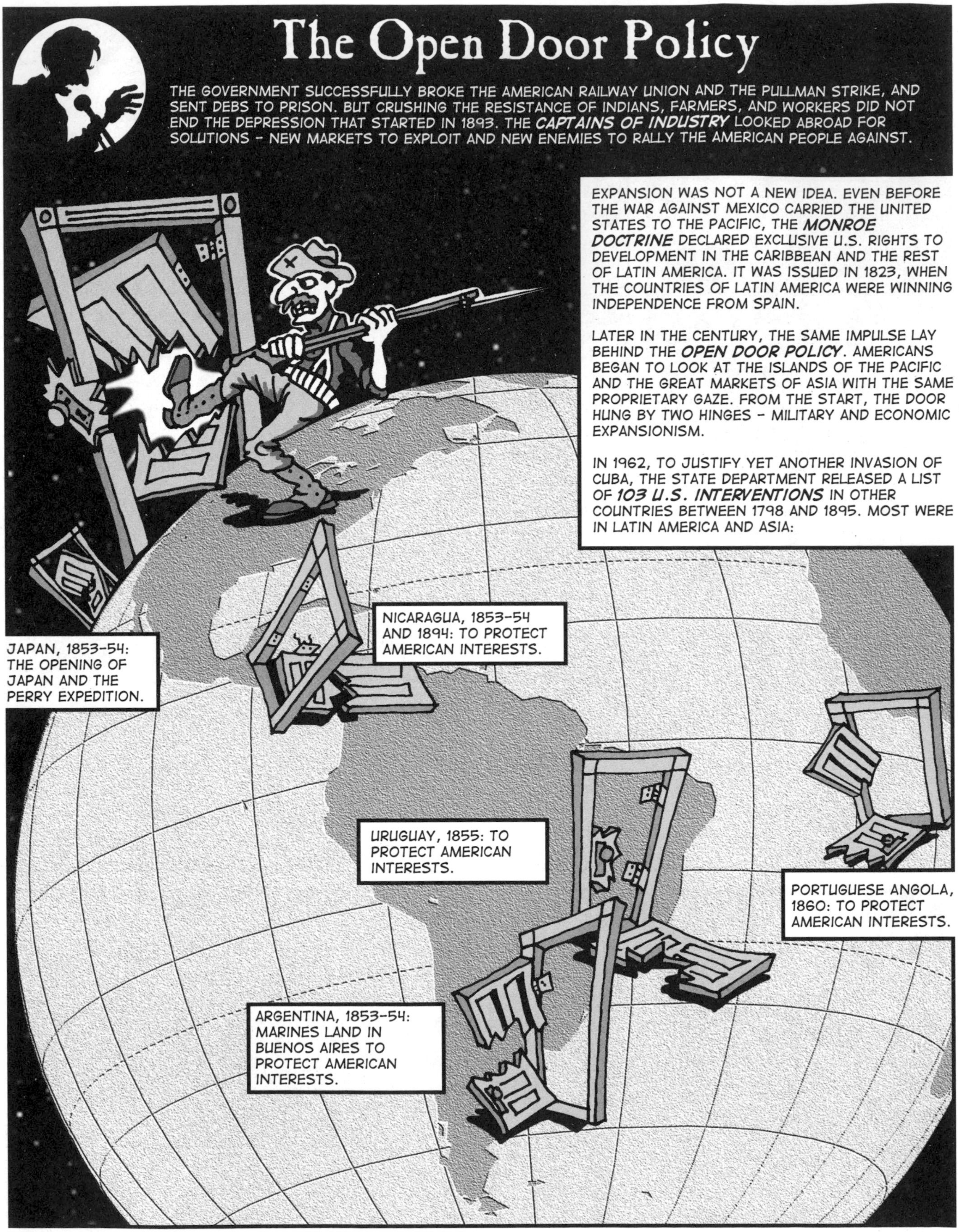
The Open Door Policy
THE GOVERNMENT SUCCESSFULLY BROKE THE AMERICAN RAILWAY UNION AND THE PULLMAN STRIKE, AND SENT DEBS TO PRISON. BUT CRUSHING THE RESISTANCE OF INDIANS, FARMERS, AND WORKERS DID NOT END THE DEPRESSION THAT STARTED IN 1893. THE CAPTAINS OF INDUSTRY LOOKED ABROAD FOR SOLUTIONS - NEW MARKETS TO EXPLOIT AND NEW ENEMIES TO RALLY THE AMERICAN PEOPLE AGAINST.
EXPANSION WAS NOT A NEW IDEA. EVEN BEFORE THE WAR AGAINST MEXICO CARRIED THE UNITED STATES TO THE PACIFIC, THE MONROE DOCTRINE DECLARED EXCLUSIVE U.S. RIGHTS TO DEVELOPMENT IN THE CARIBBEAN AND THE REST OF LATIN AMERICA. IT WAS ISSUED IN 1823, WHEN THE COUNTRIES OF LATIN AMERICA WERE WINNING INDEPENDENCE FROM SPAIN.
LATER IN THE CENTURY, THE SAME IMPULSE LAY BEHIND THE OPEN DOOR POLICY. AMERICANS BEGAN TO LOOK AT THE ISLANDS OF THE PACIFIC AND THE GREAT MARKETS OF ASIA WITH THE SAME PROPRIETARY GAZE. FROM THE START, THE DOOR HUNG BY TWO HINGES - MILITARY AND ECONOMIC EXPANSIONISM.
IN 1962, TO JUSTIFY YET ANOTHER INVASION OF CUBA, THE STATE DEPARTMENT RELEASED A LIST OF 103 U.S. INTERVENTIONS IN OTHER COUNTRIES BETWEEN 1798 AND 1895. MOST WERE IN LATIN AMERICA AND ASIA:
NICARAGUA, 1853-54 AND 1894: TO PROTECT AMERICAN INTERESTS.
JAPAN, 1853-54: THE OPENING OF JAPAN AND THE PERRY EXPEDITION.
URUGUAY, 1855: TO PROTECT AMERICAN INTERESTS.
PORTUGUESE ANGOLA, 1860: TO PROTECT AMERICAN INTERESTS.
ARGENTINA, 1853-54: MARINES LAND IN BUENOS AIRES TO PROTECT AMERICAN INTERESTS.

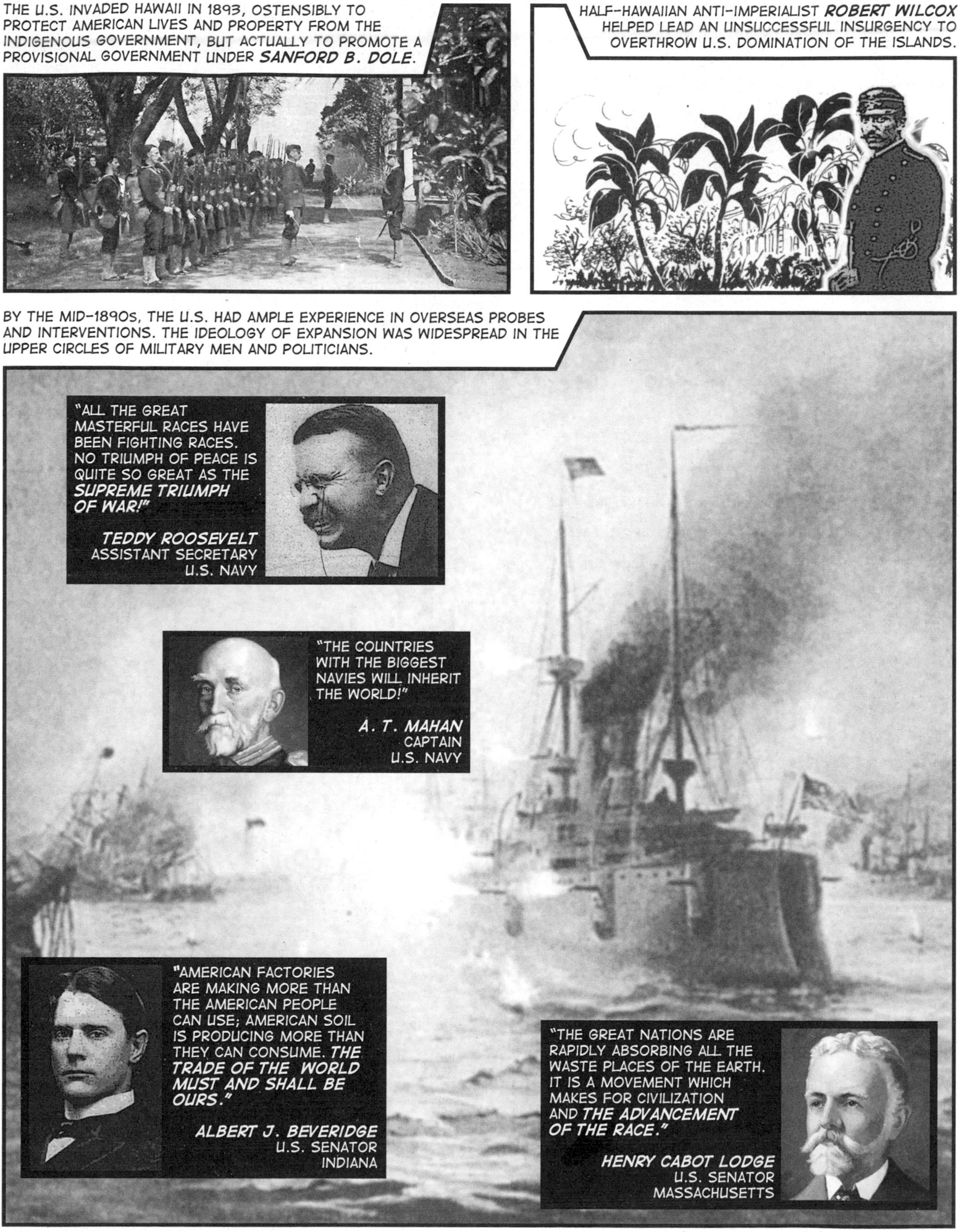
THE U.S. INVADED HAWAII IN 1893, OSTENSIBLY TO PROTECT AMERICAN LIVES AND PROPERTY FROM THE INDIGENOUS GOVERNMENT, BUT ACTUALLY TO PROMOTE A PROVISIONAL GOVERNMENT UNDER SANFORD B. DOLE.
HALF-HAWAIIAN ANTI-IMPERIALIST ROBERT WILCOX HELPED LEAD AN UNSUCCESSFUL INSURGENCY TO OVERTHROW U.S. DOMINATION OF THE ISLANDS.
BY THE MID-1890S, THE U.S. HAD AMPLE EXPERIENCE IN OVERSEAS PROBES AND INTERVENTIONS. THE IDEOLOGY OF EXPANSION WAS WIDESPREAD IN THE UPPER CIRCLES OF MILITARY MEN AND POLITICIANS.
"ALL THE GREAT MASTERFUL RACES HAVE BEEN FIGHTING RACES. NO TRIUMPH OF PEACE IS QUITE SO GREAT AS THE SUPREME TRIUMPH OF WAR!"
TEDDY ROOSEVELT
ASSISTANT SECRETARY
U.S. NAVY
"THE COUNTRIES WITH THE BIGGEST NAVIES WILL INHERIT THE WORLD!"
A. T. MAHAN
CAPTAIN
U.S. NAVY
"AMERICAN FACTORIES ARE MAKING MORE THAN THE AMERICAN PEOPLE CAN USE; AMERICAN SOIL IS PRODUCING MORE THAN THEY CAN CONSUME. THE TRADE OF THE WORLD MUST AND SHALL BE OURS."
ALBERT J. BEVERIDGE
U.S. SENATOR
INDIANA
"THE GREAT NATIONS ARE RAPIDLY ABSORBING ALL THE WASTE PLACES OF THE EARTH. IT IS A MOVEMENT WHICH MAKES FOR CIVILIZATION AND THE ADVANCEMENT OF THE RACE."
HENRY CABOT LODGE
U.S. SENATOR
MASSACHUSETTS

WOULD NOT A FOREIGN ADVENTURE DEFLECT SOME OF THE REBELLIOUS ENERGY FROM STRIKES AND PROTEST MOVEMENTS TOWARD AN EXTERNAL ENEMY? WOULD IT NOT UNITE THE PEOPLE WITH GOVERNMENT?

PATRIOTISM WAS A WAY OF DROWNING CLASS RESENTMENT. AFTER HIS ELECTION IN 1896, PRESIDENT ***WILLIAM McKINLEY*** MADE THE CONNECTION BETWEEN MONEY AND FLAG:

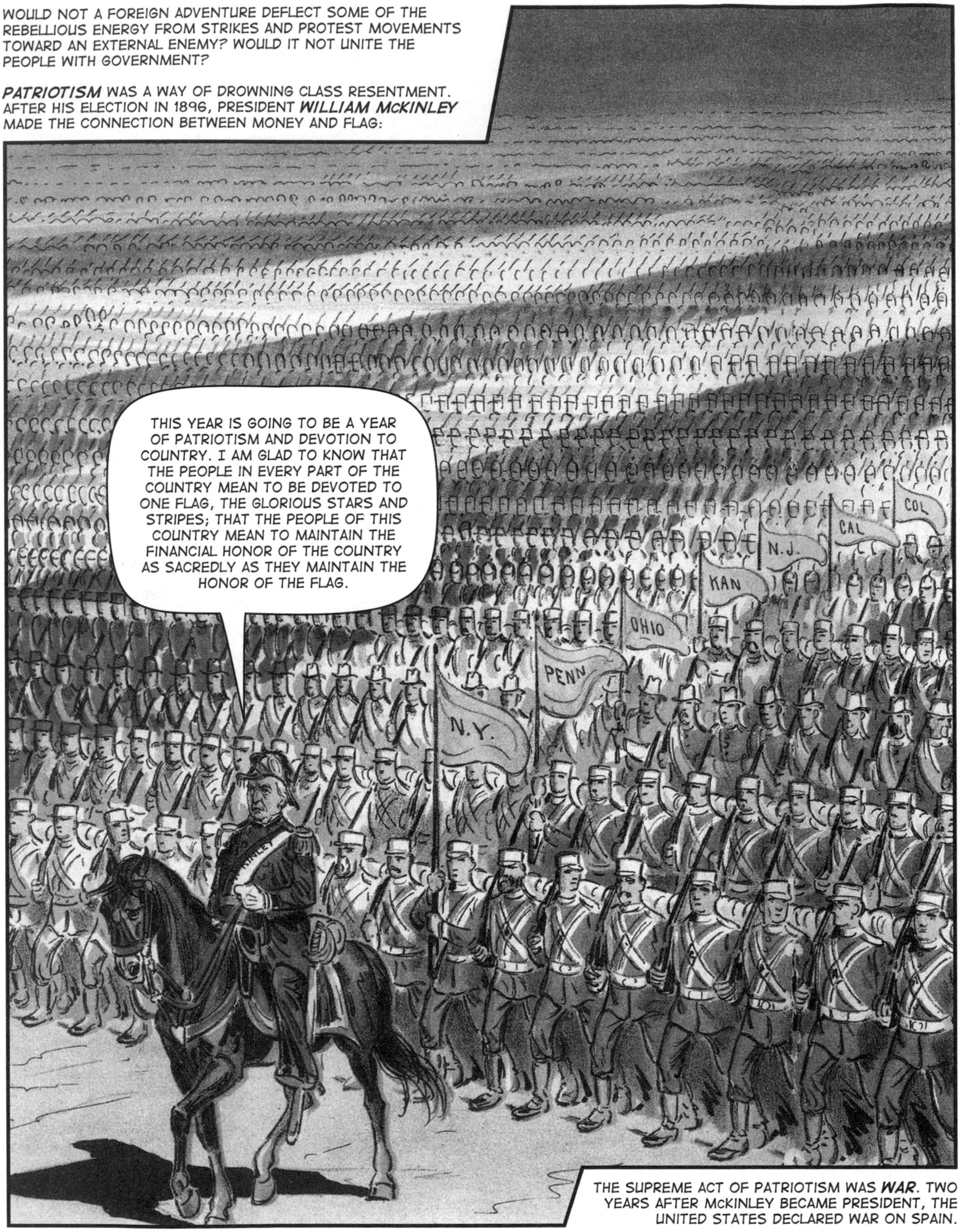

THIS YEAR IS GOING TO BE A YEAR OF PATRIOTISM AND DEVOTION TO COUNTRY. I AM GLAD TO KNOW THAT THE PEOPLE IN EVERY PART OF THE COUNTRY MEAN TO BE DEVOTED TO ONE FLAG, THE GLORIOUS STARS AND STRIPES; THAT THE PEOPLE OF THIS COUNTRY MEAN TO MAINTAIN THE FINANCIAL HONOR OF THE COUNTRY AS SACREDLY AS THEY MAINTAIN THE HONOR OF THE FLAG.
COL
CAL
N.J
KAN
OHIO
PENN
N.Y.

THE SUPREME ACT OF PATRIOTISM WAS ***WAR***. TWO YEARS AFTER McKINLEY BECAME PRESIDENT, THE UNITED STATES DECLARED WAR ON SPAIN.

Chapter II
THE SPANISH-AMERICAN WAR

"Both McKinley and the business community began to see that getting Spain out of Cuba could not be accomplished without war."

Antonio Maceo and the Cuban Revolution

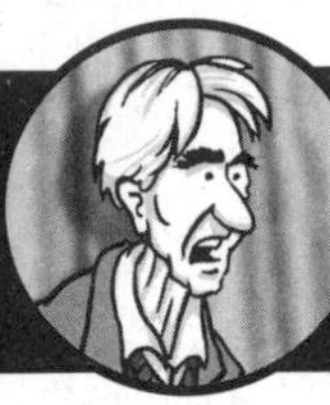

IN THE LATE 1890s, CUBA WAS A HOTBED OF REBELLION, AS POOR BLACK PEASANTS JOINED WEALTHY NATIVE-BORN WHITES TO LIBERATE THE CARIBBEAN ISLAND FROM THE GRIP OF FOUR CENTURIES OF SPANISH OCCUPATION. IT WAS AN UNEASY ALLIANCE. FREED FROM THE SHACKLES OF SLAVERY BUT NOT RACISM OR EXPLOITATION, BLACKS SAW A FREE CUBA, ***CUBA LIBRE***, AS THEIR PATH TO EQUALITY. REVOLUTIONARY WHITES FEARED A TAKEOVER BY THE BLACK MAJORITY BUT KNEW THAT INDEPENDENCE COULD NOT BE WON WITHOUT THEM.

REVOLTS HAD SPRUNG UP IN THE PAST, MOST NOTABLY THE ***TEN YEARS' WAR***, WHICH ERUPTED IN 1868 WHEN ***CARLOS MANUEL DE CESPESDES***, BACKED BY OTHER WHITE FARMERS IN ORIENTE PROVINCE, FREED HIS SLAVES AND ANNOUNCED THE ***GRITO DE YARA***,* DECLARING CUBA'S INDEPENDENCE.

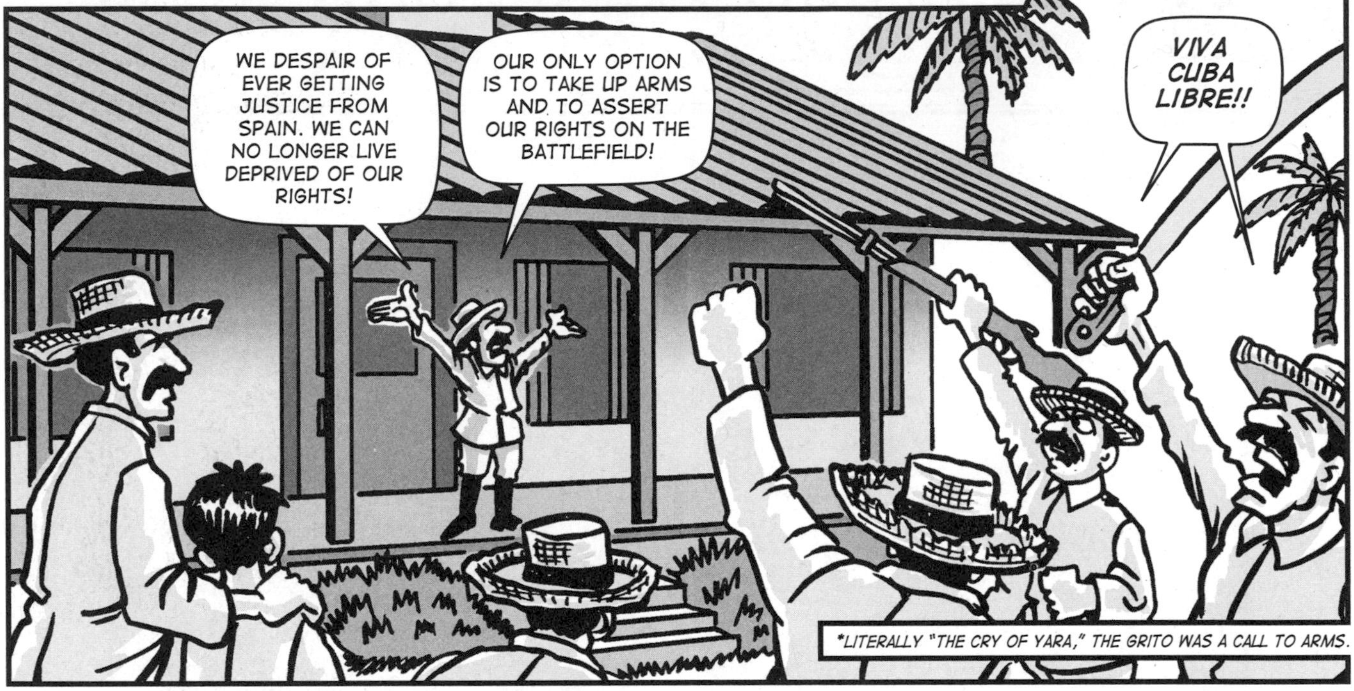
WE DESPAIR OF EVER GETTING JUSTICE FROM SPAIN. WE CAN NO LONGER LIVE DEPRIVED OF OUR RIGHTS!
OUR ONLY OPTION IS TO TAKE UP ARMS AND TO ASSERT OUR RIGHTS ON THE BATTLEFIELD!
VIVA CUBA LIBRE!!

**LITERALLY "THE CRY OF YARA," THE GRITO WAS A CALL TO ARMS.*

THE WAR ENDED WITH AN 1878 CEASE-FIRE. SPAIN RETAINED CONTROL OF CUBA. THOUGH SLAVERY WAS OFFICIALLY ABOLISHED IN 1886, LITTLE CHANGED FOR BLACKS.

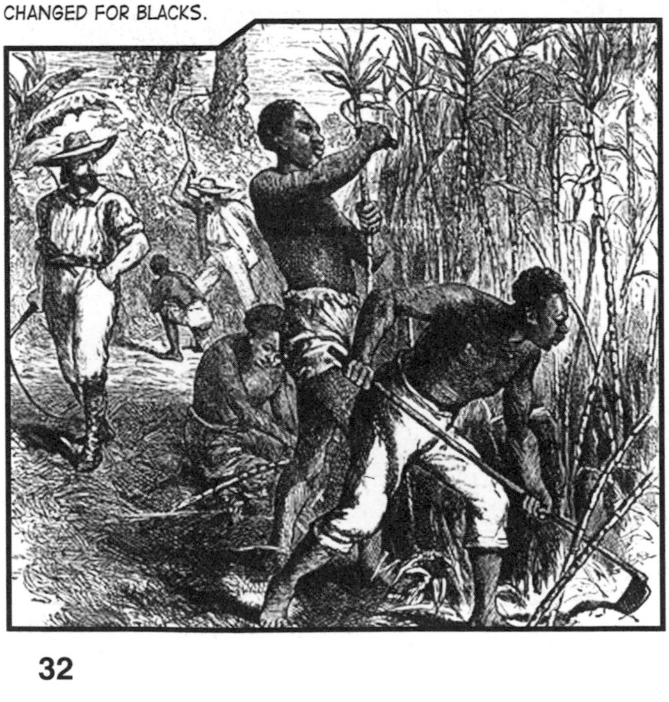

THE LIBERATION MOVEMENT CONTINUED TO FESTER ON THE HOME FRONT, WHILE EXILED LEADERS OF THE TEN YEARS' WAR LAID PLANS FOR THE NEXT WAR OF INDEPENDENCE. AMONG THEM WAS ***ANTONIO MACEO GRAJALES***, THE LEGENDARY BLACK GENERAL WHOSE EXPLOITS WOULD EARN HIM THE TITLE ***BRONZE TITAN***.

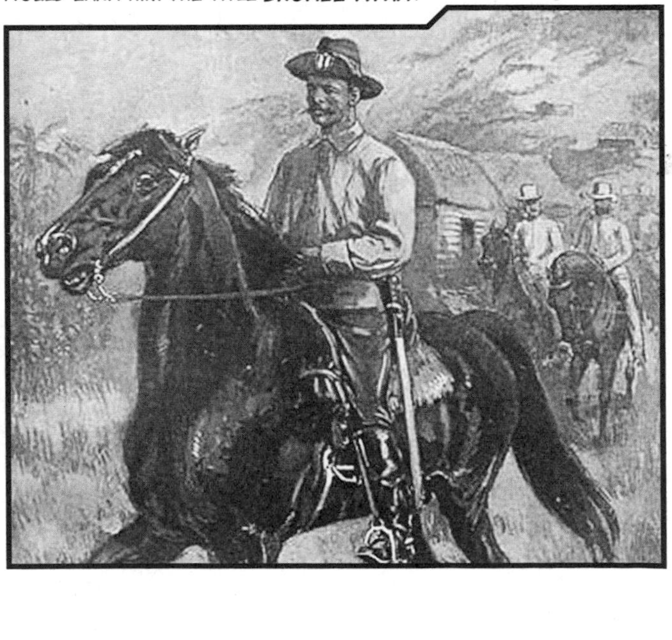

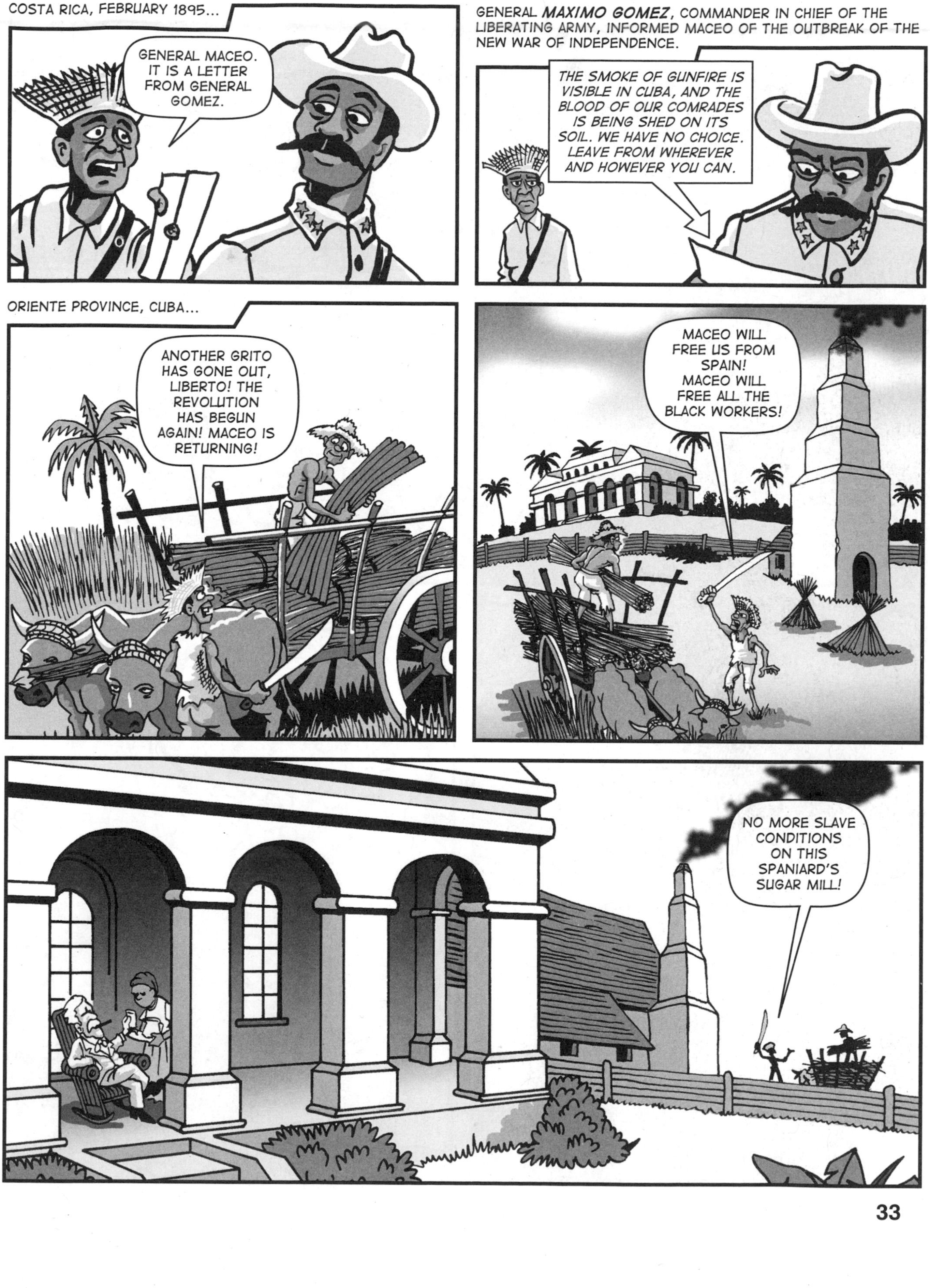
COSTA RICA, FEBRUARY 1895...
GENERAL MACEO. IT IS A LETTER FROM GENERAL GOMEZ.
GENERAL MAXIMO GOMEZ, COMMANDER IN CHIEF OF THE LIBERATING ARMY, INFORMED MACEO OF THE OUTBREAK OF THE NEW WAR OF INDEPENDENCE.
THE SMOKE OF GUNFIRE IS VISIBLE IN CUBA, AND THE BLOOD OF OUR COMRADES IS BEING SHED ON ITS SOIL. WE HAVE NO CHOICE. LEAVE FROM WHEREVER AND HOWEVER YOU CAN.
ORIENTE PROVINCE, CUBA...
ANOTHER GRITO HAS GONE OUT, LIBERTO! THE REVOLUTION HAS BEGUN AGAIN! MACEO IS RETURNING!
MACEO WILL FREE US FROM SPAIN! MACEO WILL FREE ALL THE BLACK WORKERS!
NO MORE SLAVE CONDITIONS ON THIS SPANIARD'S SUGAR MILL!

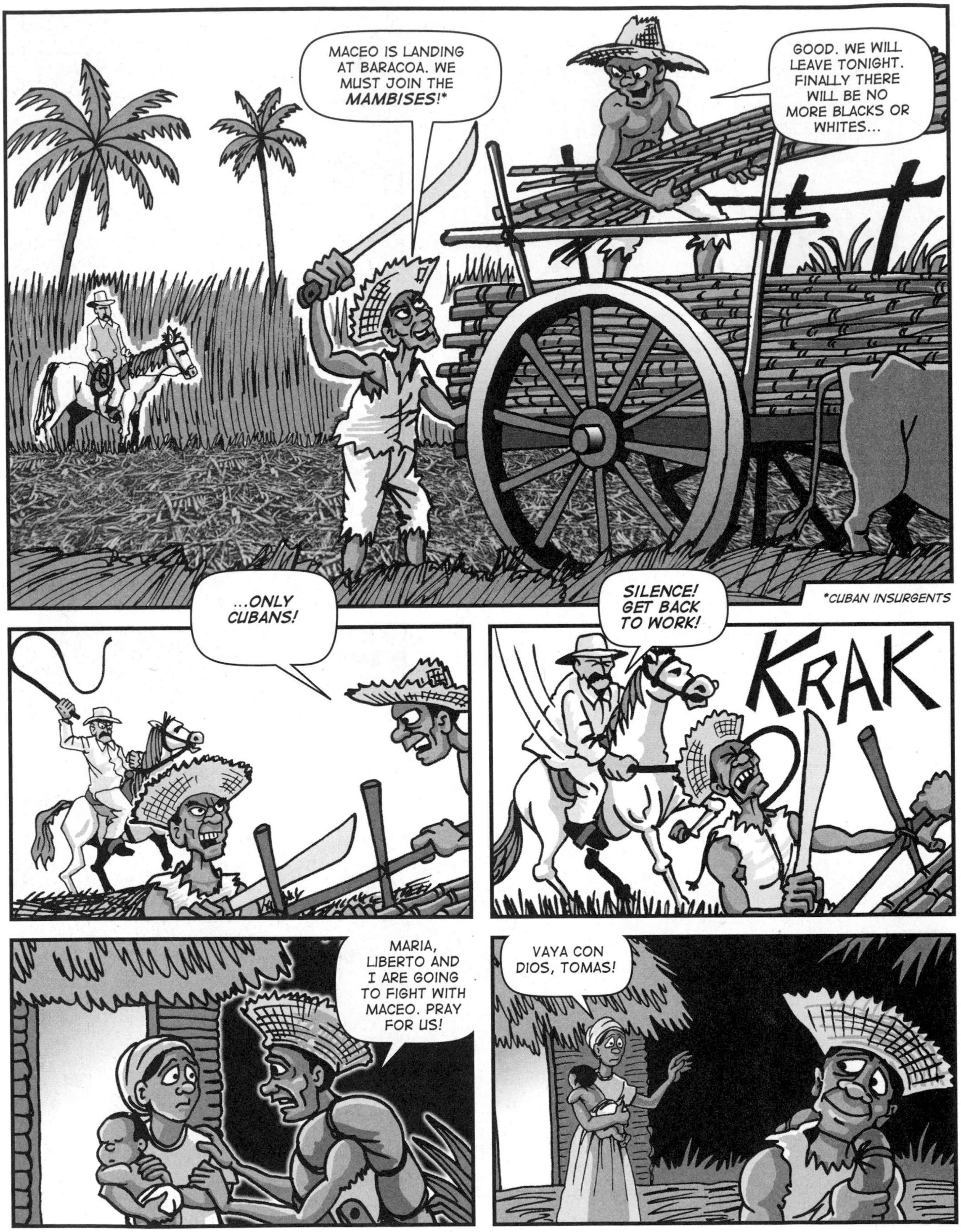
MACEO IS LANDING AT BARACOA. WE MUST JOIN THE MAMBISES!*
GOOD. WE WILL LEAVE TONIGHT. FINALLY THERE WILL BE NO MORE BLACKS OR WHITES...
*CUBAN INSURGENTS
...ONLY CUBANS!
SILENCE! GET BACK TO WORK!
KRAK
MARIA, LIBERTO AND I ARE GOING TO FIGHT WITH MACEO. PRAY FOR US!
VAYA CON DIOS, TOMAS!

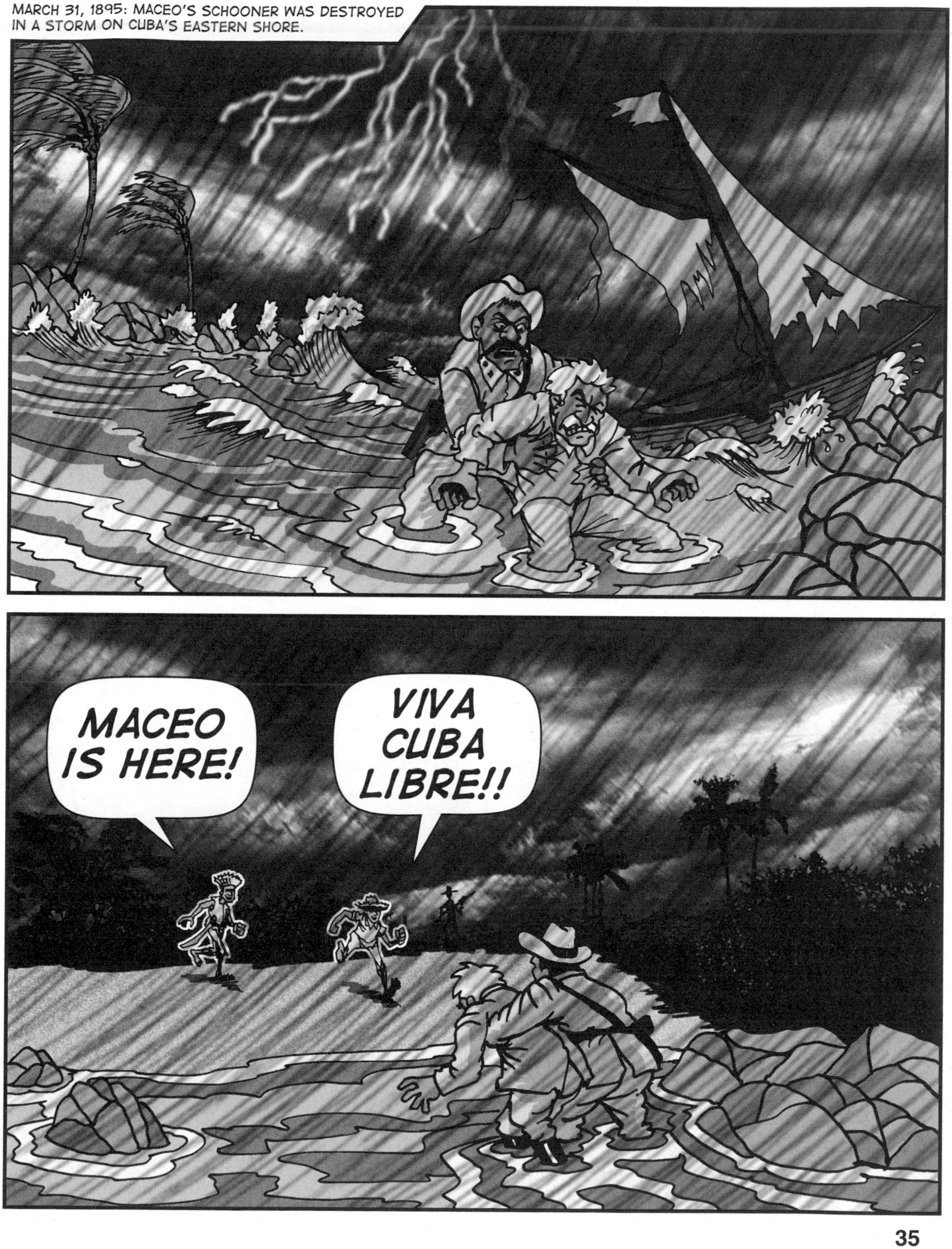
MARCH 31, 1895: MACEO'S SCHOONER WAS DESTROYED IN A STORM ON CUBA'S EASTERN SHORE.
MACEO IS HERE!
VIVA CUBA LIBRE!!

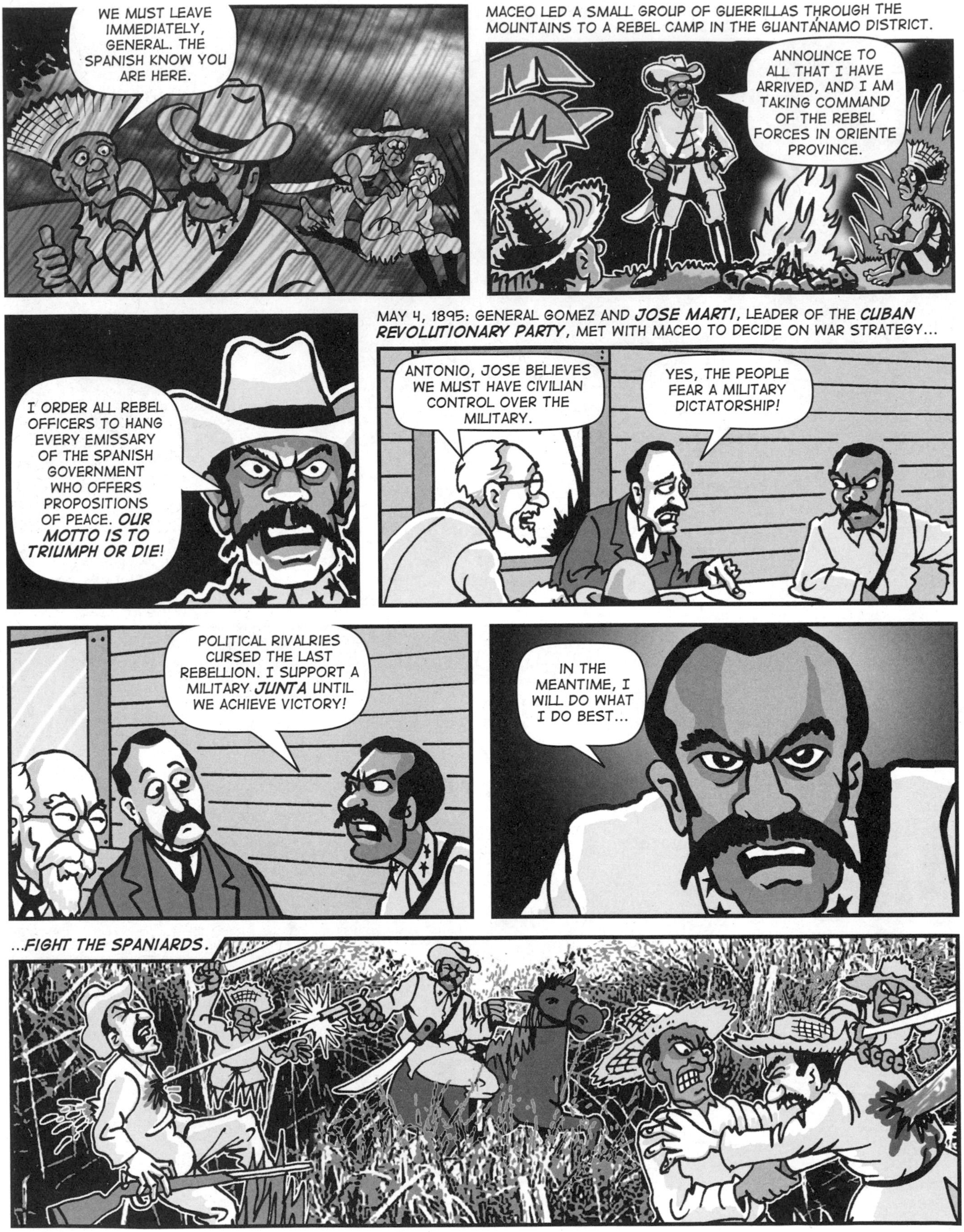
WE MUST LEAVE IMMEDIATELY, GENERAL. THE SPANISH KNOW YOU ARE HERE.
MACEO LED A SMALL GROUP OF GUERRILLAS THROUGH THE MOUNTAINS TO A REBEL CAMP IN THE GUANTÁNAMO DISTRICT.
ANNOUNCE TO ALL THAT I HAVE ARRIVED, AND I AM TAKING COMMAND OF THE REBEL FORCES IN ORIENTE PROVINCE.
I ORDER ALL REBEL OFFICERS TO HANG EVERY EMISSARY OF THE SPANISH GOVERNMENT WHO OFFERS PROPOSITIONS OF PEACE. ***OUR MOTTO IS TO TRIUMPH OR DIE***!
MAY 4, 1895: GENERAL GOMEZ AND ***JOSE MARTI***, LEADER OF THE ***CUBAN REVOLUTIONARY PARTY***, MET WITH MACEO TO DECIDE ON WAR STRATEGY...
ANTONIO, JOSE BELIEVES WE MUST HAVE CIVILIAN CONTROL OVER THE MILITARY.
YES, THE PEOPLE FEAR A MILITARY DICTATORSHIP!
POLITICAL RIVALRIES CURSED THE LAST REBELLION. I SUPPORT A MILITARY ***JUNTA*** UNTIL WE ACHIEVE VICTORY!
IN THE MEANTIME, I WILL DO WHAT I DO BEST...
...***FIGHT THE SPANIARDS***.

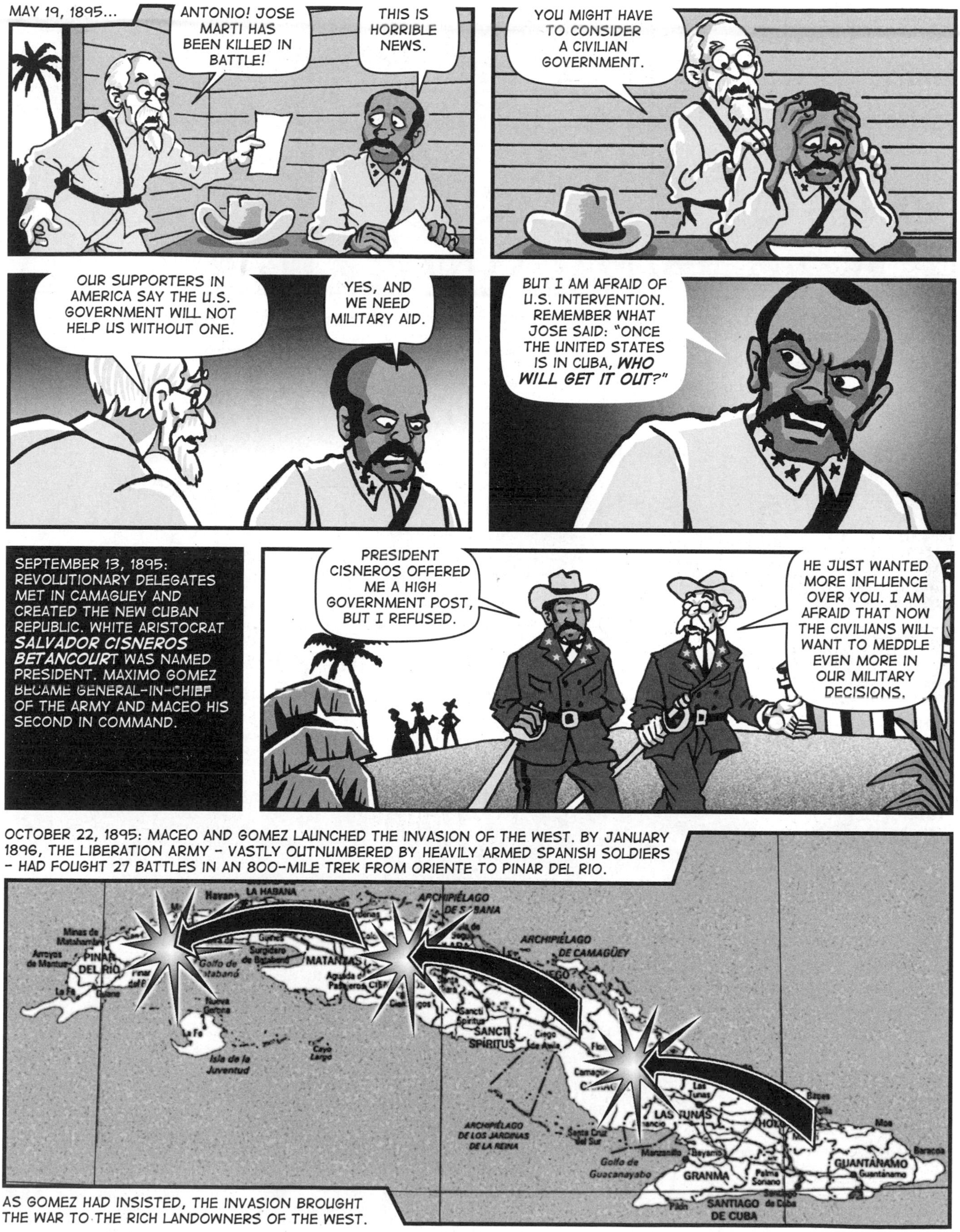

MAY 19, 1895...
ANTONIO! JOSE MARTI HAS BEEN KILLED IN BATTLE!
THIS IS HORRIBLE NEWS.
YOU MIGHT HAVE TO CONSIDER A CIVILIAN GOVERNMENT.
OUR SUPPORTERS IN AMERICA SAY THE U.S. GOVERNMENT WILL NOT HELP US WITHOUT ONE.
YES, AND WE NEED MILITARY AID.
BUT I AM AFRAID OF U.S. INTERVENTION. REMEMBER WHAT JOSE SAID: "ONCE THE UNITED STATES IS IN CUBA, *WHO WILL GET IT OUT?*"
SEPTEMBER 13, 1895: REVOLUTIONARY DELEGATES MET IN CAMAGUEY AND CREATED THE NEW CUBAN REPUBLIC. WHITE ARISTOCRAT ***SALVADOR CISNEROS BETANCOURT*** WAS NAMED PRESIDENT. MAXIMO GOMEZ BECAME GENERAL-IN-CHIEF OF THE ARMY AND MACEO HIS SECOND IN COMMAND.
PRESIDENT CISNEROS OFFERED ME A HIGH GOVERNMENT POST, BUT I REFUSED.
HE JUST WANTED MORE INFLUENCE OVER YOU. I AM AFRAID THAT NOW THE CIVILIANS WILL WANT TO MEDDLE EVEN MORE IN OUR MILITARY DECISIONS.
OCTOBER 22, 1895: MACEO AND GOMEZ LAUNCHED THE INVASION OF THE WEST. BY JANUARY 1896, THE LIBERATION ARMY – VASTLY OUTNUMBERED BY HEAVILY ARMED SPANISH SOLDIERS – HAD FOUGHT 27 BATTLES IN AN 800-MILE TREK FROM ORIENTE TO PINAR DEL RIO.
LA HABANA
ARCHIPIÉLAGO DE CAMAGÜEY
PINAR DEL RIO
MATANZAS
Isla de la Juventud
SANCTI SPIRITUS
LAS TUNAS
ARCHIPIÉLAGO DE LOS JARDINES DE LA REINA
Golfo de Guacanayabo
GRANMA
GUANTÁNAMO
SANTIAGO DE CUBA
AS GOMEZ HAD INSISTED, THE INVASION BROUGHT THE WAR TO THE RICH LANDOWNERS OF THE WEST.

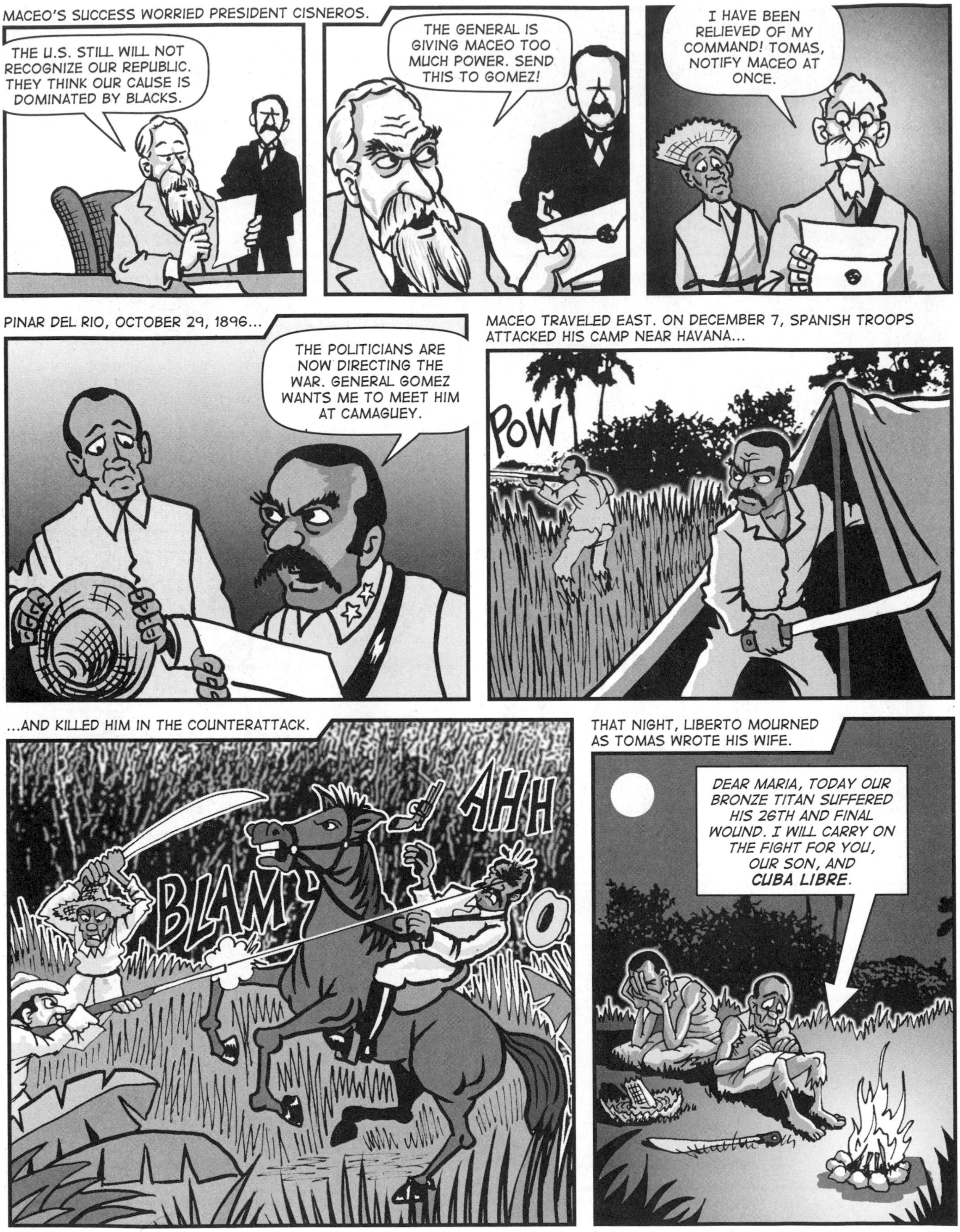
MACEO'S SUCCESS WORRIED PRESIDENT CISNEROS.
THE U.S. STILL WILL NOT RECOGNIZE OUR REPUBLIC. THEY THINK OUR CAUSE IS DOMINATED BY BLACKS.
THE GENERAL IS GIVING MACEO TOO MUCH POWER. SEND THIS TO GOMEZ!
I HAVE BEEN RELIEVED OF MY COMMAND! TOMAS, NOTIFY MACEO AT ONCE.
PINAR DEL RIO, OCTOBER 29, 1896...
THE POLITICIANS ARE NOW DIRECTING THE WAR. GENERAL GOMEZ WANTS ME TO MEET HIM AT CAMAGUEY.
MACEO TRAVELED EAST. ON DECEMBER 7, SPANISH TROOPS ATTACKED HIS CAMP NEAR HAVANA...
POW
...AND KILLED HIM IN THE COUNTERATTACK.
AHH
BLAM
THAT NIGHT, LIBERTO MOURNED AS TOMAS WROTE HIS WIFE.
DEAR MARIA, TODAY OUR BRONZE TITAN SUFFERED HIS 26TH AND FINAL WOUND. I WILL CARRY ON THE FIGHT FOR YOU, OUR SON, AND CUBA LIBRE.

The Drumbeat for War

IN THE U.S., PUBLIC SUPPORT FOR ***CUBA LIBRE*** WAS GROWING. THE DEMOCRATIC AND REPUBLICAN PARTIES DECLARED THEIR SUPPORT, BUT PRESIDENT ***GROVER CLEVELAND*** REFUSED TO AID THE REBELS.

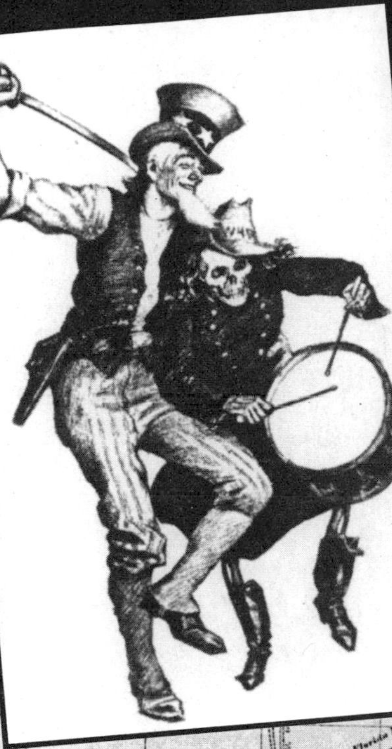

WHEN ***WILLIAM MCKINLEY*** SUCCEEDED CLEVELAND, HE ALSO REFUSED TO OFFICIALLY RECOGNIZE THE INSURGENTS. LEGAL RECOGNITION WOULD HAVE ALLOWED THE U.S. TO GIVE THE REBELS AID WITHOUT SENDING IN AN ARMY. BUT HE FEARED IF THE REBELS WON THEY WOULD KEEP THE UNITED STATES OUT.

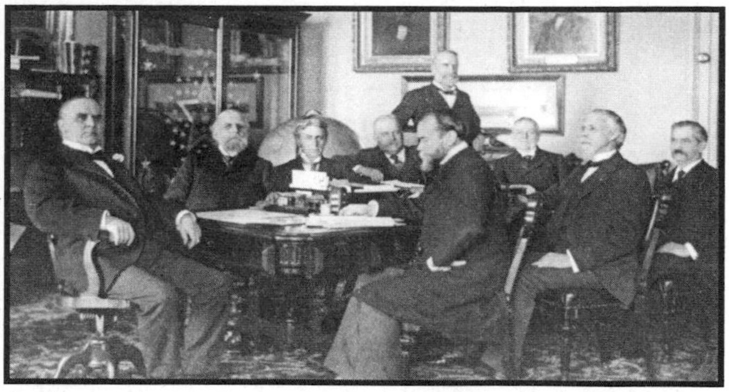

A YOUNG BRITISH OFFICER WROTE THAT SPANISH CRUELTY WAS LESS IMPORTANT THAN ***ANGLO-SAXON INTERESTS,*** WHICH REQUIRED THAT SPAIN KEEP CONTROL OF CUBA:

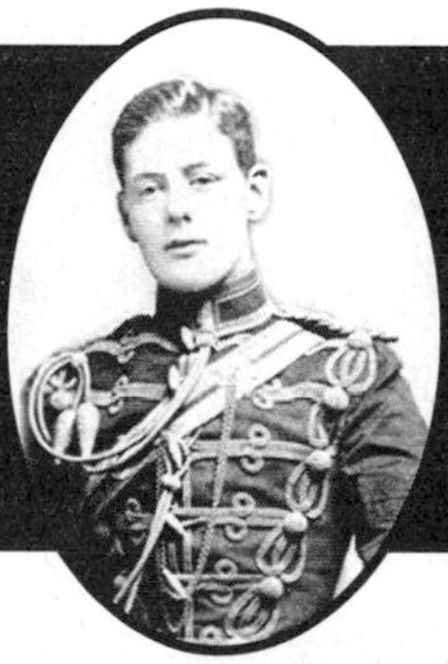

"TWO-FIFTHS OF THE INSURGENTS ARE NEGROES. THESE MEN WOULD, IN THE EVENT OF SUCCESS, DEMAND A PREDOMINANT SHARE IN THE GOVERNMENT OF THE COUNTRY, THE RESULT BEING ***ANOTHER BLACK REPUBLIC.***"

WINSTON CHURCHILL

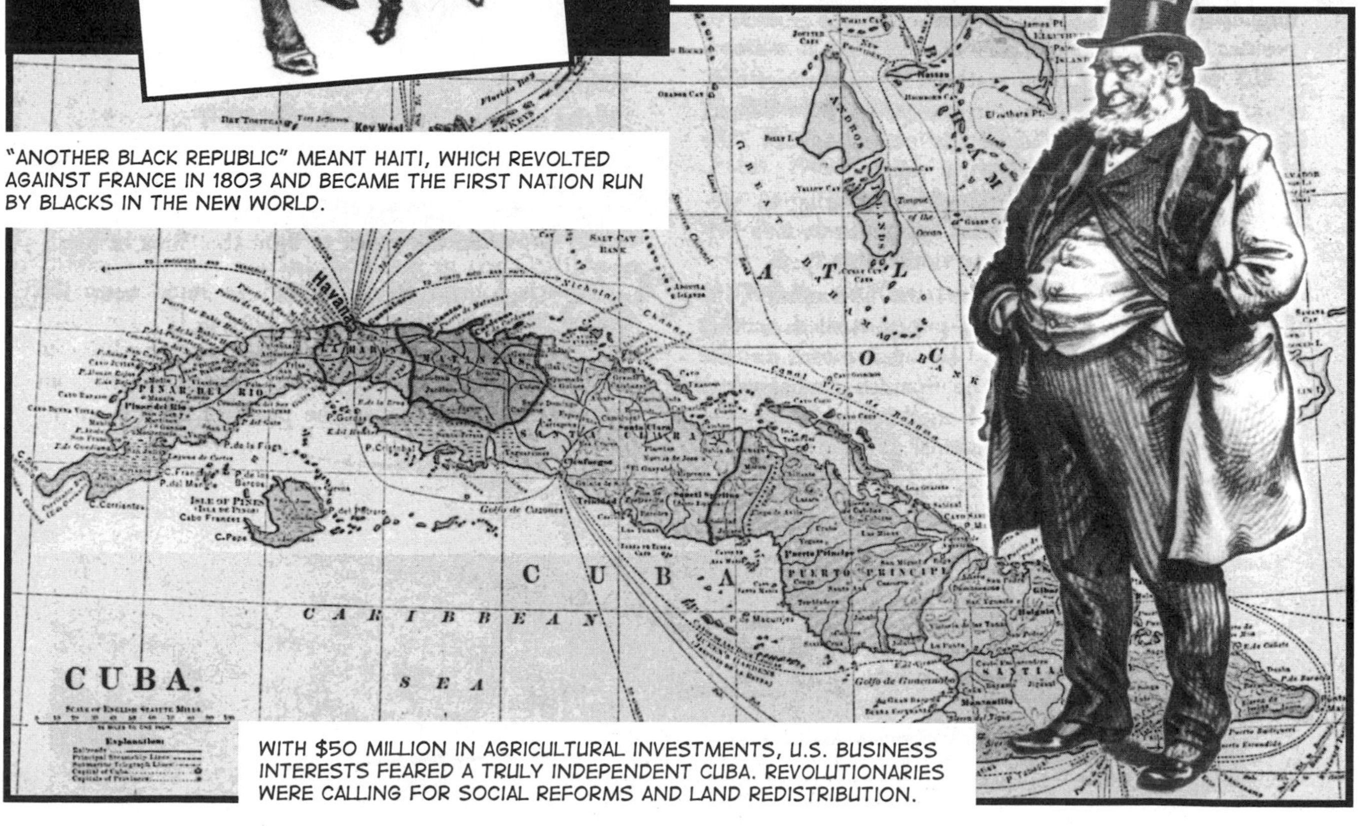
CUBA.
Havana
C U B A
C A R I B B E A N
S E A

"ANOTHER BLACK REPUBLIC" MEANT HAITI, WHICH REVOLTED AGAINST FRANCE IN 1803 AND BECAME THE FIRST NATION RUN BY BLACKS IN THE NEW WORLD.

WITH $50 MILLION IN AGRICULTURAL INVESTMENTS, U.S. BUSINESS INTERESTS FEARED A TRULY INDEPENDENT CUBA. REVOLUTIONARIES WERE CALLING FOR SOCIAL REFORMS AND LAND REDISTRIBUTION.

IN 1897, NEW YORK MEDIA MOGUL ***WILLIAM RANDOLPH HEARST*** BEGAN TO AGITATE FOR INTERVENTION IN CUBA. HE SENT CELEBRITY JOURNALIST ***RICHARD HARDING DAVIS*** AND NOTED ARTIST ***FREDERIC REMINGTON*** TO COVER THE REBELS. THEY DIDN'T STAY LONG, BUT NONETHELESS CHURNED OUT COPY FOR HEARST'S NEWSPAPER, THE ***NEW YORK JOURNAL***.

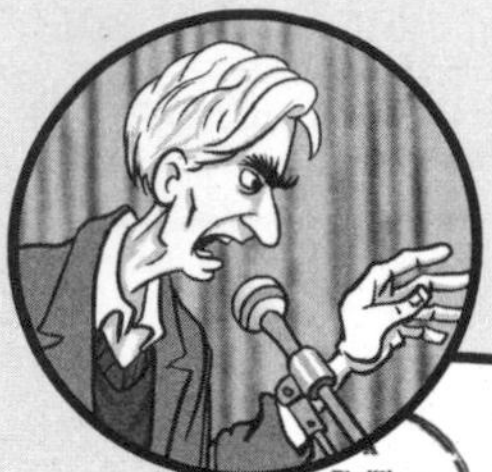

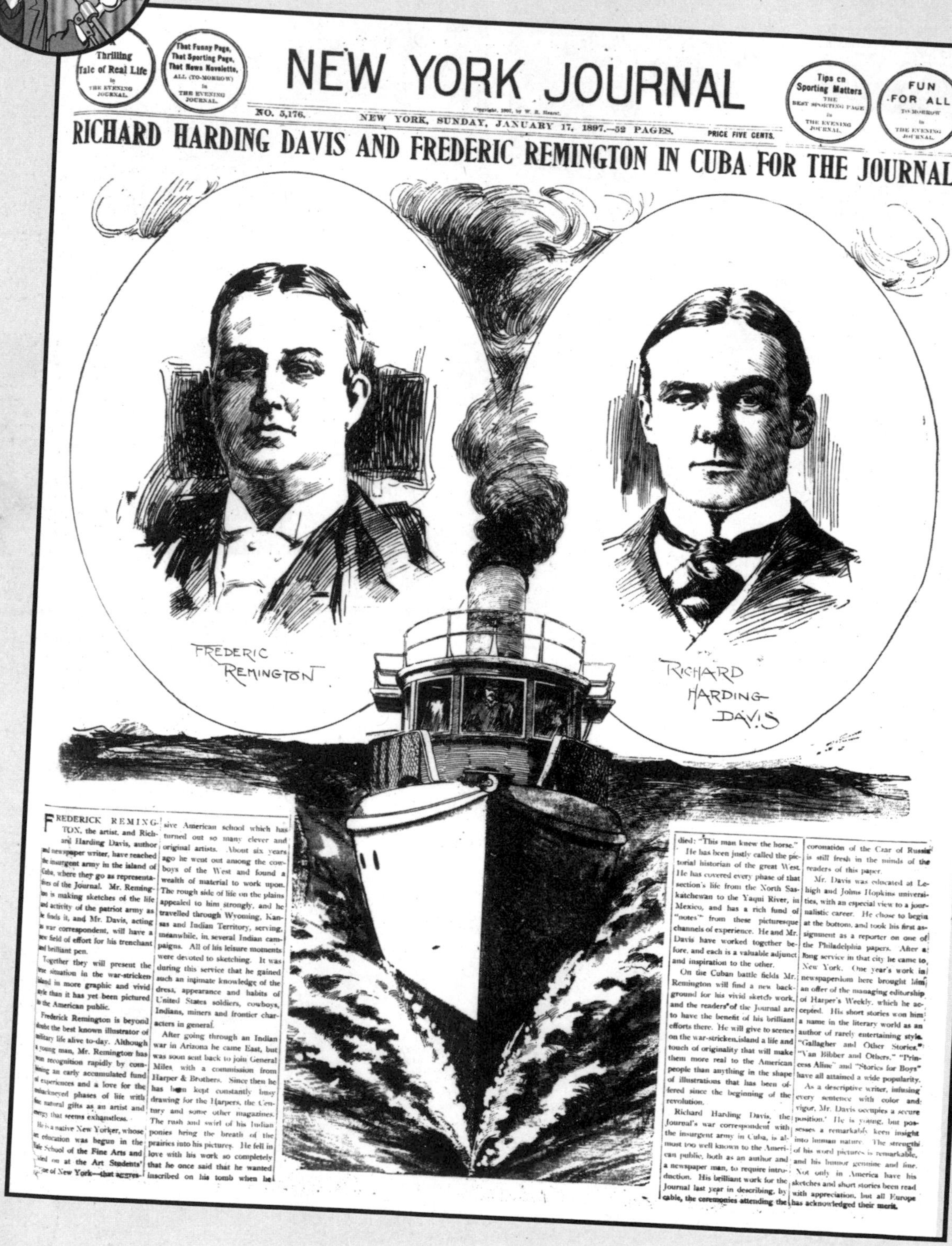

A Thrilling Tale of Real Life in THE EVENING JOURNAL.

That Funny Page, That Sporting Page, That News Novelette, ALL (TO-MORROW) in THE EVENING JOURNAL.

NEW YORK JOURNAL

Tips on Sporting Matters THE BEST SPORTING PAGE in THE EVENING JOURNAL.

FUN FOR ALL TO-MORROW in THE EVENING JOURNAL.

Copyright, 1897, by W. R. Hearst.

NO. 5,176. NEW YORK, SUNDAY, JANUARY 17, 1897.—52 PAGES. PRICE FIVE CENTS.

RICHARD HARDING DAVIS AND FREDERIC REMINGTON IN CUBA FOR THE JOURNAL.

FREDERIC REMINGTON

RICHARD HARDING DAVIS

FREDERICK REMINGTON, the artist, and Richard Harding Davis, author and newspaper writer, have reached the insurgent army in the island of Cuba, where they go as representatives of the Journal. Mr. Remington is making sketches of the life and activity of the patriot army as he finds it, and Mr. Davis, acting as war correspondent, will have a new field of effort for his trenchant and brilliant pen.

Together they will present the true situation in the war-stricken island in more graphic and vivid style than it has yet been pictured to the American public.

Frederick Remington is beyond doubt the best known illustrator of military life alive to-day. Although a young man, Mr. Remington has won recognition rapidly by combining an early accumulated fund of experiences and a love for the unhackneyed phases of life with fine natural gifts as an artist and energy that seems exhaustless.

He is a native New Yorker, whose art education was begun in the Yale School of the Fine Arts and carried on at the Art Students' League of New York—that aggressive American school which has turned out so many clever and original artists. About six years ago he went out among the cowboys of the West and found a wealth of material to work upon. The rough side of life on the plains appealed to him strongly, and he travelled through Wyoming, Kansas and Indian Territory, serving, meanwhile, in several Indian campaigns. All of his leisure moments were devoted to sketching. It was during this service that he gained such an intimate knowledge of the dress, appearance and habits of United States soldiers, cowboys, Indians, miners and frontier characters in general.

After going through an Indian war in Arizona he came East, but was soon sent back to join General Miles with a commission from Harper & Brothers. Since then he has been kept constantly busy drawing for the Harpers, the Century and some other magazines. The rush and swirl of his Indian ponies bring the breath of the prairies into his pictures. He fell in love with his work so completely that he once said that he wanted inscribed on his tomb when he died: "This man knew the horse."

He has been justly called the pictorial historian of the great West. He has covered every phase of that section's life from the North Saskatchewan to the Yaqui River, in Mexico, and has a rich fund of "notes" from these picturesque channels of experience. He and Mr. Davis have worked together before, and each is a valuable adjunct and inspiration to the other.

On the Cuban battle fields Mr. Remington will find a new background for his vivid sketch work, and the readers of the Journal are to have the benefit of his brilliant efforts there. He will give to scenes on the war-stricken island a life and touch of originality that will make them more real to the American people than anything in the shape of illustrations that has been offered since the beginning of the revolution.

Richard Harding Davis, the Journal's war correspondent with the insurgent army in Cuba, is almost too well known to the American public, both as an author and a newspaper man, to require introduction. His brilliant work for the Journal last year in describing, by cable, the ceremonies attending the coronation of the Czar of Russia is still fresh in the minds of the readers of this paper.

Mr. Davis was educated at Lehigh and Johns Hopkins universities, with an especial view to a journalistic career. He chose to begin at the bottom, and took his first assignment as a reporter on one of the Philadelphia papers. After a long service in that city he came to New York. One year's work in newspaperdom here brought him an offer of the managing editorship of Harper's Weekly, which he accepted. His short stories won him a name in the literary world as an author of rarely entertaining style. "Gallagher and Other Stories," "Van Bibber and Others," "Princess Aline" and "Stories for Boys" have all attained a wide popularity.

As a descriptive writer, infusing every sentence with color and vigor, Mr. Davis occupies a secure position. He is young, but possesses a remarkably keen insight into human nature. The strength of his word pictures is remarkable, and his humor genuine and fine. Not only in America have his sketches and short stories been read with appreciation, but all Europe has acknowledged their merit.

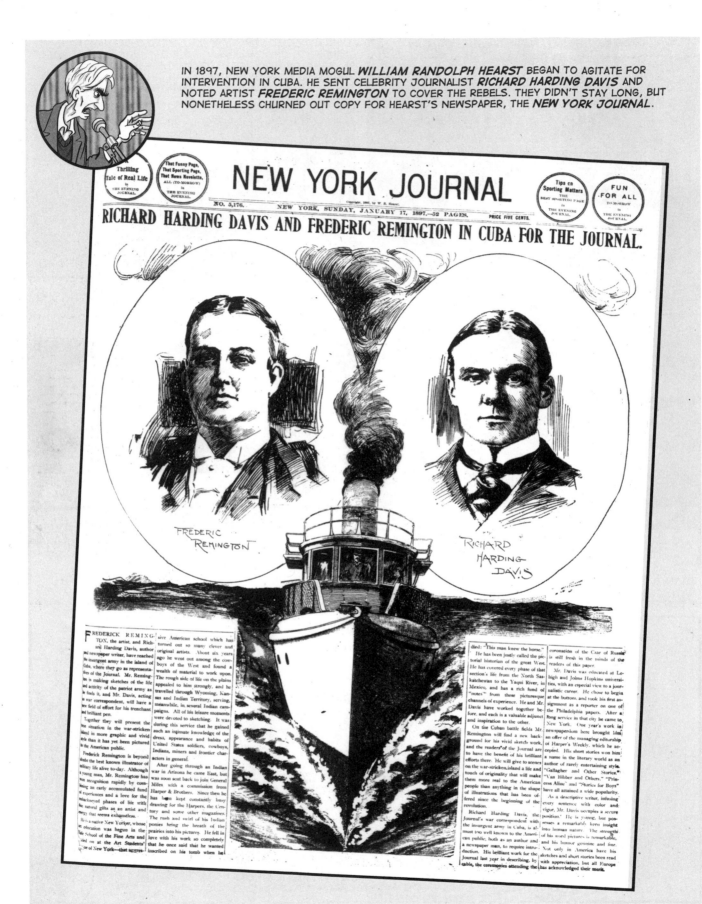

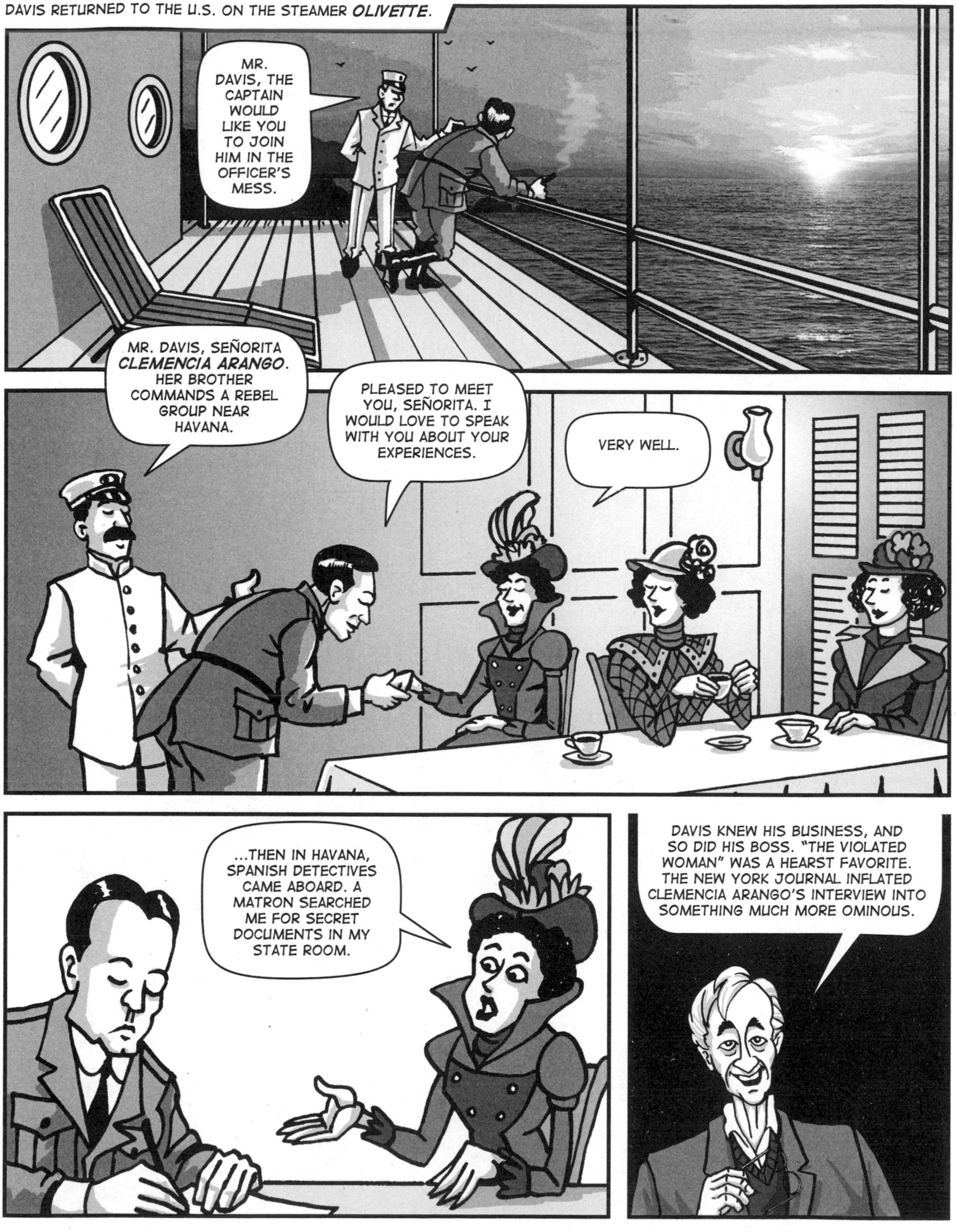
DAVIS RETURNED TO THE U.S. ON THE STEAMER *OLIVETTE*.
MR. DAVIS, THE CAPTAIN WOULD LIKE YOU TO JOIN HIM IN THE OFFICER'S MESS.
MR. DAVIS, SEÑORITA *CLEMENCIA ARANGO*. HER BROTHER COMMANDS A REBEL GROUP NEAR HAVANA.
PLEASED TO MEET YOU, SEÑORITA. I WOULD LOVE TO SPEAK WITH YOU ABOUT YOUR EXPERIENCES.
VERY WELL.
...THEN IN HAVANA, SPANISH DETECTIVES CAME ABOARD. A MATRON SEARCHED ME FOR SECRET DOCUMENTS IN MY STATE ROOM.
DAVIS KNEW HIS BUSINESS, AND SO DID HIS BOSS. "THE VIOLATED WOMAN" WAS A HEARST FAVORITE. THE NEW YORK JOURNAL INFLATED CLEMENCIA ARANGO'S INTERVIEW INTO SOMETHING MUCH MORE OMINOUS.

Fashions for Men!
Spring Designs from London and Paris in Next Sunday's Journal.

THE Yellow Kid in Ireland
Eat Blarney & Mokkery!

HEARST'S JOURNAL, IN A FURIOUS CIRCULATION WAR WITH *JOSEPH PULITZER'S NEW YORK WORLD* FOR TWO YEARS, INFLATED THE STORY BEYOND RECOGNITION. IT IMPLIED THAT THE SPANIARDS BELIEVED THE UNITED STATES WAS TOO WEAK TO DEFEND THE HONOR OF WOMEN. IT CLOSED WITH AN APPEAL TO PRESIDENT McKINLEY TO PUNISH SPAIN FOR INSULTING THE AMERICAN FLAG.

DOES OUR FLAG SHIELD WOMEN?

Indignities Practised by Spanish Officials on Board American Vessels.

Richard Harding Davis Describes Some Startling Phases of the Cuban Situation.

Refined Young Women Stripped and Searched by Brutal Spaniards While Under Our Flag on the Olivette.

By Richard Harding Davis.

TAMPA, Fla., Feb. 10.—On the boat which carried me from Cuba to Key West were three young girls who had been exiled for giving aid to the insurgents. The brother of one of them, Miss Clemencia Arango, is in command of the Cuban forces in the field near Havana. More than once the sister has joined him there and has seen fighting and carried back dispatches to the Junta in Havana. So for this she and two other young women, who were also suspected, were ordered to leave the island.

I happened to sit next to Miss Arango at table on the steamer. I found that she was not an Amazon, or a Joan of Arc, or a woman of the people, with a machete in one hand and a Cuban flag in the other. She was a well bred, well educated young person who spoke three languages and dressed as you are girls dress on Fifth avenue after church on Sunday. This is what the Spaniards did to these girls:

After ordering them to leave the island on a certain day, they sent detectives to their houses on the morning of that day and had them undressed and searched to discover if they were carrying letters to the Junta at Key West and Tampa. They then, an hour later, searched them at the Custom House as they were leaving for the steamer. They searched them thoroughly, even to the length of taking off their shoes and stockings, and fifteen minutes later, when the young ladies stood at last on the deck of an American vessel, with the American flag hanging from the stern, the Spanish officers followed them there and demanded that a cabin should be furnished them to which the girls might be taken, and they were then again undressed and searched for the third time.

Searched a Passenger on an American Ship.

Spanish officers, with red crosses for bravery on their chests and gold lace on their cuffs, strutted scowlingly about the deck while this was being done, and chancing to find a Cuban suspect among the passengers ordered him to be searched also, only they did not give him the privacy of a cabin, but stripped him of his clothes on the main deck of this American vessel before a gaping crowd of passengers and the skulking ship's captain and his crew.

In order to leave Havana it is first necessary to give notice of your wish to do so by sending your passport to the Captain-General, who looks up your record, and after twenty-four hours, if he is willing to let you go, vises your passport and, so signifies that your request is granted. After you have com...

REMINGTON "RE-IMAGINED" THE STORY FROM HIS NEW YORK STUDIO.

SPANIARDS SEARCH WOMEN ON AMERICAN STEAMERS.
DRAWN BY FREDERIC REMINGTON

Considering Him.

THE NEXT DAY, WITH A CAREFULLY CHOSEN VERB IN THE HEADLINE, THE JOURNAL FOLLOWED UP WITH REACTION FROM CONGRESS, INCLUDING A CALL FOR THE *IMMEDIATE ANNEXATION OF CUBA.*

AROUSED BY SPAIN'S ACT.

Congress Will Hear To-day of the Search Outrage on the Olivette.

LAW MAKERS INDIGNANT.

Richard Harding Davis's Story of Inhumanity to Cuban Girls Brings Forth Strong Words.

STATE DEPARTMENT HAS NO REPORT YET.

Washington, Feb. 12.—The story told by Richard Harding Davis of the outrageous manner in which Cuban girls were searched aboard the American steamer Olivette caused so much indignation here that a resolution in the House to-morrow. The fact will be argued that, while Spain technically has the right to search vessels in her ports, this in a way excuses the disgraceful conduct of officials at Havana.

State Department Stirred.

The Olivette search was the chief topic of State. It was generally agreed that such incidents afford the best opportunity this Government could have of making demands upon Spain and give the best excuse for abandoning the attitude of patience and toleration toward Madrid with regard to Cuba.

The Navy Department officials refrain from expressing themselves regarding the necessity for a warship at Havana. They say that the appearance of one vessel there would call for the entire fleet. Its ominous aspect would not be dispelled by...

SENATOR WILSON WOULD ANNEX CUBA.

Washington, Feb. 12.

Editor New York Journal:

WHEN SHE REACHED NEW YORK, CLEMENCIA ARANGO WAS ASTOUNDED AT THE FUSS THAT HAD BEEN MADE OVER HER SHIPBOARD ANECDOTE. THE RIVAL NEW YORK WORLD REPORTED THE TRUTH: THAT SHE HAD BEEN SEARCHED BY A MATRON AND WAS INDEED *CARRYING SECRET PAPERS*.

WUXTRA! WUXTRA! READ ALL ABOUT IT!

ZINNFORMATION

YEARS LATER, IRAQ WAR VETERAN *JESSICA LYNCH* SAID OF HER EXPERIENCE WITH THE PROWAR MEDIA: "IT HURT THAT PEOPLE WOULD MAKE UP STORIES THAT THEY HAD NO TRUTH ABOUT."

NEWSPAPERS CONTINUED TO STIR UP SUPPORT FOR WAR AGAINST SPAIN, BUT THE TINDER NEEDED A SPARK. IN JANUARY 1898, McKINLEY DISPATCHED THE U.S. BATTLESHIP ***MAINE*** AS A WARNING TO BOTH SIDES NOT TO THREATEN AMERICAN INTERESTS. ON FEBRUARY 15, A MYSTERIOUS EXPLOSION DESTROYED THE SHIP, KILLING 268 MEN. THE SENSATIONALIST PAPERS BLAMED IT ON THE SPANISH EVEN THOUGH THE GOVERNMENT WAS SKEPTICAL.

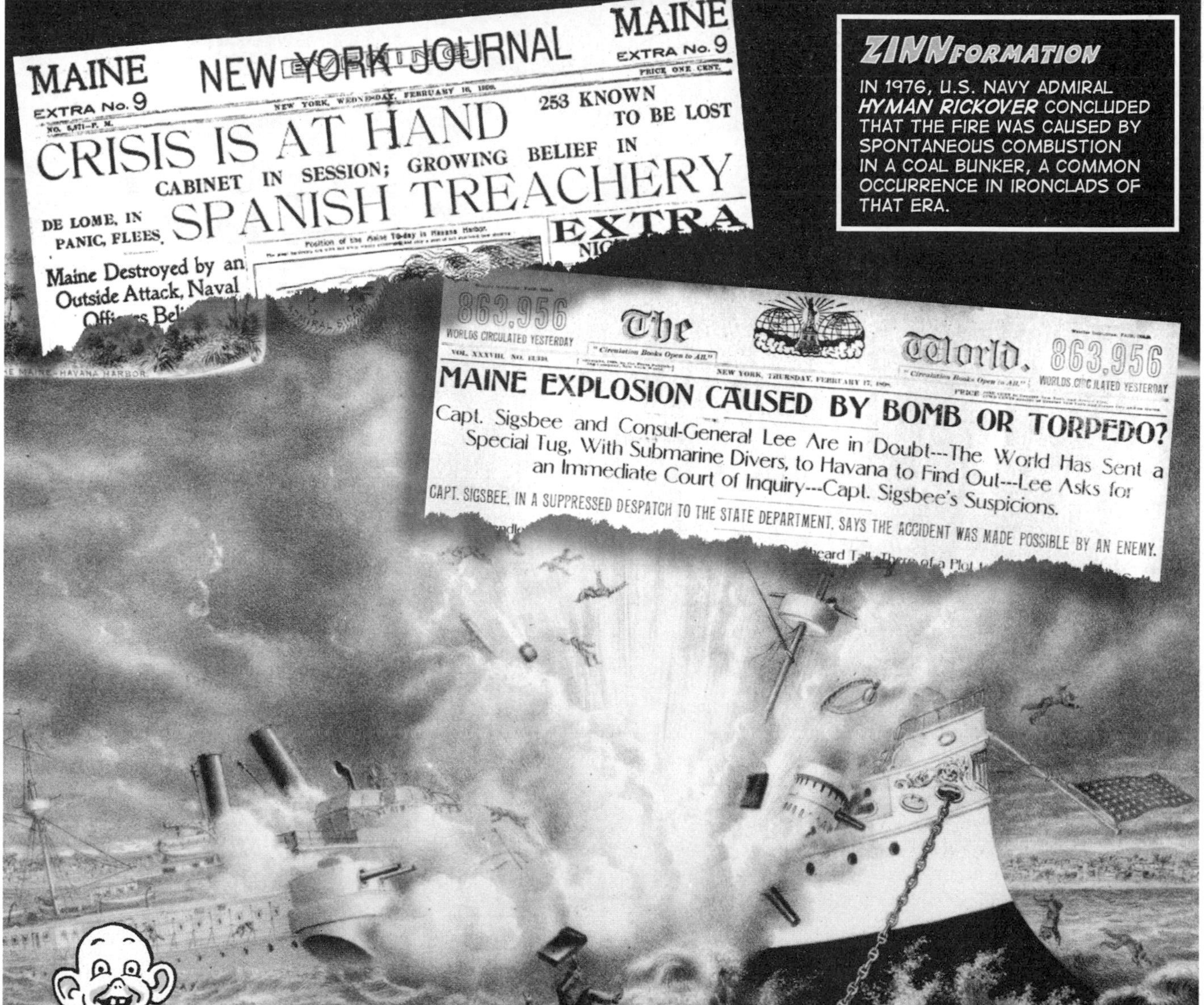
MAINE EXTRA No. 9 — NEW YORK JOURNAL — MAINE EXTRA No. 9

CRISIS IS AT HAND

253 KNOWN TO BE LOST

CABINET IN SESSION; GROWING BELIEF IN SPANISH TREACHERY

DE LOME, IN PANIC, FLEES.

EXTRA

Maine Destroyed by an Outside Attack, Naval Officers Beli...

863,956 WORLDS CIRCULATED YESTERDAY — The World. — 863,956 WORLDS CIRCULATED YESTERDAY

"Circulation Books Open to All."

MAINE EXPLOSION CAUSED BY BOMB OR TORPEDO?

Capt. Sigsbee and Consul-General Lee Are in Doubt---The World Has Sent a Special Tug, With Submarine Divers, to Havana to Find Out---Lee Asks for an Immediate Court of Inquiry---Capt. Sigsbee's Suspicions.

CAPT. SIGSBEE, IN A SUPPRESSED DESPATCH TO THE STATE DEPARTMENT, SAYS THE ACCIDENT WAS MADE POSSIBLE BY AN ENEMY.

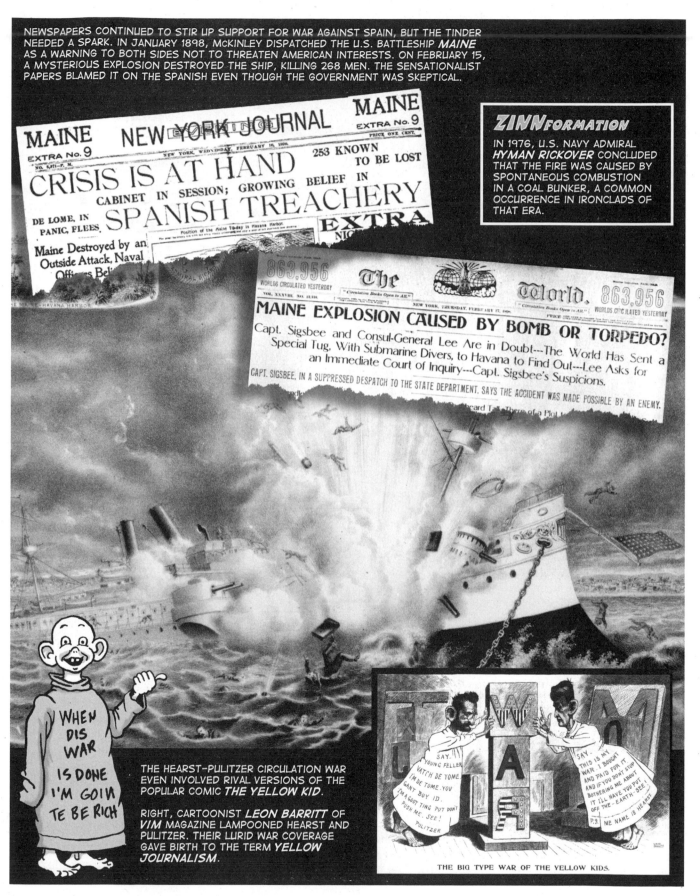

ZINNFORMATION

IN 1976, U.S. NAVY ADMIRAL ***HYMAN RICKOVER*** CONCLUDED THAT THE FIRE WAS CAUSED BY SPONTANEOUS COMBUSTION IN A COAL BUNKER, A COMMON OCCURRENCE IN IRONCLADS OF THAT ERA.

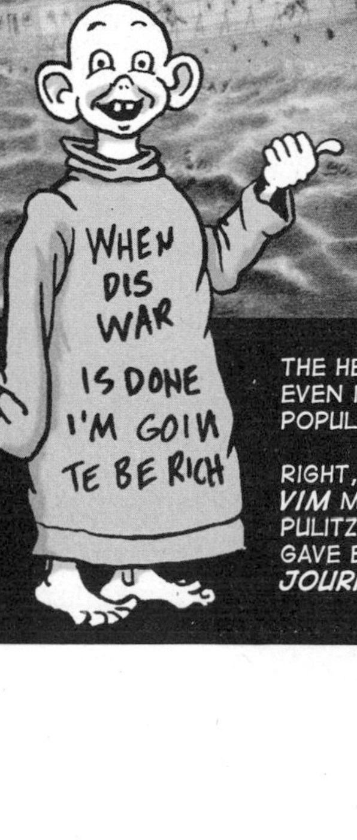
WHEN DIS WAR IS DONE I'M GOIN TE BE RICH

THE HEARST-PULITZER CIRCULATION WAR EVEN INVOLVED RIVAL VERSIONS OF THE POPULAR COMIC ***THE YELLOW KID***.

RIGHT, CARTOONIST ***LEON BARRITT*** OF ***VIM*** MAGAZINE LAMPOONED HEARST AND PULITZER. THEIR LURID WAR COVERAGE GAVE BIRTH TO THE TERM ***YELLOW JOURNALISM***.

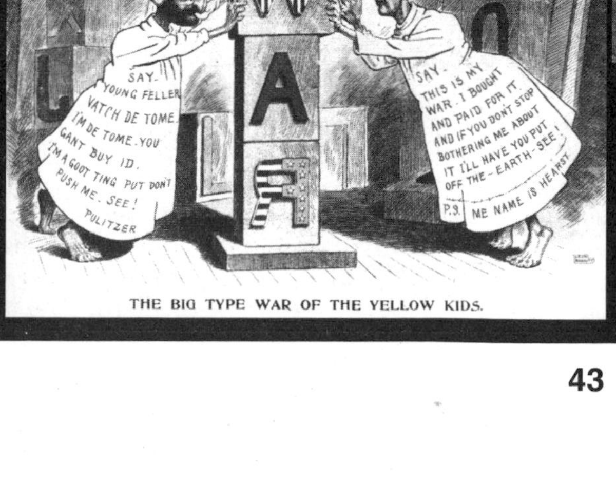
WAR
SAY. YOUNG FELLER WATCH DE TOME. I'M DE TOME. YOU CANT BUY ID. I'M A GOOT TING PUT DON'T PUSH ME. SEE! PULITZER
SAY. THIS IS MY WAR. I BOUGHT AND PAID FOR IT, AND IF YOU DON'T STOP BOTHERING ME ABOUT IT I'LL HAVE YOU PUT OFF THE EARTH. SEE! P.S. ME NAME IS HEARST
THE BIG TYPE WAR OF THE YELLOW KIDS.

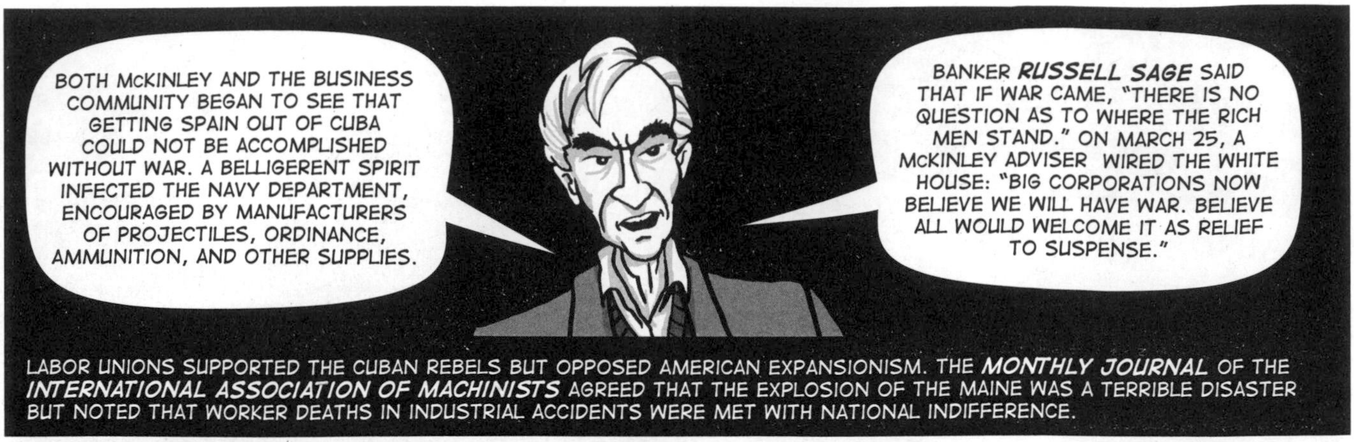
BOTH McKINLEY AND THE BUSINESS COMMUNITY BEGAN TO SEE THAT GETTING SPAIN OUT OF CUBA COULD NOT BE ACCOMPLISHED WITHOUT WAR. A BELLIGERENT SPIRIT INFECTED THE NAVY DEPARTMENT, ENCOURAGED BY MANUFACTURERS OF PROJECTILES, ORDINANCE, AMMUNITION, AND OTHER SUPPLIES.
BANKER ***RUSSELL SAGE*** SAID THAT IF WAR CAME, "THERE IS NO QUESTION AS TO WHERE THE RICH MEN STAND." ON MARCH 25, A McKINLEY ADVISER WIRED THE WHITE HOUSE: "BIG CORPORATIONS NOW BELIEVE WE WILL HAVE WAR. BELIEVE ALL WOULD WELCOME IT AS RELIEF TO SUSPENSE."
LABOR UNIONS SUPPORTED THE CUBAN REBELS BUT OPPOSED AMERICAN EXPANSIONISM. THE ***MONTHLY JOURNAL*** OF THE ***INTERNATIONAL ASSOCIATION OF MACHINISTS*** AGREED THAT THE EXPLOSION OF THE MAINE WAS A TERRIBLE DISASTER BUT NOTED THAT WORKER DEATHS IN INDUSTRIAL ACCIDENTS WERE MET WITH NATIONAL INDIFFERENCE.

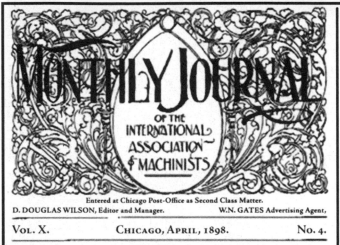

MONTHLY JOURNAL

OF THE INTERNATIONAL ASSOCIATION OF MACHINISTS

Entered at Chicago Post-Office as Second Class Matter.

D. DOUGLAS WILSON, Editor and Manager. W.N. GATES Advertising Agent,

VOL. X. CHICAGO, APRIL, 1898. NO. 4.

Death cast the shadow of his dark wings over the harbor Havana; the "Maine" sank; the nation wept, and the Journal mourns for the many poor fellows who perished with the ill-fated ship. Death in this form had not presented itself to the people in many years, so that when the evil tidings of the catastrophe came it cast a calamitous gloom over the land.

Men raved and women wept. Muttered curses "not loud but deep" were heard on every side. Spanish treachery, vengeance, retribution, were the subjects most in favor with the excited populace. Men thought awry. The great newspapers shrieked for war, for red, bloody war! The pulpit even advocated the unleashing of the war dogs. All this because there had been a great and useless sacrifice of human life.

If it could have been proven in the first moments of the excitement that it was an accident, tears and sorrow would have been manifest just the same; but the great horror that came with the thought that it was no accident and ought not to have taken place, would have been absent.

The public was horrified because it was unused to this particular form of horror. There are other forms that are just as horrible; where a hundred lives are sacrificed for every ten that went out of existence with the "Maine," but the horror has ceased to horrify, the public has grown used to the gruesome details and looks upon them with indifference and complacency.

The carnival of carnage that takes place every day, month and year in the realm of industry; the thousands of useful lives that are annually sacrificed to the Moloch of greed; the blood tribute paid by labor to capitalism, brings forth no shout for vengeance and reparation; no tear, except from the family and friends of the victims.

Trainmen and switchmen are murdered every day because of the non-equipment of the cars with a device that will reduce danger to life and limb to a minimum, and capitalism has been granted another two years to carry on the massacre. Machinists and engineers, firemen and conductors, and all other branches of the railroad service sacrifice their percentage of life and limb to the same insatiable Gorgon. Limbless children come in troops every year from factory and mine because the machinery has no protective hand rail or boxing to keep the victims from danger. Tribute is levied on old age and infancy by the corporate greed that refuses to equip street cars with a fender attachment. Death comes in thousands of instances to mill and mine, claims his victims and no popular uproar is heard, although it has been proven a thousand times that the sacrifice could have been avoided if proper and known precautions had been used.

The Journal joins in the popular sorrow for the loss of the "Maine," and regrets that so many lives, which under natural conditions would be profitably employed, have been lost with the ship. And while expressing sorrow it also expresses the hope that the day will not be far distant when it will be popularly considered that to lose life by accident in productive and distributive industry is just as noble and heroic as to lose it by accident on board a man of war. That to lose life by being drowned like a rat in a mine is just as worthy as being drowned like a rat in the hold of an ironclad. That to lose a limb by an exploding shell is no more worthy of national consideration than to lose one in a rolling mill. That to be blown up by a torpedo creates no more sorrow in the unfortunate's family than to be blown up by a boiler. That one should not be the hero of an apotheosis while the other goes to Eternity unhonored and unsung.

Smoked Yankees: The Black 25th Infantry

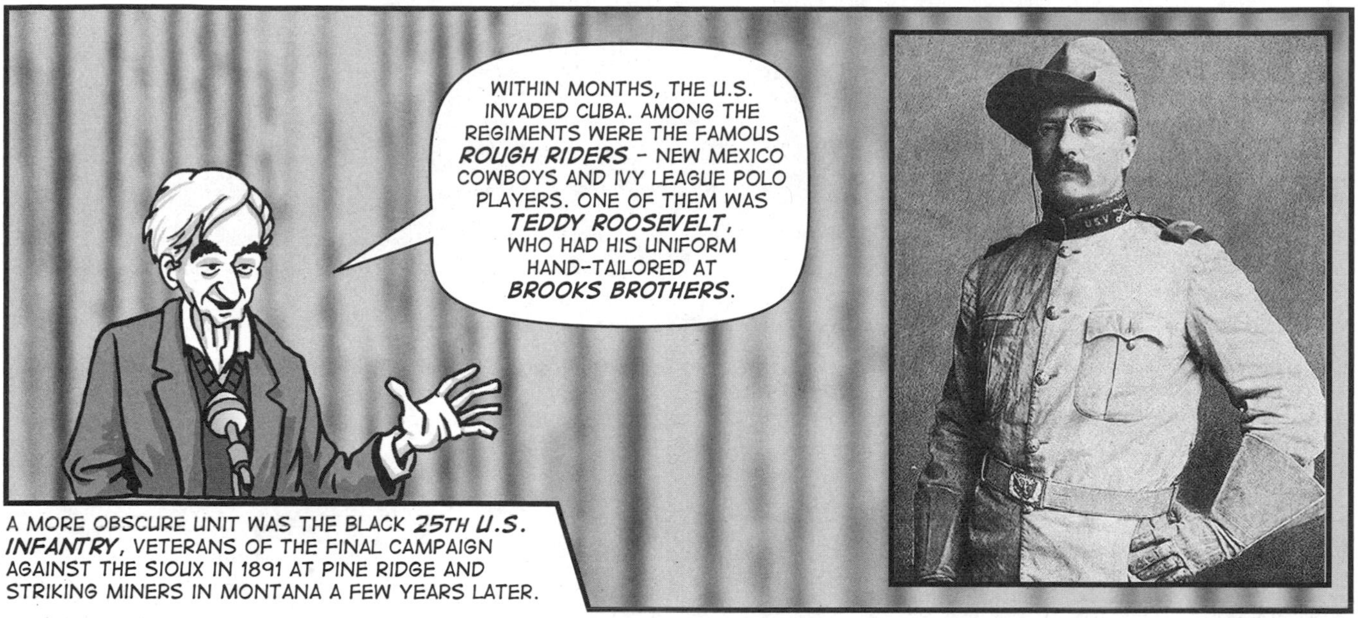
WITHIN MONTHS, THE U.S. INVADED CUBA. AMONG THE REGIMENTS WERE THE FAMOUS ROUGH RIDERS - NEW MEXICO COWBOYS AND IVY LEAGUE POLO PLAYERS. ONE OF THEM WAS TEDDY ROOSEVELT, WHO HAD HIS UNIFORM HAND-TAILORED AT BROOKS BROTHERS.
A MORE OBSCURE UNIT WAS THE BLACK 25TH U.S. INFANTRY, VETERANS OF THE FINAL CAMPAIGN AGAINST THE SIOUX IN 1891 AT PINE RIDGE AND STRIKING MINERS IN MONTANA A FEW YEARS LATER.

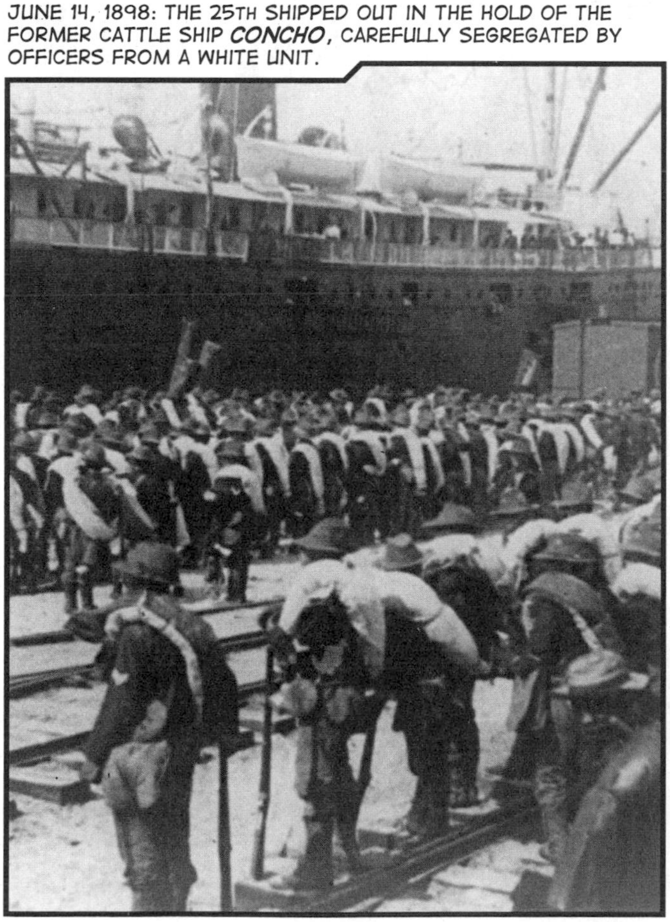
JUNE 14, 1898: THE 25TH SHIPPED OUT IN THE HOLD OF THE FORMER CATTLE SHIP CONCHO, CAREFULLY SEGREGATED BY OFFICERS FROM A WHITE UNIT.

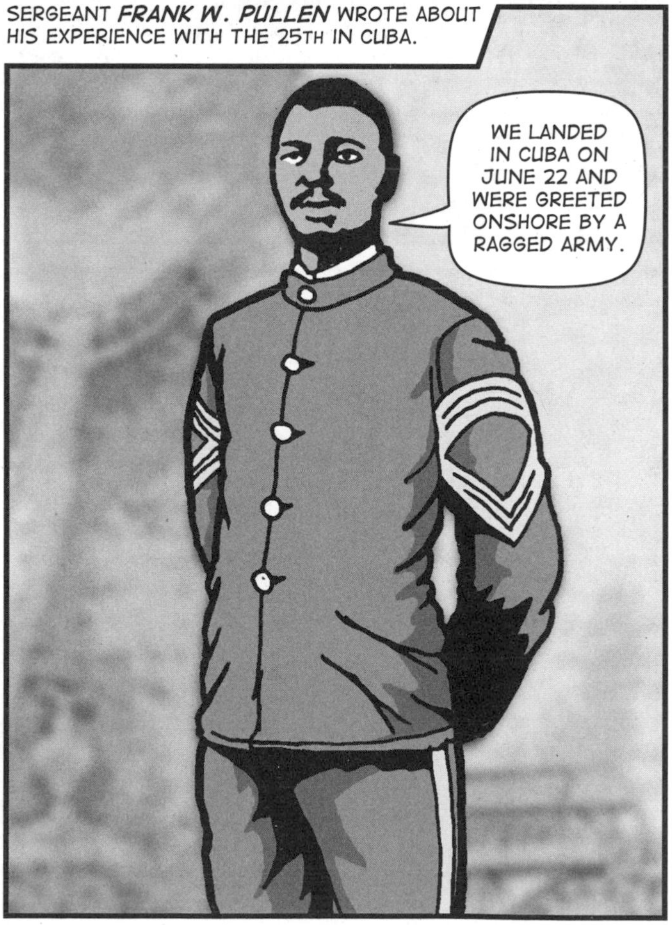
SERGEANT FRANK W. PULLEN WROTE ABOUT HIS EXPERIENCE WITH THE 25TH IN CUBA.
WE LANDED IN CUBA ON JUNE 22 AND WERE GREETED ONSHORE BY A RAGGED ARMY.

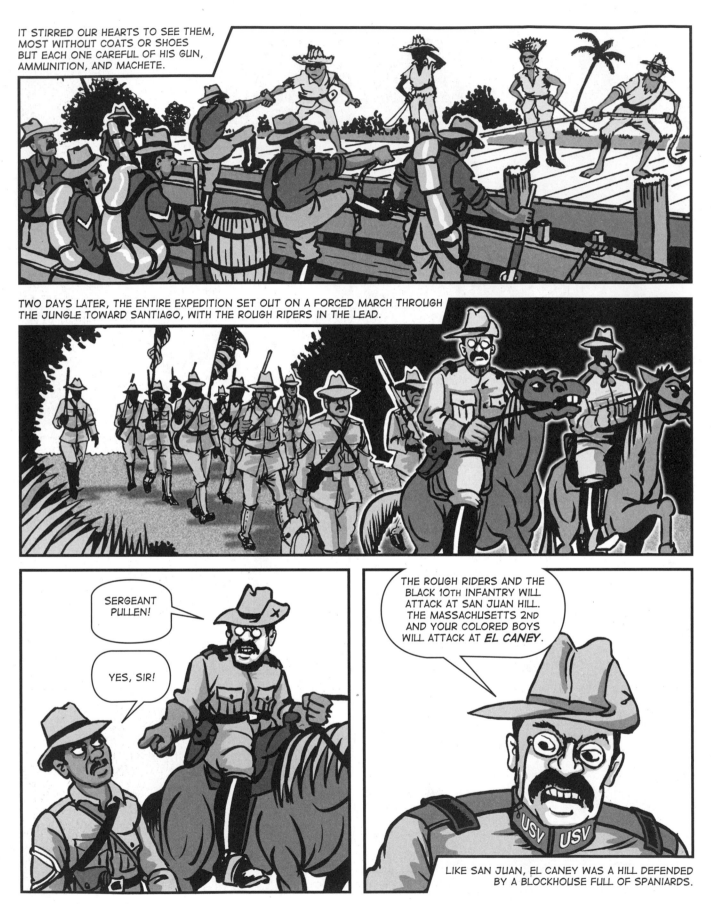

IT STIRRED OUR HEARTS TO SEE THEM, MOST WITHOUT COATS OR SHOES BUT EACH ONE CAREFUL OF HIS GUN, AMMUNITION, AND MACHETE.

TWO DAYS LATER, THE ENTIRE EXPEDITION SET OUT ON A FORCED MARCH THROUGH THE JUNGLE TOWARD SANTIAGO, WITH THE ROUGH RIDERS IN THE LEAD.

SERGEANT PULLEN!

YES, SIR!

THE ROUGH RIDERS AND THE BLACK 10TH INFANTRY WILL ATTACK AT SAN JUAN HILL. THE MASSACHUSETTS 2ND AND YOUR COLORED BOYS WILL ATTACK AT *EL CANEY*.

LIKE SAN JUAN, EL CANEY WAS A HILL DEFENDED BY A BLOCKHOUSE FULL OF SPANIARDS.

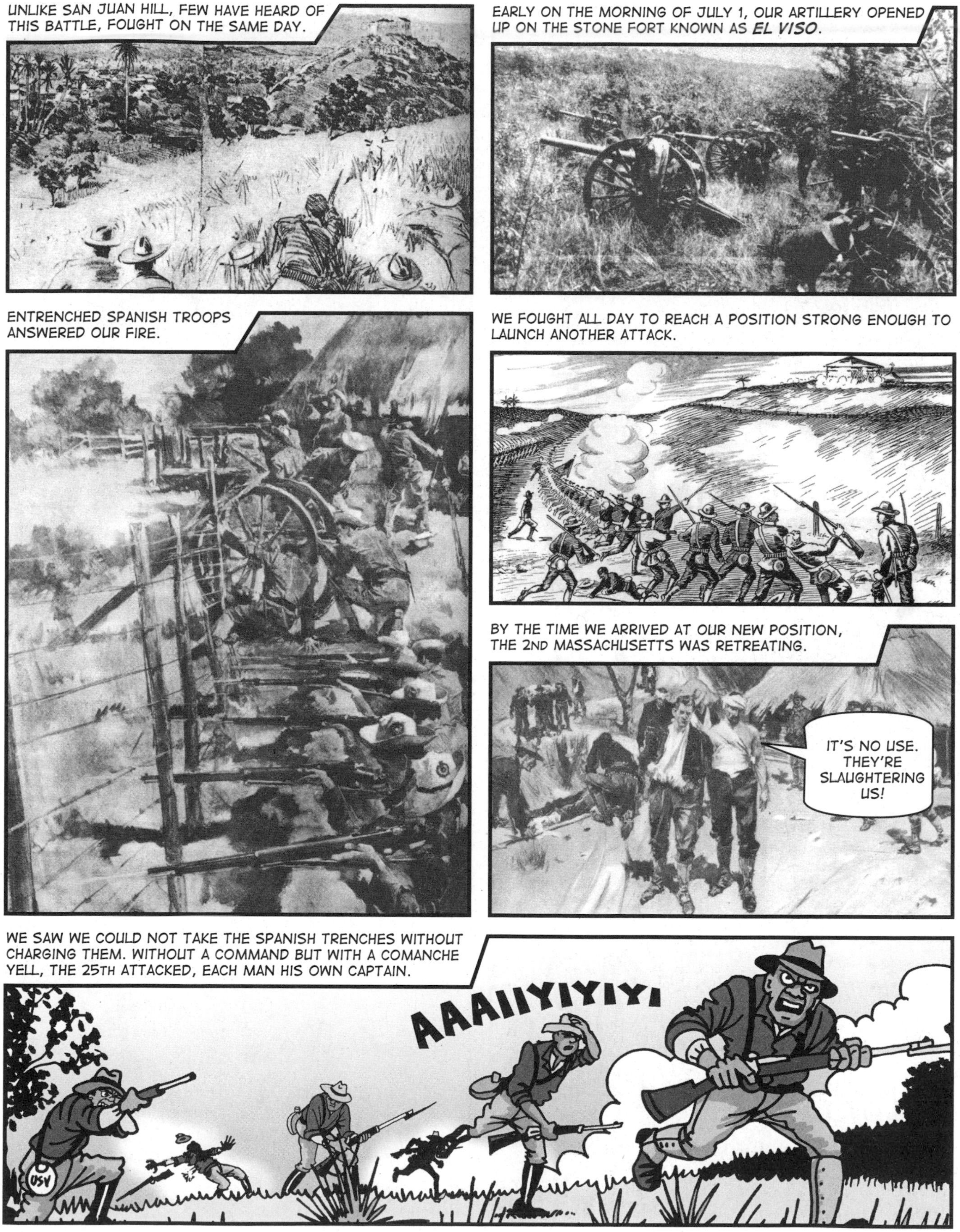
UNLIKE SAN JUAN HILL, FEW HAVE HEARD OF THIS BATTLE, FOUGHT ON THE SAME DAY.
EARLY ON THE MORNING OF JULY 1, OUR ARTILLERY OPENED UP ON THE STONE FORT KNOWN AS EL VISO.
ENTRENCHED SPANISH TROOPS ANSWERED OUR FIRE.
WE FOUGHT ALL DAY TO REACH A POSITION STRONG ENOUGH TO LAUNCH ANOTHER ATTACK.
BY THE TIME WE ARRIVED AT OUR NEW POSITION, THE 2ND MASSACHUSETTS WAS RETREATING.
IT'S NO USE. THEY'RE SLAUGHTERING US!
WE SAW WE COULD NOT TAKE THE SPANISH TRENCHES WITHOUT CHARGING THEM. WITHOUT A COMMAND BUT WITH A COMANCHE YELL, THE 25TH ATTACKED, EACH MAN HIS OWN CAPTAIN.
AAAIIYIYIYI
USV

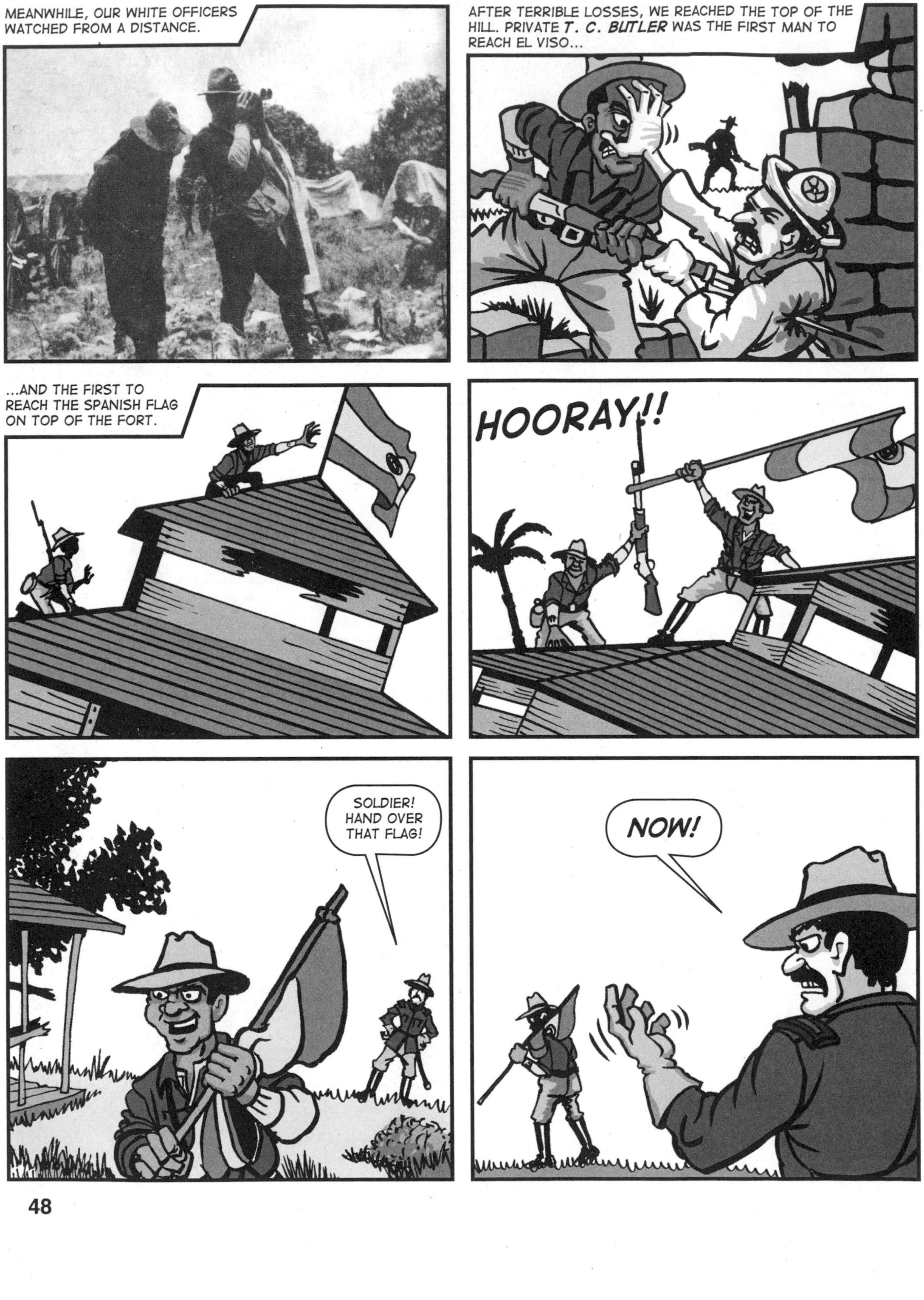
MEANWHILE, OUR WHITE OFFICERS WATCHED FROM A DISTANCE.
AFTER TERRIBLE LOSSES, WE REACHED THE TOP OF THE HILL. PRIVATE T. C. BUTLER WAS THE FIRST MAN TO REACH EL VISO...
...AND THE FIRST TO REACH THE SPANISH FLAG ON TOP OF THE FORT.
HOORAY!!
SOLDIER! HAND OVER THAT FLAG!
NOW!

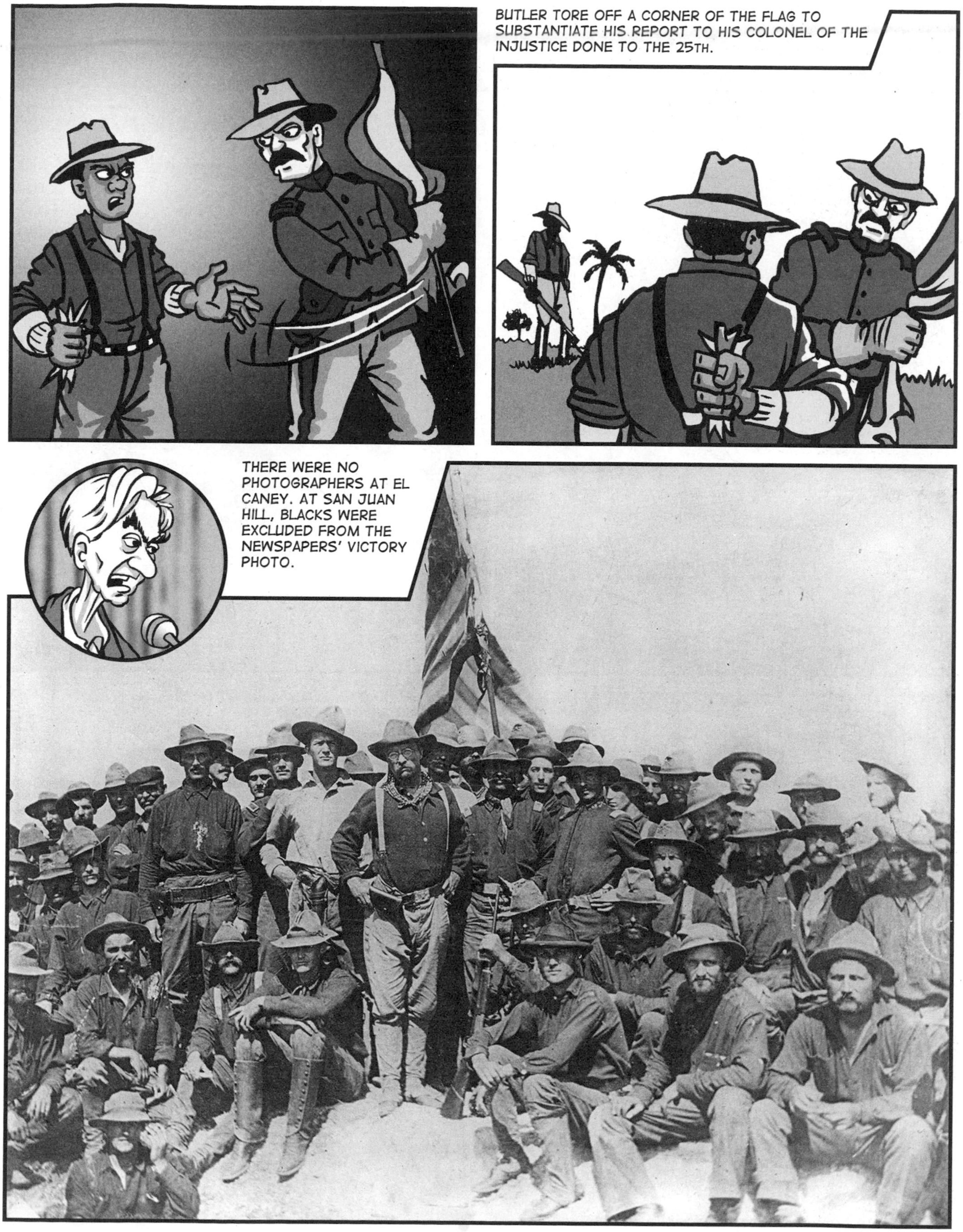
BUTLER TORE OFF A CORNER OF THE FLAG TO SUBSTANTIATE HIS REPORT TO HIS COLONEL OF THE INJUSTICE DONE TO THE 25TH.
THERE WERE NO PHOTOGRAPHERS AT EL CANEY. AT SAN JUAN HILL, BLACKS WERE EXCLUDED FROM THE NEWSPAPERS' VICTORY PHOTO.

Spoils of War

5,462 SOLDIERS AND OFFICERS DIED DURING THE WAR, BUT ONLY 379 OF THESE WERE BATTLE CASUALTIES. THE REST DIED OF DISEASE OR PUTRID FOOD, INCLUDING 500,000 POUNDS OF ROTTING CANNED MEAT SOLD TO THE ARMY BY ***ARMOUR AND CO.*** OF CHICAGO. SOME TINS WERE SO FOUL THEY HAD BURST.

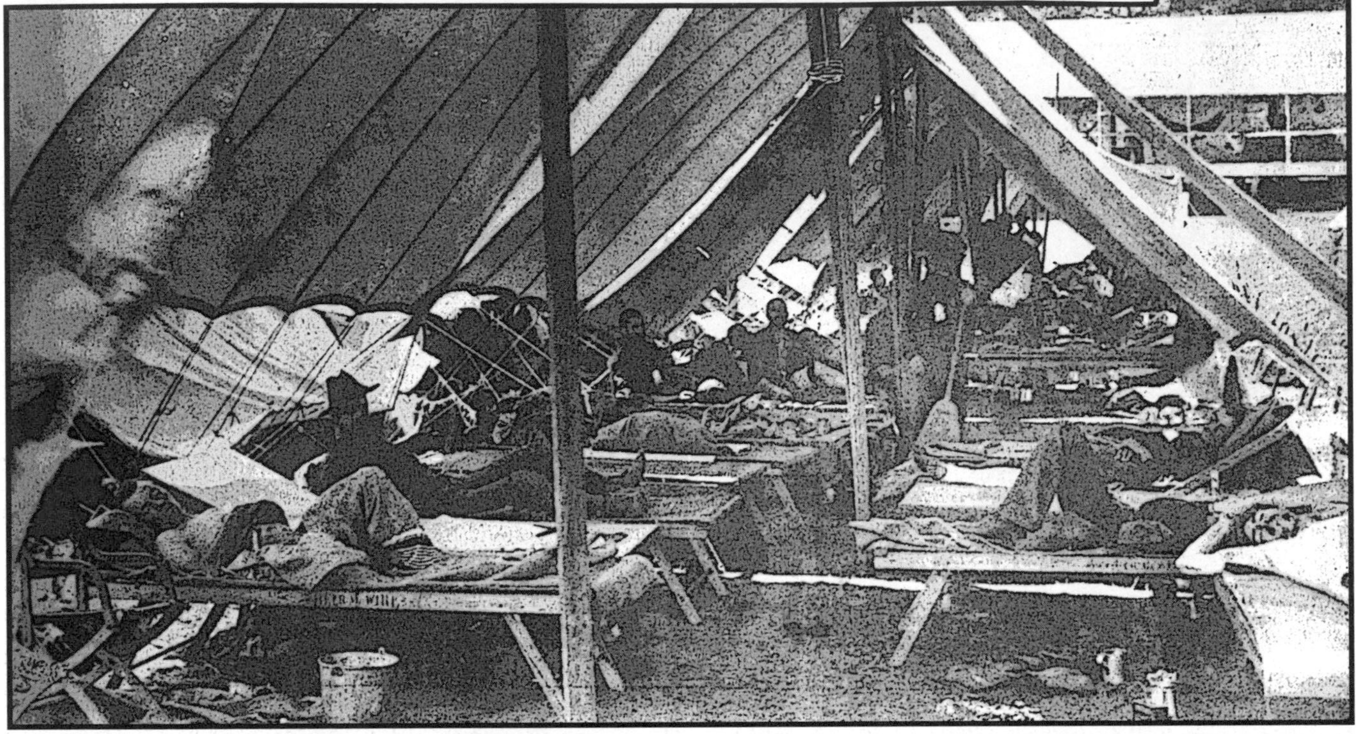

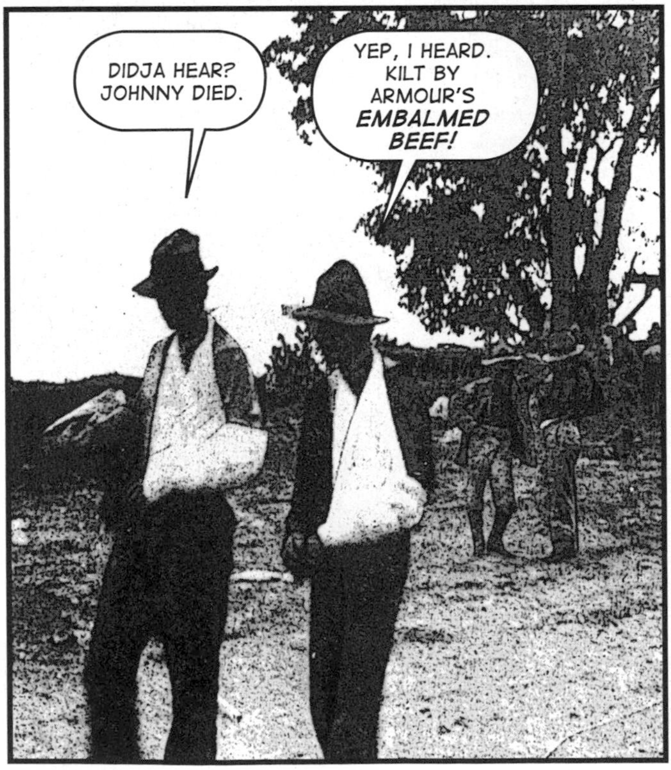
DIDJA HEAR? JOHNNY DIED.
YEP, I HEARD. KILT BY ARMOUR'S ***EMBALMED BEEF!***

AS IT TURNED OUT, BLACK AND WHITE SOLDIERS ALIKE OFTEN FACED A MORE DANGEROUS ENEMY THAN THE SPANISH – ***WAR PROFITEERING***.

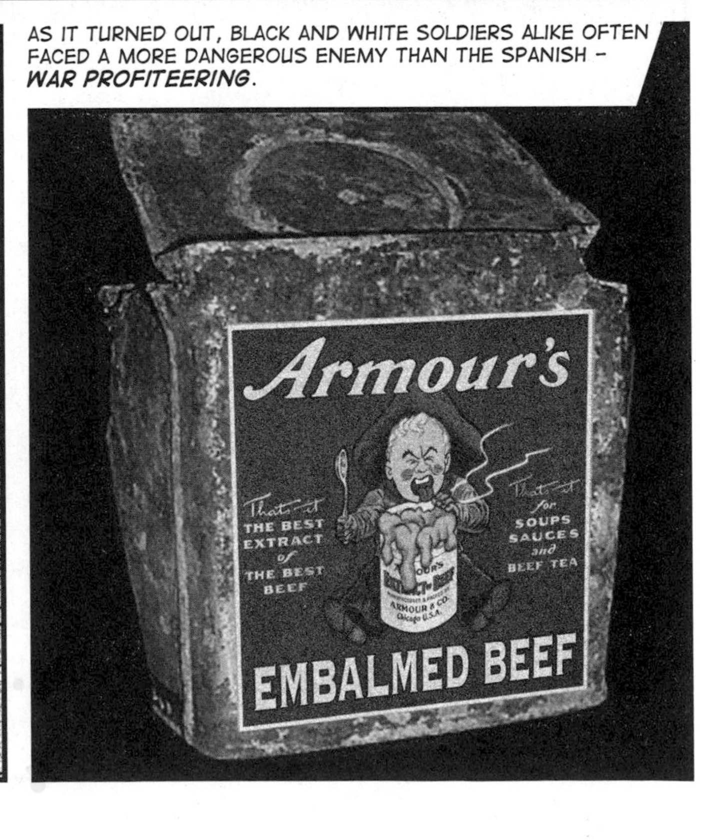
Armour's
That's it THE BEST EXTRACT of THE BEST BEEF
That's it for SOUPS SAUCES and BEEF TEA
EMBALMED BEEF

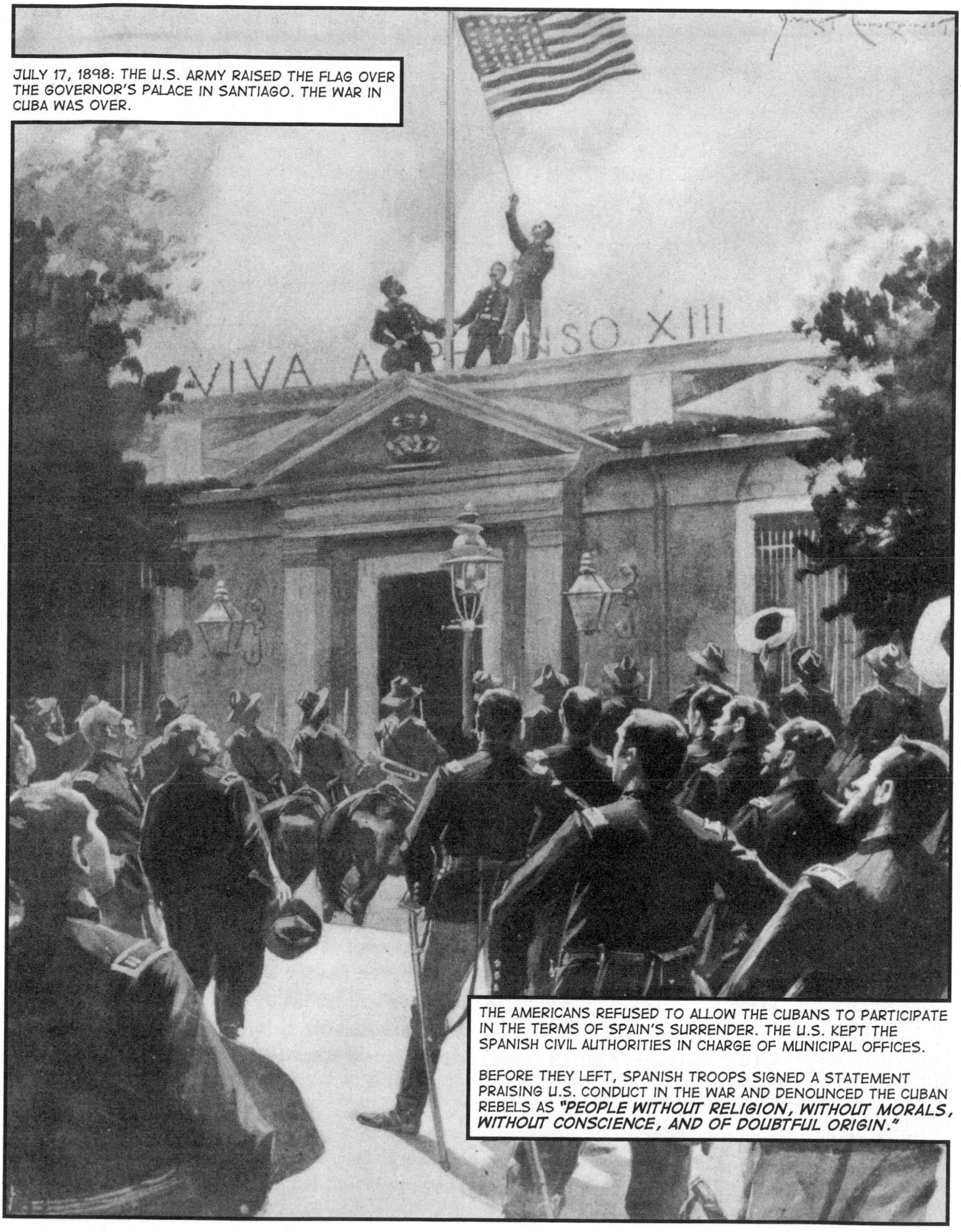
JULY 17, 1898: THE U.S. ARMY RAISED THE FLAG OVER THE GOVERNOR'S PALACE IN SANTIAGO. THE WAR IN CUBA WAS OVER.
VIVA A NSO XIII
THE AMERICANS REFUSED TO ALLOW THE CUBANS TO PARTICIPATE IN THE TERMS OF SPAIN'S SURRENDER. THE U.S. KEPT THE SPANISH CIVIL AUTHORITIES IN CHARGE OF MUNICIPAL OFFICES.
BEFORE THEY LEFT, SPANISH TROOPS SIGNED A STATEMENT PRAISING U.S. CONDUCT IN THE WAR AND DENOUNCED THE CUBAN REBELS AS ***"PEOPLE WITHOUT RELIGION, WITHOUT MORALS, WITHOUT CONSCIENCE, AND OF DOUBTFUL ORIGIN."***

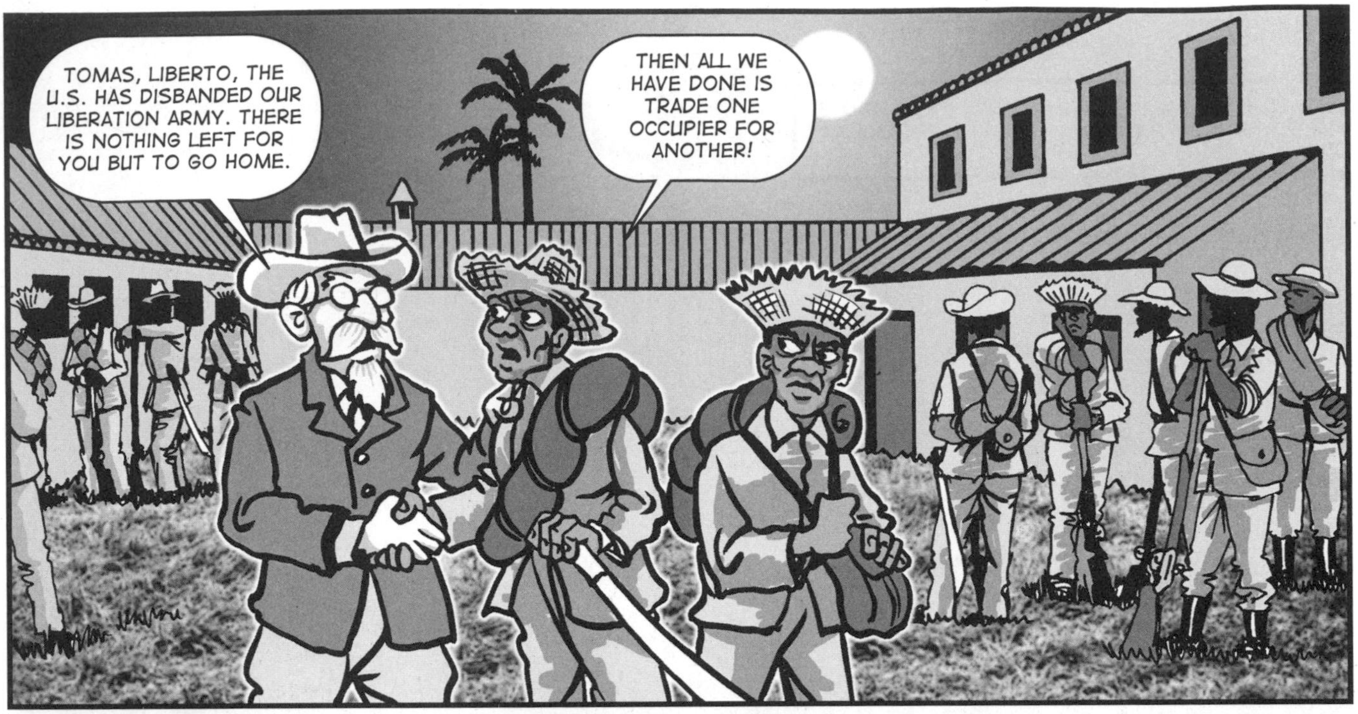
TOMAS, LIBERTO, THE U.S. HAS DISBANDED OUR LIBERATION ARMY. THERE IS NOTHING LEFT FOR YOU BUT TO GO HOME.
THEN ALL WE HAVE DONE IS TRADE ONE OCCUPIER FOR ANOTHER!

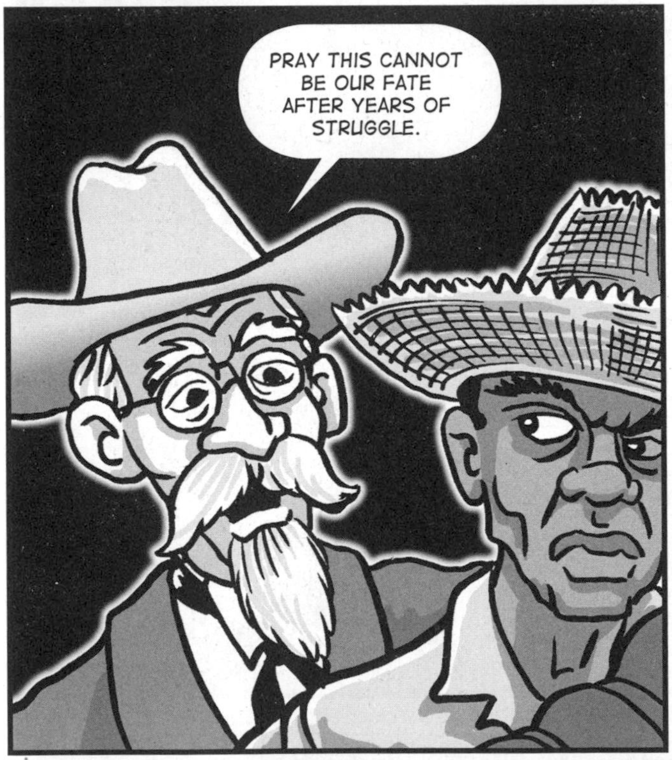
PRAY THIS CANNOT BE OUR FATE AFTER YEARS OF STRUGGLE.

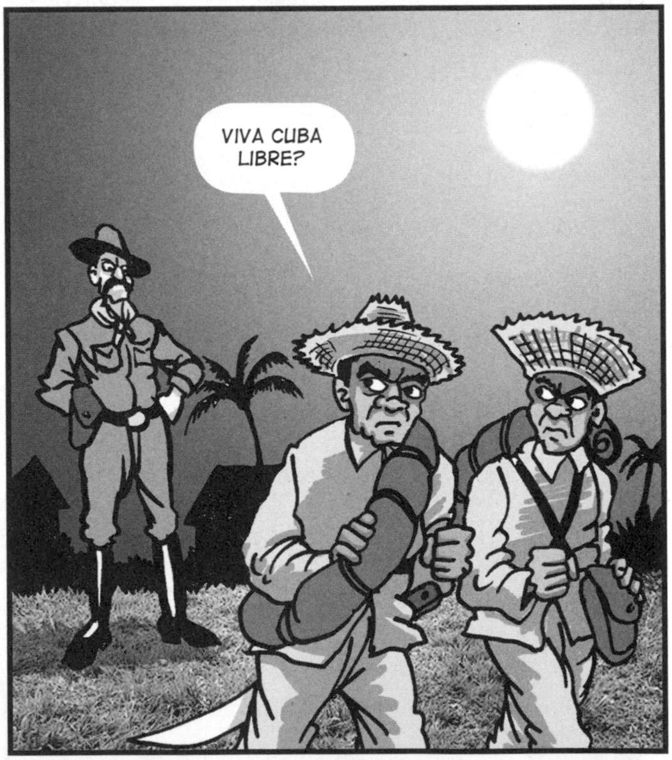
VIVA CUBA LIBRE?

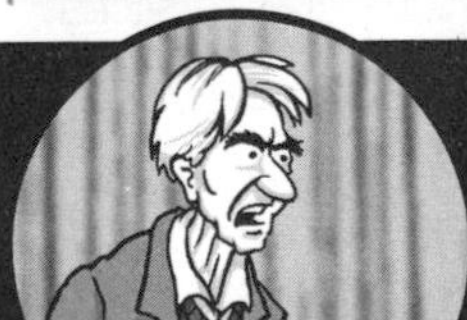

CUBA'S NEW CONSTITUTION MADE THE ISLAND A PROTECTORATE OF THE UNITED STATES. THE ***PLATT AMENDMENT*** OF 1901 ALLOWED THE U.S. TO INTERVENE AT ANY TIME IN CUBAN AFFAIRS AND REQUIRED CUBA TO PROVIDE LAND FOR AN AMERICAN BASE AT GUANTÁNAMO BAY. GENERAL ***LEONARD WOOD***, MILITARY GOVERNOR OF CUBA, WROTE TO THEODORE ROOSEVELT, "THERE IS, OF COURSE, LITTLE OR NO INDEPENDENCE LEFT IN CUBA UNDER THE PLATT AMENDMENT."

IT WASN'T UNTIL THE REVOLUTION OF 1959 THAT MARTI'S AND MACEO'S DREAM OF A CUBA FREE FROM FOREIGN DOMINATION WAS REALIZED.

Chapter III

THE INVASION OF THE PHILIPPINES

"At war's end at least 200,000 Filipinos died, many of famine; 4,000 U.S. soldiers were killed. The occupation set a pattern for future U.S. colonial adventures."

Benevolent Assimilation

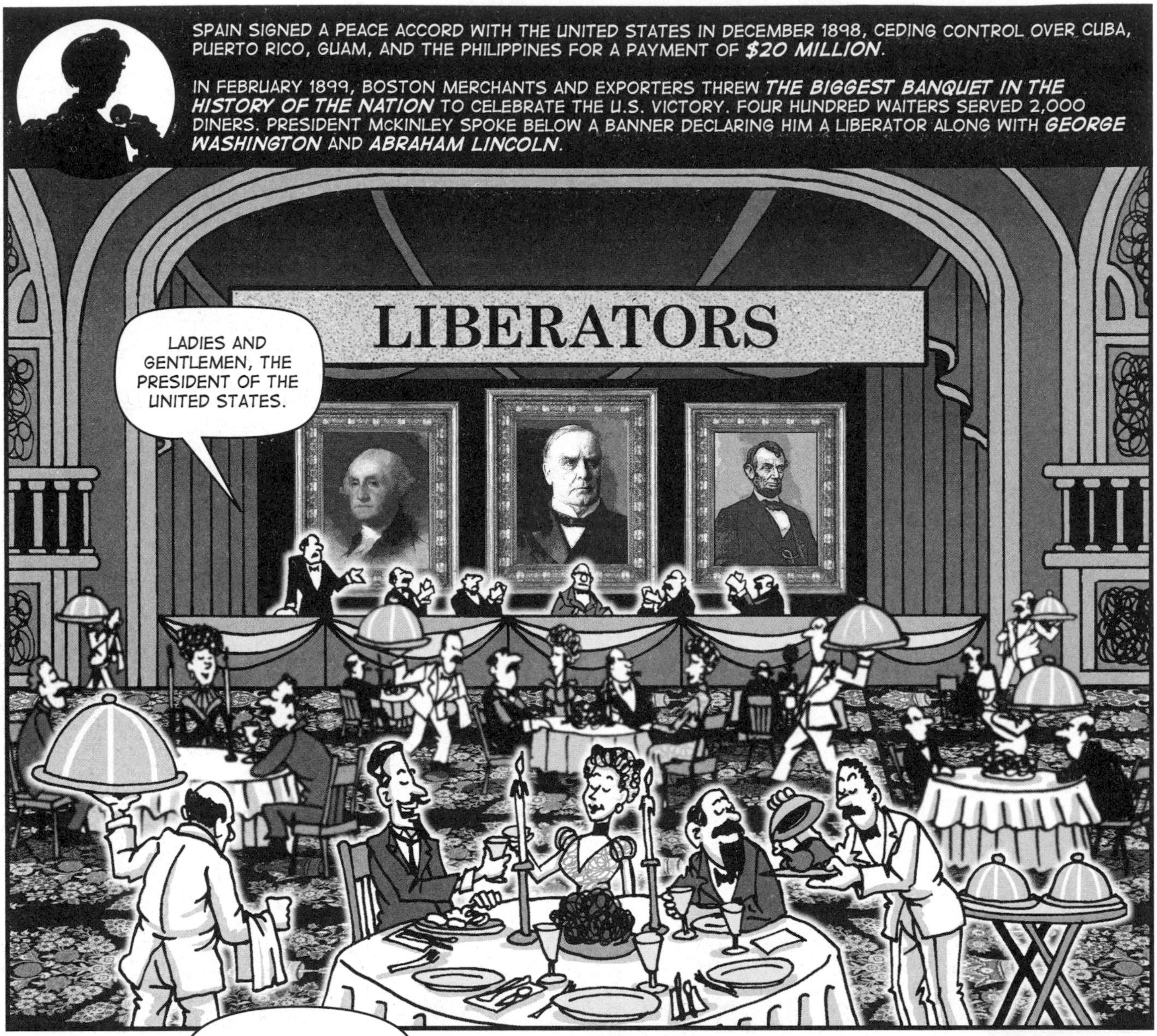

SPAIN SIGNED A PEACE ACCORD WITH THE UNITED STATES IN DECEMBER 1898, CEDING CONTROL OVER CUBA, PUERTO RICO, GUAM, AND THE PHILIPPINES FOR A PAYMENT OF *$20 MILLION*.
IN FEBRUARY 1899, BOSTON MERCHANTS AND EXPORTERS THREW ***THE BIGGEST BANQUET IN THE HISTORY OF THE NATION*** TO CELEBRATE THE U.S. VICTORY. FOUR HUNDRED WAITERS SERVED 2,000 DINERS. PRESIDENT McKINLEY SPOKE BELOW A BANNER DECLARING HIM A LIBERATOR ALONG WITH ***GEORGE WASHINGTON*** AND ***ABRAHAM LINCOLN***.
LIBERATORS
LADIES AND GENTLEMEN, THE PRESIDENT OF THE UNITED STATES.

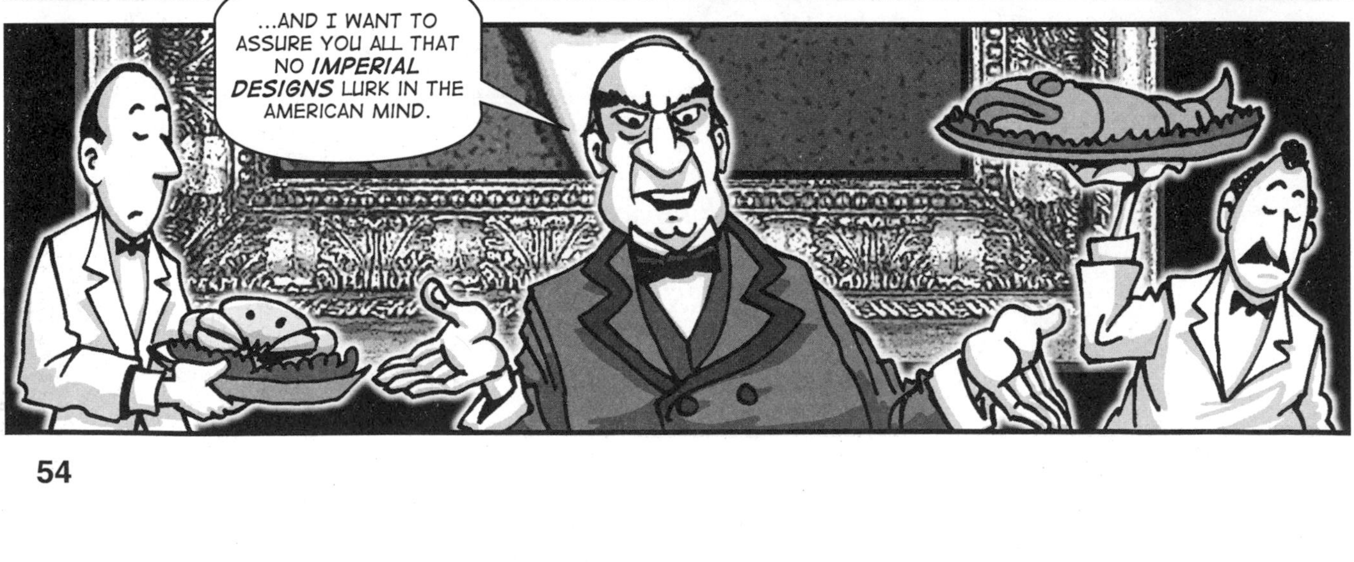

...AND I WANT TO ASSURE YOU ALL THAT NO ***IMPERIAL DESIGNS*** LURK IN THE AMERICAN MIND.

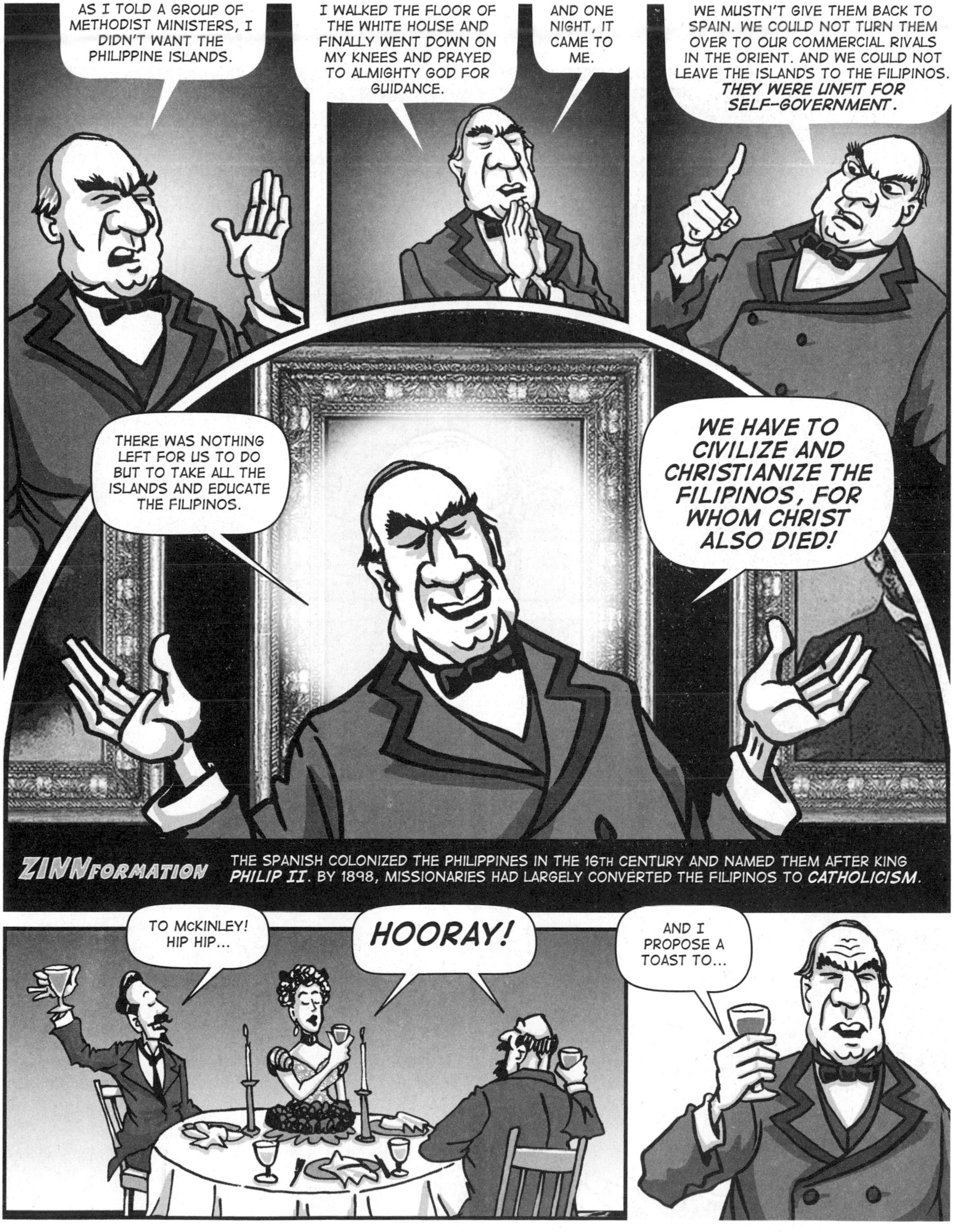
AS I TOLD A GROUP OF METHODIST MINISTERS, I DIDN'T WANT THE PHILIPPINE ISLANDS.
I WALKED THE FLOOR OF THE WHITE HOUSE AND FINALLY WENT DOWN ON MY KNEES AND PRAYED TO ALMIGHTY GOD FOR GUIDANCE.
AND ONE NIGHT, IT CAME TO ME.
WE MUSTN'T GIVE THEM BACK TO SPAIN. WE COULD NOT TURN THEM OVER TO OUR COMMERCIAL RIVALS IN THE ORIENT. AND WE COULD NOT LEAVE THE ISLANDS TO THE FILIPINOS. *THEY WERE UNFIT FOR SELF-GOVERNMENT*.
THERE WAS NOTHING LEFT FOR US TO DO BUT TO TAKE ALL THE ISLANDS AND EDUCATE THE FILIPINOS.
WE HAVE TO CIVILIZE AND CHRISTIANIZE THE FILIPINOS, FOR WHOM CHRIST ALSO DIED!
ZINNFORMATION
THE SPANISH COLONIZED THE PHILIPPINES IN THE 16TH CENTURY AND NAMED THEM AFTER KING *PHILIP II*. BY 1898, MISSIONARIES HAD LARGELY CONVERTED THE FILIPINOS TO *CATHOLICISM*.
TO McKINLEY! HIP HIP...
HOORAY!
AND I PROPOSE A TOAST TO...

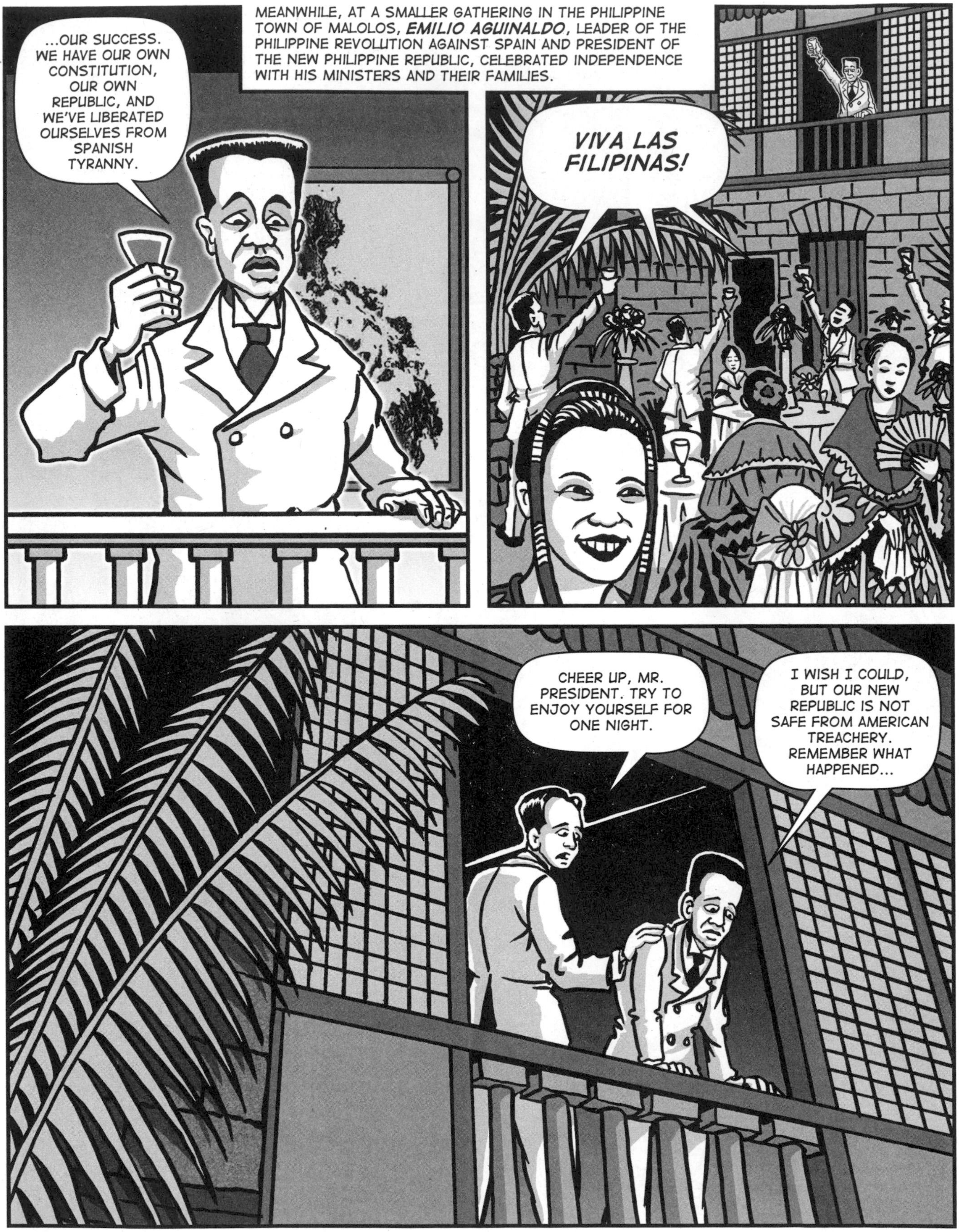
MEANWHILE, AT A SMALLER GATHERING IN THE PHILIPPINE TOWN OF MALOLOS, EMILIO AGUINALDO, LEADER OF THE PHILIPPINE REVOLUTION AGAINST SPAIN AND PRESIDENT OF THE NEW PHILIPPINE REPUBLIC, CELEBRATED INDEPENDENCE WITH HIS MINISTERS AND THEIR FAMILIES.
...OUR SUCCESS. WE HAVE OUR OWN CONSTITUTION, OUR OWN REPUBLIC, AND WE'VE LIBERATED OURSELVES FROM SPANISH TYRANNY.
VIVA LAS FILIPINAS!
CHEER UP, MR. PRESIDENT. TRY TO ENJOY YOURSELF FOR ONE NIGHT.
I WISH I COULD, BUT OUR NEW REPUBLIC IS NOT SAFE FROM AMERICAN TREACHERY. REMEMBER WHAT HAPPENED...

...THE SPANISH EXILED US TO ***HONG KONG*** AFTER OUR FAILED UPRISING OF 1896. WE USED THE TIME TO PLOT OUR RETURN. THEN IN APRIL OF 1898, AN AMERICAN DIPLOMAT MET WITH ME...

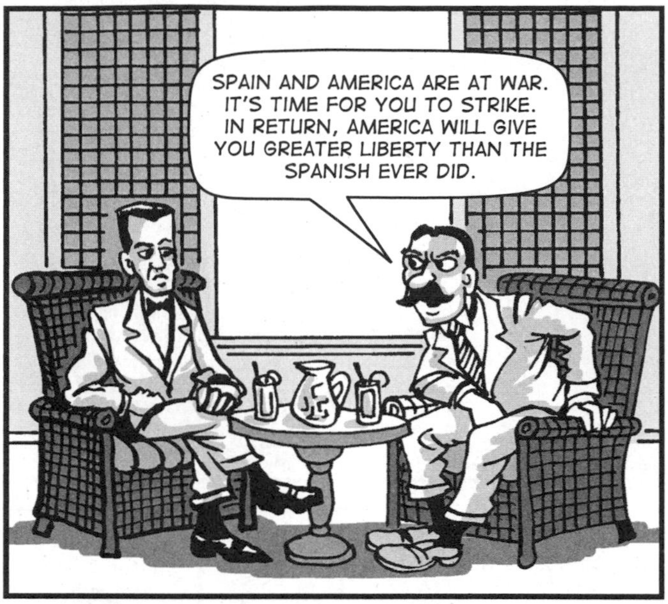
SPAIN AND AMERICA ARE AT WAR. IT'S TIME FOR YOU TO STRIKE. IN RETURN, AMERICA WILL GIVE YOU GREATER LIBERTY THAN THE SPANISH EVER DID.

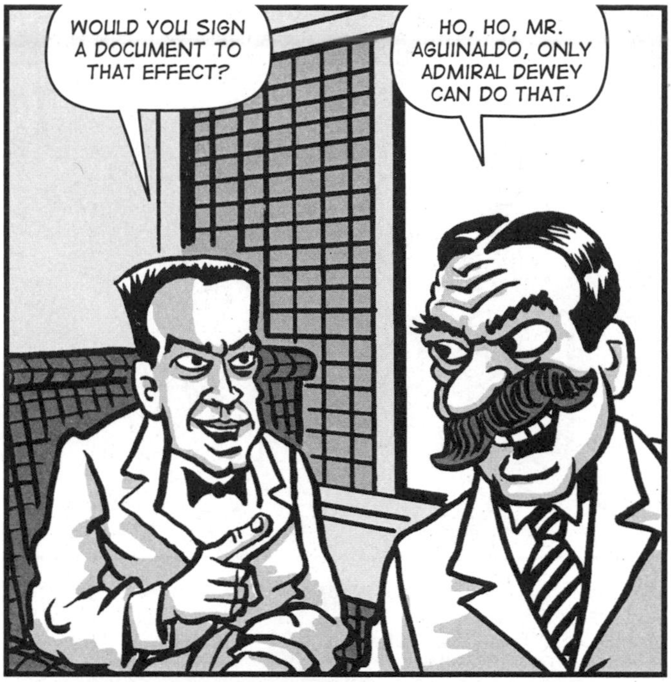
WOULD YOU SIGN A DOCUMENT TO THAT EFFECT?
HO, HO, MR. AGUINALDO, ONLY ADMIRAL DEWEY CAN DO THAT.

ON MAY 1, 1898, ADMIRAL ***GEORGE DEWEY***, COMMANDER OF THE U.S. ASIATIC SQUADRON, DESTROYED THE SPANISH FLEET IN MANILA HARBOR.

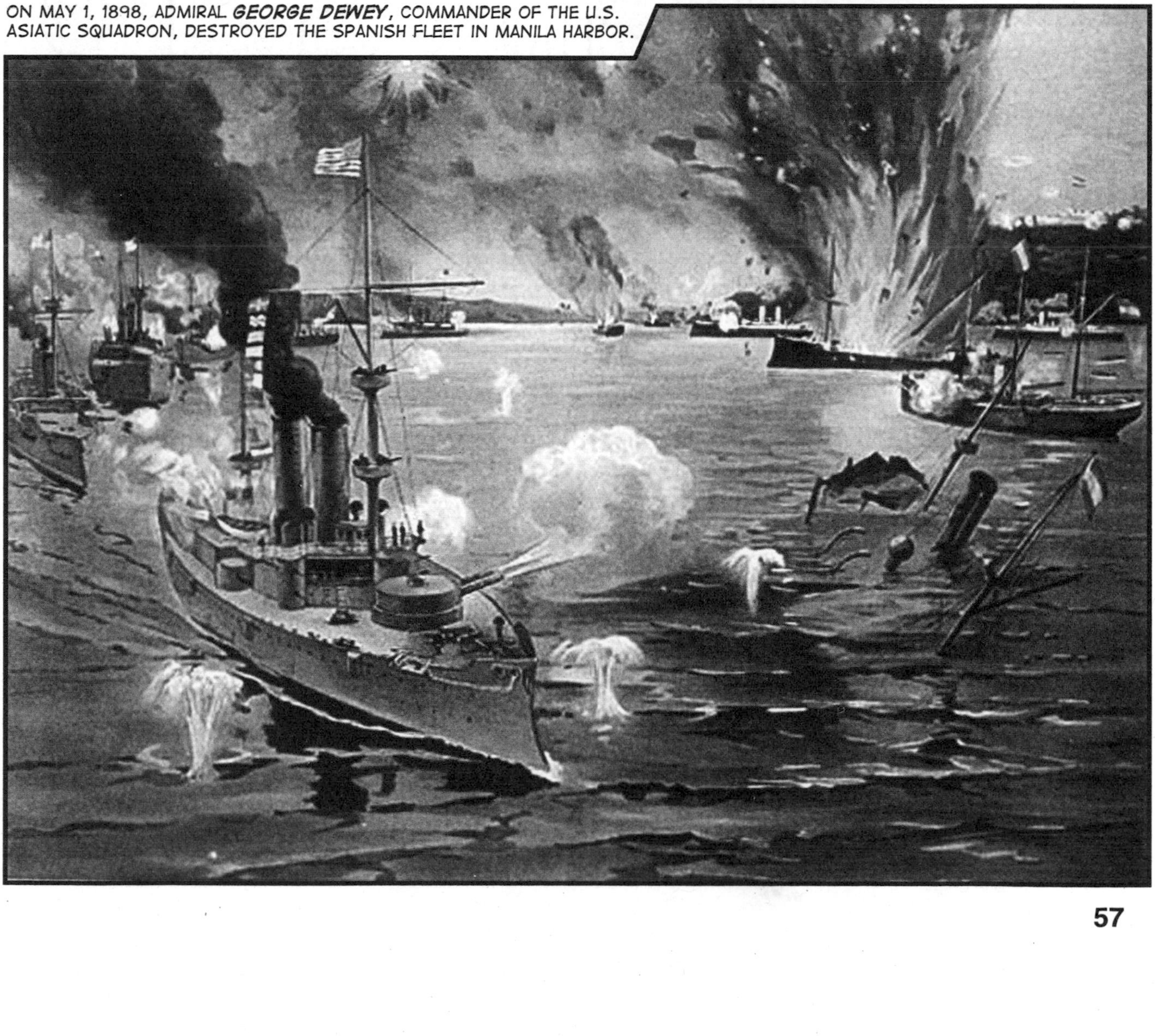

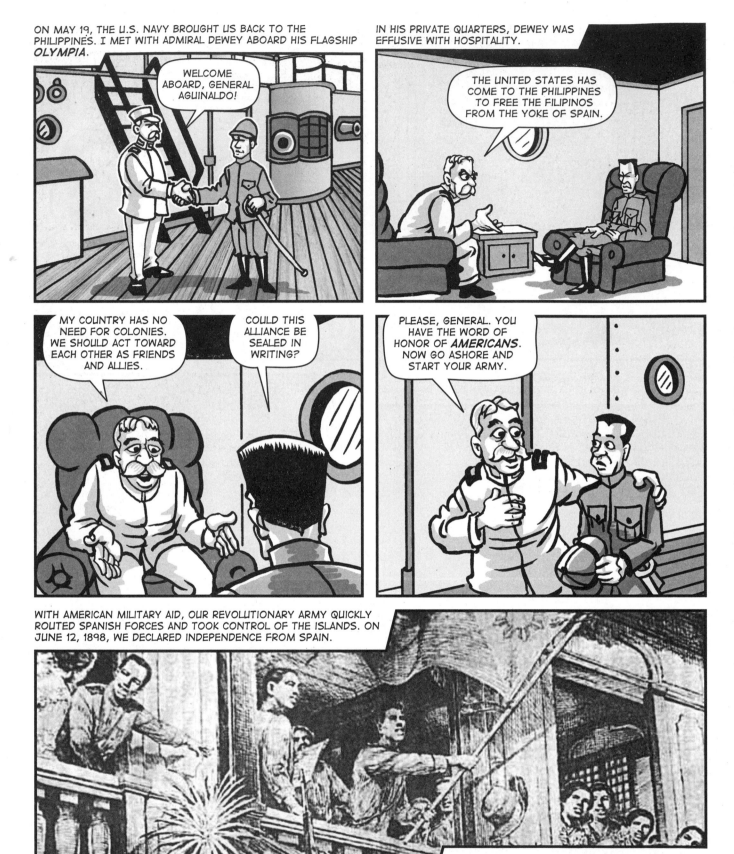

ON MAY 19, THE U.S. NAVY BROUGHT US BACK TO THE PHILIPPINES. I MET WITH ADMIRAL DEWEY ABOARD HIS FLAGSHIP *OLYMPIA*.

WELCOME ABOARD, GENERAL AGUINALDO!

IN HIS PRIVATE QUARTERS, DEWEY WAS EFFUSIVE WITH HOSPITALITY.

THE UNITED STATES HAS COME TO THE PHILIPPINES TO FREE THE FILIPINOS FROM THE YOKE OF SPAIN.

MY COUNTRY HAS NO NEED FOR COLONIES. WE SHOULD ACT TOWARD EACH OTHER AS FRIENDS AND ALLIES.

COULD THIS ALLIANCE BE SEALED IN WRITING?

PLEASE, GENERAL. YOU HAVE THE WORD OF HONOR OF *AMERICANS*. NOW GO ASHORE AND START YOUR ARMY.

WITH AMERICAN MILITARY AID, OUR REVOLUTIONARY ARMY QUICKLY ROUTED SPANISH FORCES AND TOOK CONTROL OF THE ISLANDS. ON JUNE 12, 1898, WE DECLARED INDEPENDENCE FROM SPAIN.

LITTLE DID WE KNOW THAT, ON MAY 19, MCKINLEY HAD ORDERED HIS SECRETARY OF WAR TO SEND 20,000 TROOPS TO *OCCUPY THE PHILIPPINES*.

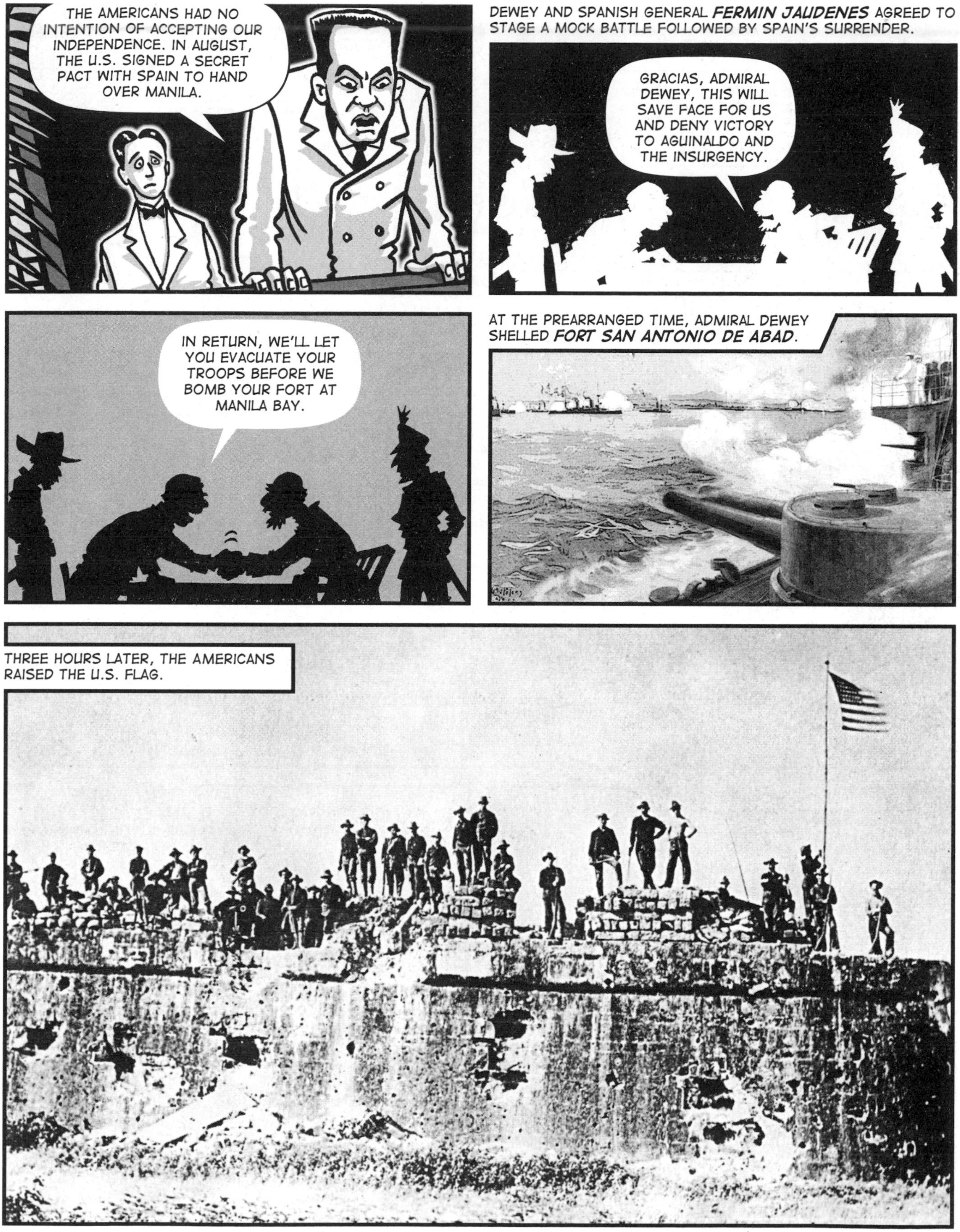
THE AMERICANS HAD NO INTENTION OF ACCEPTING OUR INDEPENDENCE. IN AUGUST, THE U.S. SIGNED A SECRET PACT WITH SPAIN TO HAND OVER MANILA.
DEWEY AND SPANISH GENERAL FERMIN JAUDENES AGREED TO STAGE A MOCK BATTLE FOLLOWED BY SPAIN'S SURRENDER.
GRACIAS, ADMIRAL DEWEY, THIS WILL SAVE FACE FOR US AND DENY VICTORY TO AGUINALDO AND THE INSURGENCY.
IN RETURN, WE'LL LET YOU EVACUATE YOUR TROOPS BEFORE WE BOMB YOUR FORT AT MANILA BAY.
AT THE PREARRANGED TIME, ADMIRAL DEWEY SHELLED FORT SAN ANTONIO DE ABAD.
THREE HOURS LATER, THE AMERICANS RAISED THE U.S. FLAG.

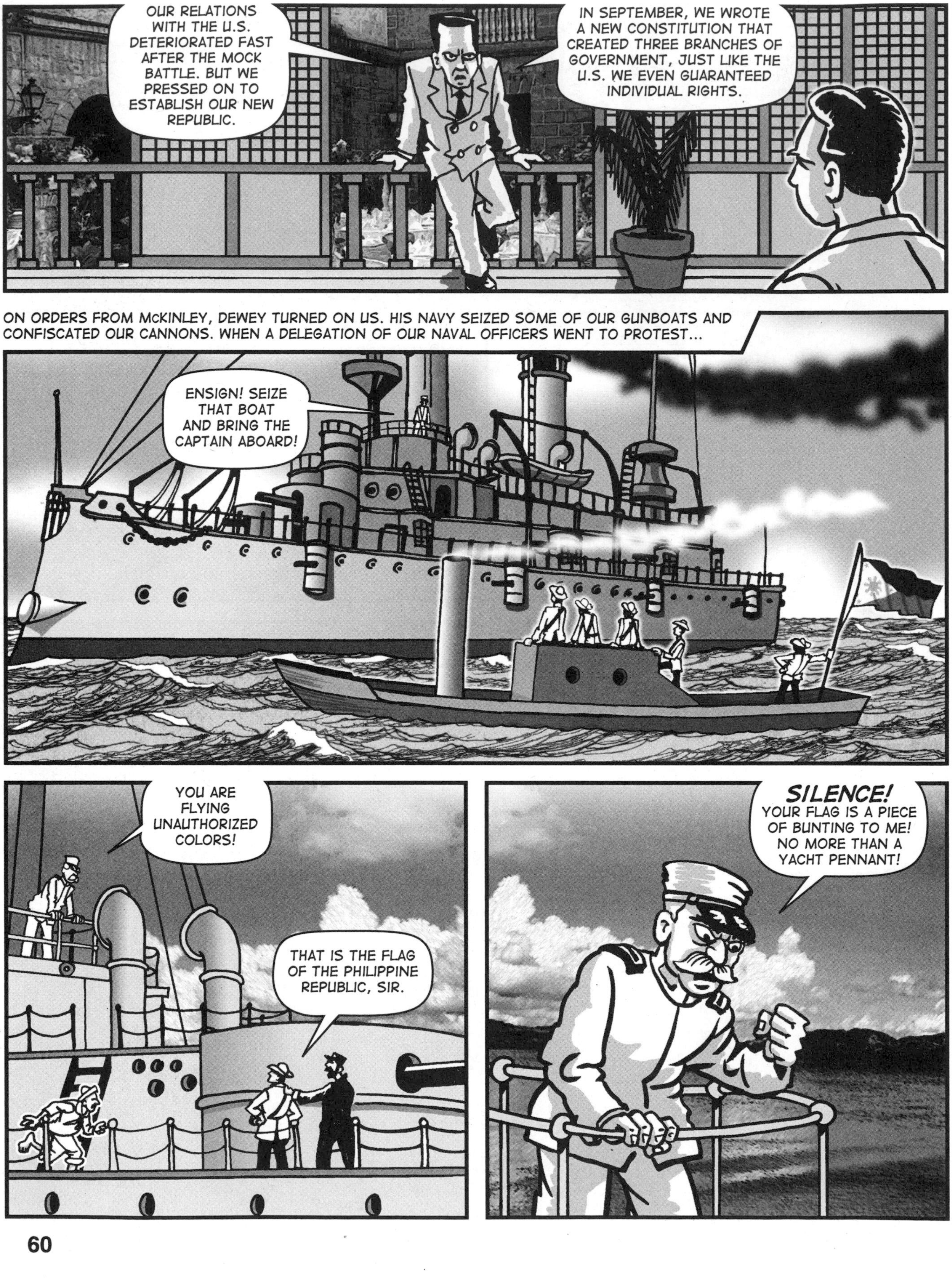
OUR RELATIONS WITH THE U.S. DETERIORATED FAST AFTER THE MOCK BATTLE. BUT WE PRESSED ON TO ESTABLISH OUR NEW REPUBLIC.
IN SEPTEMBER, WE WROTE A NEW CONSTITUTION THAT CREATED THREE BRANCHES OF GOVERNMENT, JUST LIKE THE U.S. WE EVEN GUARANTEED INDIVIDUAL RIGHTS.
ON ORDERS FROM McKINLEY, DEWEY TURNED ON US. HIS NAVY SEIZED SOME OF OUR GUNBOATS AND CONFISCATED OUR CANNONS. WHEN A DELEGATION OF OUR NAVAL OFFICERS WENT TO PROTEST...
ENSIGN! SEIZE THAT BOAT AND BRING THE CAPTAIN ABOARD!
YOU ARE FLYING UNAUTHORIZED COLORS!
THAT IS THE FLAG OF THE PHILIPPINE REPUBLIC, SIR.
SILENCE! YOUR FLAG IS A PIECE OF BUNTING TO ME! NO MORE THAN A YACHT PENNANT!

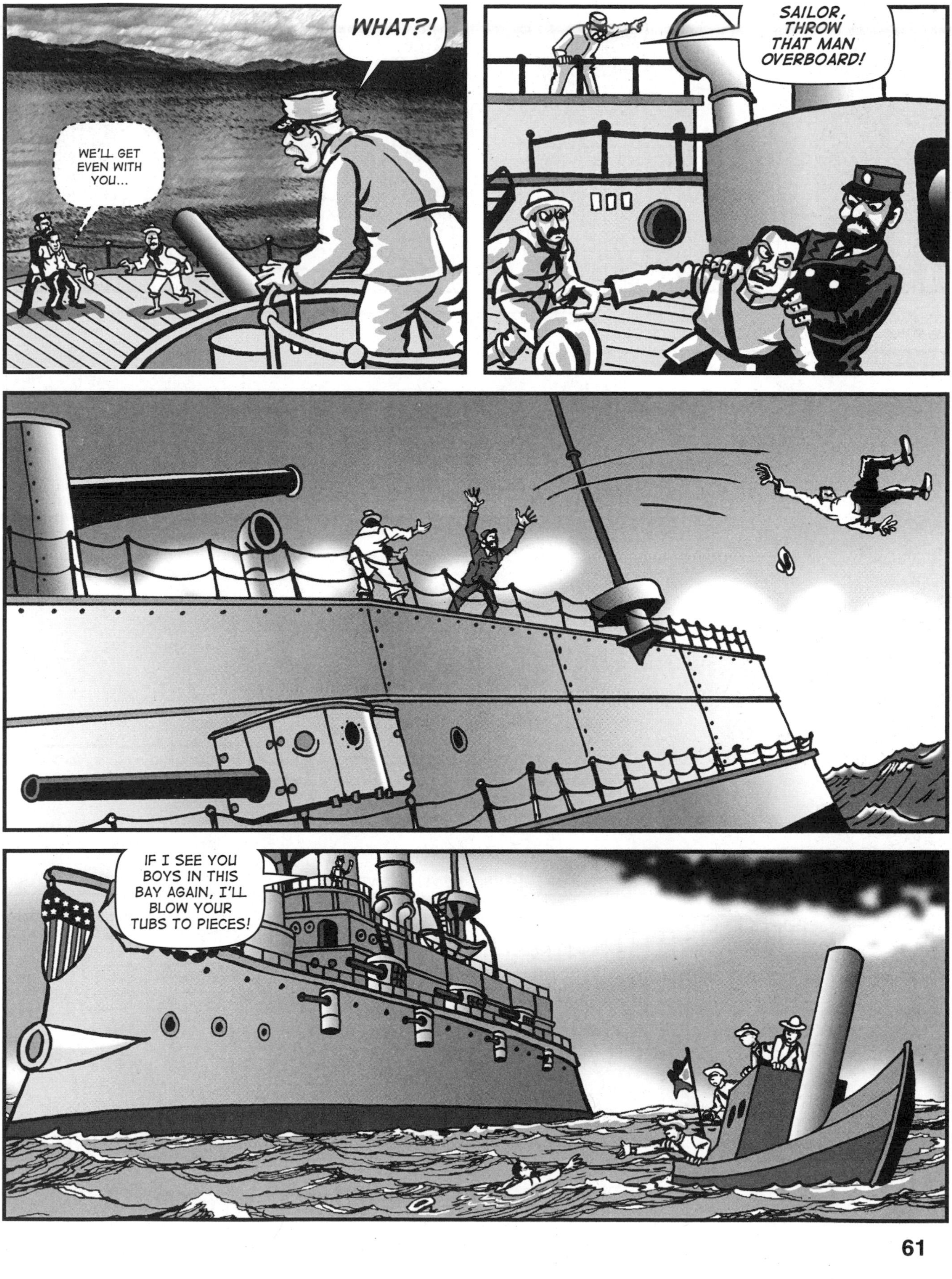
WHAT?!
WE'LL GET EVEN WITH YOU...
SAILOR, THROW THAT MAN OVERBOARD!
IF I SEE YOU BOYS IN THIS BAY AGAIN, I'LL BLOW YOUR TUBS TO PIECES!

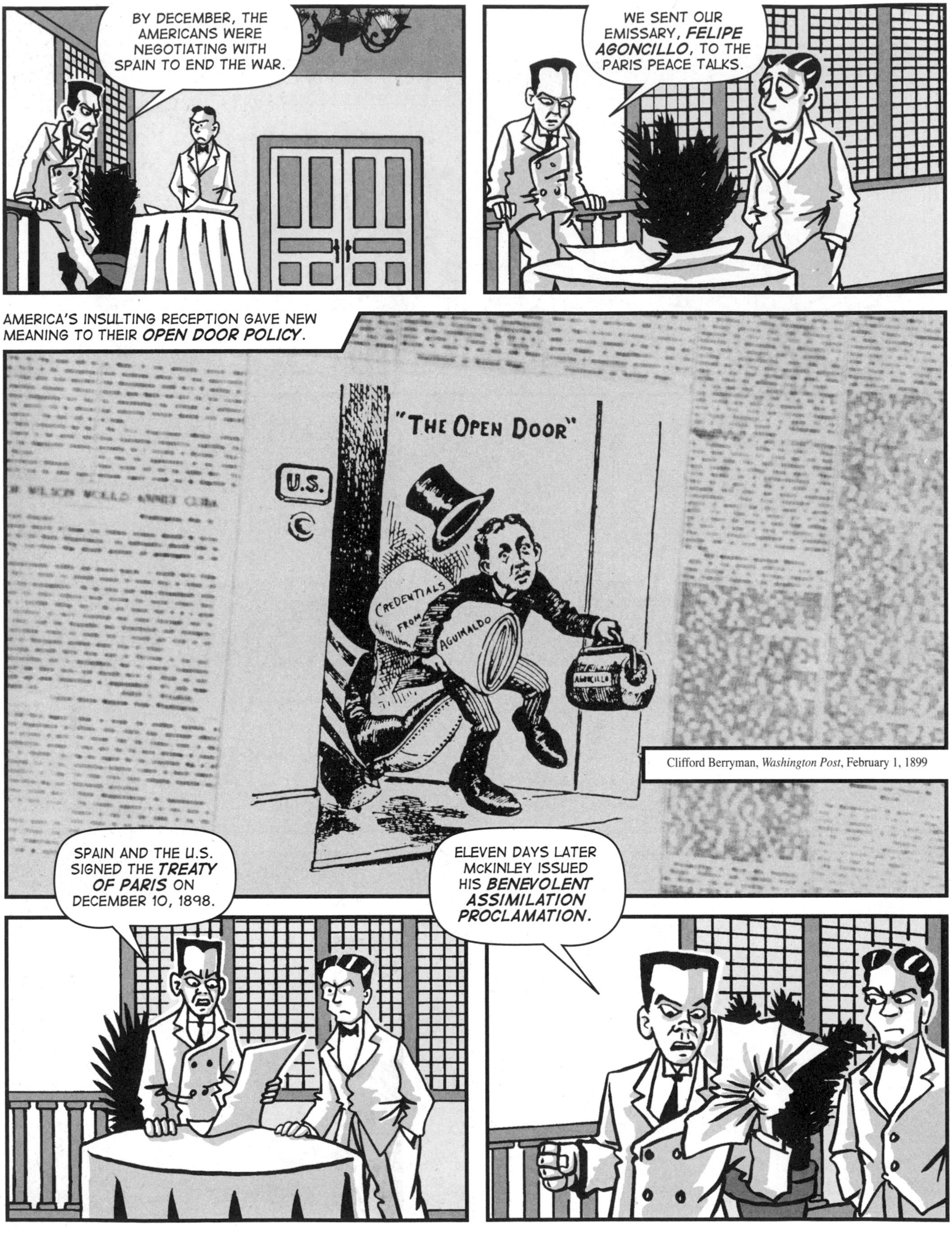
BY DECEMBER, THE AMERICANS WERE NEGOTIATING WITH SPAIN TO END THE WAR.
WE SENT OUR EMISSARY, ***FELIPE AGONCILLO***, TO THE PARIS PEACE TALKS.
AMERICA'S INSULTING RECEPTION GAVE NEW MEANING TO THEIR ***OPEN DOOR POLICY***.
"THE OPEN DOOR"
U.S.
CREDENTIALS FROM AGUINALDO
SPAIN AND THE U.S. SIGNED THE ***TREATY OF PARIS*** ON DECEMBER 10, 1898.
ELEVEN DAYS LATER McKINLEY ISSUED HIS ***BENEVOLENT ASSIMILATION PROCLAMATION***.
Clifford Berryman, *Washington Post*, February 1, 1899

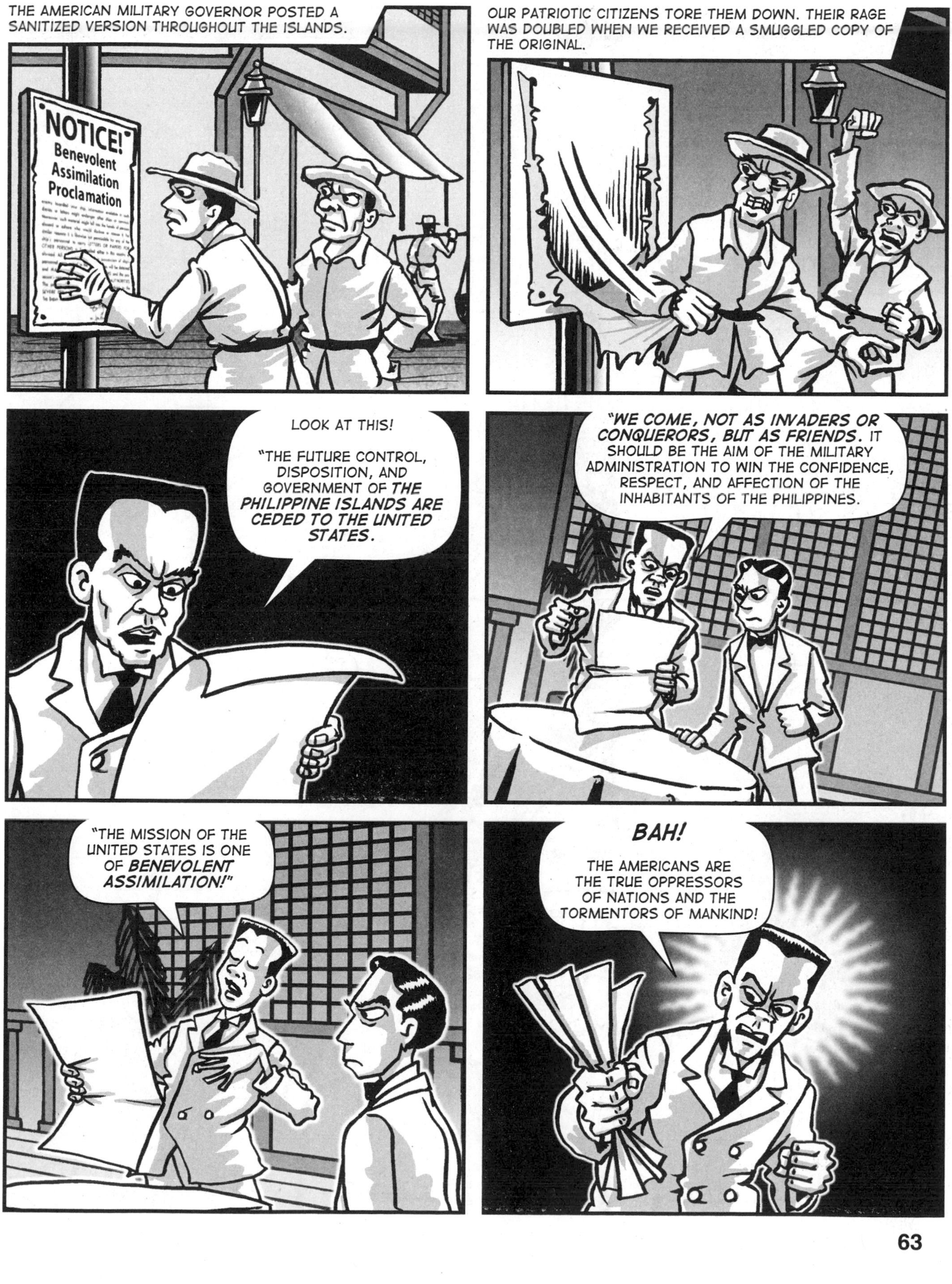
THE AMERICAN MILITARY GOVERNOR POSTED A SANITIZED VERSION THROUGHOUT THE ISLANDS.
NOTICE! Benevolent Assimilation Proclamation
OUR PATRIOTIC CITIZENS TORE THEM DOWN. THEIR RAGE WAS DOUBLED WHEN WE RECEIVED A SMUGGLED COPY OF THE ORIGINAL.
LOOK AT THIS! "THE FUTURE CONTROL, DISPOSITION, AND GOVERNMENT OF THE PHILIPPINE ISLANDS ARE CEDED TO THE UNITED STATES.
"WE COME, NOT AS INVADERS OR CONQUERORS, BUT AS FRIENDS. IT SHOULD BE THE AIM OF THE MILITARY ADMINISTRATION TO WIN THE CONFIDENCE, RESPECT, AND AFFECTION OF THE INHABITANTS OF THE PHILIPPINES.
"THE MISSION OF THE UNITED STATES IS ONE OF BENEVOLENT ASSIMILATION!"
BAH!
THE AMERICANS ARE THE TRUE OPPRESSORS OF NATIONS AND THE TORMENTORS OF MANKIND!

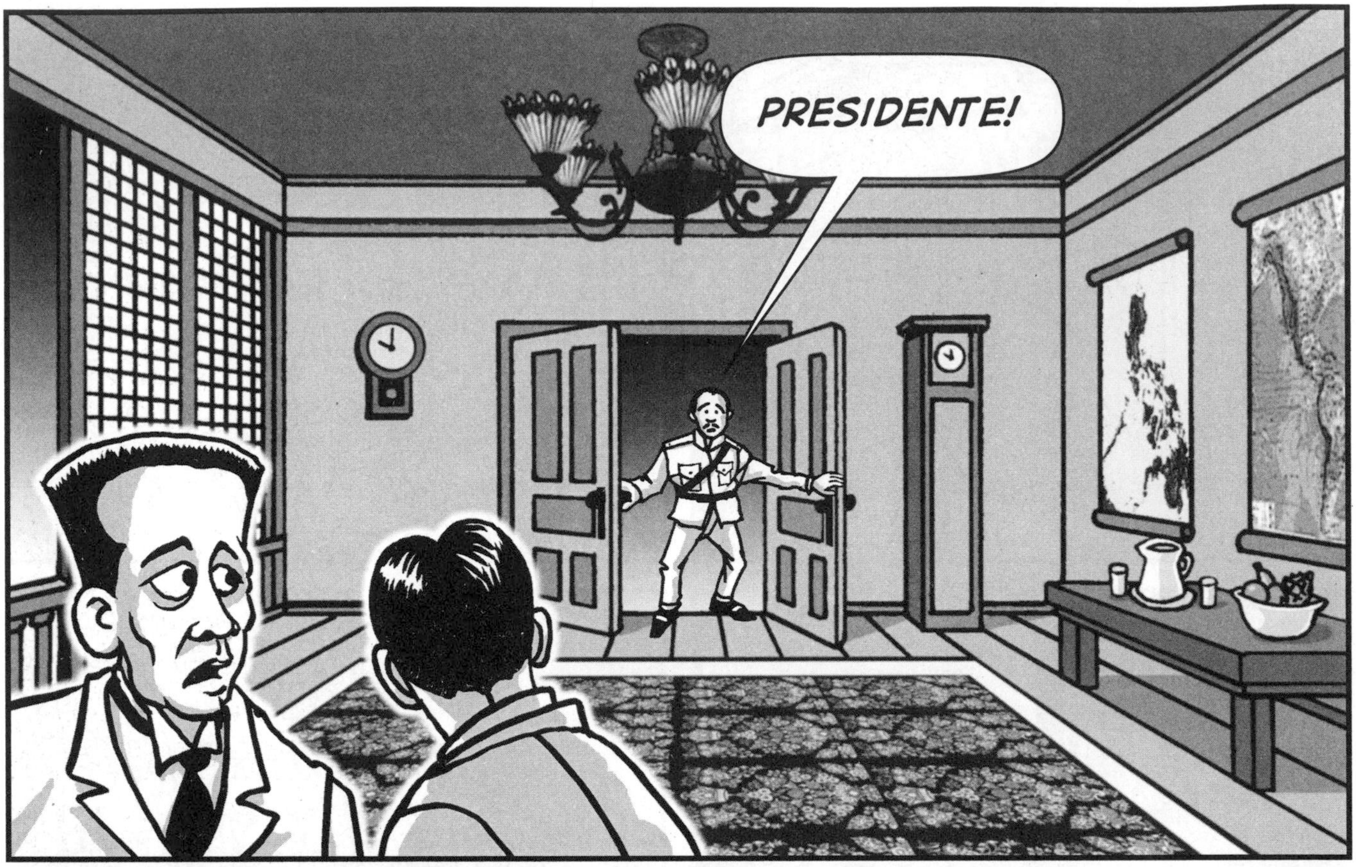
PRESIDENTE!

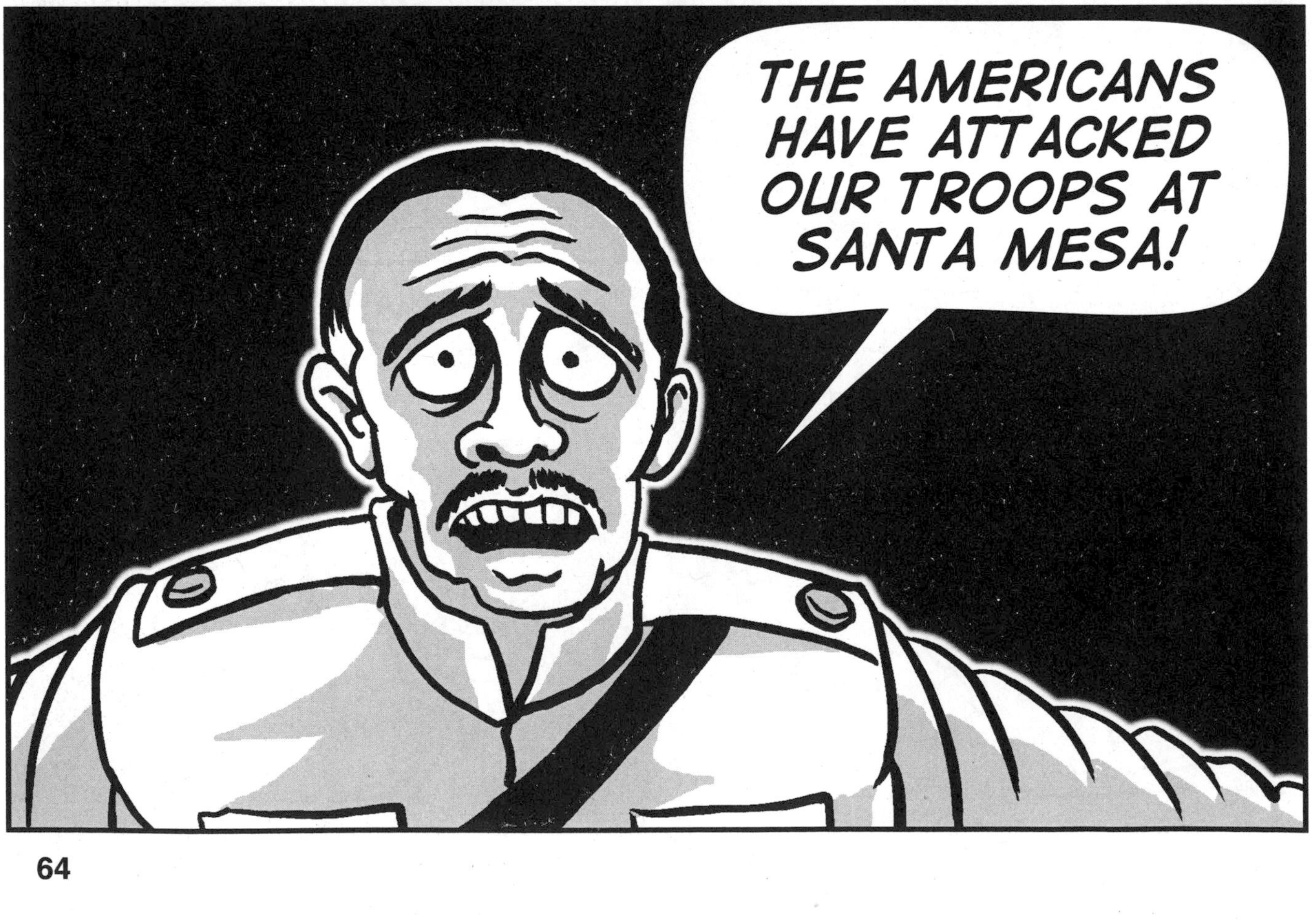
THE AMERICANS HAVE ATTACKED OUR TROOPS AT SANTA MESA!

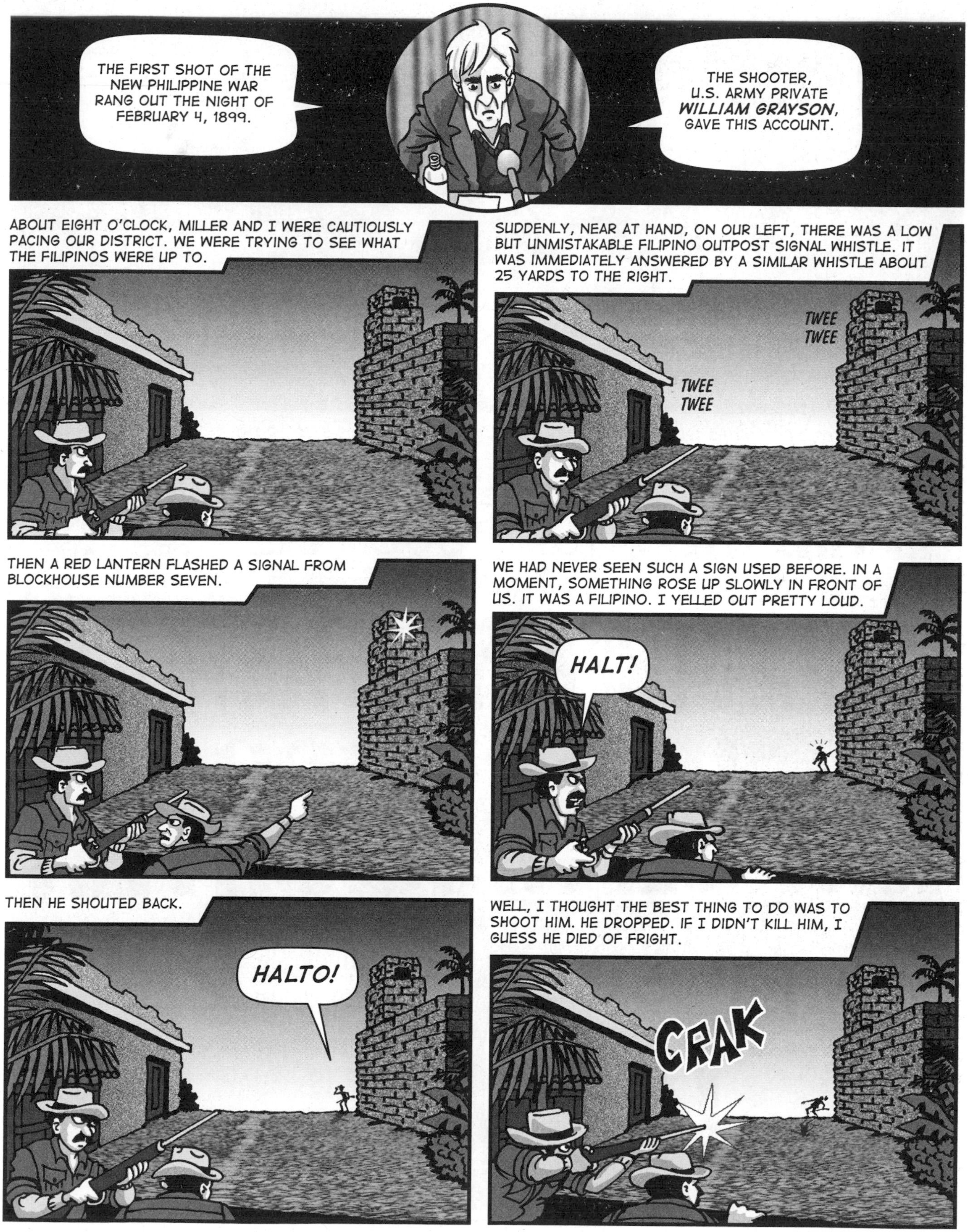
THE FIRST SHOT OF THE NEW PHILIPPINE WAR RANG OUT THE NIGHT OF FEBRUARY 4, 1899.
THE SHOOTER, U.S. ARMY PRIVATE ***WILLIAM GRAYSON,*** GAVE THIS ACCOUNT.
ABOUT EIGHT O'CLOCK, MILLER AND I WERE CAUTIOUSLY PACING OUR DISTRICT. WE WERE TRYING TO SEE WHAT THE FILIPINOS WERE UP TO.
SUDDENLY, NEAR AT HAND, ON OUR LEFT, THERE WAS A LOW BUT UNMISTAKABLE FILIPINO OUTPOST SIGNAL WHISTLE. IT WAS IMMEDIATELY ANSWERED BY A SIMILAR WHISTLE ABOUT 25 YARDS TO THE RIGHT.
TWEE TWEE
TWEE TWEE
THEN A RED LANTERN FLASHED A SIGNAL FROM BLOCKHOUSE NUMBER SEVEN.
WE HAD NEVER SEEN SUCH A SIGN USED BEFORE. IN A MOMENT, SOMETHING ROSE UP SLOWLY IN FRONT OF US. IT WAS A FILIPINO. I YELLED OUT PRETTY LOUD.
HALT!
THEN HE SHOUTED BACK.
HALTO!
WELL, I THOUGHT THE BEST THING TO DO WAS TO SHOOT HIM. HE DROPPED. IF I DIDN'T KILL HIM, I GUESS HE DIED OF FRIGHT.
CRAK

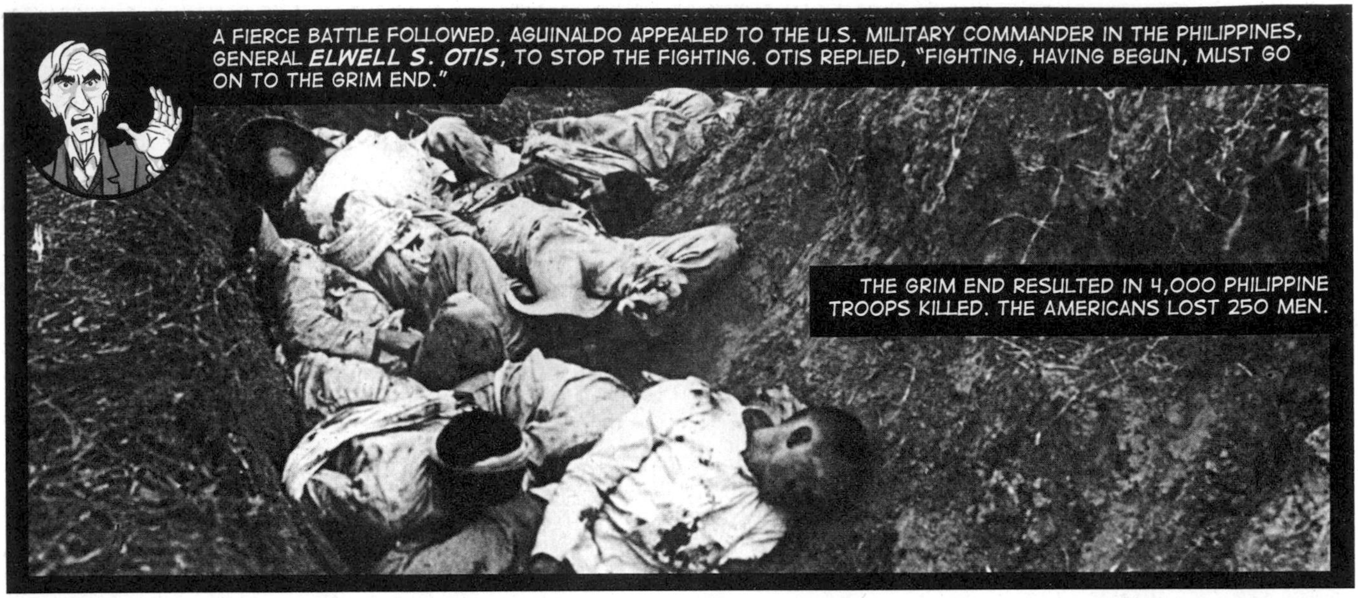
A FIERCE BATTLE FOLLOWED. AGUINALDO APPEALED TO THE U.S. MILITARY COMMANDER IN THE PHILIPPINES, GENERAL ***ELWELL S. OTIS***, TO STOP THE FIGHTING. OTIS REPLIED, "FIGHTING, HAVING BEGUN, MUST GO ON TO THE GRIM END."
THE GRIM END RESULTED IN 4,000 PHILIPPINE TROOPS KILLED. THE AMERICANS LOST 250 MEN.

THE AMERICAN PEOPLE SUPPORTED THE WAR TO LIBERATE CUBA BUT NOT TO ANNEX THE PHILIPPINES. AS A RESULT, CONGRESS CONTESTED RATIFICATION OF THE TREATY WITH SPAIN. BUT THE YELLOW JOURNALISTS FALSELY REPORTED THAT THE FILIPINOS STARTED THE WAR, CAUSING SEVERAL WAVERING SENATORS TO VOTE FOR THE TREATY. ON FEBRUARY 6, 1899, THE SENATE DELIVERED THE NECESSARY TWO-THIRDS APPROVAL BY JUST ONE VOTE.

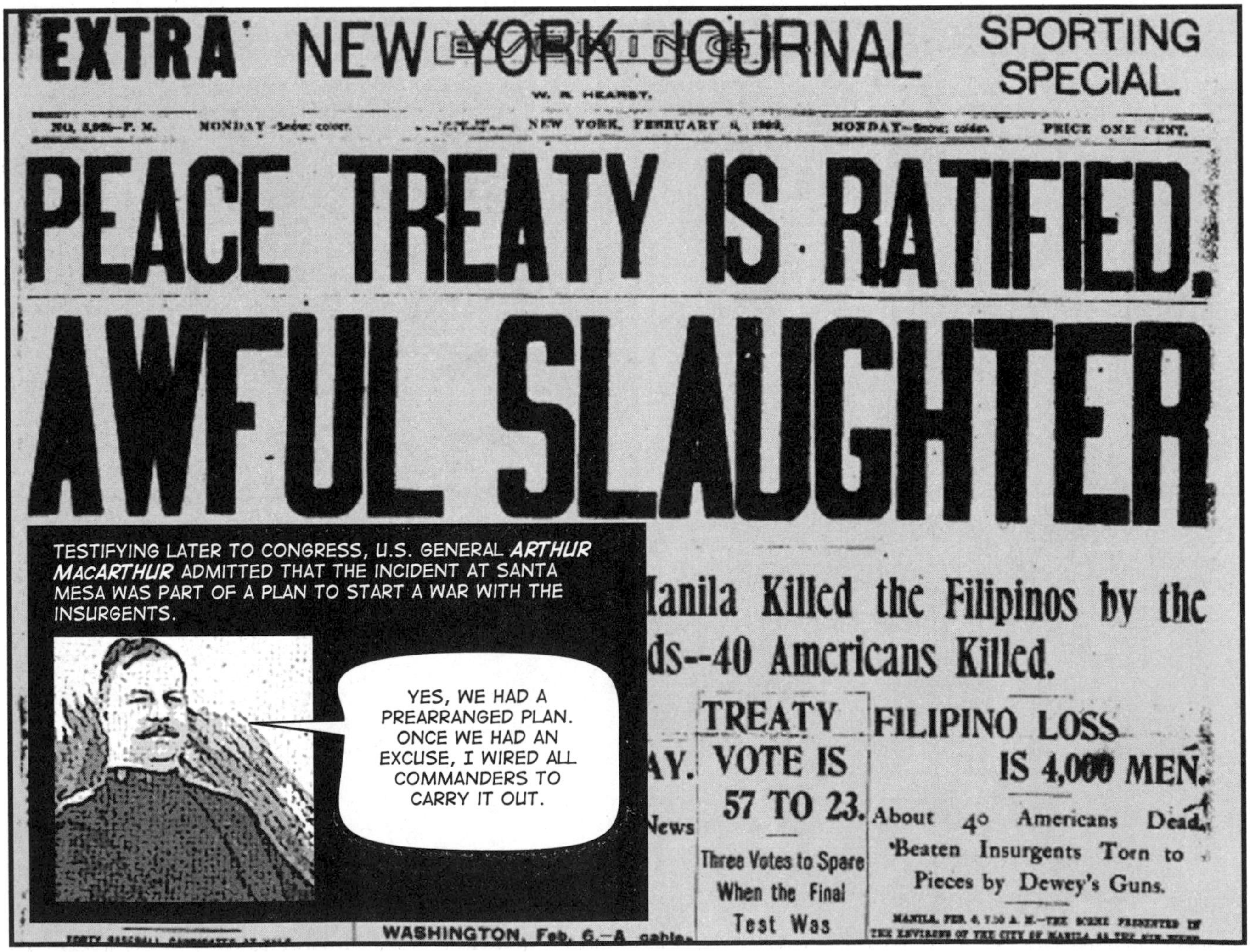
EXTRA NEW YORK JOURNAL SPORTING SPECIAL.

W. R. HEARST.

MONDAY NEW YORK, FEBRUARY 6, 1899 MONDAY PRICE ONE CENT.

PEACE TREATY IS RATIFIED. AWFUL SLAUGHTER

...Manila Killed the Filipinos by the ...ds--40 Americans Killed.

TREATY VOTE IS 57 TO 23.

Three Votes to Spare When the Final Test Was

FILIPINO LOSS IS 4,000 MEN.

About 40 Americans Dead. Beaten Insurgents Torn to Pieces by Dewey's Guns.

WASHINGTON, Feb. 6.—A cable...

TESTIFYING LATER TO CONGRESS, U.S. GENERAL ***ARTHUR MACARTHUR*** ADMITTED THAT THE INCIDENT AT SANTA MESA WAS PART OF A PLAN TO START A WAR WITH THE INSURGENTS.
YES, WE HAD A PREARRANGED PLAN. ONCE WE HAD AN EXCUSE, I WIRED ALL COMMANDERS TO CARRY IT OUT.

Republic or Empire?

THE PRESIDENTIAL ELECTION OF 1900 BECAME A BATTLE OVER AMERICA'S VIEW OF ITSELF. ***WERE WE A REPUBLIC OR AN EMPIRE?*** PRESIDENT McKINLEY, BACKED BY BUSINESS, SUPPORTED KEEPING THE PHILIPPINES. DEMOCRAT ***WILLIAM JENNINGS BRYAN***, SUPPORTED BY WORKERS AND FARMERS, RAN AS AN ANTI-IMPERIALIST AND FAVORED PHILIPPINE INDEPENDENCE. McKINLEY CONSIDERED HIS RE-ELECTION A ***MANDATE FOR EMPIRE***.

THE TASTE OF EMPIRE WAS ON THE LIPS OF POLITICIANS AND BUSINESS INTERESTS THROUGHOUT THE COUNTRY NOW. RACISM, PATERNALISM, AND TALK OF MONEY MINGLED WITH TALK OF DESTINY AND CIVILIZATION.

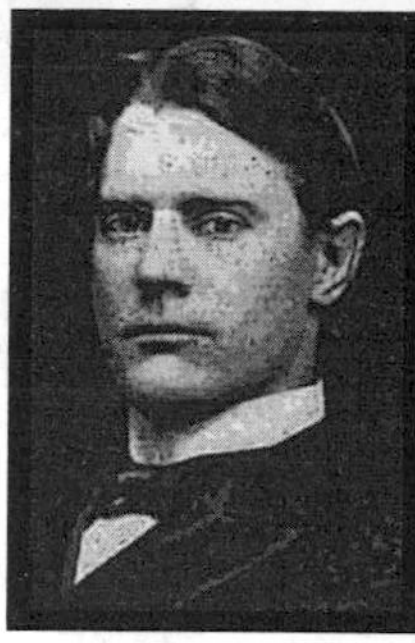

"WE WILL NOT RENOUNCE OUR PART IN THE MISSION OF OUR RACE - TRUSTEE, UNDER GOD, OF THE CIVILIZATION OF THE WORLD. THE PHILIPPINES GIVE US A BASE AT THE DOOR OF ALL THE EAST."

ALBERT J. BEVERIDGE
U.S. SENATOR
INDIANA

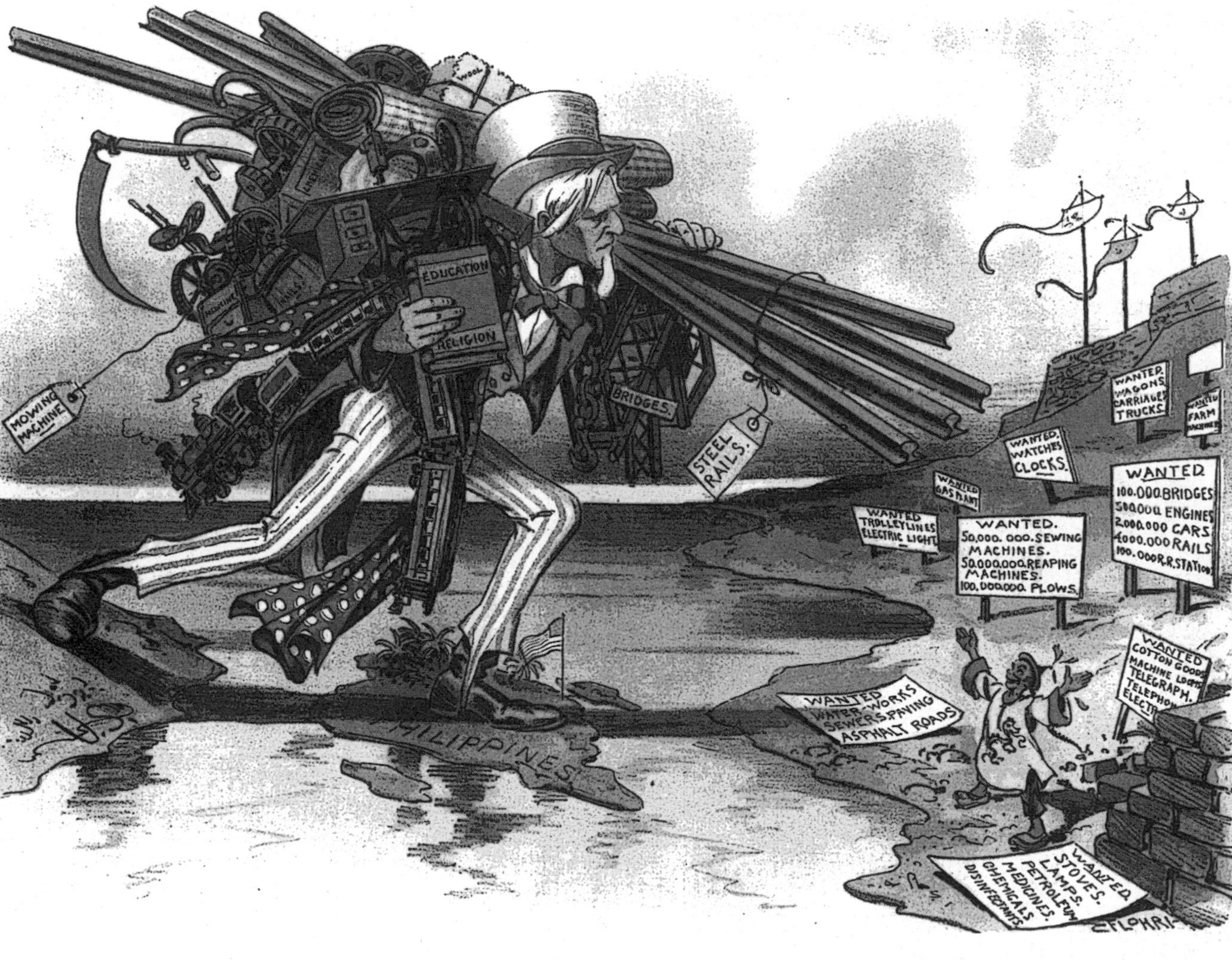
EDUCATION
RELIGION
MOWING MACHINE
BRIDGES
STEEL RAILS.
PHILIPPINES
WANTED TROLLEY LINES ELECTRIC LIGHT
WANTED GAS PLANT
WANTED. WATCHES CLOCKS.
WANTED. WAGONS CARRIAGES TRUCKS
WANTED FARM
WANTED. 50,000.000. SEWING MACHINES. 50.000.000 REAPING MACHINES. 100.000.000 PLOWS.
WANTED 100.000 BRIDGES 500.000 ENGINES 2.000.000 CARS 4000.000 RAILS 100.000 R.R.STATIONS
WANTED WATER-WORKS SEWERS PAVING ASPHALT ROADS
WANTED COTTON GOODS MACHINE LOOMS TELEGRAPH. TELEPHONE ELECTR
WANTED STOVES. LAMPS. PETROLEUM MEDICINES. CHEMICALS DISINFECTANTS
E. FLOHRI

"AND, AFTER ALL, THE PHILIPPINES ARE ONLY THE STEPPING-STONE TO CHINA."
Emil Flohri, *Judge*, March 21, 1900

The lynching of Garfield Burley and Curtis Brown, October 8, 1902, Newbern, Tennessee.

IT WAS A TIME OF INTENSE RACISM IN THE UNITED STATES. IN THE YEARS BETWEEN 1889 AND 1903, ON THE AVERAGE, EVERY WEEK, TWO NEGROES WERE LYNCHED BY MOBS – HANGED, BURNED, MUTILATED.

THE FILIPINOS WERE BROWN-SKINNED. ONE SOLDIER WROTE: "OUR FIGHTING BLOOD WAS UP, AND WE ALL WANTED TO KILL NIGGERS. *THIS SHOOTING HUMAN BEINGS BEATS RABBIT HUNTING ALL TO PIECES.*"

"THE FIRST BLACK BORED IN THE PHILIPPINES."
Grant Wallace, *Collier's Weekly*, October 7, 1899

IT WAS COMMON AMONG AMERICAN POLITICAL CARTOONISTS TO DRAW THE FILIPINOS WITH THE SAME RACIST STEREOTYPES USED TO DEPICT AFRICAN-AMERICANS.

BLACK SOLDIERS, IN FOUR REGIMENTS, FOUGHT IN THE PHILIPPINES WITH MIXED REACTIONS. MILITARY LIFE PROVIDED OPPORTUNITIES FOR SUCCESS DENIED THEM IN SOCIETY, BUT THEY WERE CONSCIOUS OF THEIR ROLE IN A BRUTAL WAR AGAINST COLORED PEOPLE. THE SOLDIERS' LETTERS HOME EXPRESSED THIS. WROTE ONE:

"OUR RACIAL SYMPATHIES WOULD NATURALLY BE WITH THE FILIPINOS, BUT WE CANNOT FOR THE SAKE OF SENTIMENT TURN OUR BACK UPON OUR OWN COUNTRY."

I FEEL SORRY FOR THESE PEOPLE. THEY HAVEN'T BEEN TREATED JUSTLY. AND IT REALLY MAKES ME ANGRY WHEN THE WHITE TROOPS CALL THEM *NIGGERS!*

AT HOME, PROMINENT BLACK LEADERS SPOKE OUT:

"IT IS ABOUT TIME FOR THE MINISTERS OF THE *A.M.E. CHURCH* TO TELL THE YOUNG MEN OF OUR RACE TO STAY OUT OF THE UNITED STATES ARMY. IF IT IS A WHITE MAN'S GOVERNMENT, AND WE GRANT IT IS, LET HIM TAKE CARE OF IT. THE NEGRO HAS NO FLAG TO DEFEND."

HENRY M. TURNER
SENIOR BISHOP
AFRICAN METHODIST EPISCOPAL CHURCH

W.E.B. DuBOIS BELIEVED THAT THE RACISM OF THE WAR CUT OFF THE OPTION OF ESCAPING OPPRESSION AT HOME BY EMIGRATING ABROAD.

NOTHING HAS MADE EMIGRATION SEEM MORE HOPELESS THAN THE RECENT COURSE OF THE U.S. TOWARD WEAKER AND DARKER PEOPLE IN THE WEST INDIES, HAWAII, AND THE PHILIPPINES.

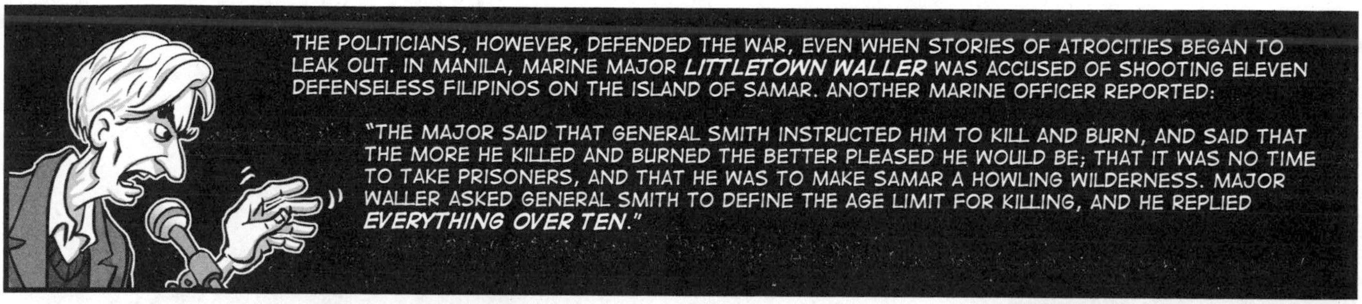
THE POLITICIANS, HOWEVER, DEFENDED THE WAR, EVEN WHEN STORIES OF ATROCITIES BEGAN TO LEAK OUT. IN MANILA, MARINE MAJOR *LITTLETOWN WALLER* WAS ACCUSED OF SHOOTING ELEVEN DEFENSELESS FILIPINOS ON THE ISLAND OF SAMAR. ANOTHER MARINE OFFICER REPORTED:
"THE MAJOR SAID THAT GENERAL SMITH INSTRUCTED HIM TO KILL AND BURN, AND SAID THAT THE MORE HE KILLED AND BURNED THE BETTER PLEASED HE WOULD BE; THAT IT WAS NO TIME TO TAKE PRISONERS, AND THAT HE WAS TO MAKE SAMAR A HOWLING WILDERNESS. MAJOR WALLER ASKED GENERAL SMITH TO DEFINE THE AGE LIMIT FOR KILLING, AND HE REPLIED *EVERYTHING OVER TEN*."

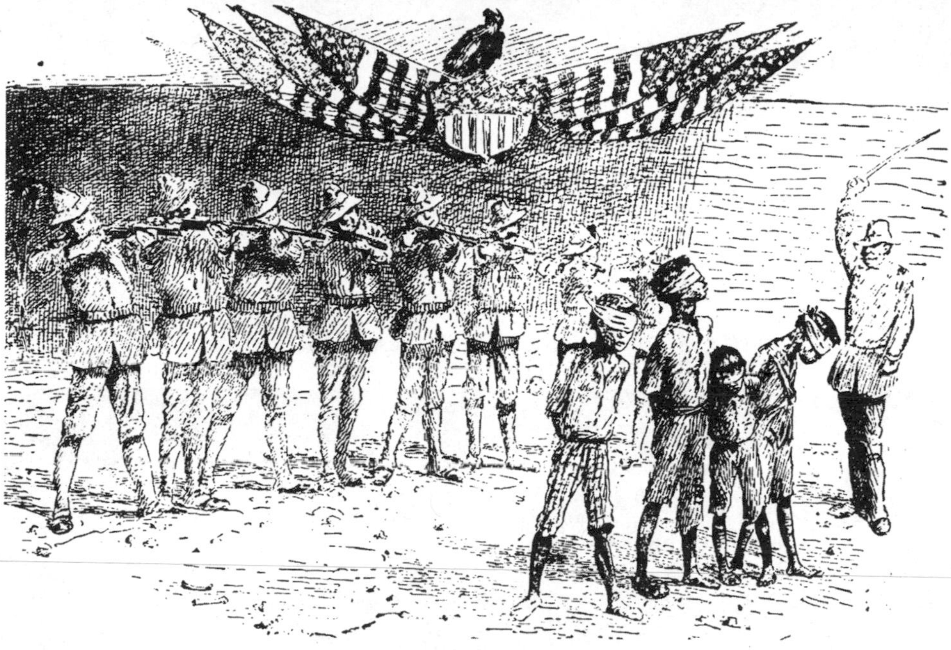

"KILL EVERYTHING OVER 10."
"CRIMINALS BECAUSE THEY WERE BORN TEN YEARS BEFORE WE TOOK THE PHILIPPINES."
Homer Davenport, *New York Evening Journal*, May 17, 1902

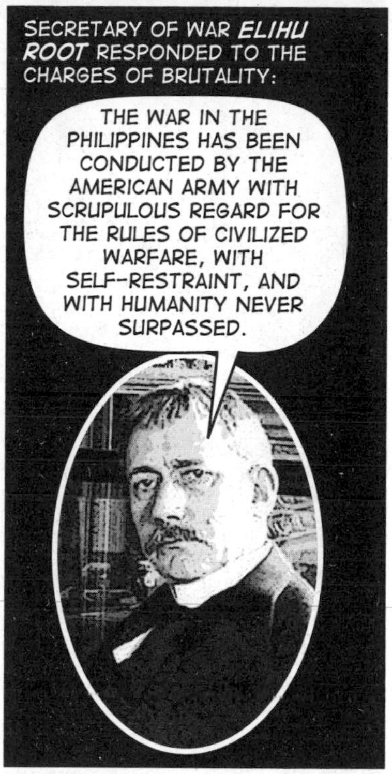
SECRETARY OF WAR *ELIHU ROOT* RESPONDED TO THE CHARGES OF BRUTALITY:
THE WAR IN THE PHILIPPINES HAS BEEN CONDUCTED BY THE AMERICAN ARMY WITH SCRUPULOUS REGARD FOR THE RULES OF CIVILIZED WARFARE, WITH SELF-RESTRAINT, AND WITH HUMANITY NEVER SURPASSED.

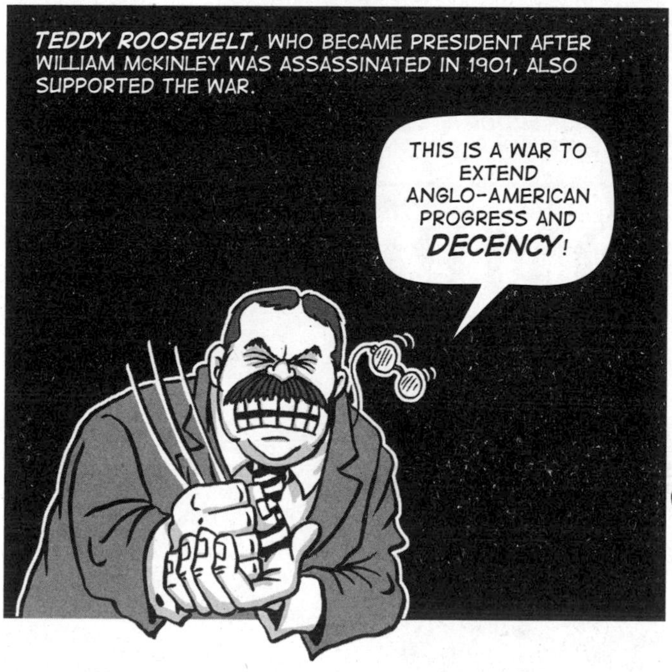
TEDDY ROOSEVELT, WHO BECAME PRESIDENT AFTER WILLIAM McKINLEY WAS ASSASSINATED IN 1901, ALSO SUPPORTED THE WAR.
THIS IS A WAR TO EXTEND ANGLO-AMERICAN PROGRESS AND *DECENCY*!

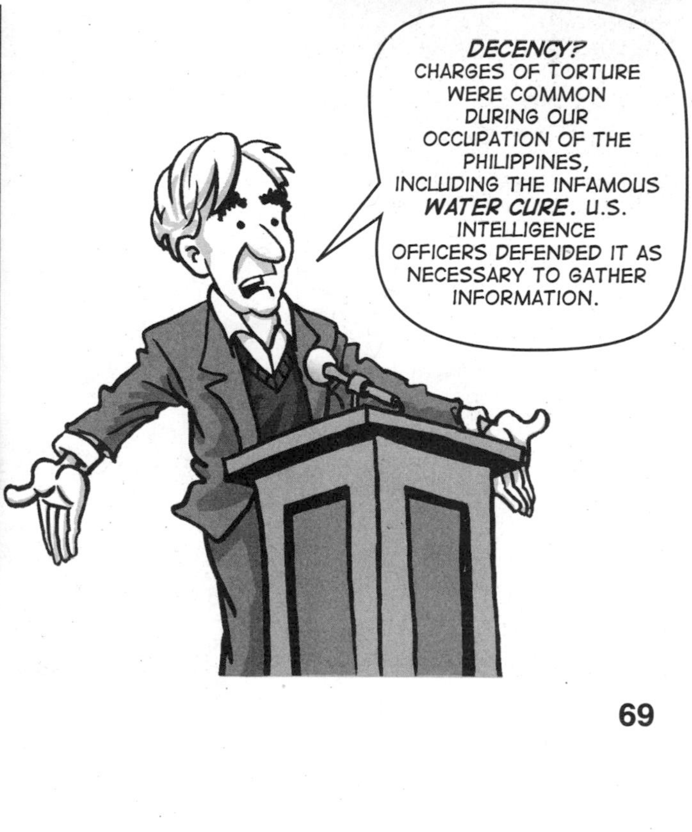
DECENCY? CHARGES OF TORTURE WERE COMMON DURING OUR OCCUPATION OF THE PHILIPPINES, INCLUDING THE INFAMOUS *WATER CURE*. U.S. INTELLIGENCE OFFICERS DEFENDED IT AS NECESSARY TO GATHER INFORMATION.

AMERICAN TROOPS USED THE WATER CURE TO INTERROGATE FILIPINO PRISONERS, FORCING WATER DOWN THEIR THROATS UNTIL THEY NEARLY DROWNED. TORTURERS THEN POUNDED THE VICTIMS' STOMACHS TO MAKE THEM TALK.

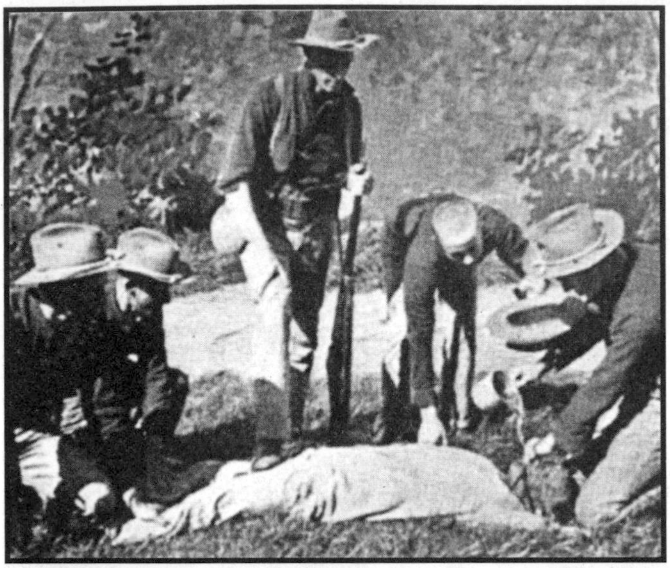

THIS EDITORIAL CARTOON RIDICULED THE PRACTICE.

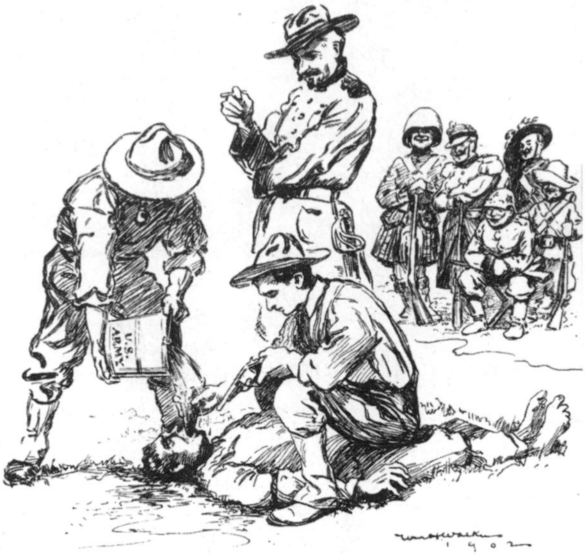

"CHORUS IN BACKGROUND: THOSE PIOUS YANKEES CAN'T THROW STONES AT US ANYMORE."
William Walker, *Life*, May 22, 1902

ZINNFORMATION

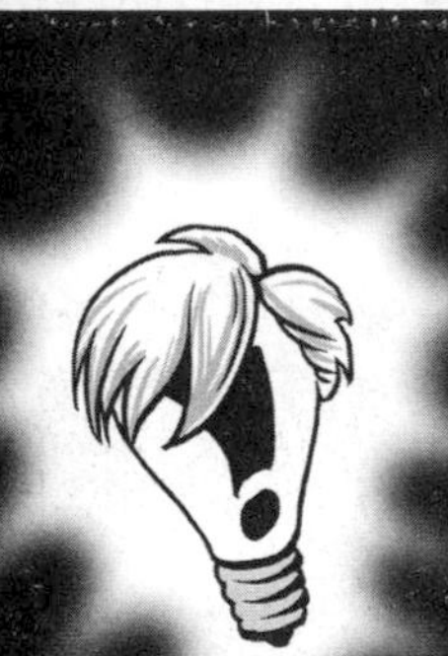

DURING THE ***WAR ON TERROR***, U.S. SOLDIERS USED BRUTAL TORTURE TECHNIQUES SUCH AS ELECTRIC SHOCK AND SEVERE BEATINGS.

ACCORDING TO ***ABC NEWS***, THEY ALSO USED ***WATER BOARDING***, WHERE THE PRISONER IS BOUND TO AN INCLINED BOARD, FEET RAISED AND HEAD SLIGHTLY BELOW THE FEET. CELLOPHANE IS WRAPPED OVER THE PRISONER'S FACE AND WATER IS POURED OVER HIM. UNAVOIDABLY, THE GAG REFLEX KICKS IN AND A TERRIFYING FEAR OF DROWNING LEADS TO ALMOST INSTANT PLEAS TO STOP THE TREATMENT.

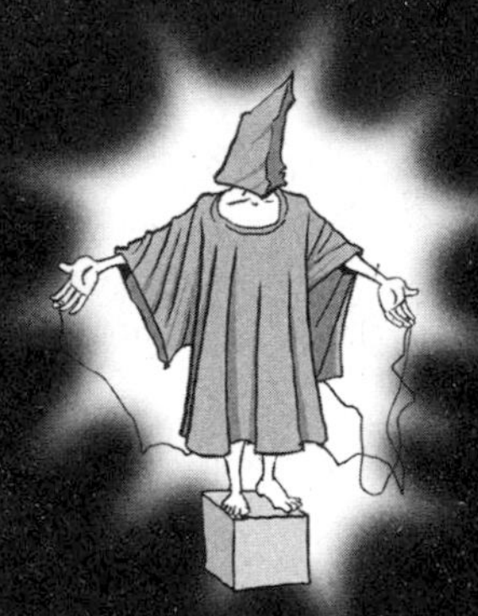

JULY 4, 1902: PRESIDENT ROOSEVELT DECLARED THE PHILIPPINE-AMERICAN WAR OVER. HOWEVER, RESISTANCE TO THE U.S. OCCUPATION CONTINUED FOR YEARS.

MAY 1, 2003: U.S. PRESIDENT ***GEORGE W. BUSH*** DECLARED THE END OF MAJOR COMBAT OPERATIONS IN THE IRAQ WAR, YET THE INSURGENCY RAGED ON.

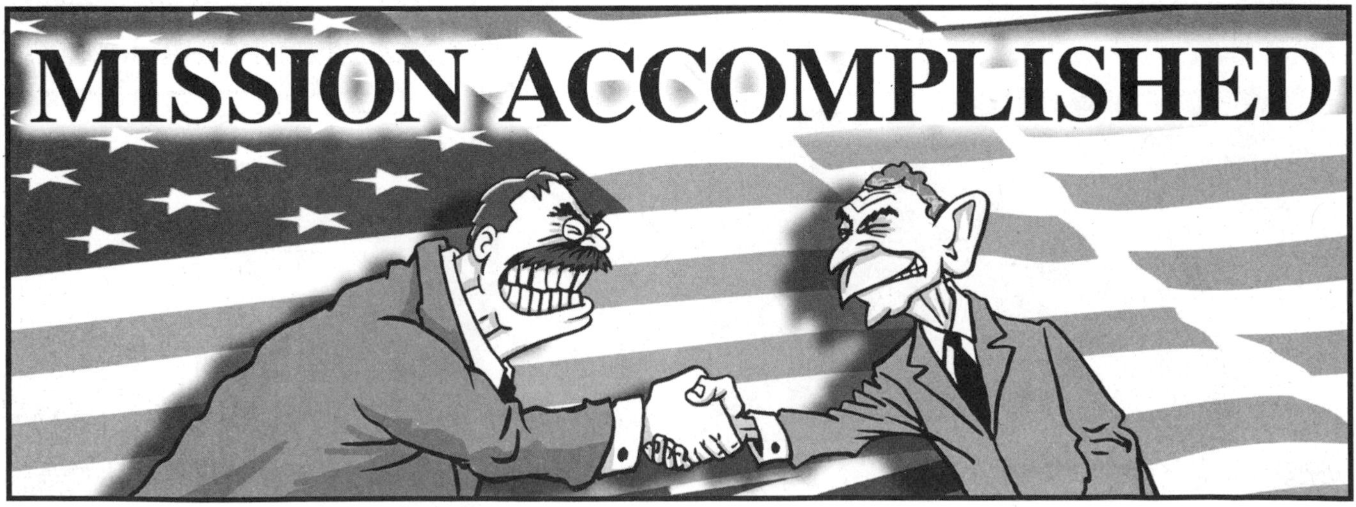
MISSION ACCOMPLISHED

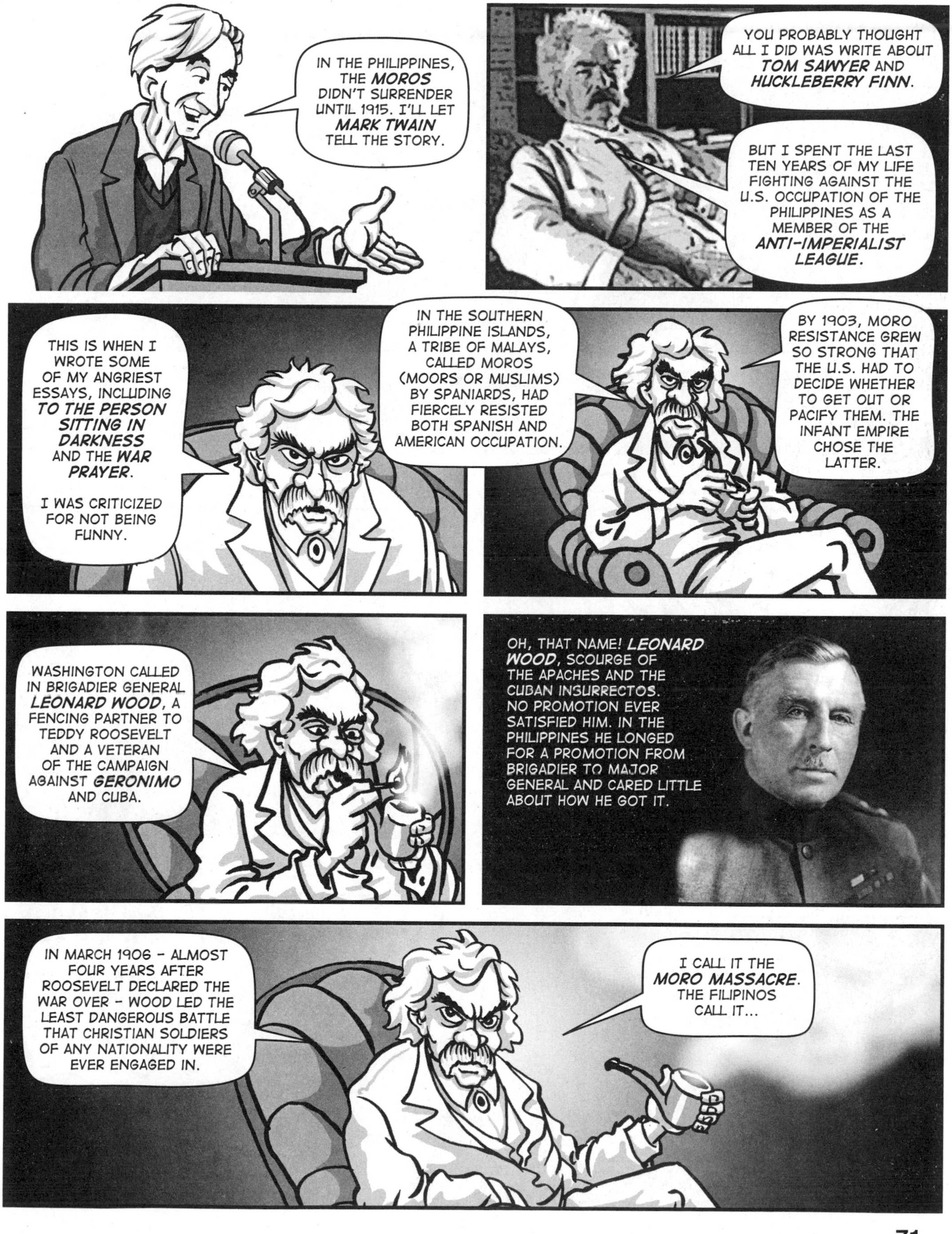
IN THE PHILIPPINES, THE MOROS DIDN'T SURRENDER UNTIL 1915. I'LL LET MARK TWAIN TELL THE STORY.
YOU PROBABLY THOUGHT ALL I DID WAS WRITE ABOUT TOM SAWYER AND HUCKLEBERRY FINN.
BUT I SPENT THE LAST TEN YEARS OF MY LIFE FIGHTING AGAINST THE U.S. OCCUPATION OF THE PHILIPPINES AS A MEMBER OF THE ANTI-IMPERIALIST LEAGUE.
THIS IS WHEN I WROTE SOME OF MY ANGRIEST ESSAYS, INCLUDING TO THE PERSON SITTING IN DARKNESS AND THE WAR PRAYER.
I WAS CRITICIZED FOR NOT BEING FUNNY.
IN THE SOUTHERN PHILIPPINE ISLANDS, A TRIBE OF MALAYS, CALLED MOROS (MOORS OR MUSLIMS) BY SPANIARDS, HAD FIERCELY RESISTED BOTH SPANISH AND AMERICAN OCCUPATION.
BY 1903, MORO RESISTANCE GREW SO STRONG THAT THE U.S. HAD TO DECIDE WHETHER TO GET OUT OR PACIFY THEM. THE INFANT EMPIRE CHOSE THE LATTER.
WASHINGTON CALLED IN BRIGADIER GENERAL LEONARD WOOD, A FENCING PARTNER TO TEDDY ROOSEVELT AND A VETERAN OF THE CAMPAIGN AGAINST GERONIMO AND CUBA.
OH, THAT NAME! LEONARD WOOD, SCOURGE OF THE APACHES AND THE CUBAN INSURRECTOS. NO PROMOTION EVER SATISFIED HIM. IN THE PHILIPPINES HE LONGED FOR A PROMOTION FROM BRIGADIER TO MAJOR GENERAL AND CARED LITTLE ABOUT HOW HE GOT IT.
IN MARCH 1906 – ALMOST FOUR YEARS AFTER ROOSEVELT DECLARED THE WAR OVER – WOOD LED THE LEAST DANGEROUS BATTLE THAT CHRISTIAN SOLDIERS OF ANY NATIONALITY WERE EVER ENGAGED IN.
I CALL IT THE MORO MASSACRE. THE FILIPINOS CALL IT...

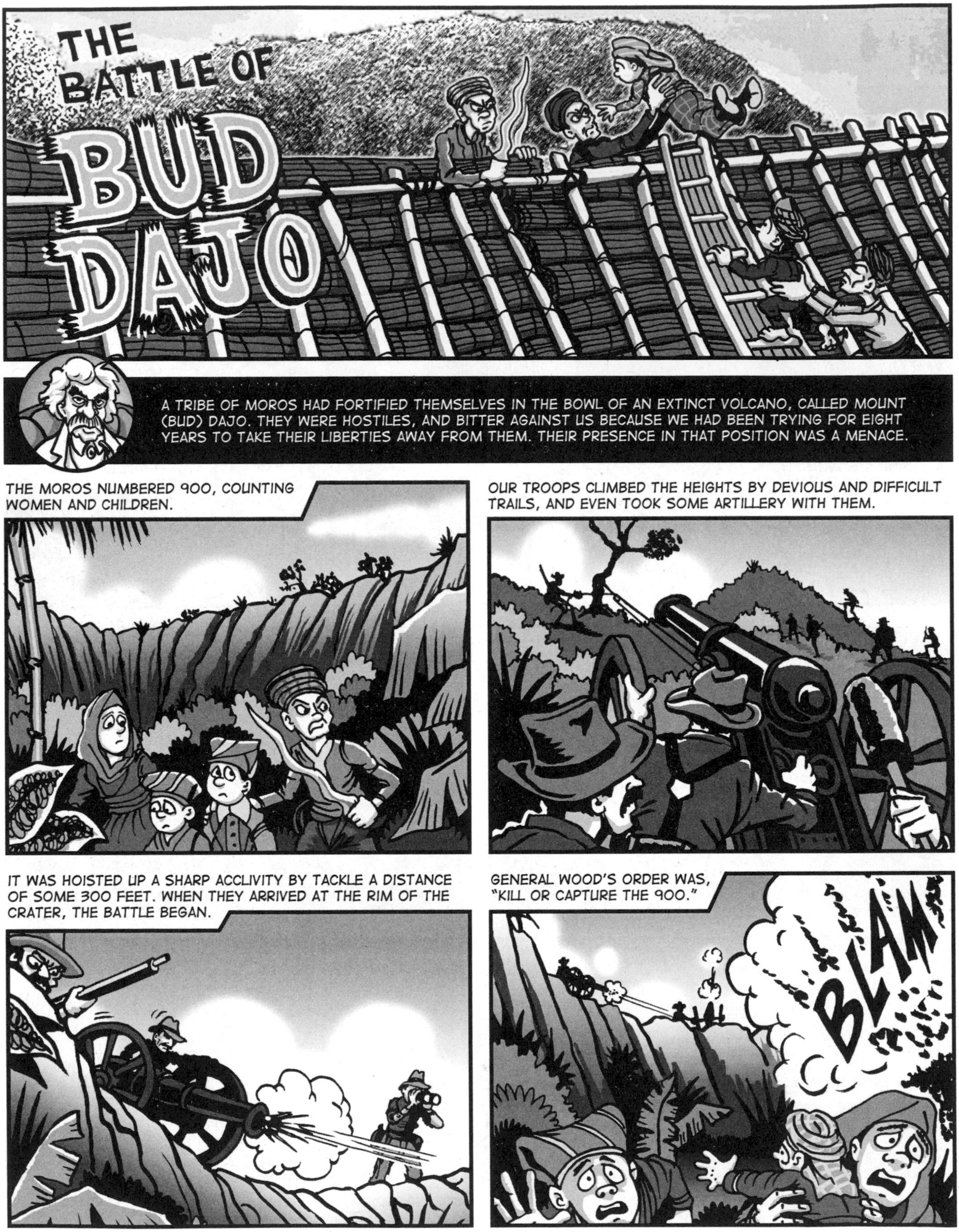
THE BATTLE OF BUD DAJO
A TRIBE OF MOROS HAD FORTIFIED THEMSELVES IN THE BOWL OF AN EXTINCT VOLCANO, CALLED MOUNT (BUD) DAJO. THEY WERE HOSTILES, AND BITTER AGAINST US BECAUSE WE HAD BEEN TRYING FOR EIGHT YEARS TO TAKE THEIR LIBERTIES AWAY FROM THEM. THEIR PRESENCE IN THAT POSITION WAS A MENACE.
THE MOROS NUMBERED 900, COUNTING WOMEN AND CHILDREN.
OUR TROOPS CLIMBED THE HEIGHTS BY DEVIOUS AND DIFFICULT TRAILS, AND EVEN TOOK SOME ARTILLERY WITH THEM.
IT WAS HOISTED UP A SHARP ACCLIVITY BY TACKLE A DISTANCE OF SOME 300 FEET. WHEN THEY ARRIVED AT THE RIM OF THE CRATER, THE BATTLE BEGAN.
GENERAL WOOD'S ORDER WAS, "KILL OR CAPTURE THE 900."
BLAM

THE "BATTLE" BEGAN – IT IS OFFICIALLY CALLED BY THAT NAME – OUR FORCES FIRING DOWN INTO THE CRATER WITH THEIR ARTILLERY AND THEIR DEADLY SMALL ARMS OF PRECISION, THE SAVAGES FURIOUSLY RETURNING THE FIRE, PROBABLY WITH BRICKBATS.

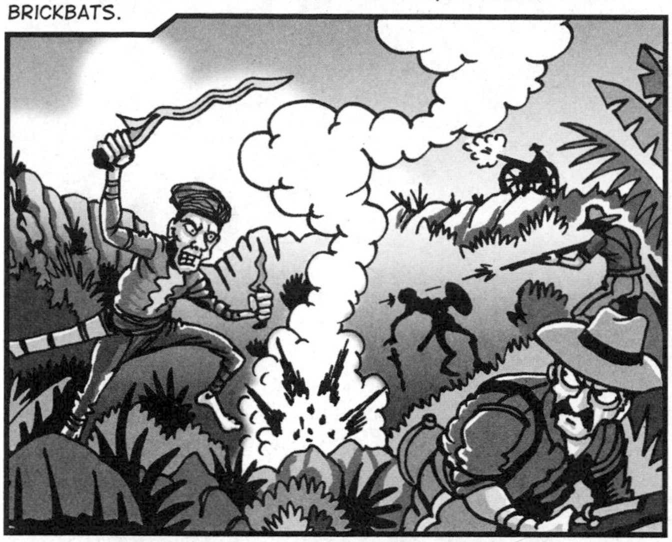

THE OFFICIAL REPORT STATED THAT THE BATTLE WAS FOUGHT WITH PRODIGIOUS ENERGY ON BOTH SIDES DURING A DAY AND A HALF, AND THAT IT ENDED WITH A COMPLETE VICTORY FOR THE AMERICAN ARMS.

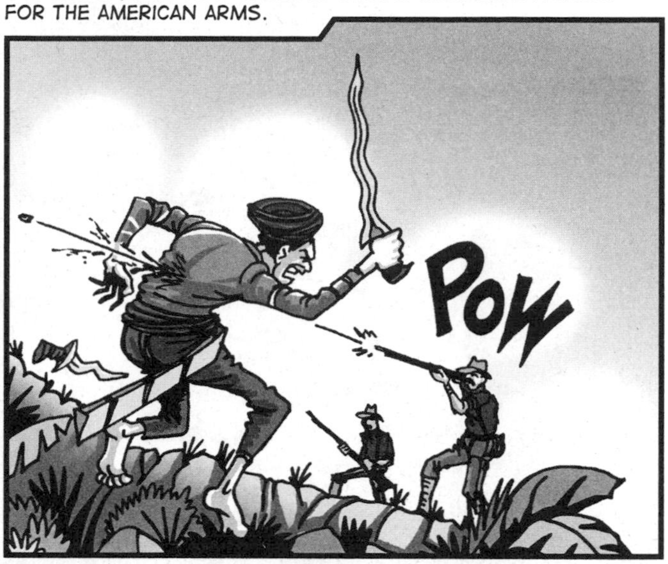
POW

OF THE 900 MOROS, NOT ONE WAS LEFT ALIVE. APPARENTLY OUR LITTLE ARMY CONSIDERED THEY WERE AUTHORIZED TO "KILL OR CAPTURE" ACCORDING TO TASTE, AND THAT THEIR TASTE HAD REMAINED WHAT IT HAD BEEN FOR EIGHT YEARS – THE TASTE OF ***CHRISTIAN BUTCHERS***.

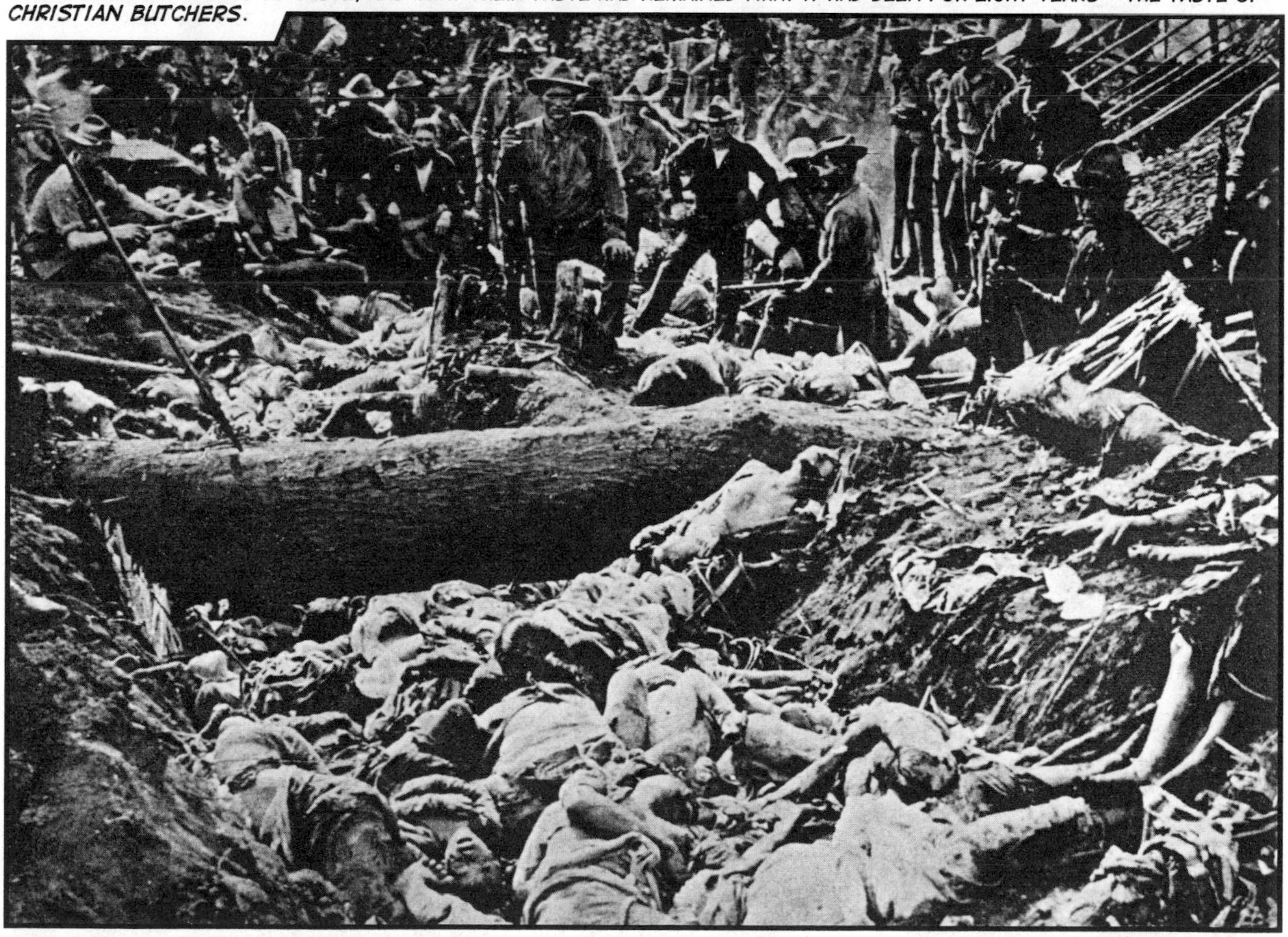

PRESIDENT ROOSEVELT COMMENDED GENERAL WOOD: "I CONGRATULATE YOU AND THE OFFICERS AND MEN OF YOUR COMMAND UPON THE ***BRILLIANT FEAT OF ARMS*** WHEREIN YOU AND THEY SO WELL ***UPHELD THE HONOR OF THE AMERICAN FLAG.***"

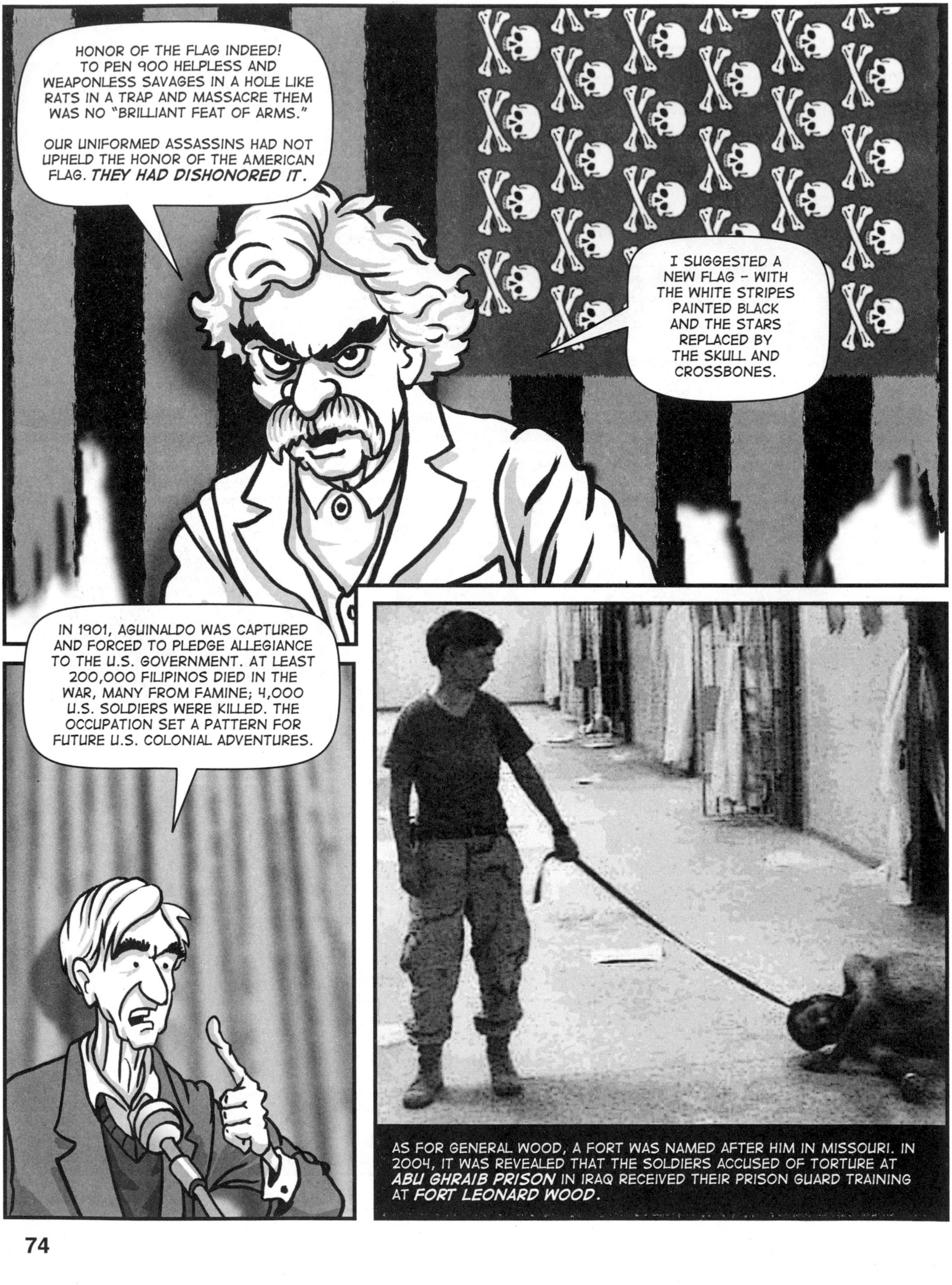
HONOR OF THE FLAG INDEED! TO PEN 900 HELPLESS AND WEAPONLESS SAVAGES IN A HOLE LIKE RATS IN A TRAP AND MASSACRE THEM WAS NO "BRILLIANT FEAT OF ARMS."
OUR UNIFORMED ASSASSINS HAD NOT UPHELD THE HONOR OF THE AMERICAN FLAG. THEY HAD DISHONORED IT.
I SUGGESTED A NEW FLAG - WITH THE WHITE STRIPES PAINTED BLACK AND THE STARS REPLACED BY THE SKULL AND CROSSBONES.
IN 1901, AGUINALDO WAS CAPTURED AND FORCED TO PLEDGE ALLEGIANCE TO THE U.S. GOVERNMENT. AT LEAST 200,000 FILIPINOS DIED IN THE WAR, MANY FROM FAMINE; 4,000 U.S. SOLDIERS WERE KILLED. THE OCCUPATION SET A PATTERN FOR FUTURE U.S. COLONIAL ADVENTURES.
AS FOR GENERAL WOOD, A FORT WAS NAMED AFTER HIM IN MISSOURI. IN 2004, IT WAS REVEALED THAT THE SOLDIERS ACCUSED OF TORTURE AT ABU GHRAIB PRISON IN IRAQ RECEIVED THEIR PRISON GUARD TRAINING AT FORT LEONARD WOOD.

Chapter IV

War Is the Health of the State

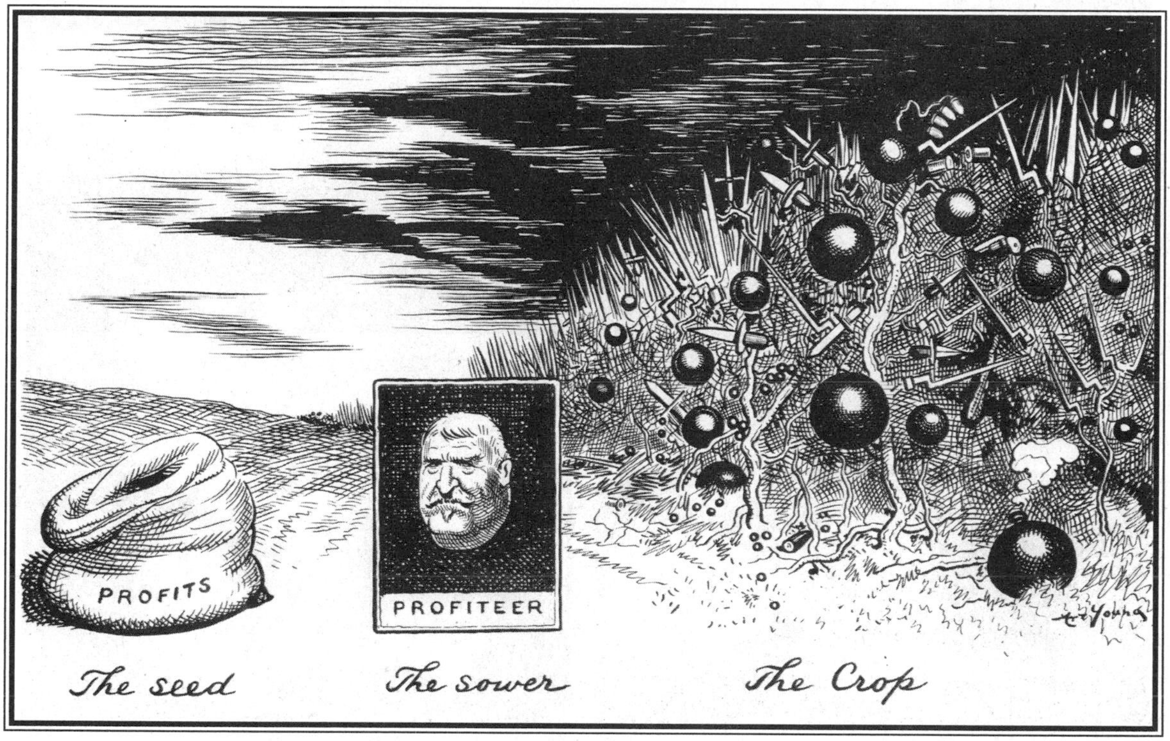
PROFITS
PROFITEER
The seed
The sower
The Crop

"World War I was a boon for U.S. goods and loans. Enormous profits tied American business interests to a British victory against Germany."

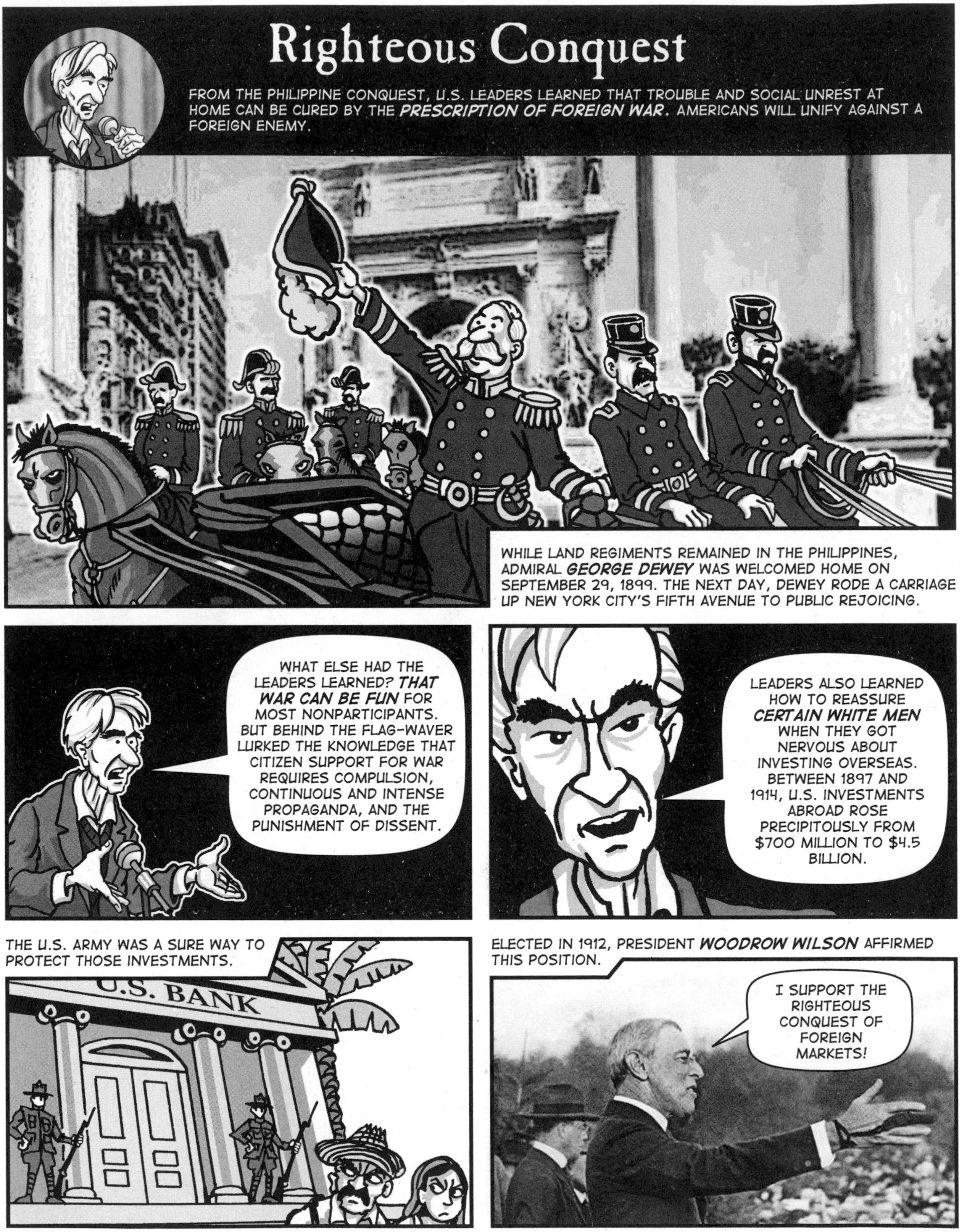
Righteous Conquest
FROM THE PHILIPPINE CONQUEST, U.S. LEADERS LEARNED THAT TROUBLE AND SOCIAL UNREST AT HOME CAN BE CURED BY THE PRESCRIPTION OF FOREIGN WAR. AMERICANS WILL UNIFY AGAINST A FOREIGN ENEMY.
WHILE LAND REGIMENTS REMAINED IN THE PHILIPPINES, ADMIRAL GEORGE DEWEY WAS WELCOMED HOME ON SEPTEMBER 29, 1899. THE NEXT DAY, DEWEY RODE A CARRIAGE UP NEW YORK CITY'S FIFTH AVENUE TO PUBLIC REJOICING.
WHAT ELSE HAD THE LEADERS LEARNED? THAT WAR CAN BE FUN FOR MOST NONPARTICIPANTS. BUT BEHIND THE FLAG-WAVER LURKED THE KNOWLEDGE THAT CITIZEN SUPPORT FOR WAR REQUIRES COMPULSION, CONTINUOUS AND INTENSE PROPAGANDA, AND THE PUNISHMENT OF DISSENT.
LEADERS ALSO LEARNED HOW TO REASSURE CERTAIN WHITE MEN WHEN THEY GOT NERVOUS ABOUT INVESTING OVERSEAS. BETWEEN 1897 AND 1914, U.S. INVESTMENTS ABROAD ROSE PRECIPITOUSLY FROM $700 MILLION TO $4.5 BILLION.
THE U.S. ARMY WAS A SURE WAY TO PROTECT THOSE INVESTMENTS.
U.S. BANK
ELECTED IN 1912, PRESIDENT WOODROW WILSON AFFIRMED THIS POSITION.
I SUPPORT THE RIGHTEOUS CONQUEST OF FOREIGN MARKETS!

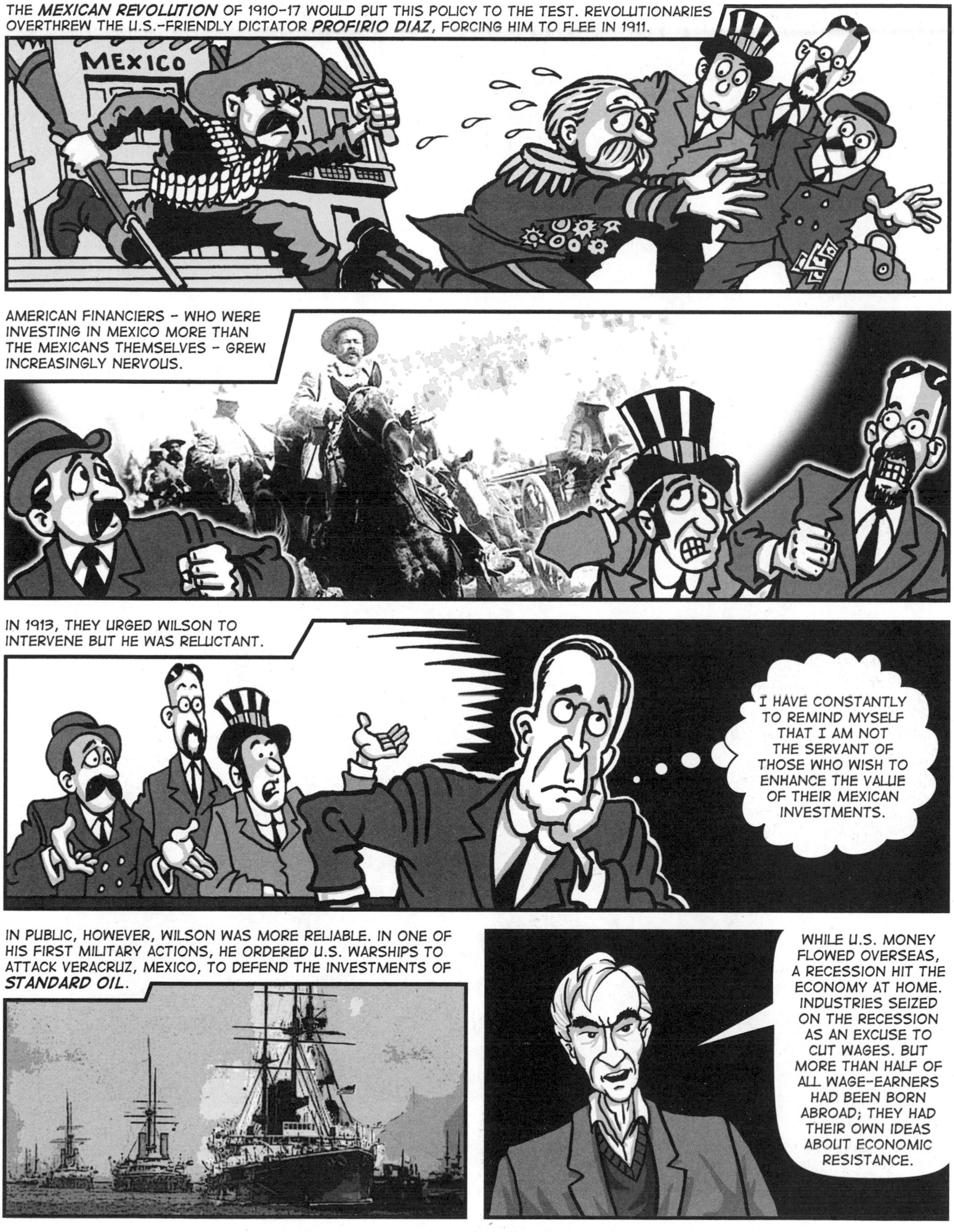
THE MEXICAN REVOLUTION OF 1910-17 WOULD PUT THIS POLICY TO THE TEST. REVOLUTIONARIES OVERTHREW THE U.S.-FRIENDLY DICTATOR PROFIRIO DIAZ, FORCING HIM TO FLEE IN 1911.
MEXICO
AMERICAN FINANCIERS - WHO WERE INVESTING IN MEXICO MORE THAN THE MEXICANS THEMSELVES - GREW INCREASINGLY NERVOUS.
IN 1913, THEY URGED WILSON TO INTERVENE BUT HE WAS RELUCTANT.
I HAVE CONSTANTLY TO REMIND MYSELF THAT I AM NOT THE SERVANT OF THOSE WHO WISH TO ENHANCE THE VALUE OF THEIR MEXICAN INVESTMENTS.
IN PUBLIC, HOWEVER, WILSON WAS MORE RELIABLE. IN ONE OF HIS FIRST MILITARY ACTIONS, HE ORDERED U.S. WARSHIPS TO ATTACK VERACRUZ, MEXICO, TO DEFEND THE INVESTMENTS OF STANDARD OIL.
WHILE U.S. MONEY FLOWED OVERSEAS, A RECESSION HIT THE ECONOMY AT HOME. INDUSTRIES SEIZED ON THE RECESSION AS AN EXCUSE TO CUT WAGES. BUT MORE THAN HALF OF ALL WAGE-EARNERS HAD BEEN BORN ABROAD; THEY HAD THEIR OWN IDEAS ABOUT ECONOMIC RESISTANCE.

The Ludlow Massacre

SHORTLY AFTER WILSON TOOK OFFICE IN 1913, THERE BEGAN ONE OF THE MOST BITTER AND VIOLENT STRUGGLES BETWEEN WORKERS AND CORPORATE CAPITAL IN THE HISTORY OF THE COUNTRY: THE STRIKE AGAINST THE ***COLORADO FUEL & IRON COMPANY*** OWNED BY THE ROCKEFELLER FAMILY.

ANGERED BY A SERIES OF MINE EXPLOSIONS AND THE FEUDAL CONDITIONS OF THE MINING CAMPS WHERE THEY LIVED, 11,000 MINERS WENT ON STRIKE. THEY SET UP TENT COLONIES AFTER THEY WERE EVICTED FROM THEIR COMPANY-OWNED HOVELS. THE LARGEST - IN LUDLOW, COLORADO - HOUSED 1,000 MINERS AND FAMILY MEMBERS.

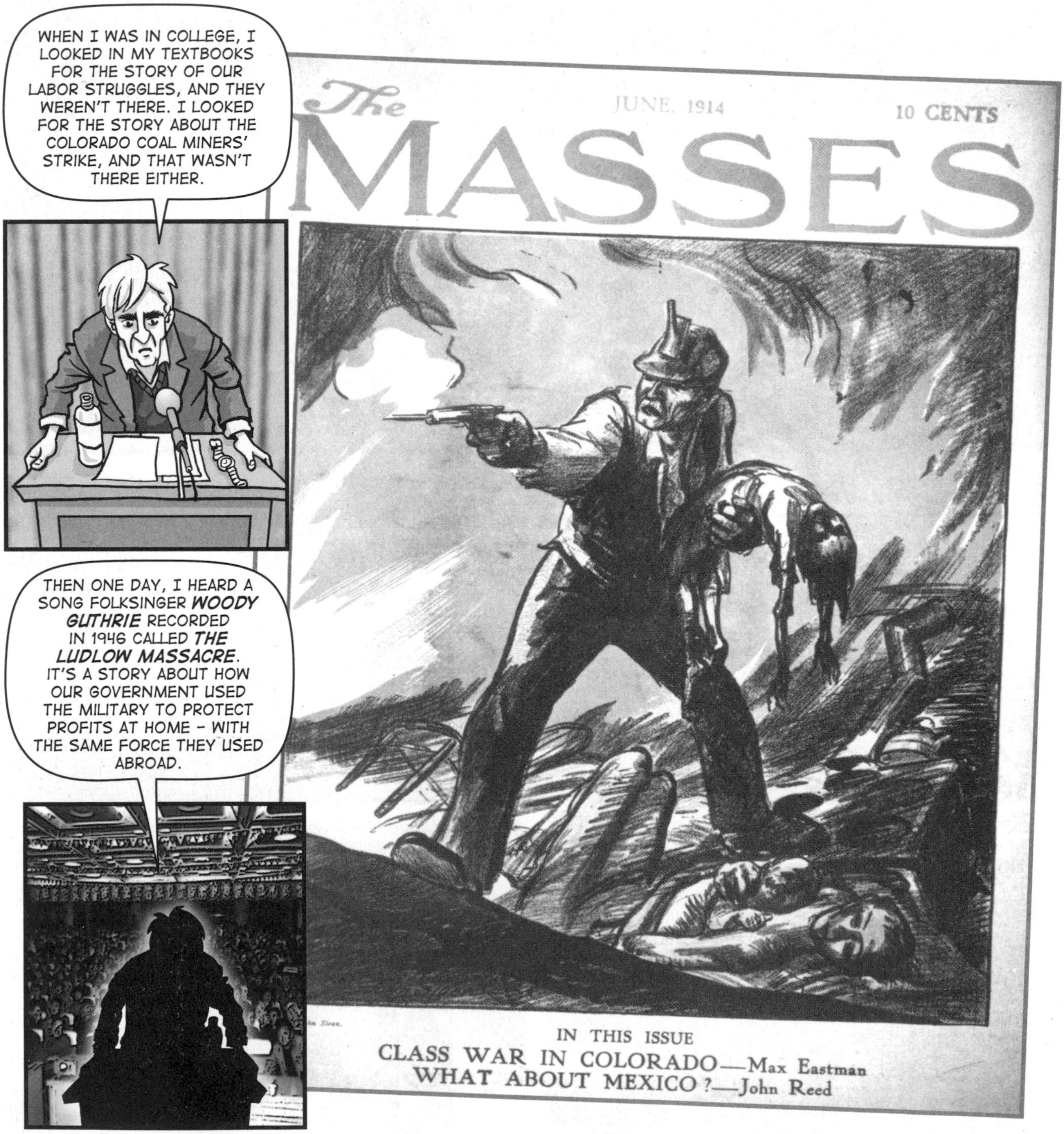
WHEN I WAS IN COLLEGE, I LOOKED IN MY TEXTBOOKS FOR THE STORY OF OUR LABOR STRUGGLES, AND THEY WEREN'T THERE. I LOOKED FOR THE STORY ABOUT THE COLORADO COAL MINERS' STRIKE, AND THAT WASN'T THERE EITHER.
THEN ONE DAY, I HEARD A SONG FOLKSINGER ***WOODY GUTHRIE*** RECORDED IN 1946 CALLED ***THE LUDLOW MASSACRE***. IT'S A STORY ABOUT HOW OUR GOVERNMENT USED THE MILITARY TO PROTECT PROFITS AT HOME - WITH THE SAME FORCE THEY USED ABROAD.
The MASSES
JUNE, 1914
10 CENTS
IN THIS ISSUE
CLASS WAR IN COLORADO—Max Eastman
WHAT ABOUT MEXICO ?—John Reed

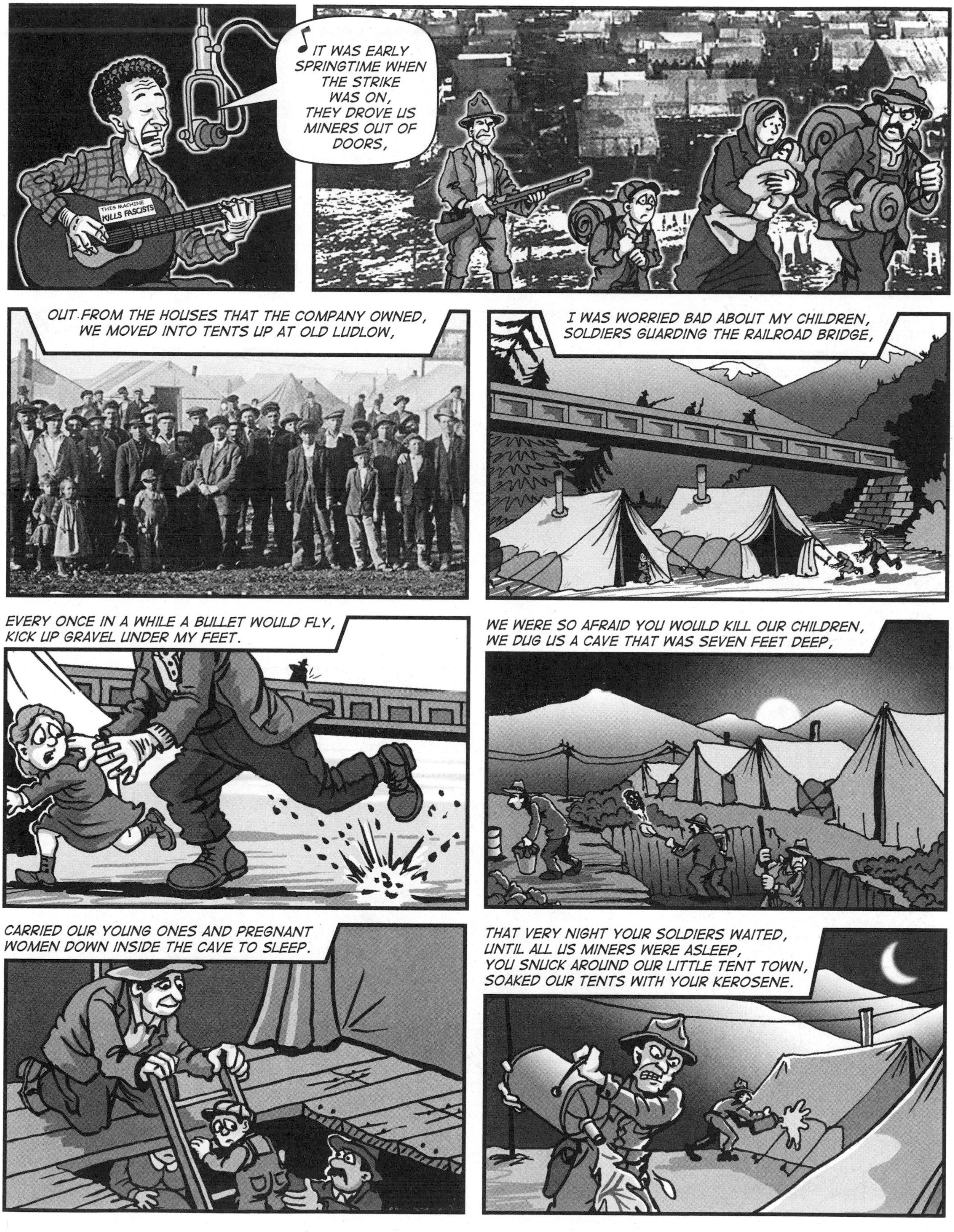

THIS MACHINE KILLS FASCISTS
IT WAS EARLY SPRINGTIME WHEN THE STRIKE WAS ON, THEY DROVE US MINERS OUT OF DOORS,
OUT FROM THE HOUSES THAT THE COMPANY OWNED, WE MOVED INTO TENTS UP AT OLD LUDLOW,
I WAS WORRIED BAD ABOUT MY CHILDREN, SOLDIERS GUARDING THE RAILROAD BRIDGE,
EVERY ONCE IN A WHILE A BULLET WOULD FLY, KICK UP GRAVEL UNDER MY FEET.
WE WERE SO AFRAID YOU WOULD KILL OUR CHILDREN, WE DUG US A CAVE THAT WAS SEVEN FEET DEEP,
CARRIED OUR YOUNG ONES AND PREGNANT WOMEN DOWN INSIDE THE CAVE TO SLEEP.
THAT VERY NIGHT YOUR SOLDIERS WAITED, UNTIL ALL US MINERS WERE ASLEEP, YOU SNUCK AROUND OUR LITTLE TENT TOWN, SOAKED OUR TENTS WITH YOUR KEROSENE.

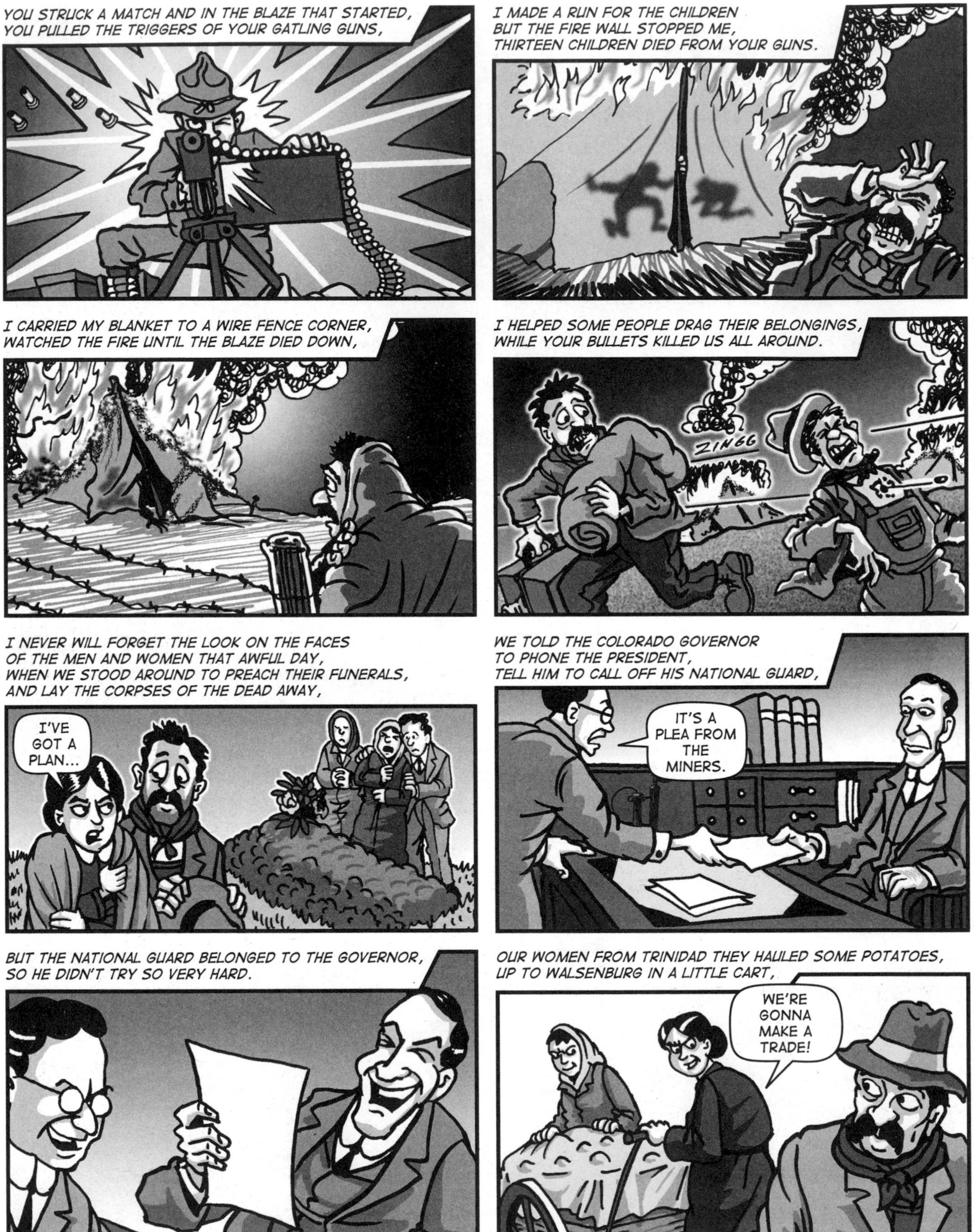
YOU STRUCK A MATCH AND IN THE BLAZE THAT STARTED,
YOU PULLED THE TRIGGERS OF YOUR GATLING GUNS,
I MADE A RUN FOR THE CHILDREN
BUT THE FIRE WALL STOPPED ME,
THIRTEEN CHILDREN DIED FROM YOUR GUNS.
I CARRIED MY BLANKET TO A WIRE FENCE CORNER,
WATCHED THE FIRE UNTIL THE BLAZE DIED DOWN,
I HELPED SOME PEOPLE DRAG THEIR BELONGINGS,
WHILE YOUR BULLETS KILLED US ALL AROUND.
ZINGG
I NEVER WILL FORGET THE LOOK ON THE FACES
OF THE MEN AND WOMEN THAT AWFUL DAY,
WHEN WE STOOD AROUND TO PREACH THEIR FUNERALS,
AND LAY THE CORPSES OF THE DEAD AWAY,
I'VE GOT A PLAN...
WE TOLD THE COLORADO GOVERNOR
TO PHONE THE PRESIDENT,
TELL HIM TO CALL OFF HIS NATIONAL GUARD,
IT'S A PLEA FROM THE MINERS.
BUT THE NATIONAL GUARD BELONGED TO THE GOVERNOR,
SO HE DIDN'T TRY SO VERY HARD.
OUR WOMEN FROM TRINIDAD THEY HAULED SOME POTATOES,
UP TO WALSENBURG IN A LITTLE CART,
WE'RE GONNA MAKE A TRADE!

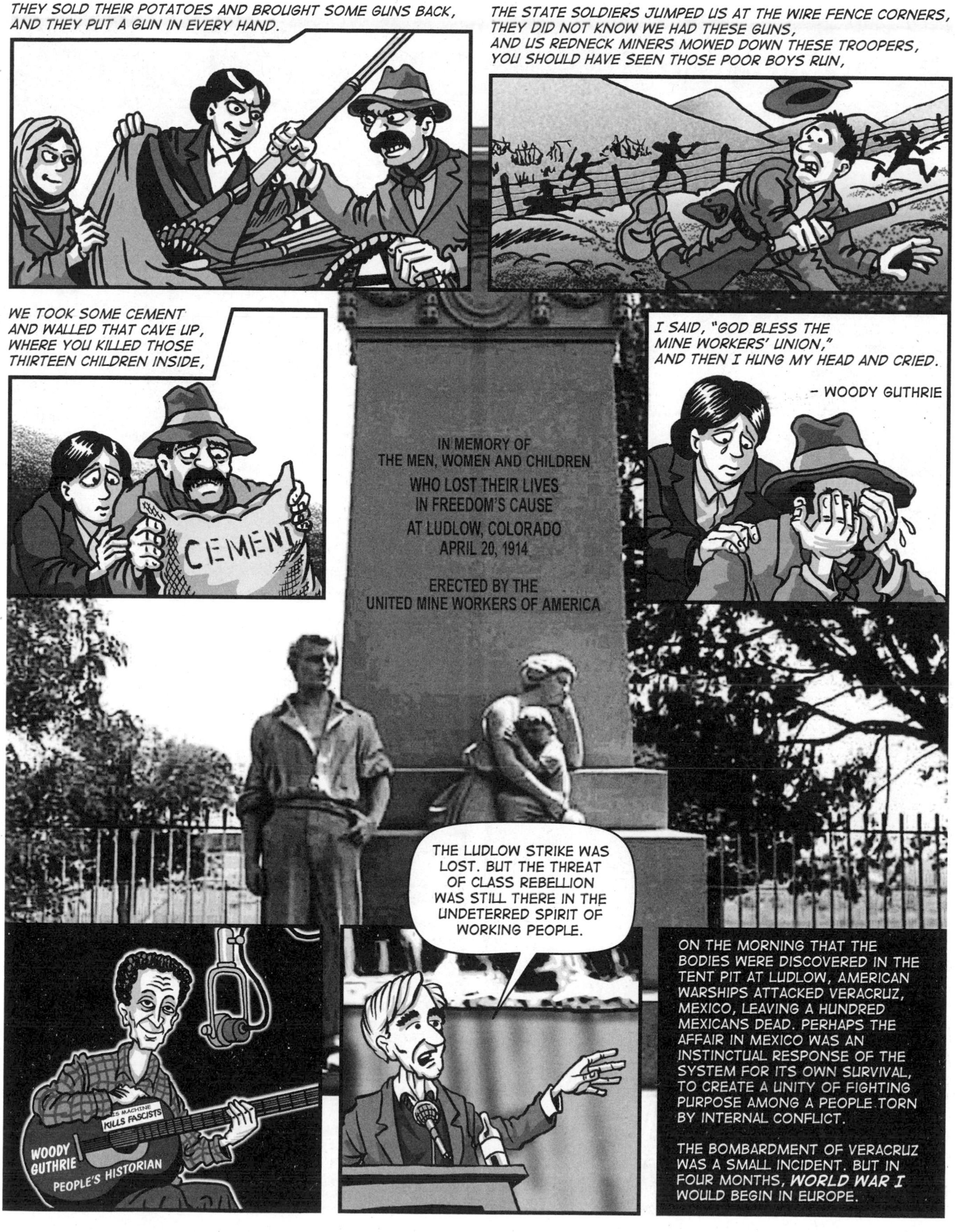
THEY SOLD THEIR POTATOES AND BROUGHT SOME GUNS BACK, AND THEY PUT A GUN IN EVERY HAND.
THE STATE SOLDIERS JUMPED US AT THE WIRE FENCE CORNERS, THEY DID NOT KNOW WE HAD THESE GUNS, AND US REDNECK MINERS MOWED DOWN THESE TROOPERS, YOU SHOULD HAVE SEEN THOSE POOR BOYS RUN,
WE TOOK SOME CEMENT AND WALLED THAT CAVE UP, WHERE YOU KILLED THOSE THIRTEEN CHILDREN INSIDE,
CEMENT
I SAID, "GOD BLESS THE MINE WORKERS' UNION," AND THEN I HUNG MY HEAD AND CRIED.
- WOODY GUTHRIE
IN MEMORY OF THE MEN, WOMEN AND CHILDREN WHO LOST THEIR LIVES IN FREEDOM'S CAUSE AT LUDLOW, COLORADO APRIL 20, 1914
ERECTED BY THE UNITED MINE WORKERS OF AMERICA
KILLS FASCISTS
WOODY GUTHRIE
PEOPLE'S HISTORIAN
THE LUDLOW STRIKE WAS LOST. BUT THE THREAT OF CLASS REBELLION WAS STILL THERE IN THE UNDETERRED SPIRIT OF WORKING PEOPLE.
ON THE MORNING THAT THE BODIES WERE DISCOVERED IN THE TENT PIT AT LUDLOW, AMERICAN WARSHIPS ATTACKED VERACRUZ, MEXICO, LEAVING A HUNDRED MEXICANS DEAD. PERHAPS THE AFFAIR IN MEXICO WAS AN INSTINCTUAL RESPONSE OF THE SYSTEM FOR ITS OWN SURVIVAL, TO CREATE A UNITY OF FIGHTING PURPOSE AMONG A PEOPLE TORN BY INTERNAL CONFLICT.
THE BOMBARDMENT OF VERACRUZ WAS A SMALL INCIDENT. BUT IN FOUR MONTHS, WORLD WAR I WOULD BEGIN IN EUROPE.

World War I

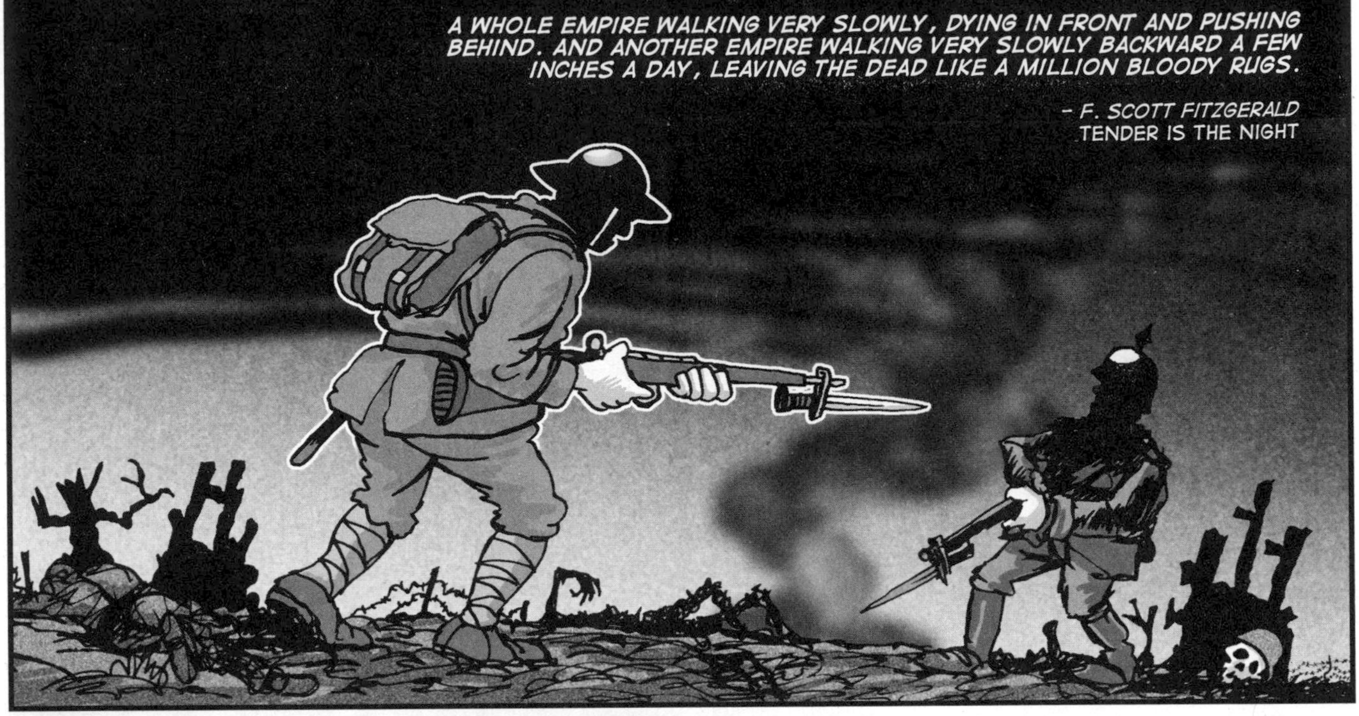
A WHOLE EMPIRE WALKING VERY SLOWLY, DYING IN FRONT AND PUSHING BEHIND. AND ANOTHER EMPIRE WALKING VERY SLOWLY BACKWARD A FEW INCHES A DAY, LEAVING THE DEAD LIKE A MILLION BLOODY RUGS.
– F. SCOTT FITZGERALD
TENDER IS THE NIGHT

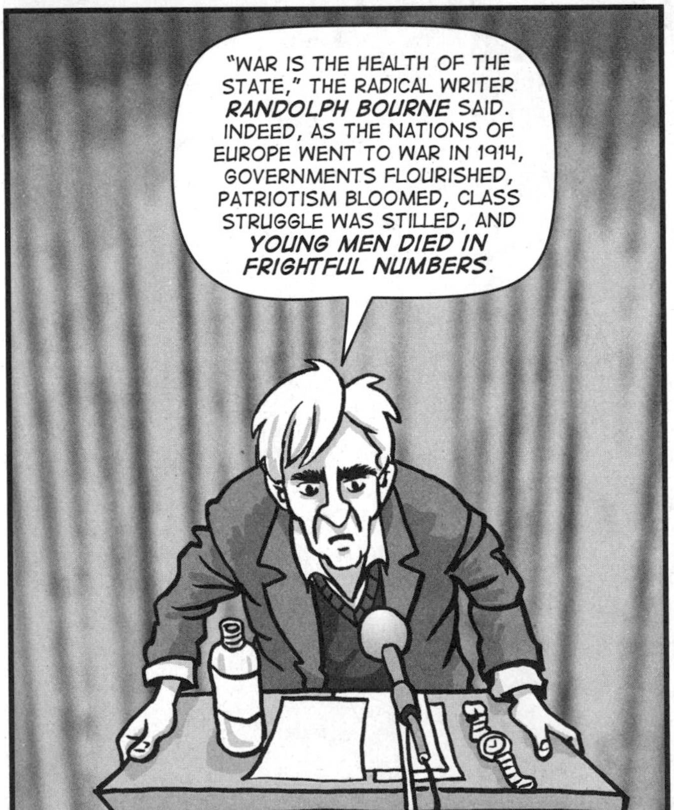
"WAR IS THE HEALTH OF THE STATE," THE RADICAL WRITER ***RANDOLPH BOURNE*** SAID. INDEED, AS THE NATIONS OF EUROPE WENT TO WAR IN 1914, GOVERNMENTS FLOURISHED, PATRIOTISM BLOOMED, CLASS STRUGGLE WAS STILLED, AND ***YOUNG MEN DIED IN FRIGHTFUL NUMBERS***.

IN THE U.S., NOT YET IN THE WAR, THERE WAS WORRY ABOUT THE HEALTH OF THE STATE. SOCIALISM WAS GROWING. CLASS CONFLICT WAS INTENSE. THE ***AMERICAN SOCIALIST PARTY*** CLAIMED THAT IT WAS AN IMPERIALIST WAR: THE ADVANCED CAPITALIST COUNTRIES OF EUROPE WERE FIGHTING OVER BOUNDARIES, COLONIES, SPHERES OF INFLUENCE; THEY WERE COMPETING FOR ALSACE-LORRAINE, THE BALKANS, AFRICA, THE MIDDLE EAST. SOCIALIST LEADER ***EUGENE DEBS*** DECLARED:

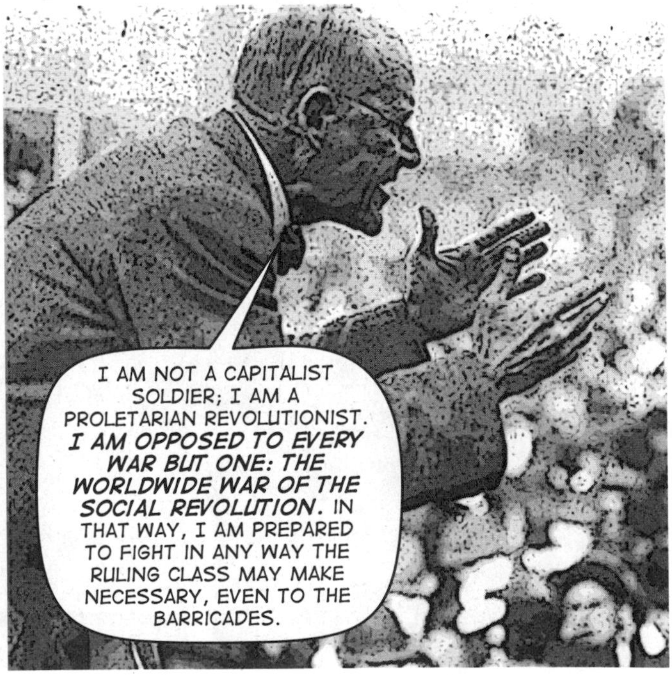
I AM NOT A CAPITALIST SOLDIER; I AM A PROLETARIAN REVOLUTIONIST. ***I AM OPPOSED TO EVERY WAR BUT ONE: THE WORLDWIDE WAR OF THE SOCIAL REVOLUTION***. IN THAT WAY, I AM PREPARED TO FIGHT IN ANY WAY THE RULING CLASS MAY MAKE NECESSARY, EVEN TO THE BARRICADES.

IN MAY 1915, THE ***ATLANTIC MONTHLY*** PUBLISHED A REMARKABLY PERCEPTIVE ARTICLE BY ***W.E.B. DU BOIS*** ENTITLED "THE AFRICAN ROOTS OF WAR." IT WAS A WAR FOR EMPIRE, HE ASSERTED, OF WHICH THE STRUGGLE BETWEEN GERMANY AND THE ALLIES OVER AFRICA WAS BOTH A SYMBOL AND REALITY:

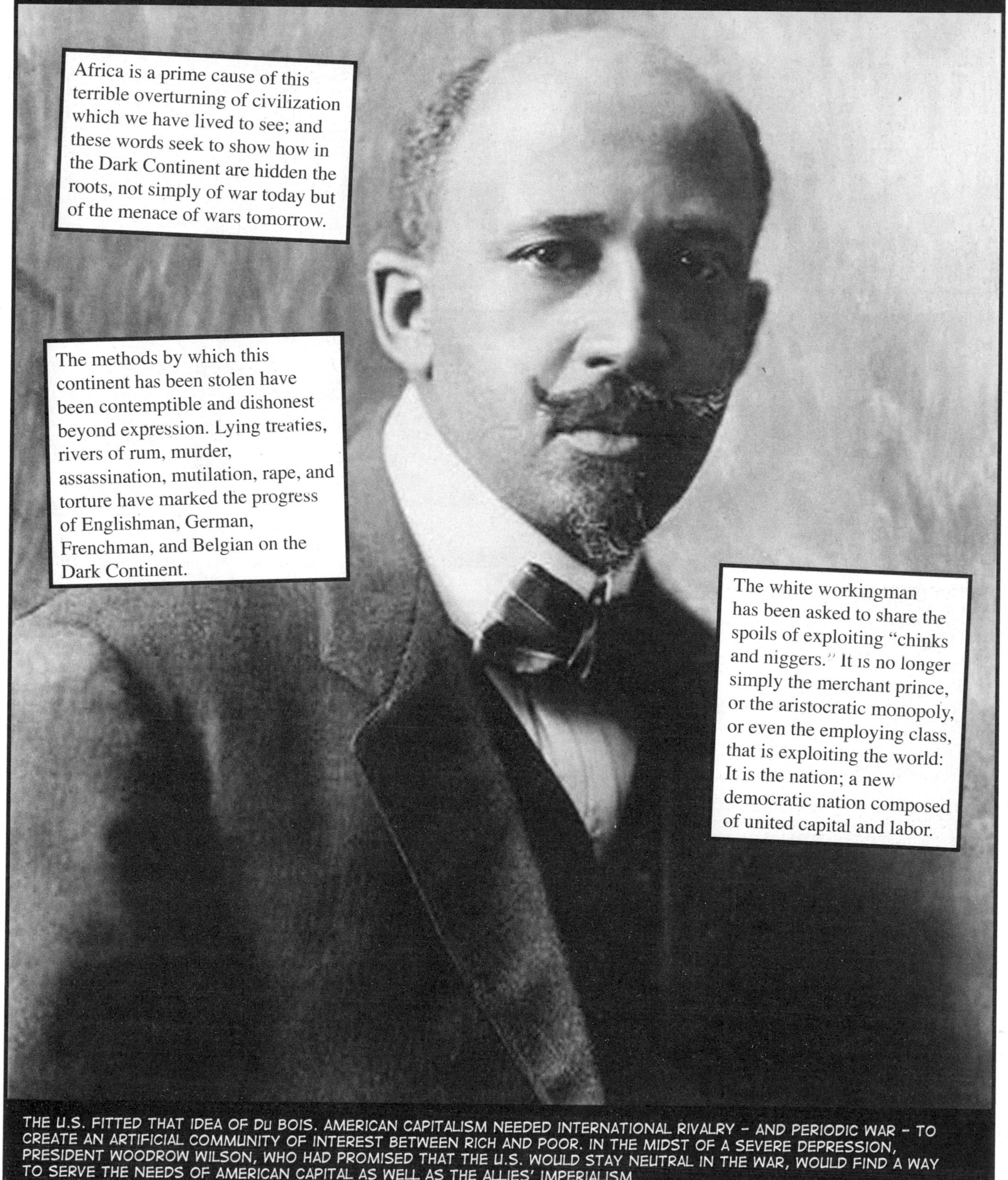
Africa is a prime cause of this terrible overturning of civilization which we have lived to see; and these words seek to show how in the Dark Continent are hidden the roots, not simply of war today but of the menace of wars tomorrow.
The methods by which this continent has been stolen have been contemptible and dishonest beyond expression. Lying treaties, rivers of rum, murder, assassination, mutilation, rape, and torture have marked the progress of Englishman, German, Frenchman, and Belgian on the Dark Continent.
The white workingman has been asked to share the spoils of exploiting "chinks and niggers." It is no longer simply the merchant prince, or the aristocratic monopoly, or even the employing class, that is exploiting the world: It is the nation; a new democratic nation composed of united capital and labor.

THE U.S. FITTED THAT IDEA OF DU BOIS. AMERICAN CAPITALISM NEEDED INTERNATIONAL RIVALRY – AND PERIODIC WAR – TO CREATE AN ARTIFICIAL COMMUNITY OF INTEREST BETWEEN RICH AND POOR. IN THE MIDST OF A SEVERE DEPRESSION, PRESIDENT WOODROW WILSON, WHO HAD PROMISED THAT THE U.S. WOULD STAY NEUTRAL IN THE WAR, WOULD FIND A WAY TO SERVE THE NEEDS OF AMERICAN CAPITAL AS WELL AS THE ALLIES' IMPERIALISM.

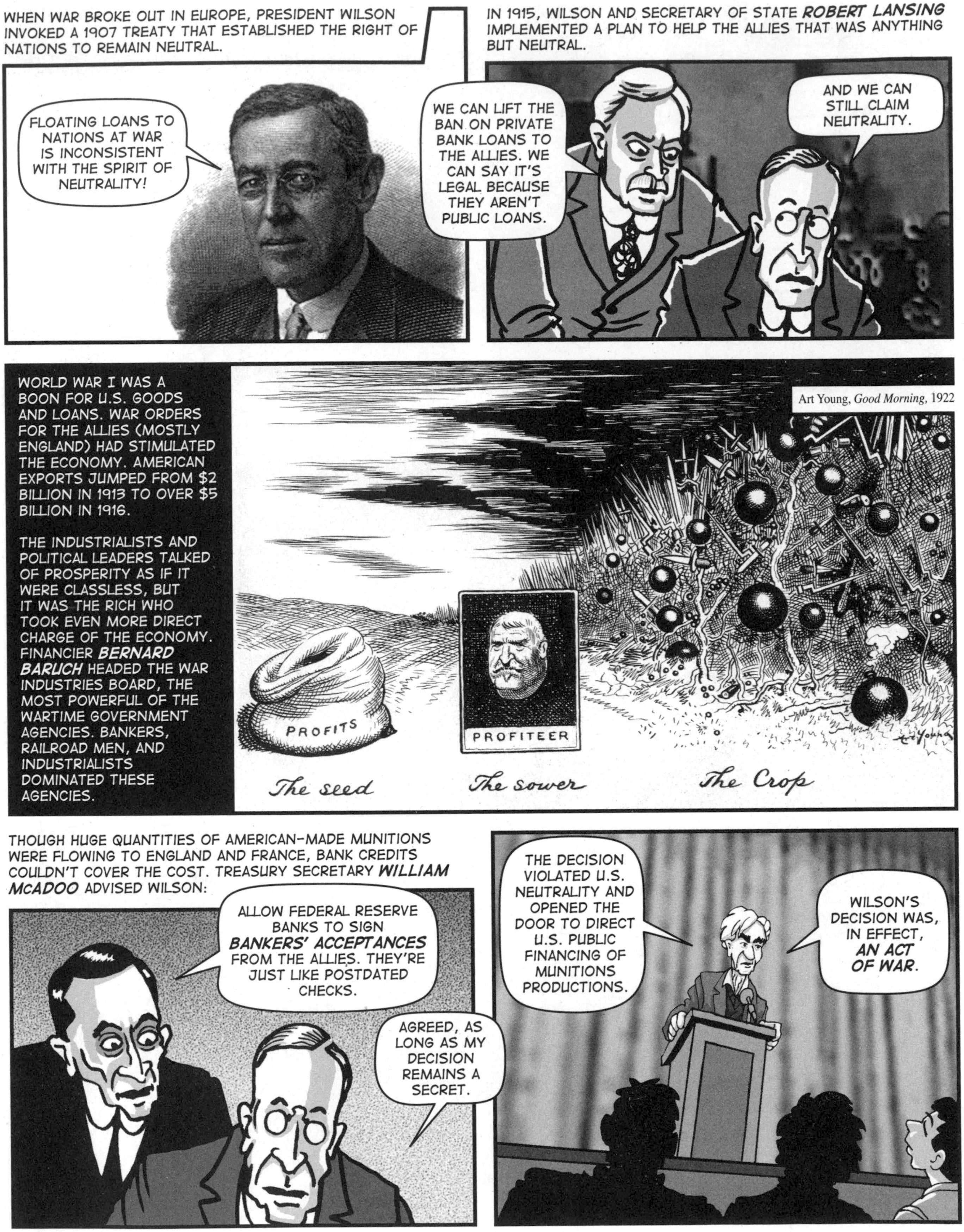
WHEN WAR BROKE OUT IN EUROPE, PRESIDENT WILSON INVOKED A 1907 TREATY THAT ESTABLISHED THE RIGHT OF NATIONS TO REMAIN NEUTRAL.
FLOATING LOANS TO NATIONS AT WAR IS INCONSISTENT WITH THE SPIRIT OF NEUTRALITY!
IN 1915, WILSON AND SECRETARY OF STATE ***ROBERT LANSING*** IMPLEMENTED A PLAN TO HELP THE ALLIES THAT WAS ANYTHING BUT NEUTRAL.
WE CAN LIFT THE BAN ON PRIVATE BANK LOANS TO THE ALLIES. WE CAN SAY IT'S LEGAL BECAUSE THEY AREN'T PUBLIC LOANS.
AND WE CAN STILL CLAIM NEUTRALITY.
WORLD WAR I WAS A BOON FOR U.S. GOODS AND LOANS. WAR ORDERS FOR THE ALLIES (MOSTLY ENGLAND) HAD STIMULATED THE ECONOMY. AMERICAN EXPORTS JUMPED FROM $2 BILLION IN 1913 TO OVER $5 BILLION IN 1916.
THE INDUSTRIALISTS AND POLITICAL LEADERS TALKED OF PROSPERITY AS IF IT WERE CLASSLESS, BUT IT WAS THE RICH WHO TOOK EVEN MORE DIRECT CHARGE OF THE ECONOMY. FINANCIER ***BERNARD BARUCH*** HEADED THE WAR INDUSTRIES BOARD, THE MOST POWERFUL OF THE WARTIME GOVERNMENT AGENCIES. BANKERS, RAILROAD MEN, AND INDUSTRIALISTS DOMINATED THESE AGENCIES.
Art Young, *Good Morning*, 1922
PROFITS
PROFITEER
The seed
The sower
The Crop
THOUGH HUGE QUANTITIES OF AMERICAN-MADE MUNITIONS WERE FLOWING TO ENGLAND AND FRANCE, BANK CREDITS COULDN'T COVER THE COST. TREASURY SECRETARY ***WILLIAM MCADOO*** ADVISED WILSON:
ALLOW FEDERAL RESERVE BANKS TO SIGN ***BANKERS' ACCEPTANCES*** FROM THE ALLIES. THEY'RE JUST LIKE POSTDATED CHECKS.
AGREED, AS LONG AS MY DECISION REMAINS A SECRET.
THE DECISION VIOLATED U.S. NEUTRALITY AND OPENED THE DOOR TO DIRECT U.S. PUBLIC FINANCING OF MUNITIONS PRODUCTIONS.
WILSON'S DECISION WAS, IN EFFECT, ***AN ACT OF WAR***.

MAY 7, 1915: A GERMAN SUBMARINE TORPEDOED THE BRITISH PASSENGER SHIP ***LUSITANIA*** EN ROUTE FROM NEW YORK TO ENGLAND. THE SHIP SANK IN 18 MINUTES; 1,198 PEOPLE DIED. WAR PASSIONS WERE ENFLAMED. THIS ENLISTMENT POSTER EXPLOITED THE CARNAGE.

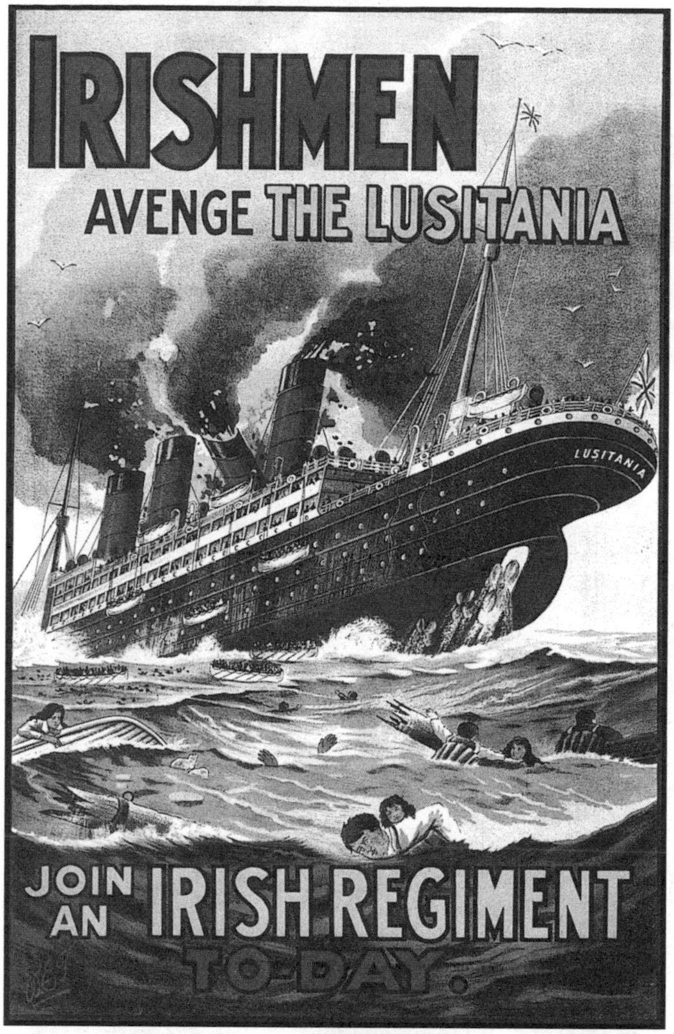

IRISHMEN
AVENGE THE LUSITANIA
LUSITANIA
JOIN AN IRISH REGIMENT
TO-DAY.

THE PUBLIC WAS NOT TOLD THAT THE SHIP WAS ARMED AND CARRYING TONS OF U.S.-MANUFACTURED WAR MATERIEL UNDER A FALSIFIED MANIFEST.

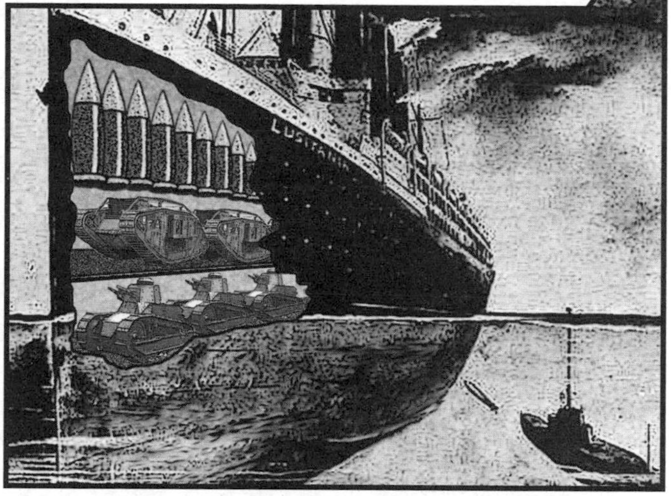

MARCH 24, 1916: GERMANY SANK THE ***SUSSEX***, AN UNARMED FRENCH PASSENGER SHIP. WILSON PROTESTED. GERMANY REPLIED THAT IT WOULD RESTRICT SUBMARINE WARFARE IF THE U.S. PERSUADED THE BRITISH TO STOP THEIR BLOCKADE OF FOOD SUPPLIES TO GERMANY...

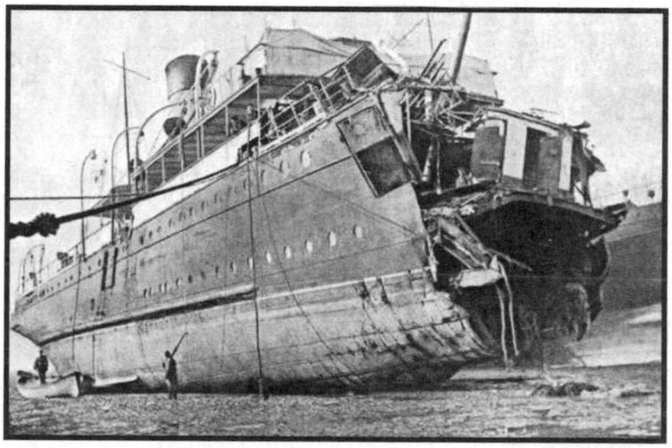

...AND IF WILSON CEASED DEFENDING ARMED BRITISH MERCHANT SHIPS. THESE SHIPS OFTEN CARRIED AMERICAN PASSENGERS.

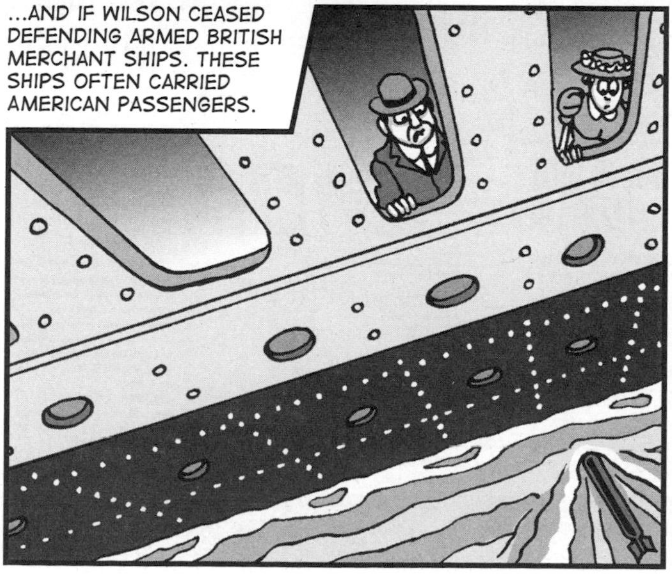

THE BRITISH REFUSED TO BREAK THEIR BLOCKADE, AND THE CAT-AND-MOUSE GAME CONTINUED.

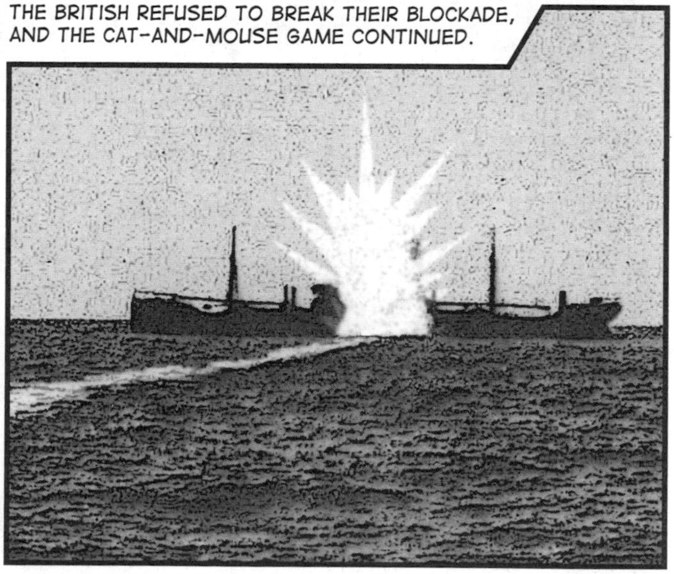

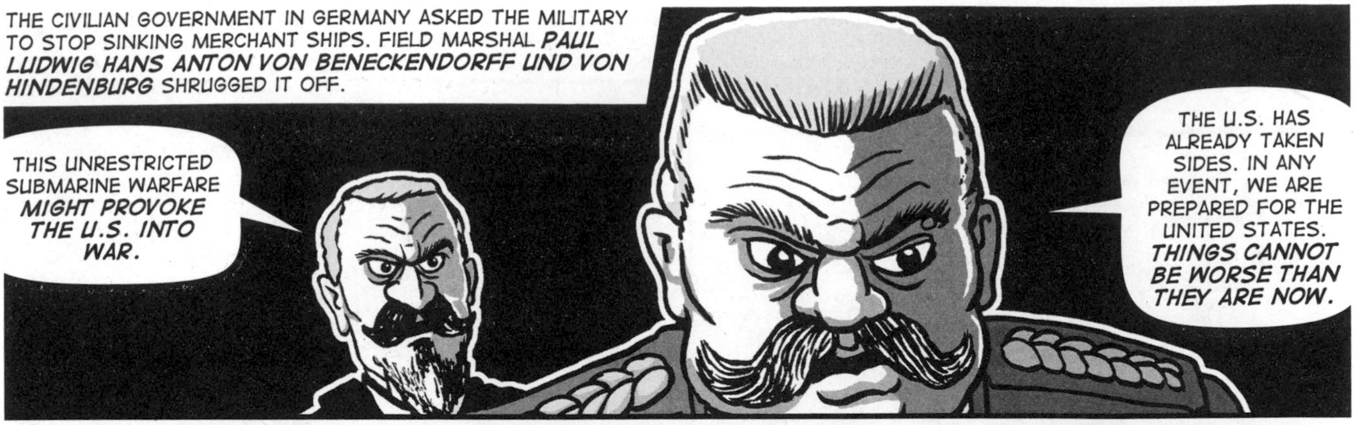
THE CIVILIAN GOVERNMENT IN GERMANY ASKED THE MILITARY TO STOP SINKING MERCHANT SHIPS. FIELD MARSHAL *PAUL LUDWIG HANS ANTON VON BENECKENDORFF UND VON HINDENBURG* SHRUGGED IT OFF.
THIS UNRESTRICTED SUBMARINE WARFARE *MIGHT PROVOKE THE U.S. INTO WAR.*
THE U.S. HAS ALREADY TAKEN SIDES. IN ANY EVENT, WE ARE PREPARED FOR THE UNITED STATES. *THINGS CANNOT BE WORSE THAN THEY ARE NOW.*

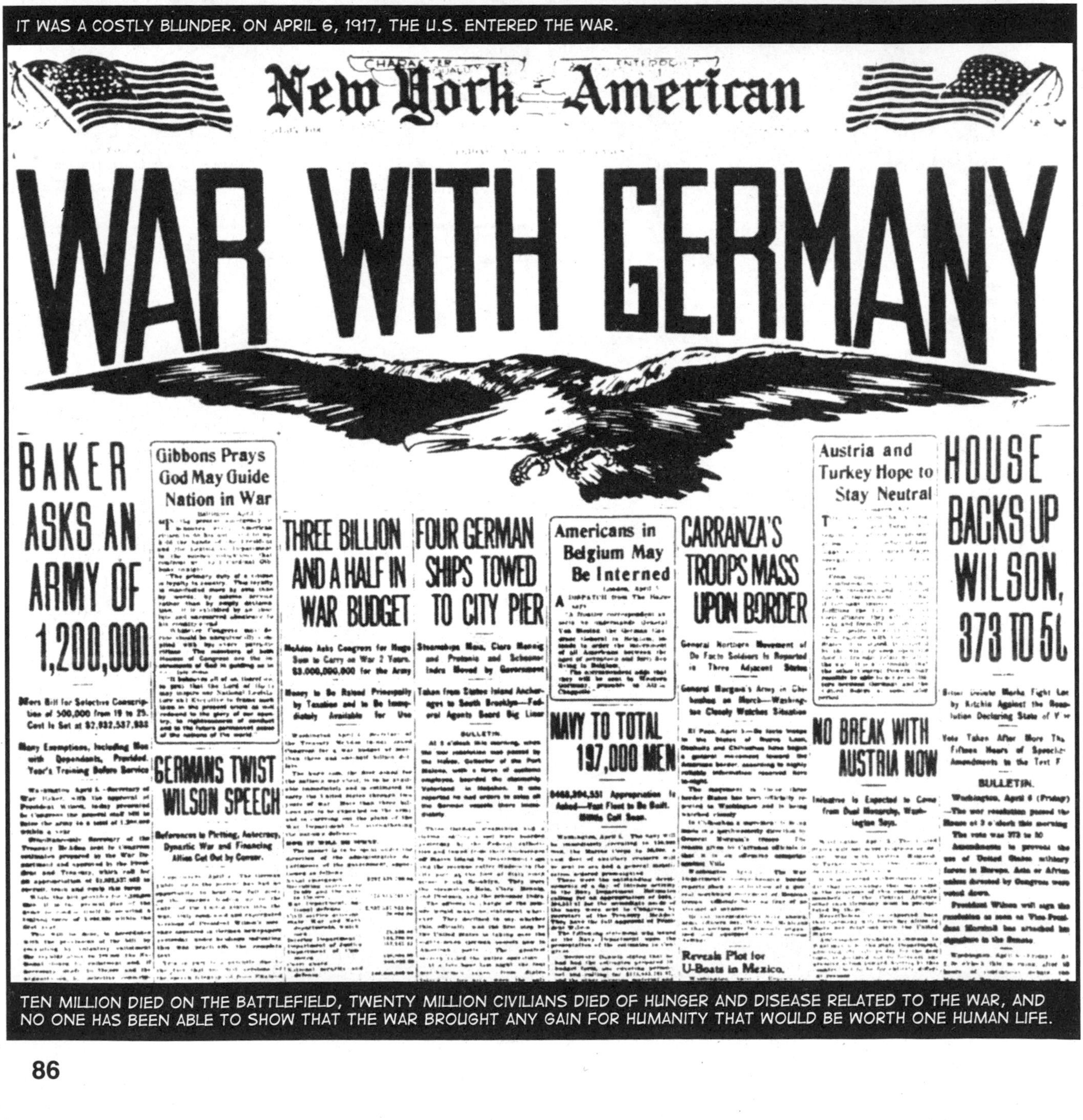
IT WAS A COSTLY BLUNDER. ON APRIL 6, 1917, THE U.S. ENTERED THE WAR.
New York American
WAR WITH GERMANY
BAKER ASKS AN ARMY OF 1,200,000
Gibbons Prays God May Guide Nation in War
THREE BILLION AND A HALF IN WAR BUDGET
FOUR GERMAN SHIPS TOWED TO CITY PIER
Americans in Belgium May Be Interned
CARRANZA'S TROOPS MASS UPON BORDER
Austria and Turkey Hope to Stay Neutral
HOUSE BACKS UP WILSON, 373 TO 50
GERMANS TWIST WILSON SPEECH
NAVY TO TOTAL 197,000 MEN
NO BREAK WITH AUSTRIA NOW
BULLETIN.
Reveals Plot for U-Boats in Mexico.
TEN MILLION DIED ON THE BATTLEFIELD, TWENTY MILLION CIVILIANS DIED OF HUNGER AND DISEASE RELATED TO THE WAR, AND NO ONE HAS BEEN ABLE TO SHOW THAT THE WAR BROUGHT ANY GAIN FOR HUMANITY THAT WOULD BE WORTH ONE HUMAN LIFE.

MAY 9, 1916: A FULL YEAR BEFORE THE U.S. ENTERED THE WAR AND MORE THAN TWO YEARS BEFORE THE WAR ENDED, BRITISH DIPLOMAT SIR *MARK SYKES* AND FRENCH NEGOTIATOR *FRANCOIS GEORGES PICOT* CARVED UP THE MIDDLE EAST.

THE *SYKES-PICOT AGREEMENT* SECRETLY PORTIONED OUT TO ENGLAND AND FRANCE THE OIL-BEARING LANDS OF THE FIVE-CENTURY-OLD *OTTOMAN EMPIRE*.

CERTAIN PORTIONS WERE ALSO ALLOTTED TO THE ITALIANS, GREEKS, RUSSIANS, ARABS, AND FLEDGLING ZIONISTS (IN AN "INTERNATIONAL ZONE"). THE ALLIED DIPLOMATS EXPRESSED THE POINT CAREFULLY: FRANCE AND GREAT BRITAIN "SHALL HAVE PRIORITY OF RIGHT OF ENTERPRISE AND LOCAL LOANS."

THE ARABS, WHO WERE LED TO BELIEVE THEY WOULD OBTAIN POSTWAR INDEPENDENCE, WERE BETRAYED.

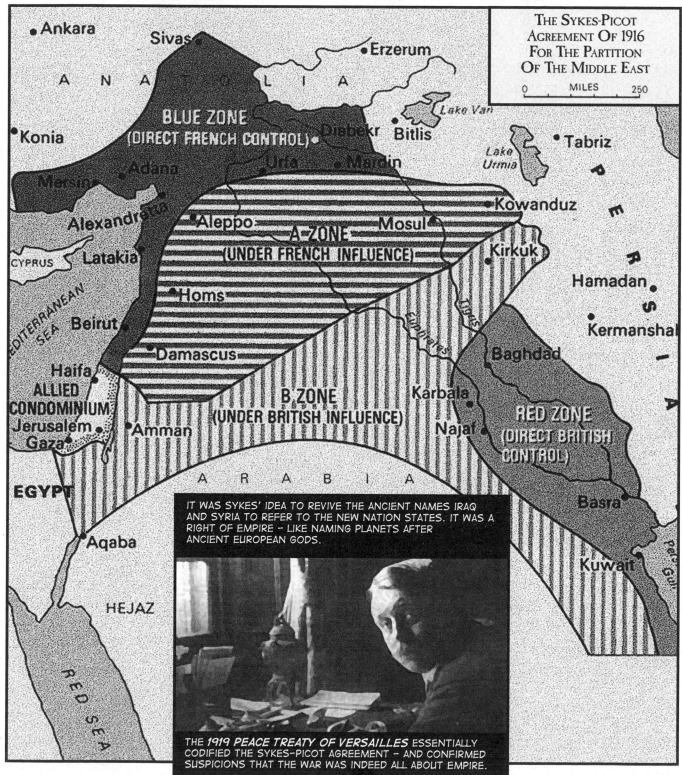

THE SYKES-PICOT AGREEMENT OF 1916 FOR THE PARTITION OF THE MIDDLE EAST

0   MILES   250

• Ankara
Sivas
• Erzerum
A N A T O L I A
Lake Van

BLUE ZONE (DIRECT FRENCH CONTROL)
• Konia
Diebekr • Bitlis
• Tabriz
Lake Urmia
• Adana
Mersin
Urfa • Mardin
Kowanduz
Alexandretta
• Aleppo   Mosul
A ZONE (UNDER FRENCH INFLUENCE)
• Kirkuk
CYPRUS   Latakia
Hamadan
MEDITERRANEAN SEA   • Homs
Tigris   Euphrates
P E R S I A
Beirut
• Kermanshal
• Damascus
Baghdad
Haifa
ALLIED CONDOMINIUM
B ZONE (UNDER BRITISH INFLUENCE)
• Karbala
RED ZONE (DIRECT BRITISH CONTROL)
Jerusalem
Gaza   • Amman
Najaf
EGYPT
A R A B I A
• Aqaba
Basra
HEJAZ
Kuwait
Persian Gulf

IT WAS SYKES' IDEA TO REVIVE THE ANCIENT NAMES IRAQ AND SYRIA TO REFER TO THE NEW NATION STATES. IT WAS A RIGHT OF EMPIRE – LIKE NAMING PLANETS AFTER ANCIENT EUROPEAN GODS.

THE *1919 PEACE TREATY OF VERSAILLES* ESSENTIALLY CODIFIED THE SYKES-PICOT AGREEMENT – AND CONFIRMED SUSPICIONS THAT THE WAR WAS INDEED ALL ABOUT EMPIRE.

Resistance to War

THE DAY AFTER THE DECLARATION OF WAR, THE ***SOCIALIST PARTY U.S.A.*** MET IN AN EMERGENCY SESSION IN ST. LOUIS AND CALLED IT "A CRIME AGAINST THE PEOPLE OF THE UNITED STATES."

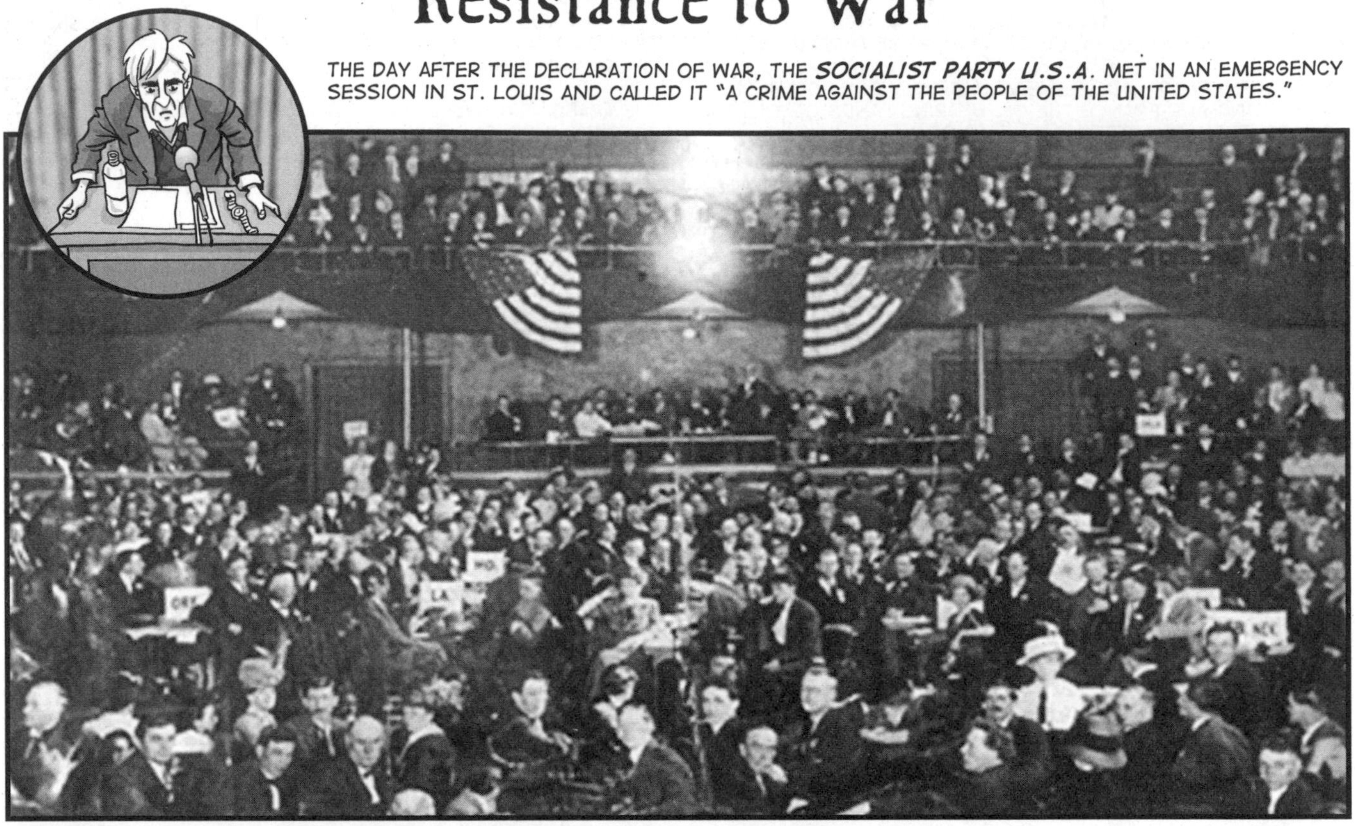

THE GENERAL PUBLIC WAS ALSO FIRMLY AGAINST THE WAR AND ELECTED MANY ANTIWAR SOCIALISTS IN THE 1917 STATE AND LOCAL ELECTIONS.

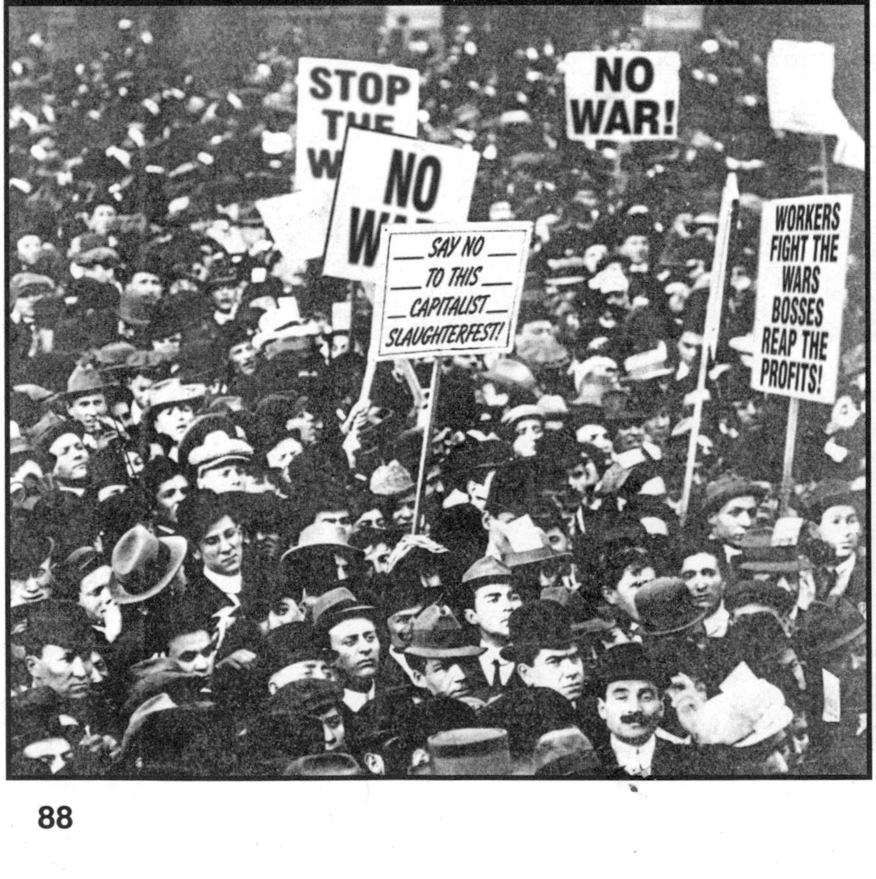
STOP
NO WAR!
NO
SAY NO TO THIS CAPITALIST SLAUGHTERFEST!
WORKERS FIGHT THE WARS BOSSES REAP THE PROFITS!

BUT PROWAR ADVOCATES ALSO RALLIED. RELIGIOUS CONSERVATIVES, LIKE THE NATION'S MOST FAMOUS EVANGELIST, ***BILLY SUNDAY***, CALLED UPON THE FAITHFUL TO SUPPORT THE WAR.

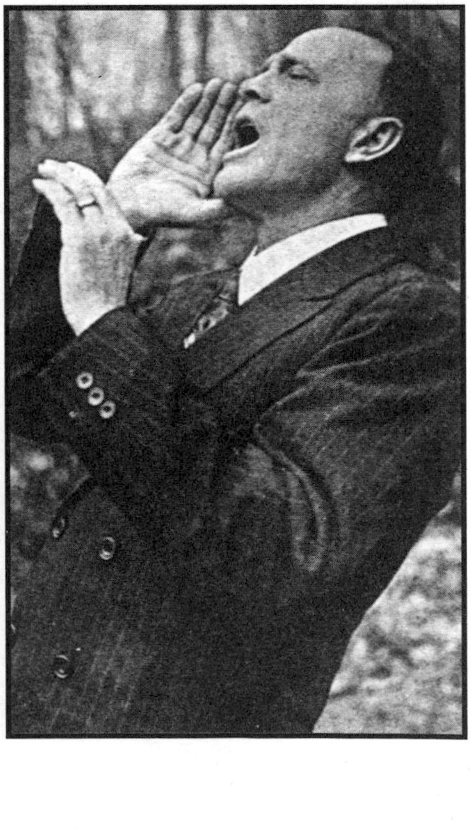

DESPITE THE ROUSING WORDS OF WILSON ABOUT A WAR "TO END ALL WARS" AND "TO MAKE THE WORLD SAFE FOR DEMOCRACY," AMERICANS DID NOT RUSH TO ENLIST. A MILLION MEN WERE NEEDED, BUT ONLY 73,000 VOLUNTEERED.

ON MAY 18, 1917, CONGRESS PASSED THE *CONSCRIPTION ACT*, I.E. A COMPULSORY DRAFT. TO MAKE SURE CONSCRIPTION WAS NOT VIEWED CASUALLY BY THE PUBLIC, IT ALSO PASSED THE *ESPIONAGE ACT* ON JUNE 25 TO CRIMINALIZE ALL BUT THE MOST INNOCUOUS DISSENT AGAINST THE WAR.

I WANT YOU FOR U.S. ARMY

NEAREST RECRUITING STATION

NO CONSCRIPTION

FREEDOM OF CONSCIENCE AT ALL COSTS!

FRIDAY, MAY 18, 8 P. M.
HARLEM RIVER CASINO
127th Street & Second Avenue

SPEAKERS: Emma Goldman; Harry Weinberger; Leonora O'Reilly; Alexander Berkman; Jacob Panken; Alex Cohen [in Yiddish] Carlo Tresca [in Italian] and others. Leonard D. Abbott, Chairman

Auspices of No-Conscription League of New York

Admission Free

A *PROPAGANDA CAMPAIGN* WAS QUICKLY ORGANIZED. TENS OF THOUSANDS OF ORATORS, DRILLED TO DELIVER A PROWAR SPEECH IN FOUR MINUTES, VISITED 5,000 CITIES AND TOWNS.

OPPOSITION TO THE WAR IS *TREASON!*

FORMER PRESIDENT *TEDDY ROOSEVELT* INTRODUCED A NEW THEME TO DESCRIBE WAR CRITICS IN A SPEECH TO THE HARVARD CLUB.

PEOPLE WHO OPPOSE THE WAR ARE JUST A RAFT OF *SEXLESS CREATURES!*

ZINNFORMATION

FORTY YEARS LATER, FORMER SPECIAL ASSISTANT FOR LATIN AMERICAN AFFAIRS IN THE KENNEDY ADMINISTRATION AND KENNEDY BIOGRAPHER *ARTHUR M. SCHLESINGER JR.* FOLLOWED SUIT, ACCUSING CRITICS OF THE COLD WAR OF SHOWING "A FEMININE FASCINATION WITH THE RUDE AND MUSCULAR POWER OF THE PROLETARIAT."

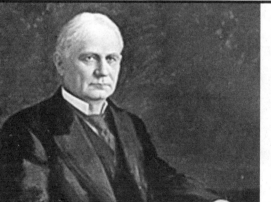

SPEAKER OF THE HOUSE *CHAMP CLARK*, A MISSOURI PROGRESSIVE, DENOUNCED THE DRAFT.

"IN THE ESTIMATION OF MISSOURIANS," HE TOLD THE HOUSE, "THERE IS PRECIOUS LITTLE DIFFERENCE BETWEEN A CONSCRIPT AND A CONVICT."

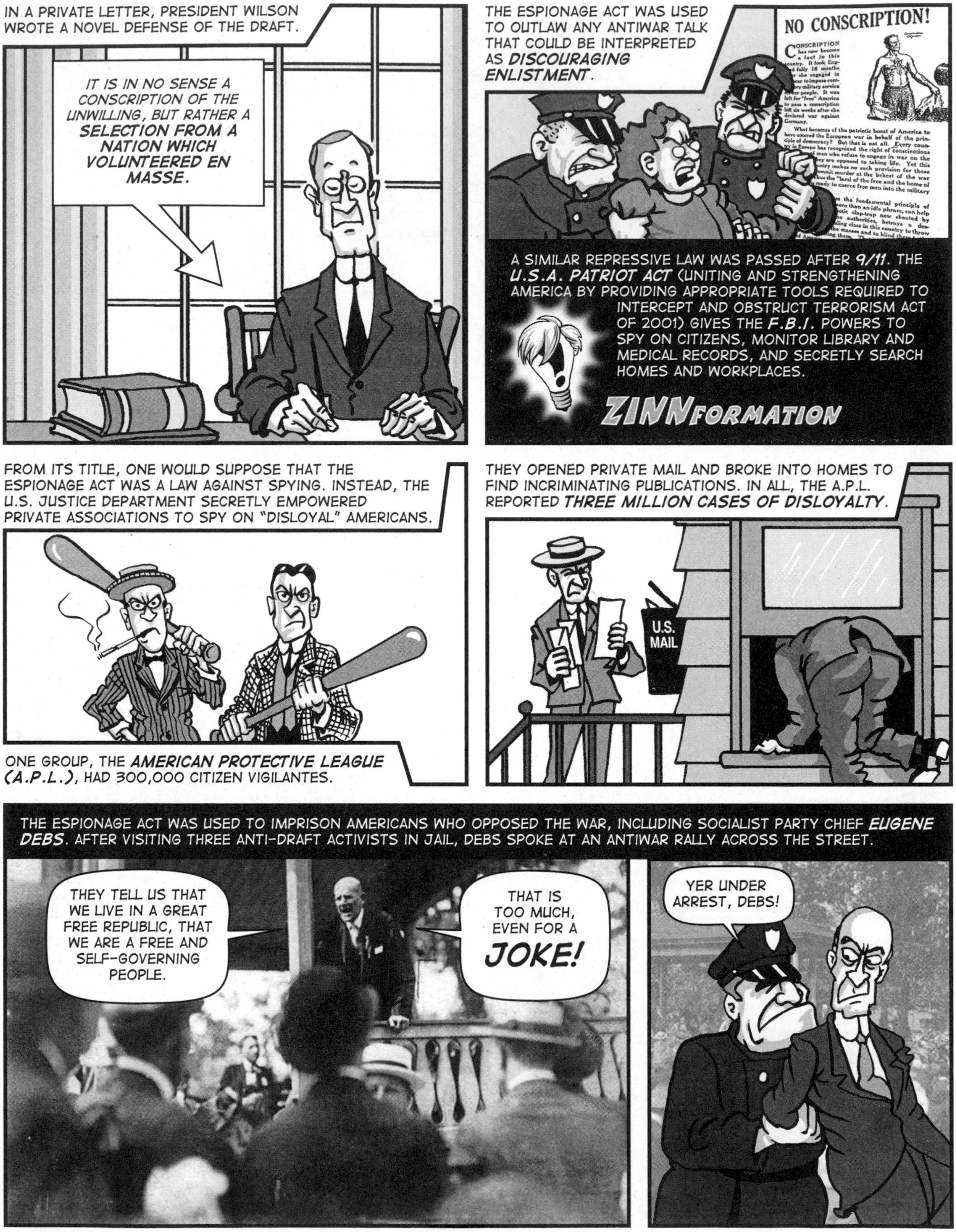
IN A PRIVATE LETTER, PRESIDENT WILSON WROTE A NOVEL DEFENSE OF THE DRAFT.
IT IS IN NO SENSE A CONSCRIPTION OF THE UNWILLING, BUT RATHER A SELECTION FROM A NATION WHICH VOLUNTEERED EN MASSE.
THE ESPIONAGE ACT WAS USED TO OUTLAW ANY ANTIWAR TALK THAT COULD BE INTERPRETED AS DISCOURAGING ENLISTMENT.
NO CONSCRIPTION!
A SIMILAR REPRESSIVE LAW WAS PASSED AFTER 9/11. THE U.S.A. PATRIOT ACT (UNITING AND STRENGTHENING AMERICA BY PROVIDING APPROPRIATE TOOLS REQUIRED TO INTERCEPT AND OBSTRUCT TERRORISM ACT OF 2001) GIVES THE F.B.I. POWERS TO SPY ON CITIZENS, MONITOR LIBRARY AND MEDICAL RECORDS, AND SECRETLY SEARCH HOMES AND WORKPLACES.
ZINNFORMATION
FROM ITS TITLE, ONE WOULD SUPPOSE THAT THE ESPIONAGE ACT WAS A LAW AGAINST SPYING. INSTEAD, THE U.S. JUSTICE DEPARTMENT SECRETLY EMPOWERED PRIVATE ASSOCIATIONS TO SPY ON "DISLOYAL" AMERICANS.
ONE GROUP, THE AMERICAN PROTECTIVE LEAGUE (A.P.L.), HAD 300,000 CITIZEN VIGILANTES.
THEY OPENED PRIVATE MAIL AND BROKE INTO HOMES TO FIND INCRIMINATING PUBLICATIONS. IN ALL, THE A.P.L. REPORTED THREE MILLION CASES OF DISLOYALTY.
U.S. MAIL
THE ESPIONAGE ACT WAS USED TO IMPRISON AMERICANS WHO OPPOSED THE WAR, INCLUDING SOCIALIST PARTY CHIEF EUGENE DEBS. AFTER VISITING THREE ANTI-DRAFT ACTIVISTS IN JAIL, DEBS SPOKE AT AN ANTIWAR RALLY ACROSS THE STREET.
THEY TELL US THAT WE LIVE IN A GREAT FREE REPUBLIC, THAT WE ARE A FREE AND SELF-GOVERNING PEOPLE.
THAT IS TOO MUCH, EVEN FOR A JOKE!
YER UNDER ARREST, DEBS!

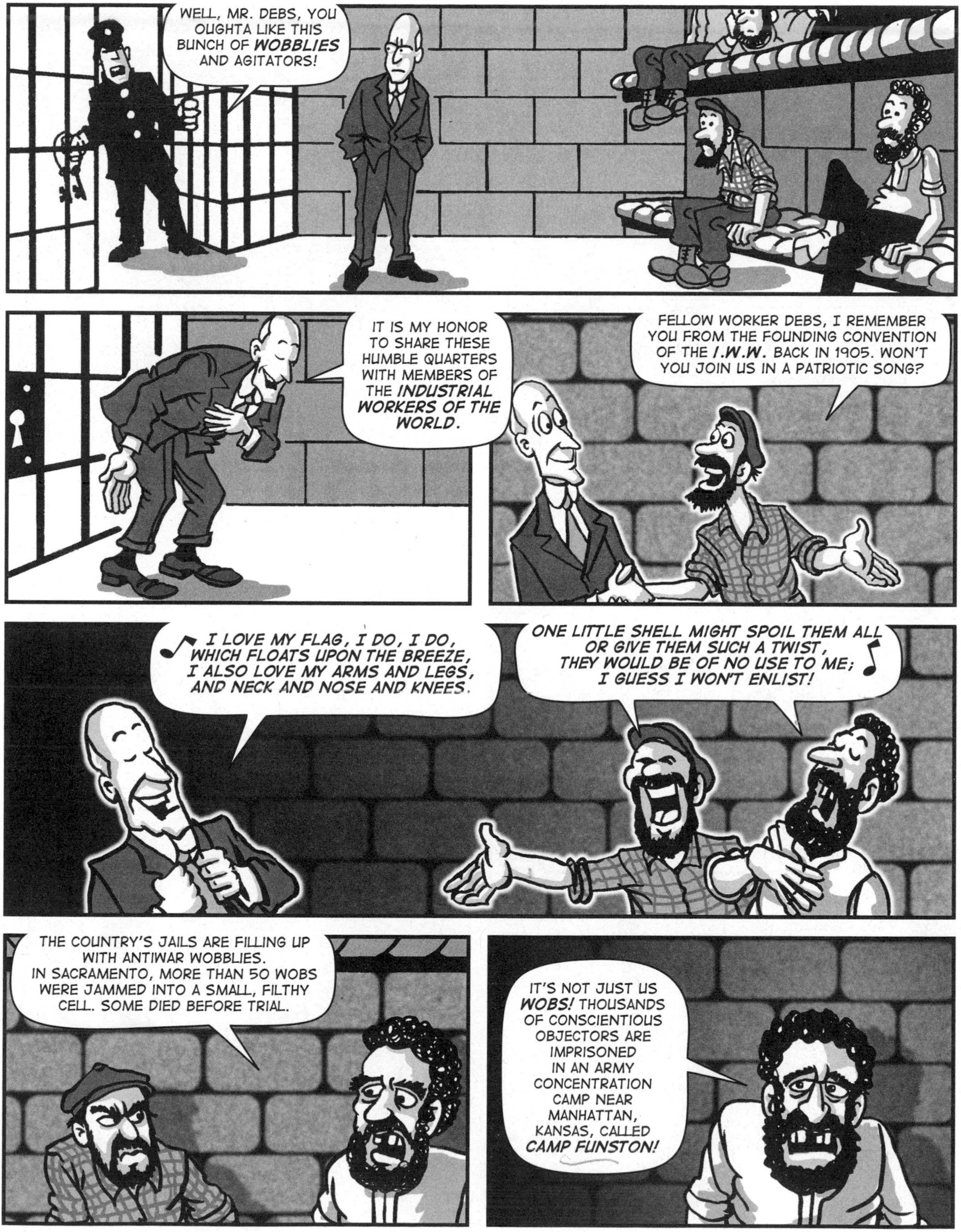
WELL, MR. DEBS, YOU OUGHTA LIKE THIS BUNCH OF WOBBLIES AND AGITATORS!
IT IS MY HONOR TO SHARE THESE HUMBLE QUARTERS WITH MEMBERS OF THE INDUSTRIAL WORKERS OF THE WORLD.
FELLOW WORKER DEBS, I REMEMBER YOU FROM THE FOUNDING CONVENTION OF THE I.W.W. BACK IN 1905. WON'T YOU JOIN US IN A PATRIOTIC SONG?
I LOVE MY FLAG, I DO, I DO, WHICH FLOATS UPON THE BREEZE, I ALSO LOVE MY ARMS AND LEGS, AND NECK AND NOSE AND KNEES.
ONE LITTLE SHELL MIGHT SPOIL THEM ALL OR GIVE THEM SUCH A TWIST, THEY WOULD BE OF NO USE TO ME; I GUESS I WON'T ENLIST!
THE COUNTRY'S JAILS ARE FILLING UP WITH ANTIWAR WOBBLIES. IN SACRAMENTO, MORE THAN 50 WOBS WERE JAMMED INTO A SMALL, FILTHY CELL. SOME DIED BEFORE TRIAL.
IT'S NOT JUST US WOBS! THOUSANDS OF CONSCIENTIOUS OBJECTORS ARE IMPRISONED IN AN ARMY CONCENTRATION CAMP NEAR MANHATTAN, KANSAS, CALLED CAMP FUNSTON!

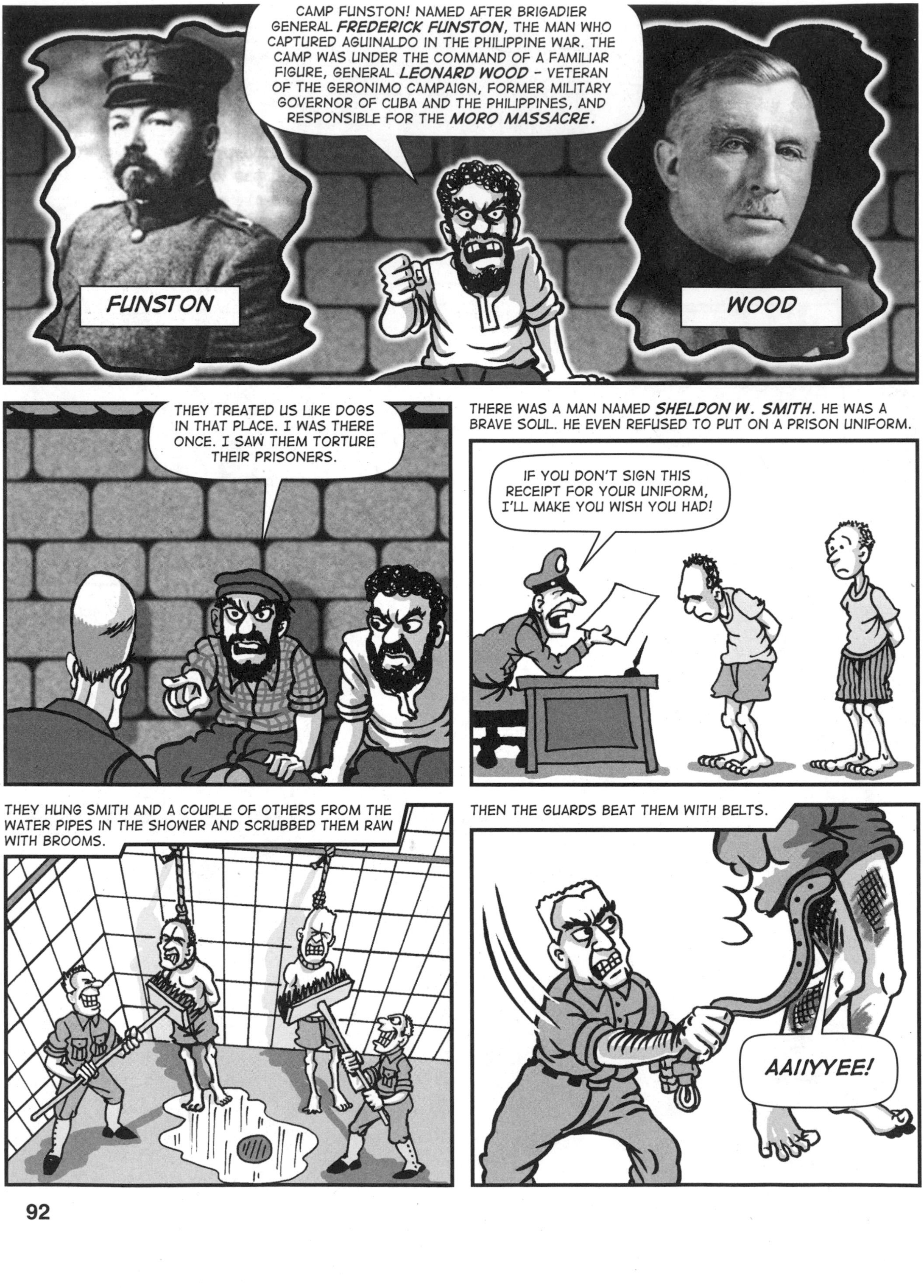

CAMP FUNSTON! NAMED AFTER BRIGADIER GENERAL FREDERICK FUNSTON, THE MAN WHO CAPTURED AGUINALDO IN THE PHILIPPINE WAR. THE CAMP WAS UNDER THE COMMAND OF A FAMILIAR FIGURE, GENERAL LEONARD WOOD - VETERAN OF THE GERONIMO CAMPAIGN, FORMER MILITARY GOVERNOR OF CUBA AND THE PHILIPPINES, AND RESPONSIBLE FOR THE MORO MASSACRE.
FUNSTON
WOOD
THEY TREATED US LIKE DOGS IN THAT PLACE. I WAS THERE ONCE. I SAW THEM TORTURE THEIR PRISONERS.
THERE WAS A MAN NAMED SHELDON W. SMITH. HE WAS A BRAVE SOUL. HE EVEN REFUSED TO PUT ON A PRISON UNIFORM.
IF YOU DON'T SIGN THIS RECEIPT FOR YOUR UNIFORM, I'LL MAKE YOU WISH YOU HAD!
THEY HUNG SMITH AND A COUPLE OF OTHERS FROM THE WATER PIPES IN THE SHOWER AND SCRUBBED THEM RAW WITH BROOMS.
THEN THE GUARDS BEAT THEM WITH BELTS.
AAIIYYEE!

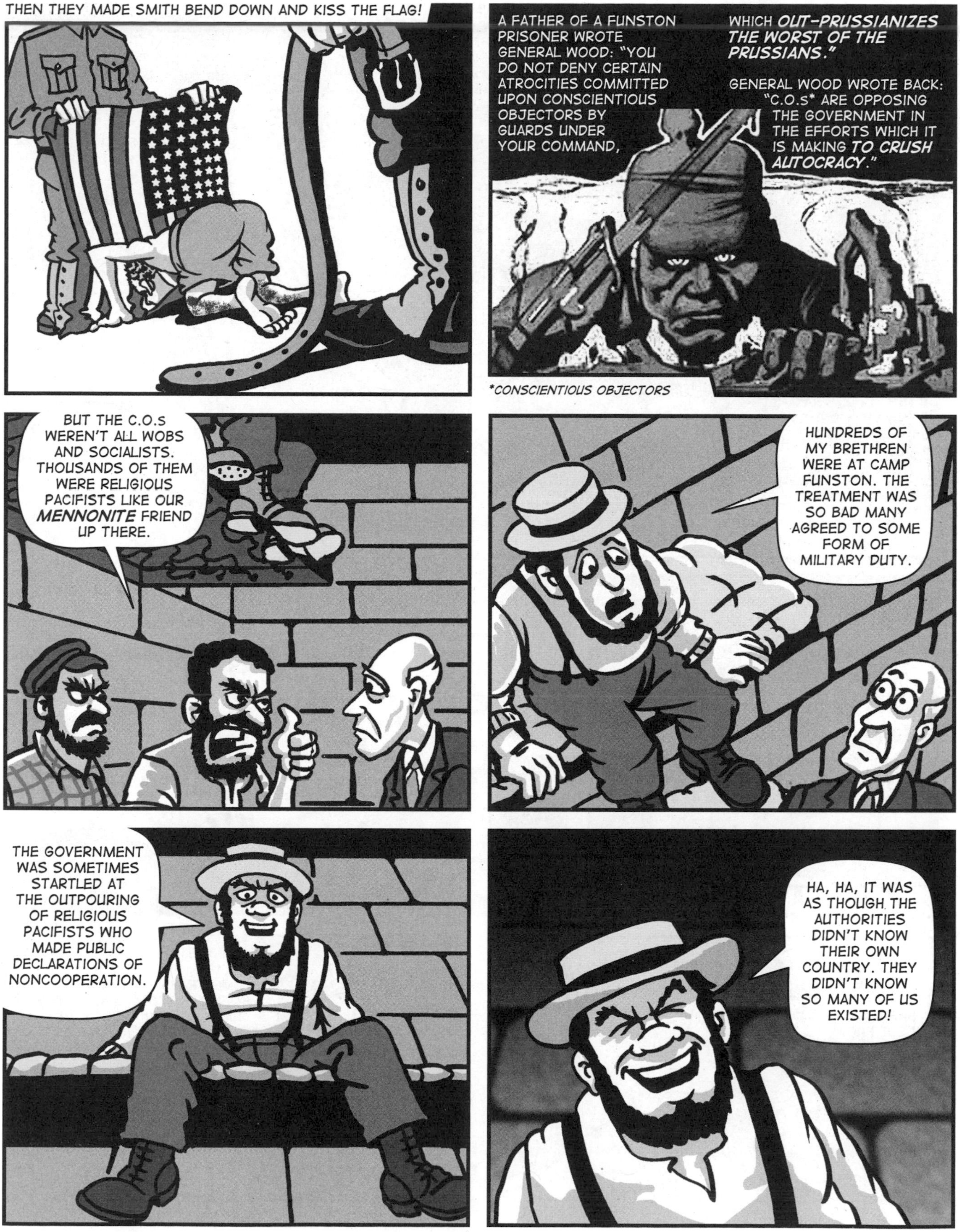
THEN THEY MADE SMITH BEND DOWN AND KISS THE FLAG!
A FATHER OF A FUNSTON PRISONER WROTE GENERAL WOOD: "YOU DO NOT DENY CERTAIN ATROCITIES COMMITTED UPON CONSCIENTIOUS OBJECTORS BY GUARDS UNDER YOUR COMMAND,
WHICH *OUT-PRUSSIANIZES THE WORST OF THE PRUSSIANS.*"
GENERAL WOOD WROTE BACK: "C.O.s* ARE OPPOSING THE GOVERNMENT IN THE EFFORTS WHICH IT IS MAKING *TO CRUSH AUTOCRACY*."
*CONSCIENTIOUS OBJECTORS
BUT THE C.O.s WEREN'T ALL WOBS AND SOCIALISTS. THOUSANDS OF THEM WERE RELIGIOUS PACIFISTS LIKE OUR *MENNONITE* FRIEND UP THERE.
HUNDREDS OF MY BRETHREN WERE AT CAMP FUNSTON. THE TREATMENT WAS SO BAD MANY AGREED TO SOME FORM OF MILITARY DUTY.
THE GOVERNMENT WAS SOMETIMES STARTLED AT THE OUTPOURING OF RELIGIOUS PACIFISTS WHO MADE PUBLIC DECLARATIONS OF NONCOOPERATION.
HA, HA, IT WAS AS THOUGH THE AUTHORITIES DIDN'T KNOW THEIR OWN COUNTRY. THEY DIDN'T KNOW SO MANY OF US EXISTED!

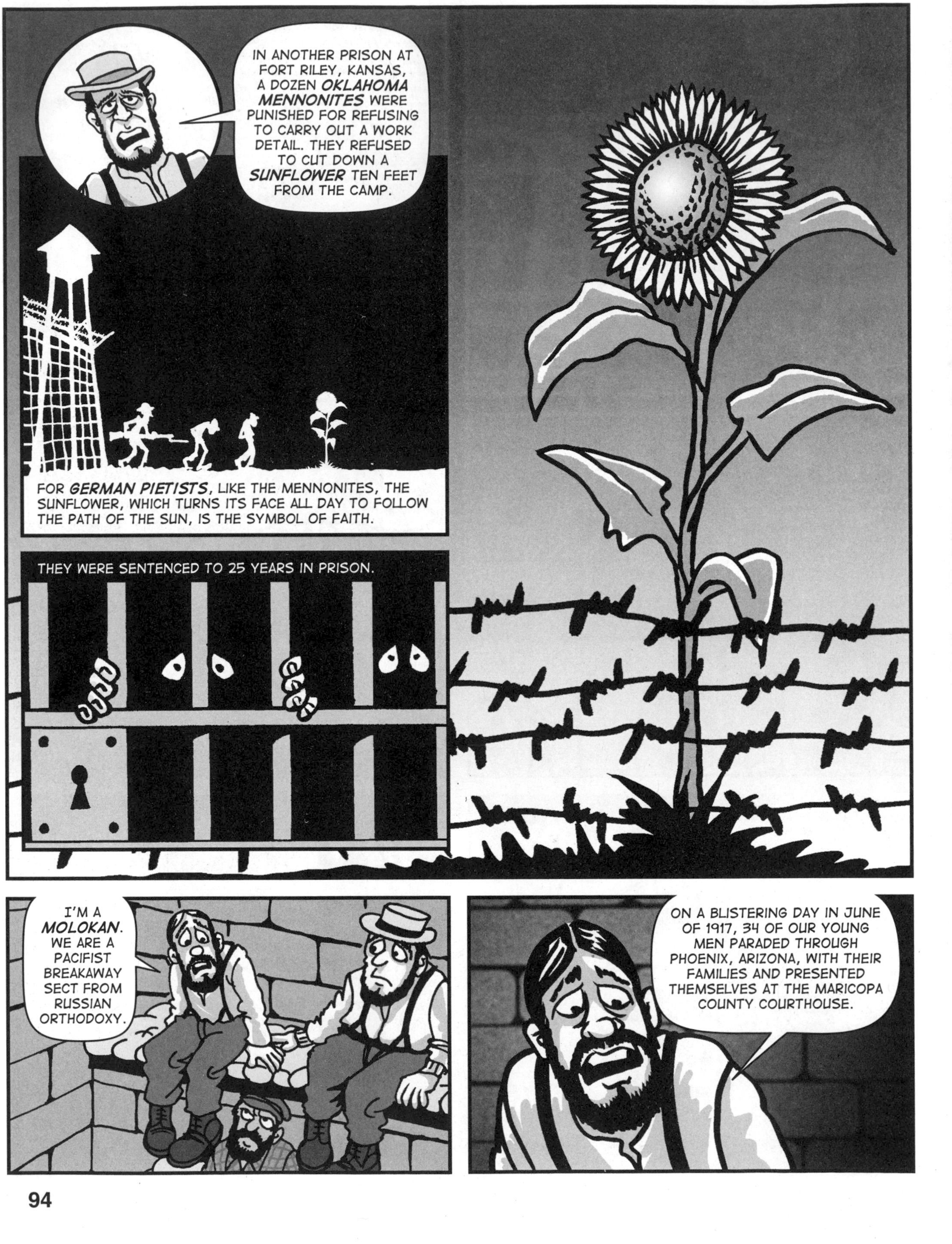
IN ANOTHER PRISON AT FORT RILEY, KANSAS, A DOZEN OKLAHOMA MENNONITES WERE PUNISHED FOR REFUSING TO CARRY OUT A WORK DETAIL. THEY REFUSED TO CUT DOWN A SUNFLOWER TEN FEET FROM THE CAMP.
FOR GERMAN PIETISTS, LIKE THE MENNONITES, THE SUNFLOWER, WHICH TURNS ITS FACE ALL DAY TO FOLLOW THE PATH OF THE SUN, IS THE SYMBOL OF FAITH.
THEY WERE SENTENCED TO 25 YEARS IN PRISON.
I'M A MOLOKAN. WE ARE A PACIFIST BREAKAWAY SECT FROM RUSSIAN ORTHODOXY.
ON A BLISTERING DAY IN JUNE OF 1917, 34 OF OUR YOUNG MEN PARADED THROUGH PHOENIX, ARIZONA, WITH THEIR FAMILIES AND PRESENTED THEMSELVES AT THE MARICOPA COUNTY COURTHOUSE.

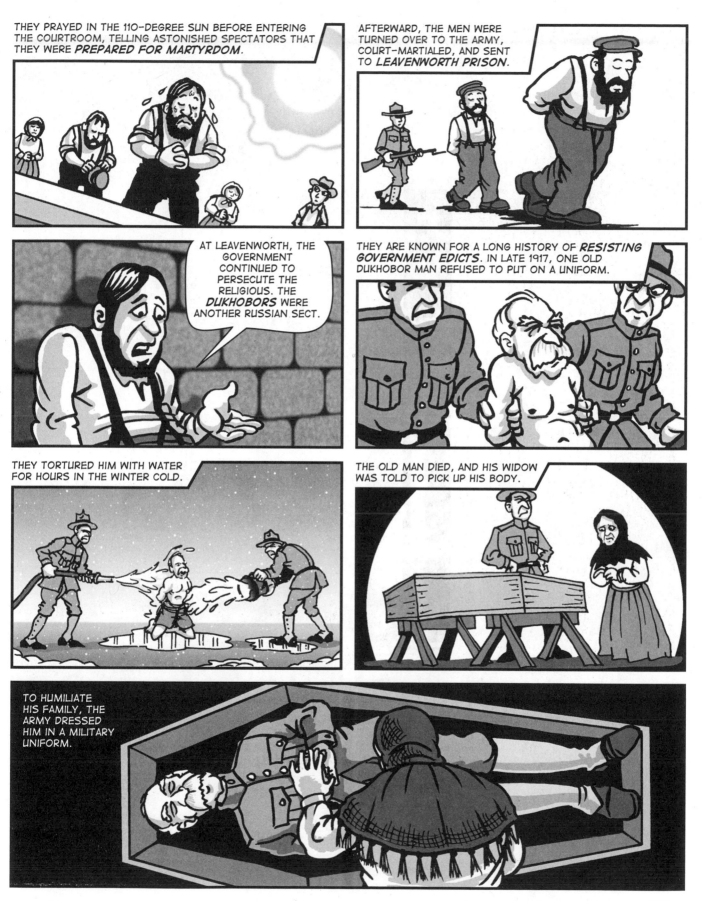

THEY PRAYED IN THE 110-DEGREE SUN BEFORE ENTERING THE COURTROOM, TELLING ASTONISHED SPECTATORS THAT THEY WERE *PREPARED FOR MARTYRDOM*.

AFTERWARD, THE MEN WERE TURNED OVER TO THE ARMY, COURT-MARTIALED, AND SENT TO *LEAVENWORTH PRISON*.

AT LEAVENWORTH, THE GOVERNMENT CONTINUED TO PERSECUTE THE RELIGIOUS. THE *DUKHOBORS* WERE ANOTHER RUSSIAN SECT.

THEY ARE KNOWN FOR A LONG HISTORY OF *RESISTING GOVERNMENT EDICTS*. IN LATE 1917, ONE OLD DUKHOBOR MAN REFUSED TO PUT ON A UNIFORM.

THEY TORTURED HIM WITH WATER FOR HOURS IN THE WINTER COLD.

THE OLD MAN DIED, AND HIS WIDOW WAS TOLD TO PICK UP HIS BODY.

TO HUMILIATE HIS FAMILY, THE ARMY DRESSED HIM IN A MILITARY UNIFORM.

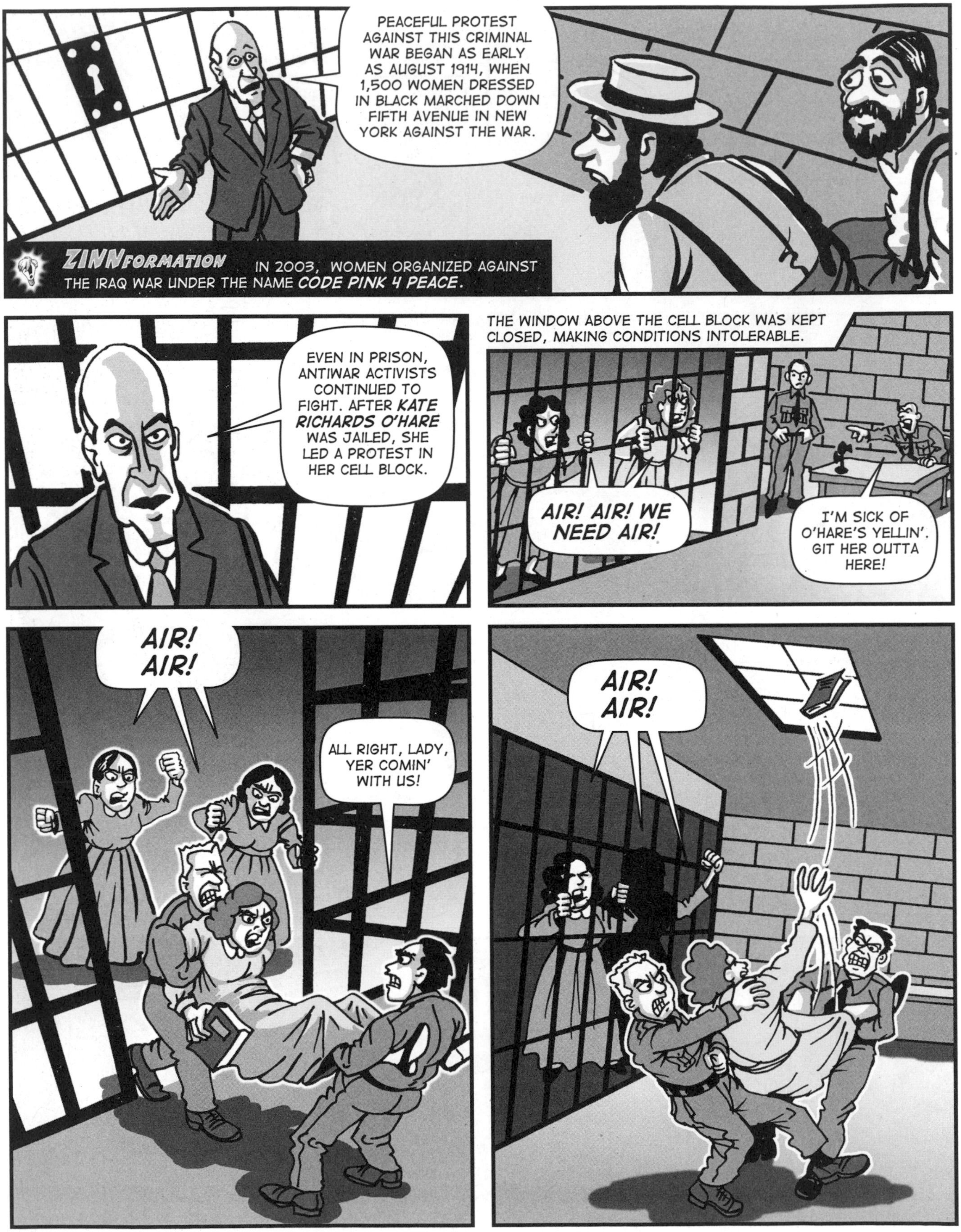
PEACEFUL PROTEST AGAINST THIS CRIMINAL WAR BEGAN AS EARLY AS AUGUST 1914, WHEN 1,500 WOMEN DRESSED IN BLACK MARCHED DOWN FIFTH AVENUE IN NEW YORK AGAINST THE WAR.
ZINNFORMATION IN 2003, WOMEN ORGANIZED AGAINST THE IRAQ WAR UNDER THE NAME CODE PINK 4 PEACE.
EVEN IN PRISON, ANTIWAR ACTIVISTS CONTINUED TO FIGHT. AFTER KATE RICHARDS O'HARE WAS JAILED, SHE LED A PROTEST IN HER CELL BLOCK.
THE WINDOW ABOVE THE CELL BLOCK WAS KEPT CLOSED, MAKING CONDITIONS INTOLERABLE.
AIR! AIR! WE NEED AIR!
I'M SICK OF O'HARE'S YELLIN'. GIT HER OUTTA HERE!
AIR! AIR!
ALL RIGHT, LADY, YER COMIN' WITH US!
AIR! AIR!

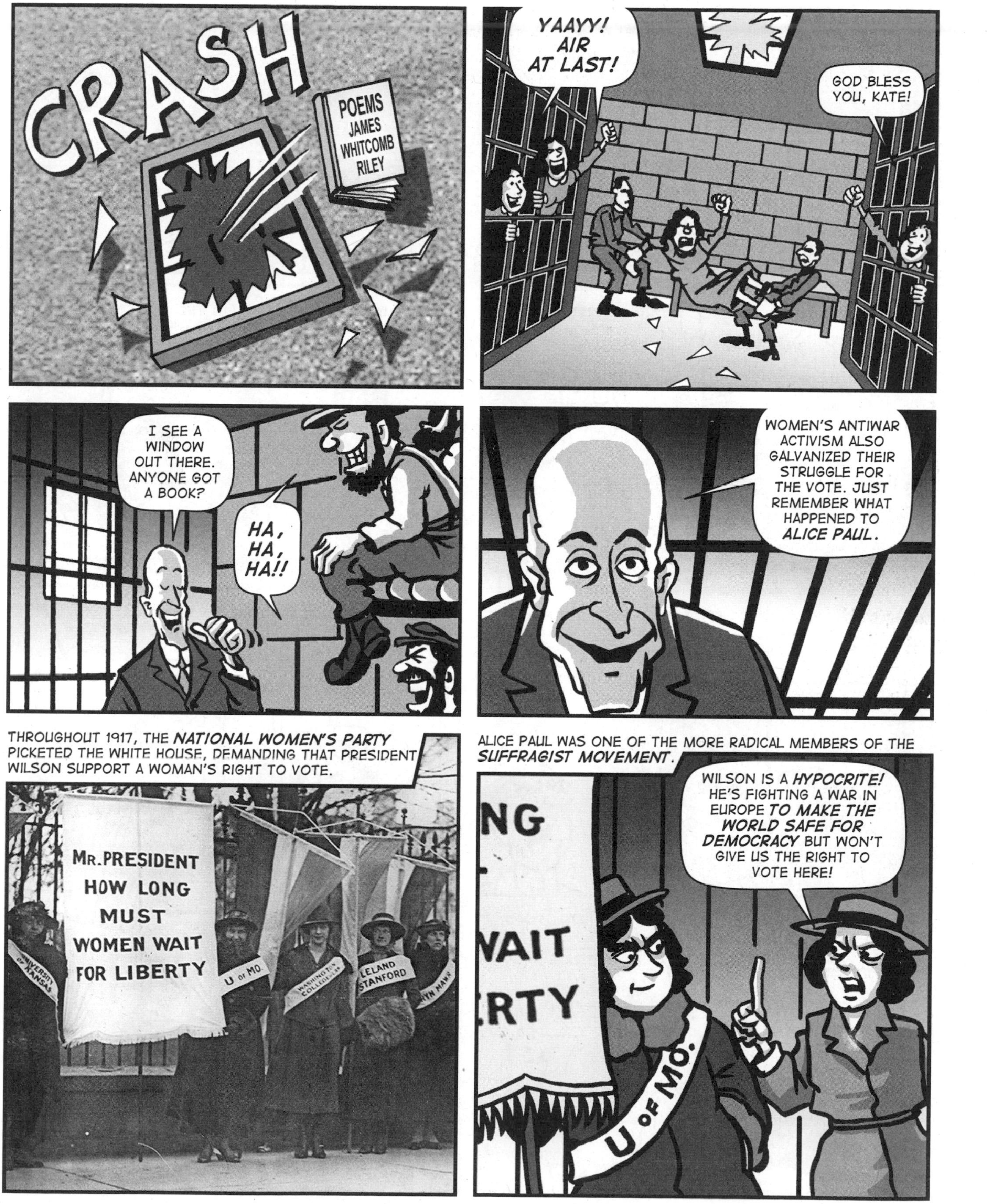
CRASH
POEMS
JAMES
WHITCOMB
RILEY
YAAYY! AIR AT LAST!
GOD BLESS YOU, KATE!
I SEE A WINDOW OUT THERE. ANYONE GOT A BOOK?
HA, HA, HA!!
WOMEN'S ANTIWAR ACTIVISM ALSO GALVANIZED THEIR STRUGGLE FOR THE VOTE. JUST REMEMBER WHAT HAPPENED TO ALICE PAUL.
THROUGHOUT 1917, THE NATIONAL WOMEN'S PARTY PICKETED THE WHITE HOUSE, DEMANDING THAT PRESIDENT WILSON SUPPORT A WOMAN'S RIGHT TO VOTE.
MR. PRESIDENT HOW LONG MUST WOMEN WAIT FOR LIBERTY
UNIVERSITY OF KANSAS
U OF MO.
LELAND STANFORD
ALICE PAUL WAS ONE OF THE MORE RADICAL MEMBERS OF THE SUFFRAGIST MOVEMENT.
WILSON IS A HYPOCRITE! HE'S FIGHTING A WAR IN EUROPE TO MAKE THE WORLD SAFE FOR DEMOCRACY BUT WON'T GIVE US THE RIGHT TO VOTE HERE!
U OF MO.

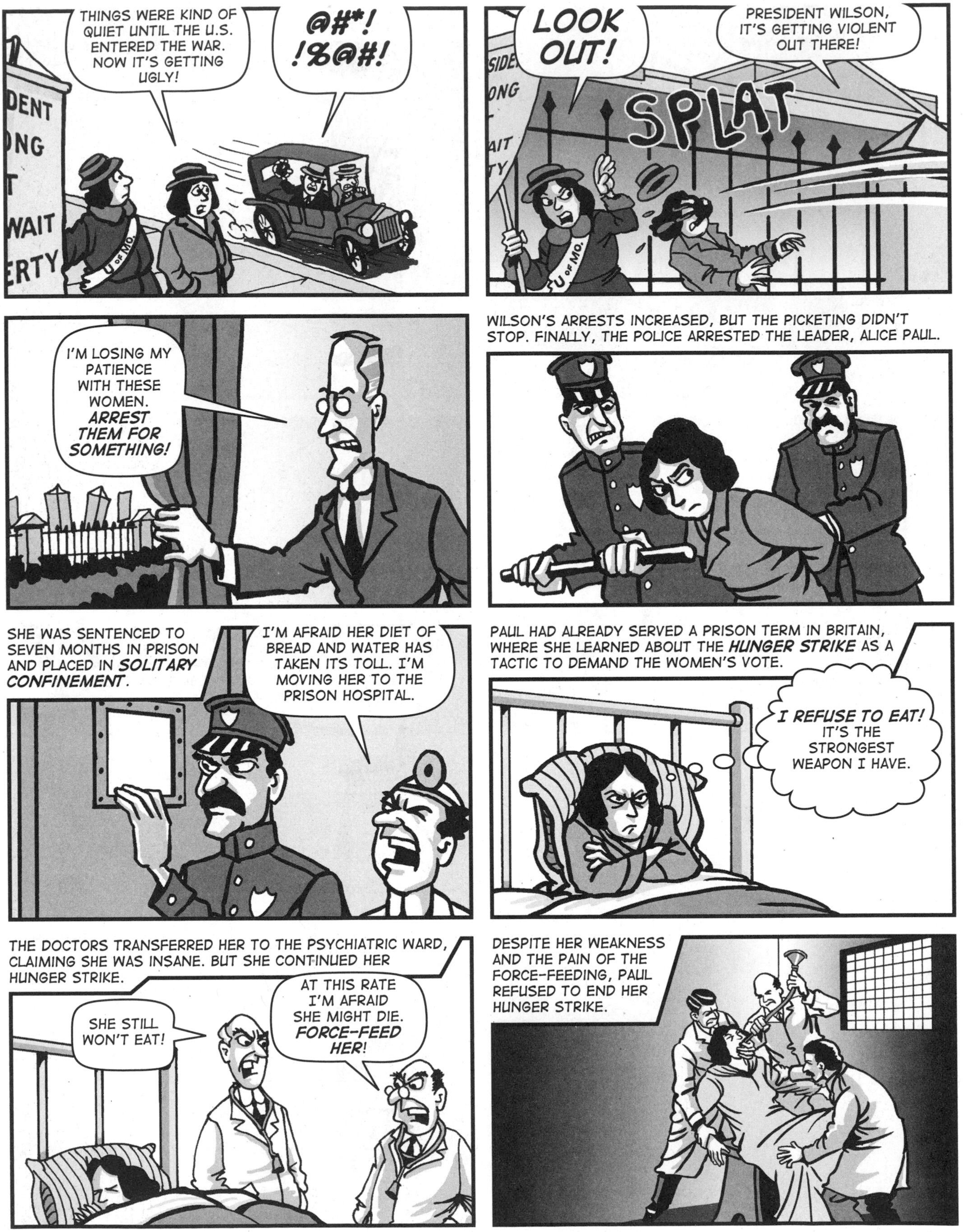
THINGS WERE KIND OF QUIET UNTIL THE U.S. ENTERED THE WAR. NOW IT'S GETTING UGLY!
@#*! !%@#!
LOOK OUT!
PRESIDENT WILSON, IT'S GETTING VIOLENT OUT THERE!
SPLAT
I'M LOSING MY PATIENCE WITH THESE WOMEN. ARREST THEM FOR SOMETHING!
WILSON'S ARRESTS INCREASED, BUT THE PICKETING DIDN'T STOP. FINALLY, THE POLICE ARRESTED THE LEADER, ALICE PAUL.
SHE WAS SENTENCED TO SEVEN MONTHS IN PRISON AND PLACED IN SOLITARY CONFINEMENT.
I'M AFRAID HER DIET OF BREAD AND WATER HAS TAKEN ITS TOLL. I'M MOVING HER TO THE PRISON HOSPITAL.
PAUL HAD ALREADY SERVED A PRISON TERM IN BRITAIN, WHERE SHE LEARNED ABOUT THE HUNGER STRIKE AS A TACTIC TO DEMAND THE WOMEN'S VOTE.
I REFUSE TO EAT! IT'S THE STRONGEST WEAPON I HAVE.
THE DOCTORS TRANSFERRED HER TO THE PSYCHIATRIC WARD, CLAIMING SHE WAS INSANE. BUT SHE CONTINUED HER HUNGER STRIKE.
SHE STILL WON'T EAT!
AT THIS RATE I'M AFRAID SHE MIGHT DIE. FORCE-FEED HER!
DESPITE HER WEAKNESS AND THE PAIN OF THE FORCE-FEEDING, PAUL REFUSED TO END HER HUNGER STRIKE.

Last name:

BLE

First name:

LA

Phone number:

7660

Title:

A people's history of

Hold until:

Tue Jun 20 2023

Pickup   Central Library

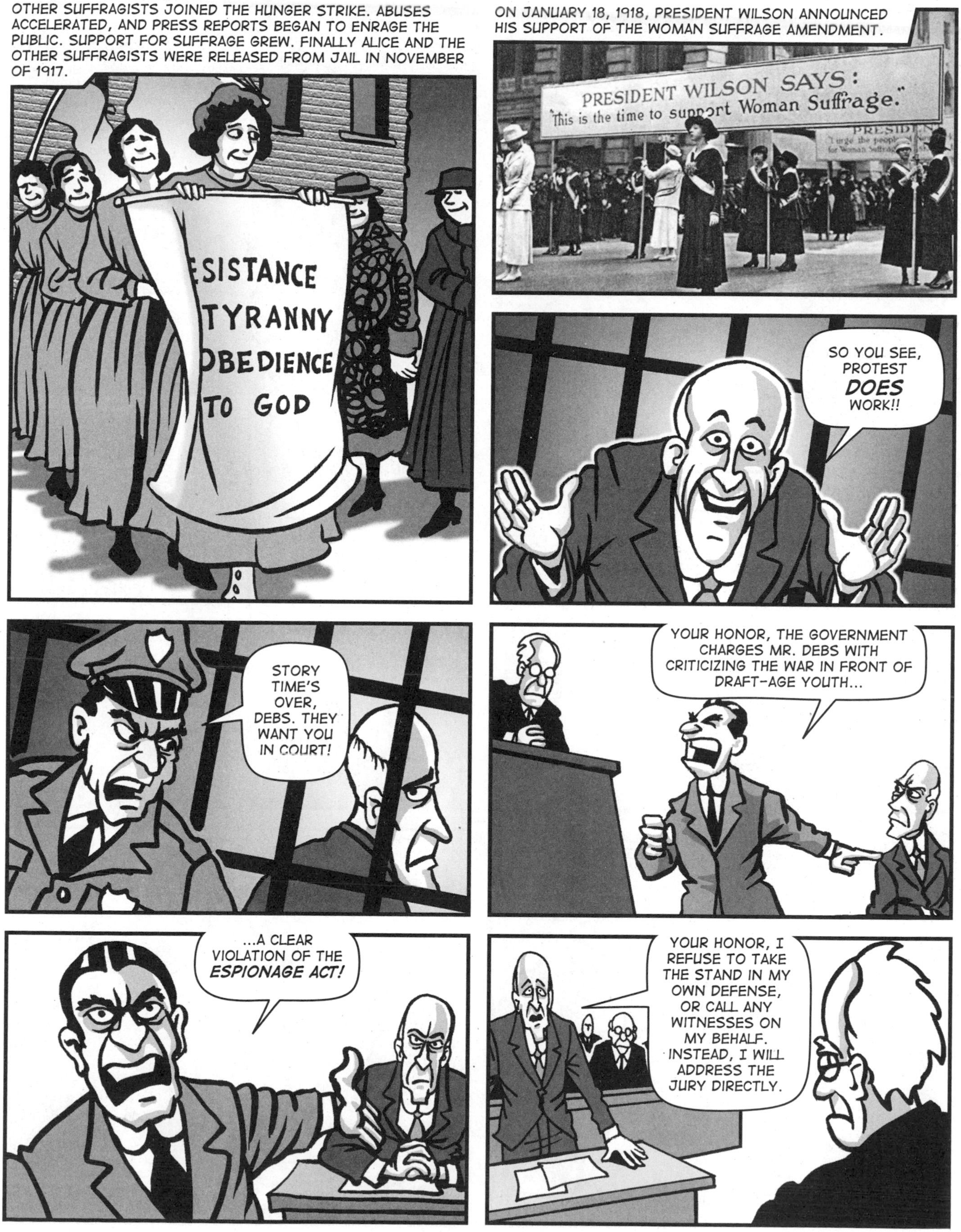
OTHER SUFFRAGISTS JOINED THE HUNGER STRIKE. ABUSES ACCELERATED, AND PRESS REPORTS BEGAN TO ENRAGE THE PUBLIC. SUPPORT FOR SUFFRAGE GREW. FINALLY ALICE AND THE OTHER SUFFRAGISTS WERE RELEASED FROM JAIL IN NOVEMBER OF 1917.
ESISTANCE
TYRANNY
OBEDIENCE
TO GOD
ON JANUARY 18, 1918, PRESIDENT WILSON ANNOUNCED HIS SUPPORT OF THE WOMAN SUFFRAGE AMENDMENT.
PRESIDENT WILSON SAYS:
"This is the time to support Woman Suffrage."
SO YOU SEE, PROTEST ***DOES*** WORK!!
STORY TIME'S OVER, DEBS. THEY WANT YOU IN COURT!
YOUR HONOR, THE GOVERNMENT CHARGES MR. DEBS WITH CRITICIZING THE WAR IN FRONT OF DRAFT-AGE YOUTH...
...A CLEAR VIOLATION OF THE ***ESPIONAGE ACT!***
YOUR HONOR, I REFUSE TO TAKE THE STAND IN MY OWN DEFENSE, OR CALL ANY WITNESSES ON MY BEHALF. INSTEAD, I WILL ADDRESS THE JURY DIRECTLY.

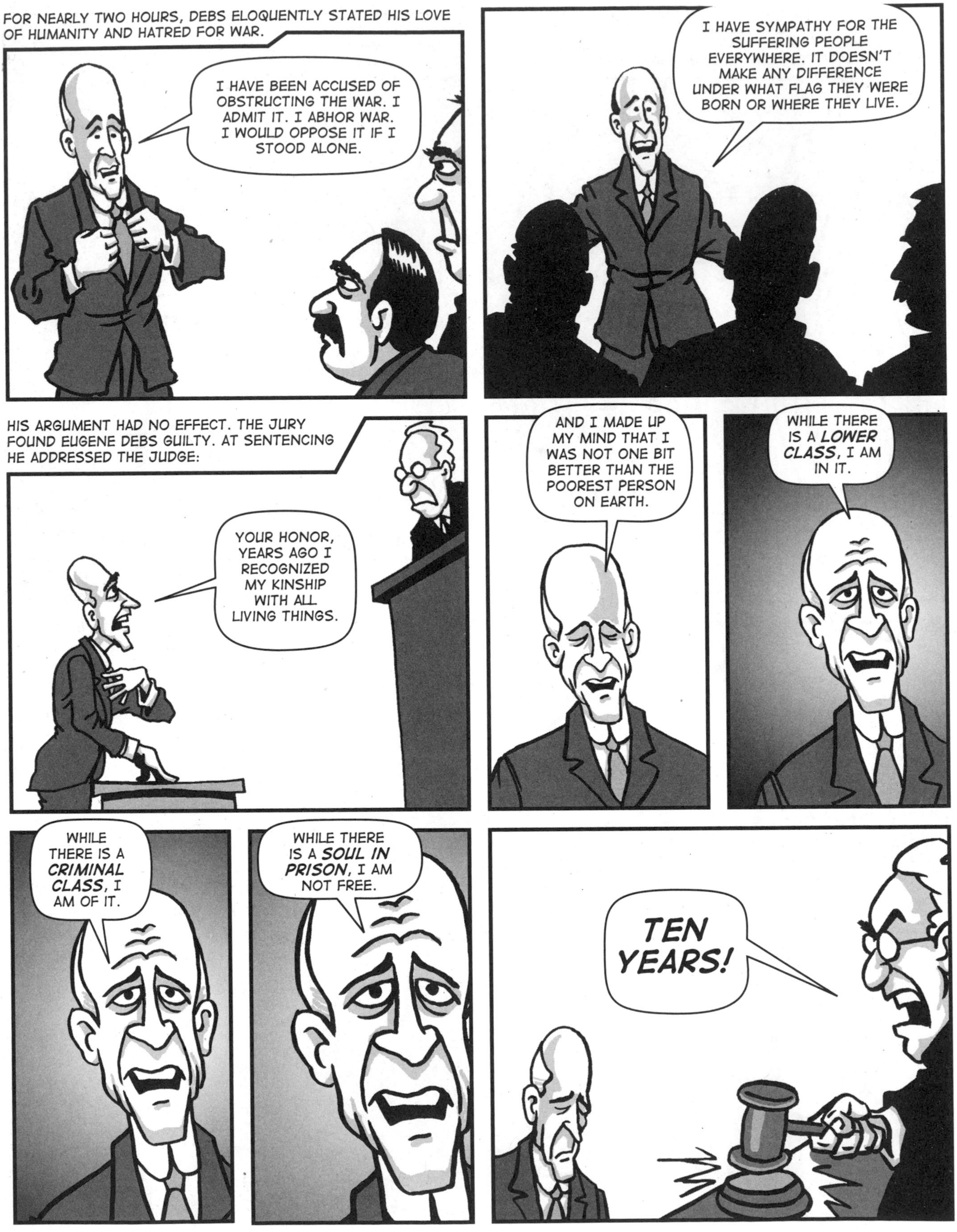
FOR NEARLY TWO HOURS, DEBS ELOQUENTLY STATED HIS LOVE OF HUMANITY AND HATRED FOR WAR.
I HAVE BEEN ACCUSED OF OBSTRUCTING THE WAR. I ADMIT IT. I ABHOR WAR. I WOULD OPPOSE IT IF I STOOD ALONE.
I HAVE SYMPATHY FOR THE SUFFERING PEOPLE EVERYWHERE. IT DOESN'T MAKE ANY DIFFERENCE UNDER WHAT FLAG THEY WERE BORN OR WHERE THEY LIVE.
HIS ARGUMENT HAD NO EFFECT. THE JURY FOUND EUGENE DEBS GUILTY. AT SENTENCING HE ADDRESSED THE JUDGE:
YOUR HONOR, YEARS AGO I RECOGNIZED MY KINSHIP WITH ALL LIVING THINGS.
AND I MADE UP MY MIND THAT I WAS NOT ONE BIT BETTER THAN THE POOREST PERSON ON EARTH.
WHILE THERE IS A LOWER CLASS, I AM IN IT.
WHILE THERE IS A CRIMINAL CLASS, I AM OF IT.
WHILE THERE IS A SOUL IN PRISON, I AM NOT FREE.
TEN YEARS!

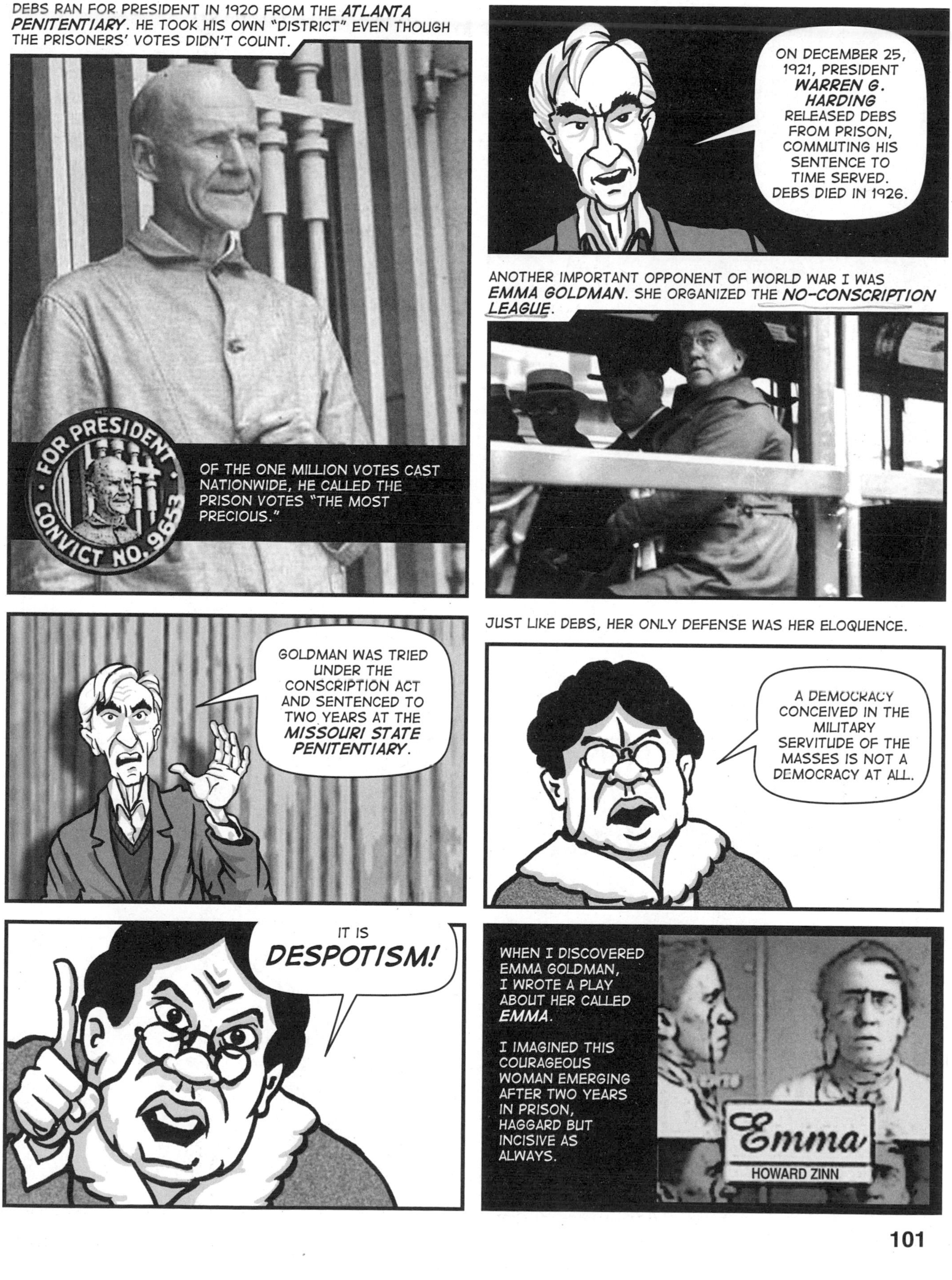
DEBS RAN FOR PRESIDENT IN 1920 FROM THE ***ATLANTA PENITENTIARY***. HE TOOK HIS OWN "DISTRICT" EVEN THOUGH THE PRISONERS' VOTES DIDN'T COUNT.
FOR PRESIDENT
CONVICT NO. 9653
OF THE ONE MILLION VOTES CAST NATIONWIDE, HE CALLED THE PRISON VOTES "THE MOST PRECIOUS."
ON DECEMBER 25, 1921, PRESIDENT ***WARREN G. HARDING*** RELEASED DEBS FROM PRISON, COMMUTING HIS SENTENCE TO TIME SERVED. DEBS DIED IN 1926.
ANOTHER IMPORTANT OPPONENT OF WORLD WAR I WAS ***EMMA GOLDMAN***. SHE ORGANIZED THE ***NO-CONSCRIPTION LEAGUE***.
GOLDMAN WAS TRIED UNDER THE CONSCRIPTION ACT AND SENTENCED TO TWO YEARS AT THE ***MISSOURI STATE PENITENTIARY***.
JUST LIKE DEBS, HER ONLY DEFENSE WAS HER ELOQUENCE.
A DEMOCRACY CONCEIVED IN THE MILITARY SERVITUDE OF THE MASSES IS NOT A DEMOCRACY AT ALL.
IT IS ***DESPOTISM!***
WHEN I DISCOVERED EMMA GOLDMAN, I WROTE A PLAY ABOUT HER CALLED ***EMMA***.
I IMAGINED THIS COURAGEOUS WOMAN EMERGING AFTER TWO YEARS IN PRISON, HAGGARD BUT INCISIVE AS ALWAYS.
Emma
HOWARD ZINN

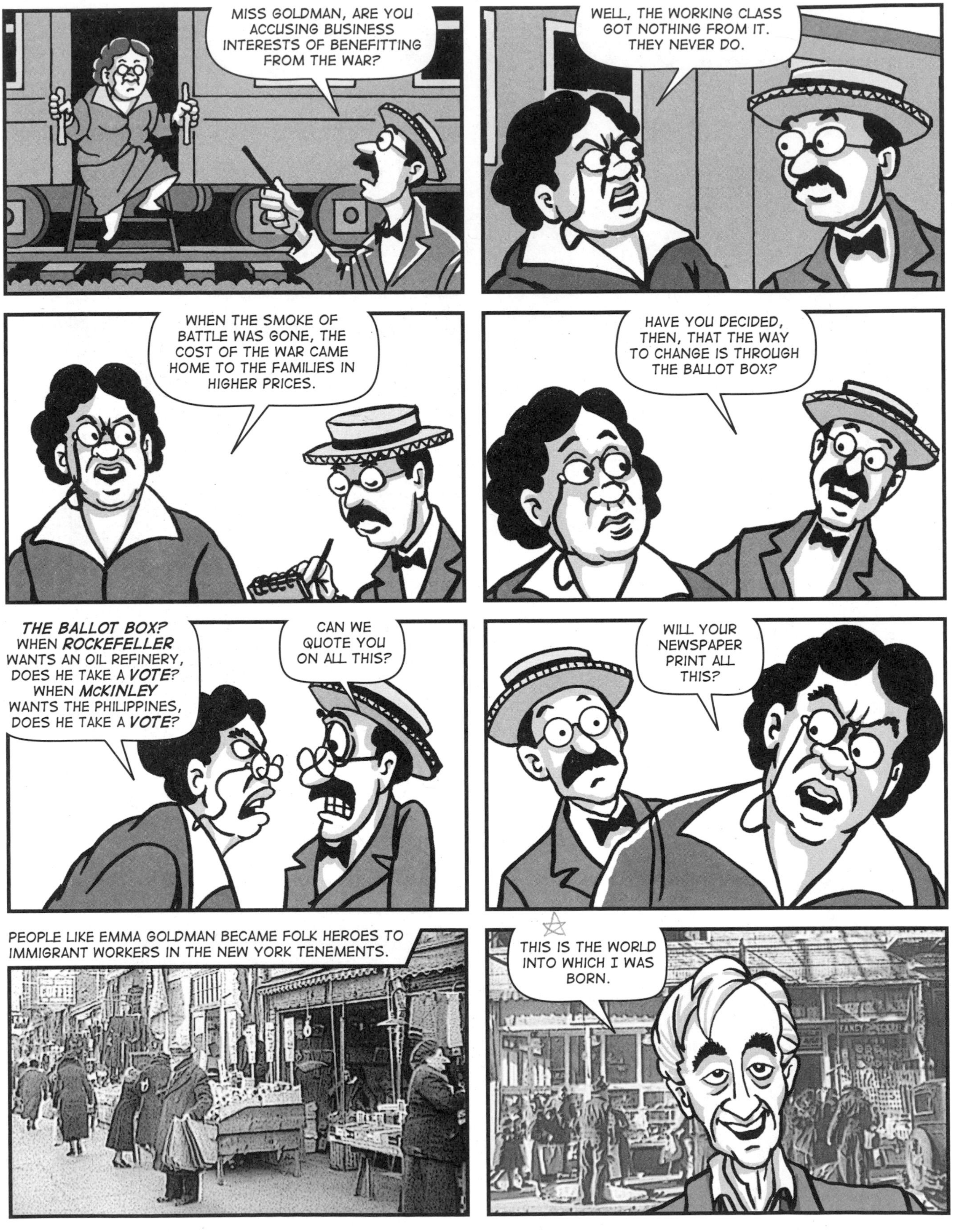
MISS GOLDMAN, ARE YOU ACCUSING BUSINESS INTERESTS OF BENEFITTING FROM THE WAR?
WELL, THE WORKING CLASS GOT NOTHING FROM IT. THEY NEVER DO.
WHEN THE SMOKE OF BATTLE WAS GONE, THE COST OF THE WAR CAME HOME TO THE FAMILIES IN HIGHER PRICES.
HAVE YOU DECIDED, THEN, THAT THE WAY TO CHANGE IS THROUGH THE BALLOT BOX?
THE BALLOT BOX? WHEN ROCKEFELLER WANTS AN OIL REFINERY, DOES HE TAKE A VOTE? WHEN McKINLEY WANTS THE PHILIPPINES, DOES HE TAKE A VOTE?
CAN WE QUOTE YOU ON ALL THIS?
WILL YOUR NEWSPAPER PRINT ALL THIS?
PEOPLE LIKE EMMA GOLDMAN BECAME FOLK HEROES TO IMMIGRANT WORKERS IN THE NEW YORK TENEMENTS.
THIS IS THE WORLD INTO WHICH I WAS BORN.

Chapter V

GROWING UP CLASS-CONSCIOUS

"What child who is loved knows he is poor?"

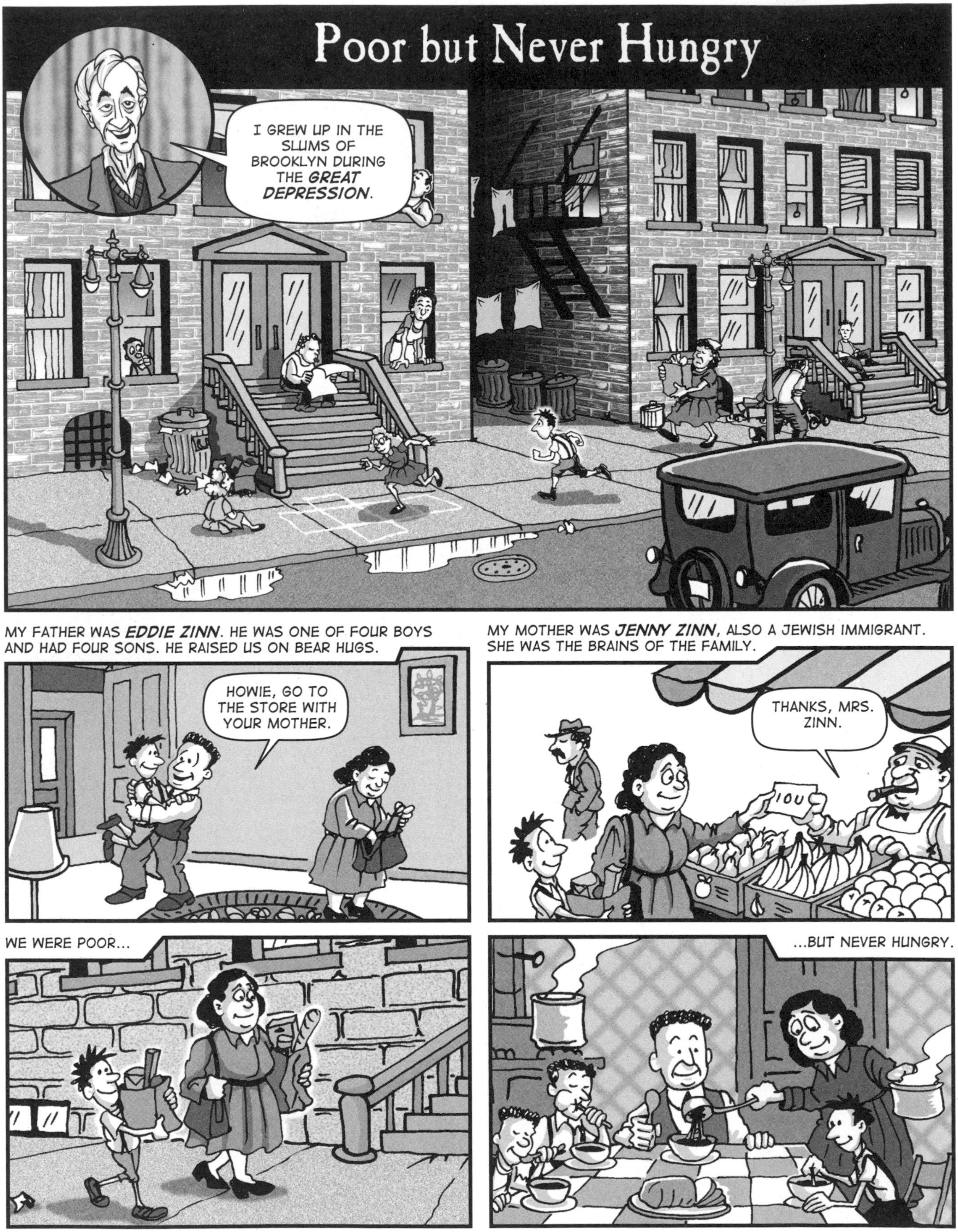
Poor but Never Hungry
I GREW UP IN THE SLUMS OF BROOKLYN DURING THE GREAT DEPRESSION.
MY FATHER WAS EDDIE ZINN. HE WAS ONE OF FOUR BOYS AND HAD FOUR SONS. HE RAISED US ON BEAR HUGS.
HOWIE, GO TO THE STORE WITH YOUR MOTHER.
MY MOTHER WAS JENNY ZINN, ALSO A JEWISH IMMIGRANT. SHE WAS THE BRAINS OF THE FAMILY.
THANKS, MRS. ZINN.
IOU
WE WERE POOR...
...BUT NEVER HUNGRY.

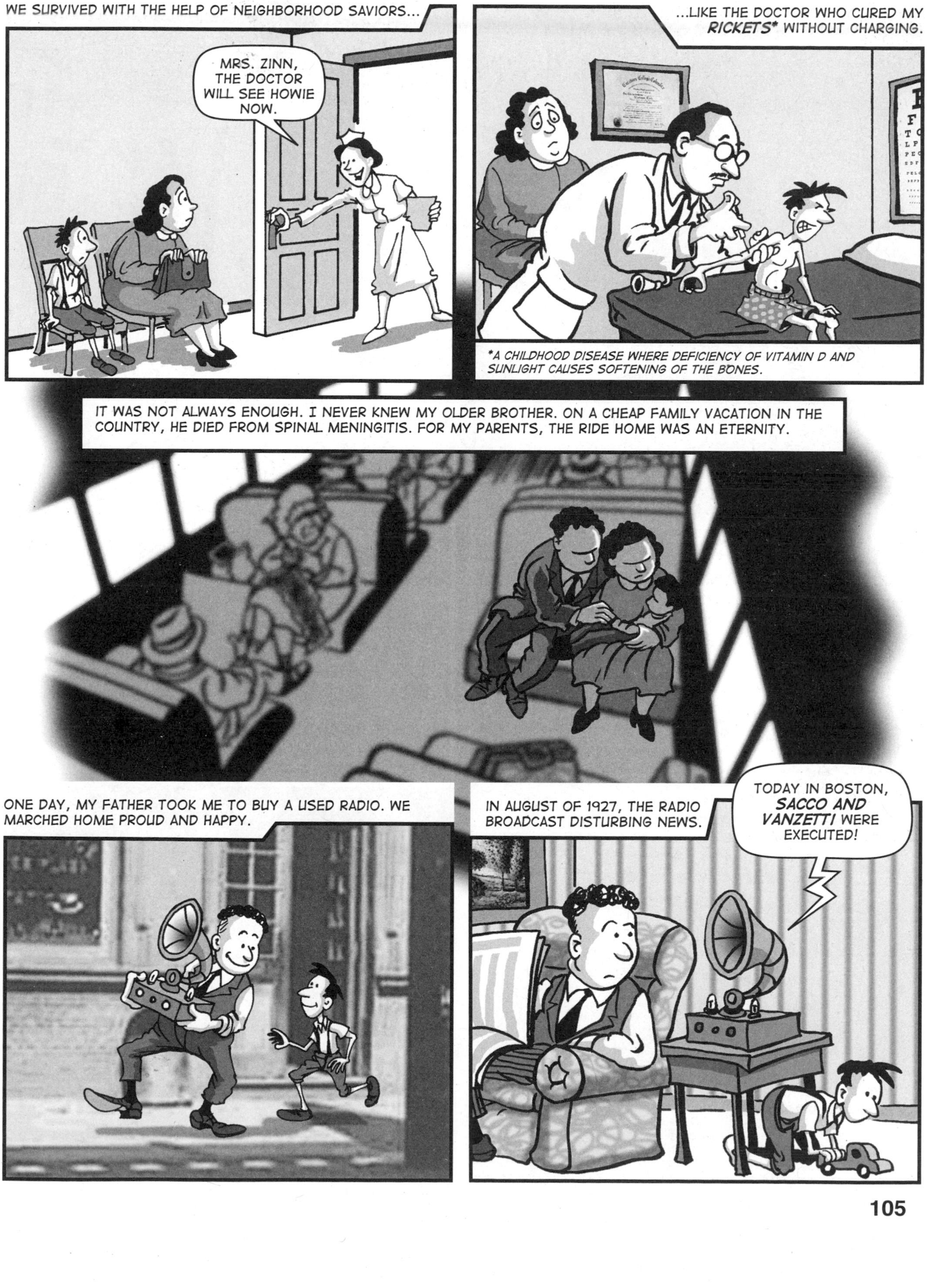

WE SURVIVED WITH THE HELP OF NEIGHBORHOOD SAVIORS...
MRS. ZINN, THE DOCTOR WILL SEE HOWIE NOW.
...LIKE THE DOCTOR WHO CURED MY RICKETS* WITHOUT CHARGING.
*A CHILDHOOD DISEASE WHERE DEFICIENCY OF VITAMIN D AND SUNLIGHT CAUSES SOFTENING OF THE BONES.
IT WAS NOT ALWAYS ENOUGH. I NEVER KNEW MY OLDER BROTHER. ON A CHEAP FAMILY VACATION IN THE COUNTRY, HE DIED FROM SPINAL MENINGITIS. FOR MY PARENTS, THE RIDE HOME WAS AN ETERNITY.
ONE DAY, MY FATHER TOOK ME TO BUY A USED RADIO. WE MARCHED HOME PROUD AND HAPPY.
IN AUGUST OF 1927, THE RADIO BROADCAST DISTURBING NEWS.
TODAY IN BOSTON, SACCO AND VANZETTI WERE EXECUTED!

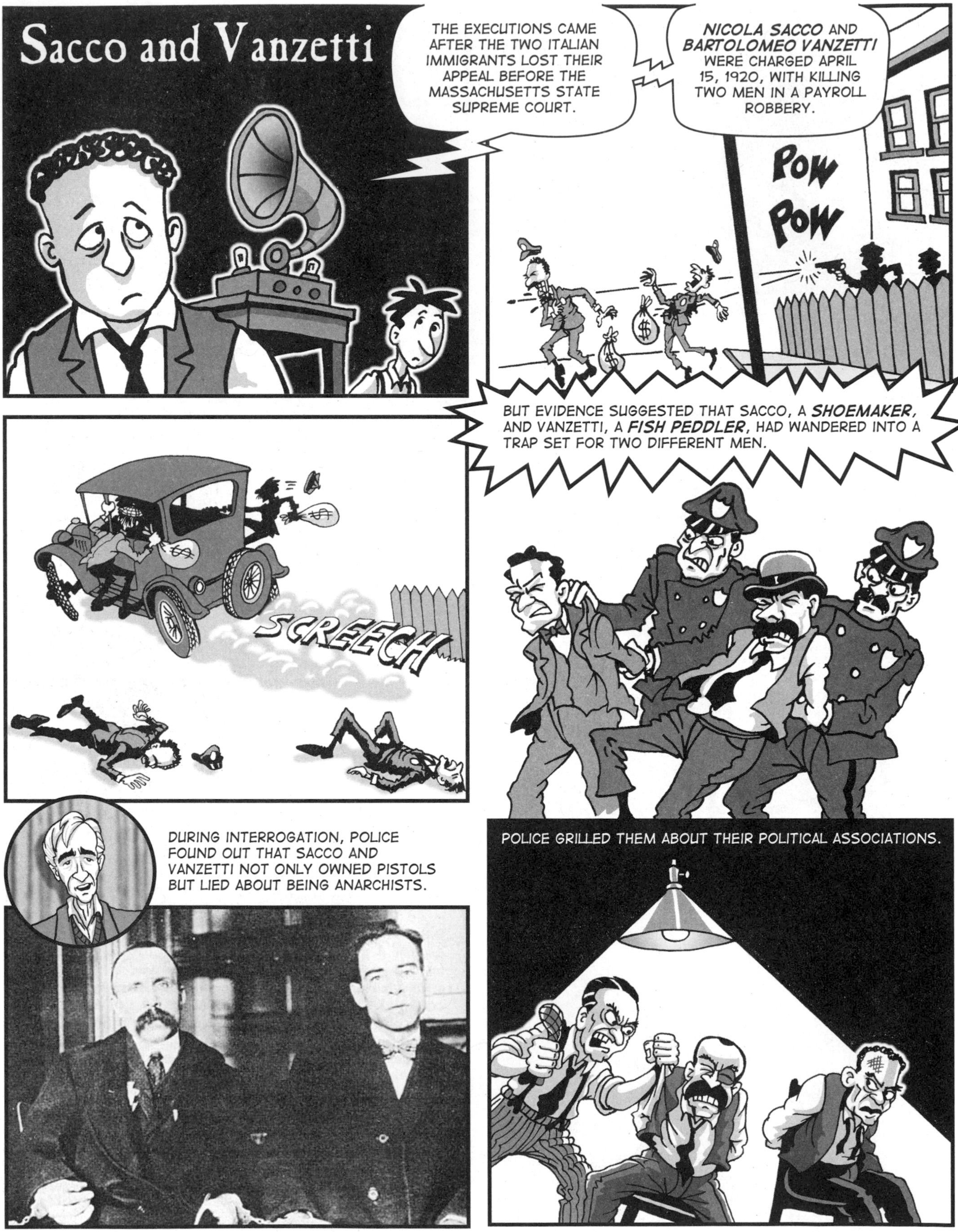
Sacco and Vanzetti
THE EXECUTIONS CAME AFTER THE TWO ITALIAN IMMIGRANTS LOST THEIR APPEAL BEFORE THE MASSACHUSETTS STATE SUPREME COURT.
NICOLA SACCO AND BARTOLOMEO VANZETTI WERE CHARGED APRIL 15, 1920, WITH KILLING TWO MEN IN A PAYROLL ROBBERY.
POW
POW
SCREECH
BUT EVIDENCE SUGGESTED THAT SACCO, A SHOEMAKER, AND VANZETTI, A FISH PEDDLER, HAD WANDERED INTO A TRAP SET FOR TWO DIFFERENT MEN.
DURING INTERROGATION, POLICE FOUND OUT THAT SACCO AND VANZETTI NOT ONLY OWNED PISTOLS BUT LIED ABOUT BEING ANARCHISTS.
POLICE GRILLED THEM ABOUT THEIR POLITICAL ASSOCIATIONS.

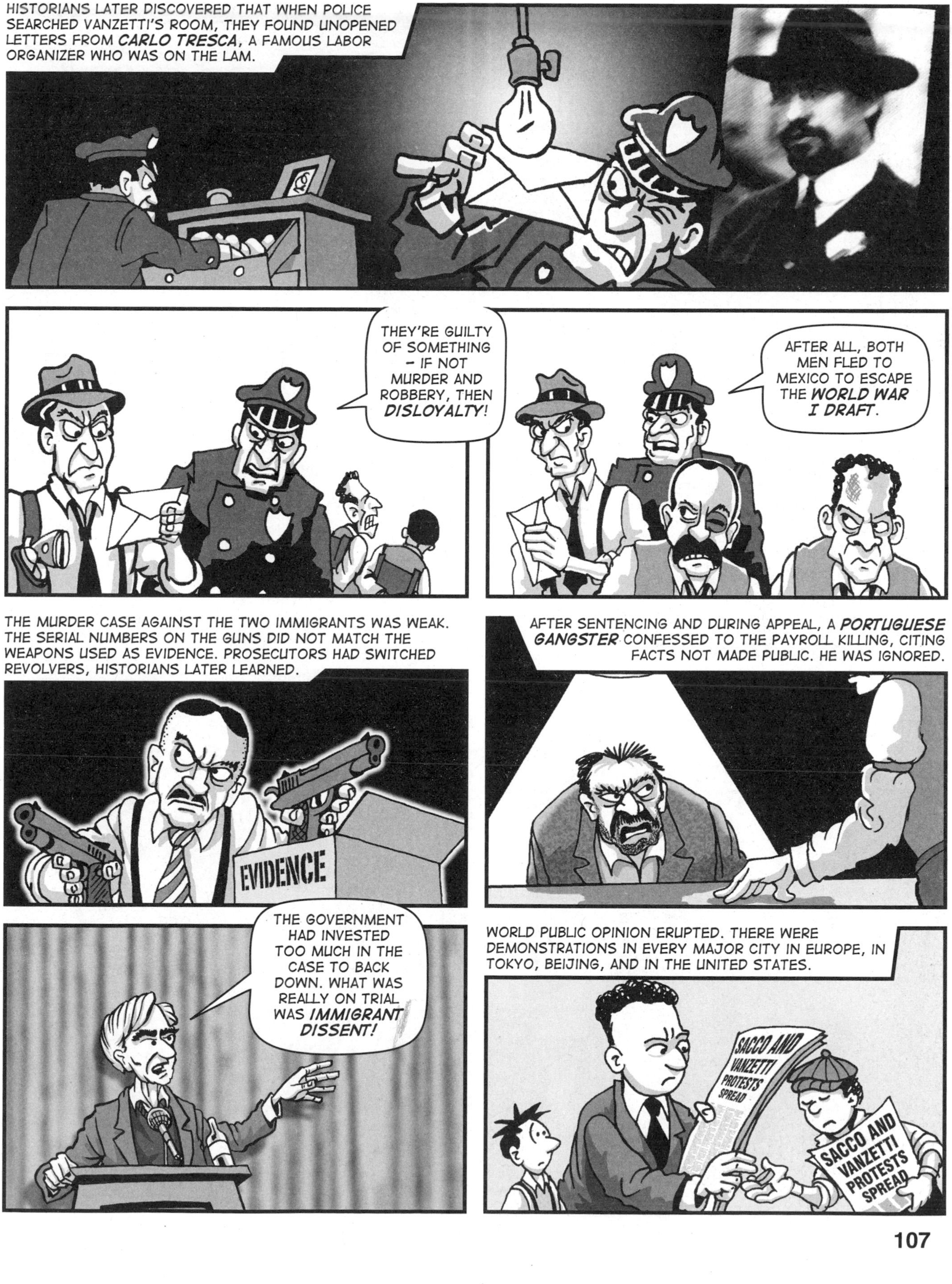
HISTORIANS LATER DISCOVERED THAT WHEN POLICE SEARCHED VANZETTI'S ROOM, THEY FOUND UNOPENED LETTERS FROM *CARLO TRESCA*, A FAMOUS LABOR ORGANIZER WHO WAS ON THE LAM.
THEY'RE GUILTY OF SOMETHING – IF NOT MURDER AND ROBBERY, THEN *DISLOYALTY*!
AFTER ALL, BOTH MEN FLED TO MEXICO TO ESCAPE THE *WORLD WAR I DRAFT*.
THE MURDER CASE AGAINST THE TWO IMMIGRANTS WAS WEAK. THE SERIAL NUMBERS ON THE GUNS DID NOT MATCH THE WEAPONS USED AS EVIDENCE. PROSECUTORS HAD SWITCHED REVOLVERS, HISTORIANS LATER LEARNED.
EVIDENCE
AFTER SENTENCING AND DURING APPEAL, A *PORTUGUESE GANGSTER* CONFESSED TO THE PAYROLL KILLING, CITING FACTS NOT MADE PUBLIC. HE WAS IGNORED.
THE GOVERNMENT HAD INVESTED TOO MUCH IN THE CASE TO BACK DOWN. WHAT WAS REALLY ON TRIAL WAS *IMMIGRANT DISSENT*!
WORLD PUBLIC OPINION ERUPTED. THERE WERE DEMONSTRATIONS IN EVERY MAJOR CITY IN EUROPE, IN TOKYO, BEIJING, AND IN THE UNITED STATES.
SACCO AND VANZETTI PROTESTS SPREAD
SACCO AND VANZETTI PROTESTS SPREAD

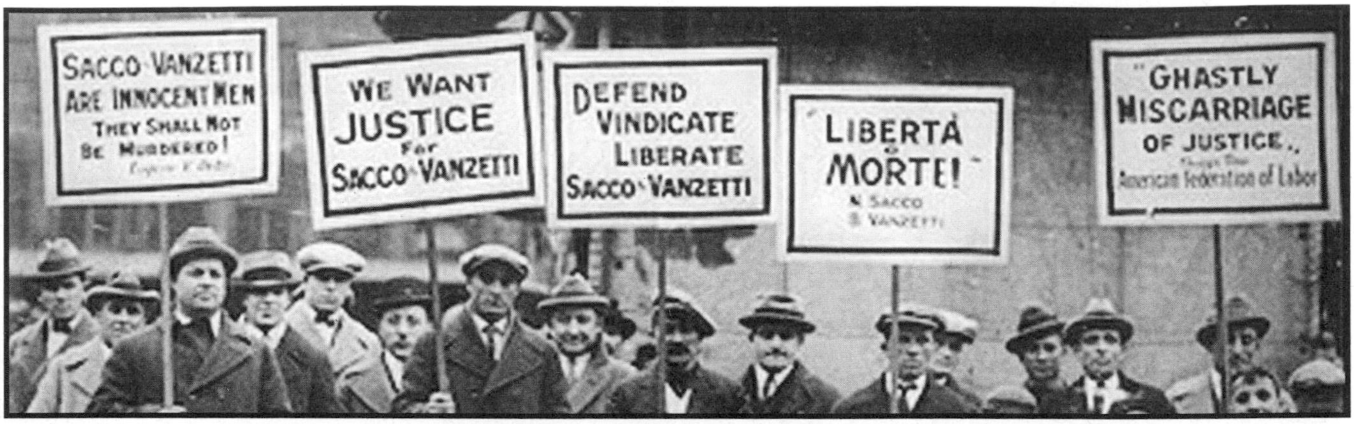
SACCO-VANZETTI ARE INNOCENT MEN THEY SHALL NOT BE MURDERED!
WE WANT JUSTICE FOR SACCO-VANZETTI
DEFEND VINDICATE LIBERATE SACCO-VANZETTI
LIBERTÀ O MORTE! N. SACCO B. VANZETTI
"GHASTLY MISCARRIAGE OF JUSTICE."
American Federation of Labor

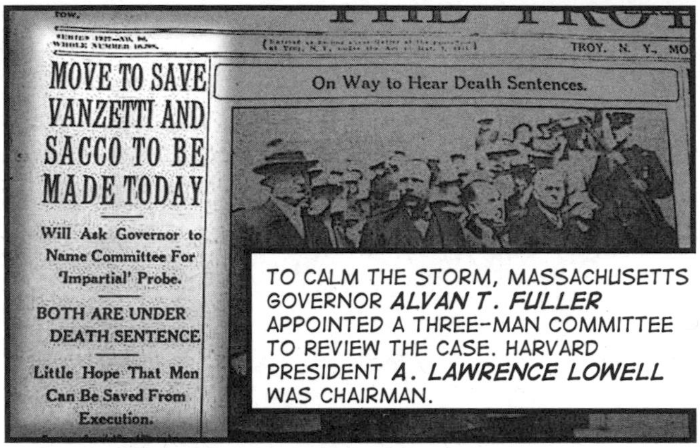
TROY, N. Y.
MOVE TO SAVE VANZETTI AND SACCO TO BE MADE TODAY
Will Ask Governor to Name Committee For 'Impartial' Probe.
BOTH ARE UNDER DEATH SENTENCE
Little Hope That Men Can Be Saved From Execution.
On Way to Hear Death Sentences.
TO CALM THE STORM, MASSACHUSETTS GOVERNOR ALVAN T. FULLER APPOINTED A THREE-MAN COMMITTEE TO REVIEW THE CASE. HARVARD PRESIDENT A. LAWRENCE LOWELL WAS CHAIRMAN.

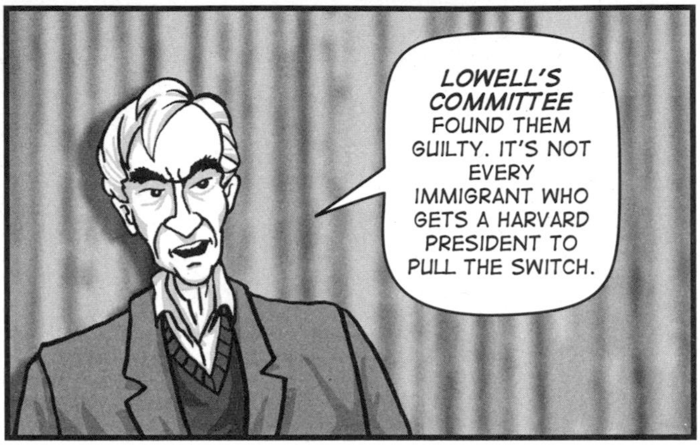
LOWELL'S COMMITTEE FOUND THEM GUILTY. IT'S NOT EVERY IMMIGRANT WHO GETS A HARVARD PRESIDENT TO PULL THE SWITCH.

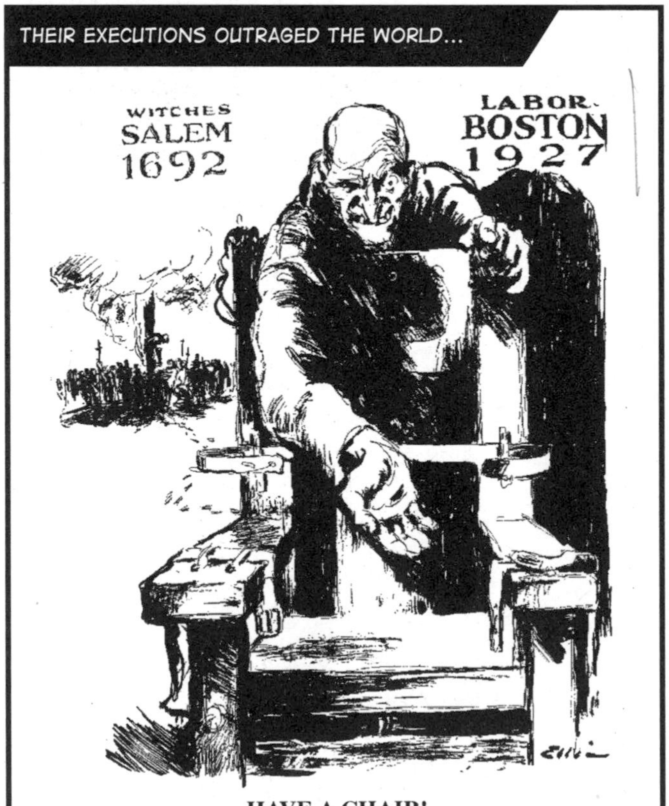
THEIR EXECUTIONS OUTRAGED THE WORLD...
WITCHES SALEM 1692
LABOR BOSTON 1927
HAVE A CHAIR!
Fred Ellis, *Daily Worker*, 1927

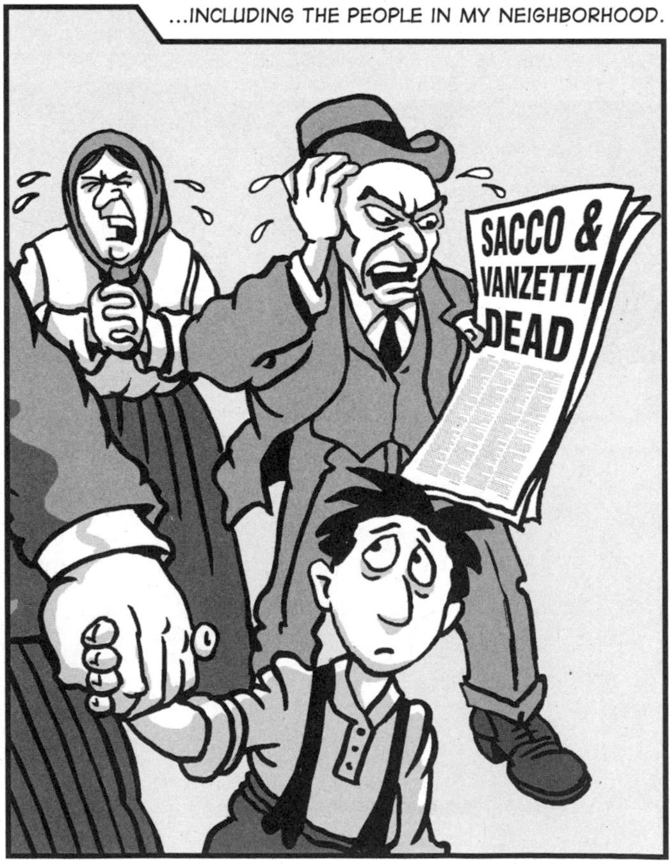
...INCLUDING THE PEOPLE IN MY NEIGHBORHOOD.
SACCO & VANZETTI DEAD

Street Smarts

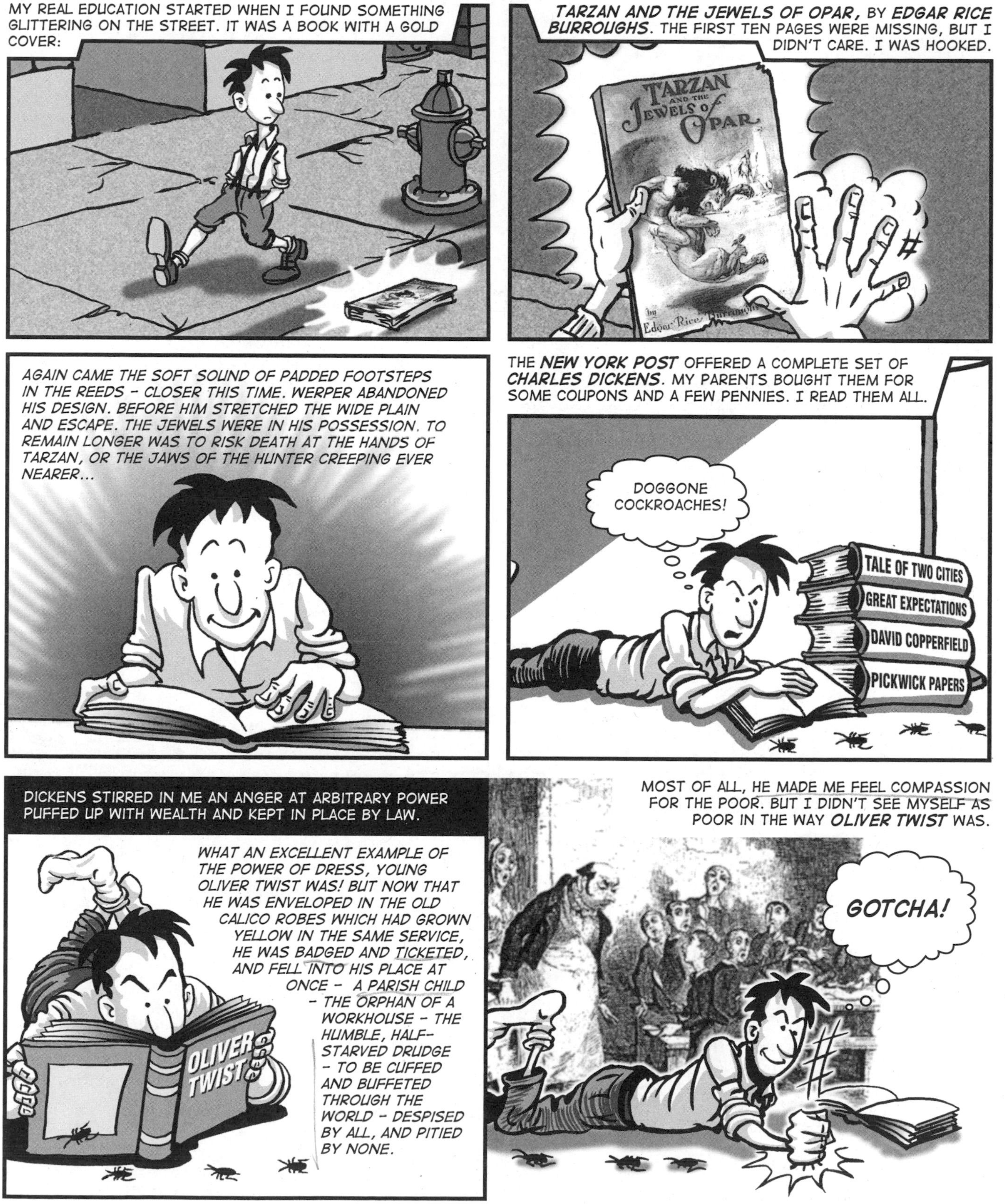
MY REAL EDUCATION STARTED WHEN I FOUND SOMETHING GLITTERING ON THE STREET. IT WAS A BOOK WITH A GOLD COVER:
TARZAN AND THE JEWELS OF OPAR, BY *EDGAR RICE BURROUGHS*. THE FIRST TEN PAGES WERE MISSING, BUT I DIDN'T CARE. I WAS HOOKED.
TARZAN AND THE JEWELS OF OPAR
by Edgar Rice Burroughs
AGAIN CAME THE SOFT SOUND OF PADDED FOOTSTEPS IN THE REEDS – CLOSER THIS TIME. WERPER ABANDONED HIS DESIGN. BEFORE HIM STRETCHED THE WIDE PLAIN AND ESCAPE. THE JEWELS WERE IN HIS POSSESSION. TO REMAIN LONGER WAS TO RISK DEATH AT THE HANDS OF TARZAN, OR THE JAWS OF THE HUNTER CREEPING EVER NEARER...
THE *NEW YORK POST* OFFERED A COMPLETE SET OF *CHARLES DICKENS*. MY PARENTS BOUGHT THEM FOR SOME COUPONS AND A FEW PENNIES. I READ THEM ALL.
DOGGONE COCKROACHES!
TALE OF TWO CITIES
GREAT EXPECTATIONS
DAVID COPPERFIELD
PICKWICK PAPERS
DICKENS STIRRED IN ME AN ANGER AT ARBITRARY POWER PUFFED UP WITH WEALTH AND KEPT IN PLACE BY LAW.
WHAT AN EXCELLENT EXAMPLE OF THE POWER OF DRESS, YOUNG OLIVER TWIST WAS! BUT NOW THAT HE WAS ENVELOPED IN THE OLD CALICO ROBES WHICH HAD GROWN YELLOW IN THE SAME SERVICE, HE WAS BADGED AND TICKETED, AND FELL INTO HIS PLACE AT ONCE – A PARISH CHILD – THE ORPHAN OF A WORKHOUSE – THE HUMBLE, HALF-STARVED DRUDGE – TO BE CUFFED AND BUFFETED THROUGH THE WORLD – DESPISED BY ALL, AND PITIED BY NONE.
OLIVER TWIST
MOST OF ALL, HE MADE ME FEEL COMPASSION FOR THE POOR. BUT I DIDN'T SEE MYSELF AS POOR IN THE WAY *OLIVER TWIST* WAS.
GOTCHA!

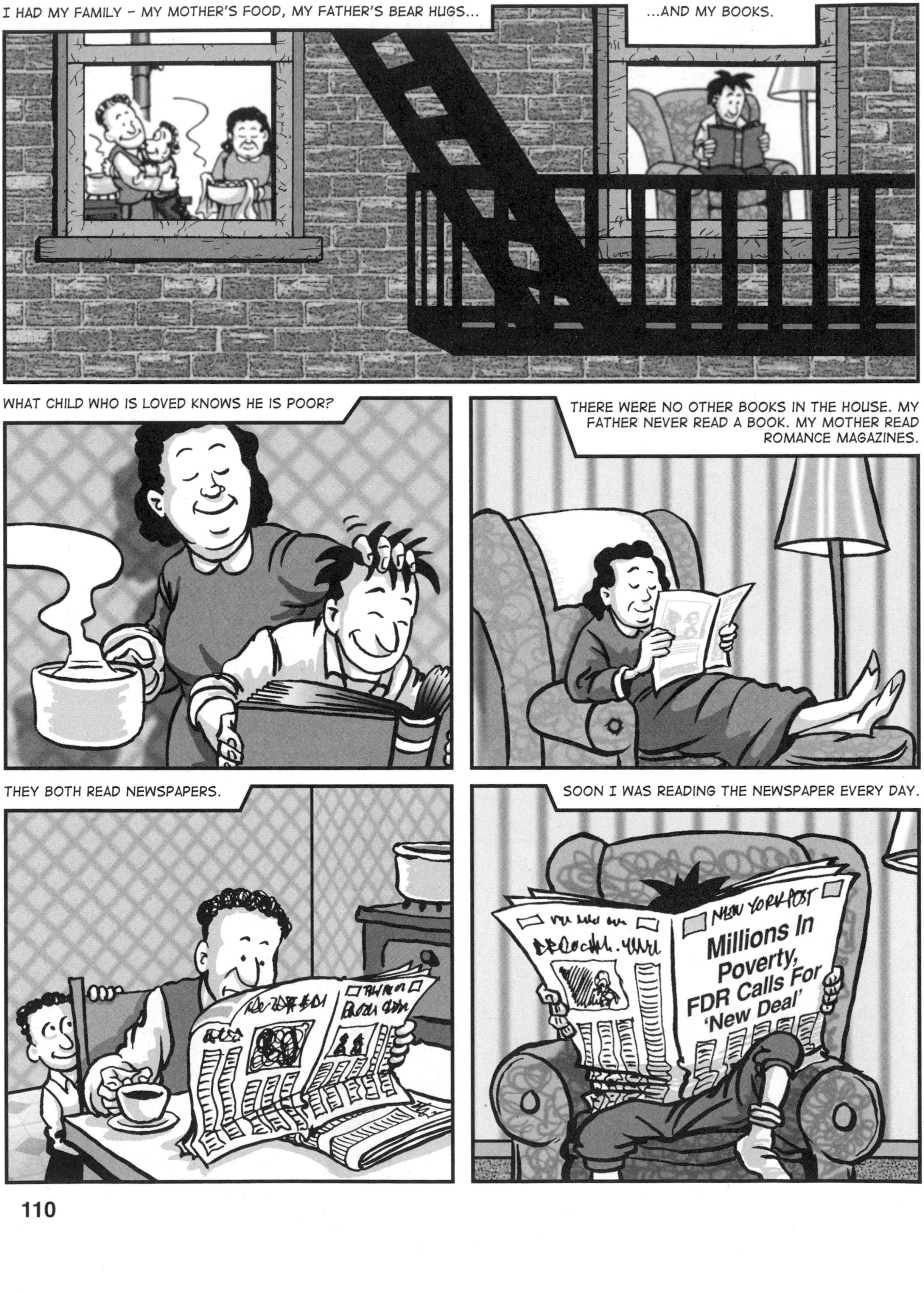
I HAD MY FAMILY - MY MOTHER'S FOOD, MY FATHER'S BEAR HUGS...
...AND MY BOOKS.
WHAT CHILD WHO IS LOVED KNOWS HE IS POOR?
THERE WERE NO OTHER BOOKS IN THE HOUSE. MY FATHER NEVER READ A BOOK. MY MOTHER READ ROMANCE MAGAZINES.
THEY BOTH READ NEWSPAPERS.
SOON I WAS READING THE NEWSPAPER EVERY DAY.
NEW YORK POST
Millions In Poverty, FDR Calls For 'New Deal'

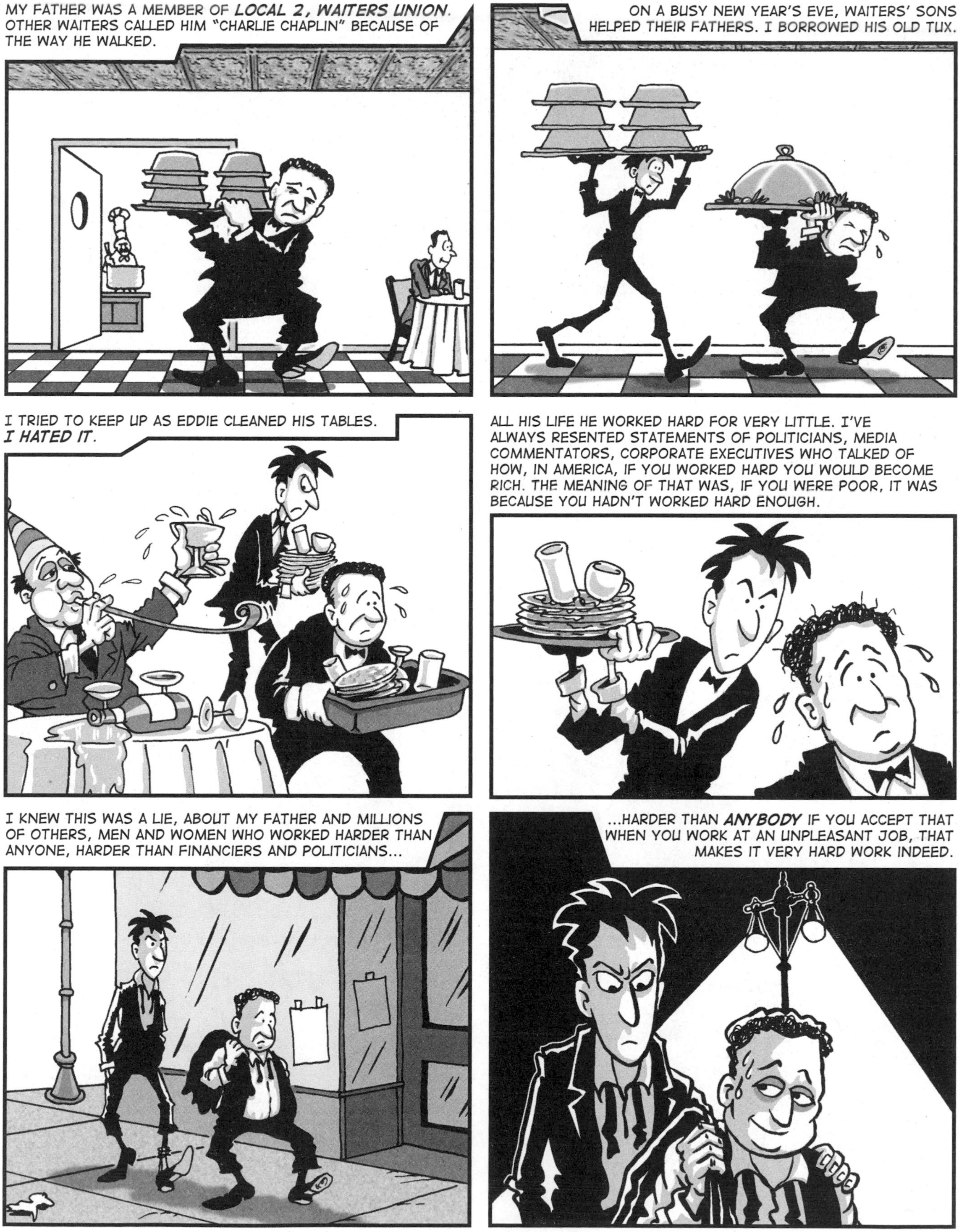
MY FATHER WAS A MEMBER OF ***LOCAL 2, WAITERS UNION***. OTHER WAITERS CALLED HIM "CHARLIE CHAPLIN" BECAUSE OF THE WAY HE WALKED.
ON A BUSY NEW YEAR'S EVE, WAITERS' SONS HELPED THEIR FATHERS. I BORROWED HIS OLD TUX.
I TRIED TO KEEP UP AS EDDIE CLEANED HIS TABLES. ***I HATED IT***.
ALL HIS LIFE HE WORKED HARD FOR VERY LITTLE. I'VE ALWAYS RESENTED STATEMENTS OF POLITICIANS, MEDIA COMMENTATORS, CORPORATE EXECUTIVES WHO TALKED OF HOW, IN AMERICA, IF YOU WORKED HARD YOU WOULD BECOME RICH. THE MEANING OF THAT WAS, IF YOU WERE POOR, IT WAS BECAUSE YOU HADN'T WORKED HARD ENOUGH.
I KNEW THIS WAS A LIE, ABOUT MY FATHER AND MILLIONS OF OTHERS, MEN AND WOMEN WHO WORKED HARDER THAN ANYONE, HARDER THAN FINANCIERS AND POLITICIANS...
...HARDER THAN ***ANYBODY*** IF YOU ACCEPT THAT WHEN YOU WORK AT AN UNPLEASANT JOB, THAT MAKES IT VERY HARD WORK INDEED.

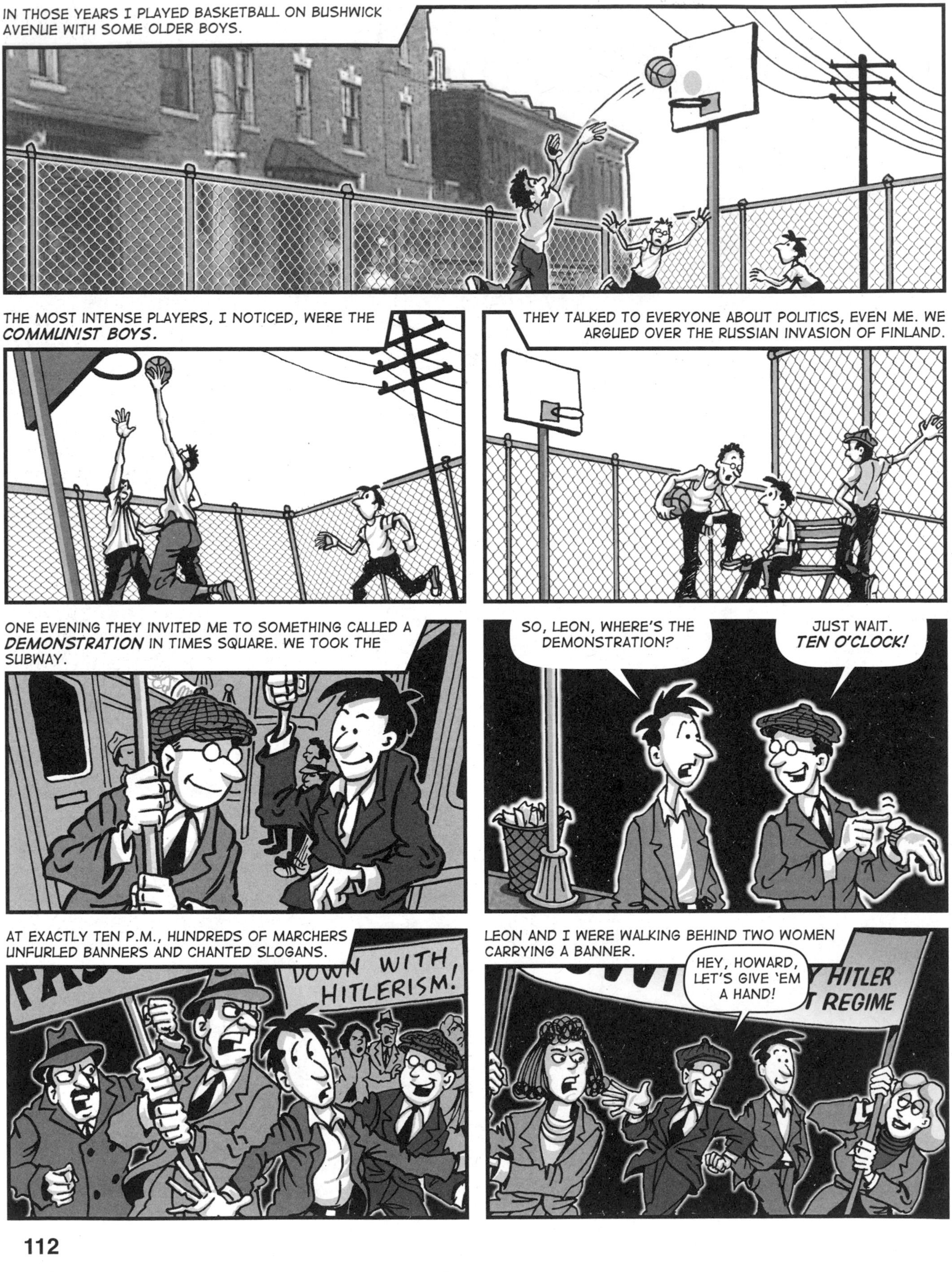
IN THOSE YEARS I PLAYED BASKETBALL ON BUSHWICK AVENUE WITH SOME OLDER BOYS.
THE MOST INTENSE PLAYERS, I NOTICED, WERE THE *COMMUNIST BOYS.*
THEY TALKED TO EVERYONE ABOUT POLITICS, EVEN ME. WE ARGUED OVER THE RUSSIAN INVASION OF FINLAND.
ONE EVENING THEY INVITED ME TO SOMETHING CALLED A *DEMONSTRATION* IN TIMES SQUARE. WE TOOK THE SUBWAY.
SO, LEON, WHERE'S THE DEMONSTRATION?
JUST WAIT. *TEN O'CLOCK!*
AT EXACTLY TEN P.M., HUNDREDS OF MARCHERS UNFURLED BANNERS AND CHANTED SLOGANS.
DOWN WITH HITLERISM!
LEON AND I WERE WALKING BEHIND TWO WOMEN CARRYING A BANNER.
HEY, HOWARD, LET'S GIVE 'EM A HAND!
HITLER
REGIME

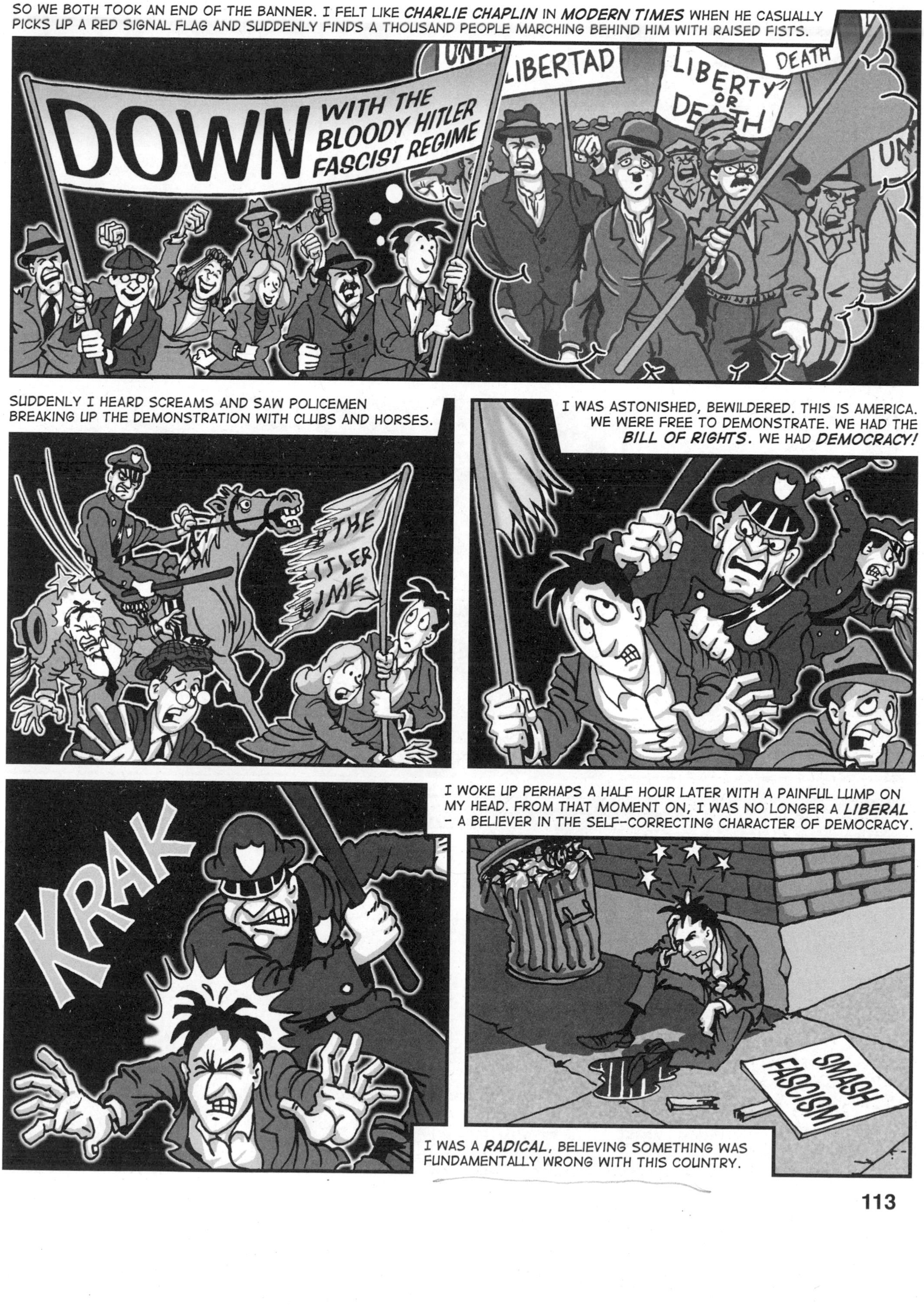
SO WE BOTH TOOK AN END OF THE BANNER. I FELT LIKE *CHARLIE CHAPLIN* IN *MODERN TIMES* WHEN HE CASUALLY PICKS UP A RED SIGNAL FLAG AND SUDDENLY FINDS A THOUSAND PEOPLE MARCHING BEHIND HIM WITH RAISED FISTS.
DOWN WITH THE BLOODY HITLER FASCIST REGIME
LIBERTAD
LIBERTY OR DEATH
DEATH
SUDDENLY I HEARD SCREAMS AND SAW POLICEMEN BREAKING UP THE DEMONSTRATION WITH CLUBS AND HORSES.
I WAS ASTONISHED, BEWILDERED. THIS IS AMERICA. WE WERE FREE TO DEMONSTRATE. WE HAD THE *BILL OF RIGHTS*. WE HAD *DEMOCRACY!*
KRAK
I WOKE UP PERHAPS A HALF HOUR LATER WITH A PAINFUL LUMP ON MY HEAD. FROM THAT MOMENT ON, I WAS NO LONGER A *LIBERAL* - A BELIEVER IN THE SELF-CORRECTING CHARACTER OF DEMOCRACY.
SMASH FASCISM
I WAS A *RADICAL*, BELIEVING SOMETHING WAS FUNDAMENTALLY WRONG WITH THIS COUNTRY.

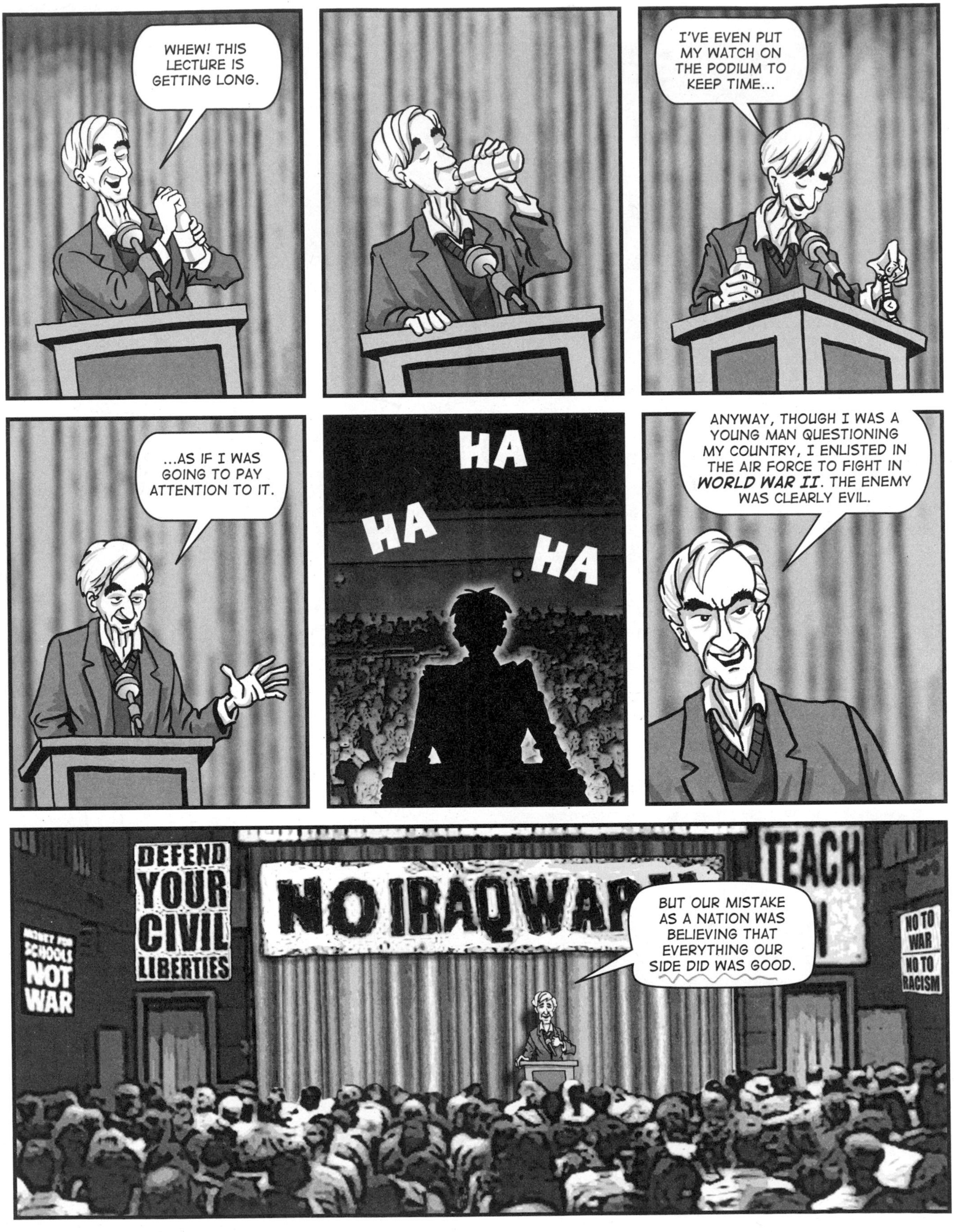
WHEW! THIS LECTURE IS GETTING LONG.
I'VE EVEN PUT MY WATCH ON THE PODIUM TO KEEP TIME...
...AS IF I WAS GOING TO PAY ATTENTION TO IT.
HA
HA
HA
ANYWAY, THOUGH I WAS A YOUNG MAN QUESTIONING MY COUNTRY, I ENLISTED IN THE AIR FORCE TO FIGHT IN ***WORLD WAR II***. THE ENEMY WAS CLEARLY EVIL.
DEFEND YOUR CIVIL LIBERTIES
NO IRAQ WAR
TEACH
SCHOOLS NOT WAR
NO TO WAR
NO TO RACISM
BUT OUR MISTAKE AS A NATION WAS BELIEVING THAT EVERYTHING OUR SIDE DID WAS GOOD.

Chapter VI

WORLD WAR II: A PEOPLE'S WAR?

"More and more it seemed that WWII had been waged by a government whose chief beneficiary was a wealthy elite."

Questioning War

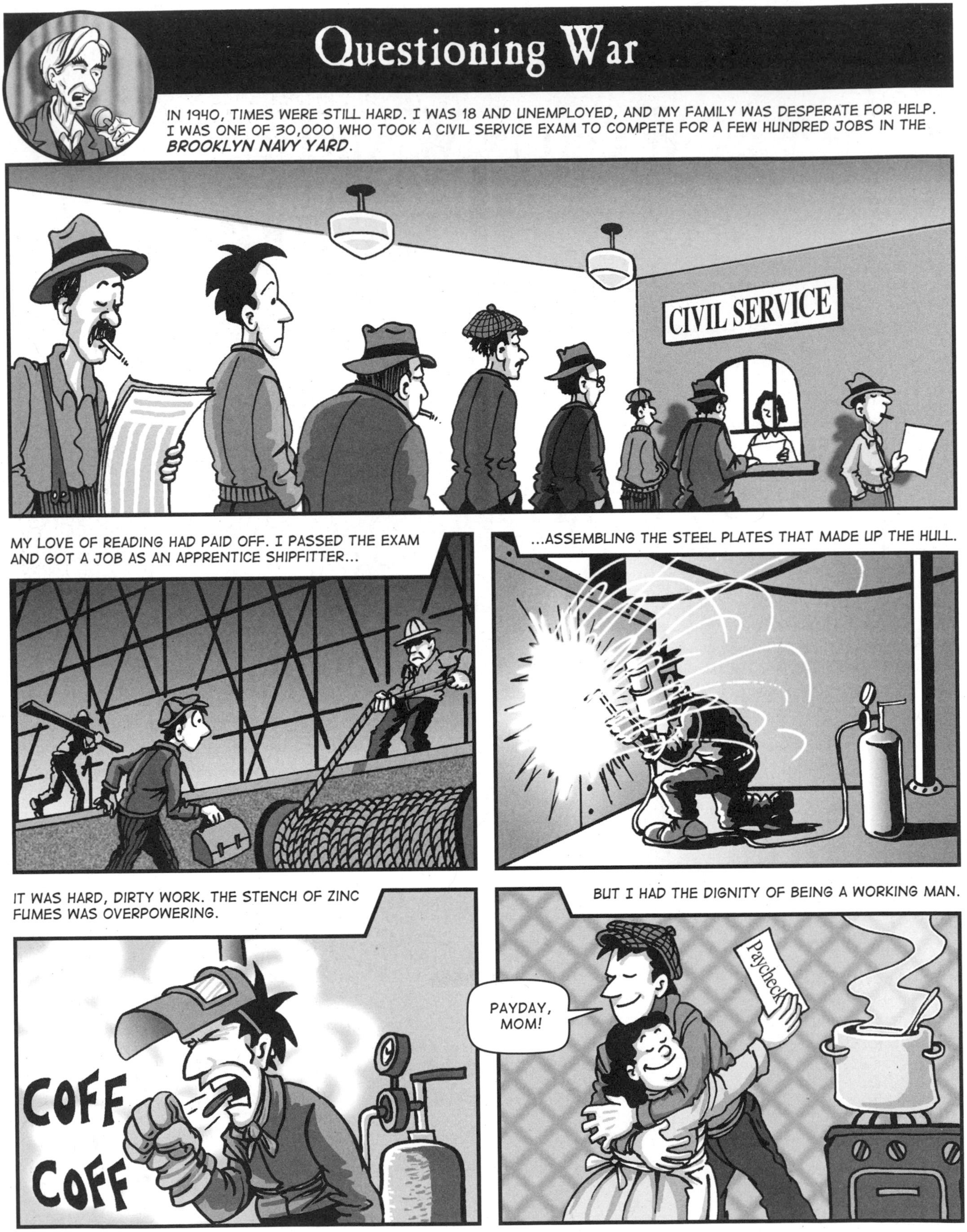

IN 1940, TIMES WERE STILL HARD. I WAS 18 AND UNEMPLOYED, AND MY FAMILY WAS DESPERATE FOR HELP. I WAS ONE OF 30,000 WHO TOOK A CIVIL SERVICE EXAM TO COMPETE FOR A FEW HUNDRED JOBS IN THE ***BROOKLYN NAVY YARD***.
CIVIL SERVICE
MY LOVE OF READING HAD PAID OFF. I PASSED THE EXAM AND GOT A JOB AS AN APPRENTICE SHIPFITTER...
...ASSEMBLING THE STEEL PLATES THAT MADE UP THE HULL.
IT WAS HARD, DIRTY WORK. THE STENCH OF ZINC FUMES WAS OVERPOWERING.
COFF
COFF
BUT I HAD THE DIGNITY OF BEING A WORKING MAN.
PAYDAY, MOM!
Paycheck

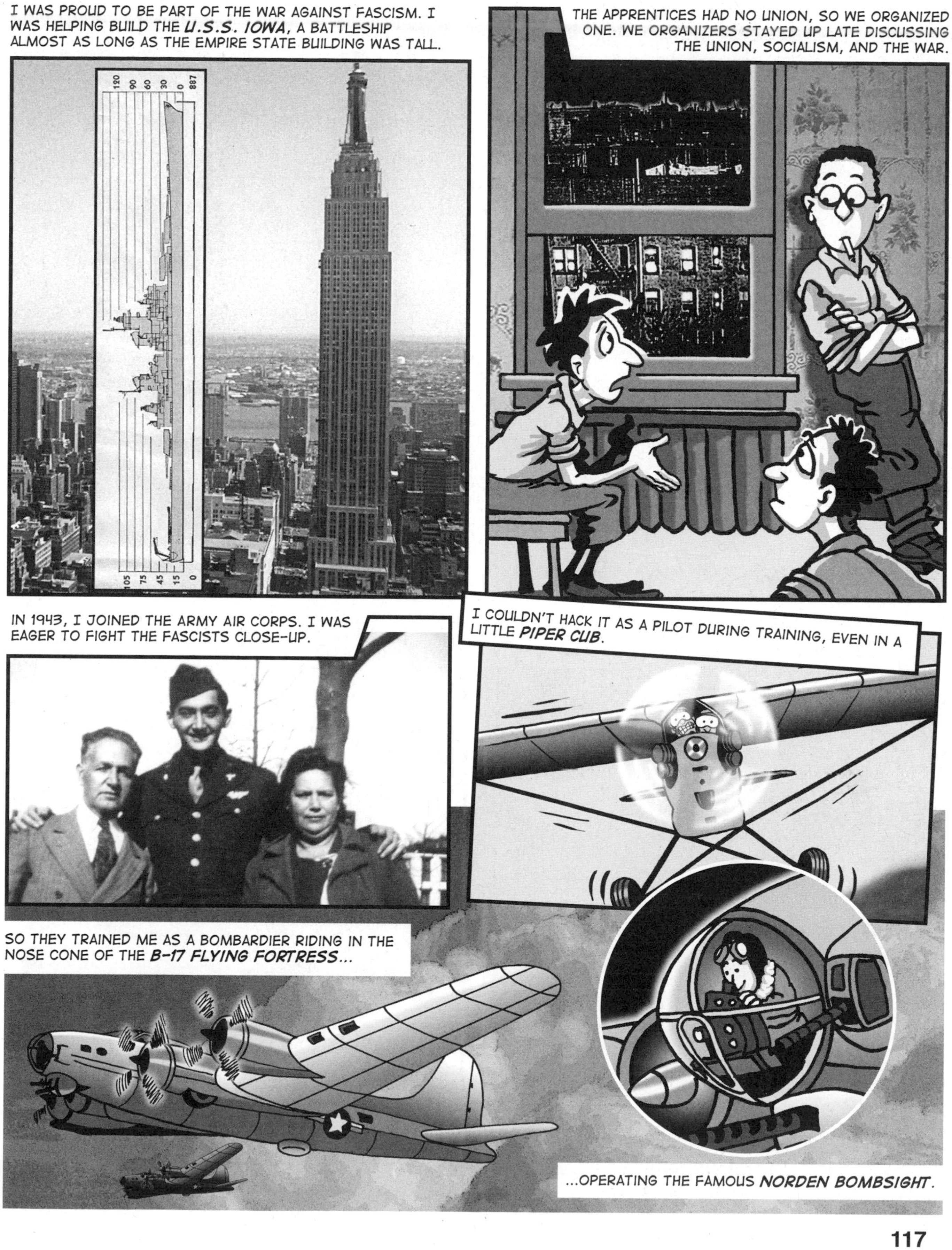
I WAS PROUD TO BE PART OF THE WAR AGAINST FASCISM. I WAS HELPING BUILD THE ***U.S.S. IOWA***, A BATTLESHIP ALMOST AS LONG AS THE EMPIRE STATE BUILDING WAS TALL.
THE APPRENTICES HAD NO UNION, SO WE ORGANIZED ONE. WE ORGANIZERS STAYED UP LATE DISCUSSING THE UNION, SOCIALISM, AND THE WAR.
IN 1943, I JOINED THE ARMY AIR CORPS. I WAS EAGER TO FIGHT THE FASCISTS CLOSE-UP.
I COULDN'T HACK IT AS A PILOT DURING TRAINING, EVEN IN A LITTLE ***PIPER CUB***.
SO THEY TRAINED ME AS A BOMBARDIER RIDING IN THE NOSE CONE OF THE ***B-17 FLYING FORTRESS***...
...OPERATING THE FAMOUS ***NORDEN BOMBSIGHT***.

WITH MY WINGS, I GOT AN 11-DAY FURLOUGH HOME. ON MY FIRST DAY BACK, I ASKED ***ROSLYN SHECHTER*** TO MARRY ME. SHE WAS A LONG-HAIRED CHESTNUT-BLONDE WITH BLUE EYES AND THE FACE OF A RUSSIAN BEAUTY.

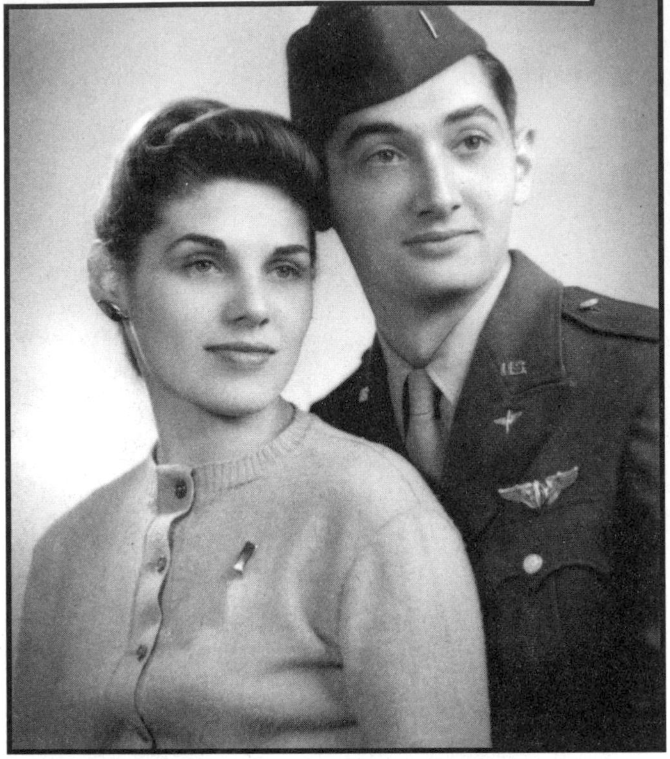

FOUR DAYS LATER, WE WERE MARRIED IN THE HOME OF A RED-HAIRED RABBI WITH NINE KIDS.

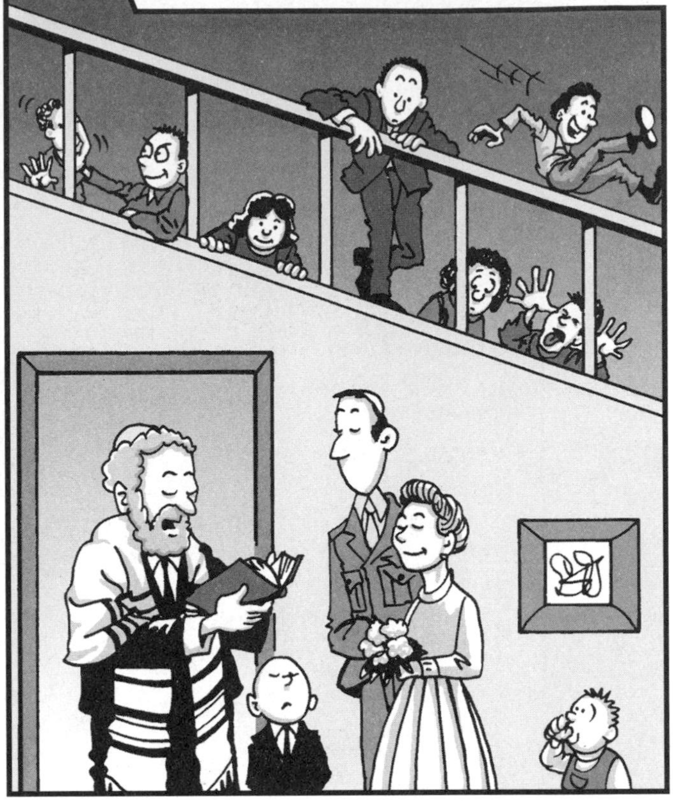

AFTER A BRIEF HONEYMOON AND MORE TRAINING, I WAS OFF TO EUROPE ON THE ***QUEEN MARY***. OF THE 16,000 TROOPS ON THE SHIP, 4,000 WERE BLACK. THEY BUNKED IN THE BOTTOM DECKS, NEXT TO THE ENGINE ROOMS.

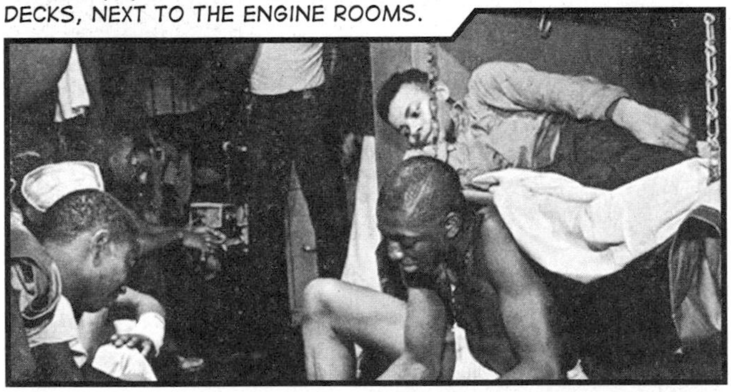

AS AN OFFICER, I WAS GIVEN A SUPERVISORY JOB TO "KEEP ORDER" DURING MEALS. USUALLY THE MESS WAS SEGREGATED, BUT ONE DAY A SHIFT MIX-UP ACCIDENTALLY INTEGRATED IT.

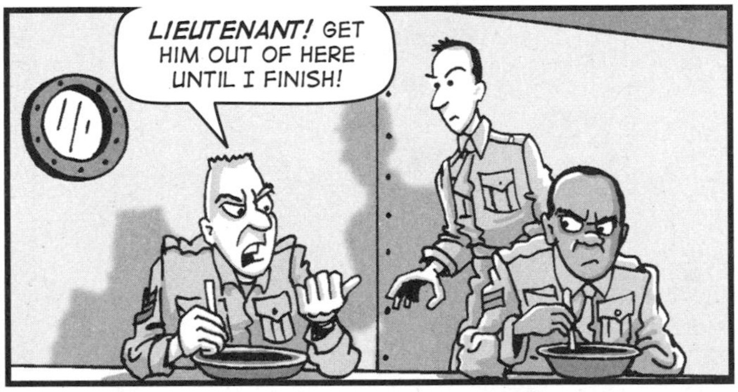
LIEUTENANT! GET HIM OUT OF HERE UNTIL I FINISH!

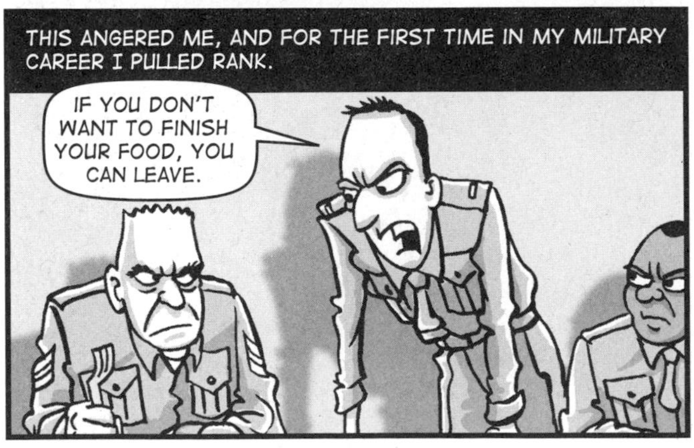
THIS ANGERED ME, AND FOR THE FIRST TIME IN MY MILITARY CAREER I PULLED RANK.
IF YOU DON'T WANT TO FINISH YOUR FOOD, YOU CAN LEAVE.

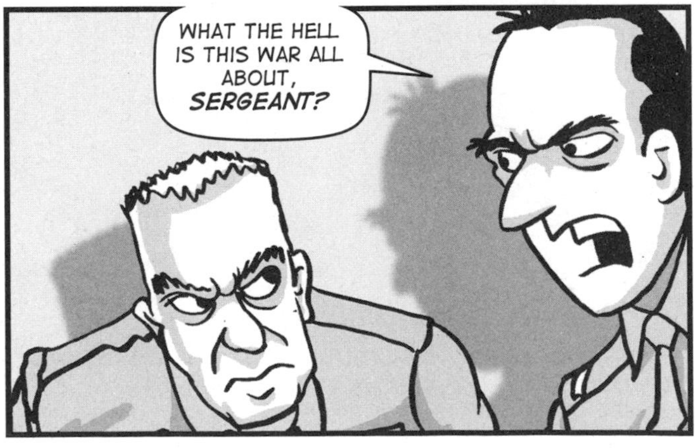
WHAT THE HELL IS THIS WAR ALL ABOUT, ***SERGEANT?***

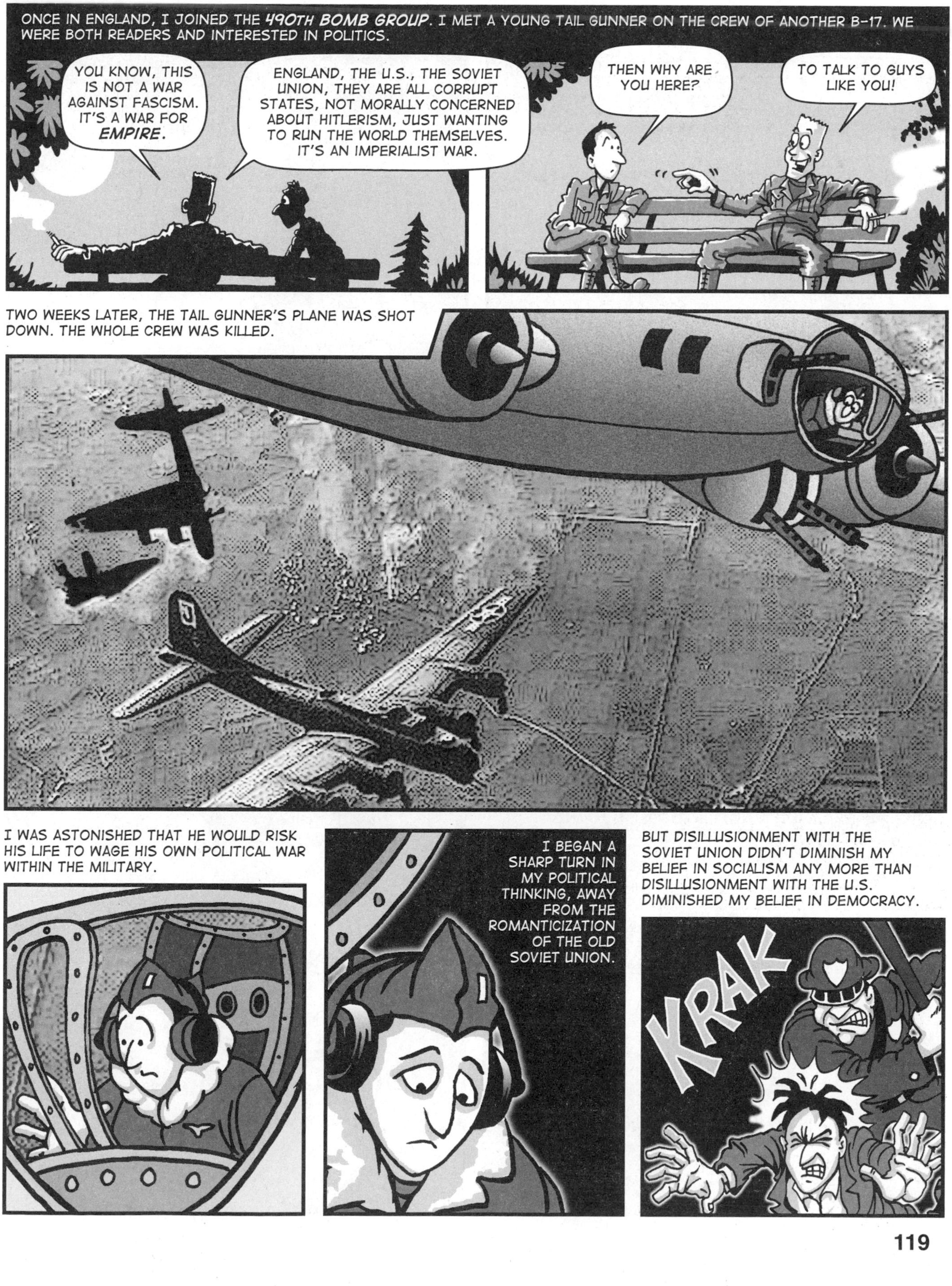
ONCE IN ENGLAND, I JOINED THE 490TH BOMB GROUP. I MET A YOUNG TAIL GUNNER ON THE CREW OF ANOTHER B-17. WE WERE BOTH READERS AND INTERESTED IN POLITICS.
YOU KNOW, THIS IS NOT A WAR AGAINST FASCISM. IT'S A WAR FOR EMPIRE.
ENGLAND, THE U.S., THE SOVIET UNION, THEY ARE ALL CORRUPT STATES, NOT MORALLY CONCERNED ABOUT HITLERISM, JUST WANTING TO RUN THE WORLD THEMSELVES. IT'S AN IMPERIALIST WAR.
THEN WHY ARE YOU HERE?
TO TALK TO GUYS LIKE YOU!
TWO WEEKS LATER, THE TAIL GUNNER'S PLANE WAS SHOT DOWN. THE WHOLE CREW WAS KILLED.
I WAS ASTONISHED THAT HE WOULD RISK HIS LIFE TO WAGE HIS OWN POLITICAL WAR WITHIN THE MILITARY.
I BEGAN A SHARP TURN IN MY POLITICAL THINKING, AWAY FROM THE ROMANTICIZATION OF THE OLD SOVIET UNION.
BUT DISILLUSIONMENT WITH THE SOVIET UNION DIDN'T DIMINISH MY BELIEF IN SOCIALISM ANY MORE THAN DISILLUSIONMENT WITH THE U.S. DIMINISHED MY BELIEF IN DEMOCRACY.
KRAK

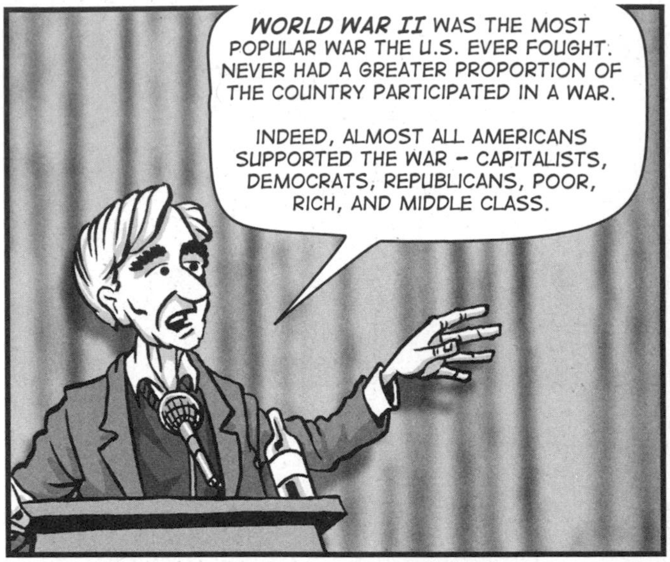
WORLD WAR II WAS THE MOST POPULAR WAR THE U.S. EVER FOUGHT. NEVER HAD A GREATER PROPORTION OF THE COUNTRY PARTICIPATED IN A WAR.
INDEED, ALMOST ALL AMERICANS SUPPORTED THE WAR – CAPITALISTS, DEMOCRATS, REPUBLICANS, POOR, RICH, AND MIDDLE CLASS.

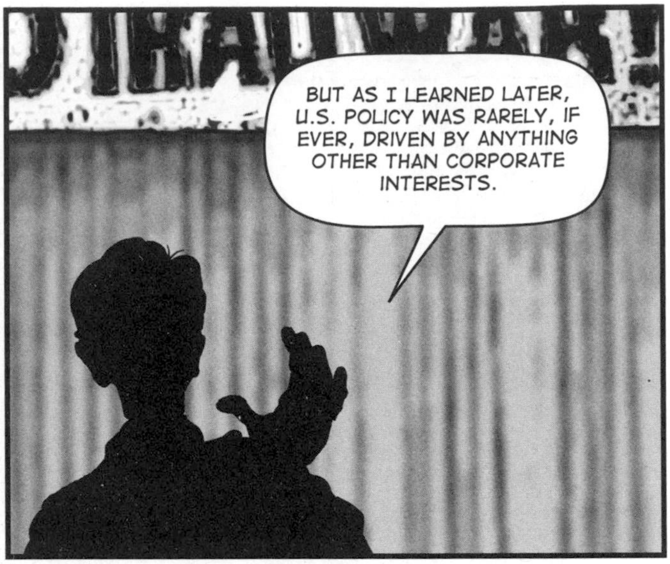
BUT AS I LEARNED LATER, U.S. POLICY WAS RARELY, IF EVER, DRIVEN BY ANYTHING OTHER THAN CORPORATE INTERESTS.

WHEN ***MUSSOLINI'S FASCISTS*** INVADED ETHIOPIA IN 1935, THE U.S. EMBARGOED THE SALE OF MUNITIONS BUT LET U.S. BUSINESSES SELL HUGE QUANTITIES OF OIL TO ITALY.

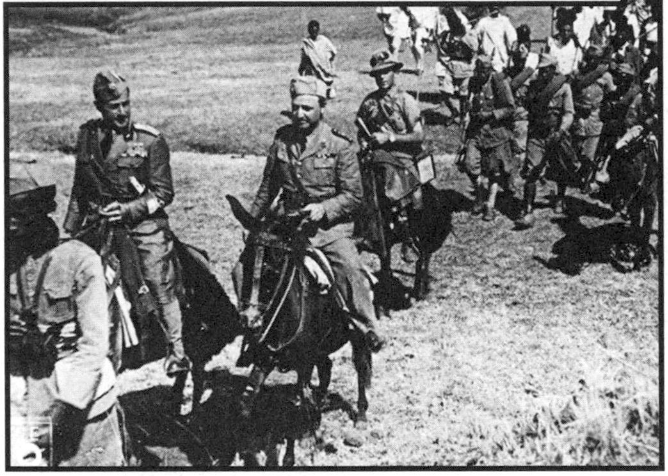

WHILE GERMANY WAS GIVING WEAPONS TO THE FASCIST REBELS IN SPAIN IN 1936, THE U.S. DOOMED THE REPUBLICAN GOVERNMENT BY SHUTTING OFF AID.

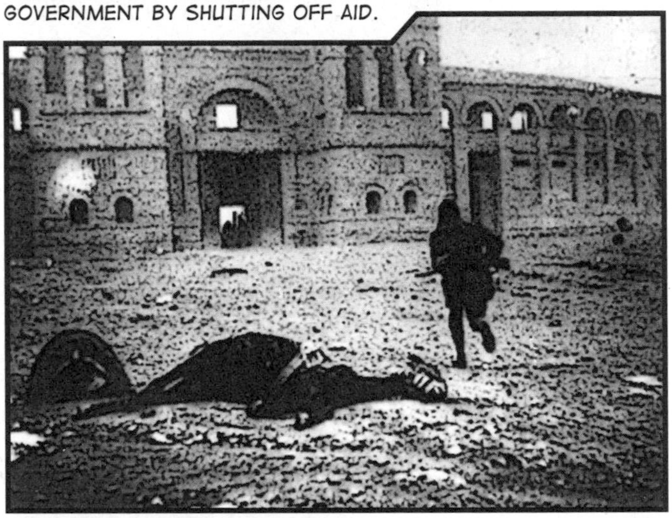

IN THE 1930S, THE U.S. DID LITTLE TO RESIST JAPAN'S INVASION OF THE ASIAN MAINLAND, TURNING AGAINST TOKYO'S FASCISTS ONLY AFTER THEY INVADED SOUTHEAST ASIA, A VITAL U.S. SOURCE FOR TIN, RUBBER, AND OIL.

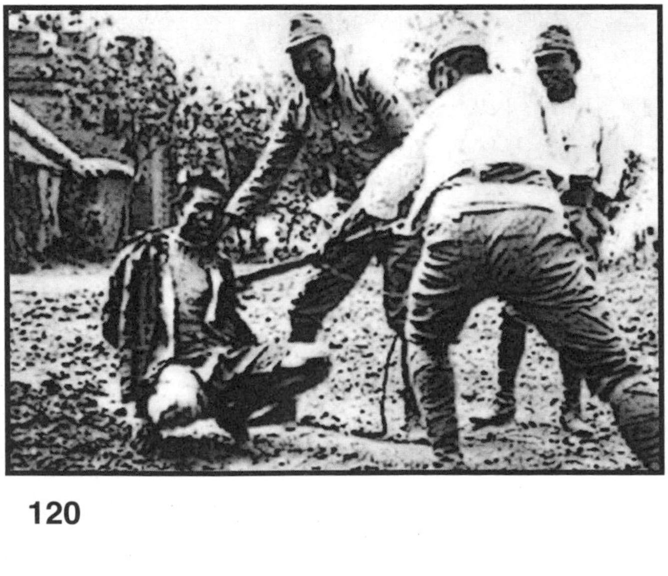

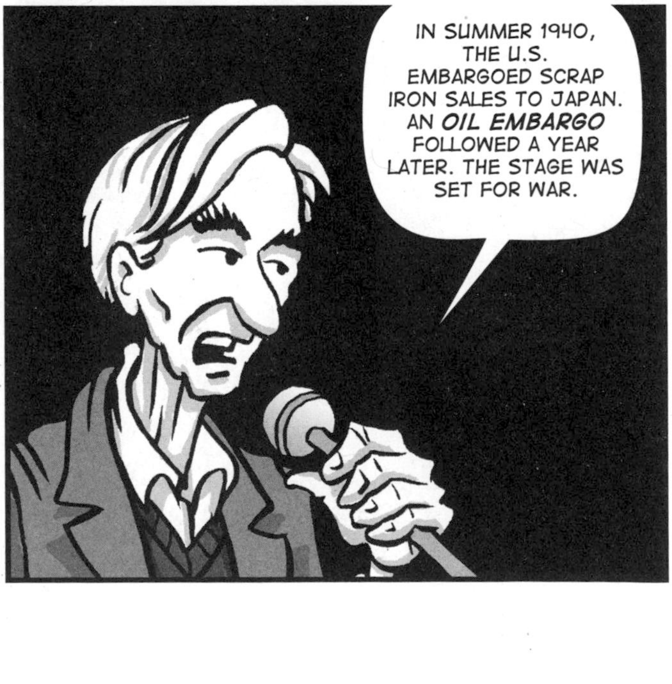
IN SUMMER 1940, THE U.S. EMBARGOED SCRAP IRON SALES TO JAPAN. AN OIL EMBARGO FOLLOWED A YEAR LATER. THE STAGE WAS SET FOR WAR.

DECEMBER 7, 1941: JAPAN BOMBED THE U.S. PACIFIC FLEET AT **PEARL HARBOR**. OUR GOVERNMENT SAID IT WAS A SNEAK ATTACK, BUT THE RECORDS SHOW THAT A WHITE HOUSE CONFERENCE TWO WEEKS BEFORE HAD ANTICIPATED A WAR WITH JAPAN, GERMANY'S ALLY.

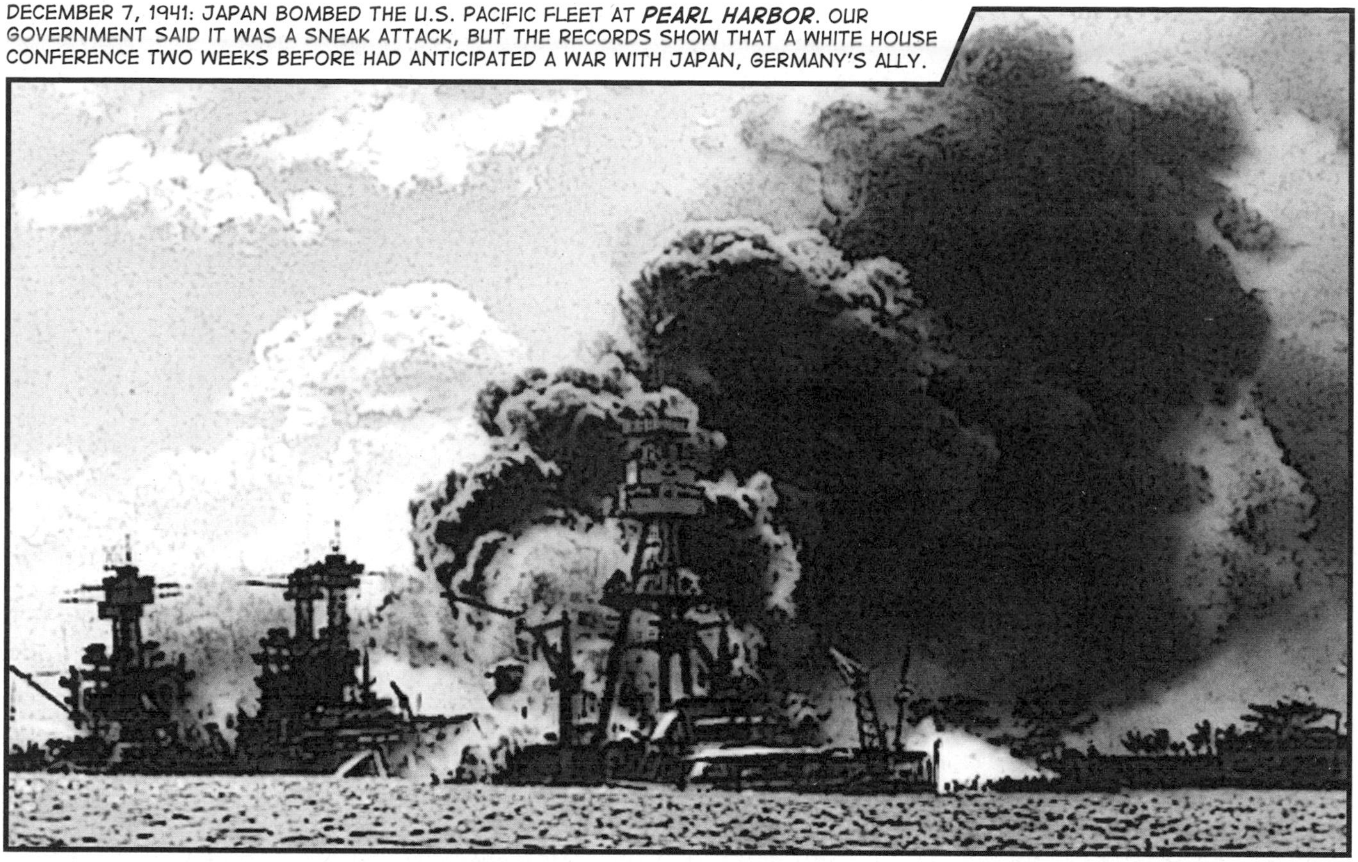

MONTHS BEFORE PEARL HARBOR, PRESIDENT ***FRANKLIN ROOSEVELT*** MISLED THE PUBLIC ABOUT CONFRONTATIONS BETWEEN U.S. WARSHIPS AND GERMAN SUBMARINES, ASSERTING THAT THE SUBS HAD LAUNCHED UNPROVOKED ATTACKS.

IN FACT, THE U.S. HAD BEEN WAGING AN UNDECLARED WAR WITH GERMANY IN THE NORTH ATLANTIC. UNDER THE MARCH 1941 ***LEND-LEASE PROGRAM*** THE U.S. BECAME "AN ARSENAL OF DEMOCRACY" TO PROTECT BRITISH AND AMERICAN MILITARY SHIPMENTS TO RUSSIA AND BRITAIN – IN VIOLATION OF THE ***NEUTRALITY ACT***.

THOMAS A. BAILEY, A HISTORIAN SYMPATHETIC TO F.D.R., WROTE THAT ROOSEVELT "REPEATEDLY DECEIVED THE AMERICAN PUBLIC... HE WAS LIKE THE PHYSICIAN WHO MUST TELL THE PATIENT LIES FOR THE PATIENT'S OWN GOOD."

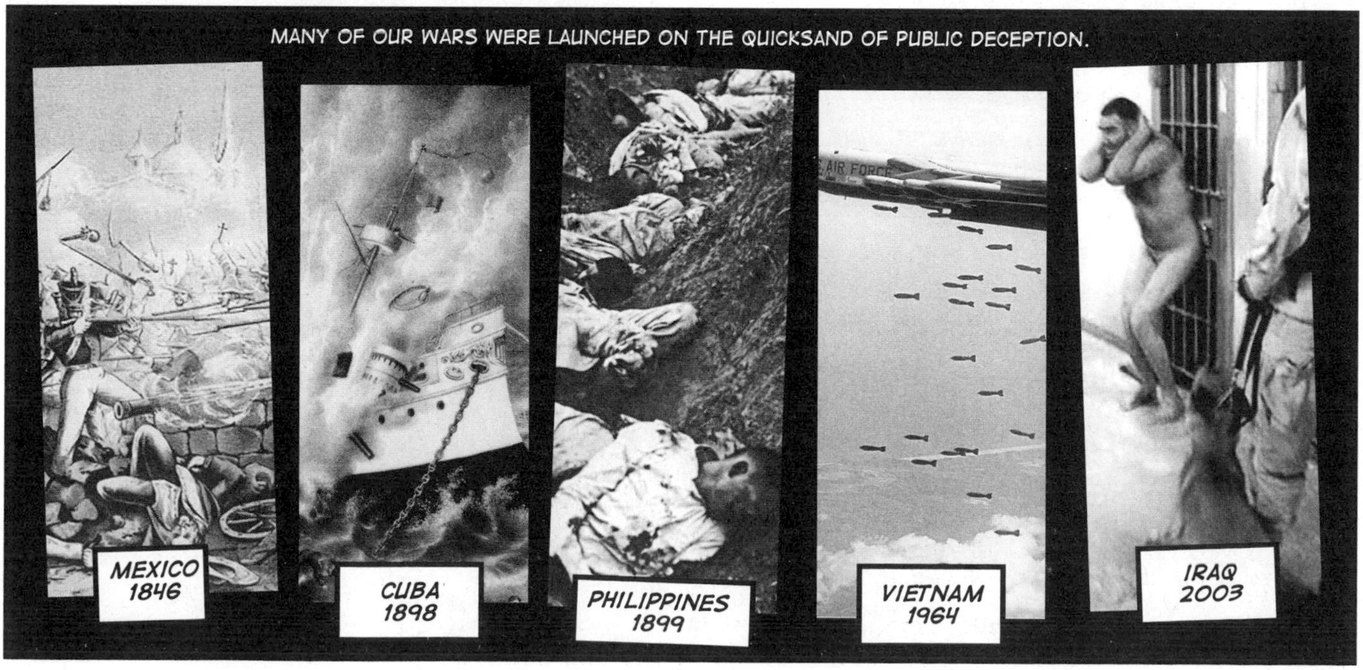
MANY OF OUR WARS WERE LAUNCHED ON THE QUICKSAND OF PUBLIC DECEPTION.
AIR FORCE
MEXICO 1846
CUBA 1898
PHILIPPINES 1899
VIETNAM 1964
IRAQ 2003

THE U.S. DID NOT ALWAYS SEE GERMANY'S ***NAZI*** GOVERNMENT AS ITS ENEMY. INDEED, IT HAD JOINED ENGLAND AND FRANCE IN APPEASING GERMAN DICTATOR ***ADOLF HITLER*** THROUGHOUT THE THIRTIES.

IN 1934, A SENATE RESOLUTION OBJECTING TO THE GERMAN TREATMENT OF JEWS WAS BURIED IN COMMITTEE AT THE REQUEST OF THE STATE DEPARTMENT.

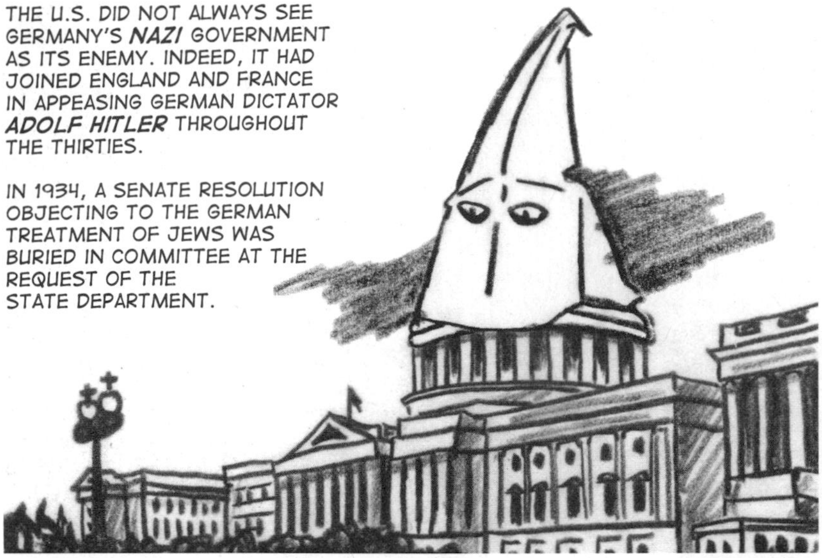

ANTI-LYNCHING LAWS WERE FILIBUSTERED IN THE SENATE. NO WONDER BLACK AMERICANS, LOOKING AT ANTI-SEMITISM IN GERMANY THAT YEAR, DID NOT SEE THEIR OWN SITUATION AS MUCH DIFFERENT.

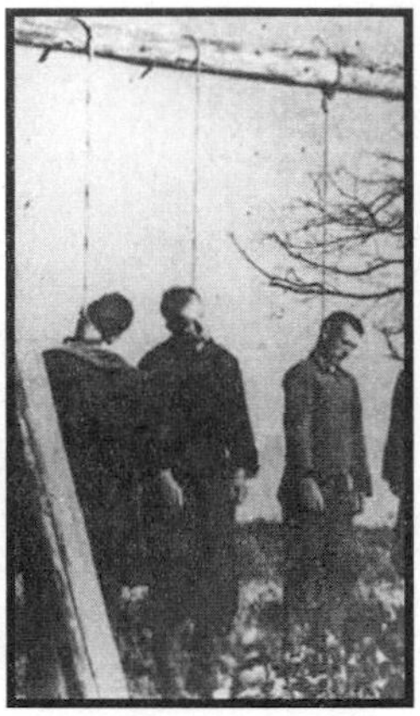

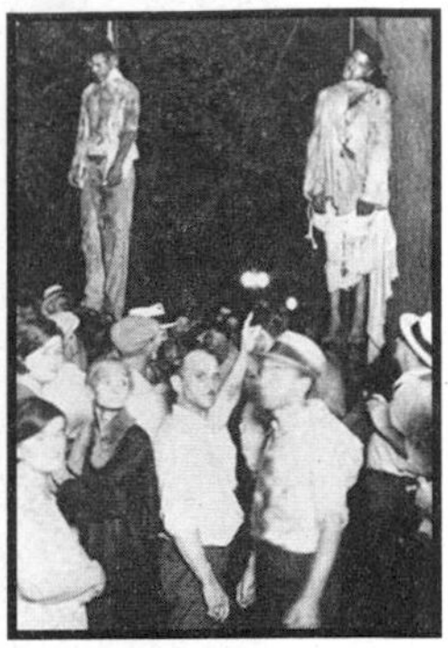

The lynching of Thomas Shipp and Abram Smith, August 7, 1930, Marion, Indiana.

THERE WAS WIDESPREAD SUPPORT FOR THE WAR, BUT ALSO WIDESPREAD WAR PROFITEERING. WAGES WERE RISING, BUT PROFITS WERE SKYROCKETING.

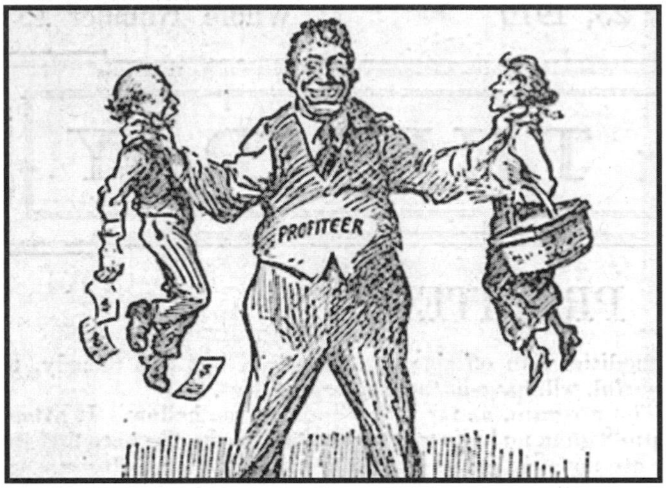
PROFITEER

IN 1941 THERE WERE OVER 4,000 STRIKES IN THE U.S. - MORE THAN AT ANY TIME SINCE 1919.

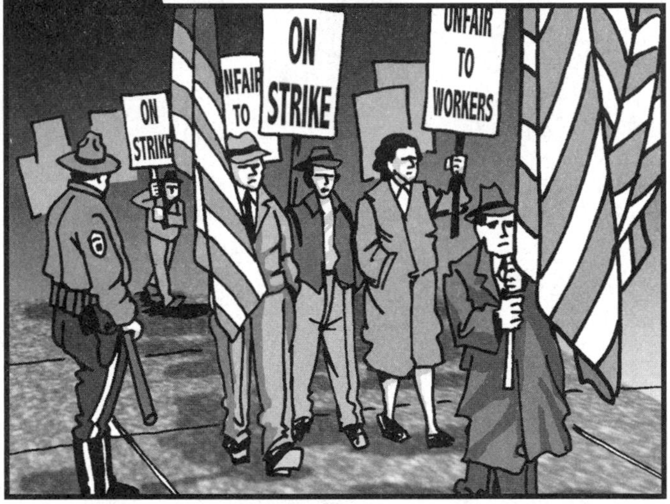
ON STRIKE
NFAIR TO
ON STRIKE
UNFAIR TO WORKERS

WORKERS REBELLED BY STRIKING AND SOMETIMES WERE PUT DOWN WITH FORCE. F.D.R. HAD TROOPS SEIZE THE MINES DURING A 1943 STRIKE, INFURIATING ***UNITED MINE WORKERS*** PRESIDENT ***JOHN L. LEWIS***.

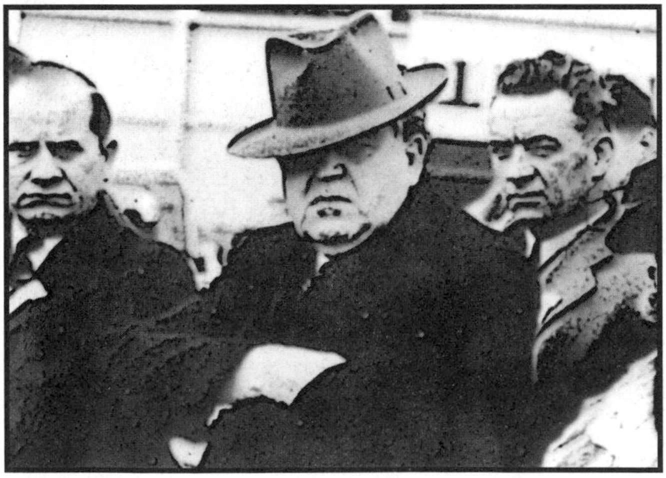

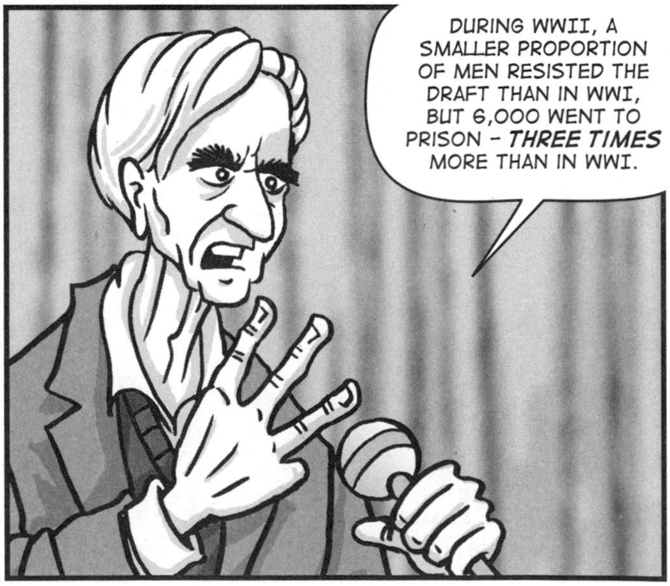
DURING WWII, A SMALLER PROPORTION OF MEN RESISTED THE DRAFT THAN IN WWI, BUT 6,000 WENT TO PRISON - THREE TIMES MORE THAN IN WWI.

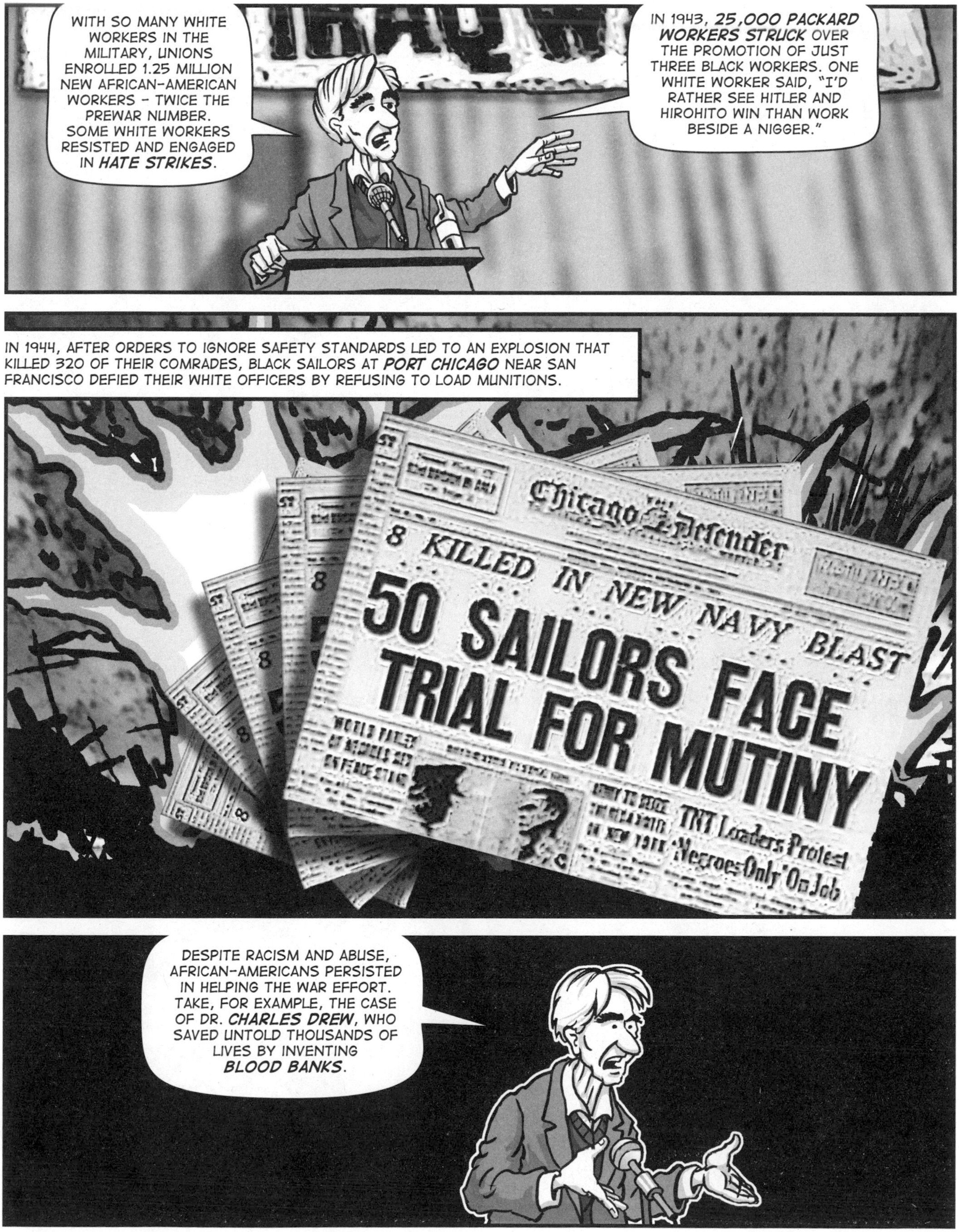

WITH SO MANY WHITE WORKERS IN THE MILITARY, UNIONS ENROLLED 1.25 MILLION NEW AFRICAN-AMERICAN WORKERS - TWICE THE PREWAR NUMBER. SOME WHITE WORKERS RESISTED AND ENGAGED IN ***HATE STRIKES***.
IN 1943, ***25,000 PACKARD WORKERS STRUCK*** OVER THE PROMOTION OF JUST THREE BLACK WORKERS. ONE WHITE WORKER SAID, "I'D RATHER SEE HITLER AND HIROHITO WIN THAN WORK BESIDE A NIGGER."
IN 1944, AFTER ORDERS TO IGNORE SAFETY STANDARDS LED TO AN EXPLOSION THAT KILLED 320 OF THEIR COMRADES, BLACK SAILORS AT ***PORT CHICAGO*** NEAR SAN FRANCISCO DEFIED THEIR WHITE OFFICERS BY REFUSING TO LOAD MUNITIONS.
Chicago Defender
8 KILLED IN NEW NAVY BLAST
50 SAILORS FACE TRIAL FOR MUTINY
TNT Loaders Protest 'Negroes Only' On Job
DESPITE RACISM AND ABUSE, AFRICAN-AMERICANS PERSISTED IN HELPING THE WAR EFFORT. TAKE, FOR EXAMPLE, THE CASE OF DR. ***CHARLES DREW***, WHO SAVED UNTOLD THOUSANDS OF LIVES BY INVENTING ***BLOOD BANKS***.

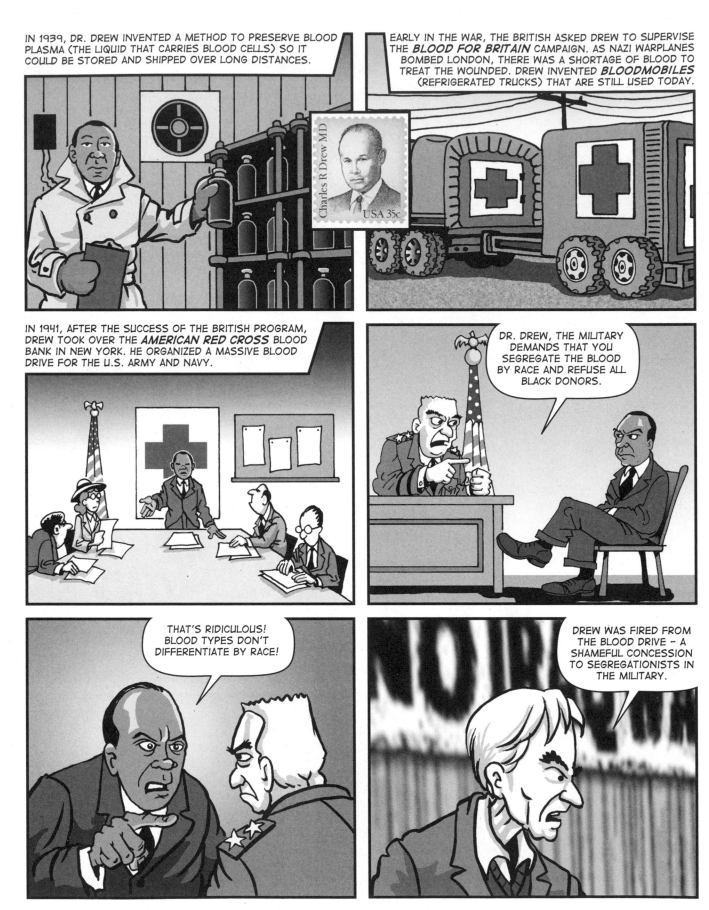

IN 1939, DR. DREW INVENTED A METHOD TO PRESERVE BLOOD PLASMA (THE LIQUID THAT CARRIES BLOOD CELLS) SO IT COULD BE STORED AND SHIPPED OVER LONG DISTANCES.

Charles R Drew MD
USA 35c

EARLY IN THE WAR, THE BRITISH ASKED DREW TO SUPERVISE THE *BLOOD FOR BRITAIN* CAMPAIGN. AS NAZI WARPLANES BOMBED LONDON, THERE WAS A SHORTAGE OF BLOOD TO TREAT THE WOUNDED. DREW INVENTED *BLOODMOBILES* (REFRIGERATED TRUCKS) THAT ARE STILL USED TODAY.

IN 1941, AFTER THE SUCCESS OF THE BRITISH PROGRAM, DREW TOOK OVER THE *AMERICAN RED CROSS* BLOOD BANK IN NEW YORK. HE ORGANIZED A MASSIVE BLOOD DRIVE FOR THE U.S. ARMY AND NAVY.

DR. DREW, THE MILITARY DEMANDS THAT YOU SEGREGATE THE BLOOD BY RACE AND REFUSE ALL BLACK DONORS.

THAT'S RIDICULOUS! BLOOD TYPES DON'T DIFFERENTIATE BY RACE!

DREW WAS FIRED FROM THE BLOOD DRIVE – A SHAMEFUL CONCESSION TO SEGREGATIONISTS IN THE MILITARY.

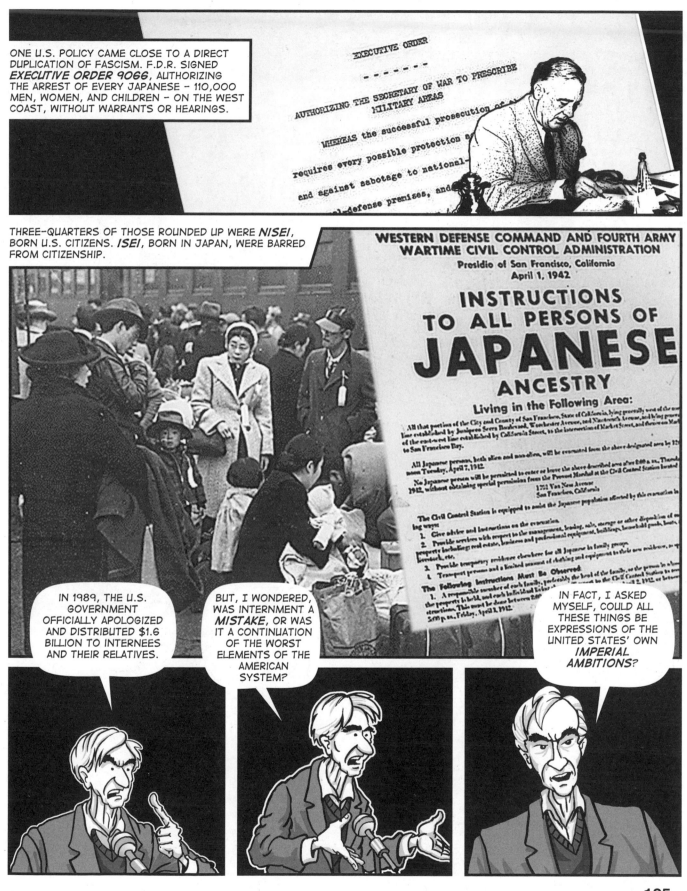

ONE U.S. POLICY CAME CLOSE TO A DIRECT DUPLICATION OF FASCISM. F.D.R. SIGNED *EXECUTIVE ORDER 9066*, AUTHORIZING THE ARREST OF EVERY JAPANESE – 110,000 MEN, WOMEN, AND CHILDREN – ON THE WEST COAST, WITHOUT WARRANTS OR HEARINGS.

THREE-QUARTERS OF THOSE ROUNDED UP WERE *NISEI*, BORN U.S. CITIZENS. *ISEI*, BORN IN JAPAN, WERE BARRED FROM CITIZENSHIP.

EXECUTIVE ORDER
- - - - - -
AUTHORIZING THE SECRETARY OF WAR TO PRESCRIBE MILITARY AREAS

WHEREAS the successful prosecution of

requires every possible protection

and against sabotage to national-

defense premises, and

WESTERN DEFENSE COMMAND AND FOURTH ARMY
WARTIME CIVIL CONTROL ADMINISTRATION
Presidio of San Francisco, California
April 1, 1942

INSTRUCTIONS TO ALL PERSONS OF JAPANESE ANCESTRY

Living in the Following Area:

IN 1989, THE U.S. GOVERNMENT OFFICIALLY APOLOGIZED AND DISTRIBUTED $1.6 BILLION TO INTERNEES AND THEIR RELATIVES.

BUT, I WONDERED, WAS INTERNMENT A *MISTAKE*, OR WAS IT A CONTINUATION OF THE WORST ELEMENTS OF THE AMERICAN SYSTEM?

IN FACT, I ASKED MYSELF, COULD ALL THESE THINGS BE EXPRESSIONS OF THE UNITED STATES' OWN *IMPERIAL AMBITIONS*?

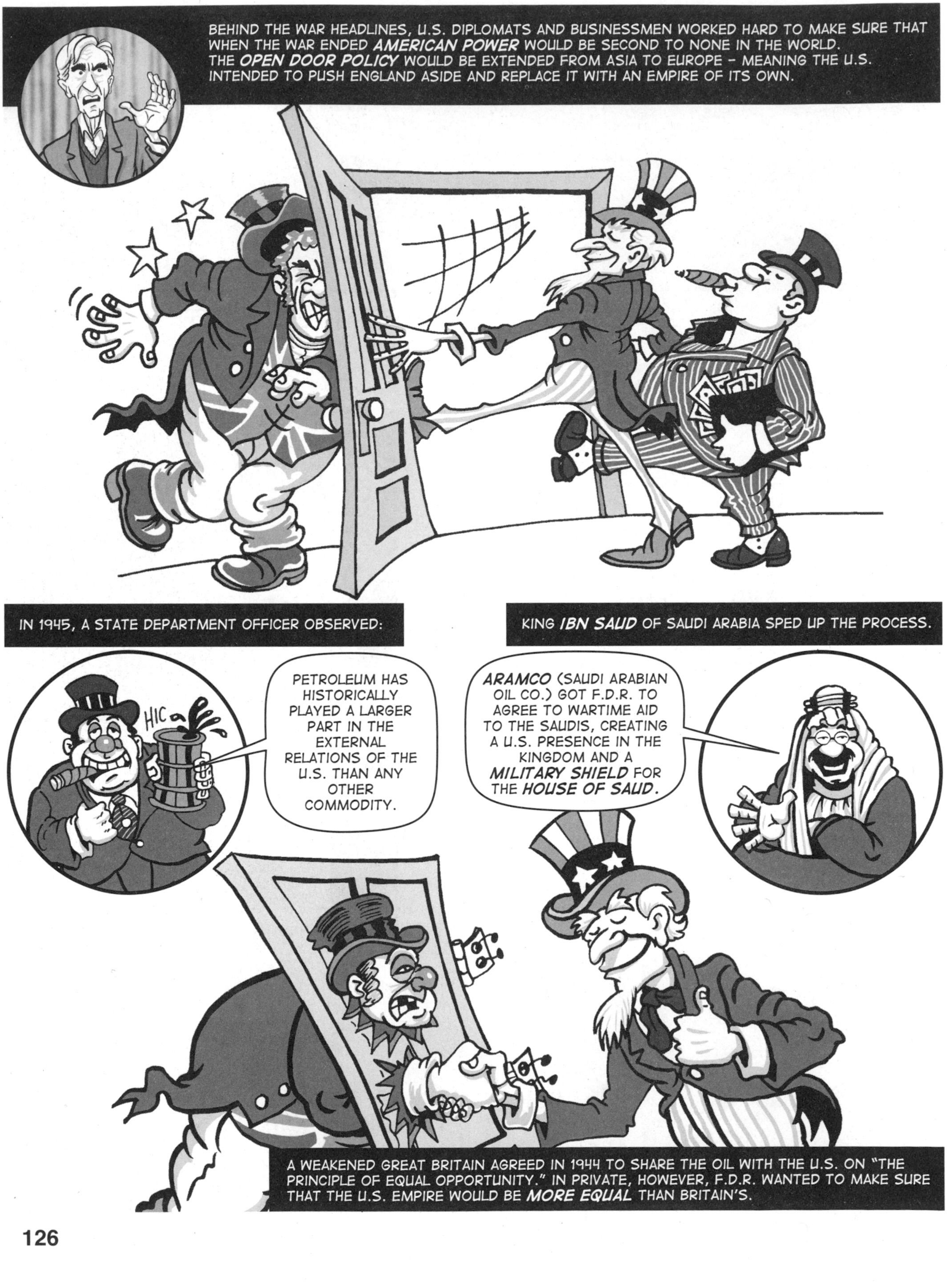
BEHIND THE WAR HEADLINES, U.S. DIPLOMATS AND BUSINESSMEN WORKED HARD TO MAKE SURE THAT WHEN THE WAR ENDED AMERICAN POWER WOULD BE SECOND TO NONE IN THE WORLD. THE OPEN DOOR POLICY WOULD BE EXTENDED FROM ASIA TO EUROPE - MEANING THE U.S. INTENDED TO PUSH ENGLAND ASIDE AND REPLACE IT WITH AN EMPIRE OF ITS OWN.
IN 1945, A STATE DEPARTMENT OFFICER OBSERVED:
HIC
PETROLEUM HAS HISTORICALLY PLAYED A LARGER PART IN THE EXTERNAL RELATIONS OF THE U.S. THAN ANY OTHER COMMODITY.
KING IBN SAUD OF SAUDI ARABIA SPED UP THE PROCESS.
ARAMCO (SAUDI ARABIAN OIL CO.) GOT F.D.R. TO AGREE TO WARTIME AID TO THE SAUDIS, CREATING A U.S. PRESENCE IN THE KINGDOM AND A MILITARY SHIELD FOR THE HOUSE OF SAUD.
A WEAKENED GREAT BRITAIN AGREED IN 1944 TO SHARE THE OIL WITH THE U.S. ON "THE PRINCIPLE OF EQUAL OPPORTUNITY." IN PRIVATE, HOWEVER, F.D.R. WANTED TO MAKE SURE THAT THE U.S. EMPIRE WOULD BE MORE EQUAL THAN BRITAIN'S.

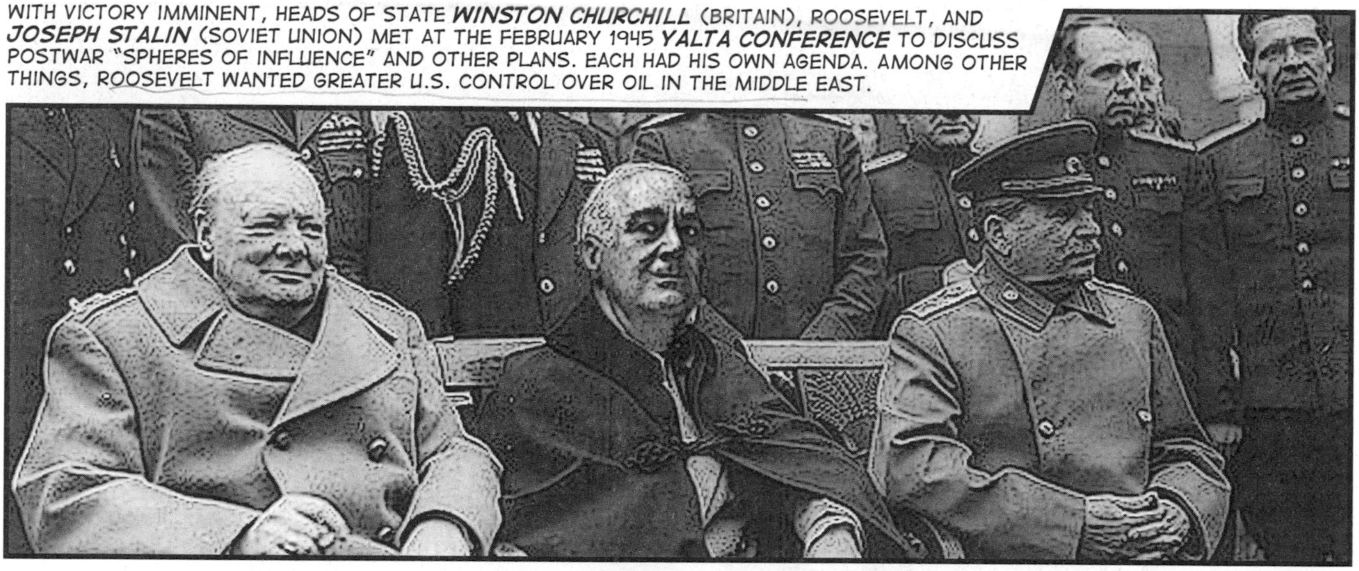
WITH VICTORY IMMINENT, HEADS OF STATE ***WINSTON CHURCHILL*** (BRITAIN), ROOSEVELT, AND ***JOSEPH STALIN*** (SOVIET UNION) MET AT THE FEBRUARY 1945 ***YALTA CONFERENCE*** TO DISCUSS POSTWAR "SPHERES OF INFLUENCE" AND OTHER PLANS. EACH HAD HIS OWN AGENDA. AMONG OTHER THINGS, ROOSEVELT WANTED GREATER U.S. CONTROL OVER OIL IN THE MIDDLE EAST.

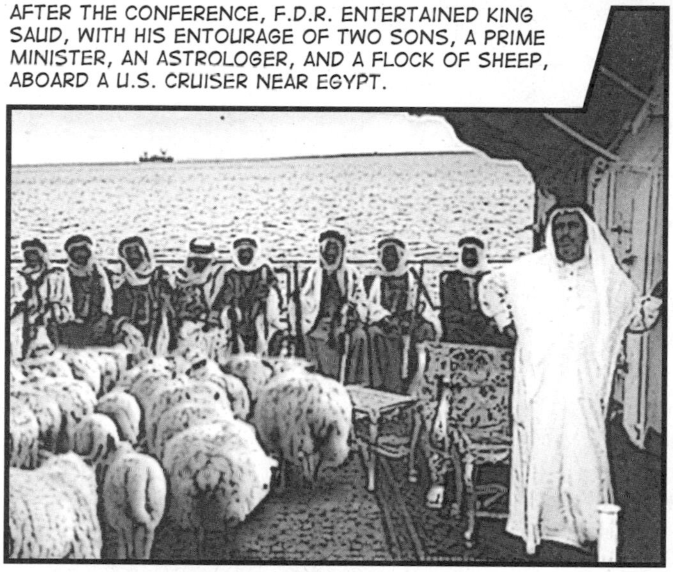
AFTER THE CONFERENCE, F.D.R. ENTERTAINED KING SAUD, WITH HIS ENTOURAGE OF TWO SONS, A PRIME MINISTER, AN ASTROLOGER, AND A FLOCK OF SHEEP, ABOARD A U.S. CRUISER NEAR EGYPT.

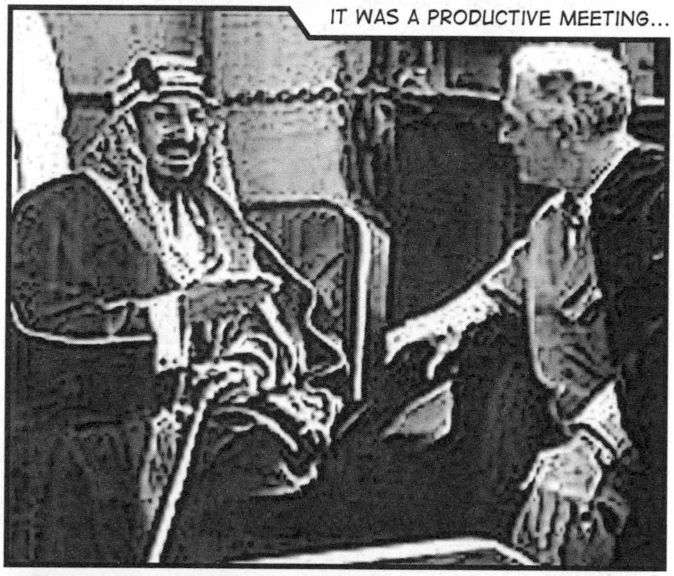
IT WAS A PRODUCTIVE MEETING...

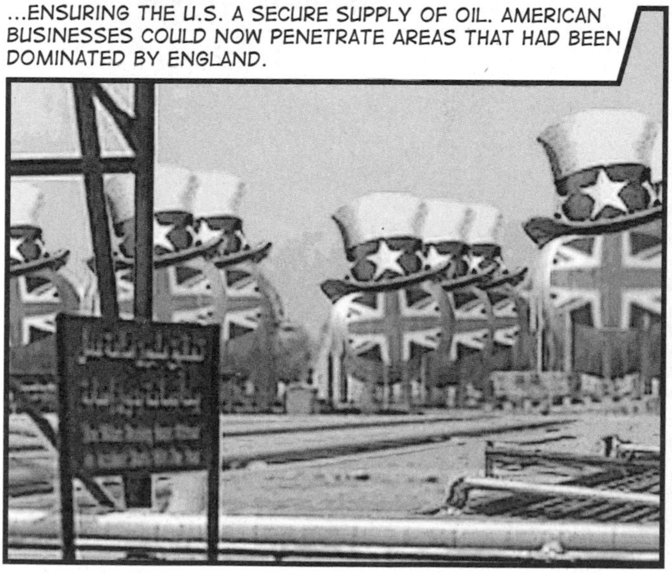
...ENSURING THE U.S. A SECURE SUPPLY OF OIL. AMERICAN BUSINESSES COULD NOW PENETRATE AREAS THAT HAD BEEN DOMINATED BY ENGLAND.

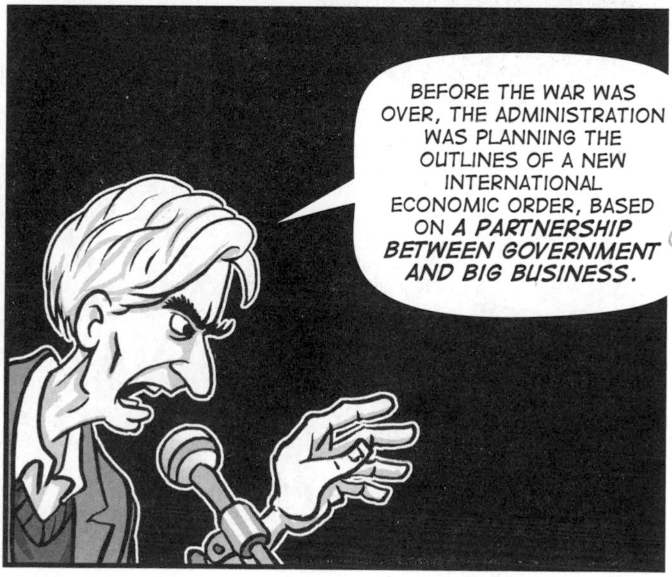
BEFORE THE WAR WAS OVER, THE ADMINISTRATION WAS PLANNING THE OUTLINES OF A NEW INTERNATIONAL ECONOMIC ORDER, BASED ON ***A PARTNERSHIP BETWEEN GOVERNMENT AND BIG BUSINESS.***

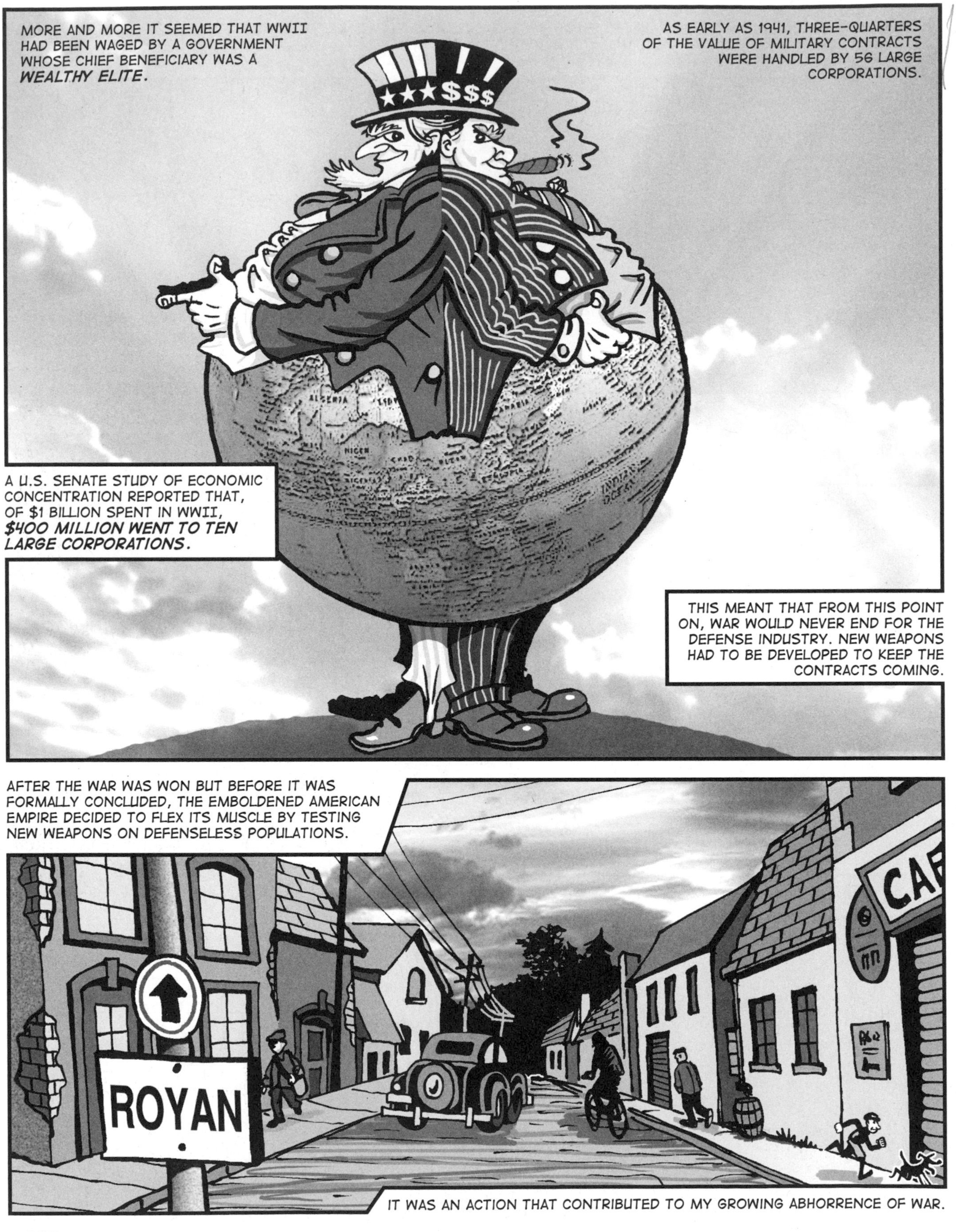
MORE AND MORE IT SEEMED THAT WWII HAD BEEN WAGED BY A GOVERNMENT WHOSE CHIEF BENEFICIARY WAS A *WEALTHY ELITE*.
AS EARLY AS 1941, THREE-QUARTERS OF THE VALUE OF MILITARY CONTRACTS WERE HANDLED BY 56 LARGE CORPORATIONS.
$$$
A U.S. SENATE STUDY OF ECONOMIC CONCENTRATION REPORTED THAT, OF $1 BILLION SPENT IN WWII, ***$400 MILLION WENT TO TEN LARGE CORPORATIONS***.
THIS MEANT THAT FROM THIS POINT ON, WAR WOULD NEVER END FOR THE DEFENSE INDUSTRY. NEW WEAPONS HAD TO BE DEVELOPED TO KEEP THE CONTRACTS COMING.
AFTER THE WAR WAS WON BUT BEFORE IT WAS FORMALLY CONCLUDED, THE EMBOLDENED AMERICAN EMPIRE DECIDED TO FLEX ITS MUSCLE BY TESTING NEW WEAPONS ON DEFENSELESS POPULATIONS.
ROYAN
IT WAS AN ACTION THAT CONTRIBUTED TO MY GROWING ABHORRENCE OF WAR.

Just Following Orders

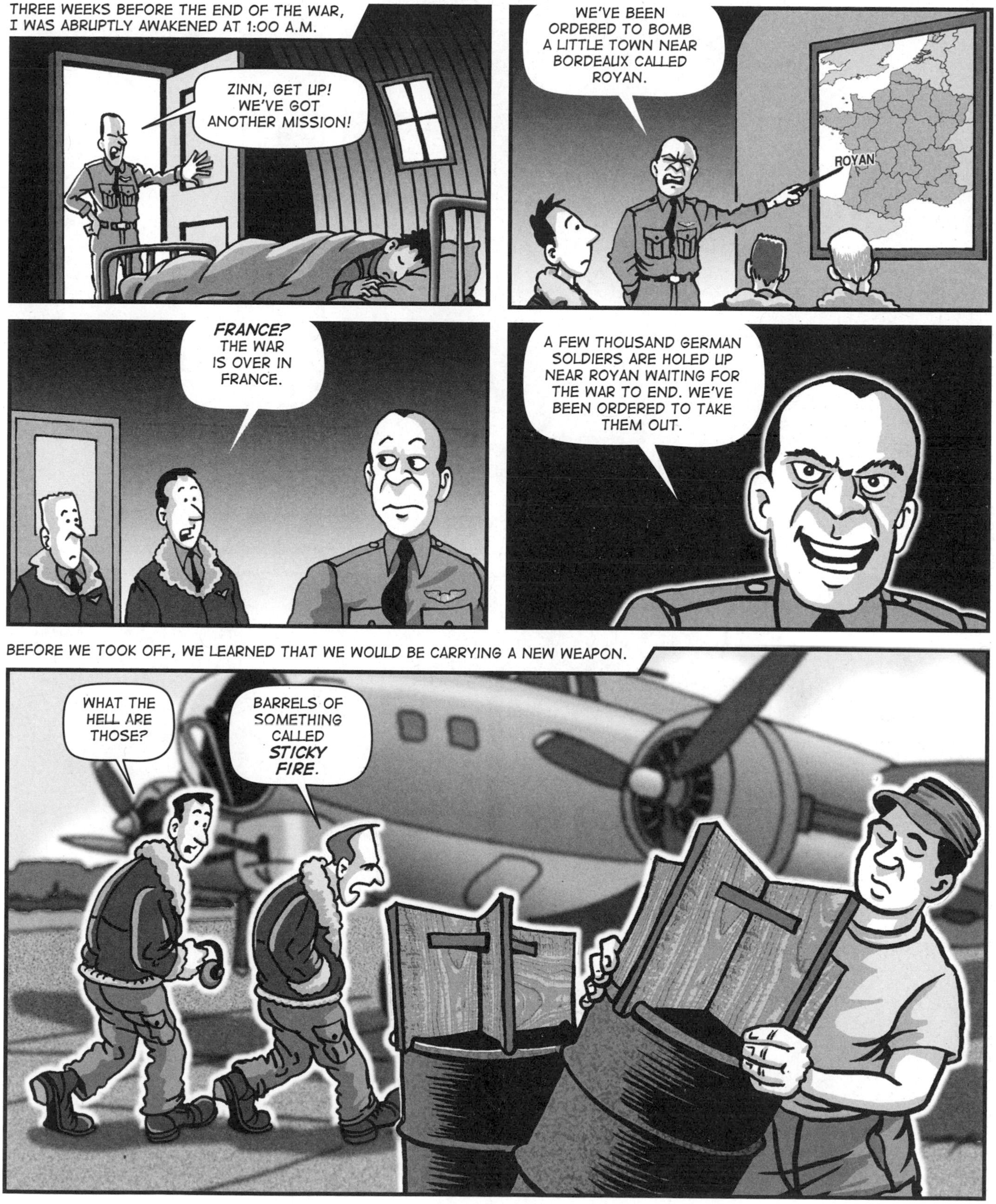
THREE WEEKS BEFORE THE END OF THE WAR, I WAS ABRUPTLY AWAKENED AT 1:00 A.M.
ZINN, GET UP! WE'VE GOT ANOTHER MISSION!
WE'VE BEEN ORDERED TO BOMB A LITTLE TOWN NEAR BORDEAUX CALLED ROYAN.
ROYAN
FRANCE? THE WAR IS OVER IN FRANCE.
A FEW THOUSAND GERMAN SOLDIERS ARE HOLED UP NEAR ROYAN WAITING FOR THE WAR TO END. WE'VE BEEN ORDERED TO TAKE THEM OUT.
BEFORE WE TOOK OFF, WE LEARNED THAT WE WOULD BE CARRYING A NEW WEAPON.
WHAT THE HELL ARE THOSE?
BARRELS OF SOMETHING CALLED *STICKY FIRE*.

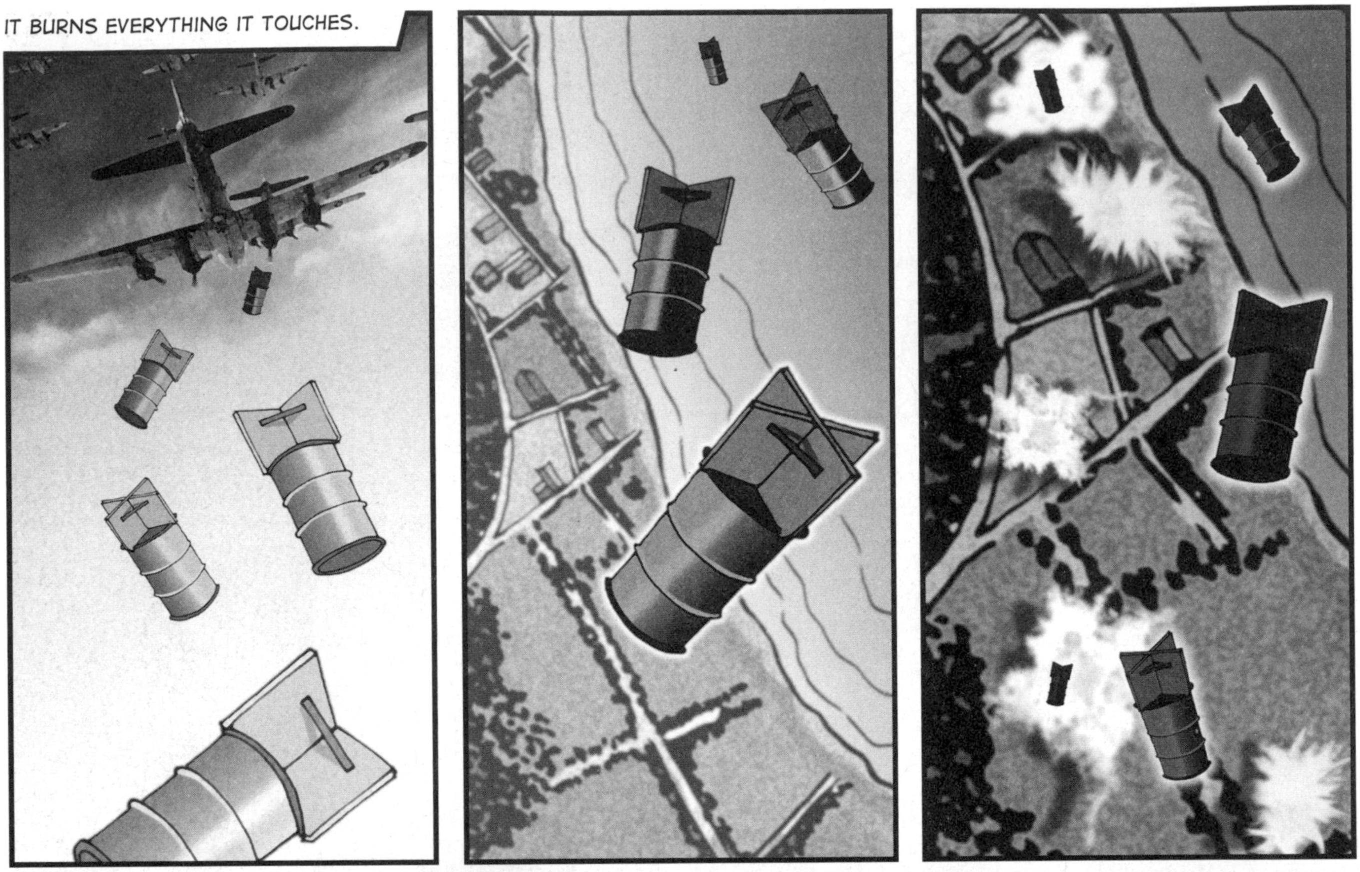
IT BURNS EVERYTHING IT TOUCHES.

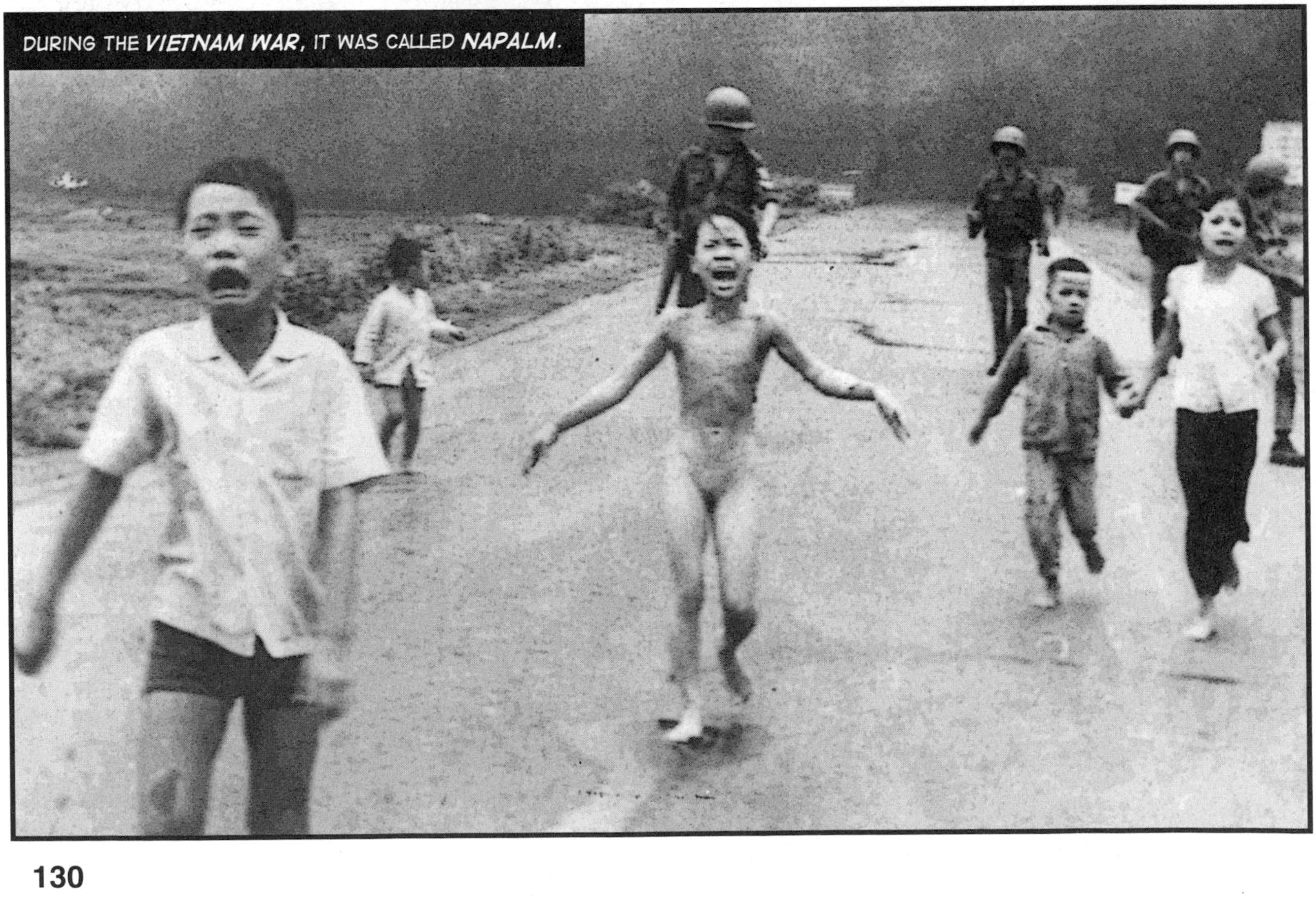
DURING THE VIETNAM WAR, IT WAS CALLED NAPALM.

THERE WERE 1,200 *FLYING FORTRESSES* OVER ROYAN THAT DAY. WE DROPPED *396,000 GALLONS OF NAPALM* ON THE TOWN. BOTH GERMAN SOLDIERS AND FRENCH CIVILIANS WERE KILLED.

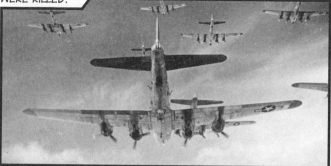

AFTER THE WAR, I READ A NEWSPAPER STORY ABOUT THAT DAY: "350 CIVILIANS CRAWLED FROM THE RUINS AND SAID THE ATTACK WAS *SUCH HELL AS WE NEVER BELIEVED POSSIBLE.*"

I REMEMBERED WHAT THE ATTACK HAD LOOKED LIKE FROM THE AIR. AS THEY HIT THE EARTH, THE DRUMS OF STICKY FIRE IGNITED BRIEFLY LIKE MATCHES FLARING.

WE SAW NO PEOPLE, HEARD NO SCREAMS, SAW NO BLOOD, NO TORN LIMBS.

I WAS JUST *FOLLOWING ORDERS.* IT IS THE ANCIENT CRY OF THE WARRIOR WHO HAS COMMITTED ATROCITIES.

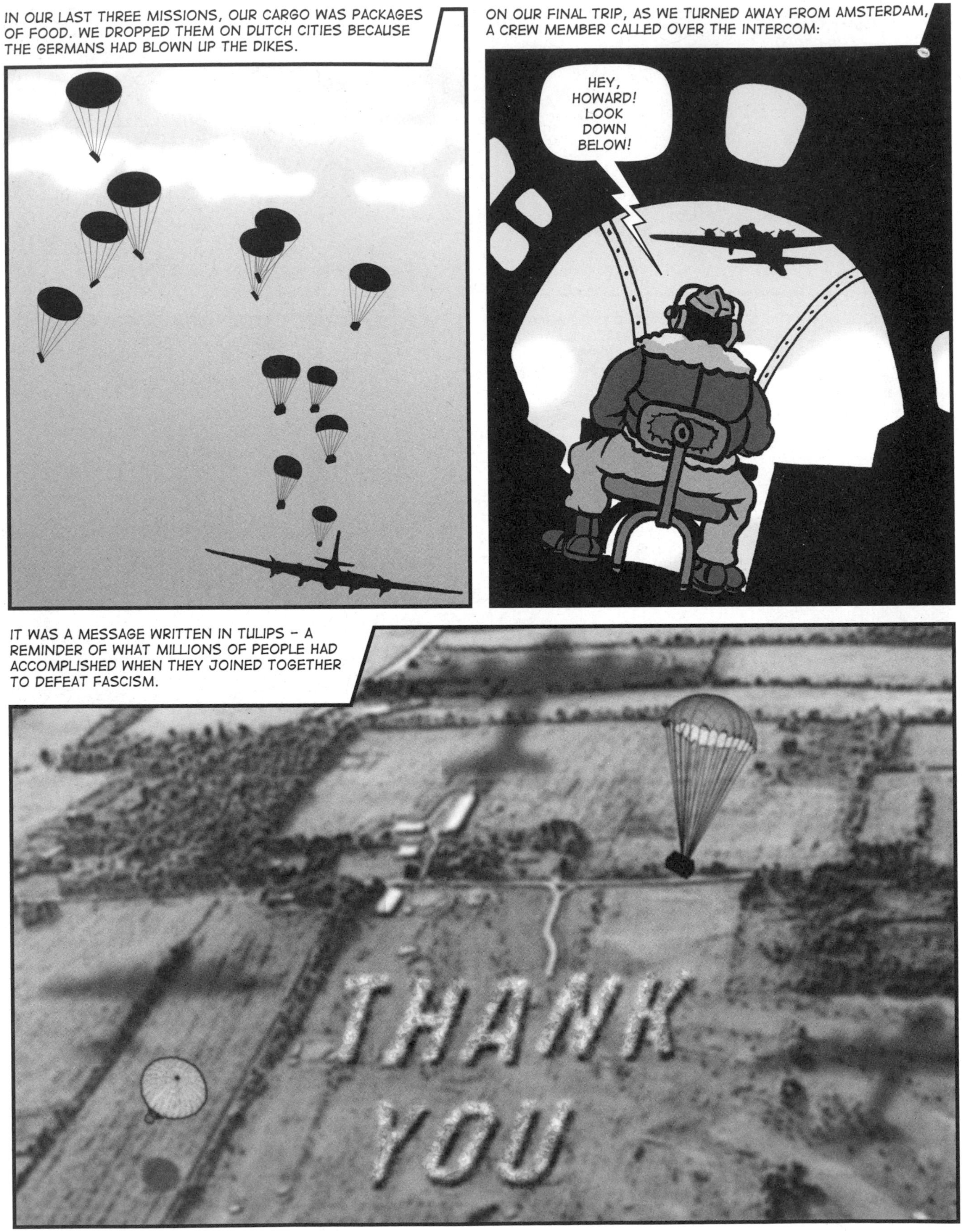
IN OUR LAST THREE MISSIONS, OUR CARGO WAS PACKAGES OF FOOD. WE DROPPED THEM ON DUTCH CITIES BECAUSE THE GERMANS HAD BLOWN UP THE DIKES.
ON OUR FINAL TRIP, AS WE TURNED AWAY FROM AMSTERDAM, A CREW MEMBER CALLED OVER THE INTERCOM:
HEY, HOWARD! LOOK DOWN BELOW!
IT WAS A MESSAGE WRITTEN IN TULIPS – A REMINDER OF WHAT MILLIONS OF PEOPLE HAD ACCOMPLISHED WHEN THEY JOINED TOGETHER TO DEFEAT FASCISM.
THANK YOU

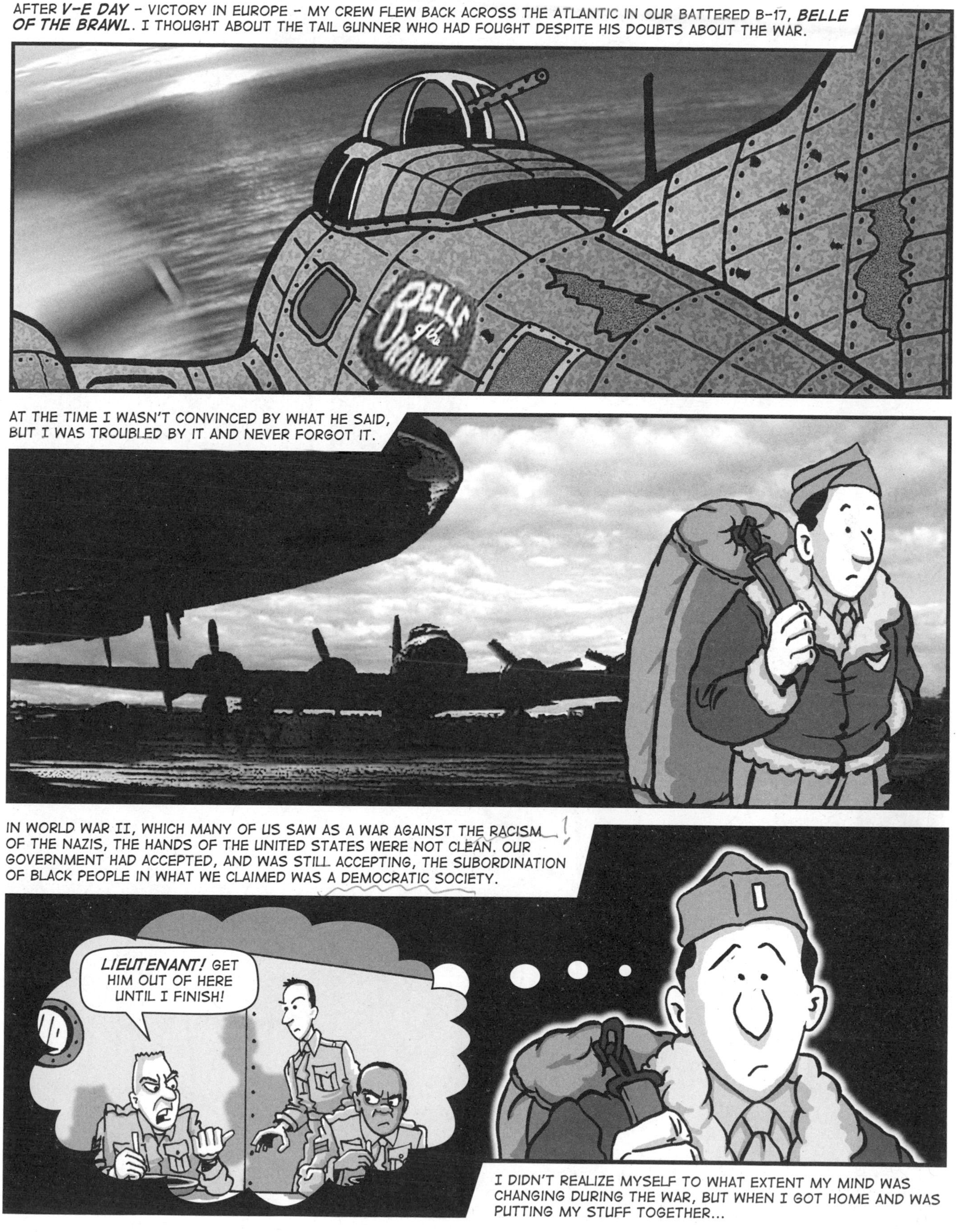
AFTER V-E DAY - VICTORY IN EUROPE - MY CREW FLEW BACK ACROSS THE ATLANTIC IN OUR BATTERED B-17, BELLE OF THE BRAWL. I THOUGHT ABOUT THE TAIL GUNNER WHO HAD FOUGHT DESPITE HIS DOUBTS ABOUT THE WAR.
BELLE of the BRAWL
AT THE TIME I WASN'T CONVINCED BY WHAT HE SAID, BUT I WAS TROUBLED BY IT AND NEVER FORGOT IT.
IN WORLD WAR II, WHICH MANY OF US SAW AS A WAR AGAINST THE RACISM OF THE NAZIS, THE HANDS OF THE UNITED STATES WERE NOT CLEAN. OUR GOVERNMENT HAD ACCEPTED, AND WAS STILL ACCEPTING, THE SUBORDINATION OF BLACK PEOPLE IN WHAT WE CLAIMED WAS A DEMOCRATIC SOCIETY.
LIEUTENANT! GET HIM OUT OF HERE UNTIL I FINISH!
I DIDN'T REALIZE MYSELF TO WHAT EXTENT MY MIND WAS CHANGING DURING THE WAR, BUT WHEN I GOT HOME AND WAS PUTTING MY STUFF TOGETHER...

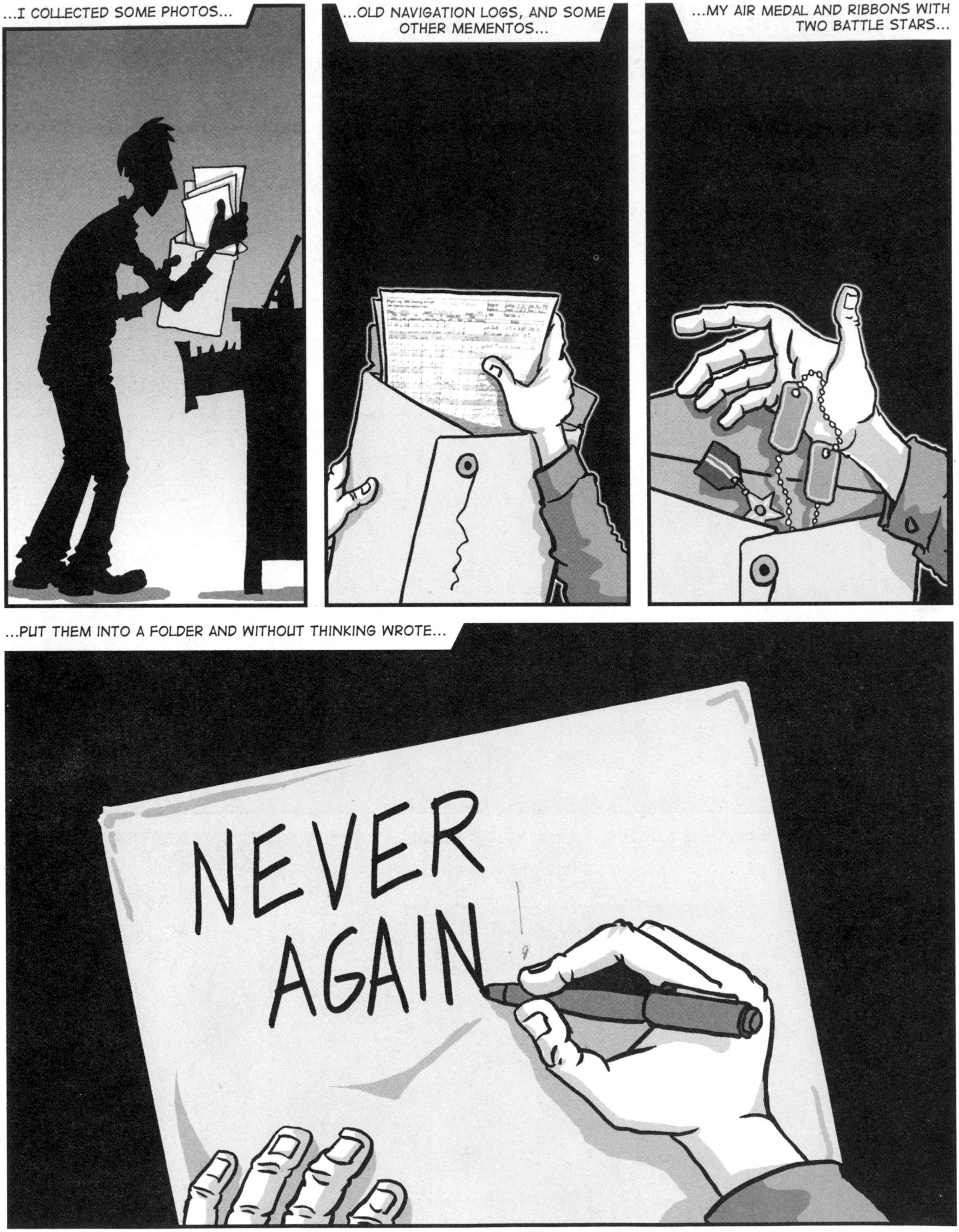
...I COLLECTED SOME PHOTOS...
...OLD NAVIGATION LOGS, AND SOME OTHER MEMENTOS...
...MY AIR MEDAL AND RIBBONS WITH TWO BATTLE STARS...
...PUT THEM INTO A FOLDER AND WITHOUT THINKING WROTE...
NEVER AGAIN

The Atomic Age

AUGUST 6, 1945, 8:15 A.M., HIROSHIMA, JAPAN...

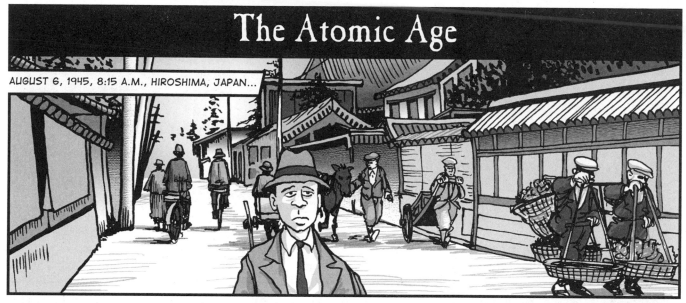

IN A BLINDING FLASH, A CITY OF 250,000 WAS REDUCED TO RUBBLE, LEAVING 100,000 DEAD AND ANOTHER 100,000 WOUNDED.

FROM THE BURNING HOMES SO MANY CRIED OUT THAT INDIVIDUAL VOICES COULD NOT BE HEARD.

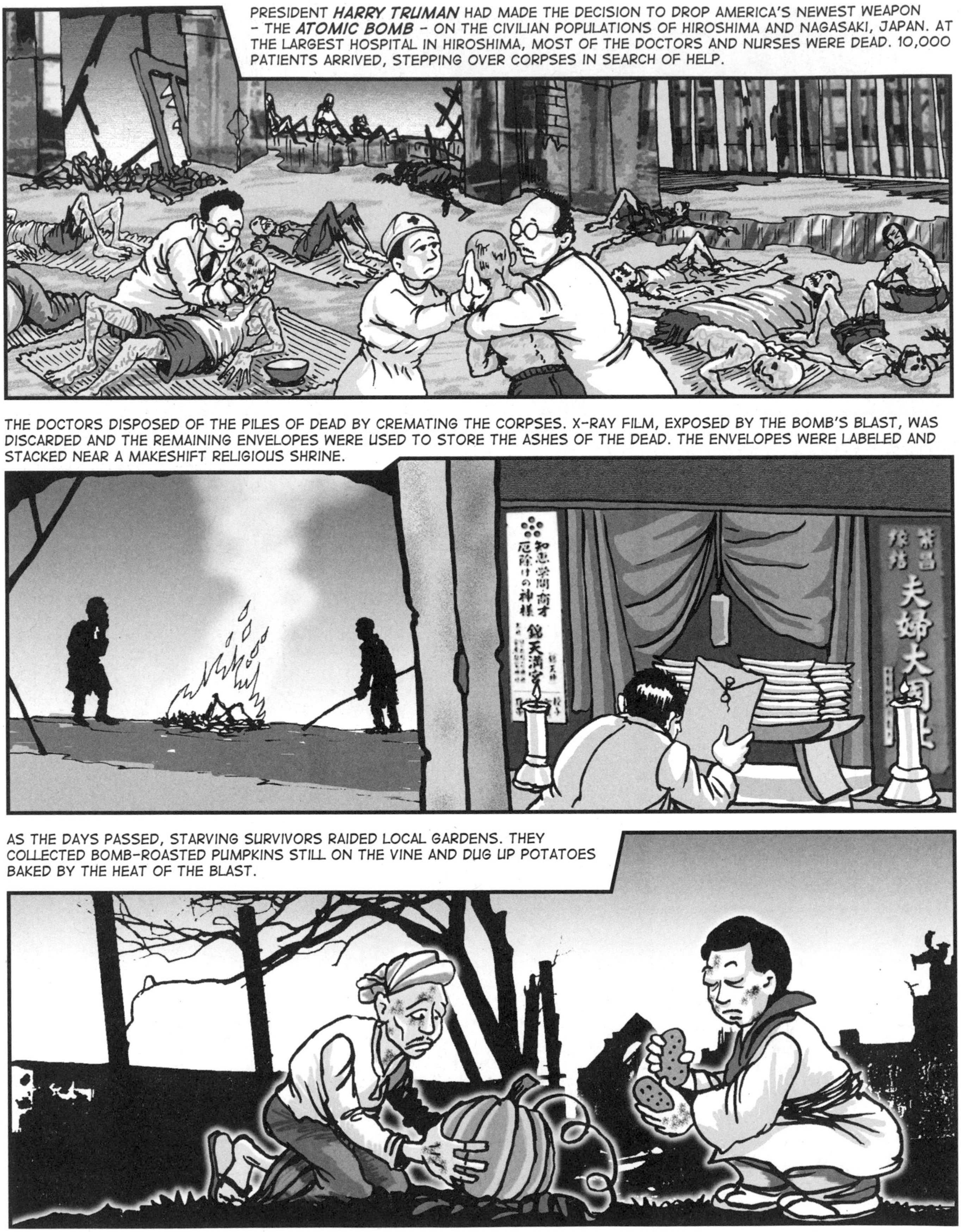
PRESIDENT HARRY TRUMAN HAD MADE THE DECISION TO DROP AMERICA'S NEWEST WEAPON - THE ATOMIC BOMB - ON THE CIVILIAN POPULATIONS OF HIROSHIMA AND NAGASAKI, JAPAN. AT THE LARGEST HOSPITAL IN HIROSHIMA, MOST OF THE DOCTORS AND NURSES WERE DEAD. 10,000 PATIENTS ARRIVED, STEPPING OVER CORPSES IN SEARCH OF HELP.
THE DOCTORS DISPOSED OF THE PILES OF DEAD BY CREMATING THE CORPSES. X-RAY FILM, EXPOSED BY THE BOMB'S BLAST, WAS DISCARDED AND THE REMAINING ENVELOPES WERE USED TO STORE THE ASHES OF THE DEAD. THE ENVELOPES WERE LABELED AND STACKED NEAR A MAKESHIFT RELIGIOUS SHRINE.
AS THE DAYS PASSED, STARVING SURVIVORS RAIDED LOCAL GARDENS. THEY COLLECTED BOMB-ROASTED PUMPKINS STILL ON THE VINE AND DUG UP POTATOES BAKED BY THE HEAT OF THE BLAST.

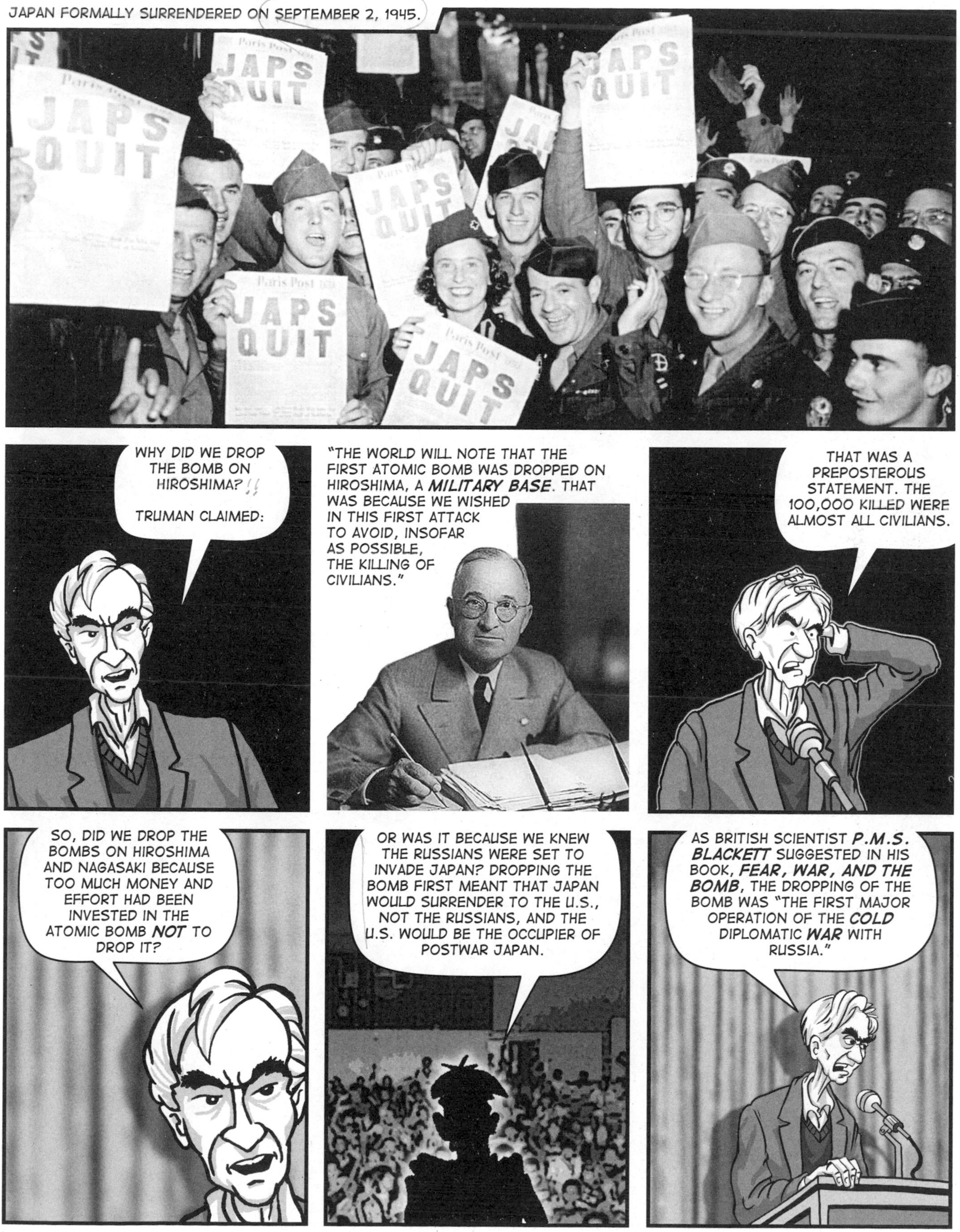
JAPAN FORMALLY SURRENDERED ON SEPTEMBER 2, 1945.
Paris Post JAPS QUIT
WHY DID WE DROP THE BOMB ON HIROSHIMA?!! TRUMAN CLAIMED:
"THE WORLD WILL NOTE THAT THE FIRST ATOMIC BOMB WAS DROPPED ON HIROSHIMA, A MILITARY BASE. THAT WAS BECAUSE WE WISHED IN THIS FIRST ATTACK TO AVOID, INSOFAR AS POSSIBLE, THE KILLING OF CIVILIANS."
THAT WAS A PREPOSTEROUS STATEMENT. THE 100,000 KILLED WERE ALMOST ALL CIVILIANS.
SO, DID WE DROP THE BOMBS ON HIROSHIMA AND NAGASAKI BECAUSE TOO MUCH MONEY AND EFFORT HAD BEEN INVESTED IN THE ATOMIC BOMB NOT TO DROP IT?
OR WAS IT BECAUSE WE KNEW THE RUSSIANS WERE SET TO INVADE JAPAN? DROPPING THE BOMB FIRST MEANT THAT JAPAN WOULD SURRENDER TO THE U.S., NOT THE RUSSIANS, AND THE U.S. WOULD BE THE OCCUPIER OF POSTWAR JAPAN.
AS BRITISH SCIENTIST P.M.S. BLACKETT SUGGESTED IN HIS BOOK, FEAR, WAR, AND THE BOMB, THE DROPPING OF THE BOMB WAS "THE FIRST MAJOR OPERATION OF THE COLD DIPLOMATIC WAR WITH RUSSIA."

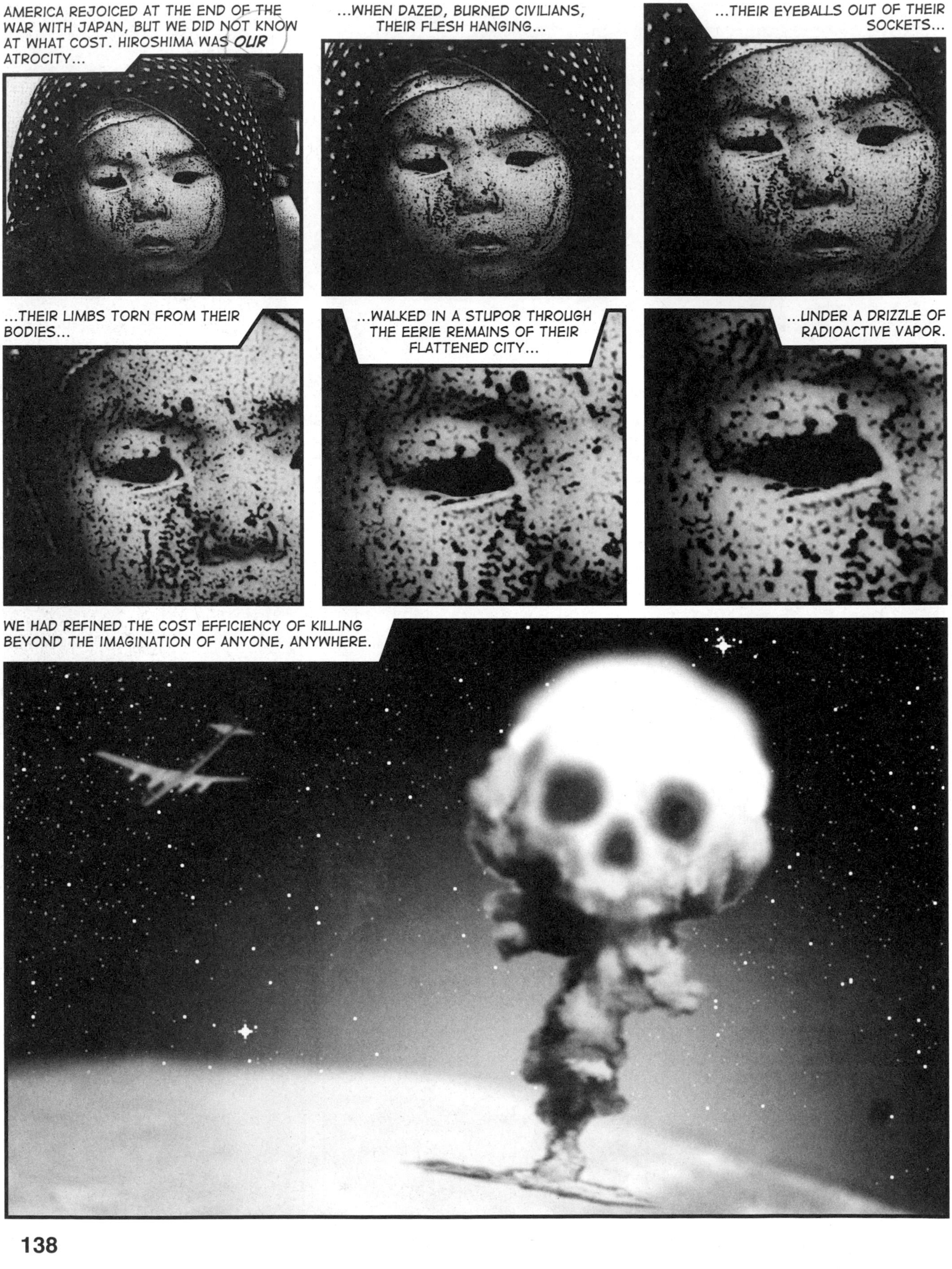
AMERICA REJOICED AT THE END OF THE WAR WITH JAPAN, BUT WE DID NOT KNOW AT WHAT COST. HIROSHIMA WAS *OUR* ATROCITY...
...WHEN DAZED, BURNED CIVILIANS, THEIR FLESH HANGING...
...THEIR EYEBALLS OUT OF THEIR SOCKETS...
...THEIR LIMBS TORN FROM THEIR BODIES...
...WALKED IN A STUPOR THROUGH THE EERIE REMAINS OF THEIR FLATTENED CITY...
...UNDER A DRIZZLE OF RADIOACTIVE VAPOR.
WE HAD REFINED THE COST EFFICIENCY OF KILLING BEYOND THE IMAGINATION OF ANYONE, ANYWHERE.

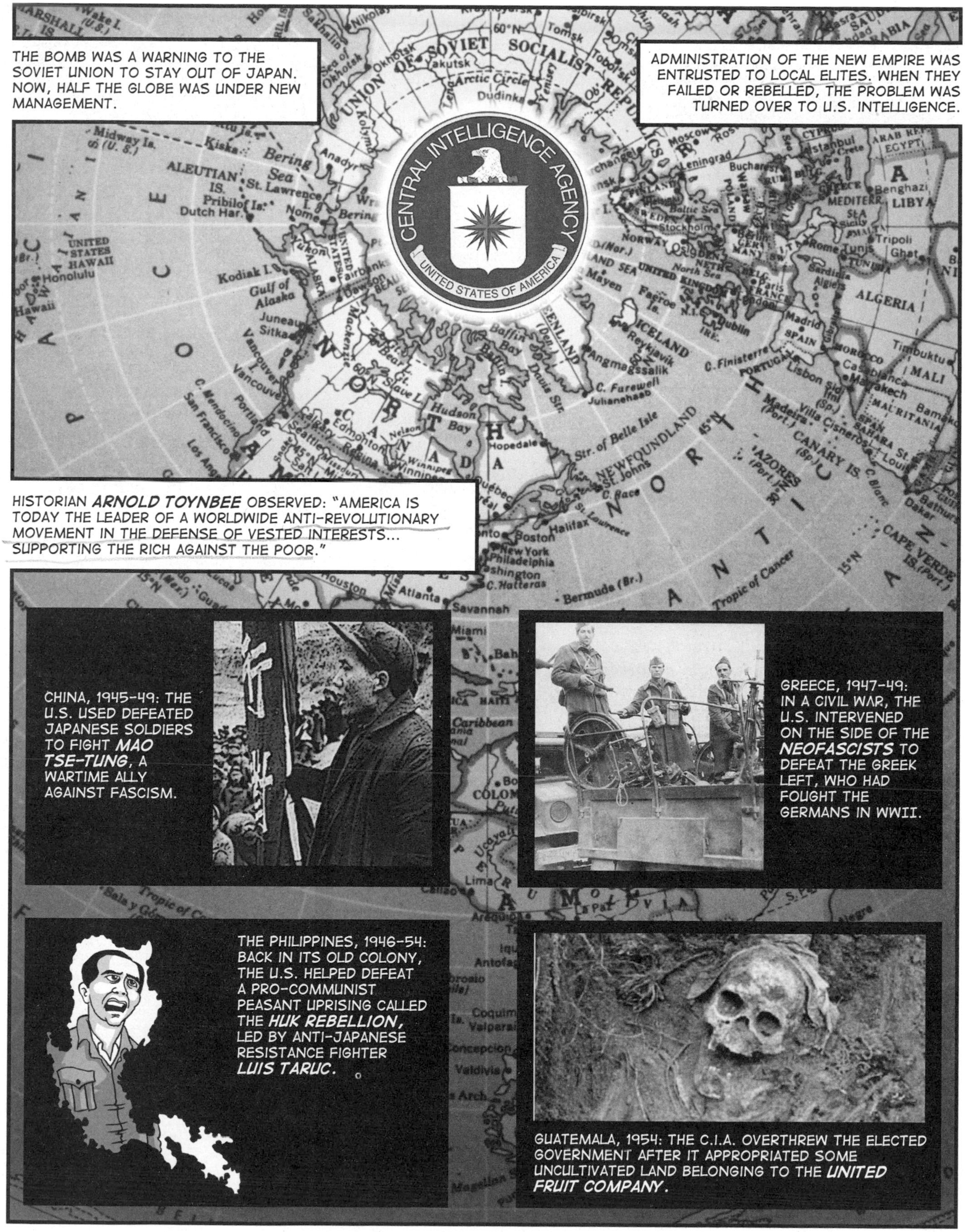
THE BOMB WAS A WARNING TO THE SOVIET UNION TO STAY OUT OF JAPAN. NOW, HALF THE GLOBE WAS UNDER NEW MANAGEMENT.
ADMINISTRATION OF THE NEW EMPIRE WAS ENTRUSTED TO LOCAL ELITES. WHEN THEY FAILED OR REBELLED, THE PROBLEM WAS TURNED OVER TO U.S. INTELLIGENCE.
CENTRAL INTELLIGENCE AGENCY
UNITED STATES OF AMERICA
HISTORIAN ARNOLD TOYNBEE OBSERVED: "AMERICA IS TODAY THE LEADER OF A WORLDWIDE ANTI-REVOLUTIONARY MOVEMENT IN THE DEFENSE OF VESTED INTERESTS... SUPPORTING THE RICH AGAINST THE POOR."
CHINA, 1945-49: THE U.S. USED DEFEATED JAPANESE SOLDIERS TO FIGHT MAO TSE-TUNG, A WARTIME ALLY AGAINST FASCISM.
GREECE, 1947-49: IN A CIVIL WAR, THE U.S. INTERVENED ON THE SIDE OF THE NEOFASCISTS TO DEFEAT THE GREEK LEFT, WHO HAD FOUGHT THE GERMANS IN WWII.
THE PHILIPPINES, 1946-54: BACK IN ITS OLD COLONY, THE U.S. HELPED DEFEAT A PRO-COMMUNIST PEASANT UPRISING CALLED THE HUK REBELLION, LED BY ANTI-JAPANESE RESISTANCE FIGHTER LUIS TARUC.
GUATEMALA, 1954: THE C.I.A. OVERTHREW THE ELECTED GOVERNMENT AFTER IT APPROPRIATED SOME UNCULTIVATED LAND BELONGING TO THE UNITED FRUIT COMPANY.

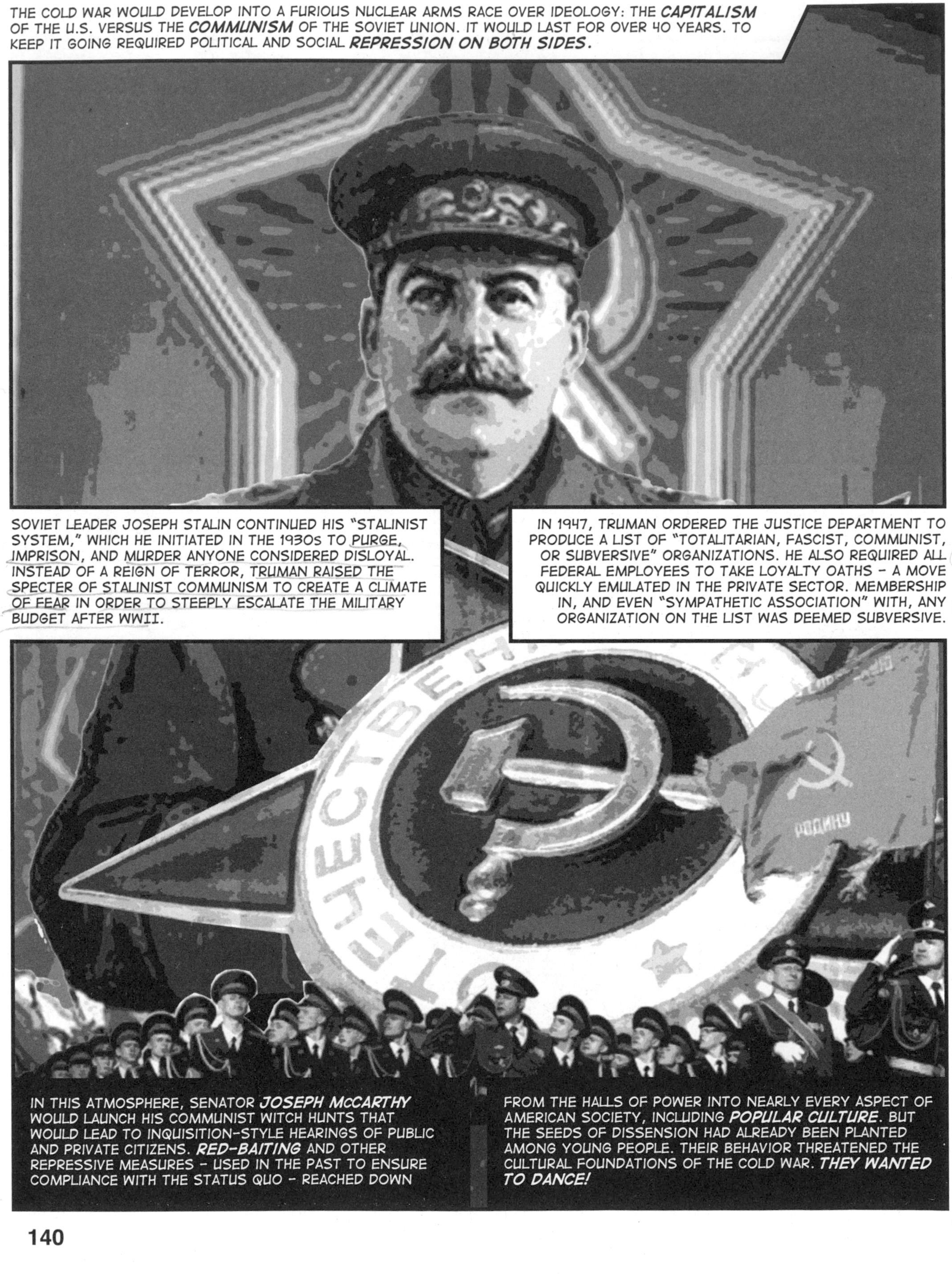
THE COLD WAR WOULD DEVELOP INTO A FURIOUS NUCLEAR ARMS RACE OVER IDEOLOGY: THE *CAPITALISM* OF THE U.S. VERSUS THE *COMMUNISM* OF THE SOVIET UNION. IT WOULD LAST FOR OVER 40 YEARS. TO KEEP IT GOING REQUIRED POLITICAL AND SOCIAL ***REPRESSION ON BOTH SIDES***.
SOVIET LEADER JOSEPH STALIN CONTINUED HIS "STALINIST SYSTEM," WHICH HE INITIATED IN THE 1930s TO PURGE, IMPRISON, AND MURDER ANYONE CONSIDERED DISLOYAL. INSTEAD OF A REIGN OF TERROR, TRUMAN RAISED THE SPECTER OF STALINIST COMMUNISM TO CREATE A CLIMATE OF FEAR IN ORDER TO STEEPLY ESCALATE THE MILITARY BUDGET AFTER WWII.
IN 1947, TRUMAN ORDERED THE JUSTICE DEPARTMENT TO PRODUCE A LIST OF "TOTALITARIAN, FASCIST, COMMUNIST, OR SUBVERSIVE" ORGANIZATIONS. HE ALSO REQUIRED ALL FEDERAL EMPLOYEES TO TAKE LOYALTY OATHS - A MOVE QUICKLY EMULATED IN THE PRIVATE SECTOR. MEMBERSHIP IN, AND EVEN "SYMPATHETIC ASSOCIATION" WITH, ANY ORGANIZATION ON THE LIST WAS DEEMED SUBVERSIVE.
РОДИНУ
IN THIS ATMOSPHERE, SENATOR ***JOSEPH McCARTHY*** WOULD LAUNCH HIS COMMUNIST WITCH HUNTS THAT WOULD LEAD TO INQUISITION-STYLE HEARINGS OF PUBLIC AND PRIVATE CITIZENS. ***RED-BAITING*** AND OTHER REPRESSIVE MEASURES - USED IN THE PAST TO ENSURE COMPLIANCE WITH THE STATUS QUO - REACHED DOWN
FROM THE HALLS OF POWER INTO NEARLY EVERY ASPECT OF AMERICAN SOCIETY, INCLUDING ***POPULAR CULTURE***. BUT THE SEEDS OF DISSENSION HAD ALREADY BEEN PLANTED AMONG YOUNG PEOPLE. THEIR BEHAVIOR THREATENED THE CULTURAL FOUNDATIONS OF THE COLD WAR. ***THEY WANTED TO DANCE!***

Chapter VII

The Cool War

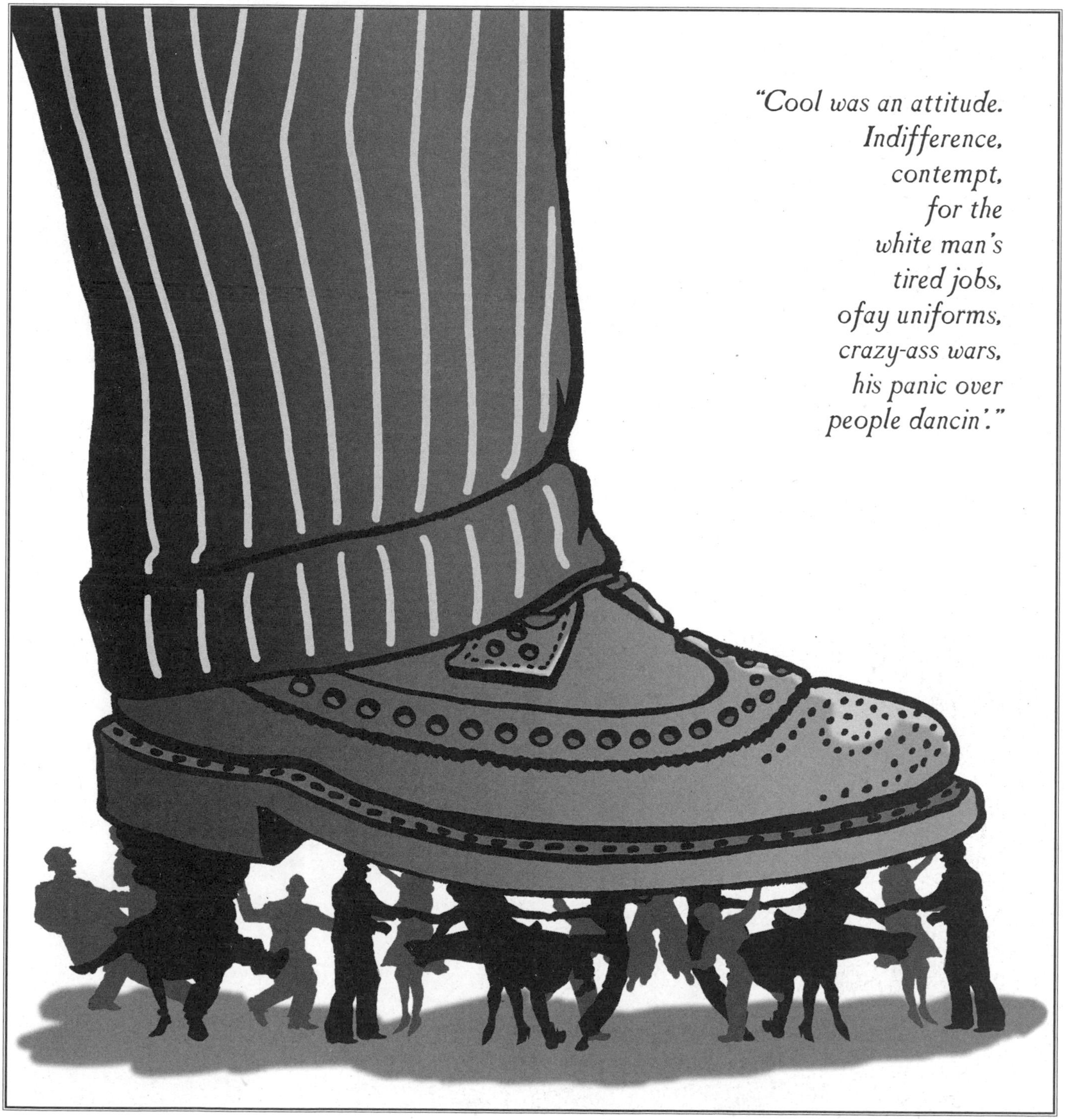

"Cool was an attitude.
Indifference,
contempt,
for the
white man's
tired jobs,
ofay uniforms,
crazy-ass wars,
his panic over
people dancin'."

The Jitterbug Riot

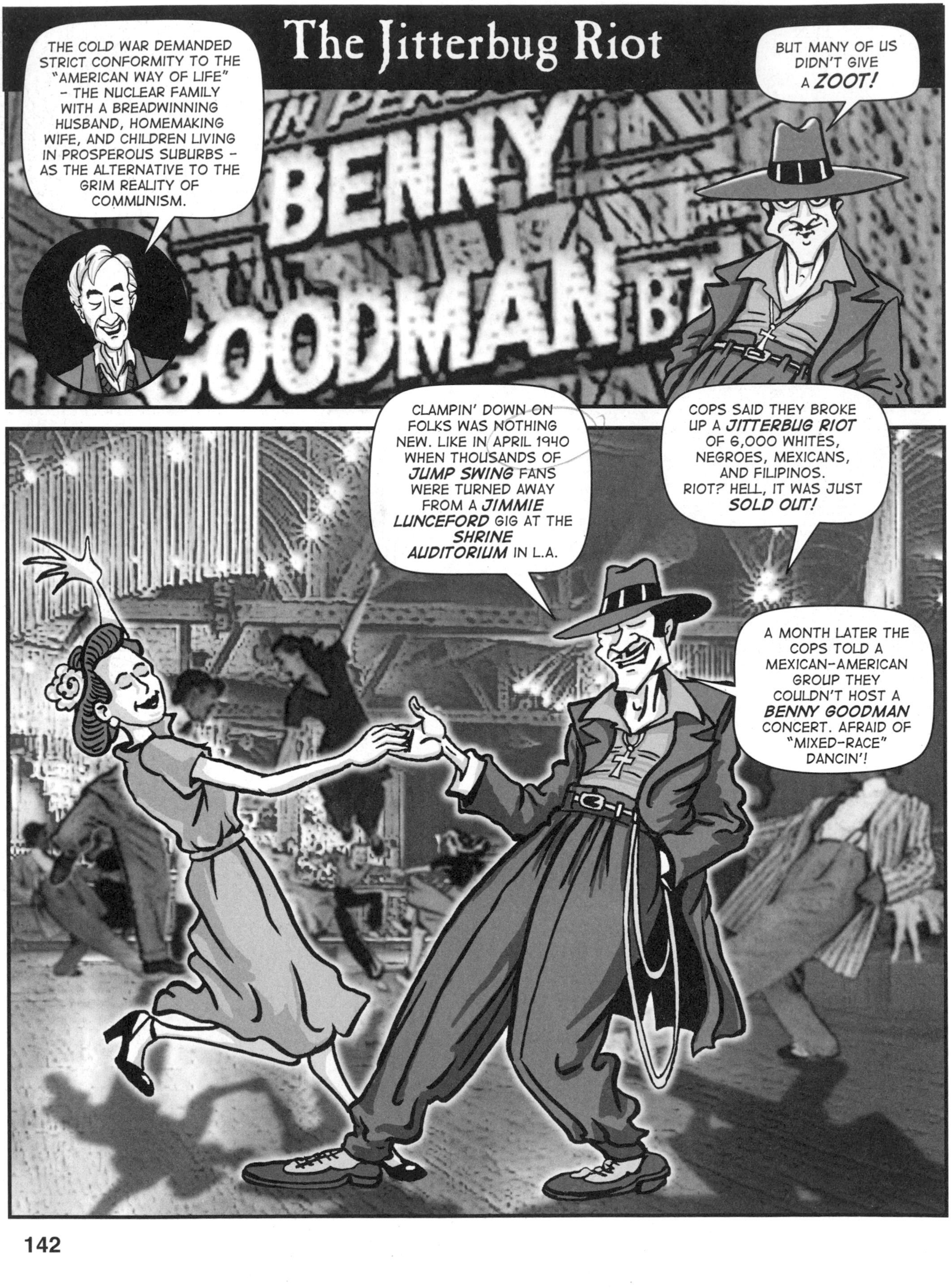
THE COLD WAR DEMANDED STRICT CONFORMITY TO THE "AMERICAN WAY OF LIFE" – THE NUCLEAR FAMILY WITH A BREADWINNING HUSBAND, HOMEMAKING WIFE, AND CHILDREN LIVING IN PROSPEROUS SUBURBS – AS THE ALTERNATIVE TO THE GRIM REALITY OF COMMUNISM.
BUT MANY OF US DIDN'T GIVE A ZOOT!
BENNY GOODMAN
CLAMPIN' DOWN ON FOLKS WAS NOTHING NEW. LIKE IN APRIL 1940 WHEN THOUSANDS OF JUMP SWING FANS WERE TURNED AWAY FROM A JIMMIE LUNCEFORD GIG AT THE SHRINE AUDITORIUM IN L.A.
COPS SAID THEY BROKE UP A JITTERBUG RIOT OF 6,000 WHITES, NEGROES, MEXICANS, AND FILIPINOS. RIOT? HELL, IT WAS JUST SOLD OUT!
A MONTH LATER THE COPS TOLD A MEXICAN-AMERICAN GROUP THEY COULDN'T HOST A BENNY GOODMAN CONCERT. AFRAID OF "MIXED-RACE" DANCIN'!

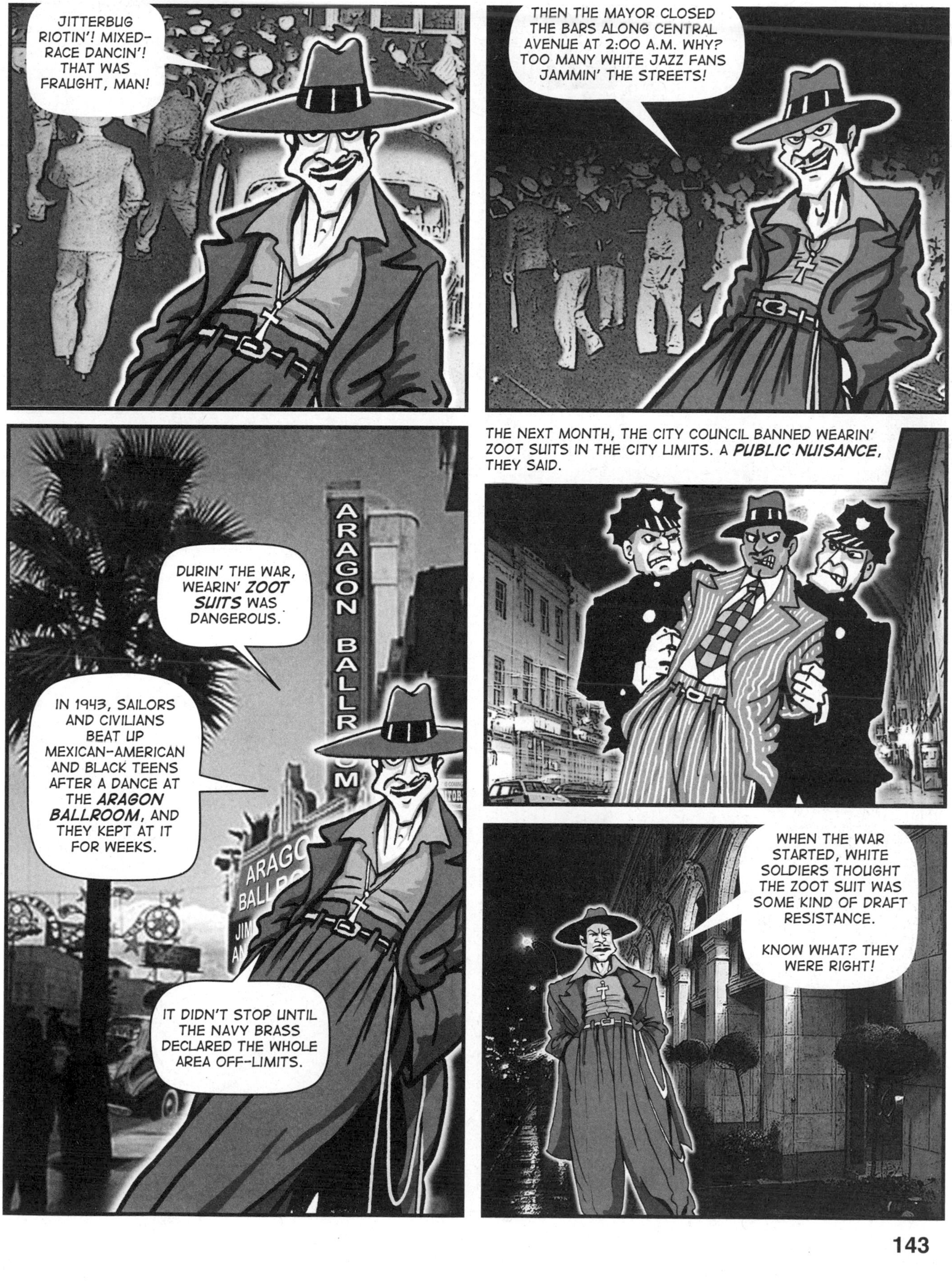
JITTERBUG RIOTIN'! MIXED-RACE DANCIN'! THAT WAS FRAUGHT, MAN!
THEN THE MAYOR CLOSED THE BARS ALONG CENTRAL AVENUE AT 2:00 A.M. WHY? TOO MANY WHITE JAZZ FANS JAMMIN' THE STREETS!
DURIN' THE WAR, WEARIN' ZOOT SUITS WAS DANGEROUS.
IN 1943, SAILORS AND CIVILIANS BEAT UP MEXICAN-AMERICAN AND BLACK TEENS AFTER A DANCE AT THE ARAGON BALLROOM, AND THEY KEPT AT IT FOR WEEKS.
IT DIDN'T STOP UNTIL THE NAVY BRASS DECLARED THE WHOLE AREA OFF-LIMITS.
ARAGON BALLROOM
THE NEXT MONTH, THE CITY COUNCIL BANNED WEARIN' ZOOT SUITS IN THE CITY LIMITS. A PUBLIC NUISANCE, THEY SAID.
WHEN THE WAR STARTED, WHITE SOLDIERS THOUGHT THE ZOOT SUIT WAS SOME KIND OF DRAFT RESISTANCE.
KNOW WHAT? THEY WERE RIGHT!

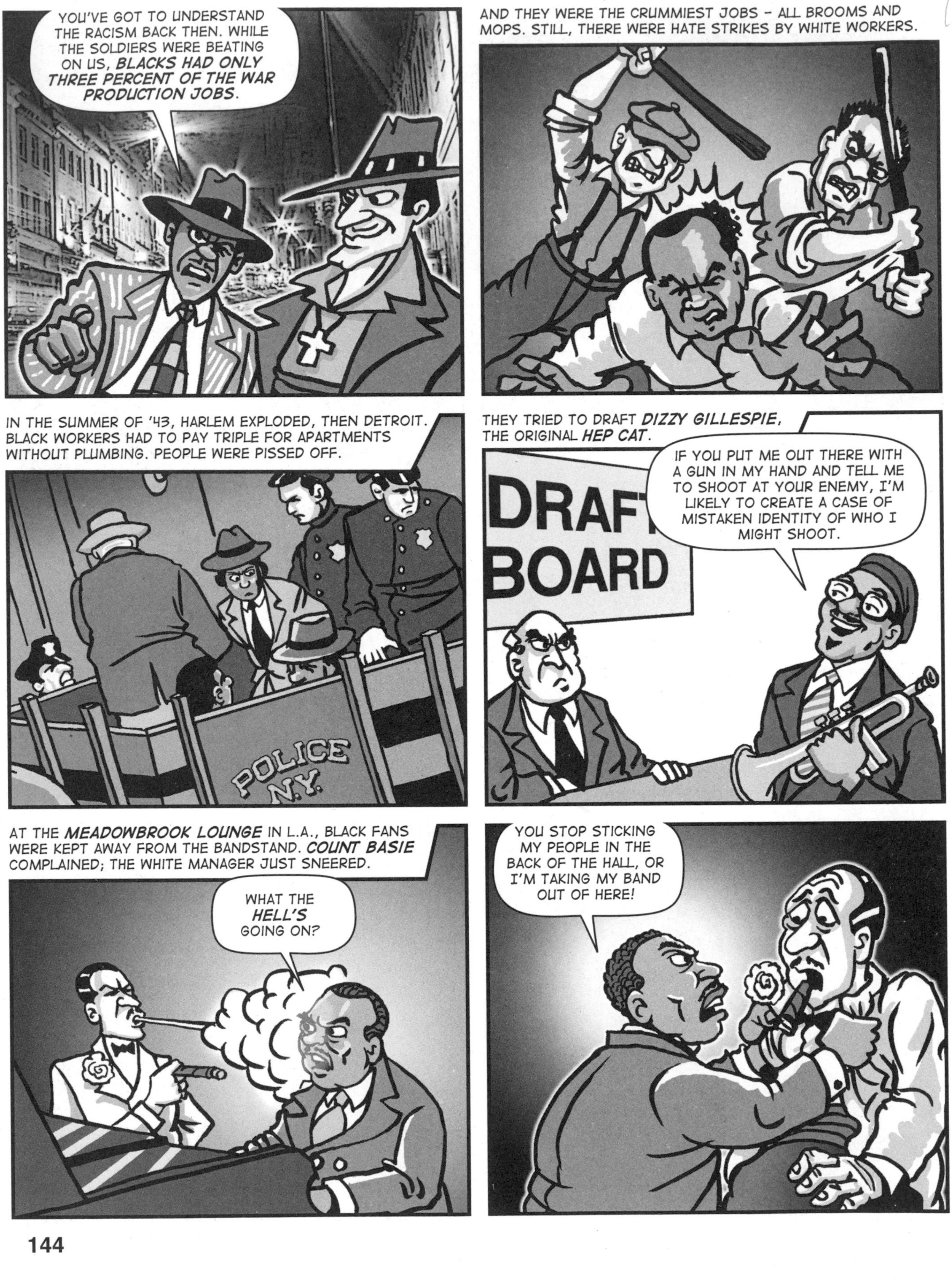
YOU'VE GOT TO UNDERSTAND THE RACISM BACK THEN. WHILE THE SOLDIERS WERE BEATING ON US, ***BLACKS HAD ONLY THREE PERCENT OF THE WAR PRODUCTION JOBS.***
AND THEY WERE THE CRUMMIEST JOBS - ALL BROOMS AND MOPS. STILL, THERE WERE HATE STRIKES BY WHITE WORKERS.
IN THE SUMMER OF '43, HARLEM EXPLODED, THEN DETROIT. BLACK WORKERS HAD TO PAY TRIPLE FOR APARTMENTS WITHOUT PLUMBING. PEOPLE WERE PISSED OFF.
POLICE N.Y.
THEY TRIED TO DRAFT ***DIZZY GILLESPIE***, THE ORIGINAL ***HEP CAT***.
DRAFT BOARD
IF YOU PUT ME OUT THERE WITH A GUN IN MY HAND AND TELL ME TO SHOOT AT YOUR ENEMY, I'M LIKELY TO CREATE A CASE OF MISTAKEN IDENTITY OF WHO I MIGHT SHOOT.
AT THE ***MEADOWBROOK LOUNGE*** IN L.A., BLACK FANS WERE KEPT AWAY FROM THE BANDSTAND. ***COUNT BASIE*** COMPLAINED; THE WHITE MANAGER JUST SNEERED.
WHAT THE ***HELL'S*** GOING ON?
YOU STOP STICKING MY PEOPLE IN THE BACK OF THE HALL, OR I'M TAKING MY BAND OUT OF HERE!

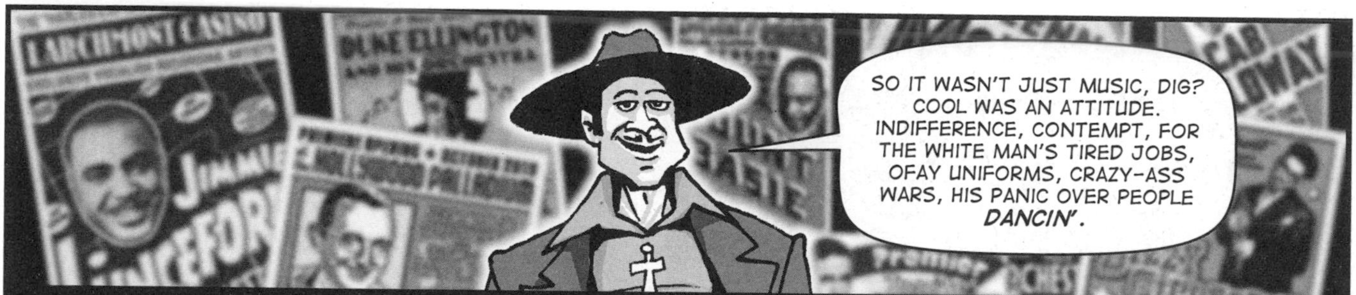
LARCHMONT CASINO
DUKE ELLINGTON
JIMMIE LUNCEFORD
SO IT WASN'T JUST MUSIC, DIG? COOL WAS AN ATTITUDE. INDIFFERENCE, CONTEMPT, FOR THE WHITE MAN'S TIRED JOBS, OFAY UNIFORMS, CRAZY-ASS WARS, HIS PANIC OVER PEOPLE ***DANCIN'***.

ZINNformation IN 2004, HISTORIAN ANTHONY MACIAS OBSERVED THAT ***BLACK SOCIAL DANCING CIRCULATED SOCIAL ENERGY***. THAT'S JUST WHAT THE WHITE URBAN ELITE OF EARLY 1940s LOS ANGELES FEARED. THE CITY CREATED THE ***BUREAU OF MUSIC*** TO "BRING PROPER MUSIC TO THE PEOPLE."

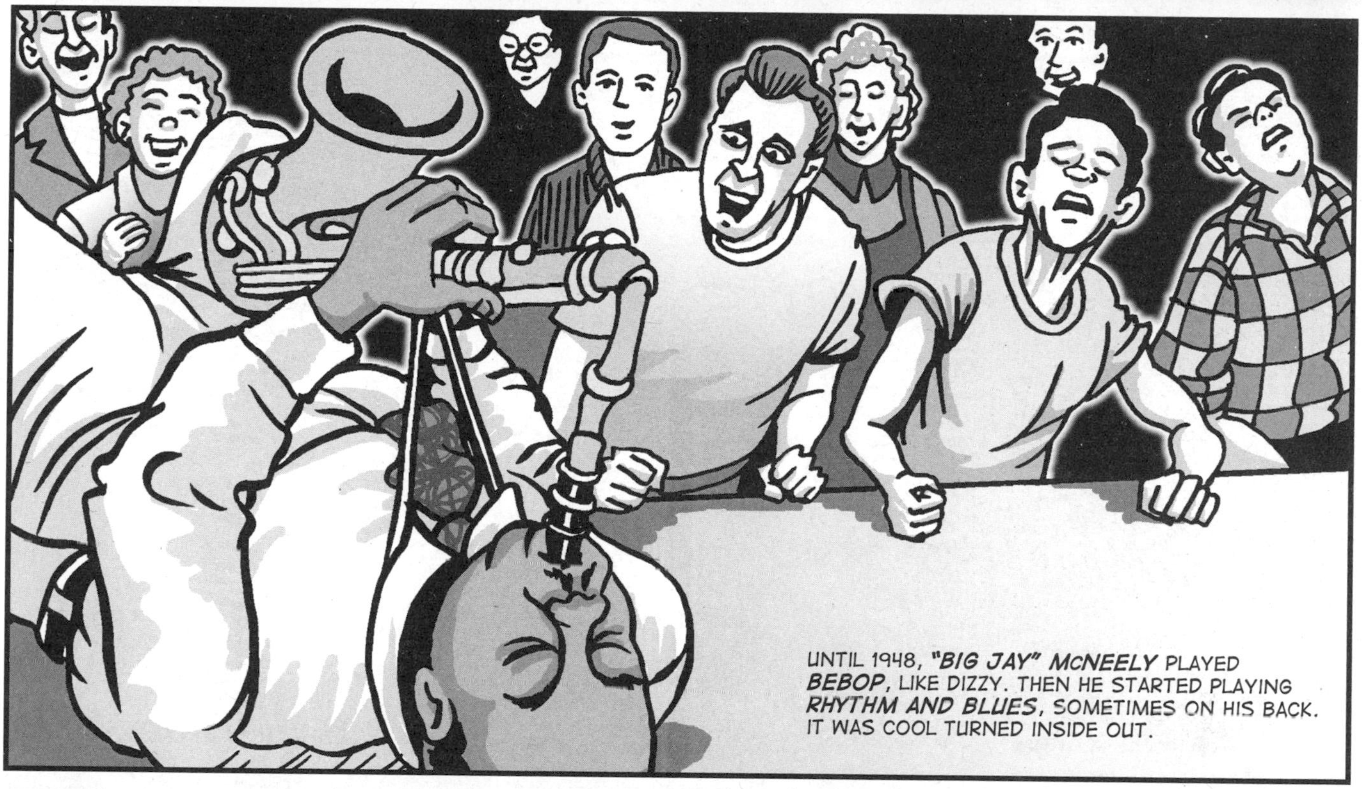
UNTIL 1948, ***"BIG JAY" McNEELY*** PLAYED ***BEBOP***, LIKE DIZZY. THEN HE STARTED PLAYING ***RHYTHM AND BLUES***, SOMETIMES ON HIS BACK. IT WAS COOL TURNED INSIDE OUT.

ONE NIGHT IN SAN DIEGO, BIG JAY PLAYED HIS SAX WHILE WALKING ACROSS THE BAR...

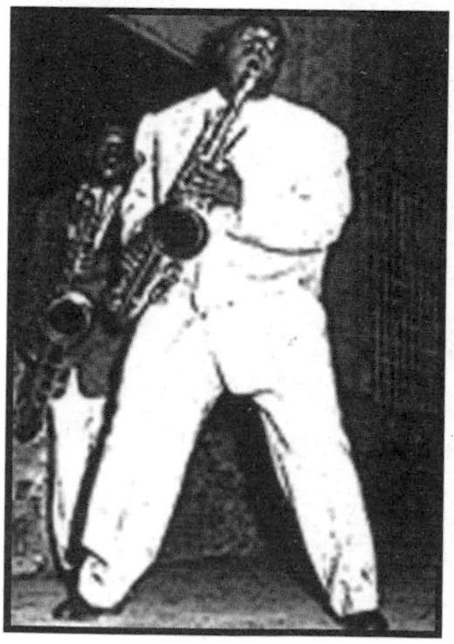

...OUT THE DOOR AND INTO THE STREET.

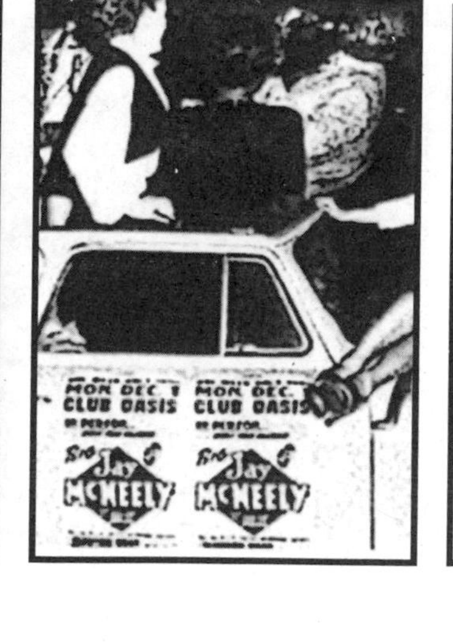
MON. DEC.
CLUB OASIS
JAY McNEELY
MON. DEC.
CLUB OASIS
JAY McNEELY

THE COPS ARRESTED HIM FOR DISTURBING THE PEACE AND BOOKED HIM DOWNTOWN.

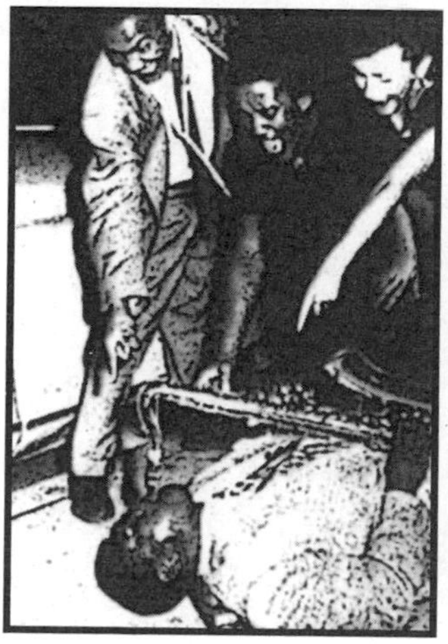

THE BAND KEPT PLAYING UNTIL SOMEONE RAN DOWN TO POST BIG JAY'S BAIL AND BRING HIM BACK TO FINISH HIS SOLO.

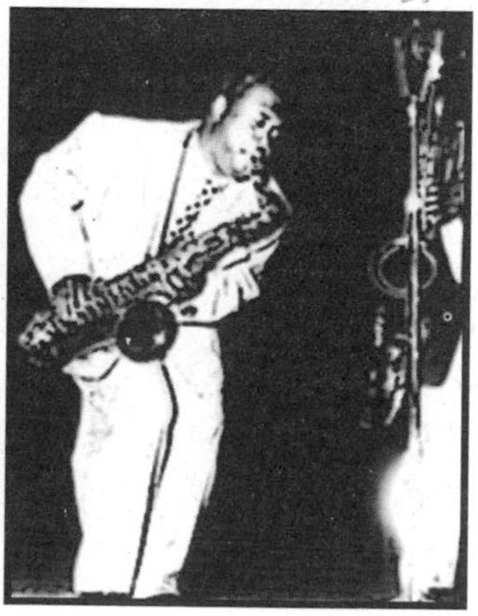

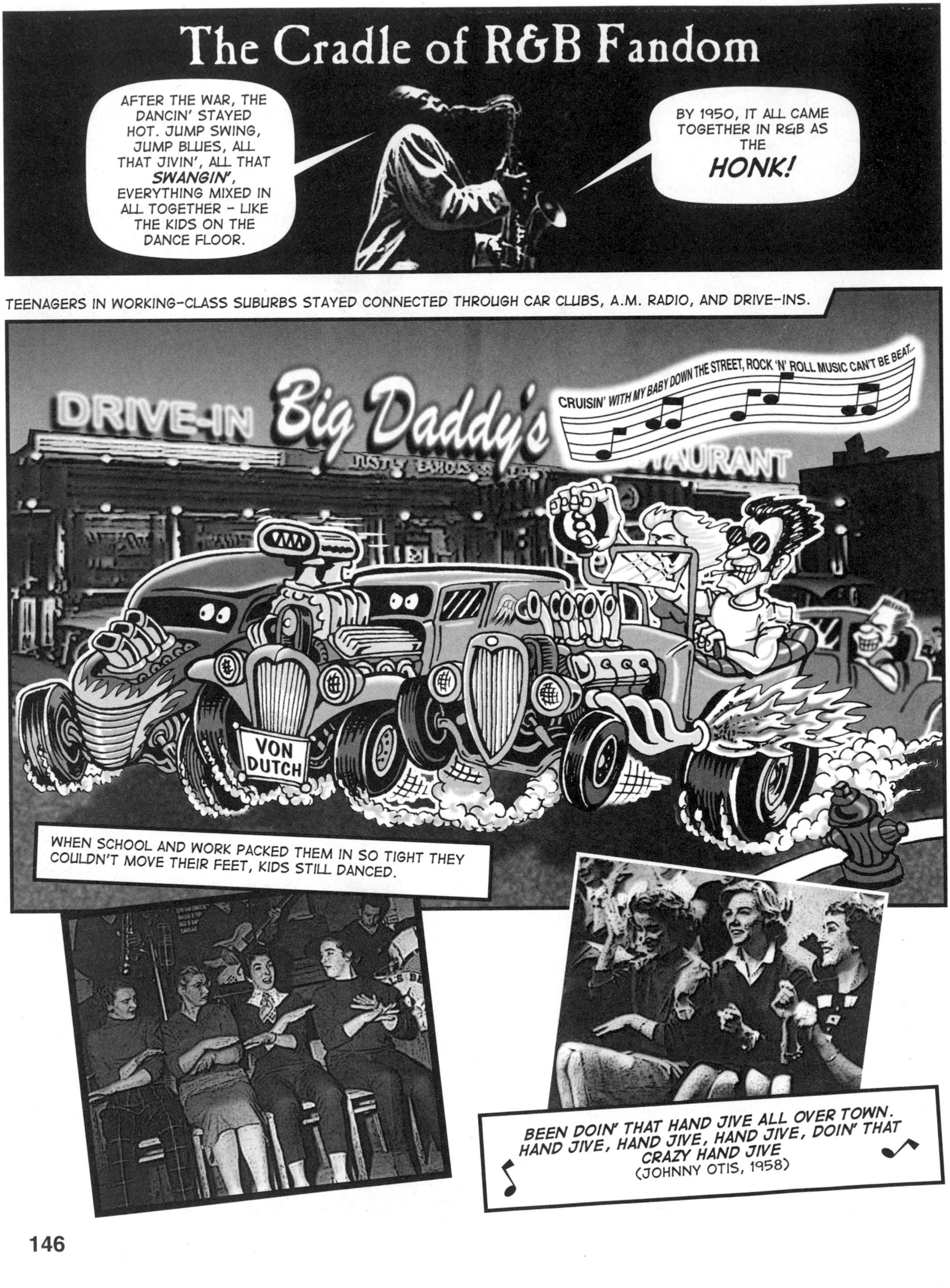

The Cradle of R&B Fandom
AFTER THE WAR, THE DANCIN' STAYED HOT. JUMP SWING, JUMP BLUES, ALL THAT JIVIN', ALL THAT ***SWANGIN'***, EVERYTHING MIXED IN ALL TOGETHER – LIKE THE KIDS ON THE DANCE FLOOR.
BY 1950, IT ALL CAME TOGETHER IN R&B AS THE ***HONK!***
TEENAGERS IN WORKING-CLASS SUBURBS STAYED CONNECTED THROUGH CAR CLUBS, A.M. RADIO, AND DRIVE-INS.
DRIVE-IN
Big Daddy's
CRUISIN' WITH MY BABY DOWN THE STREET, ROCK 'N' ROLL MUSIC CAN'T BE BEAT...
VON DUTCH
WHEN SCHOOL AND WORK PACKED THEM IN SO TIGHT THEY COULDN'T MOVE THEIR FEET, KIDS STILL DANCED.
BEEN DOIN' THAT HAND JIVE ALL OVER TOWN. HAND JIVE, HAND JIVE, HAND JIVE, DOIN' THAT CRAZY HAND JIVE
(JOHNNY OTIS, 1958)

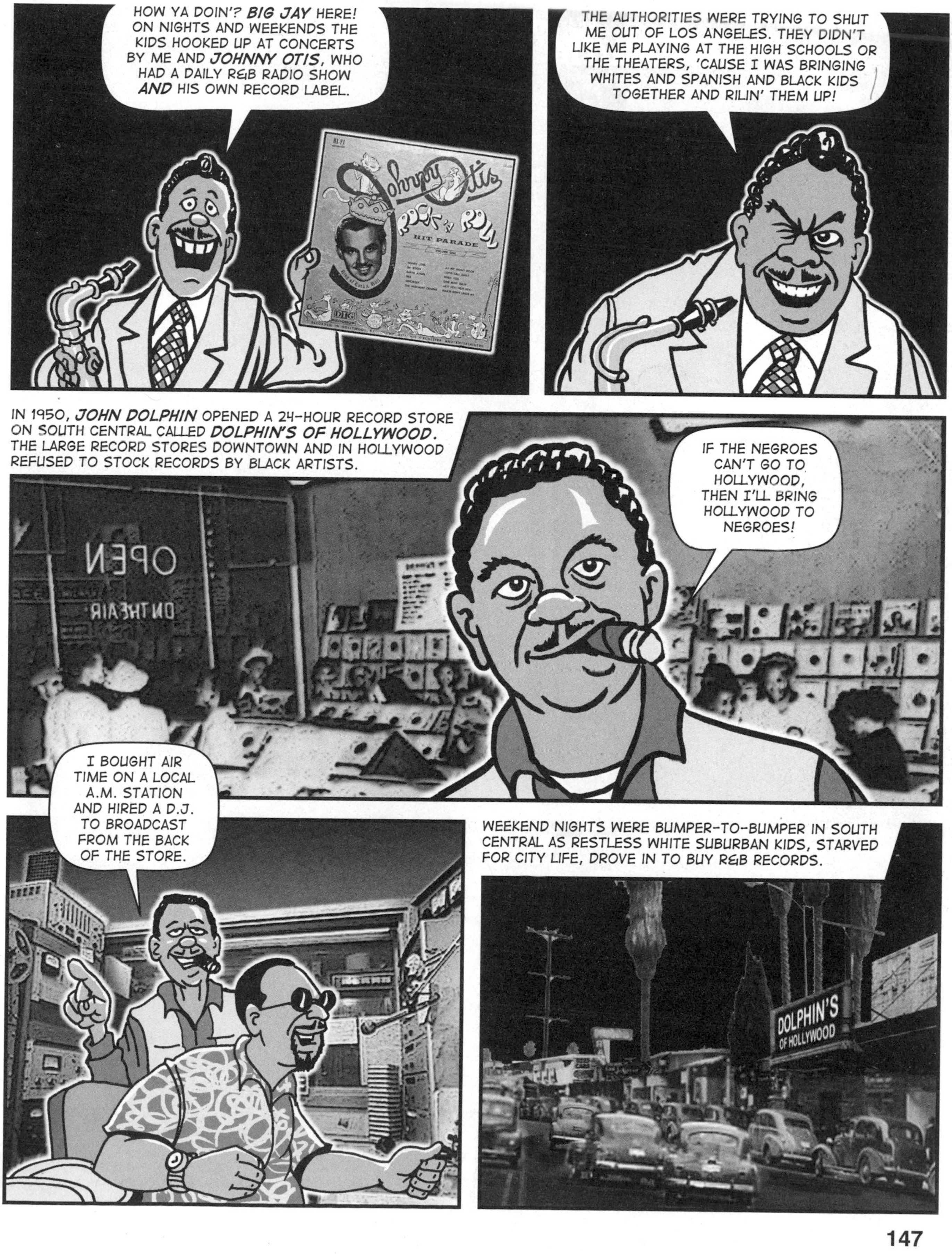
HOW YA DOIN'? **BIG JAY** HERE! ON NIGHTS AND WEEKENDS THE KIDS HOOKED UP AT CONCERTS BY ME AND **JOHNNY OTIS**, WHO HAD A DAILY R&B RADIO SHOW **AND** HIS OWN RECORD LABEL.
Johnny Otis
ROCK 'n' ROLL
HIT PARADE
THE AUTHORITIES WERE TRYING TO SHUT ME OUT OF LOS ANGELES. THEY DIDN'T LIKE ME PLAYING AT THE HIGH SCHOOLS OR THE THEATERS, 'CAUSE I WAS BRINGING WHITES AND SPANISH AND BLACK KIDS TOGETHER AND RILIN' THEM UP!
IN 1950, **JOHN DOLPHIN** OPENED A 24-HOUR RECORD STORE ON SOUTH CENTRAL CALLED **DOLPHIN'S OF HOLLYWOOD.** THE LARGE RECORD STORES DOWNTOWN AND IN HOLLYWOOD REFUSED TO STOCK RECORDS BY BLACK ARTISTS.
OPEN
ON THE AIR
IF THE NEGROES CAN'T GO TO HOLLYWOOD, THEN I'LL BRING HOLLYWOOD TO NEGROES!
I BOUGHT AIR TIME ON A LOCAL A.M. STATION AND HIRED A D.J. TO BROADCAST FROM THE BACK OF THE STORE.
WEEKEND NIGHTS WERE BUMPER-TO-BUMPER IN SOUTH CENTRAL AS RESTLESS WHITE SUBURBAN KIDS, STARVED FOR CITY LIFE, DROVE IN TO BUY R&B RECORDS.
DOLPHIN'S
OF HOLLYWOOD

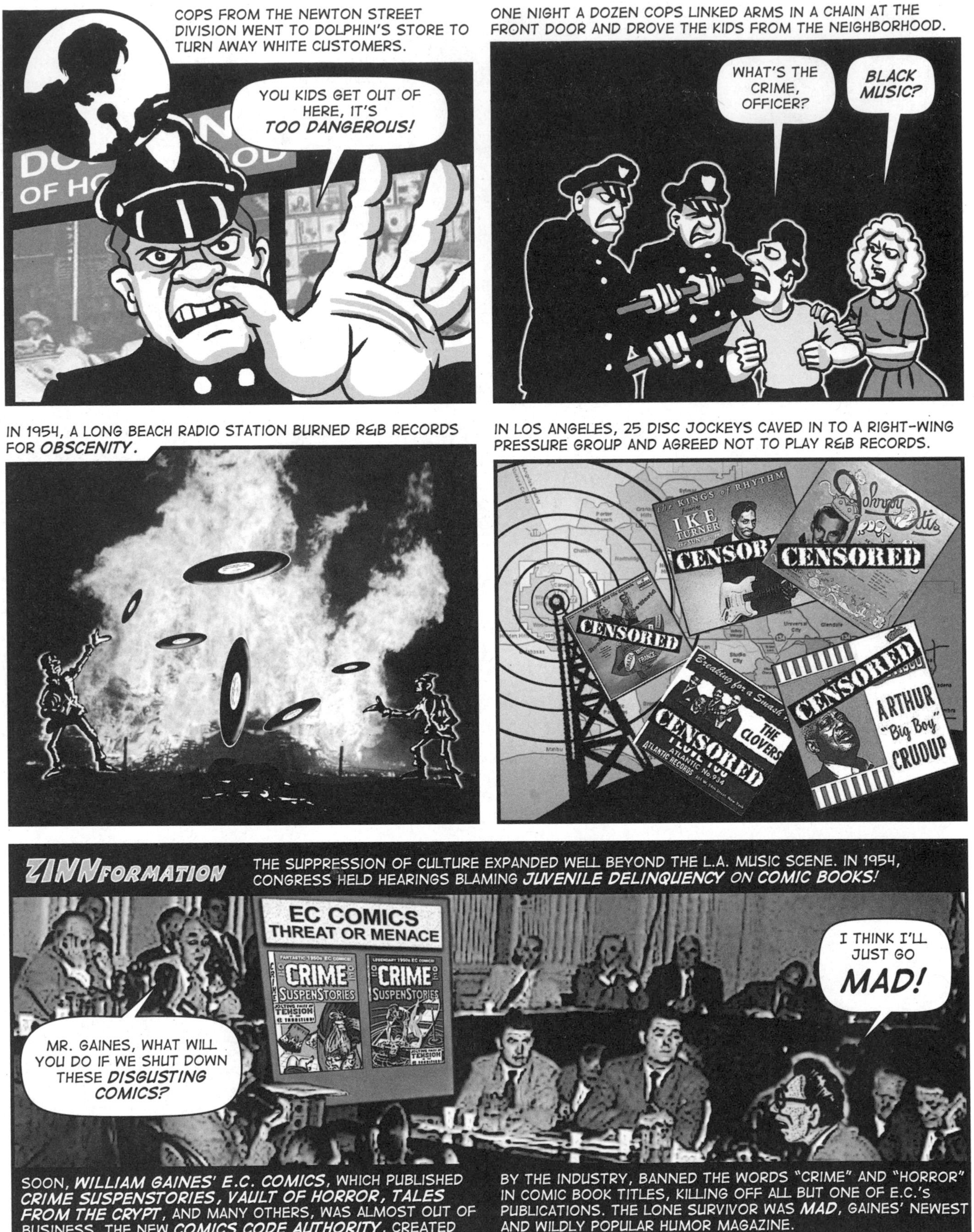
COPS FROM THE NEWTON STREET DIVISION WENT TO DOLPHIN'S STORE TO TURN AWAY WHITE CUSTOMERS.
YOU KIDS GET OUT OF HERE, IT'S *TOO DANGEROUS!*
ONE NIGHT A DOZEN COPS LINKED ARMS IN A CHAIN AT THE FRONT DOOR AND DROVE THE KIDS FROM THE NEIGHBORHOOD.
WHAT'S THE CRIME, OFFICER?
BLACK MUSIC?
IN 1954, A LONG BEACH RADIO STATION BURNED R&B RECORDS FOR *OBSCENITY.*
IN LOS ANGELES, 25 DISC JOCKEYS CAVED IN TO A RIGHT-WING PRESSURE GROUP AND AGREED NOT TO PLAY R&B RECORDS.
the KINGS of RHYTHM
IKE TURNER
CENSORED
CENSORED
CENSORED
Breaking for a Smash
THE CLOVERS
CENSORED
ATLANTIC No. 934
ATLANTIC RECORDS
CENSORED
ARTHUR "Big Boy" CRUDUP
ZINNFORMATION
THE SUPPRESSION OF CULTURE EXPANDED WELL BEYOND THE L.A. MUSIC SCENE. IN 1954, CONGRESS HELD HEARINGS BLAMING *JUVENILE DELINQUENCY* ON *COMIC BOOKS!*
EC COMICS THREAT OR MENACE
CRIME SUSPENSTORIES
CRIME SUSPENSTORIES
MR. GAINES, WHAT WILL YOU DO IF WE SHUT DOWN THESE *DISGUSTING COMICS?*
I THINK I'LL JUST GO *MAD!*
SOON, *WILLIAM GAINES' E.C. COMICS*, WHICH PUBLISHED *CRIME SUSPENSTORIES, VAULT OF HORROR, TALES FROM THE CRYPT*, AND MANY OTHERS, WAS ALMOST OUT OF BUSINESS. THE NEW *COMICS CODE AUTHORITY*, CREATED BY THE INDUSTRY, BANNED THE WORDS "CRIME" AND "HORROR" IN COMIC BOOK TITLES, KILLING OFF ALL BUT ONE OF E.C.'S PUBLICATIONS. THE LONE SURVIVOR WAS *MAD*, GAINES' NEWEST AND WILDLY POPULAR HUMOR MAGAZINE.

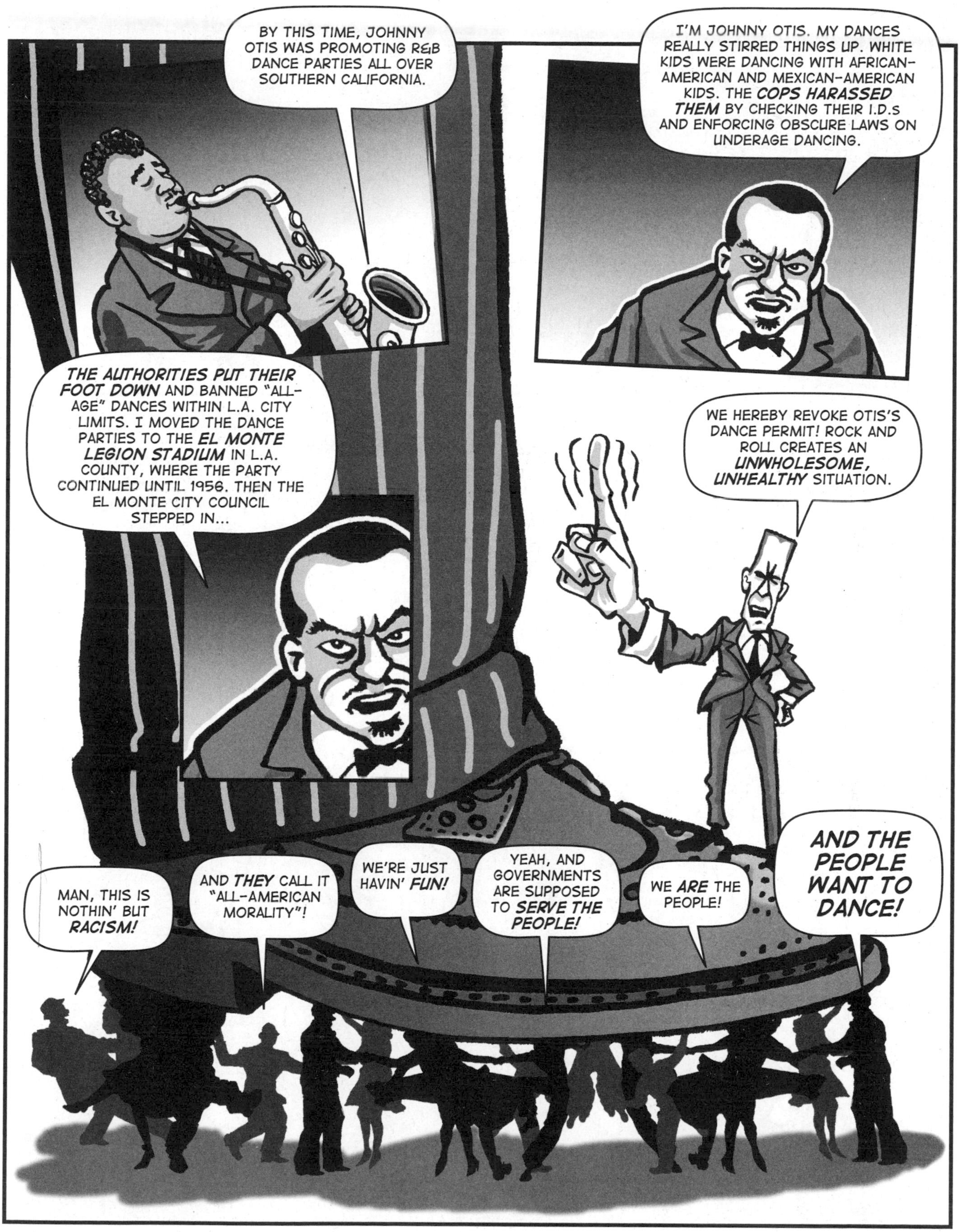
BY THIS TIME, JOHNNY OTIS WAS PROMOTING R&B DANCE PARTIES ALL OVER SOUTHERN CALIFORNIA.
I'M JOHNNY OTIS. MY DANCES REALLY STIRRED THINGS UP. WHITE KIDS WERE DANCING WITH AFRICAN-AMERICAN AND MEXICAN-AMERICAN KIDS. THE **COPS HARASSED THEM** BY CHECKING THEIR I.D.s AND ENFORCING OBSCURE LAWS ON UNDERAGE DANCING.
THE AUTHORITIES PUT THEIR FOOT DOWN AND BANNED "ALL-AGE" DANCES WITHIN L.A. CITY LIMITS. I MOVED THE DANCE PARTIES TO THE **EL MONTE LEGION STADIUM** IN L.A. COUNTY, WHERE THE PARTY CONTINUED UNTIL 1956. THEN THE EL MONTE CITY COUNCIL STEPPED IN...
WE HEREBY REVOKE OTIS'S DANCE PERMIT! ROCK AND ROLL CREATES AN ***UNWHOLESOME, UNHEALTHY*** SITUATION.
MAN, THIS IS NOTHIN' BUT ***RACISM!***
AND ***THEY*** CALL IT "ALL-AMERICAN MORALITY"!
WE'RE JUST HAVIN' ***FUN!***
YEAH, AND GOVERNMENTS ARE SUPPOSED TO ***SERVE THE PEOPLE!***
WE ***ARE*** THE PEOPLE!
AND THE PEOPLE WANT TO DANCE!

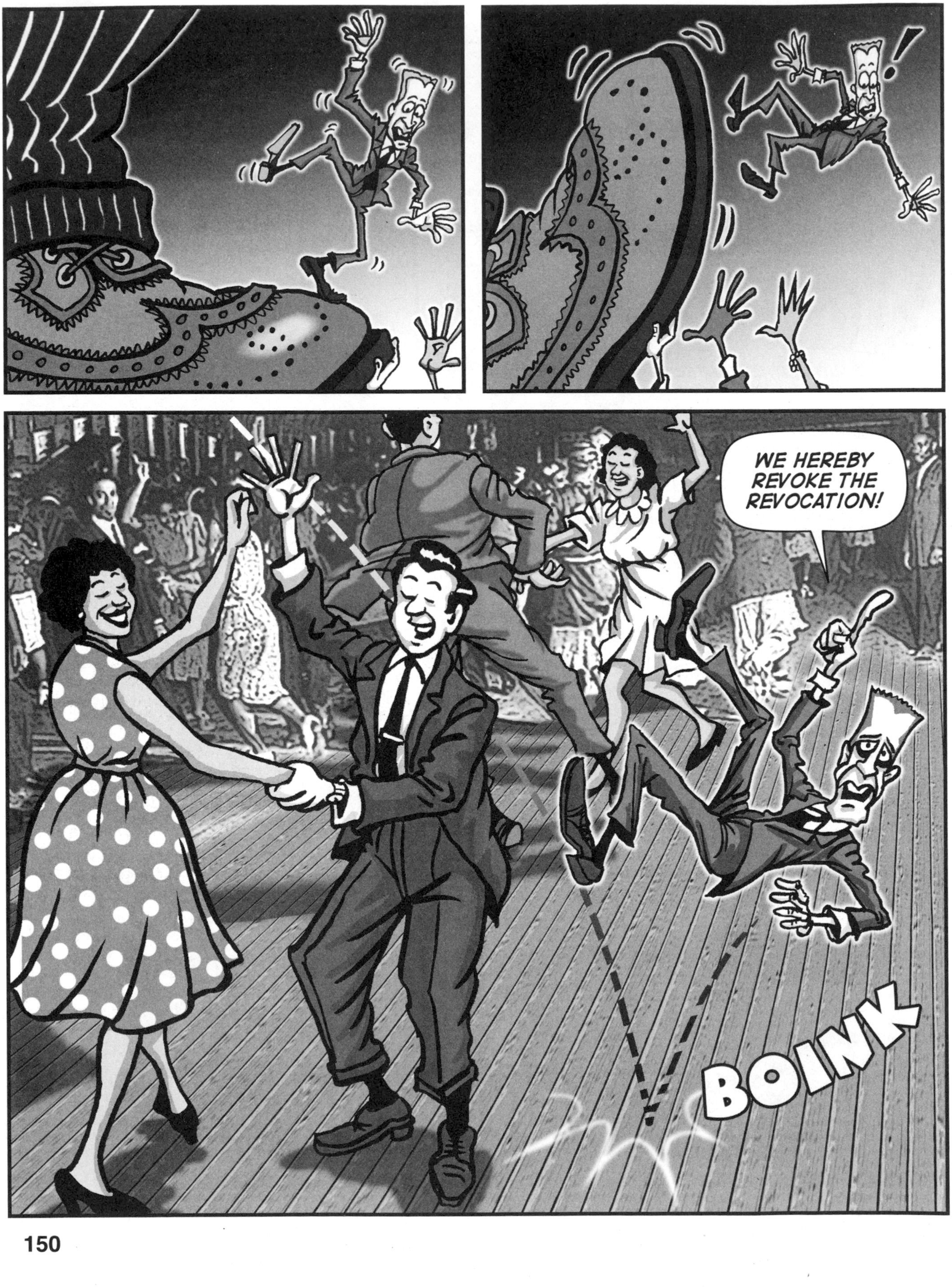
WE HEREBY REVOKE THE REVOCATION!
BOINK

Chapter VIII

Children of the Empire

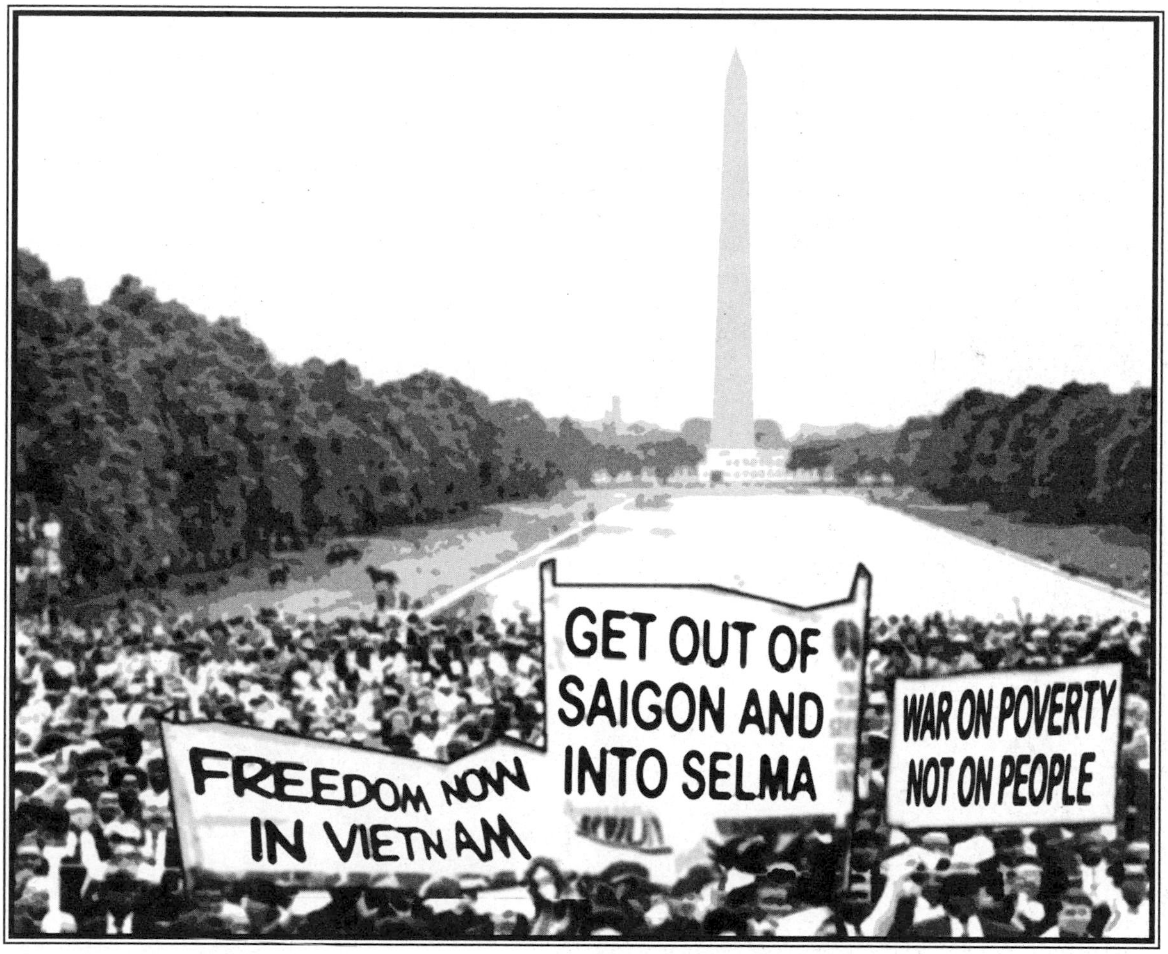
GET OUT OF
SAIGON AND
INTO SELMA
WAR ON POVERTY
NOT ON PEOPLE
FREEDOM NOW
IN VIETNAM

"Social progress is ignored when the guns of war become a national obsession. The bombs in Vietnam explode at home!"

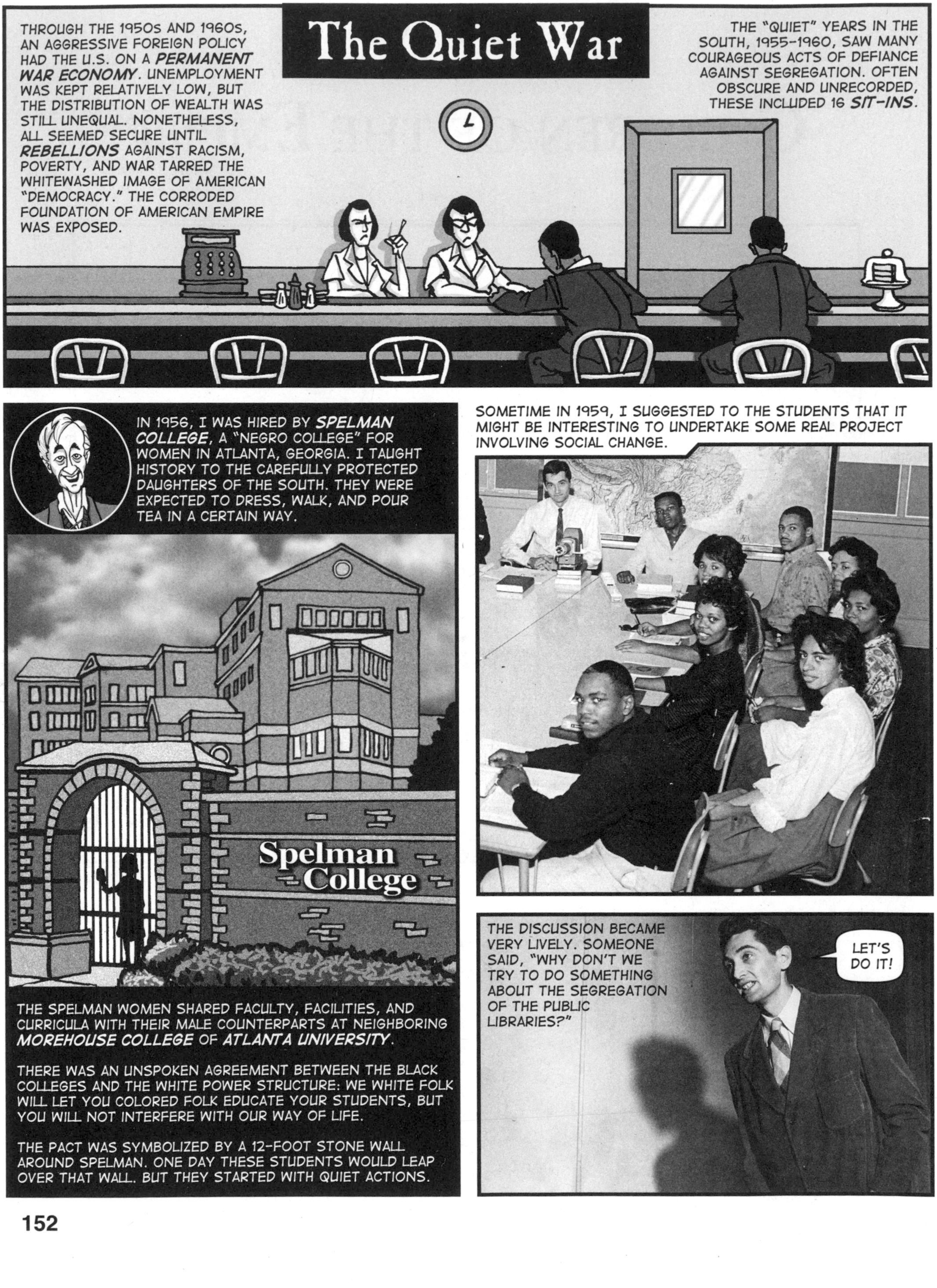
The Quiet War
THROUGH THE 1950s AND 1960s, AN AGGRESSIVE FOREIGN POLICY HAD THE U.S. ON A PERMANENT WAR ECONOMY. UNEMPLOYMENT WAS KEPT RELATIVELY LOW, BUT THE DISTRIBUTION OF WEALTH WAS STILL UNEQUAL. NONETHELESS, ALL SEEMED SECURE UNTIL REBELLIONS AGAINST RACISM, POVERTY, AND WAR TARRED THE WHITEWASHED IMAGE OF AMERICAN "DEMOCRACY." THE CORRODED FOUNDATION OF AMERICAN EMPIRE WAS EXPOSED.
THE "QUIET" YEARS IN THE SOUTH, 1955–1960, SAW MANY COURAGEOUS ACTS OF DEFIANCE AGAINST SEGREGATION. OFTEN OBSCURE AND UNRECORDED, THESE INCLUDED 16 SIT-INS.
IN 1956, I WAS HIRED BY SPELMAN COLLEGE, A "NEGRO COLLEGE" FOR WOMEN IN ATLANTA, GEORGIA. I TAUGHT HISTORY TO THE CAREFULLY PROTECTED DAUGHTERS OF THE SOUTH. THEY WERE EXPECTED TO DRESS, WALK, AND POUR TEA IN A CERTAIN WAY.
Spelman College
THE SPELMAN WOMEN SHARED FACULTY, FACILITIES, AND CURRICULA WITH THEIR MALE COUNTERPARTS AT NEIGHBORING MOREHOUSE COLLEGE OF ATLANTA UNIVERSITY.
THERE WAS AN UNSPOKEN AGREEMENT BETWEEN THE BLACK COLLEGES AND THE WHITE POWER STRUCTURE: WE WHITE FOLK WILL LET YOU COLORED FOLK EDUCATE YOUR STUDENTS, BUT YOU WILL NOT INTERFERE WITH OUR WAY OF LIFE.
THE PACT WAS SYMBOLIZED BY A 12-FOOT STONE WALL AROUND SPELMAN. ONE DAY THESE STUDENTS WOULD LEAP OVER THAT WALL. BUT THEY STARTED WITH QUIET ACTIONS.
SOMETIME IN 1959, I SUGGESTED TO THE STUDENTS THAT IT MIGHT BE INTERESTING TO UNDERTAKE SOME REAL PROJECT INVOLVING SOCIAL CHANGE.
THE DISCUSSION BECAME VERY LIVELY. SOMEONE SAID, "WHY DON'T WE TRY TO DO SOMETHING ABOUT THE SEGREGATION OF THE PUBLIC LIBRARIES?"
LET'S DO IT!

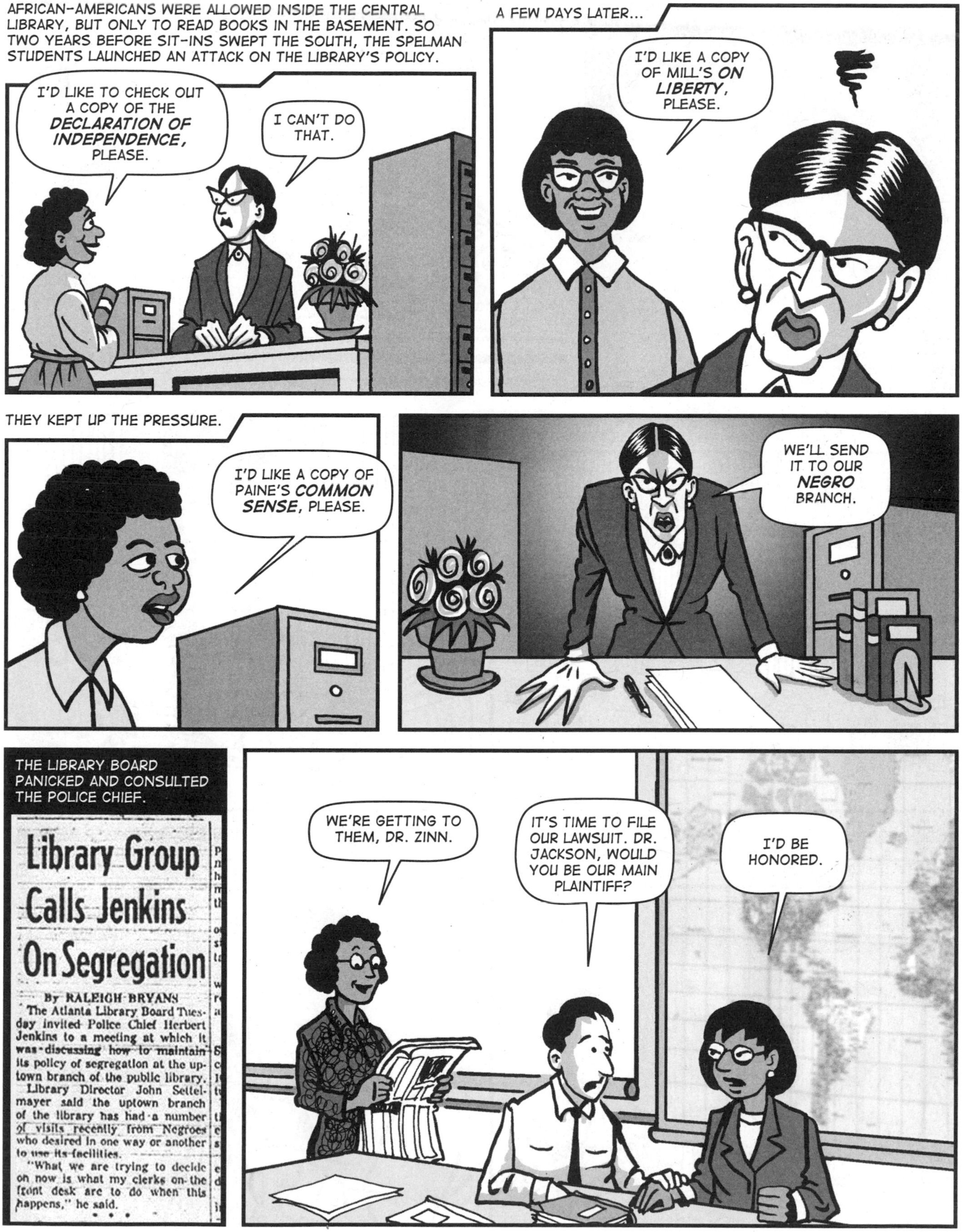
AFRICAN-AMERICANS WERE ALLOWED INSIDE THE CENTRAL LIBRARY, BUT ONLY TO READ BOOKS IN THE BASEMENT. SO TWO YEARS BEFORE SIT-INS SWEPT THE SOUTH, THE SPELMAN STUDENTS LAUNCHED AN ATTACK ON THE LIBRARY'S POLICY.
I'D LIKE TO CHECK OUT A COPY OF THE *DECLARATION OF INDEPENDENCE,* PLEASE.
I CAN'T DO THAT.
A FEW DAYS LATER...
I'D LIKE A COPY OF MILL'S *ON LIBERTY,* PLEASE.
THEY KEPT UP THE PRESSURE.
I'D LIKE A COPY OF PAINE'S *COMMON SENSE,* PLEASE.
WE'LL SEND IT TO OUR *NEGRO* BRANCH.
THE LIBRARY BOARD PANICKED AND CONSULTED THE POLICE CHIEF.
Library Group Calls Jenkins On Segregation
By RALEIGH BRYANS
The Atlanta Library Board Tuesday invited Police Chief Herbert Jenkins to a meeting at which it was discussing how to maintain its policy of segregation at the uptown branch of the public library.
Library Director John Settelmayer said the uptown branch of the library has had a number of visits recently from Negroes who desired in one way or another to use its facilities.
"What we are trying to decide on now is what my clerks on the front desk are to do when this happens," he said.
WE'RE GETTING TO THEM, DR. ZINN.
IT'S TIME TO FILE OUR LAWSUIT. DR. JACKSON, WOULD YOU BE OUR MAIN PLAINTIFF?
I'D BE HONORED.

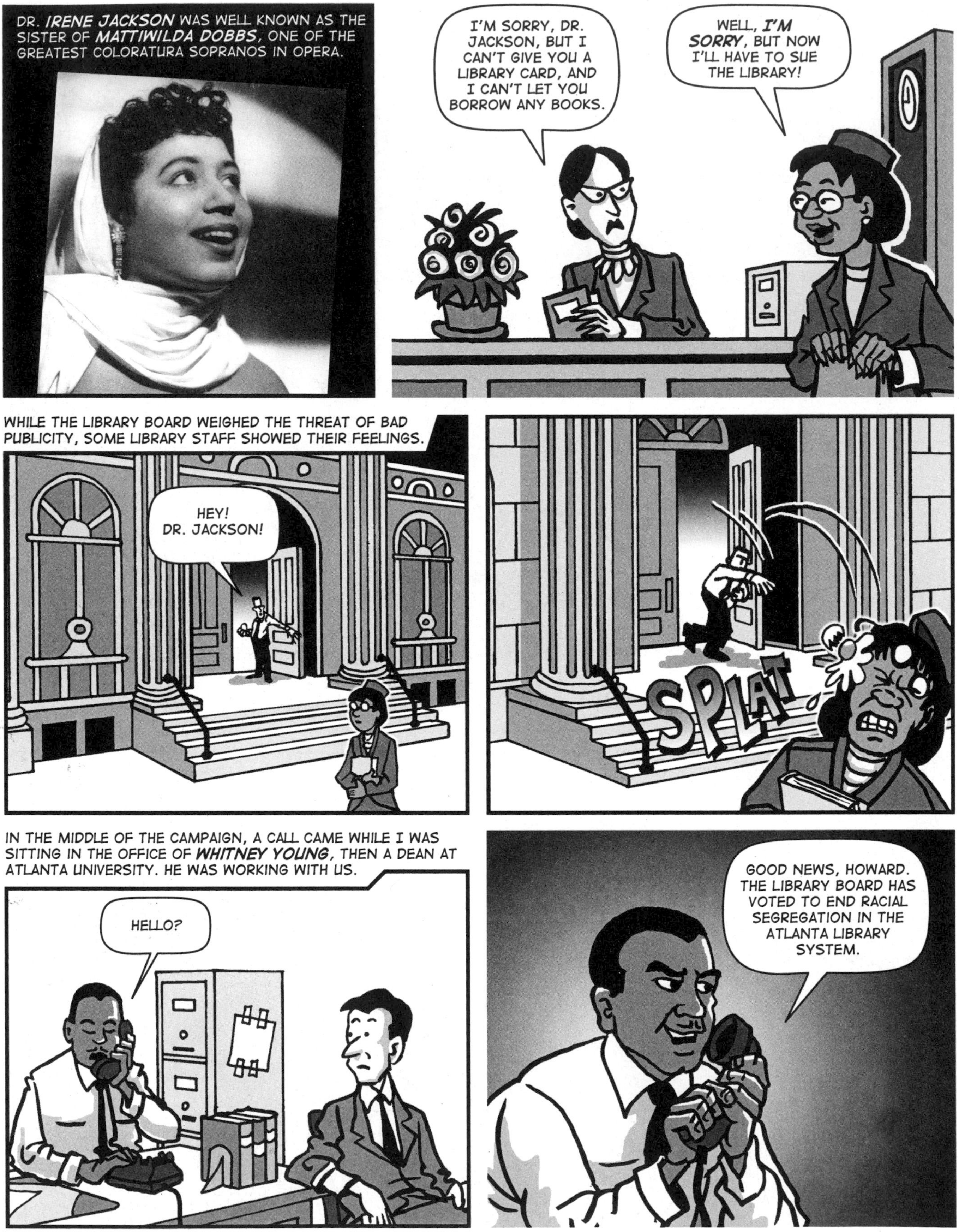
DR. IRENE JACKSON WAS WELL KNOWN AS THE SISTER OF MATTIWILDA DOBBS, ONE OF THE GREATEST COLORATURA SOPRANOS IN OPERA.
I'M SORRY, DR. JACKSON, BUT I CAN'T GIVE YOU A LIBRARY CARD, AND I CAN'T LET YOU BORROW ANY BOOKS.
WELL, I'M SORRY, BUT NOW I'LL HAVE TO SUE THE LIBRARY!
WHILE THE LIBRARY BOARD WEIGHED THE THREAT OF BAD PUBLICITY, SOME LIBRARY STAFF SHOWED THEIR FEELINGS.
HEY! DR. JACKSON!
SPLAT
IN THE MIDDLE OF THE CAMPAIGN, A CALL CAME WHILE I WAS SITTING IN THE OFFICE OF WHITNEY YOUNG, THEN A DEAN AT ATLANTA UNIVERSITY. HE WAS WORKING WITH US.
HELLO?
GOOD NEWS, HOWARD. THE LIBRARY BOARD HAS VOTED TO END RACIAL SEGREGATION IN THE ATLANTA LIBRARY SYSTEM.

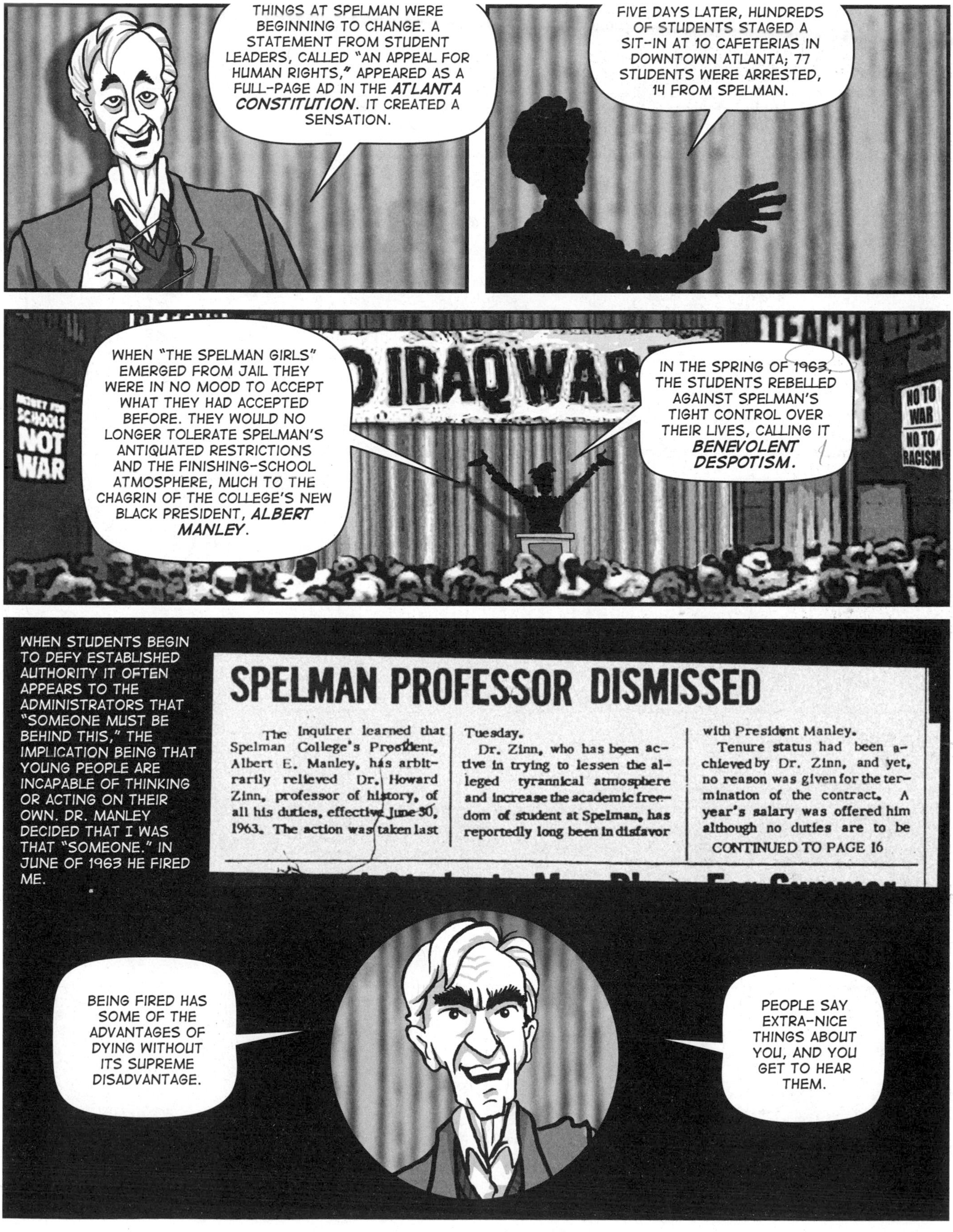
THINGS AT SPELMAN WERE BEGINNING TO CHANGE. A STATEMENT FROM STUDENT LEADERS, CALLED "AN APPEAL FOR HUMAN RIGHTS," APPEARED AS A FULL-PAGE AD IN THE *ATLANTA CONSTITUTION*. IT CREATED A SENSATION.
FIVE DAYS LATER, HUNDREDS OF STUDENTS STAGED A SIT-IN AT 10 CAFETERIAS IN DOWNTOWN ATLANTA; 77 STUDENTS WERE ARRESTED, 14 FROM SPELMAN.
WHEN "THE SPELMAN GIRLS" EMERGED FROM JAIL THEY WERE IN NO MOOD TO ACCEPT WHAT THEY HAD ACCEPTED BEFORE. THEY WOULD NO LONGER TOLERATE SPELMAN'S ANTIQUATED RESTRICTIONS AND THE FINISHING-SCHOOL ATMOSPHERE, MUCH TO THE CHAGRIN OF THE COLLEGE'S NEW BLACK PRESIDENT, ***ALBERT MANLEY***.
IN THE SPRING OF 1963, THE STUDENTS REBELLED AGAINST SPELMAN'S TIGHT CONTROL OVER THEIR LIVES, CALLING IT ***BENEVOLENT DESPOTISM***.
SCHOOLS NOT WAR
NO TO WAR
NO TO RACISM
WHEN STUDENTS BEGIN TO DEFY ESTABLISHED AUTHORITY IT OFTEN APPEARS TO THE ADMINISTRATORS THAT "SOMEONE MUST BE BEHIND THIS," THE IMPLICATION BEING THAT YOUNG PEOPLE ARE INCAPABLE OF THINKING OR ACTING ON THEIR OWN. DR. MANLEY DECIDED THAT I WAS THAT "SOMEONE." IN JUNE OF 1963 HE FIRED ME.
SPELMAN PROFESSOR DISMISSED
The Inquirer learned that Spelman College's President, Albert E. Manley, has arbitrarily relieved Dr. Howard Zinn, professor of history, of all his duties, effective June 30, 1963. The action was taken last Tuesday.
Dr. Zinn, who has been active in trying to lessen the alleged tyrannical atmosphere and increase the academic freedom of student at Spelman, has reportedly long been in disfavor with President Manley.
Tenure status had been achieved by Dr. Zinn, and yet, no reason was given for the termination of the contract. A year's salary was offered him although no duties are to be
CONTINUED TO PAGE 16
BEING FIRED HAS SOME OF THE ADVANTAGES OF DYING WITHOUT ITS SUPREME DISADVANTAGE.
PEOPLE SAY EXTRA-NICE THINGS ABOUT YOU, AND YOU GET TO HEAR THEM.

Civil Rights: Shaken to the Bone

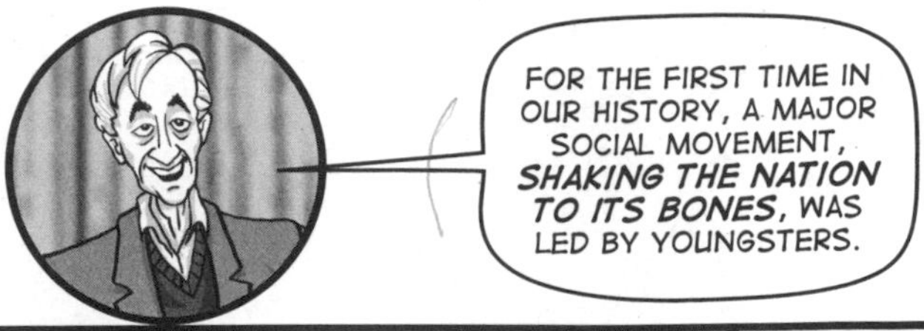

FOR THE FIRST TIME IN OUR HISTORY, A MAJOR SOCIAL MOVEMENT, ***SHAKING THE NATION TO ITS BONES***, WAS LED BY YOUNGSTERS.

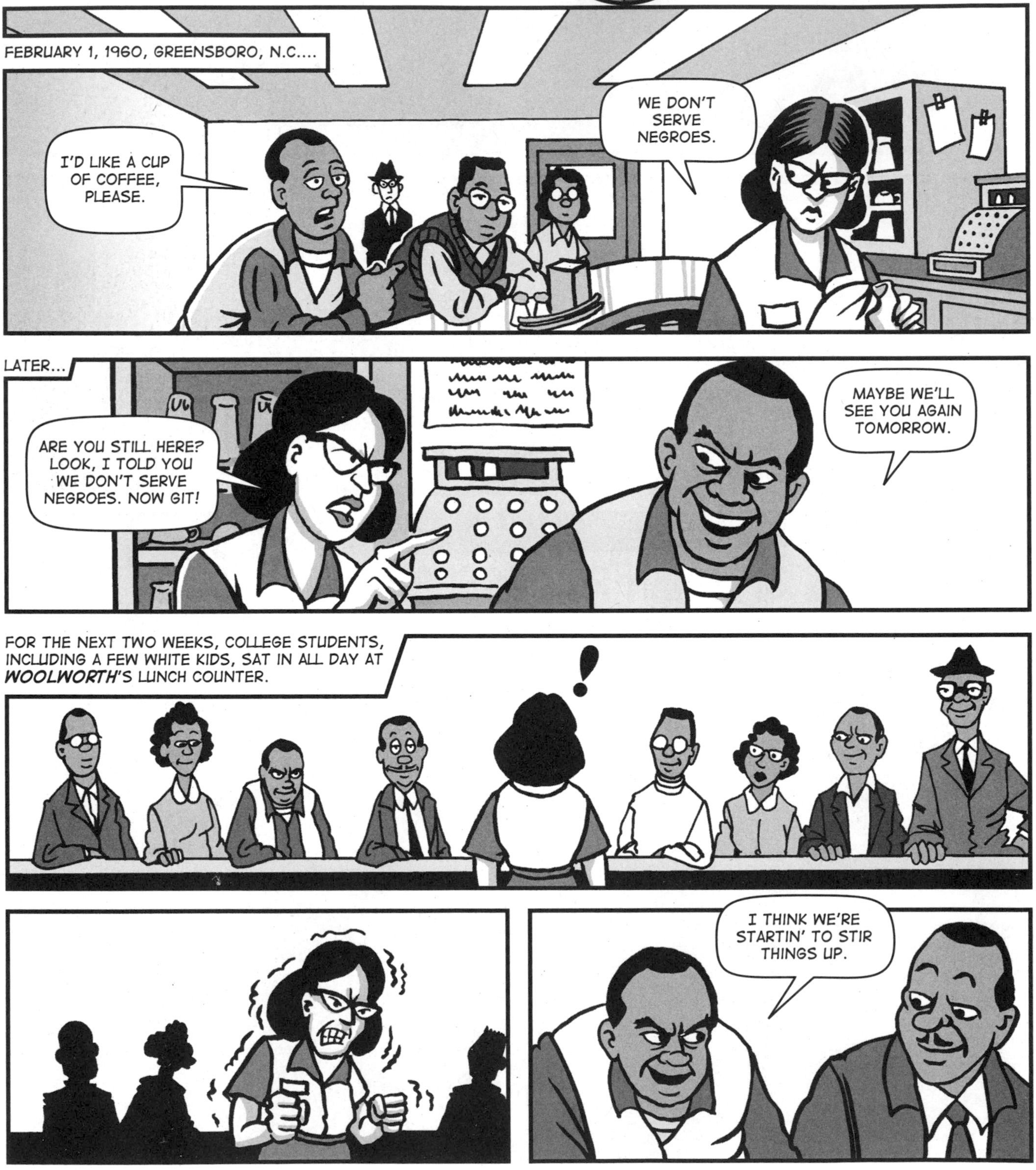

FEBRUARY 1, 1960, GREENSBORO, N.C....
I'D LIKE A CUP OF COFFEE, PLEASE.
WE DON'T SERVE NEGROES.
LATER...
ARE YOU STILL HERE? LOOK, I TOLD YOU WE DON'T SERVE NEGROES. NOW GIT!
MAYBE WE'LL SEE YOU AGAIN TOMORROW.
FOR THE NEXT TWO WEEKS, COLLEGE STUDENTS, INCLUDING A FEW WHITE KIDS, SAT IN ALL DAY AT ***WOOLWORTH***'S LUNCH COUNTER.
!
I THINK WE'RE STARTIN' TO STIR THINGS UP.

THE SIT-INS SPREAD ALL OVER THE SOUTH. WITHIN A YEAR, 50,000 PEOPLE HAD MARCHED IN 100 CITIES, AND THOUSANDS SPENT TIME IN JAIL.

SOON, THE PROTESTERS TURNED TO A NEW TACTIC: DESEGREGATING INTERSTATE BUS SERVICE.

THE ***FREEDOM RIDERS***, AS THEY WERE CALLED, LAUNCHED A MORAL REVOLUTION.

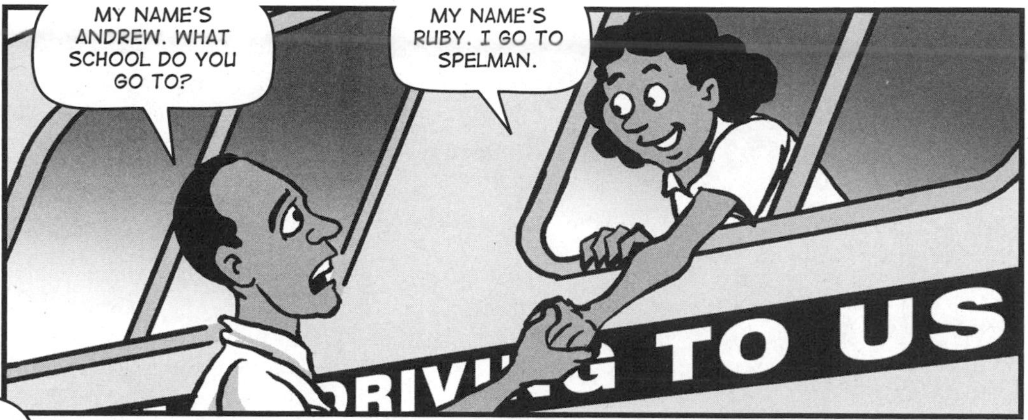
MY NAME'S ANDREW. WHAT SCHOOL DO YOU GO TO?
MY NAME'S RUBY. I GO TO SPELMAN.
TO US

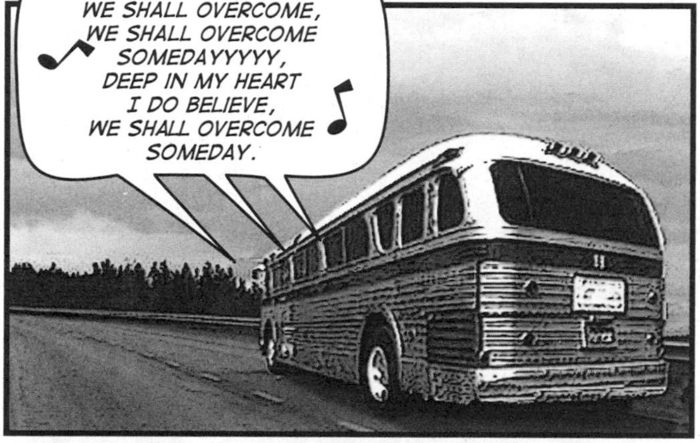
WE SHALL OVERCOME, WE SHALL OVERCOME, WE SHALL OVERCOME SOMEDAYYYYY, DEEP IN MY HEART I DO BELIEVE, WE SHALL OVERCOME SOMEDAY.

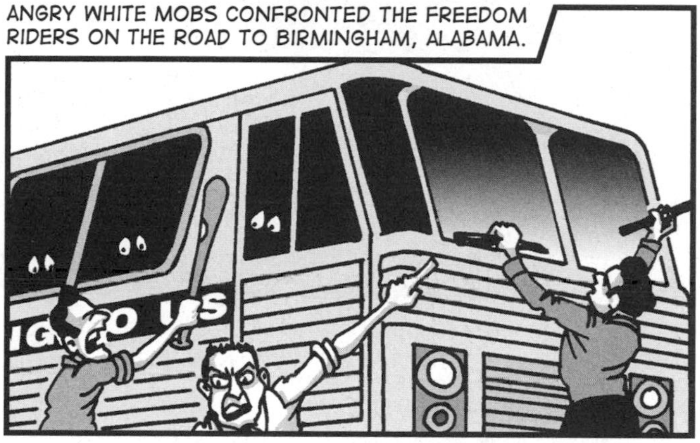
ANGRY WHITE MOBS CONFRONTED THE FREEDOM RIDERS ON THE ROAD TO BIRMINGHAM, ALABAMA.

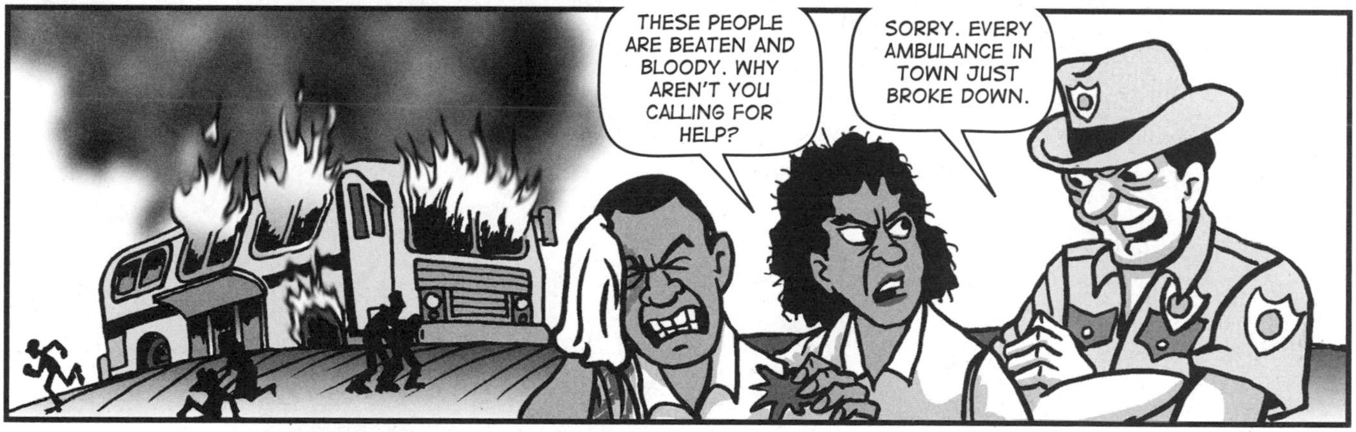
THESE PEOPLE ARE BEATEN AND BLOODY. WHY AREN'T YOU CALLING FOR HELP?
SORRY. EVERY AMBULANCE IN TOWN JUST BROKE DOWN.

IN JACKSON, MISS., 27 PEOPLE WERE ARRESTED FOR TRYING TO INTEGRATE THE BUS TERMINAL'S WHITE WAITING ROOM. THEY REFUSED TO POST BAIL AND SPENT TWO MONTHS IN PRISON.

TO PASS THE TIME, THE SPELMAN WOMEN SANG FREEDOM SONGS AND PRACTICED THEIR BALLET STEPS.

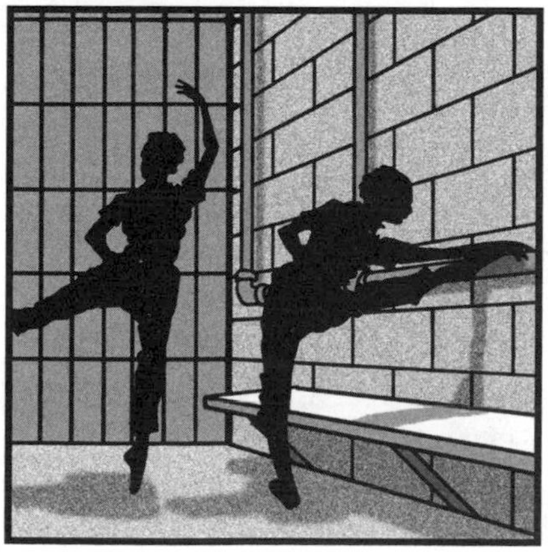

IN SOUTHERN JAILS, DISCRIMINATION AND RACISM AGAINST POOR BLACKS RADICALIZED EDUCATED, MIDDLE-CLASS ACTIVISTS FROM ATLANTA AND NEW YORK.

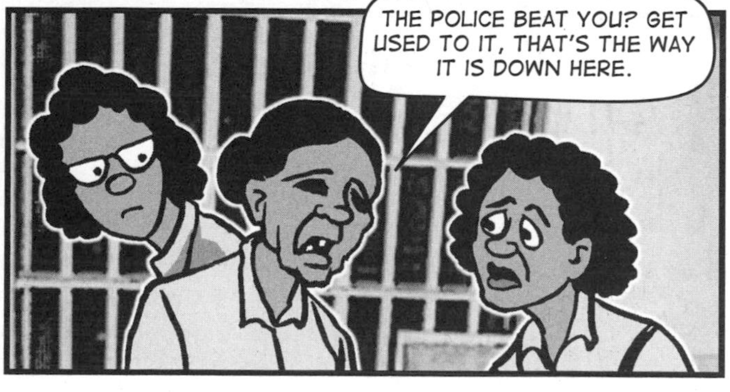
THE POLICE BEAT YOU? GET USED TO IT, THAT'S THE WAY IT IS DOWN HERE.

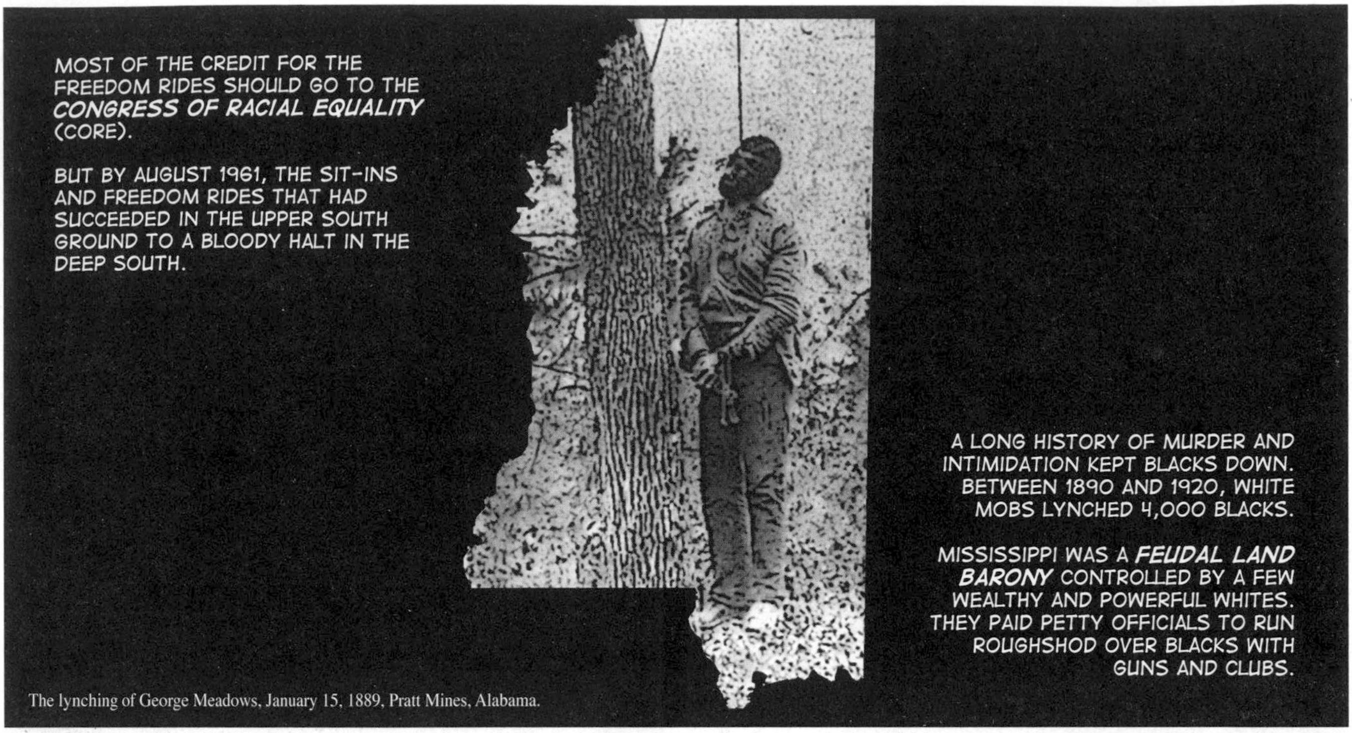
MOST OF THE CREDIT FOR THE FREEDOM RIDES SHOULD GO TO THE CONGRESS OF RACIAL EQUALITY (CORE).
BUT BY AUGUST 1961, THE SIT-INS AND FREEDOM RIDES THAT HAD SUCCEEDED IN THE UPPER SOUTH GROUND TO A BLOODY HALT IN THE DEEP SOUTH.
A LONG HISTORY OF MURDER AND INTIMIDATION KEPT BLACKS DOWN. BETWEEN 1890 AND 1920, WHITE MOBS LYNCHED 4,000 BLACKS.
MISSISSIPPI WAS A FEUDAL LAND BARONY CONTROLLED BY A FEW WEALTHY AND POWERFUL WHITES. THEY PAID PETTY OFFICIALS TO RUN ROUGHSHOD OVER BLACKS WITH GUNS AND CLUBS.
The lynching of George Meadows, January 15, 1889, Pratt Mines, Alabama.

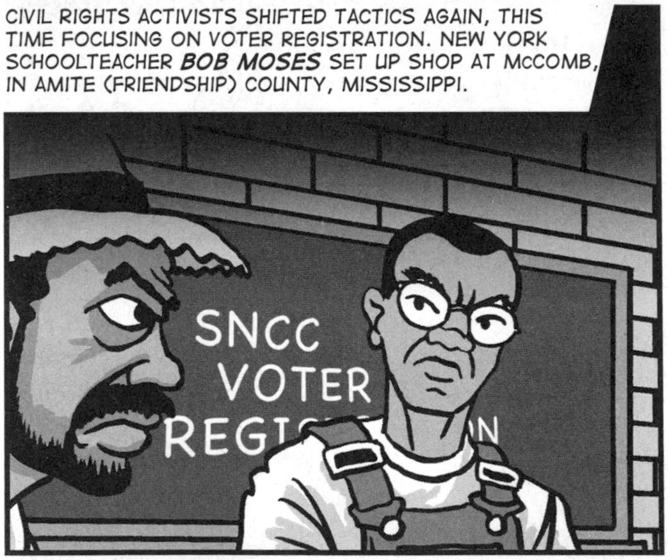
CIVIL RIGHTS ACTIVISTS SHIFTED TACTICS AGAIN, THIS TIME FOCUSING ON VOTER REGISTRATION. NEW YORK SCHOOLTEACHER BOB MOSES SET UP SHOP AT McCOMB, IN AMITE (FRIENDSHIP) COUNTY, MISSISSIPPI.
SNCC VOTER REGI

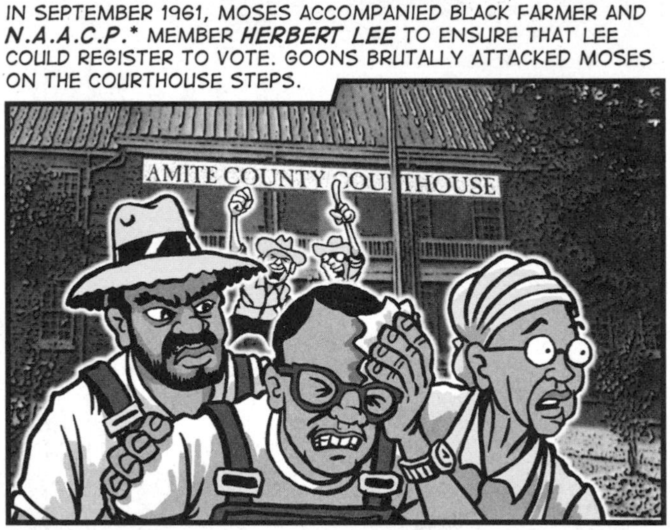
IN SEPTEMBER 1961, MOSES ACCOMPANIED BLACK FARMER AND N.A.A.C.P.* MEMBER HERBERT LEE TO ENSURE THAT LEE COULD REGISTER TO VOTE. GOONS BRUTALLY ATTACKED MOSES ON THE COURTHOUSE STEPS.
AMITE COUNTY COU THOUSE

*NATIONAL ASSOCIATION FOR THE ADVANCEMENT OF COLORED PEOPLE

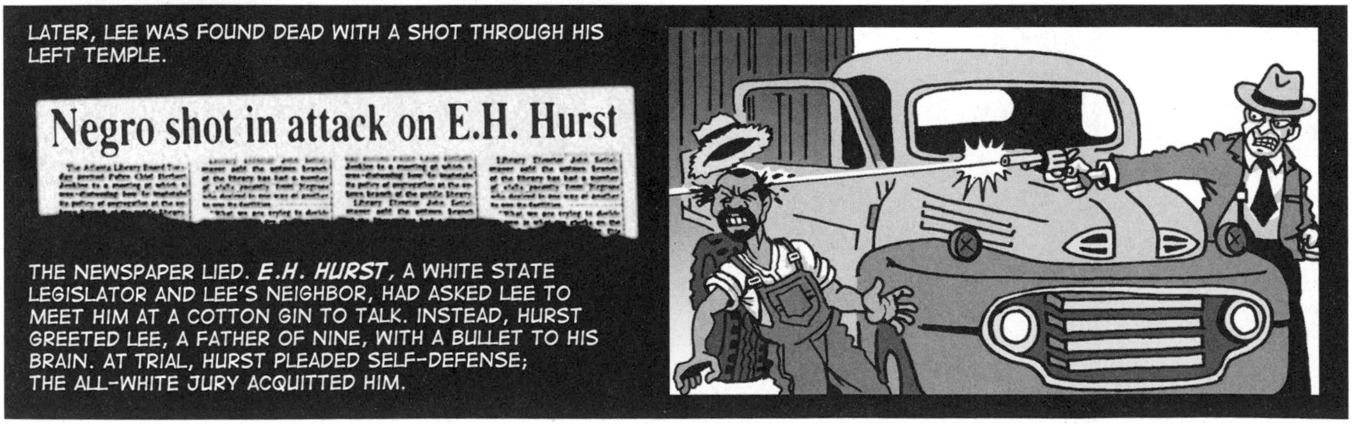
LATER, LEE WAS FOUND DEAD WITH A SHOT THROUGH HIS LEFT TEMPLE.
Negro shot in attack on E.H. Hurst
THE NEWSPAPER LIED. E.H. HURST, A WHITE STATE LEGISLATOR AND LEE'S NEIGHBOR, HAD ASKED LEE TO MEET HIM AT A COTTON GIN TO TALK. INSTEAD, HURST GREETED LEE, A FATHER OF NINE, WITH A BULLET TO HIS BRAIN. AT TRIAL, HURST PLEADED SELF-DEFENSE; THE ALL-WHITE JURY ACQUITTED HIM.

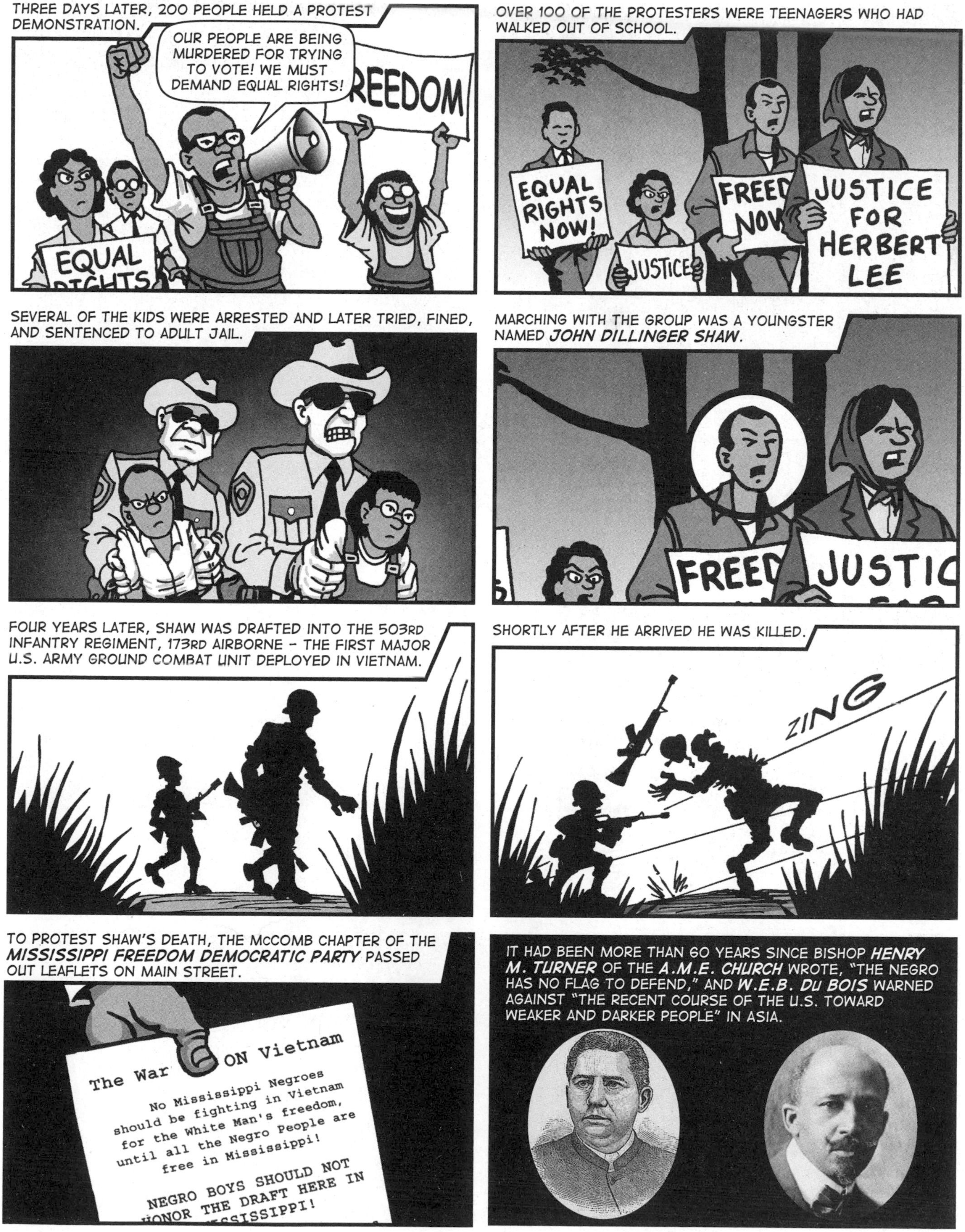
THREE DAYS LATER, 200 PEOPLE HELD A PROTEST DEMONSTRATION.
OUR PEOPLE ARE BEING MURDERED FOR TRYING TO VOTE! WE MUST DEMAND EQUAL RIGHTS!
REEDOM
EQUAL
OVER 100 OF THE PROTESTERS WERE TEENAGERS WHO HAD WALKED OUT OF SCHOOL.
EQUAL RIGHTS NOW!
JUSTICE
FREED NOW
JUSTICE FOR HERBERT LEE
SEVERAL OF THE KIDS WERE ARRESTED AND LATER TRIED, FINED, AND SENTENCED TO ADULT JAIL.
MARCHING WITH THE GROUP WAS A YOUNGSTER NAMED *JOHN DILLINGER SHAW*.
FREED
JUSTIC
FOUR YEARS LATER, SHAW WAS DRAFTED INTO THE 503RD INFANTRY REGIMENT, 173RD AIRBORNE – THE FIRST MAJOR U.S. ARMY GROUND COMBAT UNIT DEPLOYED IN VIETNAM.
SHORTLY AFTER HE ARRIVED HE WAS KILLED.
ZING
TO PROTEST SHAW'S DEATH, THE McCOMB CHAPTER OF THE *MISSISSIPPI FREEDOM DEMOCRATIC PARTY* PASSED OUT LEAFLETS ON MAIN STREET.
The War ON Vietnam
No Mississippi Negroes should be fighting in Vietnam for the White Man's freedom, until all the Negro People are free in Mississippi!
NEGRO BOYS SHOULD NOT HONOR THE DRAFT HERE IN MISSISSIPPI!
IT HAD BEEN MORE THAN 60 YEARS SINCE BISHOP *HENRY M. TURNER* OF THE *A.M.E. CHURCH* WROTE, "THE NEGRO HAS NO FLAG TO DEFEND," AND *W.E.B. DU BOIS* WARNED AGAINST "THE RECENT COURSE OF THE U.S. TOWARD WEAKER AND DARKER PEOPLE" IN ASIA.

The Bombs in Vietnam Explode at Home

AUGUST 6, 1965: ONE MONTH AFTER PVT. JOHN D. SHAW DIED, PRESIDENT ***LYNDON B. JOHNSON*** SIGNED THE ***VOTING RIGHTS ACT*** TO BREAK THE GRIP OF STATE DISFRANCHISEMENT OF MINORITIES.

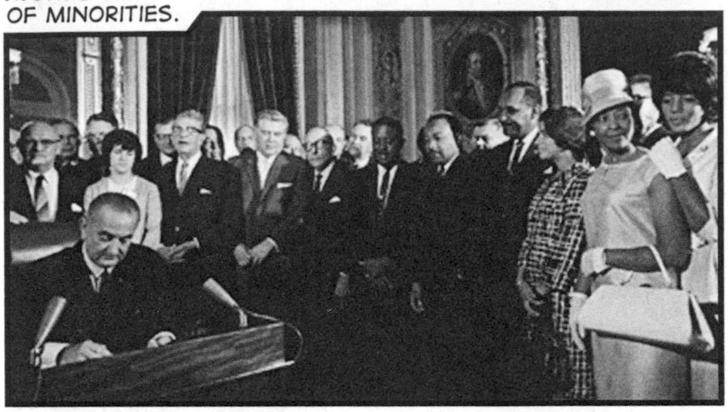

BUT THE ISSUE OF VOTING WAS ECLIPSED BY ANGER OVER POVERTY. OVER THE NEXT THREE YEARS, THERE WERE BLACK REVOLTS IN WATTS (LOS ANGELES), SAN FRANCISCO, DETROIT, BALTIMORE, NEW YORK, CHICAGO, AND CLEVELAND.

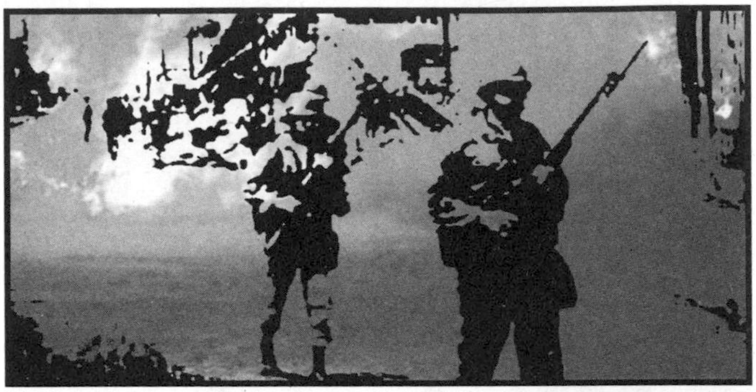

IN VIETNAM, BLACK SOLDIERS WERE BEING KILLED AT TWICE THE PERCENTAGE OF THEIR POPULATION IN THE U.S.

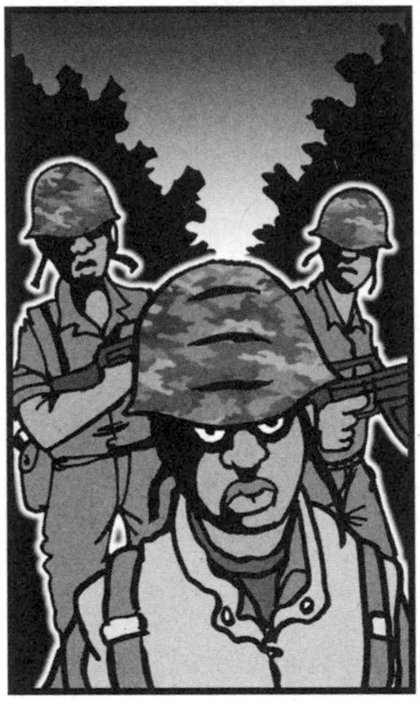

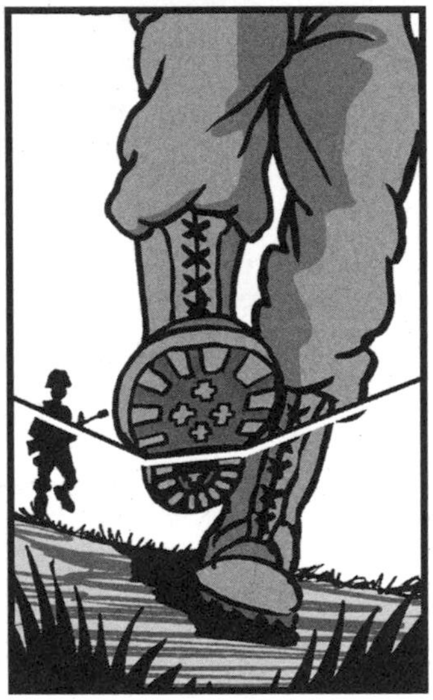

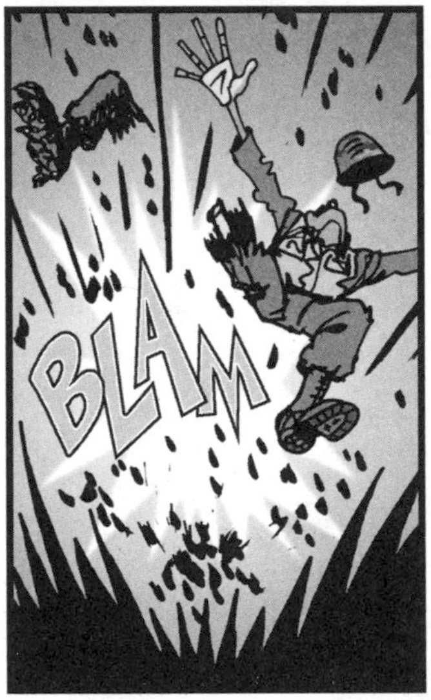
BLAM

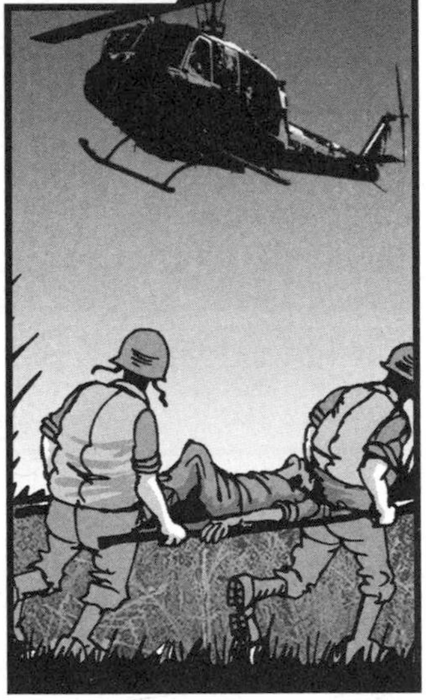

CIVIL RIGHTS LEADER ***DR. MARTIN LUTHER KING*** WAS AN OUTSPOKEN CRITIC OF THE WAR.

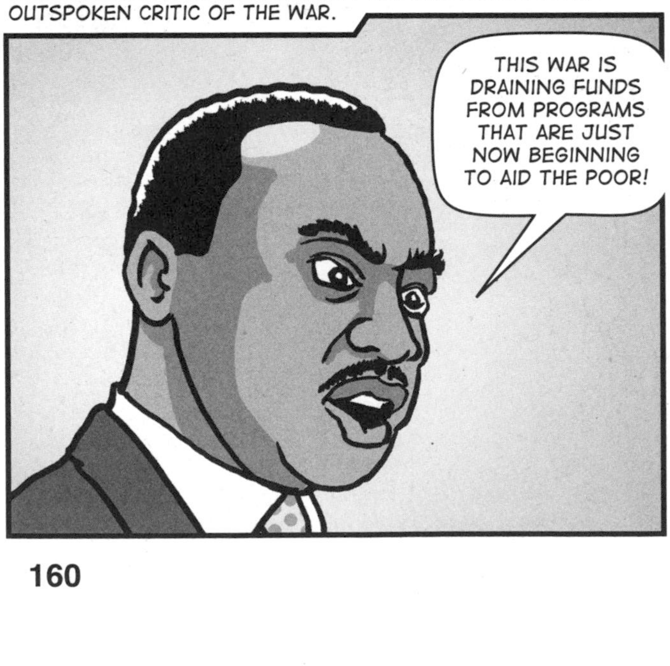
THIS WAR IS DRAINING FUNDS FROM PROGRAMS THAT ARE JUST NOW BEGINNING TO AID THE POOR!

PRESSURE MOUNTED FROM ALL SIDES TO SILENCE KING, ESPECIALLY FROM WHITE PROWAR LIBERALS.

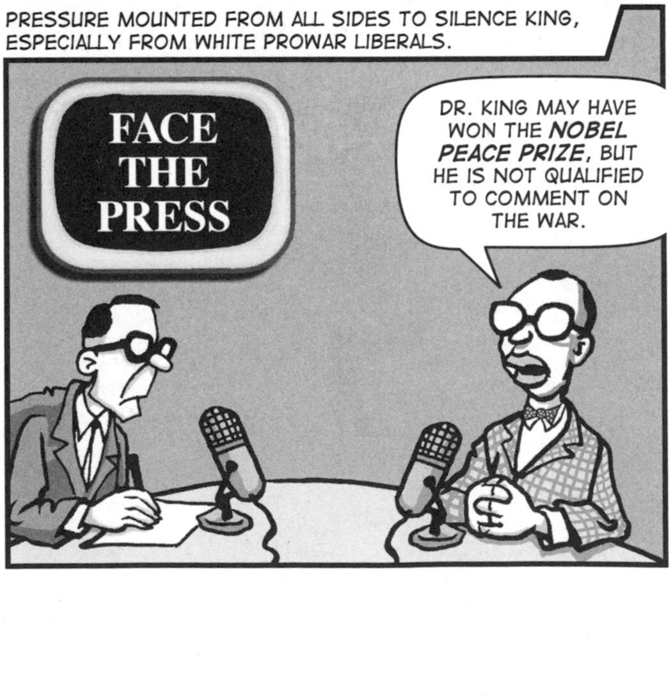
FACE THE PRESS
DR. KING MAY HAVE WON THE ***NOBEL PEACE PRIZE***, BUT HE IS NOT QUALIFIED TO COMMENT ON THE WAR.

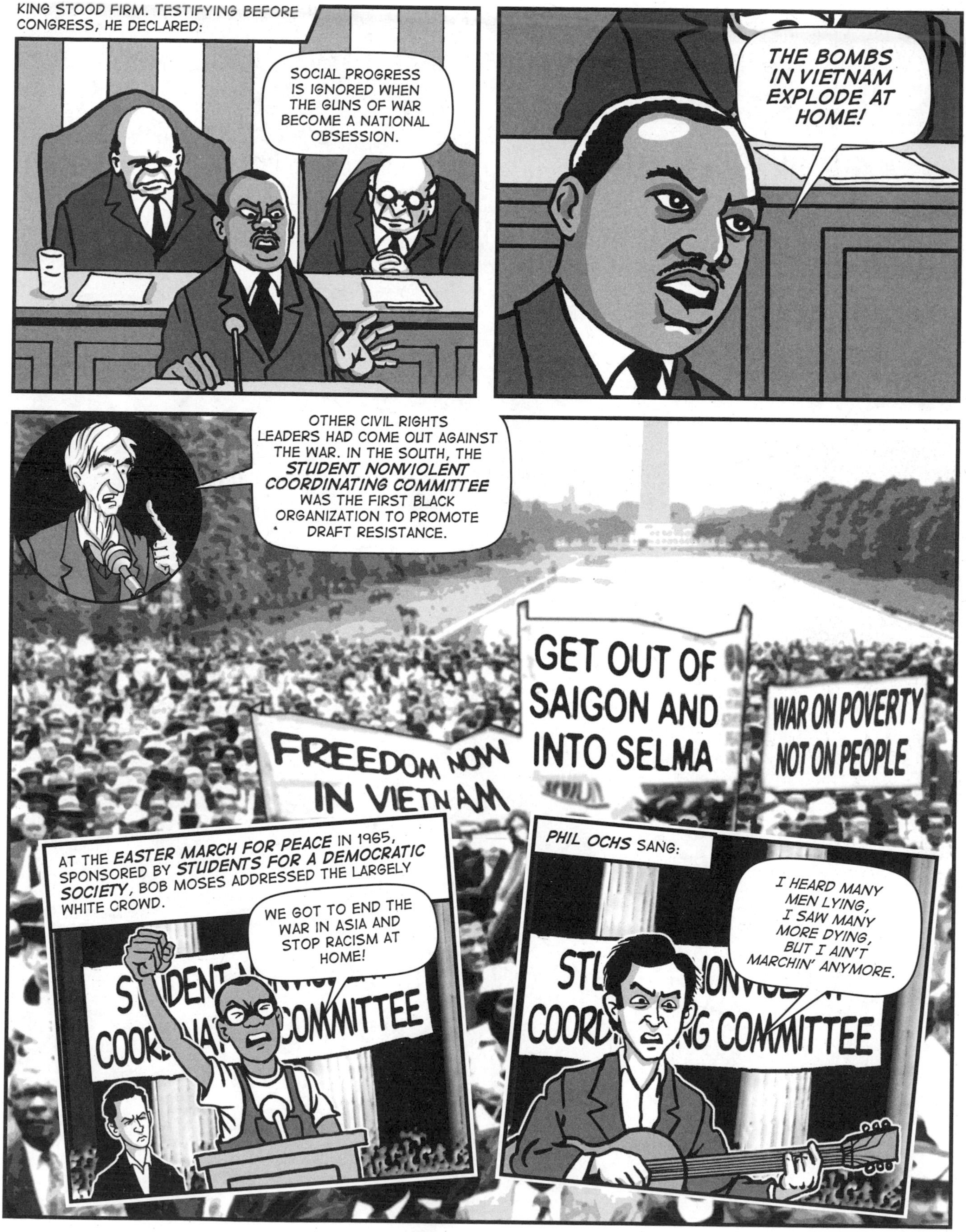
KING STOOD FIRM. TESTIFYING BEFORE CONGRESS, HE DECLARED:
SOCIAL PROGRESS IS IGNORED WHEN THE GUNS OF WAR BECOME A NATIONAL OBSESSION.
THE BOMBS IN VIETNAM EXPLODE AT HOME!
OTHER CIVIL RIGHTS LEADERS HAD COME OUT AGAINST THE WAR. IN THE SOUTH, THE STUDENT NONVIOLENT COORDINATING COMMITTEE WAS THE FIRST BLACK ORGANIZATION TO PROMOTE DRAFT RESISTANCE.
GET OUT OF SAIGON AND INTO SELMA
WAR ON POVERTY NOT ON PEOPLE
FREEDOM NOW IN VIETNAM
AT THE EASTER MARCH FOR PEACE IN 1965, SPONSORED BY STUDENTS FOR A DEMOCRATIC SOCIETY, BOB MOSES ADDRESSED THE LARGELY WHITE CROWD.
WE GOT TO END THE WAR IN ASIA AND STOP RACISM AT HOME!
COMMITTEE
PHIL OCHS SANG:
I HEARD MANY MEN LYING, I SAW MANY MORE DYING, BUT I AIN'T MARCHIN' ANYMORE.
COMMITTEE

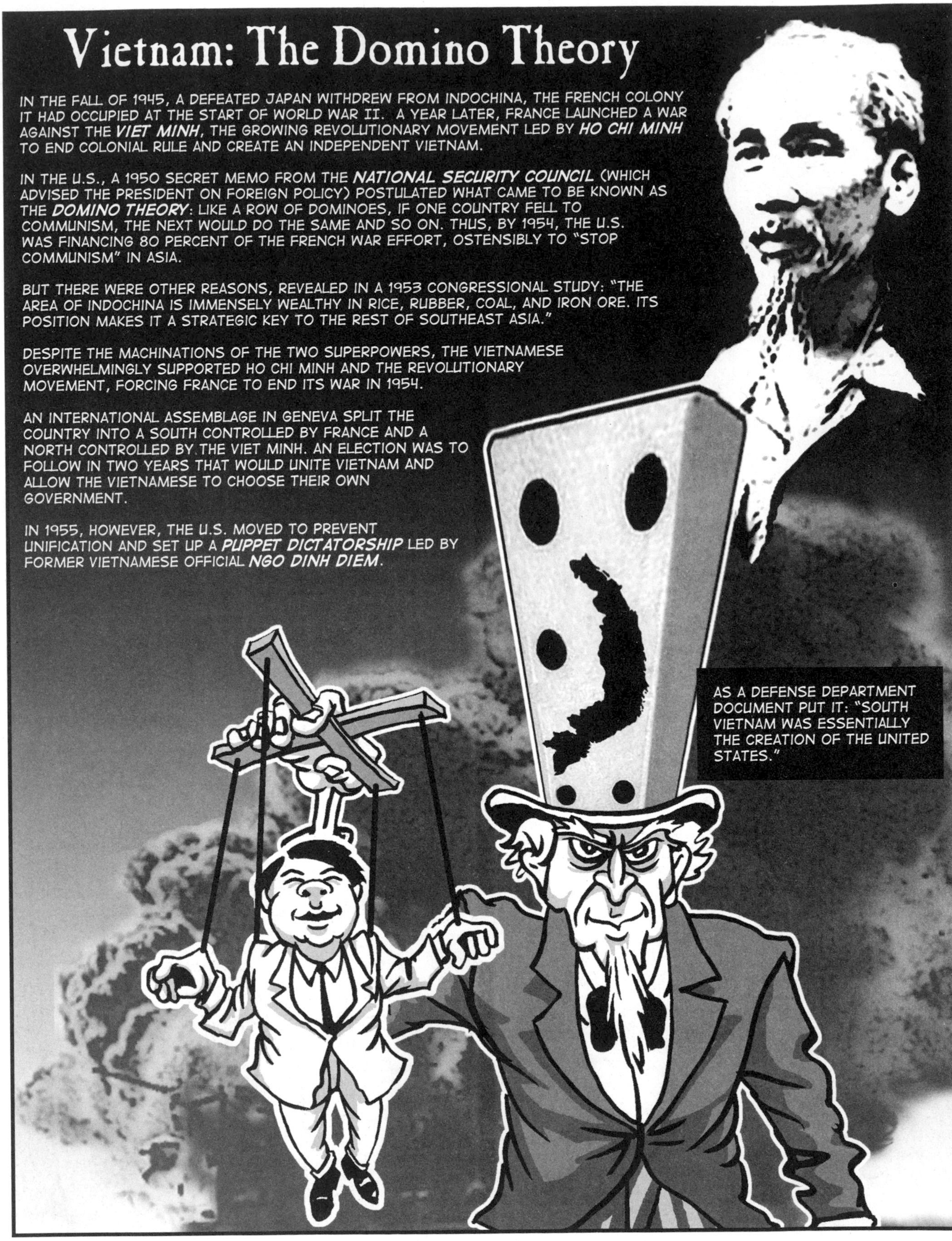
Vietnam: The Domino Theory
IN THE FALL OF 1945, A DEFEATED JAPAN WITHDREW FROM INDOCHINA, THE FRENCH COLONY IT HAD OCCUPIED AT THE START OF WORLD WAR II. A YEAR LATER, FRANCE LAUNCHED A WAR AGAINST THE VIET MINH, THE GROWING REVOLUTIONARY MOVEMENT LED BY HO CHI MINH TO END COLONIAL RULE AND CREATE AN INDEPENDENT VIETNAM.
IN THE U.S., A 1950 SECRET MEMO FROM THE NATIONAL SECURITY COUNCIL (WHICH ADVISED THE PRESIDENT ON FOREIGN POLICY) POSTULATED WHAT CAME TO BE KNOWN AS THE DOMINO THEORY: LIKE A ROW OF DOMINOES, IF ONE COUNTRY FELL TO COMMUNISM, THE NEXT WOULD DO THE SAME AND SO ON. THUS, BY 1954, THE U.S. WAS FINANCING 80 PERCENT OF THE FRENCH WAR EFFORT, OSTENSIBLY TO "STOP COMMUNISM" IN ASIA.
BUT THERE WERE OTHER REASONS, REVEALED IN A 1953 CONGRESSIONAL STUDY: "THE AREA OF INDOCHINA IS IMMENSELY WEALTHY IN RICE, RUBBER, COAL, AND IRON ORE. ITS POSITION MAKES IT A STRATEGIC KEY TO THE REST OF SOUTHEAST ASIA."
DESPITE THE MACHINATIONS OF THE TWO SUPERPOWERS, THE VIETNAMESE OVERWHELMINGLY SUPPORTED HO CHI MINH AND THE REVOLUTIONARY MOVEMENT, FORCING FRANCE TO END ITS WAR IN 1954.
AN INTERNATIONAL ASSEMBLAGE IN GENEVA SPLIT THE COUNTRY INTO A SOUTH CONTROLLED BY FRANCE AND A NORTH CONTROLLED BY THE VIET MINH. AN ELECTION WAS TO FOLLOW IN TWO YEARS THAT WOULD UNITE VIETNAM AND ALLOW THE VIETNAMESE TO CHOOSE THEIR OWN GOVERNMENT.
IN 1955, HOWEVER, THE U.S. MOVED TO PREVENT UNIFICATION AND SET UP A PUPPET DICTATORSHIP LED BY FORMER VIETNAMESE OFFICIAL NGO DINH DIEM.
AS A DEFENSE DEPARTMENT DOCUMENT PUT IT: "SOUTH VIETNAM WAS ESSENTIALLY THE CREATION OF THE UNITED STATES."

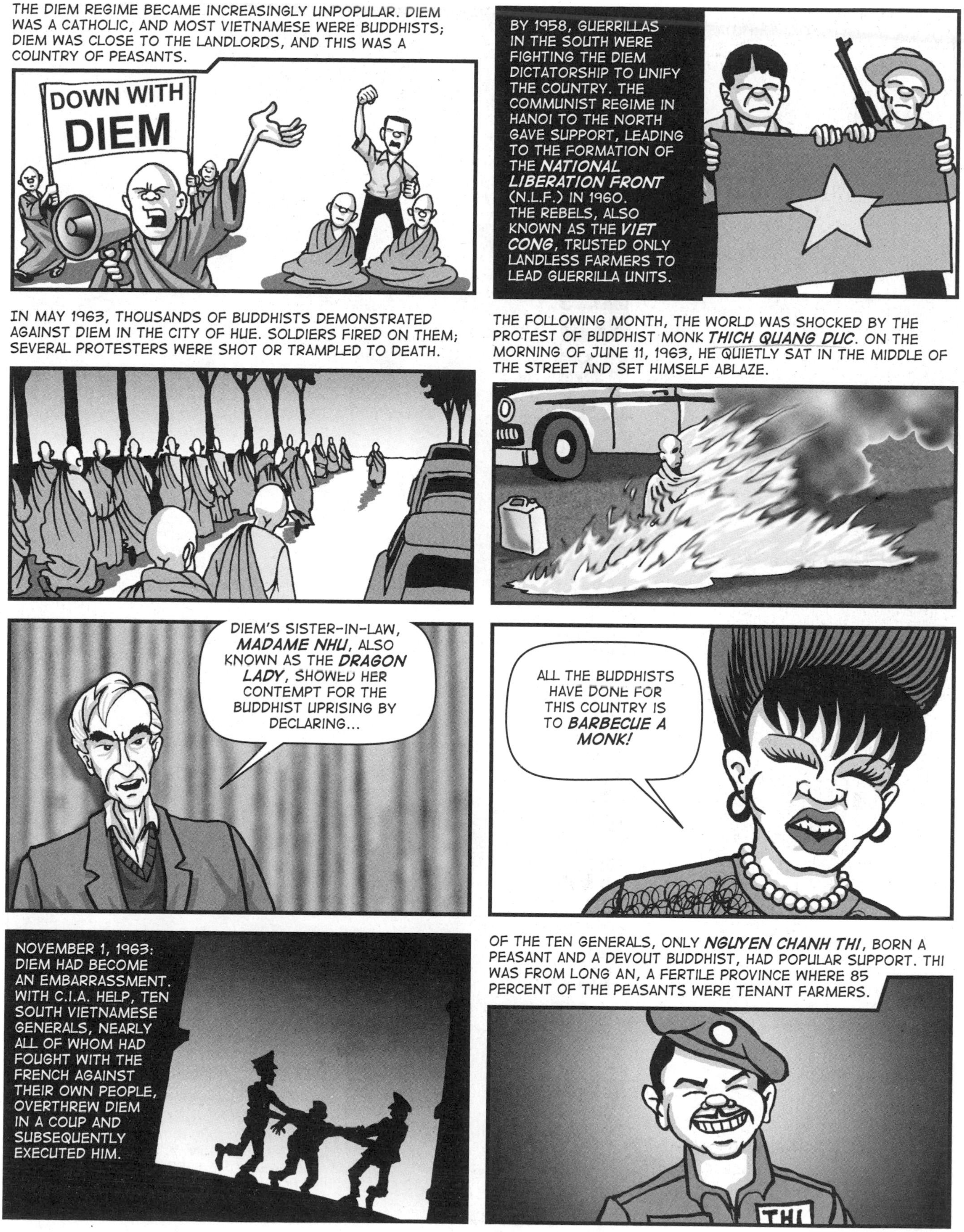
THE DIEM REGIME BECAME INCREASINGLY UNPOPULAR. DIEM WAS A CATHOLIC, AND MOST VIETNAMESE WERE BUDDHISTS; DIEM WAS CLOSE TO THE LANDLORDS, AND THIS WAS A COUNTRY OF PEASANTS.
DOWN WITH DIEM
BY 1958, GUERRILLAS IN THE SOUTH WERE FIGHTING THE DIEM DICTATORSHIP TO UNIFY THE COUNTRY. THE COMMUNIST REGIME IN HANOI TO THE NORTH GAVE SUPPORT, LEADING TO THE FORMATION OF THE NATIONAL LIBERATION FRONT (N.L.F.) IN 1960. THE REBELS, ALSO KNOWN AS THE VIET CONG, TRUSTED ONLY LANDLESS FARMERS TO LEAD GUERRILLA UNITS.
IN MAY 1963, THOUSANDS OF BUDDHISTS DEMONSTRATED AGAINST DIEM IN THE CITY OF HUE. SOLDIERS FIRED ON THEM; SEVERAL PROTESTERS WERE SHOT OR TRAMPLED TO DEATH.
THE FOLLOWING MONTH, THE WORLD WAS SHOCKED BY THE PROTEST OF BUDDHIST MONK THICH QUANG DUC. ON THE MORNING OF JUNE 11, 1963, HE QUIETLY SAT IN THE MIDDLE OF THE STREET AND SET HIMSELF ABLAZE.
DIEM'S SISTER-IN-LAW, MADAME NHU, ALSO KNOWN AS THE DRAGON LADY, SHOWED HER CONTEMPT FOR THE BUDDHIST UPRISING BY DECLARING...
ALL THE BUDDHISTS HAVE DONE FOR THIS COUNTRY IS TO BARBECUE A MONK!
NOVEMBER 1, 1963: DIEM HAD BECOME AN EMBARRASSMENT. WITH C.I.A. HELP, TEN SOUTH VIETNAMESE GENERALS, NEARLY ALL OF WHOM HAD FOUGHT WITH THE FRENCH AGAINST THEIR OWN PEOPLE, OVERTHREW DIEM IN A COUP AND SUBSEQUENTLY EXECUTED HIM.
OF THE TEN GENERALS, ONLY NGUYEN CHANH THI, BORN A PEASANT AND A DEVOUT BUDDHIST, HAD POPULAR SUPPORT. THI WAS FROM LONG AN, A FERTILE PROVINCE WHERE 85 PERCENT OF THE PEASANTS WERE TENANT FARMERS.
THI

IN EARLY AUGUST 1964, PRESIDENT JOHNSON USED A MURKY SET OF EVENTS IN THE ***GULF OF TONKIN***, OFF THE COAST OF NORTH VIETNAM, TO LAUNCH FULL-SCALE WAR.

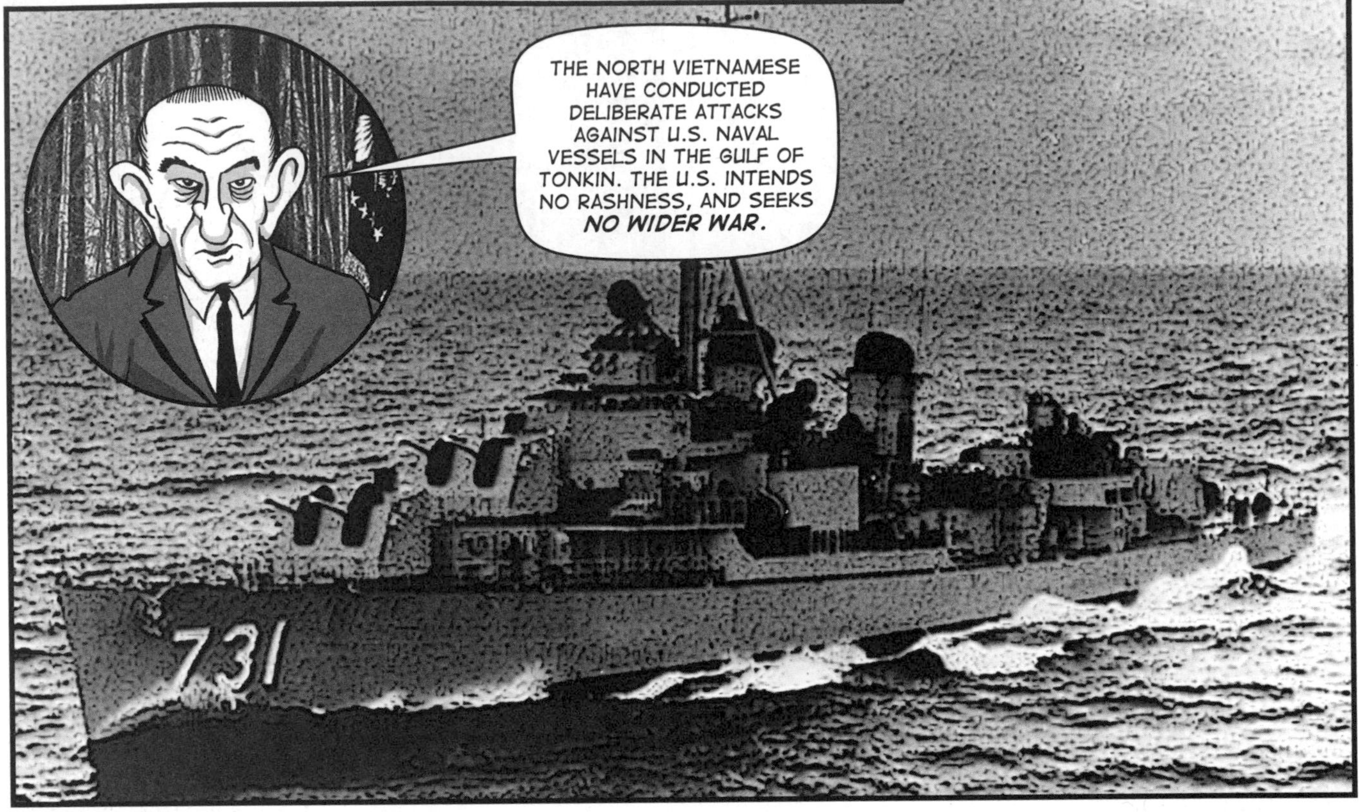
THE NORTH VIETNAMESE HAVE CONDUCTED DELIBERATE ATTACKS AGAINST U.S. NAVAL VESSELS IN THE GULF OF TONKIN. THE U.S. INTENDS NO RASHNESS, AND SEEKS ***NO WIDER WAR***.
731

IMMEDIATELY AFTER THE TONKIN AFFAIR, AMERICAN WARPLANES BEGAN BOMBARDING NORTH VIETNAM.

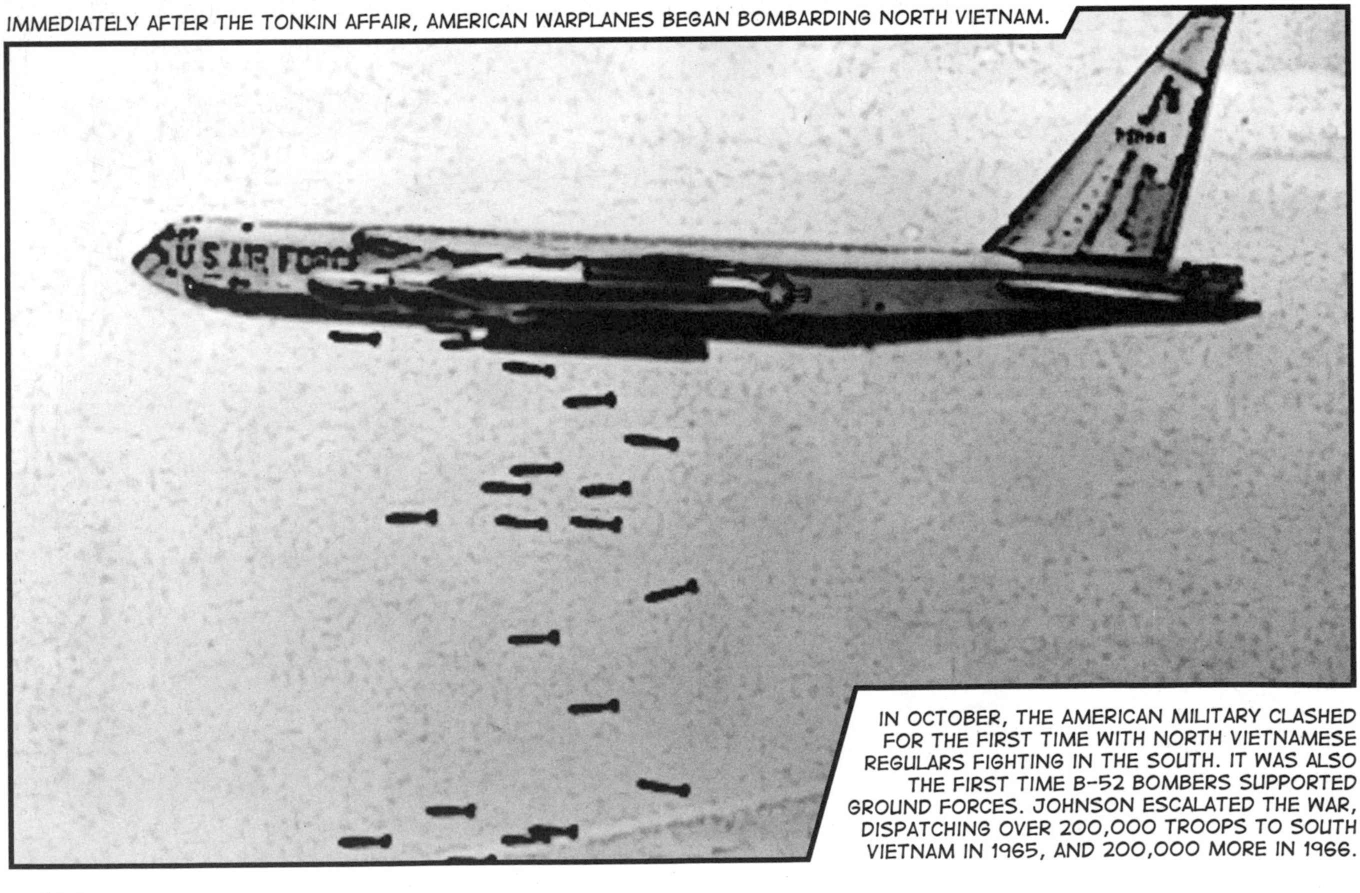
U.S. AIR FORCE

IN OCTOBER, THE AMERICAN MILITARY CLASHED FOR THE FIRST TIME WITH NORTH VIETNAMESE REGULARS FIGHTING IN THE SOUTH. IT WAS ALSO THE FIRST TIME B-52 BOMBERS SUPPORTED GROUND FORCES. JOHNSON ESCALATED THE WAR, DISPATCHING OVER 200,000 TROOPS TO SOUTH VIETNAM IN 1965, AND 200,000 MORE IN 1966.

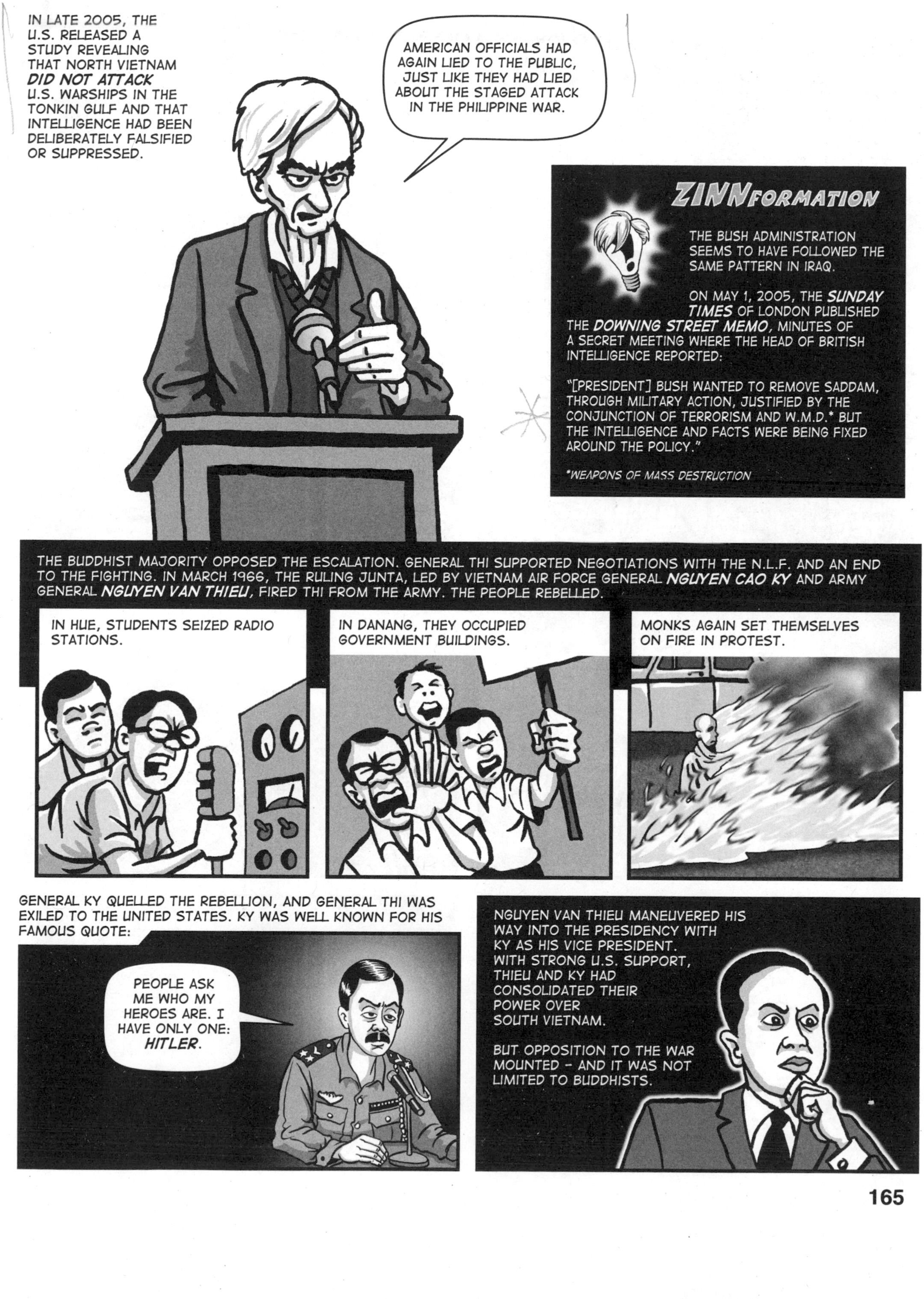
IN LATE 2005, THE U.S. RELEASED A STUDY REVEALING THAT NORTH VIETNAM ***DID NOT ATTACK*** U.S. WARSHIPS IN THE TONKIN GULF AND THAT INTELLIGENCE HAD BEEN DELIBERATELY FALSIFIED OR SUPPRESSED.
AMERICAN OFFICIALS HAD AGAIN LIED TO THE PUBLIC, JUST LIKE THEY HAD LIED ABOUT THE STAGED ATTACK IN THE PHILIPPINE WAR.
ZINNFORMATION
THE BUSH ADMINISTRATION SEEMS TO HAVE FOLLOWED THE SAME PATTERN IN IRAQ.
ON MAY 1, 2005, THE ***SUNDAY TIMES*** OF LONDON PUBLISHED THE ***DOWNING STREET MEMO,*** MINUTES OF A SECRET MEETING WHERE THE HEAD OF BRITISH INTELLIGENCE REPORTED:
"[PRESIDENT] BUSH WANTED TO REMOVE SADDAM, THROUGH MILITARY ACTION, JUSTIFIED BY THE CONJUNCTION OF TERRORISM AND W.M.D.* BUT THE INTELLIGENCE AND FACTS WERE BEING FIXED AROUND THE POLICY."
*WEAPONS OF MASS DESTRUCTION
THE BUDDHIST MAJORITY OPPOSED THE ESCALATION. GENERAL THI SUPPORTED NEGOTIATIONS WITH THE N.L.F. AND AN END TO THE FIGHTING. IN MARCH 1966, THE RULING JUNTA, LED BY VIETNAM AIR FORCE GENERAL ***NGUYEN CAO KY*** AND ARMY GENERAL ***NGUYEN VAN THIEU,*** FIRED THI FROM THE ARMY. THE PEOPLE REBELLED.
IN HUE, STUDENTS SEIZED RADIO STATIONS.
IN DANANG, THEY OCCUPIED GOVERNMENT BUILDINGS.
MONKS AGAIN SET THEMSELVES ON FIRE IN PROTEST.
GENERAL KY QUELLED THE REBELLION, AND GENERAL THI WAS EXILED TO THE UNITED STATES. KY WAS WELL KNOWN FOR HIS FAMOUS QUOTE:
PEOPLE ASK ME WHO MY HEROES ARE. I HAVE ONLY ONE: ***HITLER***.
NGUYEN VAN THIEU MANEUVERED HIS WAY INTO THE PRESIDENCY WITH KY AS HIS VICE PRESIDENT. WITH STRONG U.S. SUPPORT, THIEU AND KY HAD CONSOLIDATED THEIR POWER OVER SOUTH VIETNAM.
BUT OPPOSITION TO THE WAR MOUNTED - AND IT WAS NOT LIMITED TO BUDDHISTS.

From Resistance to Revolt

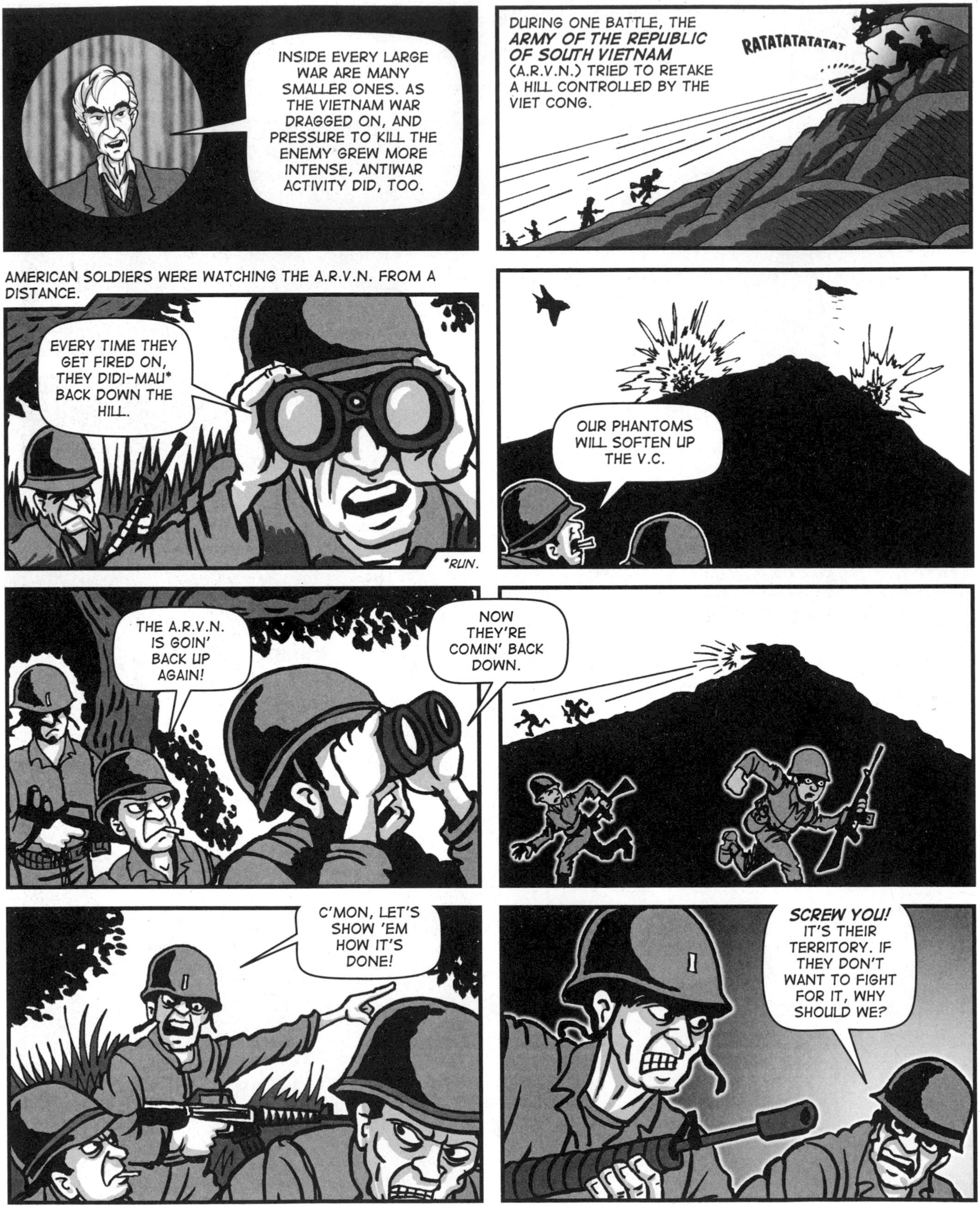
INSIDE EVERY LARGE WAR ARE MANY SMALLER ONES. AS THE VIETNAM WAR DRAGGED ON, AND PRESSURE TO KILL THE ENEMY GREW MORE INTENSE, ANTIWAR ACTIVITY DID, TOO.
DURING ONE BATTLE, THE ARMY OF THE REPUBLIC OF SOUTH VIETNAM (A.R.V.N.) TRIED TO RETAKE A HILL CONTROLLED BY THE VIET CONG.
RATATATATATAT
AMERICAN SOLDIERS WERE WATCHING THE A.R.V.N. FROM A DISTANCE.
EVERY TIME THEY GET FIRED ON, THEY DIDI-MAU* BACK DOWN THE HILL.
*RUN.
OUR PHANTOMS WILL SOFTEN UP THE V.C.
THE A.R.V.N. IS GOIN' BACK UP AGAIN!
NOW THEY'RE COMIN' BACK DOWN.
C'MON, LET'S SHOW 'EM HOW IT'S DONE!
SCREW YOU! IT'S THEIR TERRITORY. IF THEY DON'T WANT TO FIGHT FOR IT, WHY SHOULD WE?

U.S. SOLDIERS WERE APT TO BE SOUTHERN BLACK DRAFTEES. AS IN ALL OF THE COUNTRY'S EARLIER WARS, BLACK SOLDIERS FROM THE POOR AND WORKING CLASS WOULD BE THE FIRST TO REBEL. SOMETIMES THEIR ANTIWAR ACTIVITY WAS PEACEFUL.

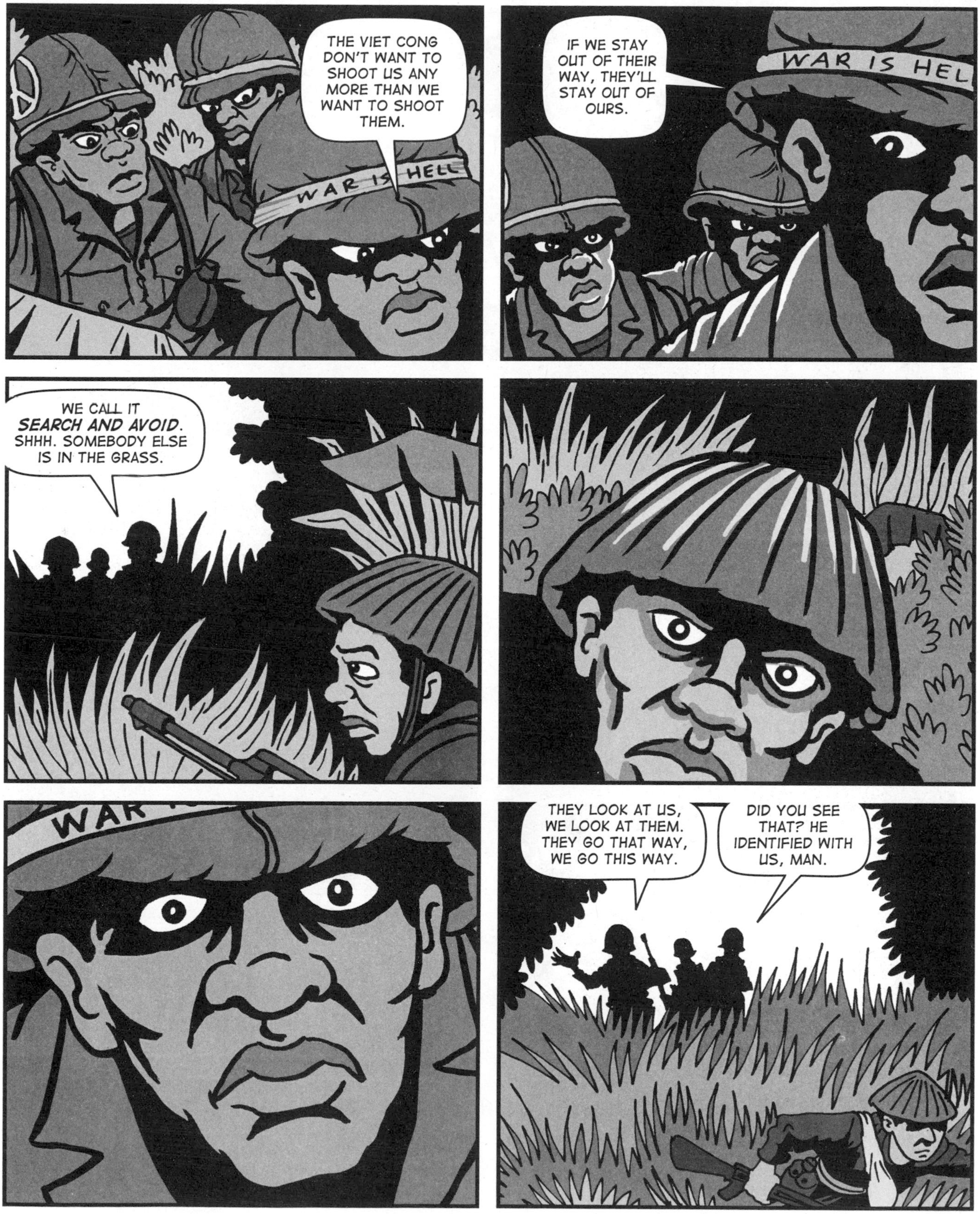

THE VIET CONG DON'T WANT TO SHOOT US ANY MORE THAN WE WANT TO SHOOT THEM.
WAR IS HELL
IF WE STAY OUT OF THEIR WAY, THEY'LL STAY OUT OF OURS.
WAR IS HEL
WE CALL IT *SEARCH AND AVOID*. SHHH. SOMEBODY ELSE IS IN THE GRASS.
WAR
THEY LOOK AT US, WE LOOK AT THEM. THEY GO THAT WAY, WE GO THIS WAY.
DID YOU SEE THAT? HE IDENTIFIED WITH US, MAN.

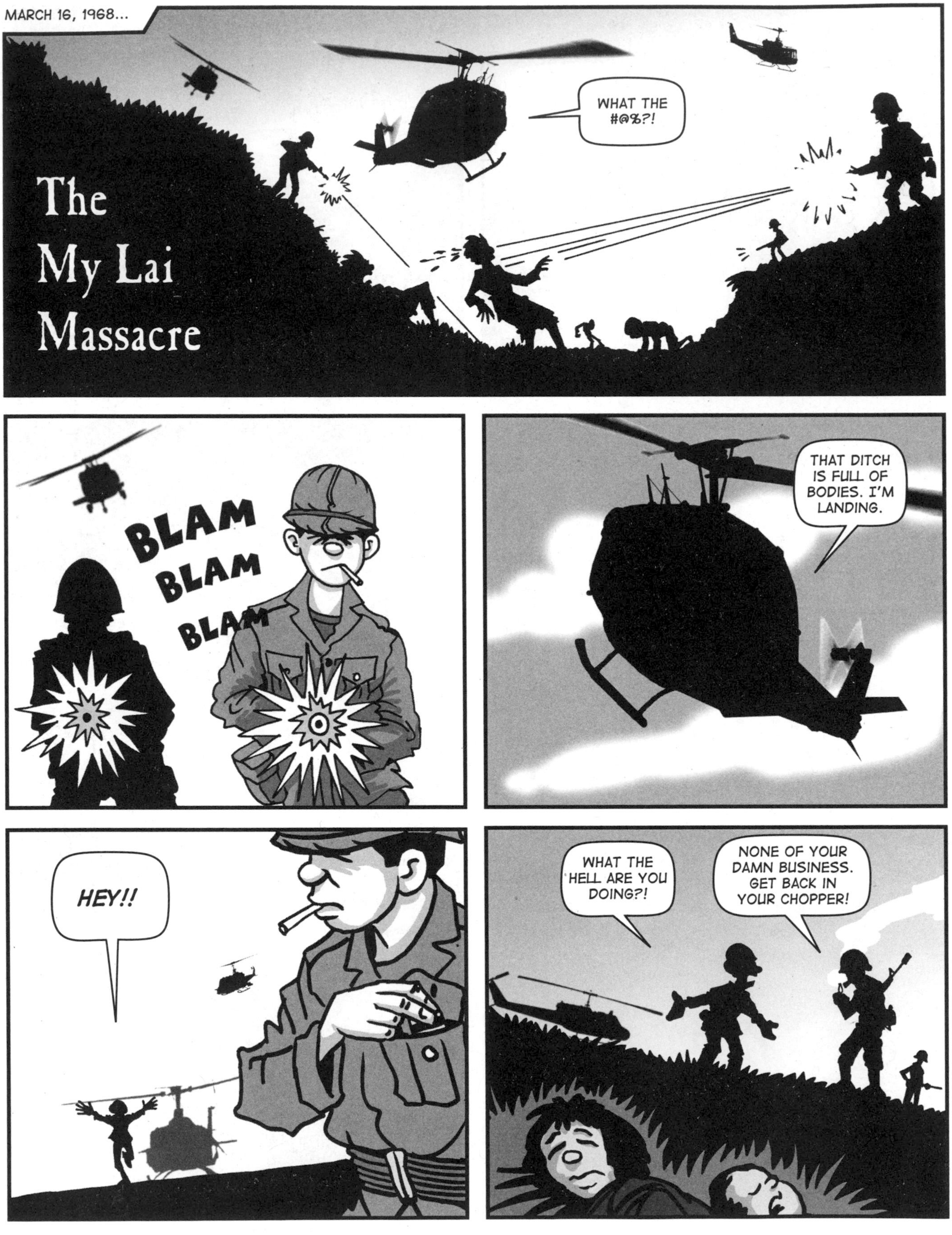
MARCH 16, 1968...
The My Lai Massacre
WHAT THE #@%?!
BLAM
BLAM
BLAM
THAT DITCH IS FULL OF BODIES. I'M LANDING.
HEY!!
WHAT THE HELL ARE YOU DOING?!
NONE OF YOUR DAMN BUSINESS. GET BACK IN YOUR CHOPPER!

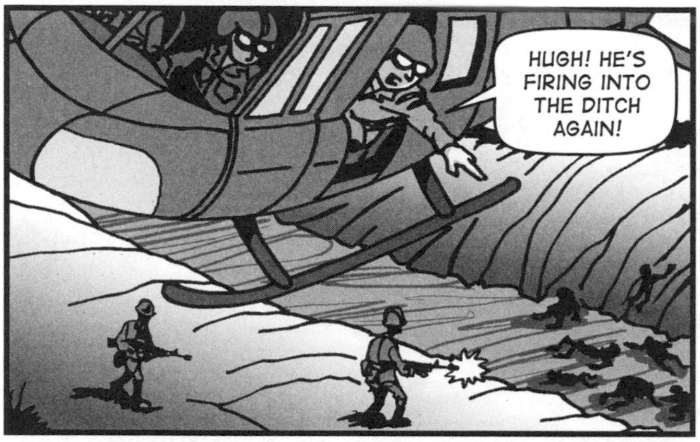
HUGH! HE'S FIRING INTO THE DITCH AGAIN!

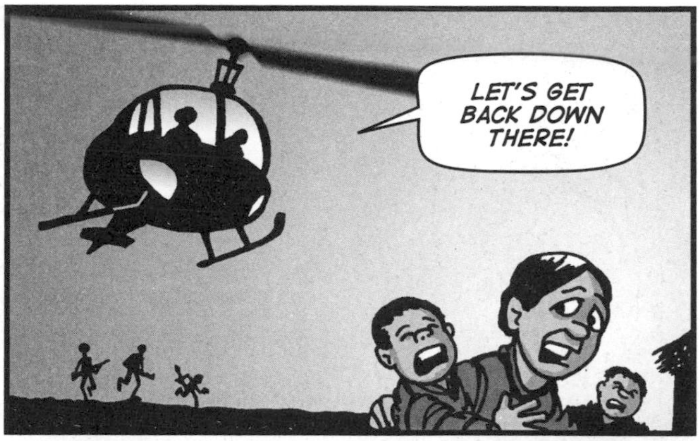
LET'S GET BACK DOWN THERE!

PILOT ***HUGH THOMPSON*** JUMPED FROM HIS CHOPPER, OUTRAGED AT WHAT HE WAS SEEING.

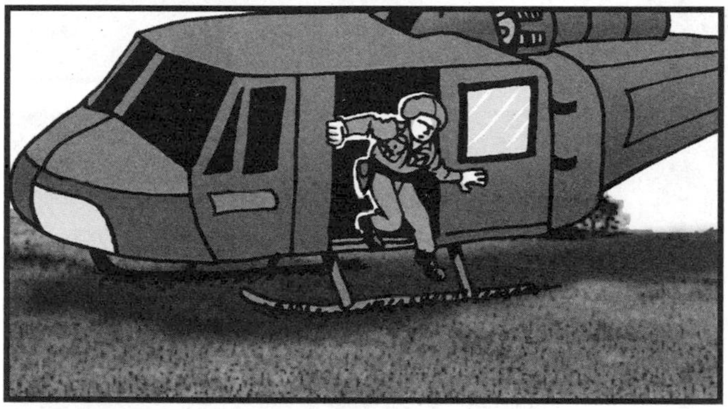

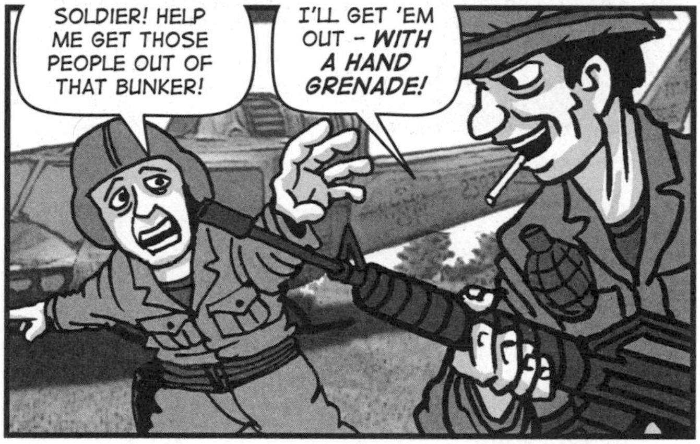
SOLDIER! HELP ME GET THOSE PEOPLE OUT OF THAT BUNKER!
I'LL GET 'EM OUT - ***WITH A HAND GRENADE!***

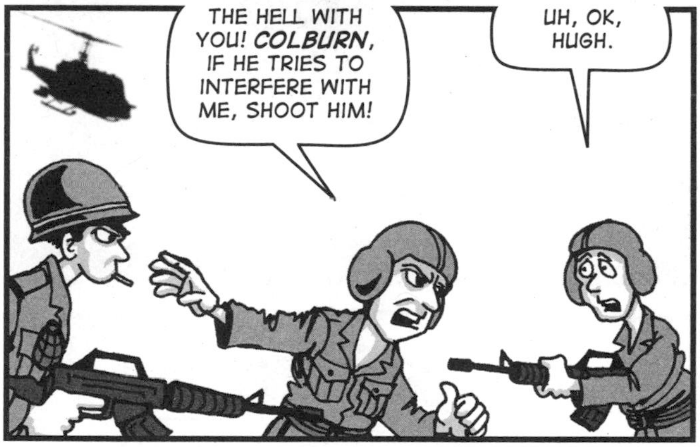
THE HELL WITH YOU! ***COLBURN***, IF HE TRIES TO INTERFERE WITH ME, SHOOT HIM!
UH, OK, HUGH.

THOMPSON AND HIS CREW RESCUED FOUR ADULTS AND FIVE CHILDREN FROM THE VILLAGE OF MY LAI.

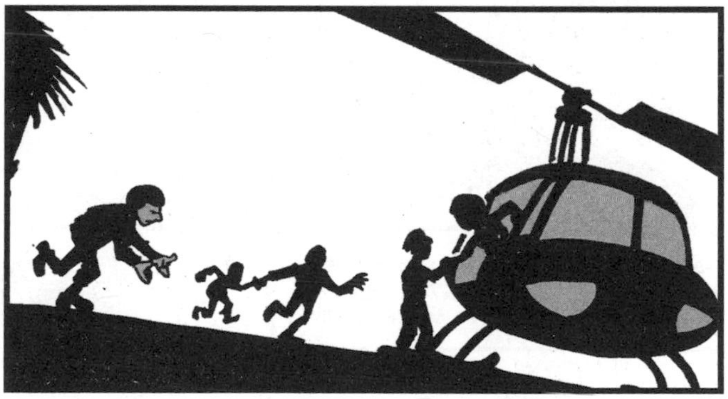

A SHORT WHILE LATER, THEY WENT BACK TO THE DITCH.

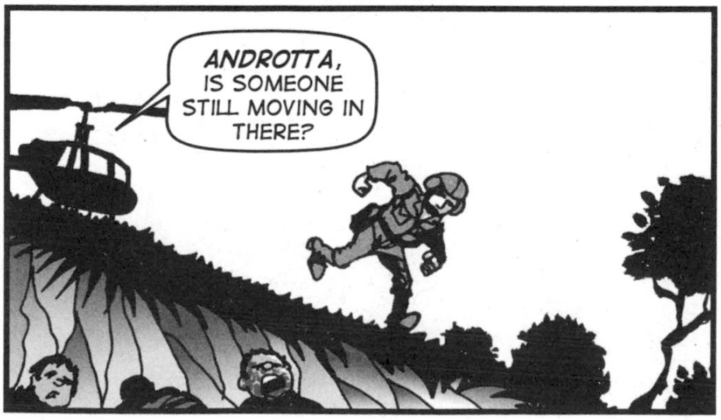
ANDROTTA, IS SOMEONE STILL MOVING IN THERE?

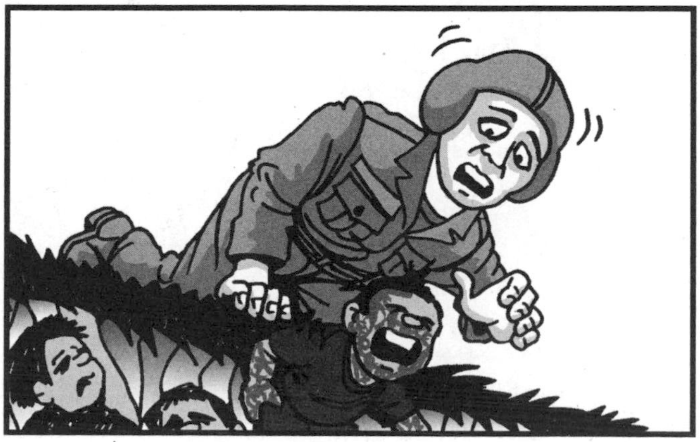

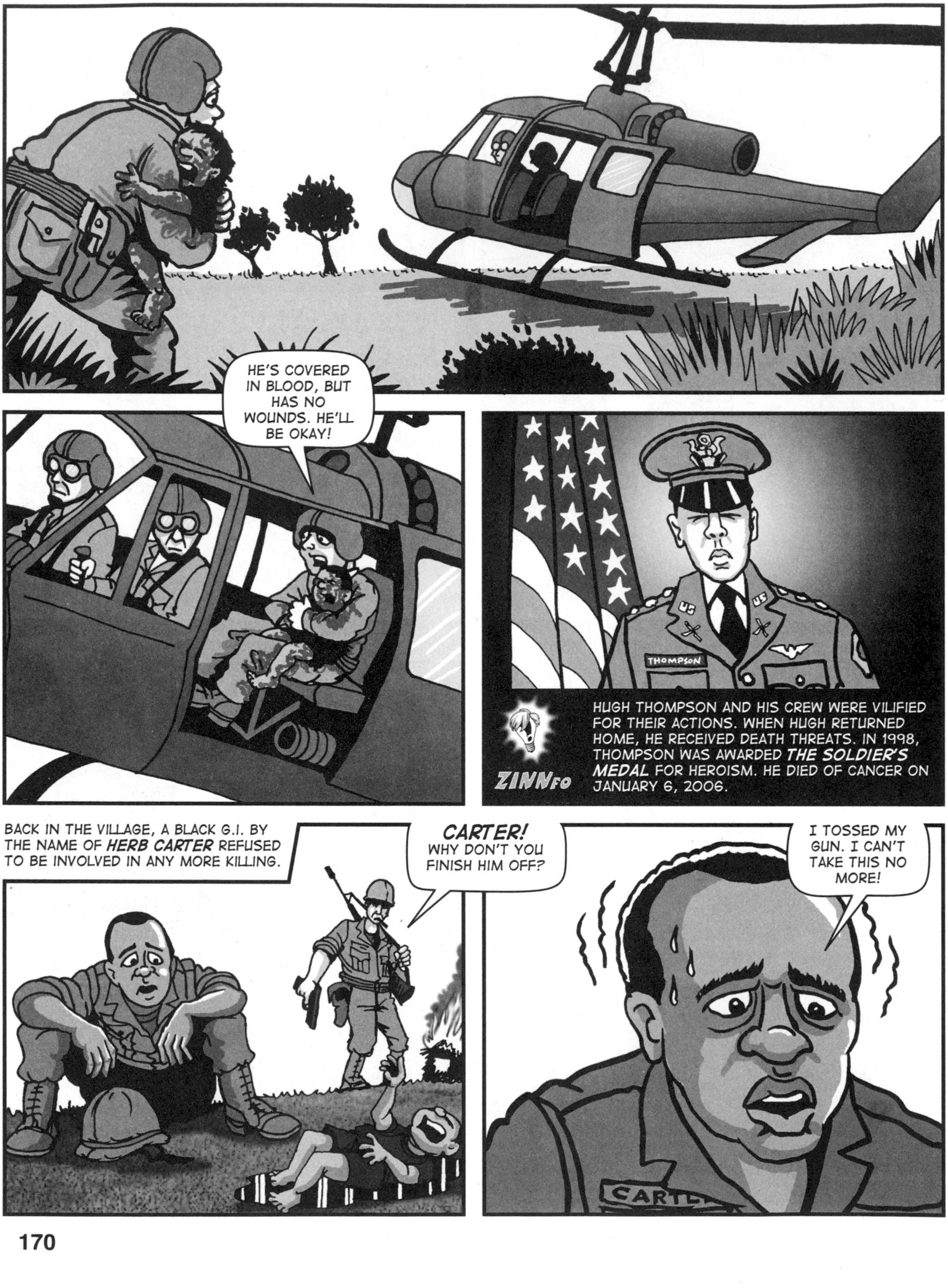
HE'S COVERED IN BLOOD, BUT HAS NO WOUNDS. HE'LL BE OKAY!
THOMPSON
ZINNFO
HUGH THOMPSON AND HIS CREW WERE VILIFIED FOR THEIR ACTIONS. WHEN HUGH RETURNED HOME, HE RECEIVED DEATH THREATS. IN 1998, THOMPSON WAS AWARDED ***THE SOLDIER'S MEDAL*** FOR HEROISM. HE DIED OF CANCER ON JANUARY 6, 2006.
BACK IN THE VILLAGE, A BLACK G.I. BY THE NAME OF ***HERB CARTER*** REFUSED TO BE INVOLVED IN ANY MORE KILLING.
CARTER! WHY DON'T YOU FINISH HIM OFF?
I TOSSED MY GUN. I CAN'T TAKE THIS NO MORE!

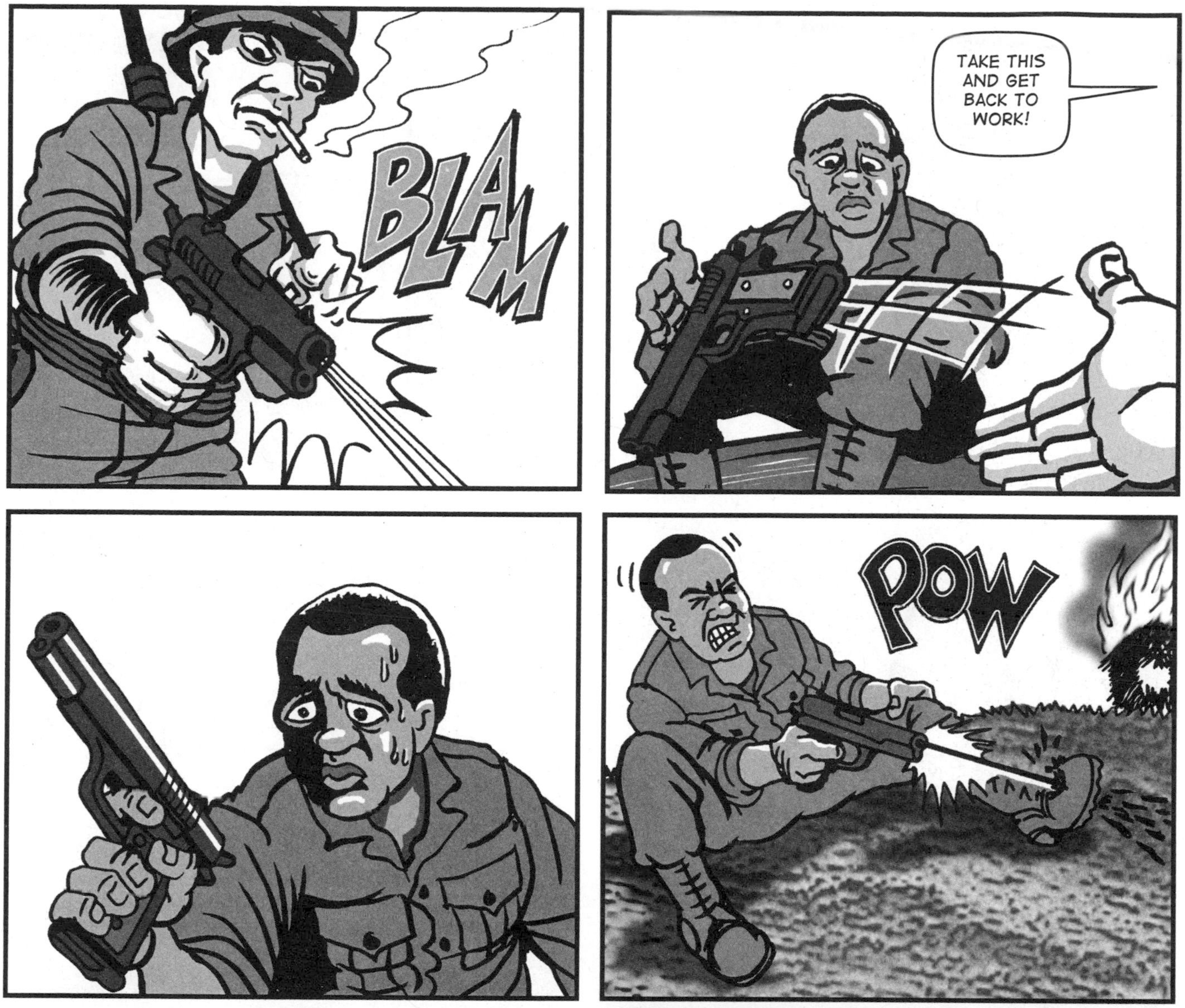
BLAM
TAKE THIS AND GET BACK TO WORK!
POW

THE BUTCHERY WAS WHOLESALE. EVEN THE PEASANTS' ANIMALS WERE SHOT BECAUSE THEY WERE CONSIDERED VIET CONG SUPPORT UNITS.

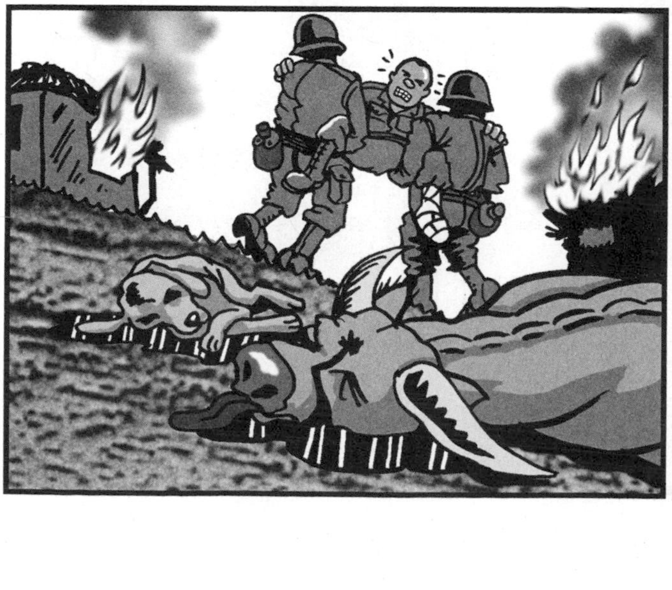

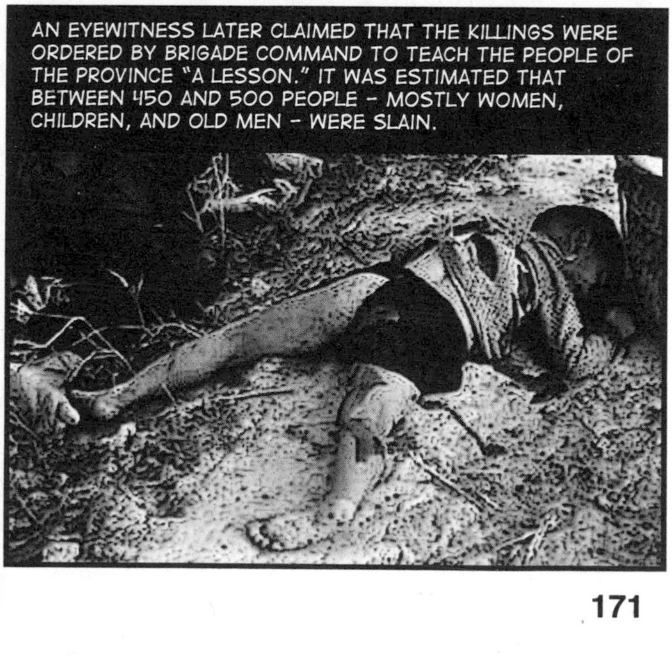
AN EYEWITNESS LATER CLAIMED THAT THE KILLINGS WERE ORDERED BY BRIGADE COMMAND TO TEACH THE PEOPLE OF THE PROVINCE "A LESSON." IT WAS ESTIMATED THAT BETWEEN 450 AND 500 PEOPLE - MOSTLY WOMEN, CHILDREN, AND OLD MEN - WERE SLAIN.

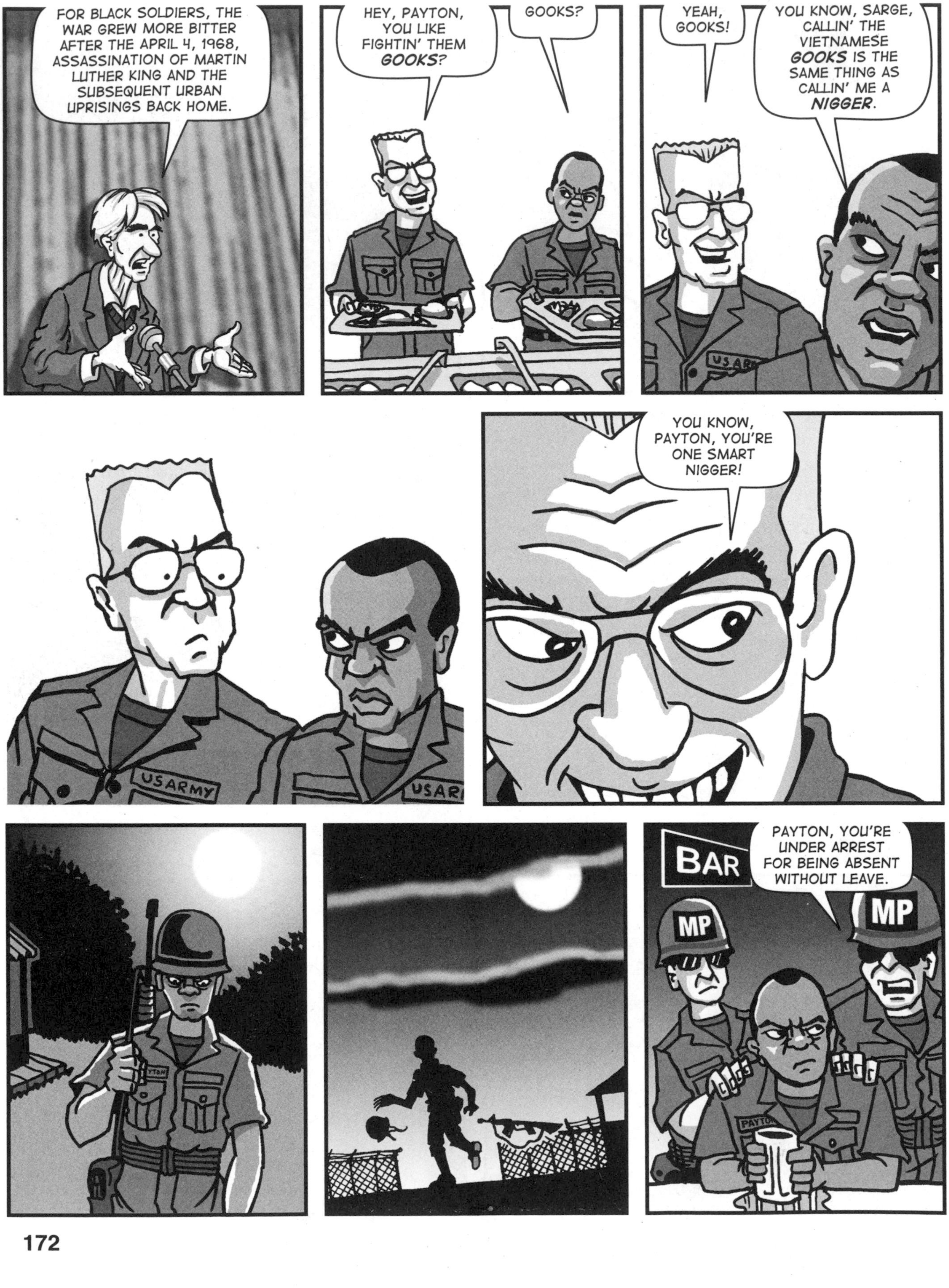
FOR BLACK SOLDIERS, THE WAR GREW MORE BITTER AFTER THE APRIL 4, 1968, ASSASSINATION OF MARTIN LUTHER KING AND THE SUBSEQUENT URBAN UPRISINGS BACK HOME.
HEY, PAYTON, YOU LIKE FIGHTIN' THEM *GOOKS*?
GOOKS?
YEAH, GOOKS!
YOU KNOW, SARGE, CALLIN' THE VIETNAMESE *GOOKS* IS THE SAME THING AS CALLIN' ME A *NIGGER*.
YOU KNOW, PAYTON, YOU'RE ONE SMART NIGGER!
BAR
PAYTON, YOU'RE UNDER ARREST FOR BEING ABSENT WITHOUT LEAVE.
MP
MP

G.I. ***GARY PAYTON*** WAS CONVICTED AND SENTENCED TO SIX MONTHS IN THE ***LONG BINH JAIL*** FOR GOING AWOL.

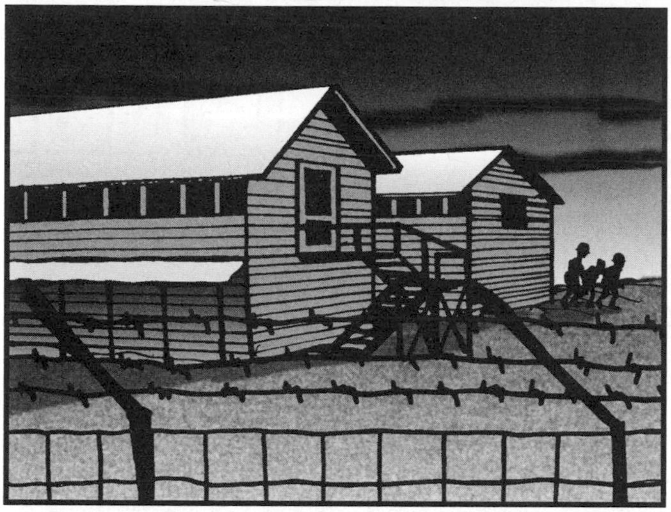

PRISONERS CALLED THE STOCKADE "L.B.J." FOR SHORT. IT WAS NOTORIOUS FOR ITS SQUALOR AND THE SADISM OF ITS GUARDS. PAYTON SPENT TIME IN "THE BOX," WITH TWO 15-MINUTE BREAKS A DAY AND FREQUENT MEALS OF LETTUCE LEAVES ROLLED IN WATER.

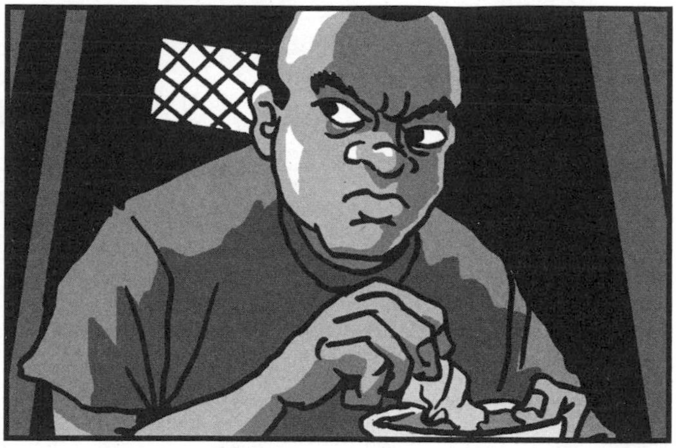

NINETY PERCENT OF THE PRISONERS IN LONG BINH JAIL WERE BLACK. SOME DEVELOPED AN INTENSE AFRICANIST NATIONALISM. IT WAS HERE THAT THE ***DAP**** WAS CREATED - A COMPLICATED HANDSHAKE THAT COULD TAKE TWO MINUTES OR LONGER .

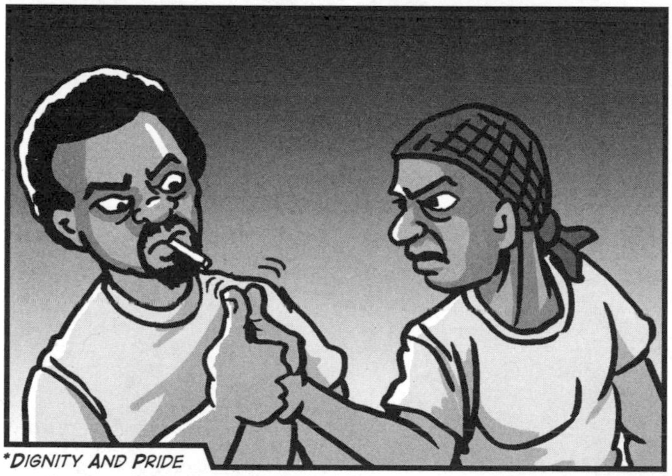

**DIGNITY AND PRIDE*

ALTHOUGH A FEW MOVES WERE STANDARDIZED, MUCH OF THE DAP WAS IMPROVISED - JAZZ FOR THE HANDS. IT HAS SURVIVED TO THIS DAY.

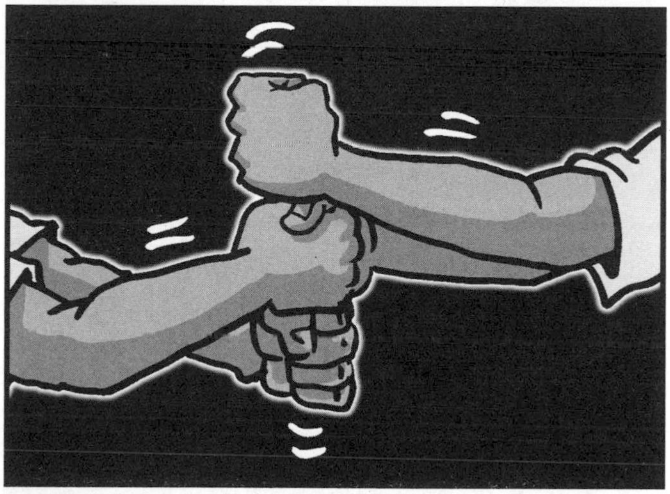

WHEN HE WAS FREED FROM THE BOX, PAYTON PULLED "GOOD DUTY," DRIVING A TRUCK OUTSIDE THE STOCKADE.

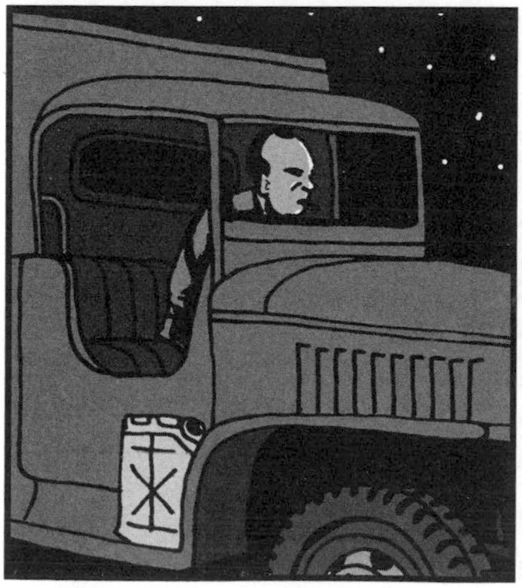

HIS JOB WAS TO USE ***KEROSENE*** TO BURN THE CAMP FECES.

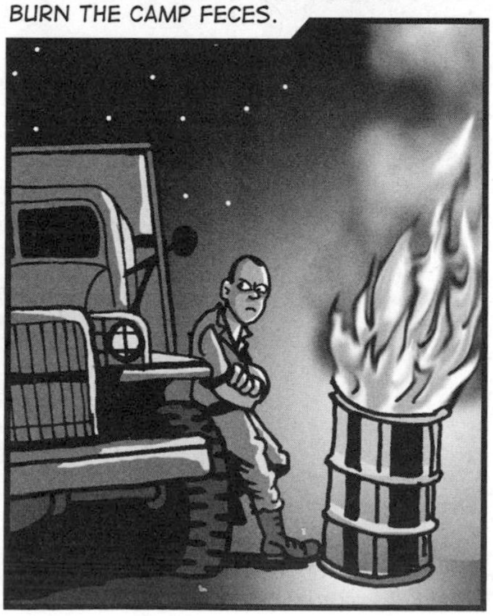

SOON AFTER, A GROUP OF INMATES PERSUADED HIM TO BRING AN EXTRA CAN INTO CAMP EVERY OTHER NIGHT.

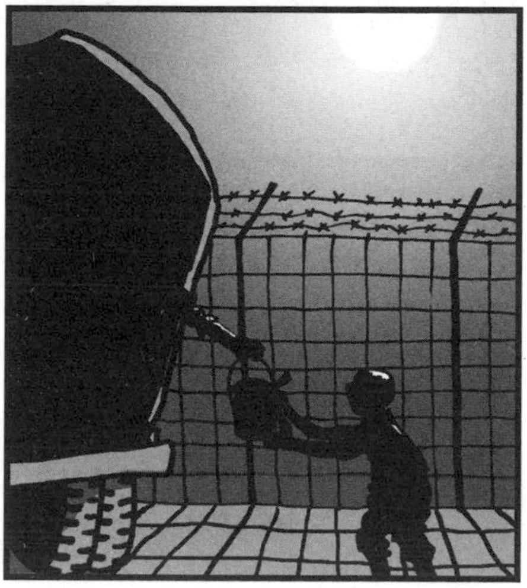

MIDNIGHT, AUGUST 29, 1968...

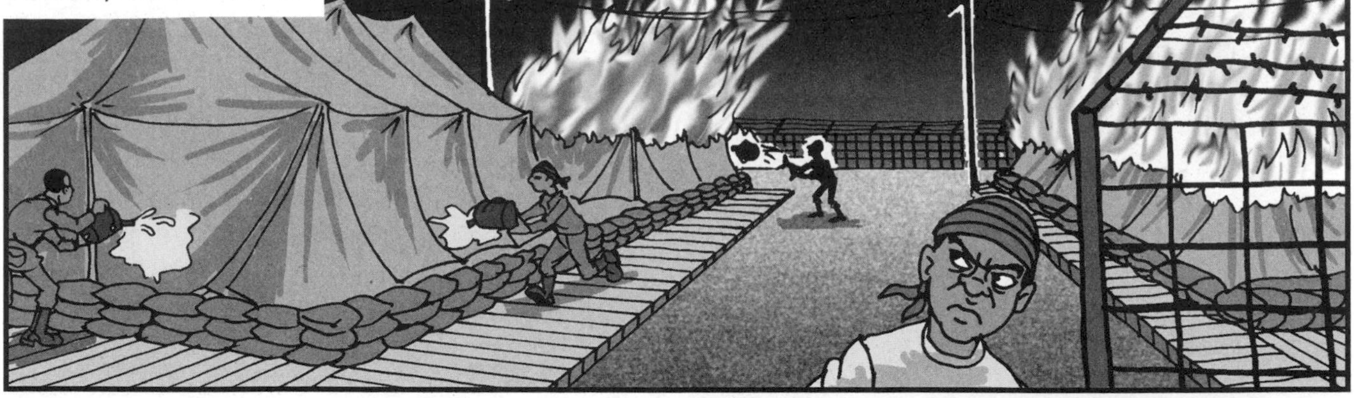

ONE MAN WAS KILLED. SEVEN BUILDINGS AND 19 TENTS WERE DESTROYED. THE ***LONG BINH JAIL REBELLION*** WAS THE SINGLE LARGEST SOLDIER REVOLT IN VIETNAM.

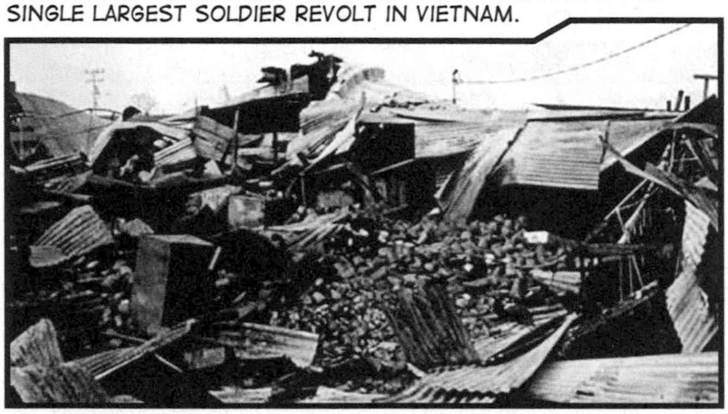

BUT OFFICERS IN THE FIELD HAD MORE PRESSING WORRIES THAN ARSON.

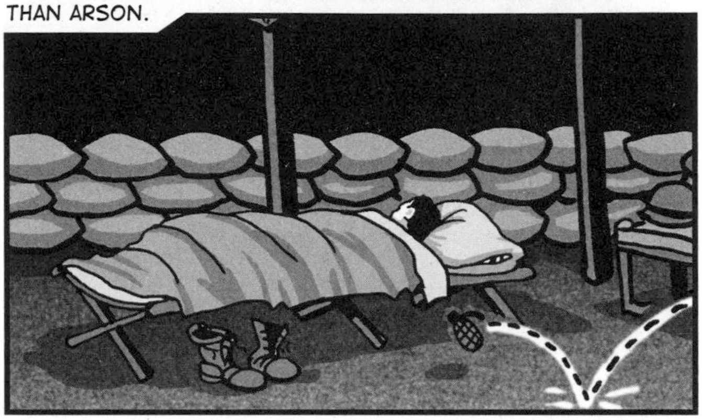

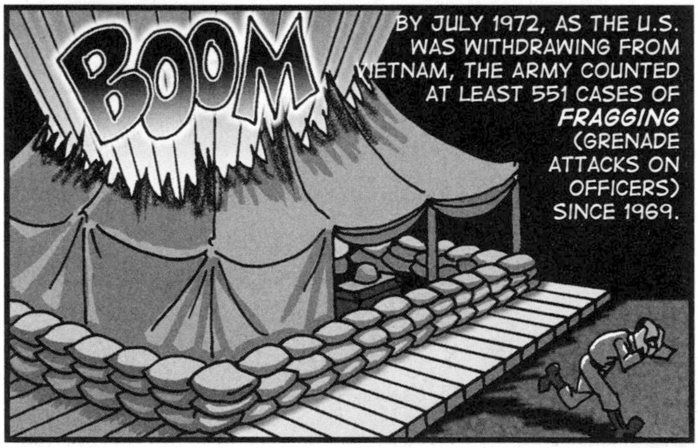
BOOM
BY JULY 1972, AS THE U.S. WAS WITHDRAWING FROM VIETNAM, THE ARMY COUNTED AT LEAST 551 CASES OF ***FRAGGING*** (GRENADE ATTACKS ON OFFICERS) SINCE 1969.

AS THE BATTLES WITH THE VIET CONG AND NORTH VIETNAMESE ARMY BECAME BLOODIER AND MORE POINTLESS, LIFERS* WERE ALSO SEEN AS THE ENEMY.

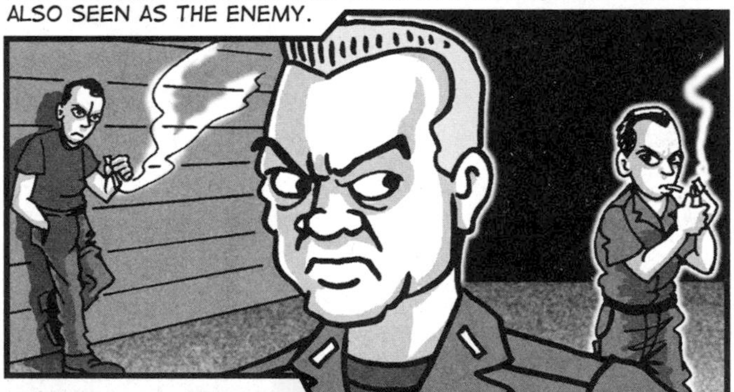

**CAREER MILITARY OFFICERS*

ONE MARINE REPORTED THAT WHEN A LIFER WAS SEEN NEAR THE FENCE, SOME MARINES CALLED OUT...

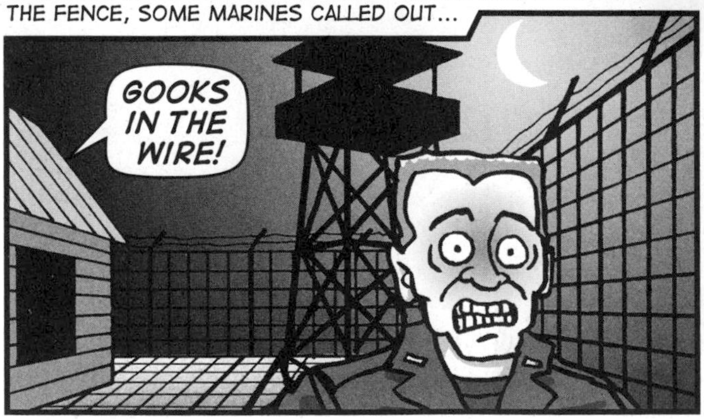
GOOKS IN THE WIRE!

"THEN YOU TRY TO KILL ANY OF THE LIFERS YOU DON'T LIKE."

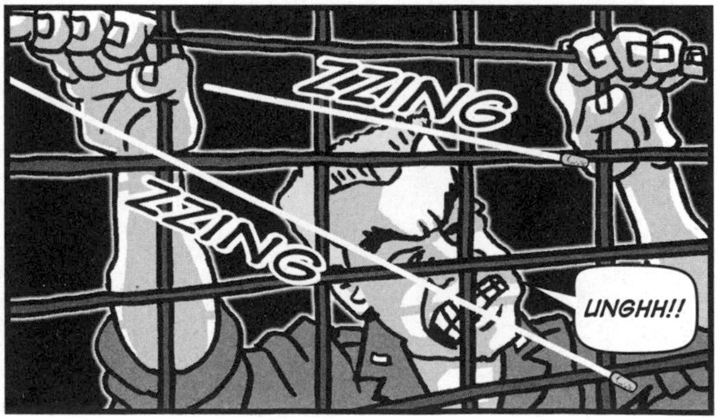
ZZING
ZZING
UNGHH!!

A Peace Mission

IN JANUARY 1968, THE YEAR AFTER I PUBLISHED A BOOK ON VIETNAM, I GOT A CALL FROM *DAVID DELLINGER*, VETERAN PACIFIST AND ONE OF THE NATIONAL LEADERS OF THE ANTIWAR MOVEMENT.

THE NORTH VIETNAMESE ARE WILLING TO RELEASE THREE CAPTURED U.S. PILOTS IF THE PEACE MOVEMENT SENDS A RESPONSIBLE REPRESENTATIVE. WILL YOU GO?

THE NEXT MORNING IN MANHATTAN, I MET WITH *DANIEL BERRIGAN*, PEACE ACTIVIST AND JESUIT PRIEST. HE HAD ALREADY AGREED TO GO.

I'M SO GLAD WE ARE GOING TOGETHER, HOWARD.

THE TRIP TO NORTH VIETNAM TOOK 28 HOURS – THROUGH COPENHAGEN, FRANKFURT, TEHRAN, CALCUTTA, AND BANGKOK – BEFORE WE LANDED IN LAOS TO MAKE THE FINAL LEG TO HANOI.

WHILE COOLING OUR HEELS IN A SEEDY HOTEL IN VIENTIANE, LAOS, THE VIET CONG IN SOUTH VIETNAM IGNITED THE *TET OFFENSIVE*, A TURNING POINT AGAINST THE U.S. OCCUPATION.

WHEN WE WERE FINALLY ABLE TO FLY INTO NORTH VIETNAM, THE ROAD TO HANOI WAS A SCENE OF BOMBED-OUT BUILDINGS AND PEOPLE EVERYWHERE ON FOOT AND BICYCLES.

WE FELL ASLEEP, EXHAUSTED. AMERICAN BOMBS AND NORTH VIETNAMESE ANTIAIRCRAFT GUNS WOKE US UP.

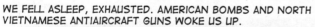

THE NEXT DAY, WE DISCOVERED A CITY WITHOUT CHILDREN. LIKE LONDON DURING THE BLITZ, ALMOST ALL HAD BEEN SENT TO THE COUNTRYSIDE.

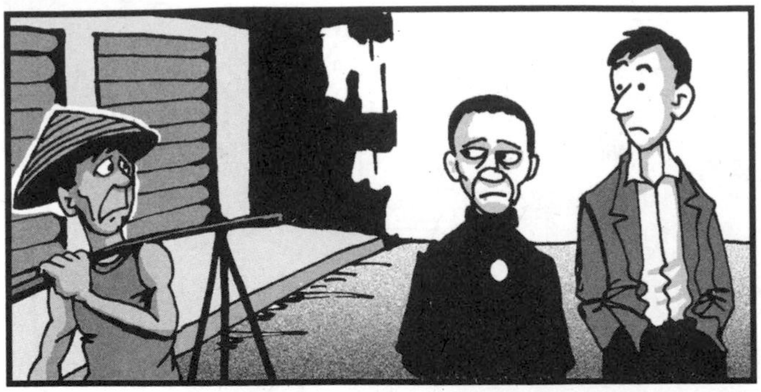

AT THE ZOO, THE MONKEY CAGES WERE EMPTY. THEY, TOO, HAD BEEN SENT AWAY. HANOI WAS UNSAFE FOR CHILDREN - AND MONKEYS.

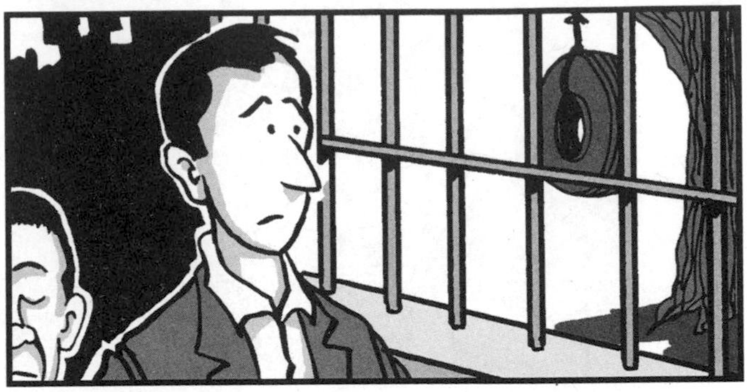

Why these 3 men?

AFTER AN UNEVENTFUL PRESS CONFERENCE, WE "RECEIVED" THE THREE FLIERS: MAJOR ***NORRIS OVERLY***, CAPTAIN ***JOHN BLACK***, AND LIEUTENANT J. G. ***DAVID METHANY***. WE ALL FLEW BACK TO VIENTIANE AND THEN HOME TO A DIFFERENT KIND OF WAR.

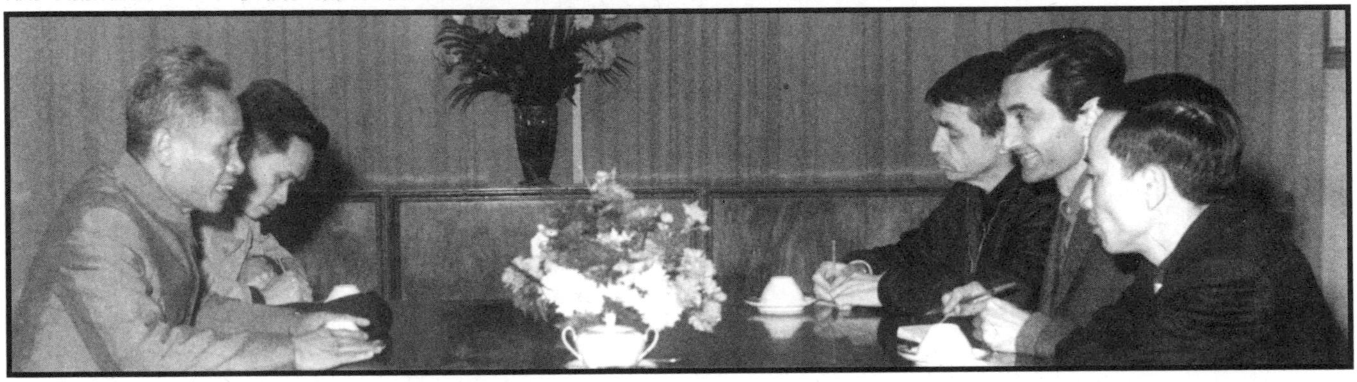

AS WE LEFT VIETNAM, I LOOKED OVER THE SCARRED COUNTRYSIDE AND THOUGHT HOW THE WORLD HAD CHANGED SINCE I SAW "THANK YOU" SPELLED OUT IN TULIPS ON OUR LAST MISSION IN EUROPE. A FEW YEARS LATER I RECALLED THAT MOMENT WHEN I CAME ACROSS A PHOTO OF THE HUGE PEACE SYMBOL BULLDOZED INTO THE POCKMARKED EARTH OF VIETNAM BY ANTIWAR G.I.s OF THE 101ST AIRBORNE. IT WAS MY TURN TO SAY TO THEM, "THANK YOU."

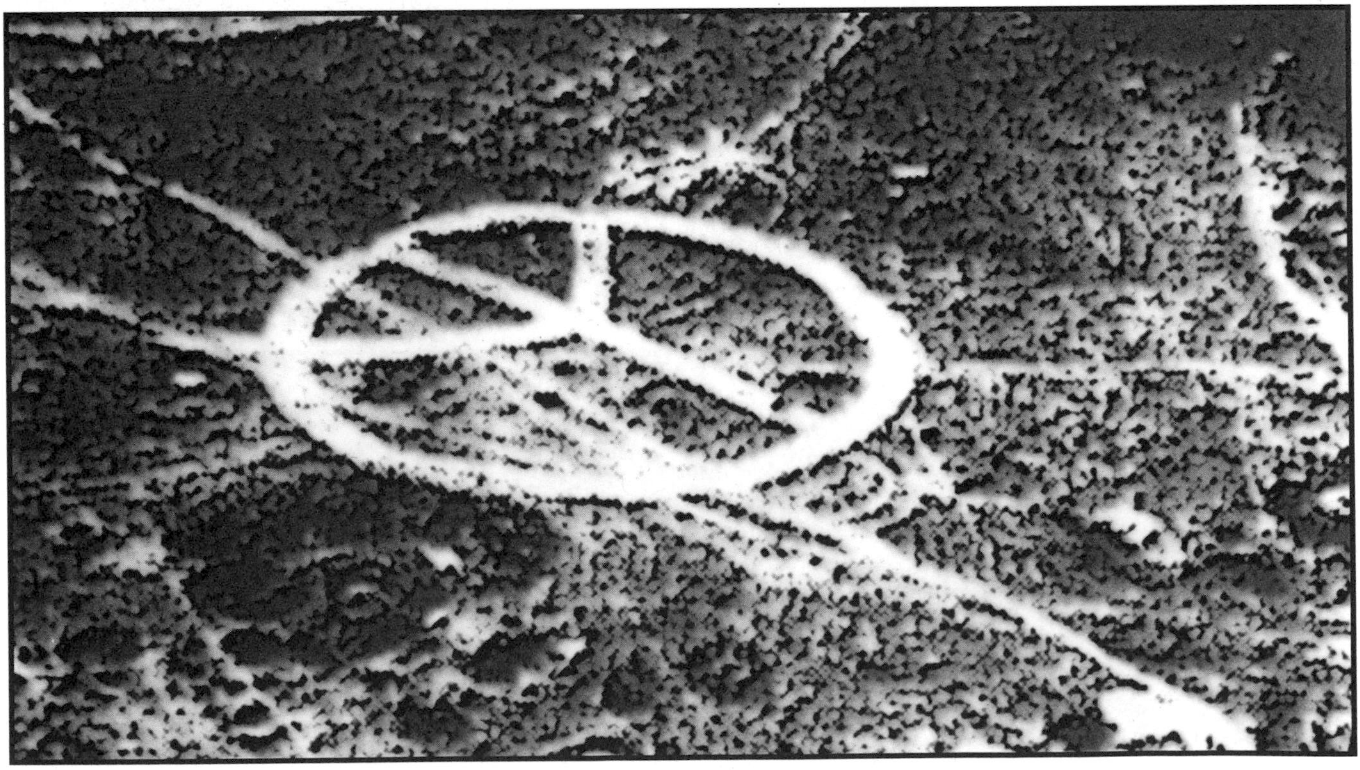

Chapter IX

LAND OF BURNING CHILDREN

"We could not, so help us God, do otherwise. For we are sick at heart, our hearts give us no rest for thinking of the land of burning children."

What Happens to a Dream Deferred?

DOES IT DRY UP LIKE A RAISIN IN THE SUN? OR FESTER LIKE A SORE – AND THEN RUN? DOES IT STINK LIKE ROTTEN MEAT? OR CRUST AND SUGAR OVER – LIKE A SYRUPY SWEET? MAYBE IT JUST SAGS LIKE A HEAVY LOAD. ***OR DOES IT EXPLODE?***

– LANGSTON HUGHES, "HARLEM"

IN HIS BOOK ***A THOUSAND DAYS***, WHITE HOUSE ADVISER ***ARTHUR SCHLESINGER, JR.*** TELLS HOW PRESIDENT ***JOHN F. KENNEDY*** MET WITH CIVIL RIGHTS LEADERS AND PERSUADED THEM NOT TO LAY SIEGE TO CAPITOL HILL DURING THE 1963 MARCH ON WASHINGTON.

Why tell them not to do something they never planned to do

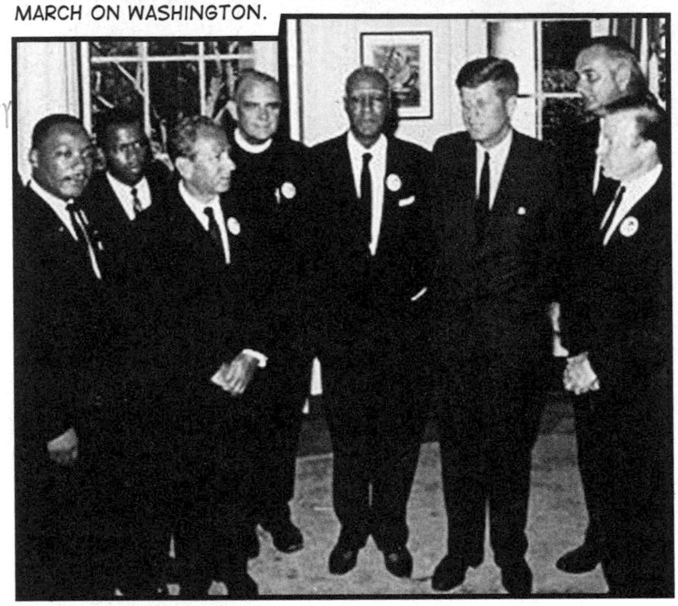

THE MARCH ATTRACTED 200,000 PEACEFUL DEMONSTRATORS. THE REVEREND ***MARTIN LUTHER KING, JR.***'S ELOQUENT SPEECH GAVE HOPE AND IMPETUS TO THE BURGEONING CIVIL RIGHTS MOVEMENT.

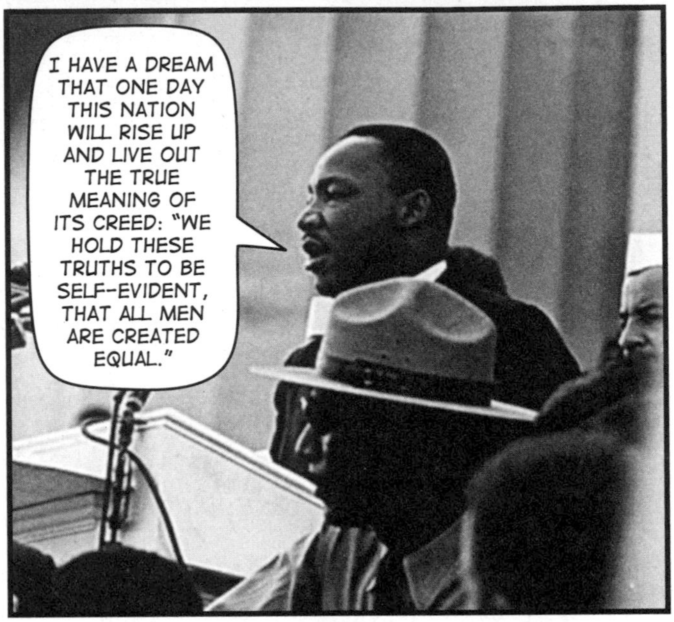
I HAVE A DREAM THAT ONE DAY THIS NATION WILL RISE UP AND LIVE OUT THE TRUE MEANING OF ITS CREED: "WE HOLD THESE TRUTHS TO BE SELF-EVIDENT, THAT ALL MEN ARE CREATED EQUAL."

SCHLESINGER'S BOOK DESCRIBES THE MARCH ADMIRINGLY, NOTING: "SO IN 1963 KENNEDY MOVED TO INCORPORATE THE NEGRO REVOLUTION INTO THE DEMOCRATIC COALITION."

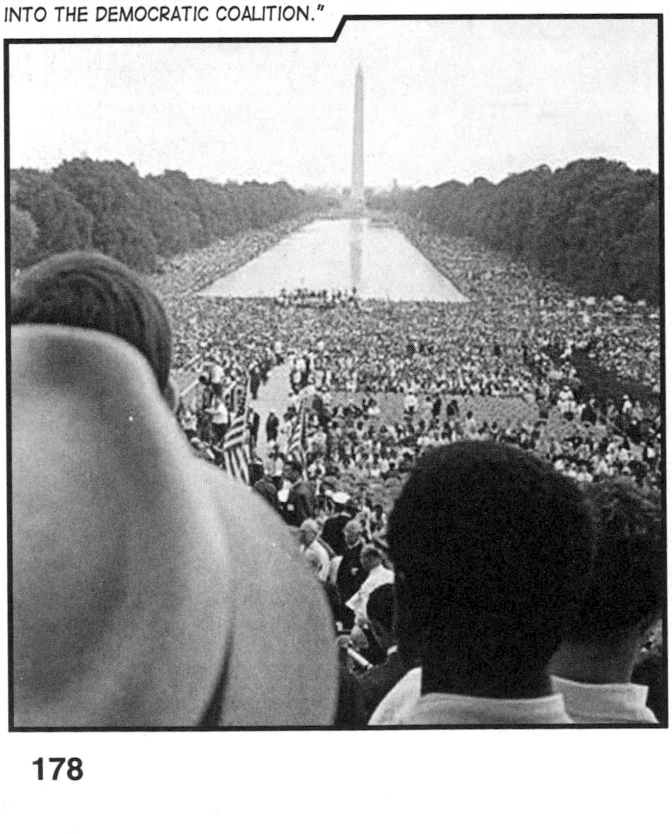

IT DIDN'T WORK, EVEN WITH THE PASSAGE OF THE GROUNDBREAKING ***1964 CIVIL RIGHTS ACT*** AND THE ***1965 VOTING RIGHTS ACT***. IT BECAME CLEAR THAT BLACKS COULD NOT BE EASILY BROUGHT INTO THE DEMOCRATIC COALITION WHEN BOMBS KEPT EXPLODING IN CHURCHES...

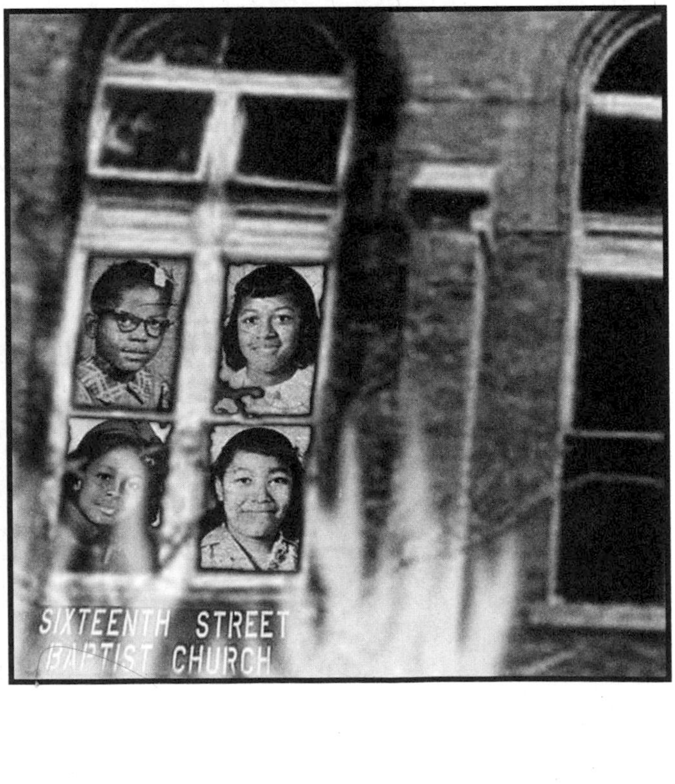
SIXTEENTH STREET
BAPTIST CHURCH

...WHEN NEW CIVIL RIGHTS LAWS DID NOT CHANGE THE ROOT CONDITION OF BLACK PEOPLE...

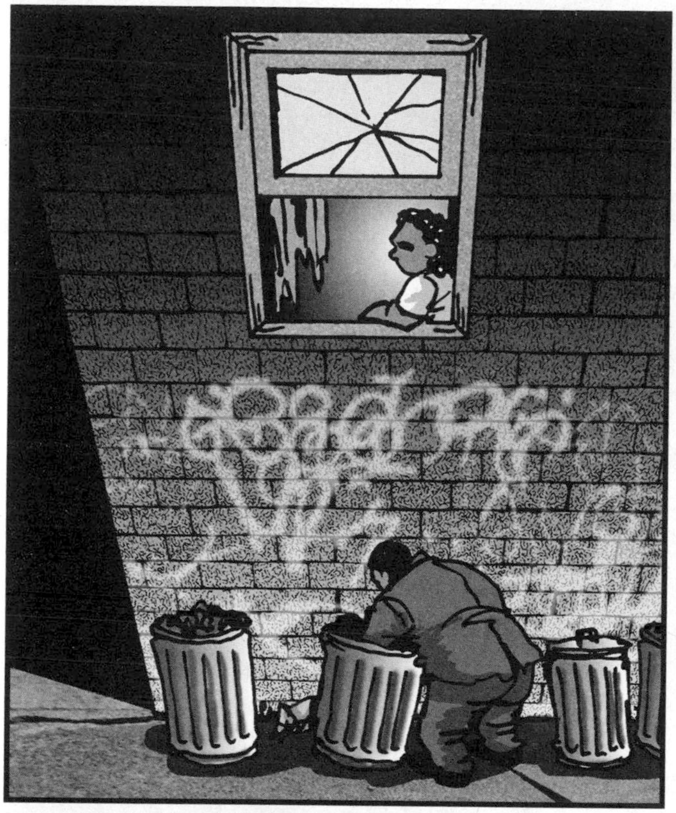

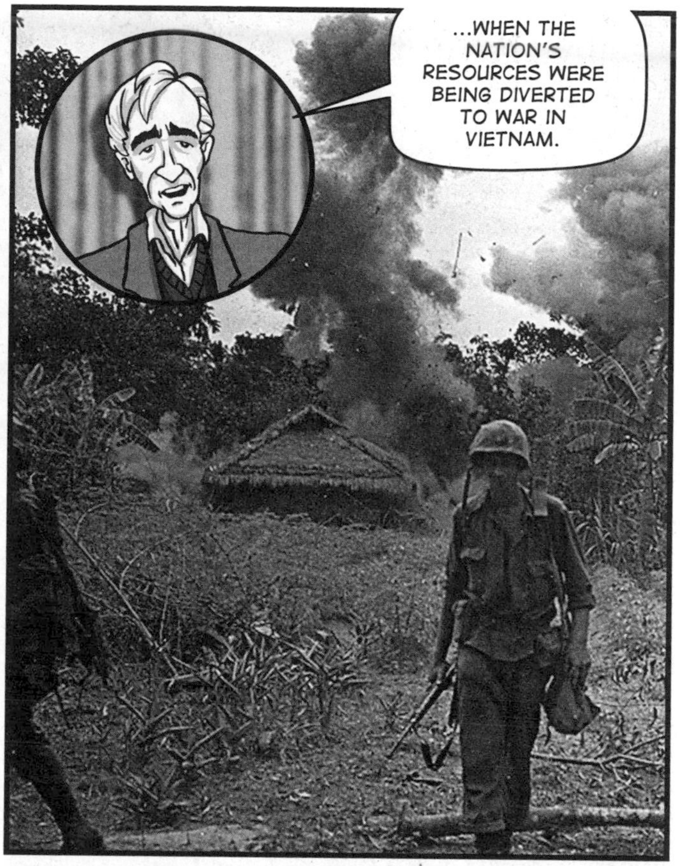

...WHEN THE NATION'S RESOURCES WERE BEING DIVERTED TO WAR IN VIETNAM.

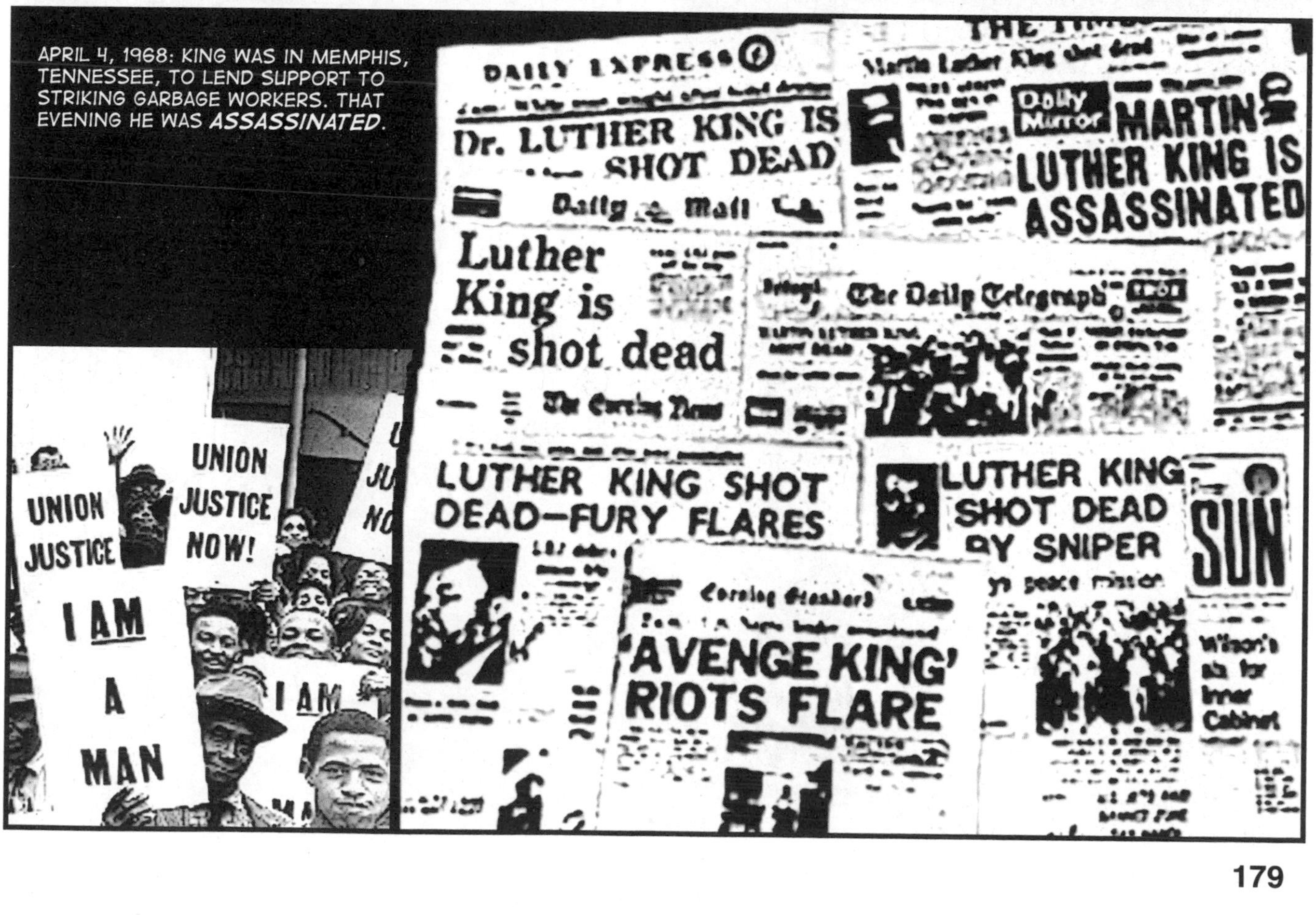

APRIL 4, 1968: KING WAS IN MEMPHIS, TENNESSEE, TO LEND SUPPORT TO STRIKING GARBAGE WORKERS. THAT EVENING HE WAS *ASSASSINATED*.
UNION JUSTICE
I AM A MAN
UNION JUSTICE NOW!
I AM
DAILY EXPRESS
Dr. LUTHER KING IS SHOT DEAD
Daily Mail
Daily Mirror
MARTIN LUTHER KING IS ASSASSINATED
Luther King is shot dead
The Evening News
The Daily Telegraph
LUTHER KING SHOT DEAD—FURY FLARES
LUTHER KING SHOT DEAD BY SNIPER
SUN
Evening Standard
'AVENGE KING' RIOTS FLARE
Wilson's ... for Inner Cabinet

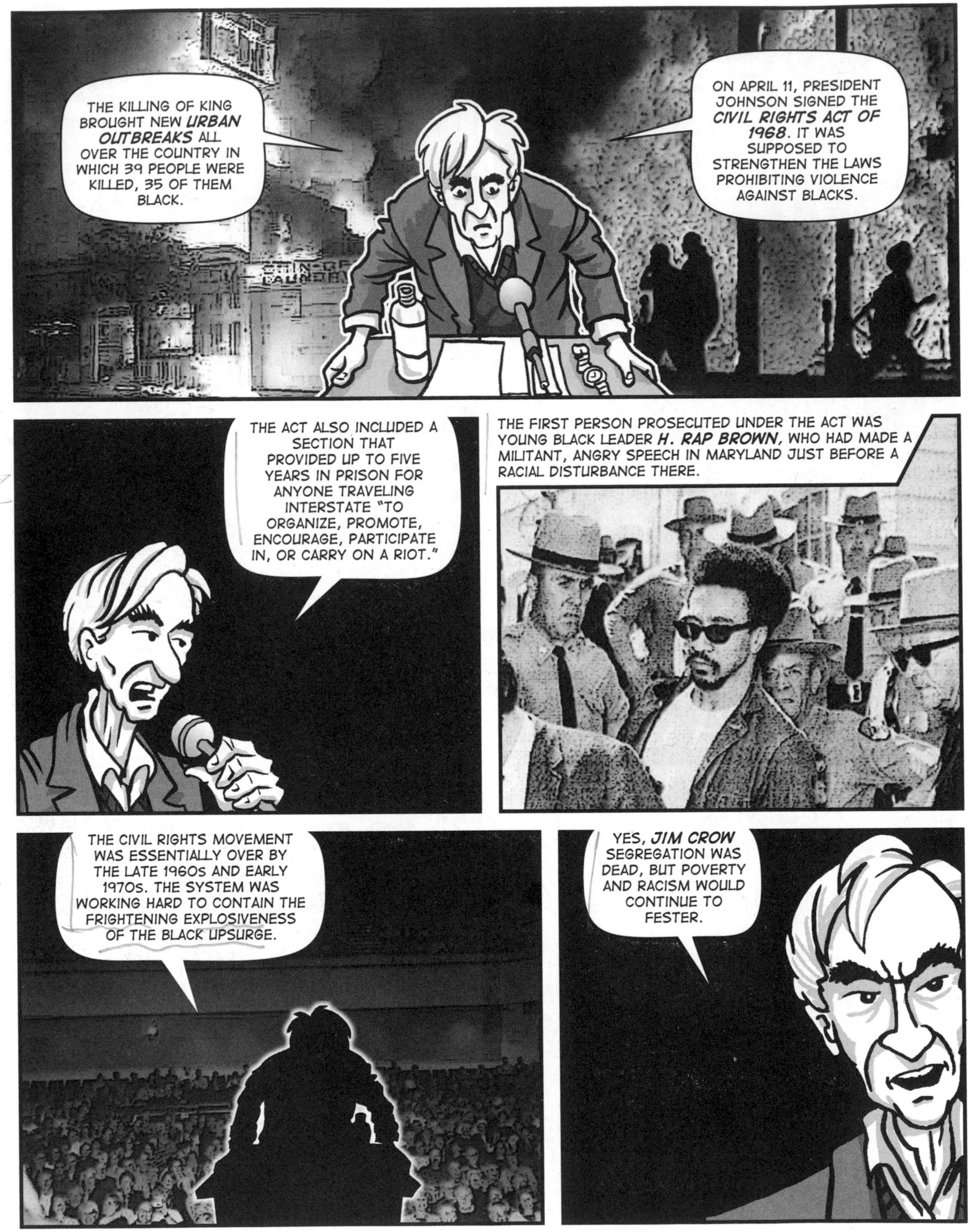
THE KILLING OF KING BROUGHT NEW URBAN OUTBREAKS ALL OVER THE COUNTRY IN WHICH 39 PEOPLE WERE KILLED, 35 OF THEM BLACK.
ON APRIL 11, PRESIDENT JOHNSON SIGNED THE CIVIL RIGHTS ACT OF 1968. IT WAS SUPPOSED TO STRENGTHEN THE LAWS PROHIBITING VIOLENCE AGAINST BLACKS.
THE ACT ALSO INCLUDED A SECTION THAT PROVIDED UP TO FIVE YEARS IN PRISON FOR ANYONE TRAVELING INTERSTATE "TO ORGANIZE, PROMOTE, ENCOURAGE, PARTICIPATE IN, OR CARRY ON A RIOT."
THE FIRST PERSON PROSECUTED UNDER THE ACT WAS YOUNG BLACK LEADER H. RAP BROWN, WHO HAD MADE A MILITANT, ANGRY SPEECH IN MARYLAND JUST BEFORE A RACIAL DISTURBANCE THERE.
THE CIVIL RIGHTS MOVEMENT WAS ESSENTIALLY OVER BY THE LATE 1960s AND EARLY 1970s. THE SYSTEM WAS WORKING HARD TO CONTAIN THE FRIGHTENING EXPLOSIVENESS OF THE BLACK UPSURGE.
YES, JIM CROW SEGREGATION WAS DEAD, BUT POVERTY AND RACISM WOULD CONTINUE TO FESTER.

War Resistance at Home

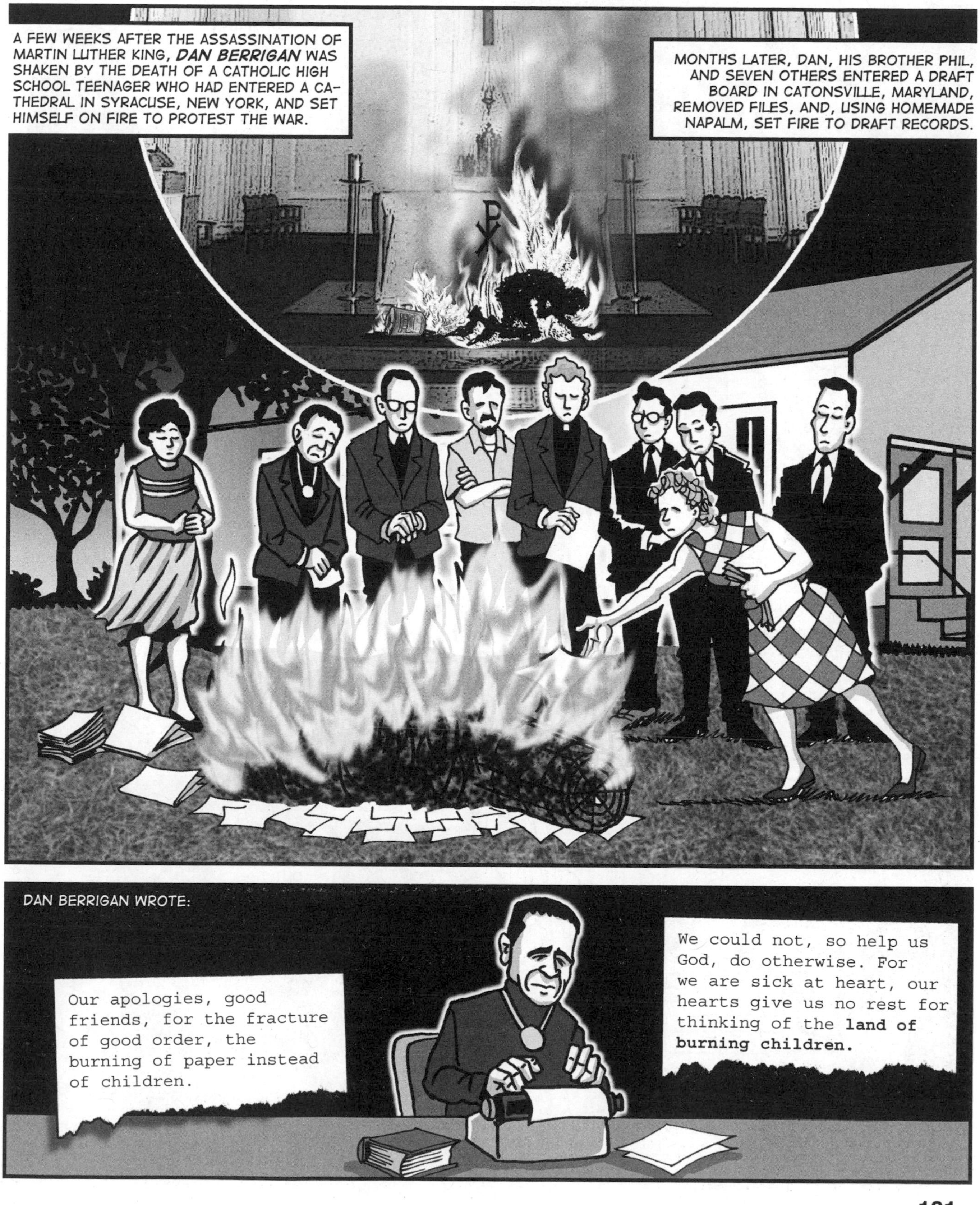
A FEW WEEKS AFTER THE ASSASSINATION OF MARTIN LUTHER KING, ***DAN BERRIGAN*** WAS SHAKEN BY THE DEATH OF A CATHOLIC HIGH SCHOOL TEENAGER WHO HAD ENTERED A CATHEDRAL IN SYRACUSE, NEW YORK, AND SET HIMSELF ON FIRE TO PROTEST THE WAR.
MONTHS LATER, DAN, HIS BROTHER PHIL, AND SEVEN OTHERS ENTERED A DRAFT BOARD IN CATONSVILLE, MARYLAND, REMOVED FILES, AND, USING HOMEMADE NAPALM, SET FIRE TO DRAFT RECORDS.
DAN BERRIGAN WROTE:
Our apologies, good friends, for the fracture of good order, the burning of paper instead of children.
We could not, so help us God, do otherwise. For we are sick at heart, our hearts give us no rest for thinking of the **land of burning children.**

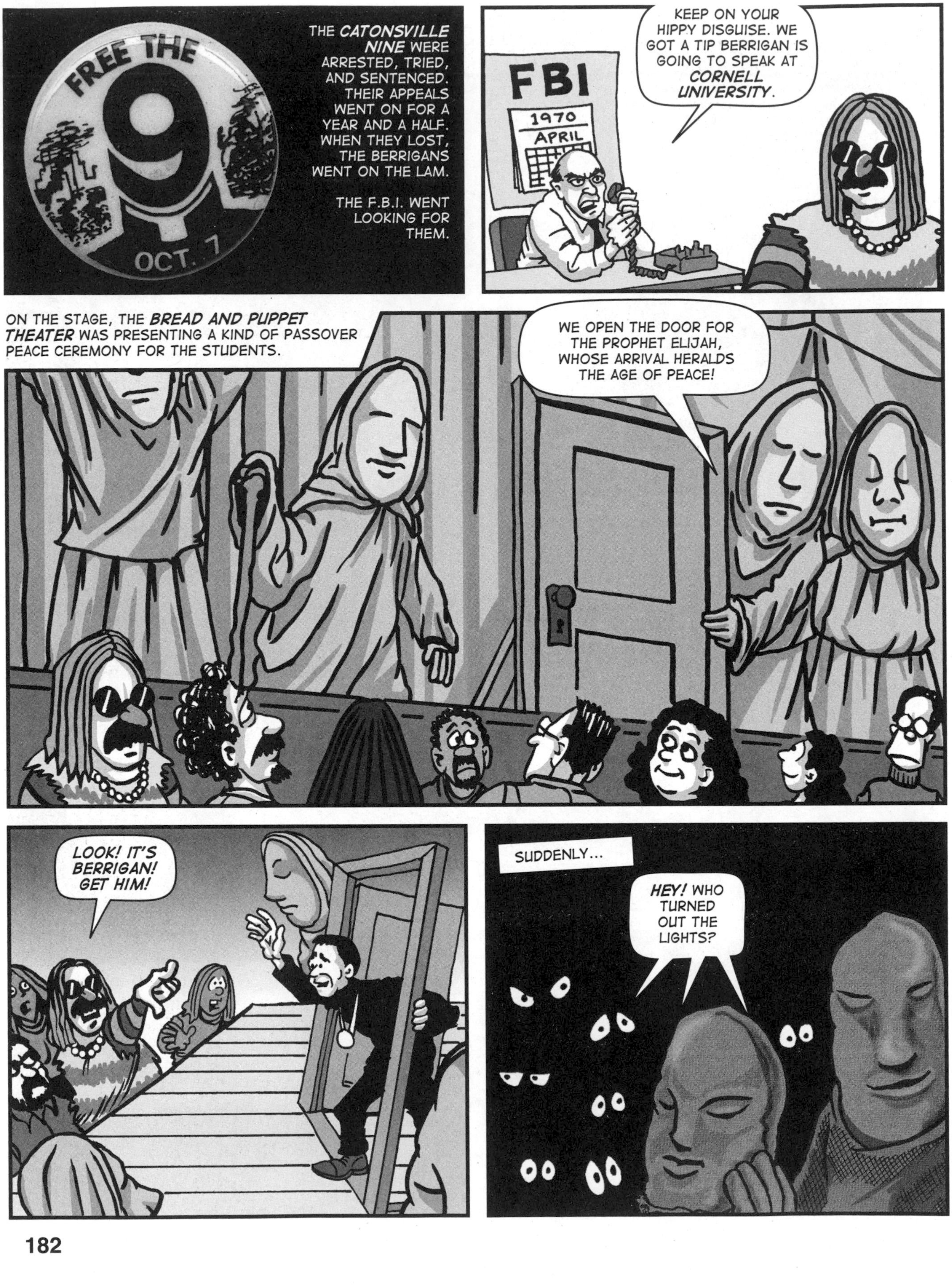
FREE THE 9 OCT. 7
THE CATONSVILLE NINE WERE ARRESTED, TRIED, AND SENTENCED. THEIR APPEALS WENT ON FOR A YEAR AND A HALF. WHEN THEY LOST, THE BERRIGANS WENT ON THE LAM.
THE F.B.I. WENT LOOKING FOR THEM.
FBI
1970 APRIL
KEEP ON YOUR HIPPY DISGUISE. WE GOT A TIP BERRIGAN IS GOING TO SPEAK AT CORNELL UNIVERSITY.
ON THE STAGE, THE BREAD AND PUPPET THEATER WAS PRESENTING A KIND OF PASSOVER PEACE CEREMONY FOR THE STUDENTS.
WE OPEN THE DOOR FOR THE PROPHET ELIJAH, WHOSE ARRIVAL HERALDS THE AGE OF PEACE!
LOOK! IT'S BERRIGAN! GET HIM!
SUDDENLY...
HEY! WHO TURNED OUT THE LIGHTS?

DAN WAS HIDDEN IN A LARGE PUPPET, CARRIED OUT TO A WAITING CAR, AND ESCAPED TO A NEARBY FARMHOUSE.

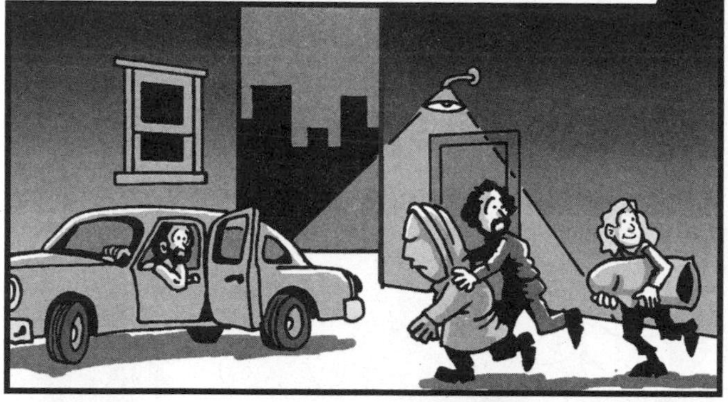

HE STAYED UNDERGROUND FOR FOUR MONTHS, WRITING POEMS, ISSUING STATEMENTS...

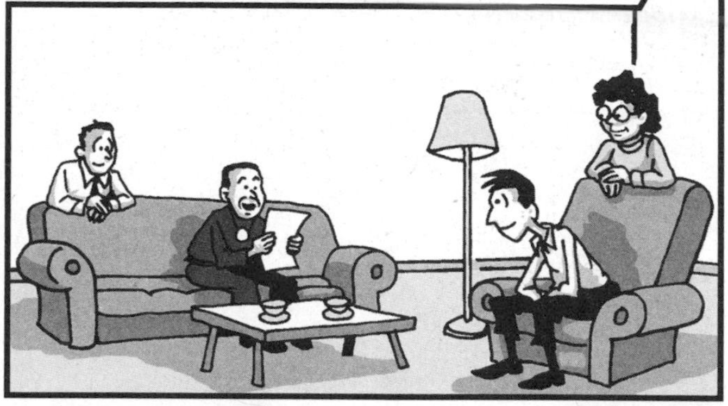

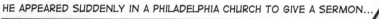

...AND GIVING SECRET INTERVIEWS.

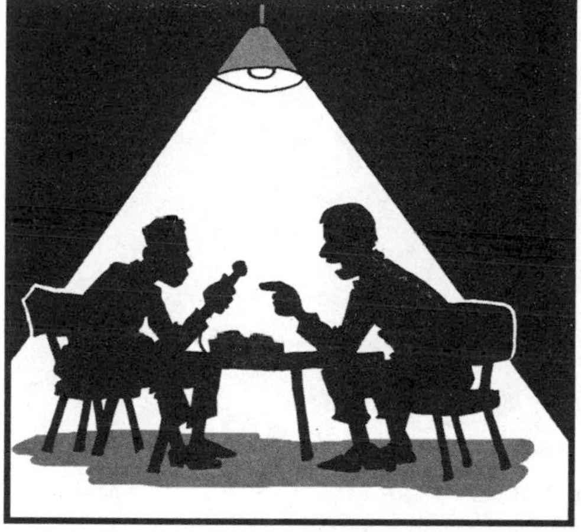

HE APPEARED SUDDENLY IN A PHILADELPHIA CHURCH TO GIVE A SERMON...

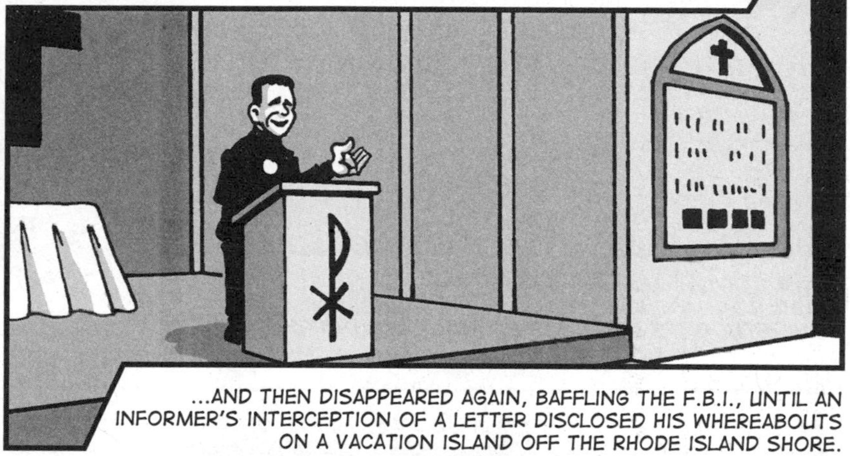

...AND THEN DISAPPEARED AGAIN, BAFFLING THE F.B.I., UNTIL AN INFORMER'S INTERCEPTION OF A LETTER DISCLOSED HIS WHEREABOUTS ON A VACATION ISLAND OFF THE RHODE ISLAND SHORE.

F.B.I. AGENTS, POSING AS BIRD-WATCHERS, WERE IN THE BUSHES. DAN WAS THE BIRD THEY WERE WATCHING. THEY ARRESTED HIM AND TOOK HIM BY BOAT TO THE MAINLAND. THE SEA WAS ROUGH, AND THE F.B.I. MEN GOT SICK.

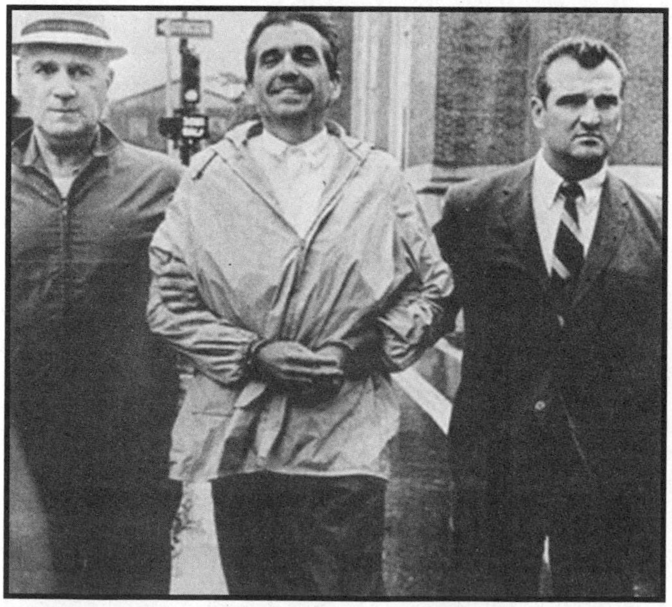

THERE'S A FUNNY PHOTOGRAPH OF DAN HANDCUFFED, AN F.B.I. MAN ON EITHER SIDE OF HIM, ARRIVING ONSHORE. THE CAPTURED FUGITIVE HAS A BROAD SMILE ON HIS FACE; HIS CAPTORS LOOK QUITE MISERABLE.

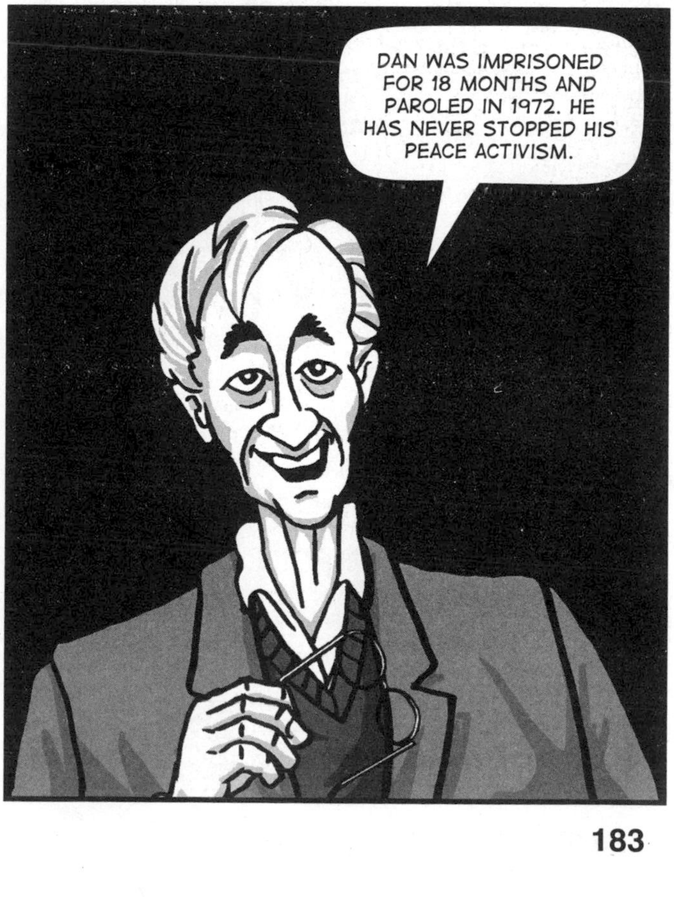
DAN WAS IMPRISONED FOR 18 MONTHS AND PAROLED IN 1972. HE HAS NEVER STOPPED HIS PEACE ACTIVISM.

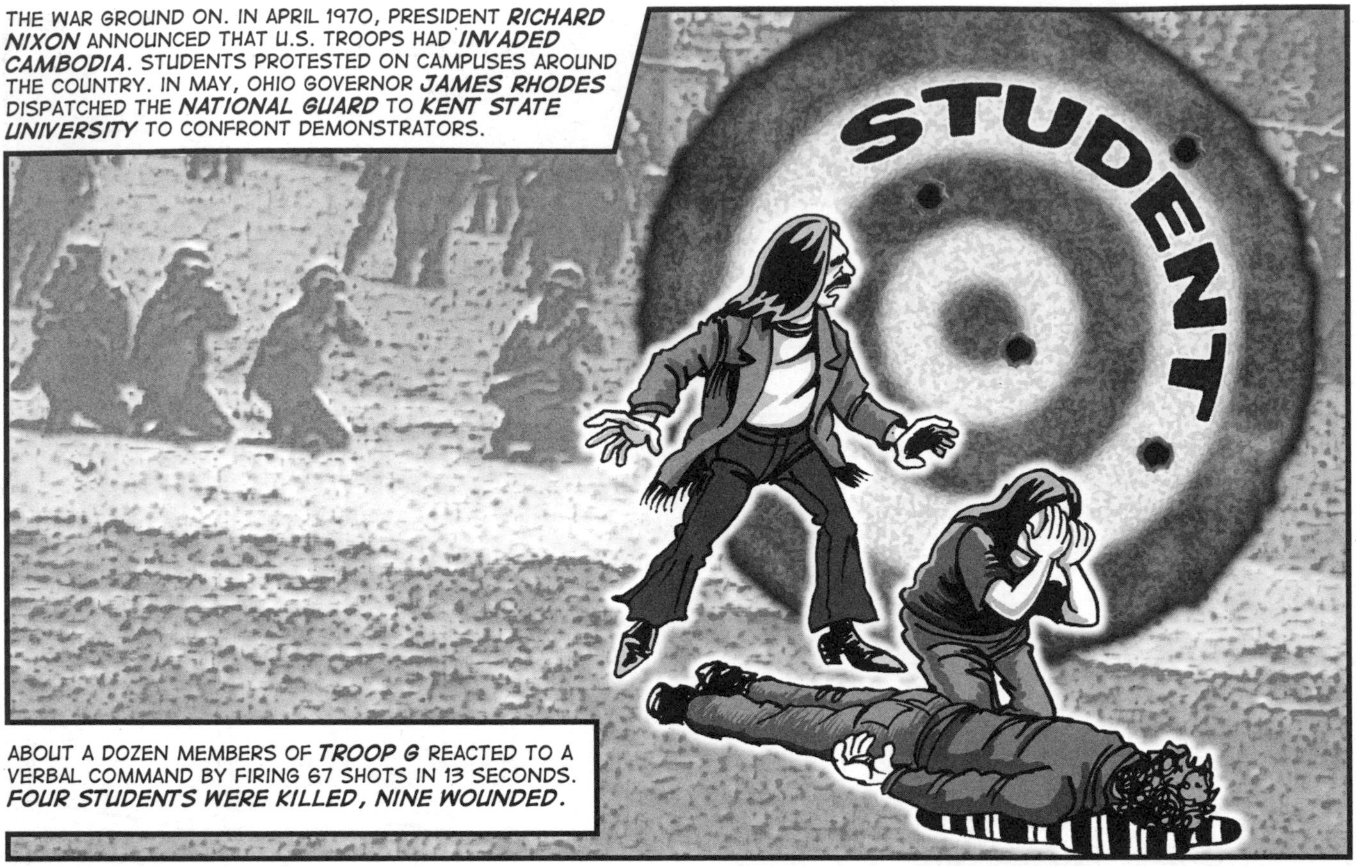
THE WAR GROUND ON. IN APRIL 1970, PRESIDENT RICHARD NIXON ANNOUNCED THAT U.S. TROOPS HAD INVADED CAMBODIA. STUDENTS PROTESTED ON CAMPUSES AROUND THE COUNTRY. IN MAY, OHIO GOVERNOR JAMES RHODES DISPATCHED THE NATIONAL GUARD TO KENT STATE UNIVERSITY TO CONFRONT DEMONSTRATORS.
STUDENT
ABOUT A DOZEN MEMBERS OF TROOP G REACTED TO A VERBAL COMMAND BY FIRING 67 SHOTS IN 13 SECONDS. FOUR STUDENTS WERE KILLED, NINE WOUNDED.

MAY 15, 1970, JACKSON, MISSISSIPPI: ON THE CAMPUS OF ***JACKSON STATE,*** A NEGRO COLLEGE, POLICE LAID DOWN A 28-SECOND BARRAGE OF GUNFIRE, USING SHOTGUNS, RIFLES, AND A SUBMACHINE GUN. FOUR HUNDRED BULLETS OR PIECES OF BUCKSHOT STRUCK THE GIRLS' DORMITORY, KILLING TWO BLACK STUDENTS.

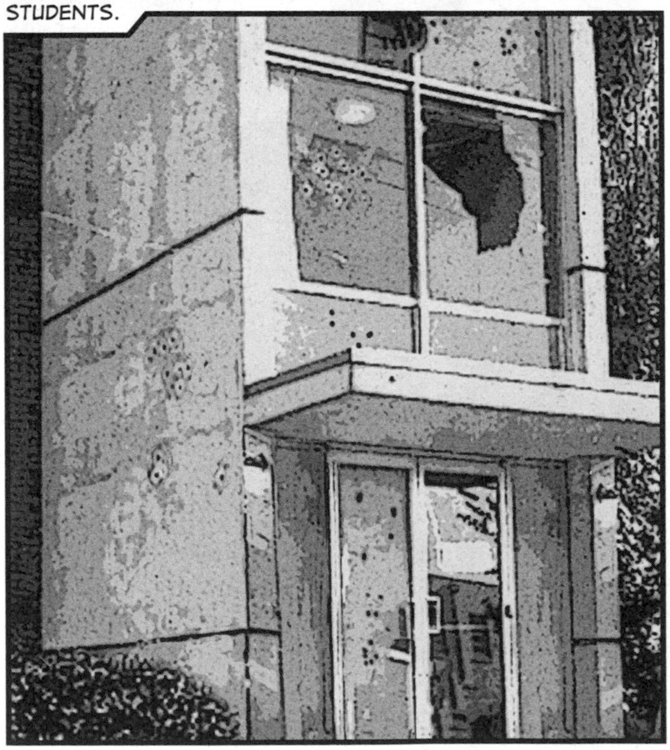

A LOCAL GRAND JURY FOUND THE ATTACK "JUSTIFIED" AND U.S. DISTRICT COURT JUDGE ***HAROLD COX*** (A KENNEDY APPOINTEE) DECLARED:

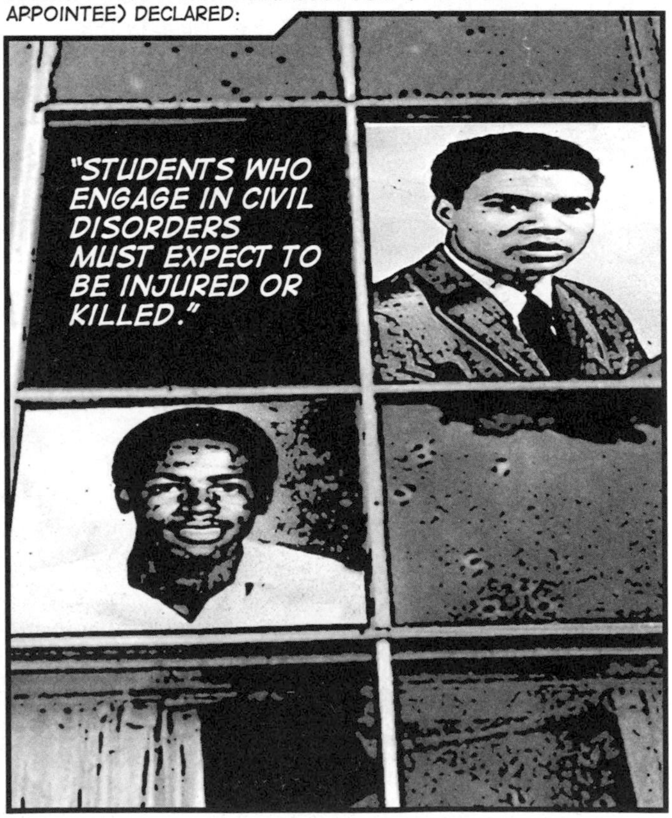
"STUDENTS WHO ENGAGE IN CIVIL DISORDERS MUST EXPECT TO BE INJURED OR KILLED."

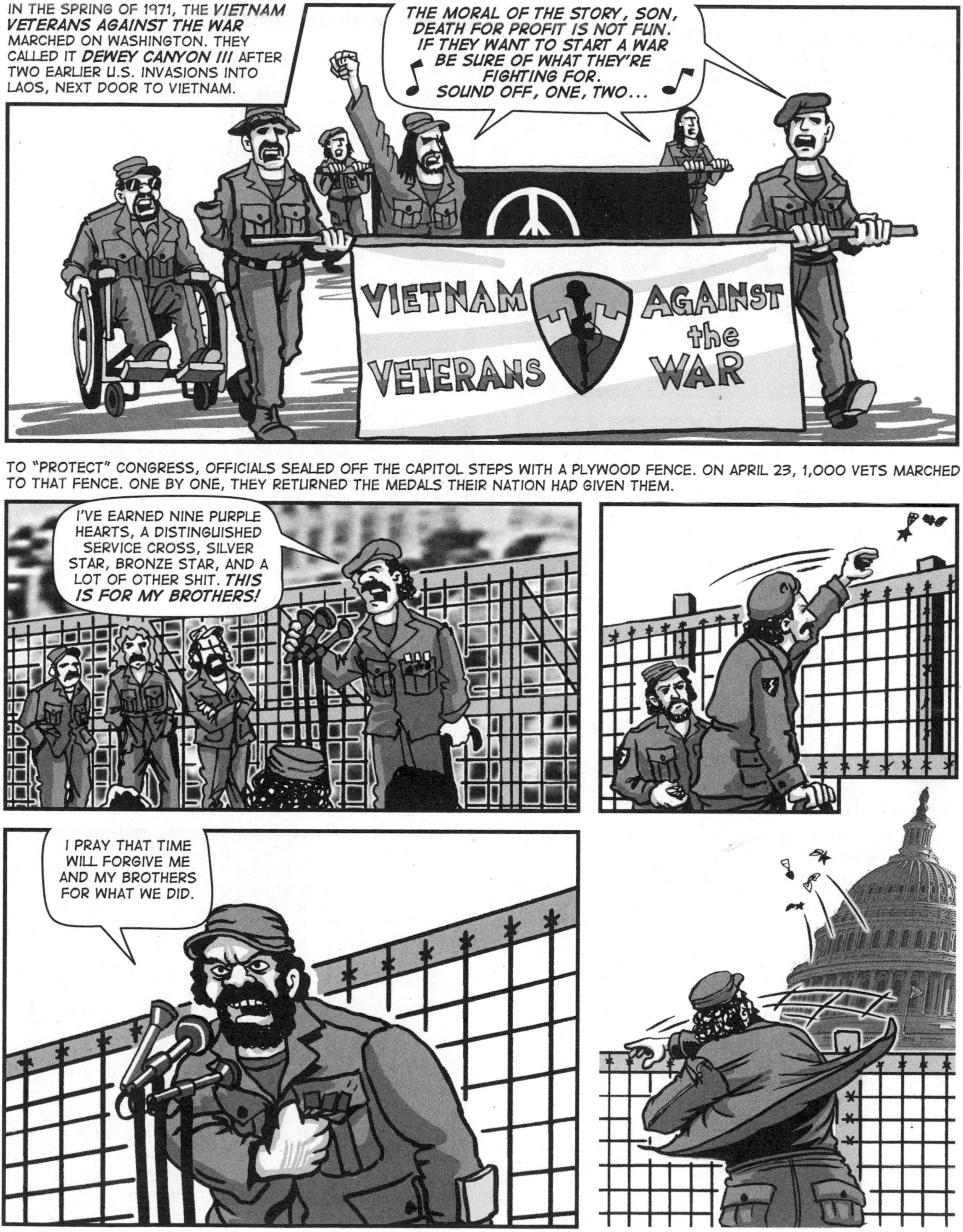
IN THE SPRING OF 1971, THE *VIETNAM VETERANS AGAINST THE WAR* MARCHED ON WASHINGTON. THEY CALLED IT *DEWEY CANYON III* AFTER TWO EARLIER U.S. INVASIONS INTO LAOS, NEXT DOOR TO VIETNAM.
THE MORAL OF THE STORY, SON, DEATH FOR PROFIT IS NOT FUN. IF THEY WANT TO START A WAR BE SURE OF WHAT THEY'RE FIGHTING FOR. SOUND OFF, ONE, TWO...
VIETNAM VETERANS AGAINST the WAR
TO "PROTECT" CONGRESS, OFFICIALS SEALED OFF THE CAPITOL STEPS WITH A PLYWOOD FENCE. ON APRIL 23, 1,000 VETS MARCHED TO THAT FENCE. ONE BY ONE, THEY RETURNED THE MEDALS THEIR NATION HAD GIVEN THEM.
I'VE EARNED NINE PURPLE HEARTS, A DISTINGUISHED SERVICE CROSS, SILVER STAR, BRONZE STAR, AND A LOT OF OTHER SHIT. *THIS IS FOR MY BROTHERS!*
I PRAY THAT TIME WILL FORGIVE ME AND MY BROTHERS FOR WHAT WE DID.

AS THE VETERANS MARCHED, A HALF MILLION PROTESTERS FILTERED INTO THE CAPITAL FROM AROUND THE COUNTRY.

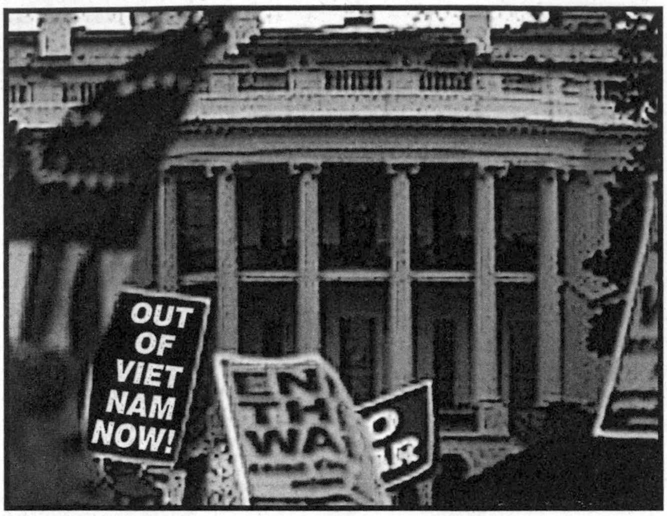
OUT OF VIET NAM NOW!

ONE OF THEM WAS ME. AT 49, I WAS NO SPRING CHICKEN. BUT I HAD TO BE THERE, AND SO DID THE REST OF MY NEW ENGLAND AFFINITY GROUP...

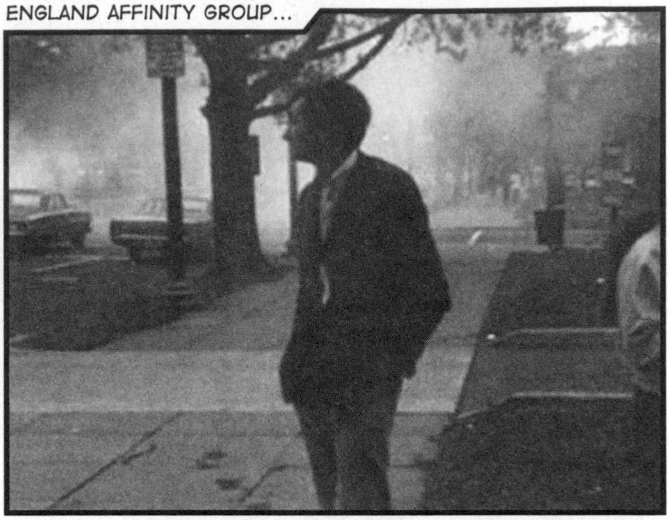

...WRITERS AND PROFESSORS ***NOAM CHOMSKY, DAN ELLSBERG, MARILYN YOUNG, ZEE GAMSON, FRED BRANFMAN, MARK PTASHNE, CYNTHIA FREDERICK,*** AND ***MITCH GOODMAN.***

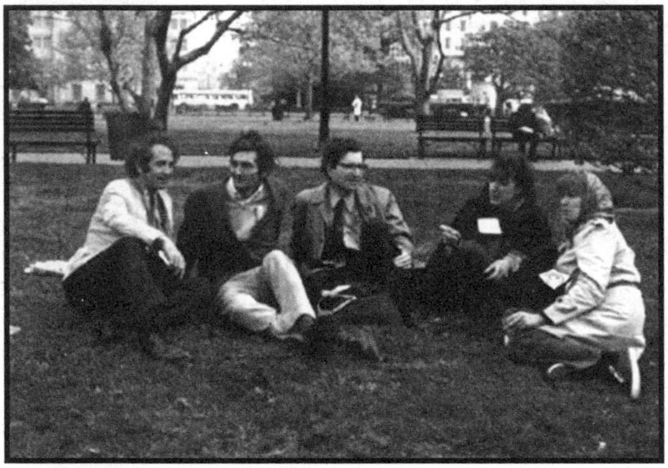

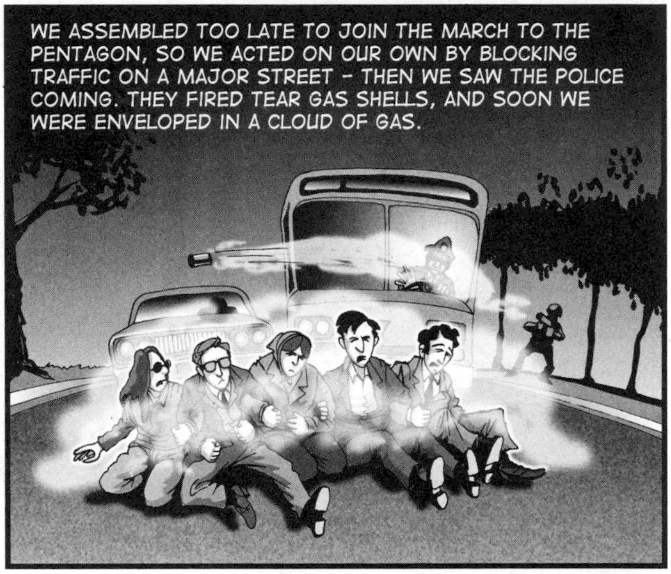
WE ASSEMBLED TOO LATE TO JOIN THE MARCH TO THE PENTAGON, SO WE ACTED ON OUR OWN BY BLOCKING TRAFFIC ON A MAJOR STREET - THEN WE SAW THE POLICE COMING. THEY FIRED TEAR GAS SHELLS, AND SOON WE WERE ENVELOPED IN A CLOUD OF GAS.

WE RAN AND THEN REGROUPED, AND LOOKED FOR ANOTHER STREET TO BLOCK.

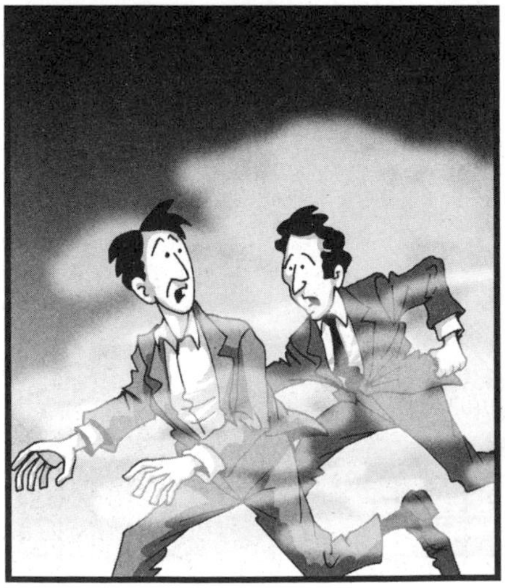

DURING ONE OF OUR REGROUPINGS, A COP WALKED UP TO US AND BLASTED DAN ELLSBERG AND ME WITH MACE. WE WERE BLINDED FOR 10 MINUTES. WE RECOVERED, BUT OUR ACTION WAS OVER.

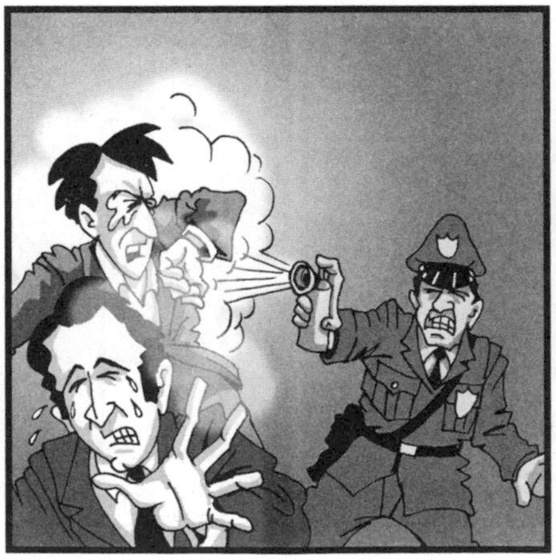

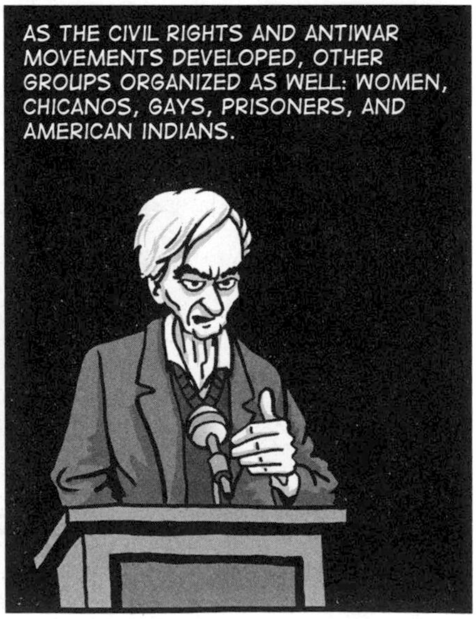
AS THE CIVIL RIGHTS AND ANTIWAR MOVEMENTS DEVELOPED, OTHER GROUPS ORGANIZED AS WELL: WOMEN, CHICANOS, GAYS, PRISONERS, AND AMERICAN INDIANS.

EIGHTY YEARS AFTER THE FIRST BATTLE OF WOUNDED KNEE, THE ***VANISHING RED MAN*** (AS AMERICAN INDIANS WERE LONG DESCRIBED) HAD REFUSED TO VANISH. ENCOURAGED BY THE ANTIWAR, BLACK POWER, AND OTHER MOVEMENTS AGAINST AMERICAN EMPIRE, INDIANS JOINED THE REBELLION.

IN THE 1970S, CONDITIONS ON THE ***PINE RIDGE RESERVATION*** WERE SQUALID.

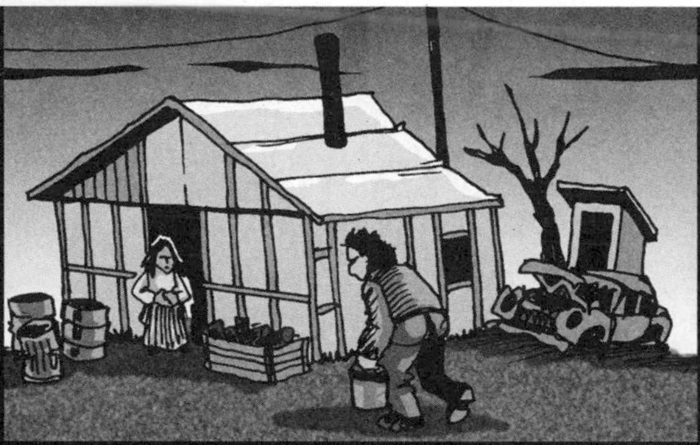

THE PEOPLE OF PINE RIDGE TRIED TO OUST TRIBAL PRESIDENT ***DICKY WILSON,*** WHO RULED THE RESERVATION WITH AN IRON FIST. HE ABOLISHED ALL CONSTITUTIONAL RIGHTS AND WAS PROTECTED BY THE F.B.I. AND FEDERAL MARSHALS.

THIS DESPERATE SITUATION CAME TO A HEAD IN 1973, FOLLOWING A RIGGED ELECTION. IT WAS THE SPARK THAT SET OFF...

The Second Battle of Wounded Knee

FEBRUARY 27, 1973: A LARGE CROWD OF ANGRY ***OGLALA SIOUX*** MET AT THE CALICO, S.D., COMMUNITY CENTER. AMONG THEM WERE MEMBERS OF A NEW MILITANT ORGANIZATION CALLED THE ***AMERICAN INDIAN MOVEMENT (AIM)***.

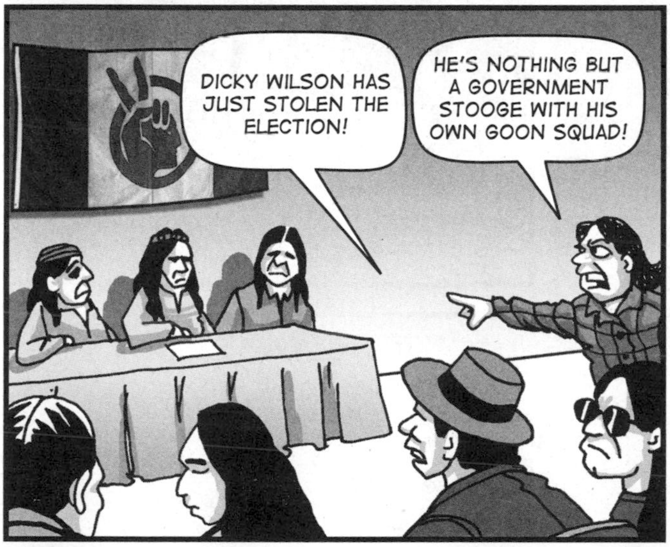
DICKY WILSON HAS JUST STOLEN THE ELECTION!
HE'S NOTHING BUT A GOVERNMENT STOOGE WITH HIS OWN GOON SQUAD!

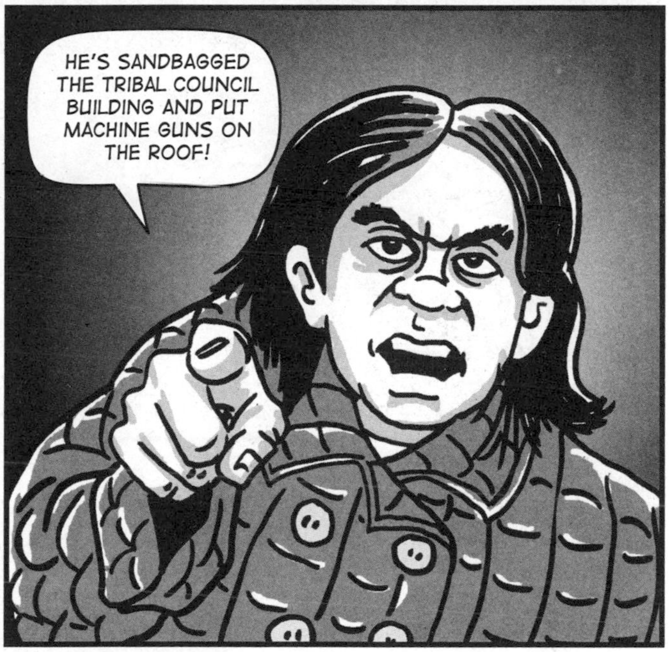
HE'S SANDBAGGED THE TRIBAL COUNCIL BUILDING AND PUT MACHINE GUNS ON THE ROOF!

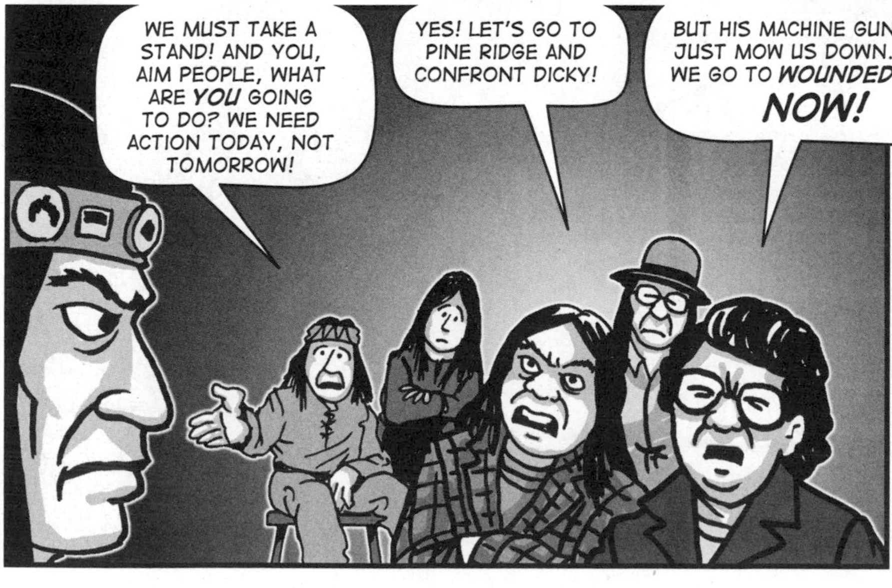
WE MUST TAKE A STAND! AND YOU, AIM PEOPLE, WHAT ARE *YOU* GOING TO DO? WE NEED ACTION TODAY, NOT TOMORROW!
YES! LET'S GO TO PINE RIDGE AND CONFRONT DICKY!
BUT HIS MACHINE GUNS WILL JUST MOW US DOWN. I SAY WE GO TO ***WOUNDED KNEE NOW!***

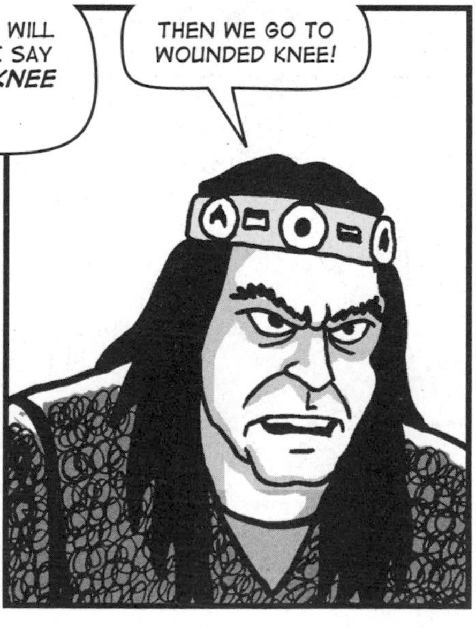
THEN WE GO TO WOUNDED KNEE!

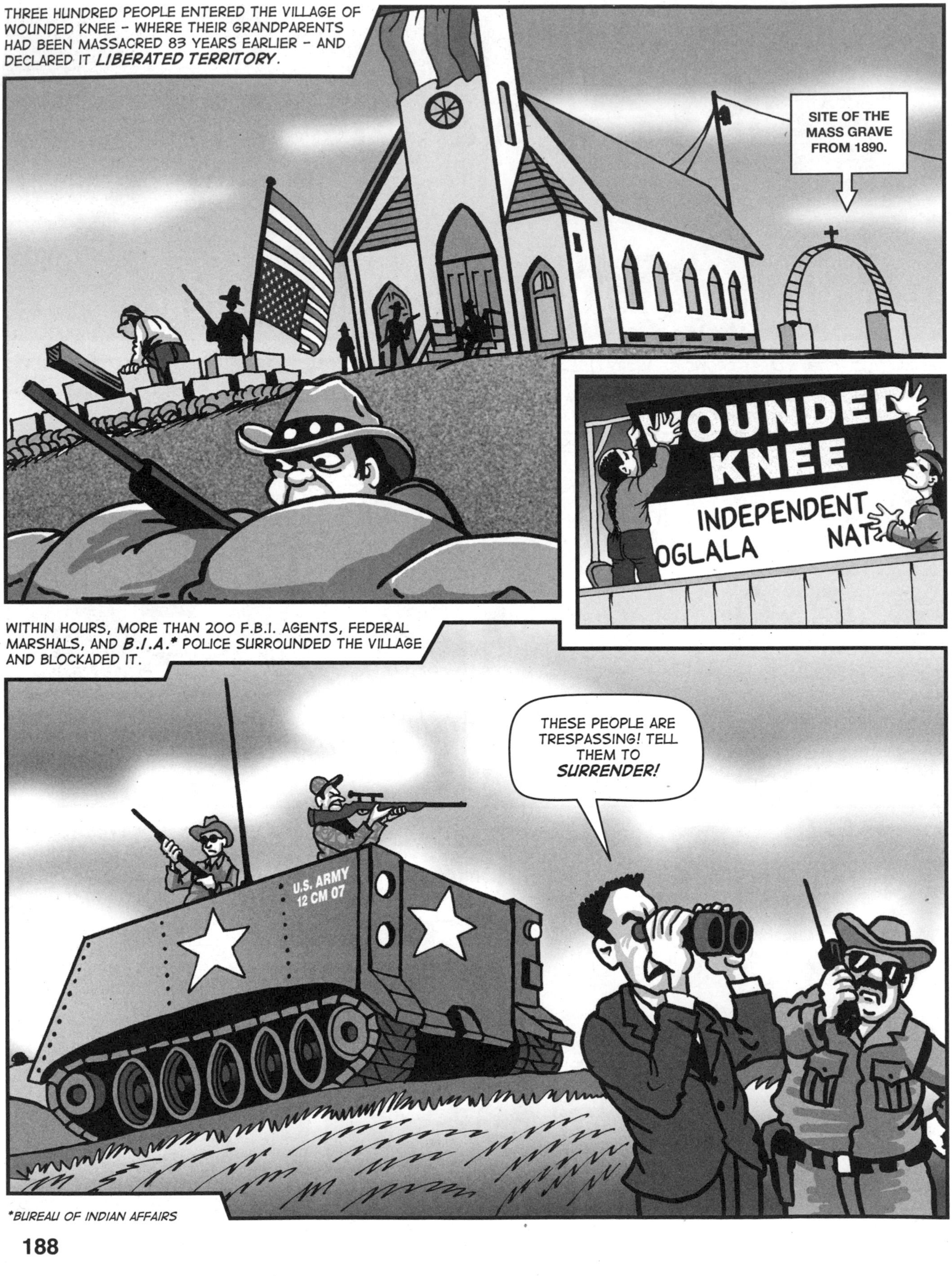
THREE HUNDRED PEOPLE ENTERED THE VILLAGE OF WOUNDED KNEE - WHERE THEIR GRANDPARENTS HAD BEEN MASSACRED 83 YEARS EARLIER - AND DECLARED IT LIBERATED TERRITORY.
SITE OF THE MASS GRAVE FROM 1890.
WOUNDED KNEE
INDEPENDENT
OGLALA NAT
WITHIN HOURS, MORE THAN 200 F.B.I. AGENTS, FEDERAL MARSHALS, AND B.I.A.* POLICE SURROUNDED THE VILLAGE AND BLOCKADED IT.
U.S. ARMY 12 CM 07
THESE PEOPLE ARE TRESPASSING! TELL THEM TO SURRENDER!

*BUREAU OF INDIAN AFFAIRS

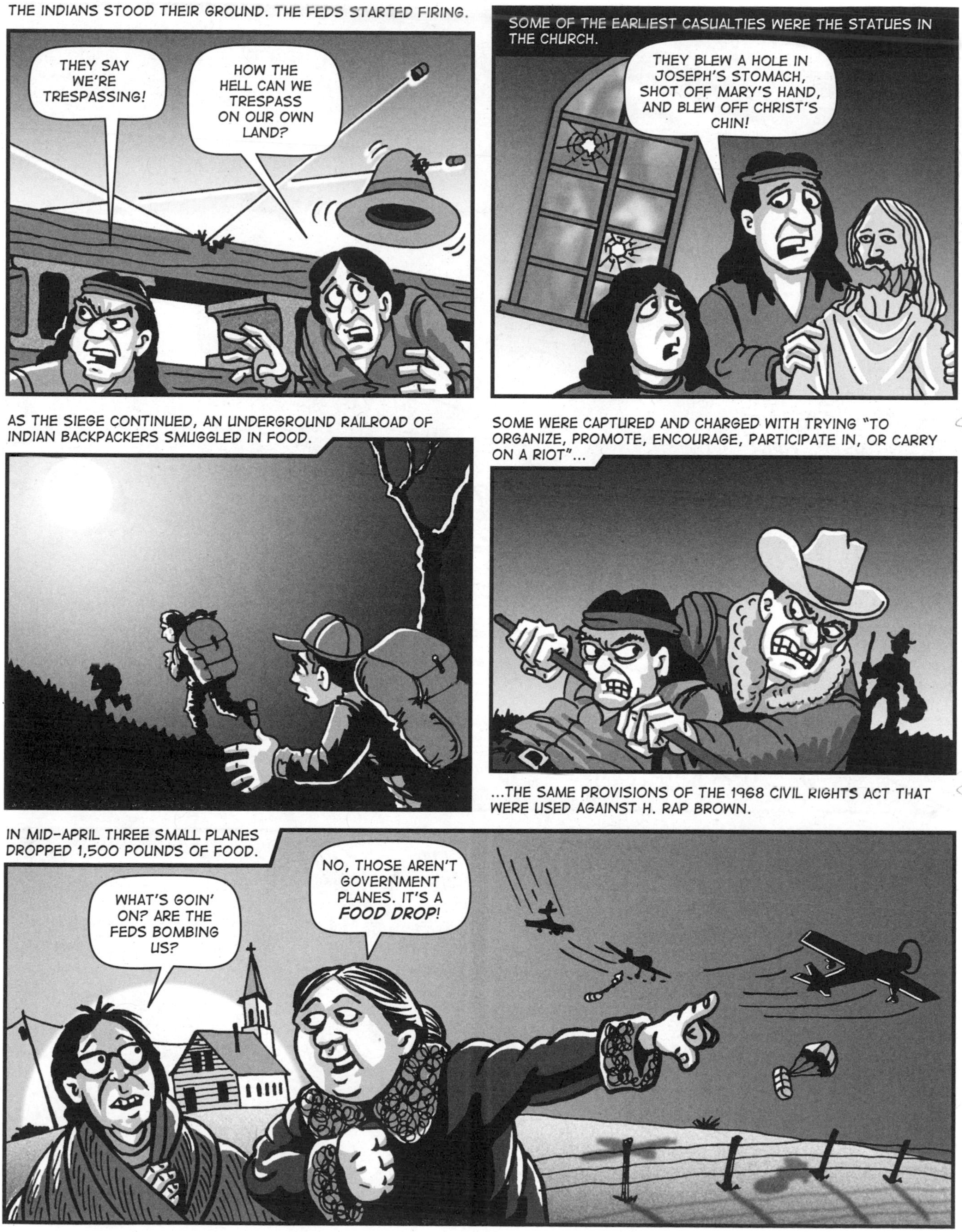
THE INDIANS STOOD THEIR GROUND. THE FEDS STARTED FIRING.
THEY SAY WE'RE TRESPASSING!
HOW THE HELL CAN WE TRESPASS ON OUR OWN LAND?
SOME OF THE EARLIEST CASUALTIES WERE THE STATUES IN THE CHURCH.
THEY BLEW A HOLE IN JOSEPH'S STOMACH, SHOT OFF MARY'S HAND, AND BLEW OFF CHRIST'S CHIN!
AS THE SIEGE CONTINUED, AN UNDERGROUND RAILROAD OF INDIAN BACKPACKERS SMUGGLED IN FOOD.
SOME WERE CAPTURED AND CHARGED WITH TRYING "TO ORGANIZE, PROMOTE, ENCOURAGE, PARTICIPATE IN, OR CARRY ON A RIOT"...
...THE SAME PROVISIONS OF THE 1968 CIVIL RIGHTS ACT THAT WERE USED AGAINST H. RAP BROWN.
IN MID-APRIL THREE SMALL PLANES DROPPED 1,500 POUNDS OF FOOD.
WHAT'S GOIN' ON? ARE THE FEDS BOMBING US?
NO, THOSE AREN'T GOVERNMENT PLANES. IT'S A *FOOD DROP*!

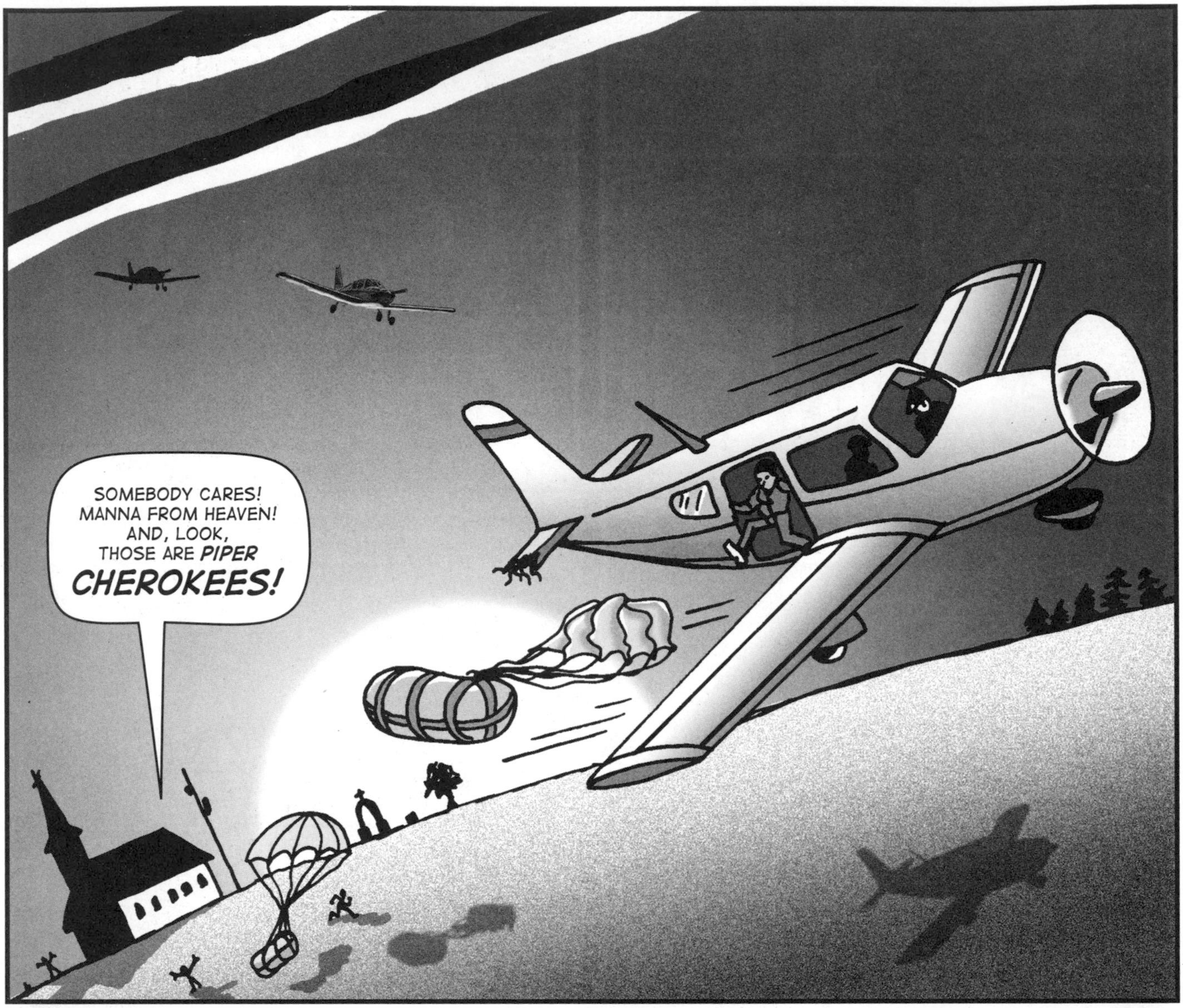
SOMEBODY CARES! MANNA FROM HEAVEN! AND, LOOK, THOSE ARE *PIPER* **CHEROKEES!**

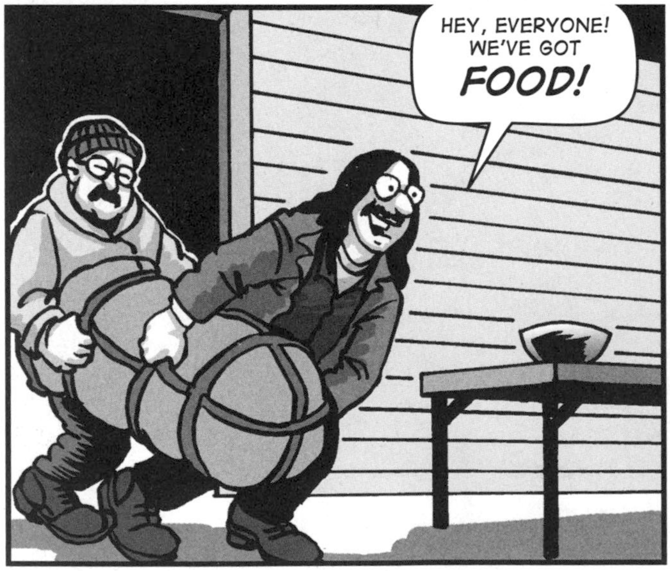
HEY, EVERYONE! WE'VE GOT **FOOD!**

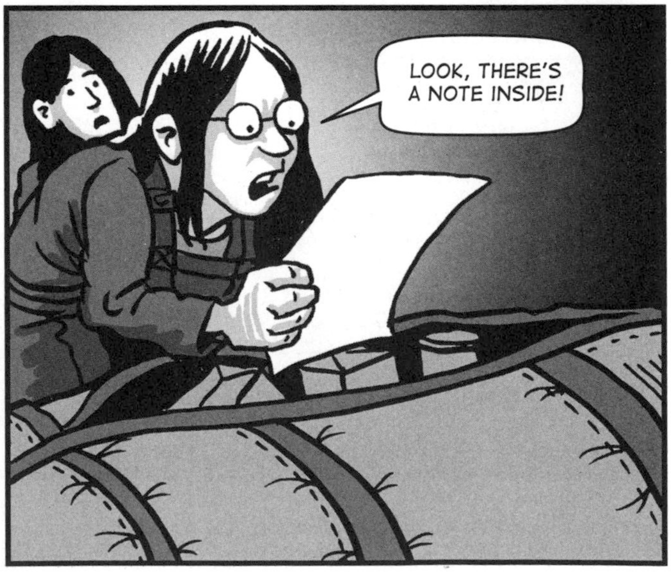
LOOK, THERE'S A NOTE INSIDE!

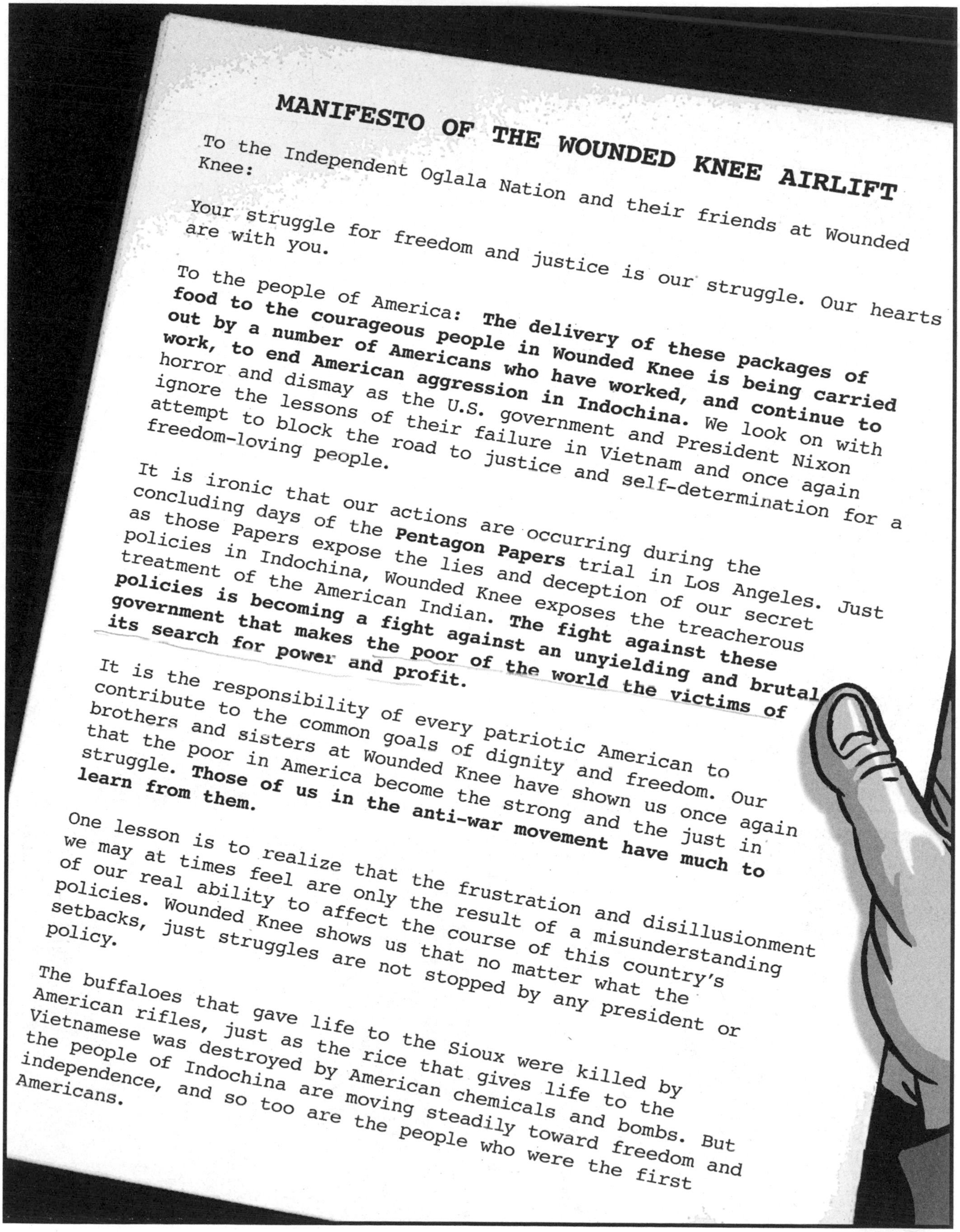

MANIFESTO OF THE WOUNDED KNEE AIRLIFT

To the Independent Oglala Nation and their friends at Wounded Knee:

Your struggle for freedom and justice is our struggle. Our hearts are with you.

To the people of America: **The delivery of these packages of food to the courageous people in Wounded Knee is being carried out by a number of Americans who have worked, and continue to work, to end American aggression in Indochina.** We look on with horror and dismay as the U.S. government and President Nixon ignore the lessons of their failure in Vietnam and once again attempt to block the road to justice and self-determination for a freedom-loving people.

It is ironic that our actions are occurring during the concluding days of the **Pentagon Papers** trial in Los Angeles. Just as those Papers expose the lies and deception of our secret policies in Indochina, Wounded Knee exposes the treacherous treatment of the American Indian. **The fight against these policies is becoming a fight against an unyielding and brutal government that makes the poor of the world the victims of its search for power and profit.**

It is the responsibility of every patriotic American to contribute to the common goals of dignity and freedom. Our brothers and sisters at Wounded Knee have shown us once again that the poor in America become the strong and the just in struggle. **Those of us in the anti-war movement have much to learn from them.**

One lesson is to realize that the frustration and disillusionment we may at times feel are only the result of a misunderstanding of our real ability to affect the course of this country's policies. Wounded Knee shows us that no matter what the setbacks, just struggles are not stopped by any president or policy.

The buffaloes that gave life to the Sioux were killed by American rifles, just as the rice that gives life to the Vietnamese was destroyed by American chemicals and bombs. But the people of Indochina are moving steadily toward freedom and independence, and so too are the people who were the first Americans.

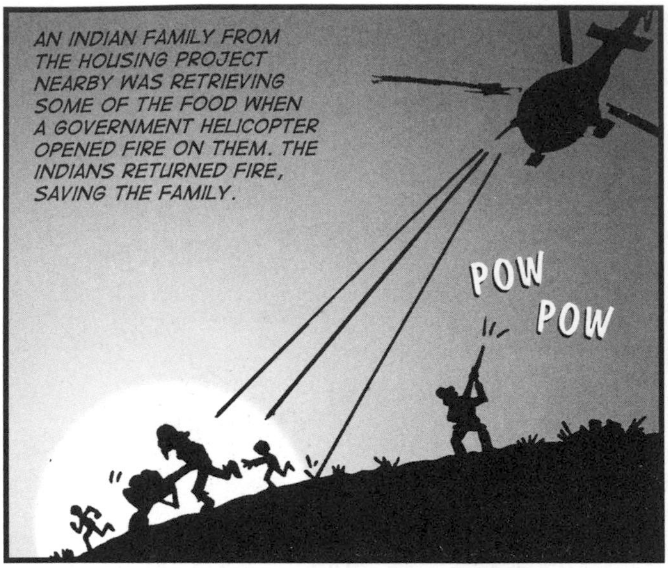
AN INDIAN FAMILY FROM THE HOUSING PROJECT NEARBY WAS RETRIEVING SOME OF THE FOOD WHEN A GOVERNMENT HELICOPTER OPENED FIRE ON THEM. THE INDIANS RETURNED FIRE, SAVING THE FAMILY.
POW
POW

IN RETALIATION, THE FEDS OPENED UP WITH ONE OF THE DEADLIEST BARRAGES OF THE SIEGE. ***FRANK CLEARWATER***, AN APACHE FROM NORTH CAROLINA, WAS SHOT AND LATER DIED.

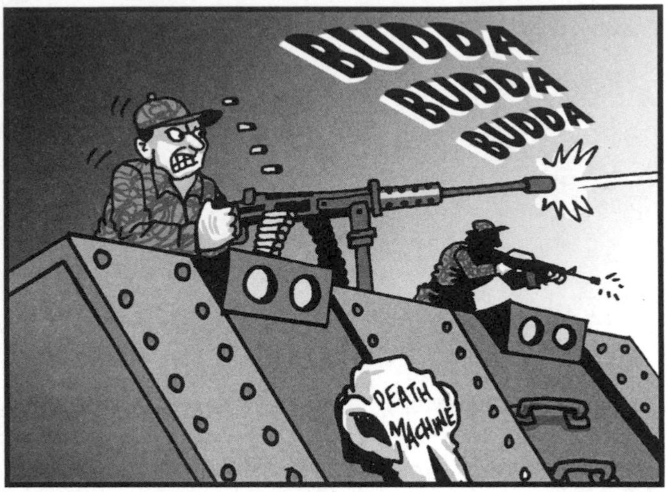
BUDDA
BUDDA
BUDDA
DEATH MACHINE

FINALLY, ON MAY 8, A NEGOTIATED PEACE WAS SIGNED. BOTH SIDES AGREED TO DISARM. THE SIEGE WAS OVER, AND 120 OCCUPIERS WERE ARRESTED.

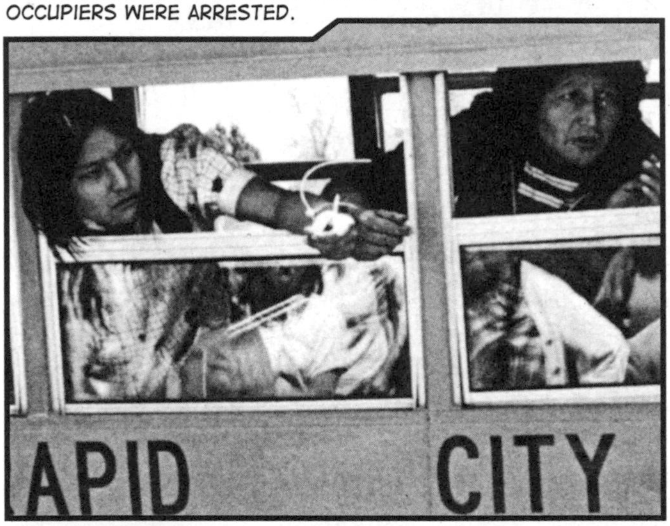
APID
CITY

THE OGLALA HAD HELD OUT FOR 71 DAYS, EXTRACTING A PROMISE THAT A PRESIDENTIAL COMMISSION WOULD REASSESS THE ***SIOUX TREATY OF 1868***.

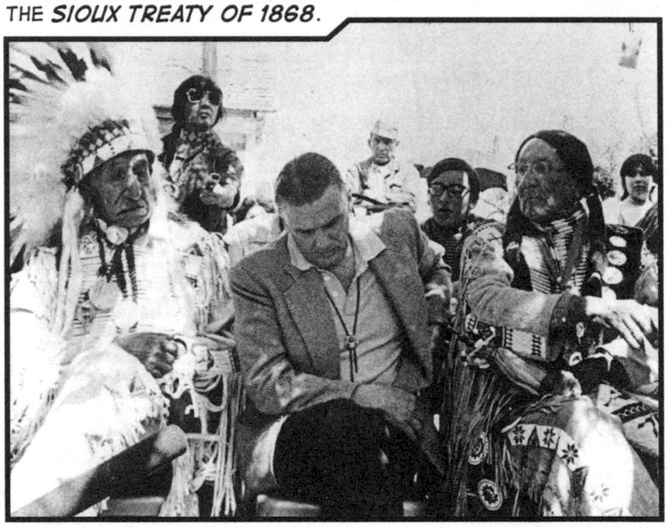

THE PRESIDENTIAL COMMISSION WAS NEVER FORMED, BUT THE FEDS REVIEWED THE TREATY AND DETERMINED THAT IT HAD BEEN ***SUPERSEDED*** BY THE U.S. POWER OF "EMINENT DOMAIN" – THE GOVERNMENT'S POWER TO TAKE LAND.

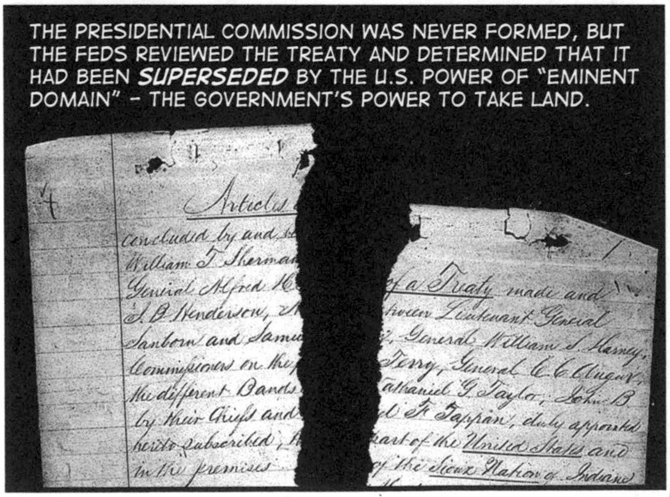
William T. Sherman
a Treaty made and
Lieutenant General
General William S. Harney
Terry, General C. C. Augur
Nathaniel G. Taylor, John B.
Tappan, duly appointed
part of the United States and
of the Sioux Nation of Indians

IT WAS A PERFECT RECORD: THE U.S. HAD VIOLATED EACH OF THE MORE THAN 400 TREATIES IT SIGNED WITH NORTH AMERICAN TRIBES SINCE 1775.

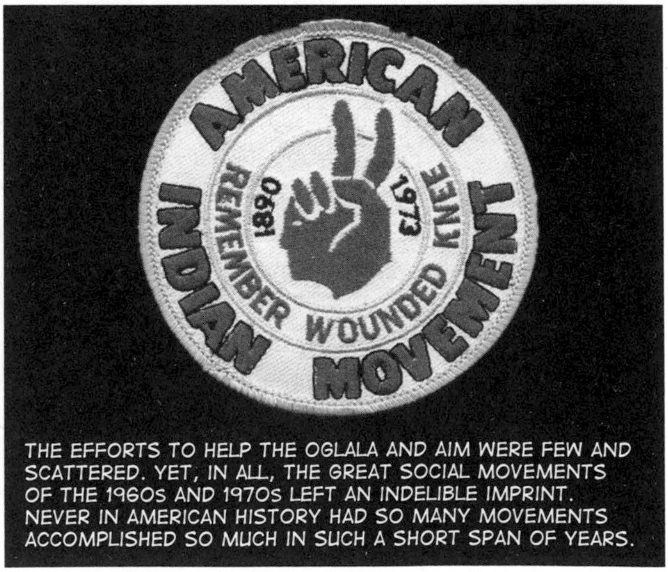
AMERICAN
INDIAN
MOVEMENT
REMEMBER WOUNDED KNEE
1890
1973

THE EFFORTS TO HELP THE OGLALA AND AIM WERE FEW AND SCATTERED. YET, IN ALL, THE GREAT SOCIAL MOVEMENTS OF THE 1960S AND 1970S LEFT AN INDELIBLE IMPRINT. NEVER IN AMERICAN HISTORY HAD SO MANY MOVEMENTS ACCOMPLISHED SO MUCH IN SUCH A SHORT SPAN OF YEARS.

Chapter X

The Same Rotting Barrel

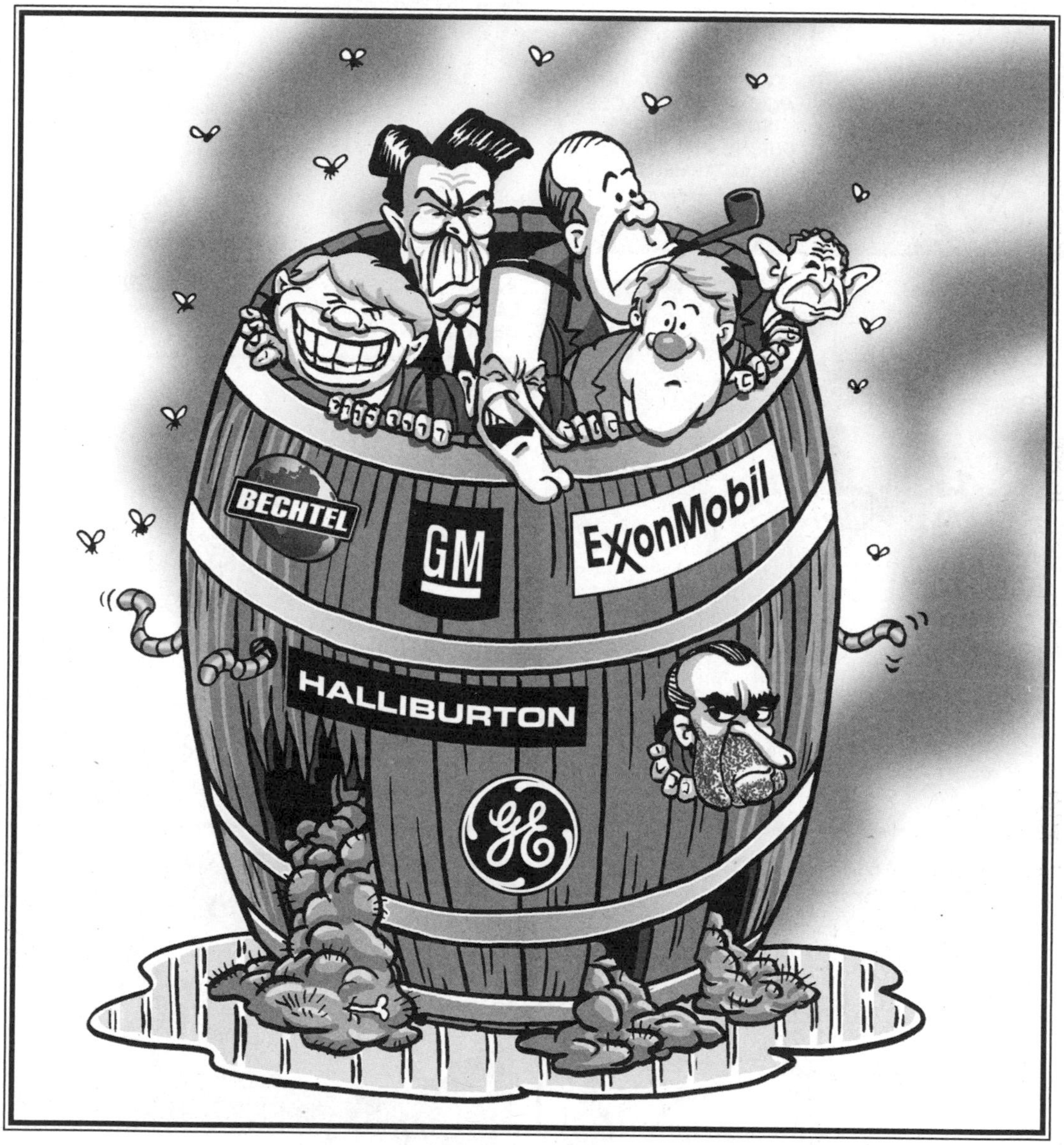
BECHTEL
GM
ExxonMobil
HALLIBURTON

"The underlying causes of the gross misconduct of our law-enforcement system are largely personal, not institutional. All the rotten apples should be thrown out. But save the barrel."

Daniel Ellsberg and the Pentagon Papers

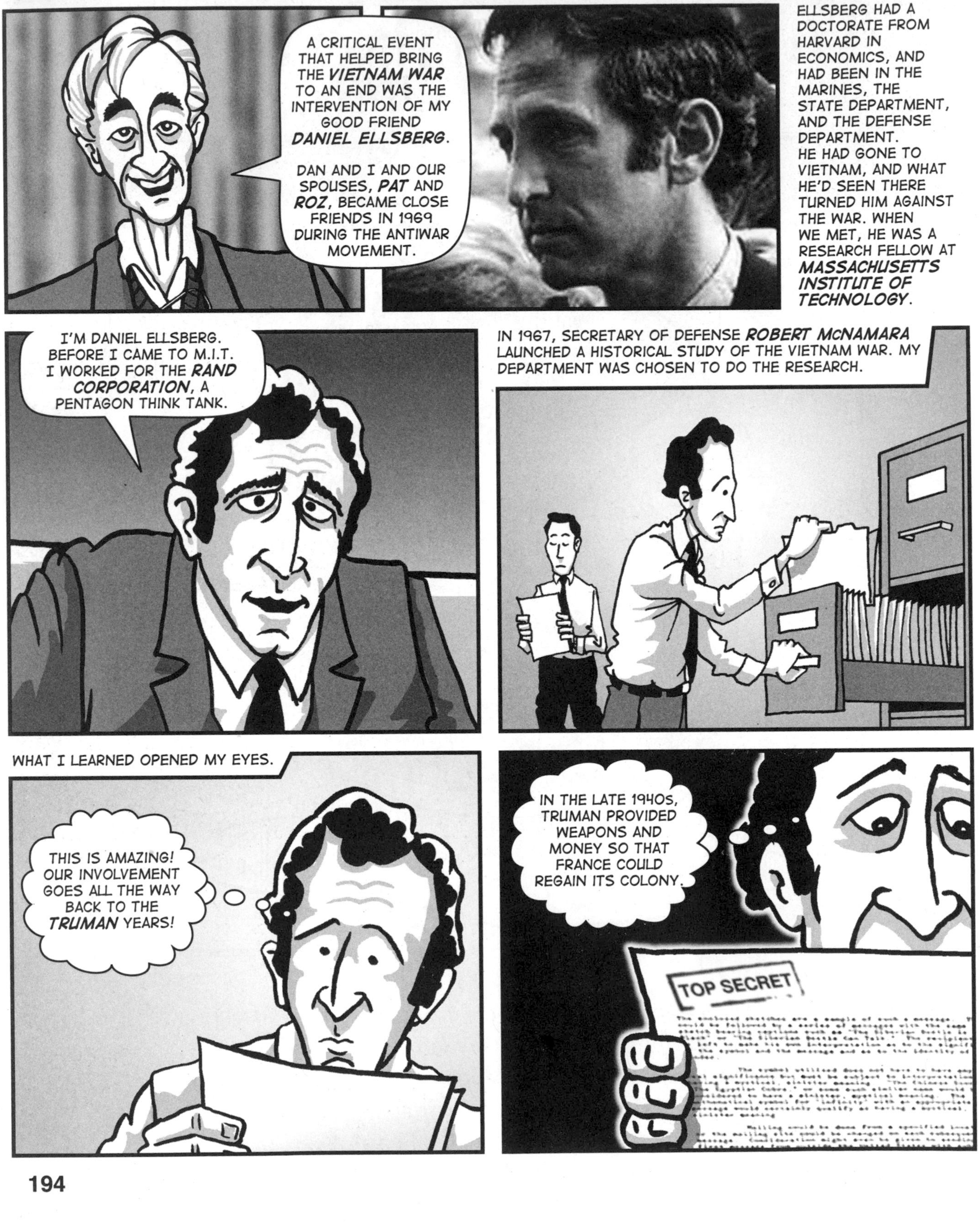
A CRITICAL EVENT THAT HELPED BRING THE VIETNAM WAR TO AN END WAS THE INTERVENTION OF MY GOOD FRIEND DANIEL ELLSBERG.
DAN AND I AND OUR SPOUSES, PAT AND ROZ, BECAME CLOSE FRIENDS IN 1969 DURING THE ANTIWAR MOVEMENT.
ELLSBERG HAD A DOCTORATE FROM HARVARD IN ECONOMICS, AND HAD BEEN IN THE MARINES, THE STATE DEPARTMENT, AND THE DEFENSE DEPARTMENT. HE HAD GONE TO VIETNAM, AND WHAT HE'D SEEN THERE TURNED HIM AGAINST THE WAR. WHEN WE MET, HE WAS A RESEARCH FELLOW AT MASSACHUSETTS INSTITUTE OF TECHNOLOGY.
I'M DANIEL ELLSBERG. BEFORE I CAME TO M.I.T. I WORKED FOR THE RAND CORPORATION, A PENTAGON THINK TANK.
IN 1967, SECRETARY OF DEFENSE ROBERT McNAMARA LAUNCHED A HISTORICAL STUDY OF THE VIETNAM WAR. MY DEPARTMENT WAS CHOSEN TO DO THE RESEARCH.
WHAT I LEARNED OPENED MY EYES.
THIS IS AMAZING! OUR INVOLVEMENT GOES ALL THE WAY BACK TO THE TRUMAN YEARS!
IN THE LATE 1940S, TRUMAN PROVIDED WEAPONS AND MONEY SO THAT FRANCE COULD REGAIN ITS COLONY.
TOP SECRET

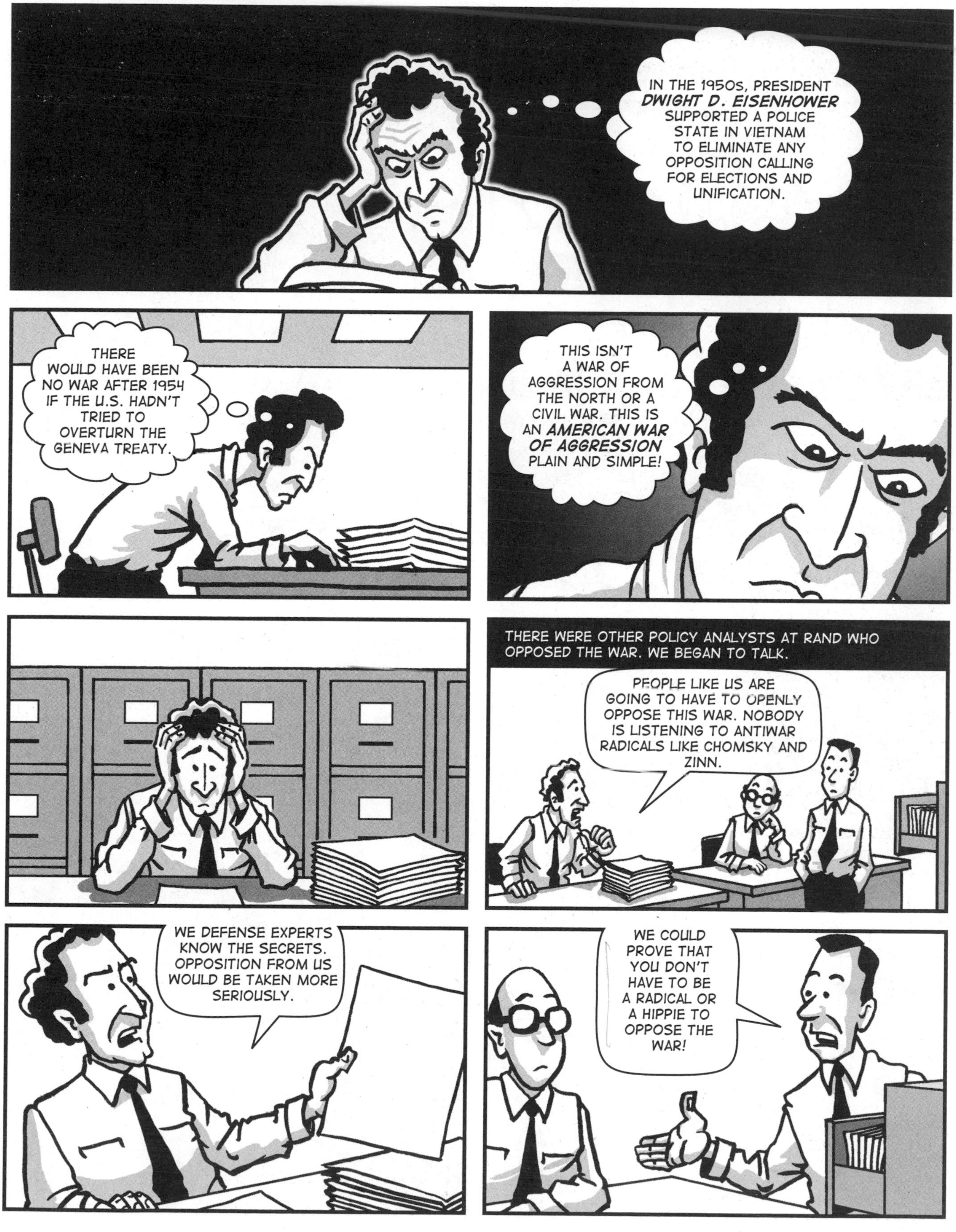
IN THE 1950s, PRESIDENT DWIGHT D. EISENHOWER SUPPORTED A POLICE STATE IN VIETNAM TO ELIMINATE ANY OPPOSITION CALLING FOR ELECTIONS AND UNIFICATION.
THERE WOULD HAVE BEEN NO WAR AFTER 1954 IF THE U.S. HADN'T TRIED TO OVERTURN THE GENEVA TREATY.
THIS ISN'T A WAR OF AGGRESSION FROM THE NORTH OR A CIVIL WAR. THIS IS AN AMERICAN WAR OF AGGRESSION PLAIN AND SIMPLE!
THERE WERE OTHER POLICY ANALYSTS AT RAND WHO OPPOSED THE WAR. WE BEGAN TO TALK.
PEOPLE LIKE US ARE GOING TO HAVE TO OPENLY OPPOSE THIS WAR. NOBODY IS LISTENING TO ANTIWAR RADICALS LIKE CHOMSKY AND ZINN.
WE DEFENSE EXPERTS KNOW THE SECRETS. OPPOSITION FROM US WOULD BE TAKEN MORE SERIOUSLY.
WE COULD PROVE THAT YOU DON'T HAVE TO BE A RADICAL OR A HIPPIE TO OPPOSE THE WAR!

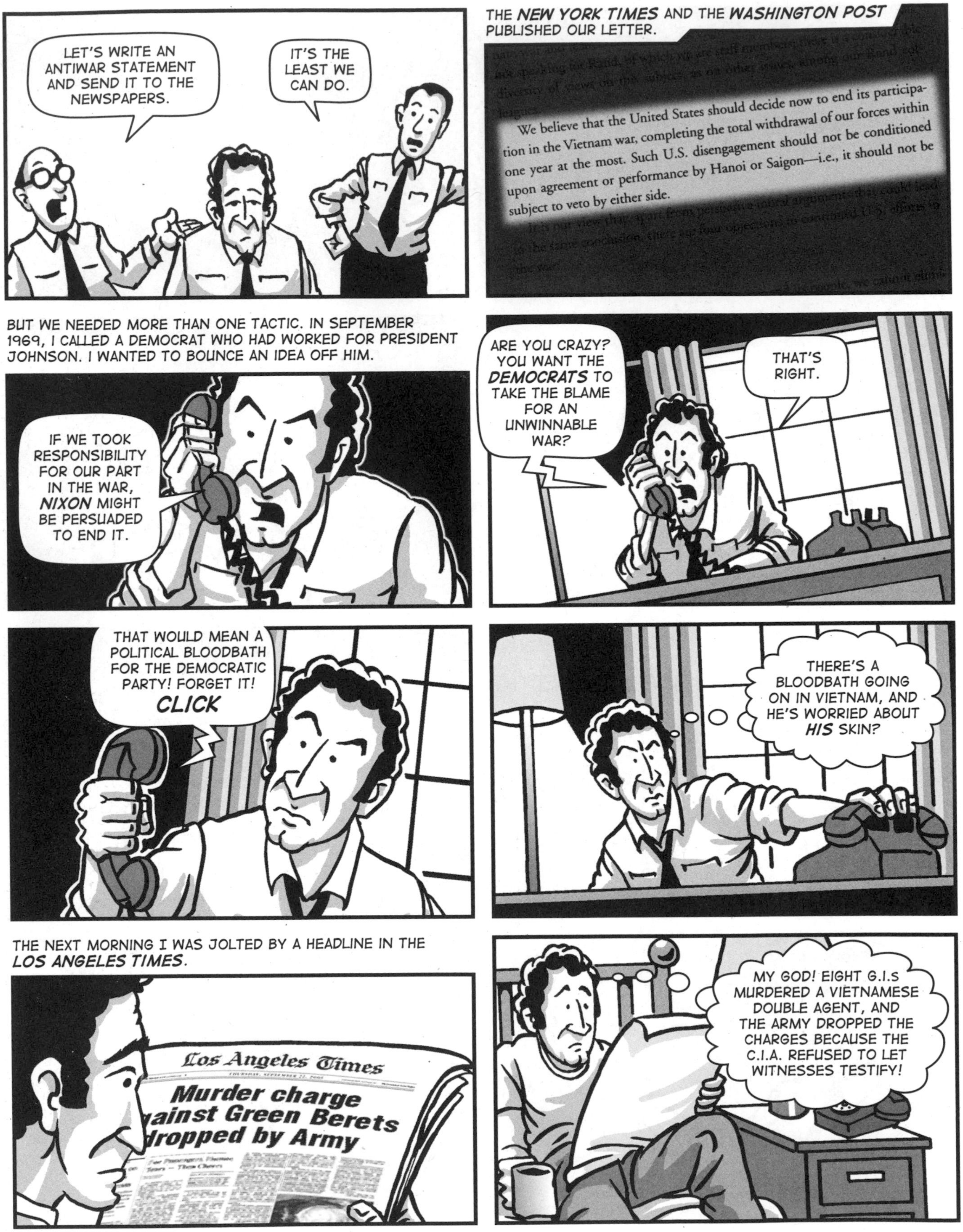

LET'S WRITE AN ANTIWAR STATEMENT AND SEND IT TO THE NEWSPAPERS.
IT'S THE LEAST WE CAN DO.
THE *NEW YORK TIMES* AND THE *WASHINGTON POST* PUBLISHED OUR LETTER.
We believe that the United States should decide now to end its participation in the Vietnam war, completing the total withdrawal of our forces within one year at the most. Such U.S. disengagement should not be conditioned upon agreement or performance by Hanoi or Saigon—i.e., it should not be subject to veto by either side.
BUT WE NEEDED MORE THAN ONE TACTIC. IN SEPTEMBER 1969, I CALLED A DEMOCRAT WHO HAD WORKED FOR PRESIDENT JOHNSON. I WANTED TO BOUNCE AN IDEA OFF HIM.
IF WE TOOK RESPONSIBILITY FOR OUR PART IN THE WAR, *NIXON* MIGHT BE PERSUADED TO END IT.
ARE YOU CRAZY? YOU WANT THE *DEMOCRATS* TO TAKE THE BLAME FOR AN UNWINNABLE WAR?
THAT'S RIGHT.
THAT WOULD MEAN A POLITICAL BLOODBATH FOR THE DEMOCRATIC PARTY! FORGET IT!
CLICK
THERE'S A BLOODBATH GOING ON IN VIETNAM, AND HE'S WORRIED ABOUT *HIS* SKIN?
THE NEXT MORNING I WAS JOLTED BY A HEADLINE IN THE *LOS ANGELES TIMES*.
Los Angeles Times
Murder charge
ainst Green Berets
dropped by Army
MY GOD! EIGHT G.I.s MURDERED A VIETNAMESE DOUBLE AGENT, AND THE ARMY DROPPED THE CHARGES BECAUSE THE C.I.A. REFUSED TO LET WITNESSES TESTIFY!

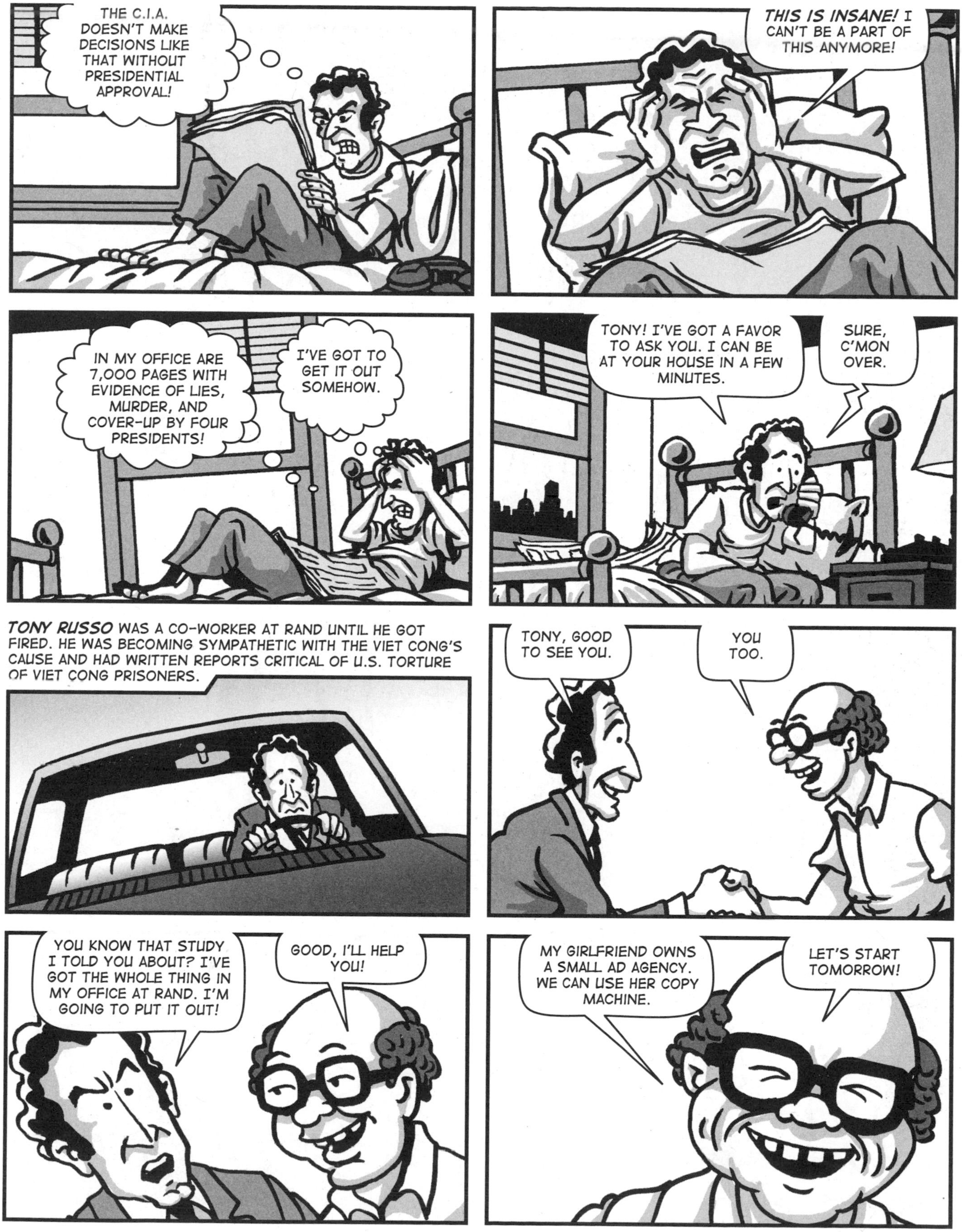
THE C.I.A. DOESN'T MAKE DECISIONS LIKE THAT WITHOUT PRESIDENTIAL APPROVAL!
THIS IS INSANE! I CAN'T BE A PART OF THIS ANYMORE!
IN MY OFFICE ARE 7,000 PAGES WITH EVIDENCE OF LIES, MURDER, AND COVER-UP BY FOUR PRESIDENTS!
I'VE GOT TO GET IT OUT SOMEHOW.
TONY! I'VE GOT A FAVOR TO ASK YOU. I CAN BE AT YOUR HOUSE IN A FEW MINUTES.
SURE, C'MON OVER.
TONY RUSSO WAS A CO-WORKER AT RAND UNTIL HE GOT FIRED. HE WAS BECOMING SYMPATHETIC WITH THE VIET CONG'S CAUSE AND HAD WRITTEN REPORTS CRITICAL OF U.S. TORTURE OF VIET CONG PRISONERS.
TONY, GOOD TO SEE YOU.
YOU TOO.
YOU KNOW THAT STUDY I TOLD YOU ABOUT? I'VE GOT THE WHOLE THING IN MY OFFICE AT RAND. I'M GOING TO PUT IT OUT!
GOOD, I'LL HELP YOU!
MY GIRLFRIEND OWNS A SMALL AD AGENCY. WE CAN USE HER COPY MACHINE.
LET'S START TOMORROW!

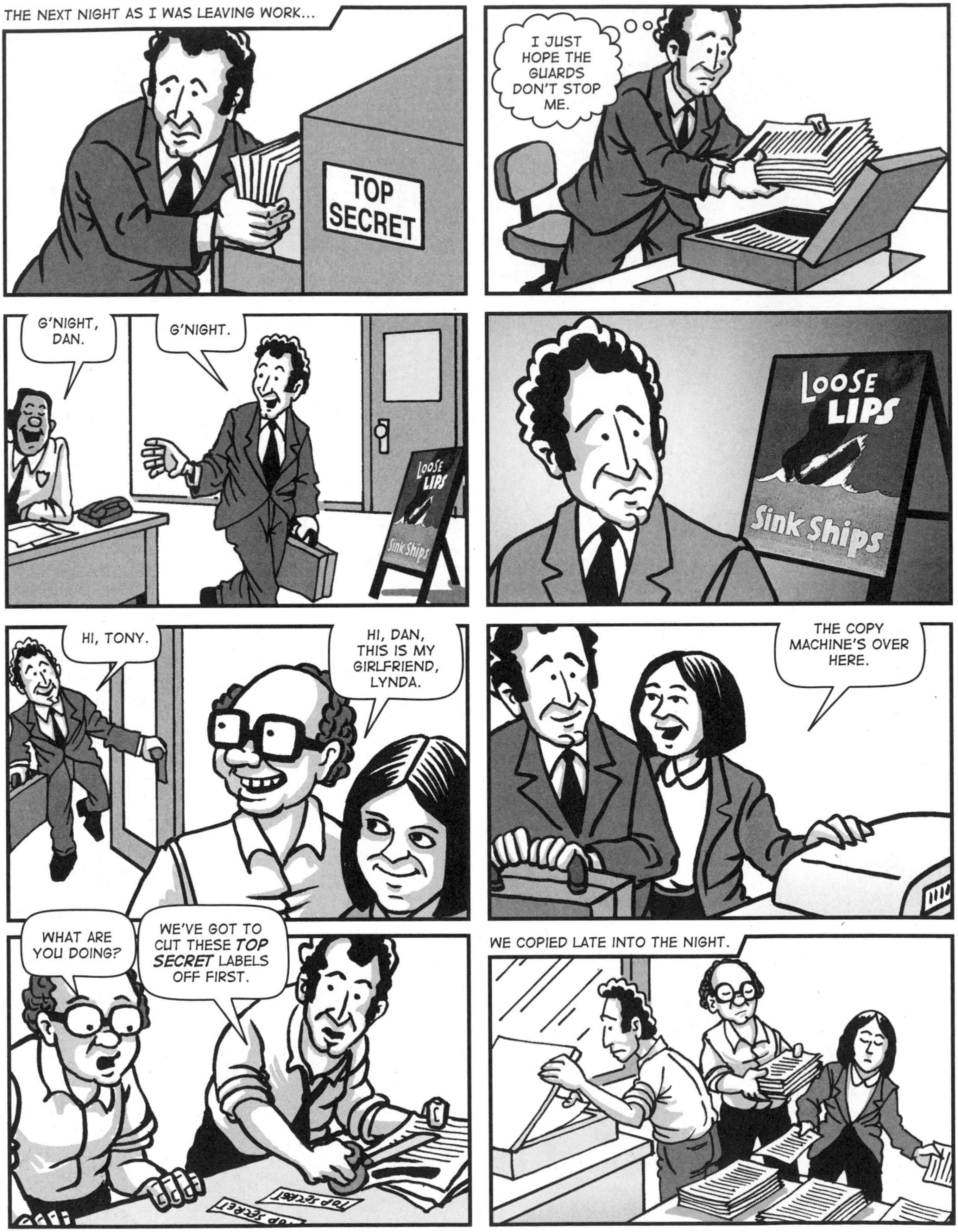
THE NEXT NIGHT AS I WAS LEAVING WORK...
TOP SECRET
I JUST HOPE THE GUARDS DON'T STOP ME.
G'NIGHT, DAN.
G'NIGHT.
LOOSE LIPS Sink Ships
LOOSE LIPS Sink Ships
HI, TONY.
HI, DAN, THIS IS MY GIRLFRIEND, LYNDA.
THE COPY MACHINE'S OVER HERE.
WHAT ARE YOU DOING?
WE'VE GOT TO CUT THESE *TOP SECRET* LABELS OFF FIRST.
TOP SECRET
WE COPIED LATE INTO THE NIGHT.

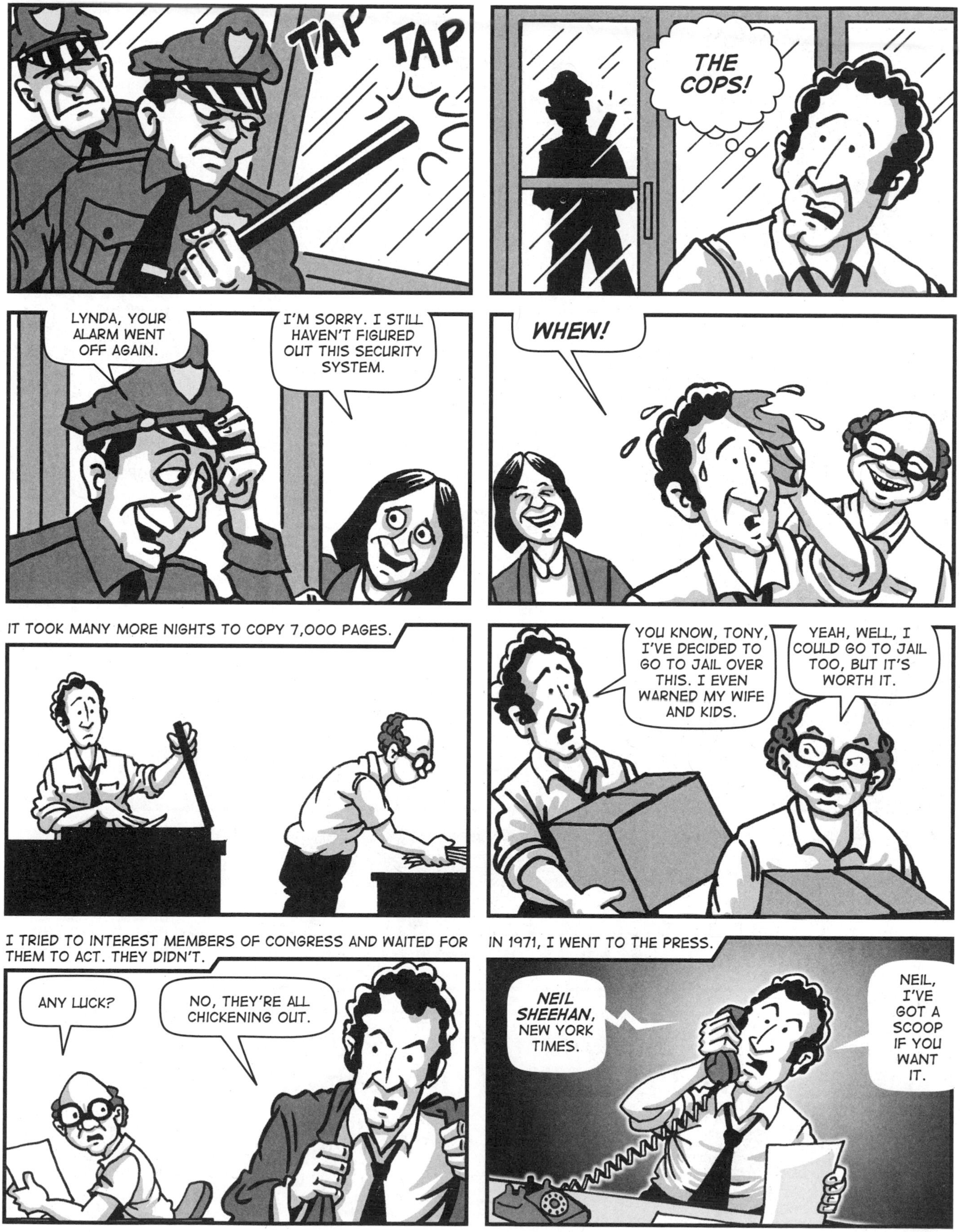
TAP TAP
THE COPS!
LYNDA, YOUR ALARM WENT OFF AGAIN.
I'M SORRY. I STILL HAVEN'T FIGURED OUT THIS SECURITY SYSTEM.
WHEW!
IT TOOK MANY MORE NIGHTS TO COPY 7,000 PAGES.
YOU KNOW, TONY, I'VE DECIDED TO GO TO JAIL OVER THIS. I EVEN WARNED MY WIFE AND KIDS.
YEAH, WELL, I COULD GO TO JAIL TOO, BUT IT'S WORTH IT.
I TRIED TO INTEREST MEMBERS OF CONGRESS AND WAITED FOR THEM TO ACT. THEY DIDN'T.
ANY LUCK?
NO, THEY'RE ALL CHICKENING OUT.
IN 1971, I WENT TO THE PRESS.
NEIL SHEEHAN, NEW YORK TIMES.
NEIL, I'VE GOT A SCOOP IF YOU WANT IT.

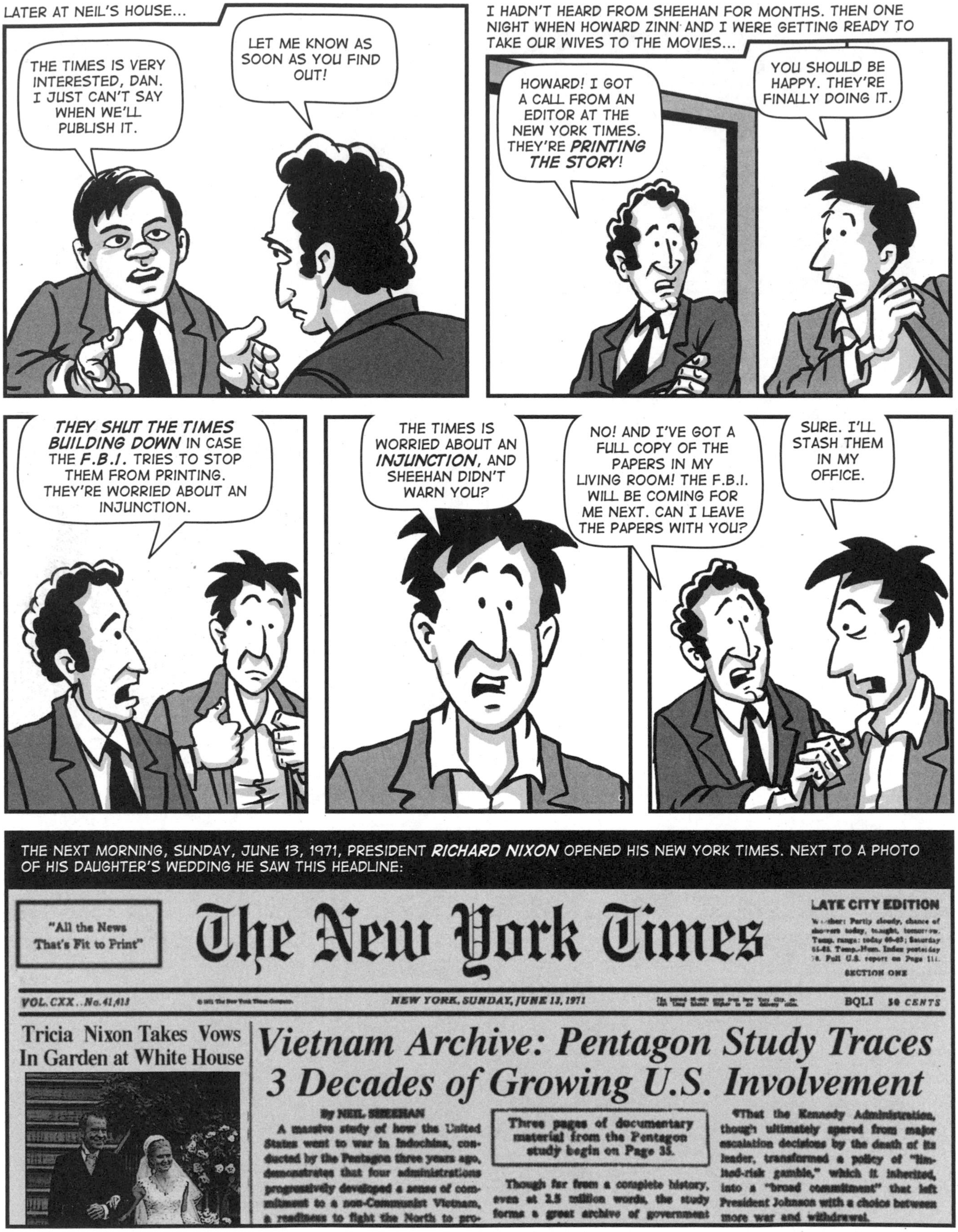
LATER AT NEIL'S HOUSE...
THE TIMES IS VERY INTERESTED, DAN. I JUST CAN'T SAY WHEN WE'LL PUBLISH IT.
LET ME KNOW AS SOON AS YOU FIND OUT!
I HADN'T HEARD FROM SHEEHAN FOR MONTHS. THEN ONE NIGHT WHEN HOWARD ZINN AND I WERE GETTING READY TO TAKE OUR WIVES TO THE MOVIES...
HOWARD! I GOT A CALL FROM AN EDITOR AT THE NEW YORK TIMES. THEY'RE PRINTING THE STORY!
YOU SHOULD BE HAPPY. THEY'RE FINALLY DOING IT.
THEY SHUT THE TIMES BUILDING DOWN IN CASE THE F.B.I. TRIES TO STOP THEM FROM PRINTING. THEY'RE WORRIED ABOUT AN INJUNCTION.
THE TIMES IS WORRIED ABOUT AN INJUNCTION, AND SHEEHAN DIDN'T WARN YOU?
NO! AND I'VE GOT A FULL COPY OF THE PAPERS IN MY LIVING ROOM! THE F.B.I. WILL BE COMING FOR ME NEXT. CAN I LEAVE THE PAPERS WITH YOU?
SURE. I'LL STASH THEM IN MY OFFICE.
THE NEXT MORNING, SUNDAY, JUNE 13, 1971, PRESIDENT RICHARD NIXON OPENED HIS NEW YORK TIMES. NEXT TO A PHOTO OF HIS DAUGHTER'S WEDDING HE SAW THIS HEADLINE:
"All the News That's Fit to Print"
The New York Times
LATE CITY EDITION
SECTION ONE
VOL. CXX..No. 41,413
NEW YORK, SUNDAY, JUNE 13, 1971
BQLI 50 CENTS
Tricia Nixon Takes Vows In Garden at White House
Vietnam Archive: Pentagon Study Traces 3 Decades of Growing U.S. Involvement
By NEIL SHEEHAN
A massive study of how the United States went to war in Indochina, conducted by the Pentagon three years ago, demonstrates that four administrations progressively developed a sense of commitment to a non-Communist Vietnam, a readiness to fight the North to pro-
Three pages of documentary material from the Pentagon study begin on Page 35.
Though far from a complete history, even at 2.5 million words, the study forms a great archive of government
¶That the Kennedy Administration, though ultimately spared from major escalation decisions by the death of its leader, transformed a policy of "limited-risk gamble," which it inherited, into a "broad commitment" that left President Johnson with a choice between more war and withdrawal.

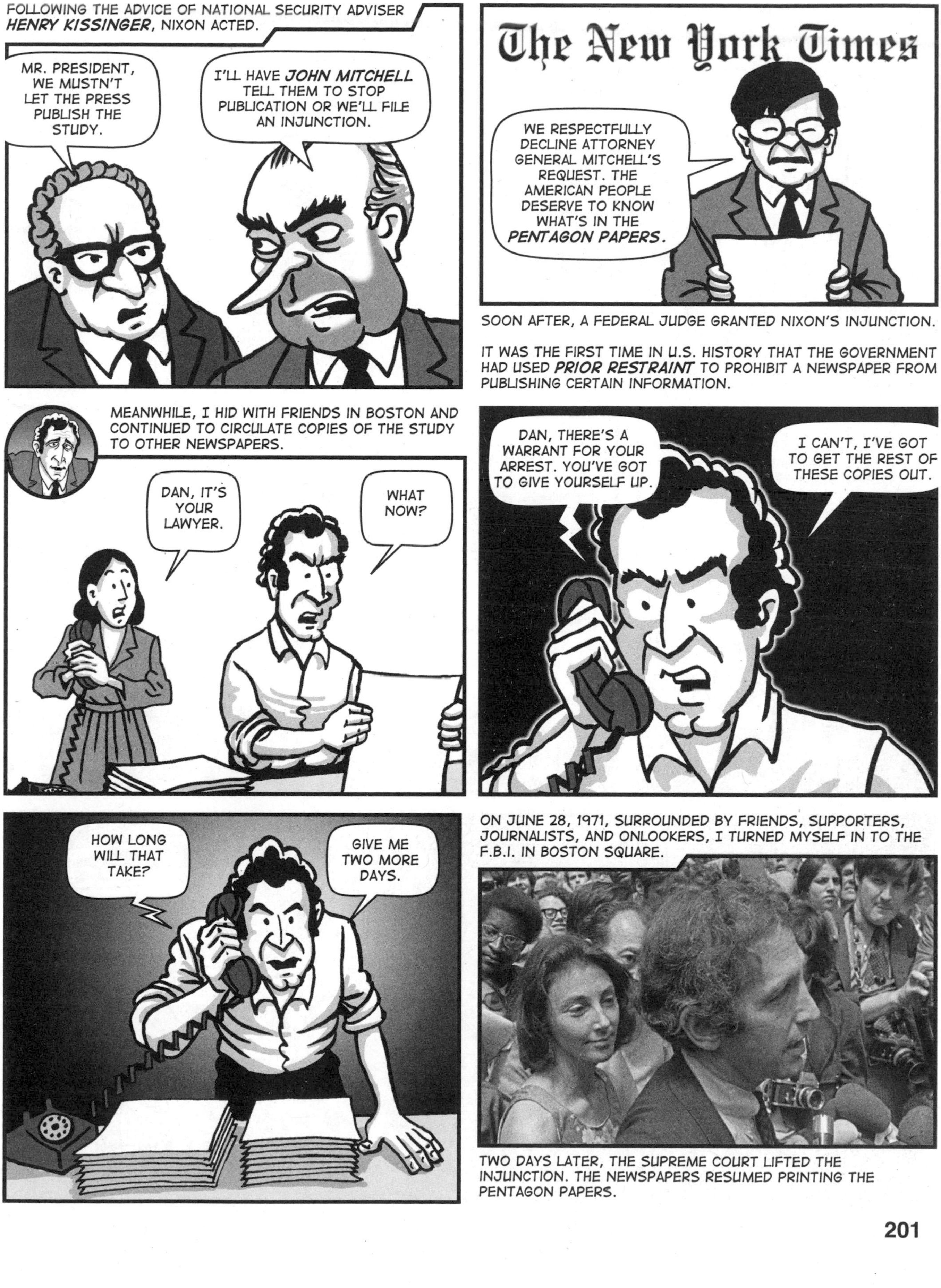
FOLLOWING THE ADVICE OF NATIONAL SECURITY ADVISER HENRY KISSINGER, NIXON ACTED.
MR. PRESIDENT, WE MUSTN'T LET THE PRESS PUBLISH THE STUDY.
I'LL HAVE JOHN MITCHELL TELL THEM TO STOP PUBLICATION OR WE'LL FILE AN INJUNCTION.
The New York Times
WE RESPECTFULLY DECLINE ATTORNEY GENERAL MITCHELL'S REQUEST. THE AMERICAN PEOPLE DESERVE TO KNOW WHAT'S IN THE PENTAGON PAPERS.
SOON AFTER, A FEDERAL JUDGE GRANTED NIXON'S INJUNCTION.
IT WAS THE FIRST TIME IN U.S. HISTORY THAT THE GOVERNMENT HAD USED PRIOR RESTRAINT TO PROHIBIT A NEWSPAPER FROM PUBLISHING CERTAIN INFORMATION.
MEANWHILE, I HID WITH FRIENDS IN BOSTON AND CONTINUED TO CIRCULATE COPIES OF THE STUDY TO OTHER NEWSPAPERS.
DAN, IT'S YOUR LAWYER.
WHAT NOW?
DAN, THERE'S A WARRANT FOR YOUR ARREST. YOU'VE GOT TO GIVE YOURSELF UP.
I CAN'T, I'VE GOT TO GET THE REST OF THESE COPIES OUT.
HOW LONG WILL THAT TAKE?
GIVE ME TWO MORE DAYS.
ON JUNE 28, 1971, SURROUNDED BY FRIENDS, SUPPORTERS, JOURNALISTS, AND ONLOOKERS, I TURNED MYSELF IN TO THE F.B.I. IN BOSTON SQUARE.
TWO DAYS LATER, THE SUPREME COURT LIFTED THE INJUNCTION. THE NEWSPAPERS RESUMED PRINTING THE PENTAGON PAPERS.

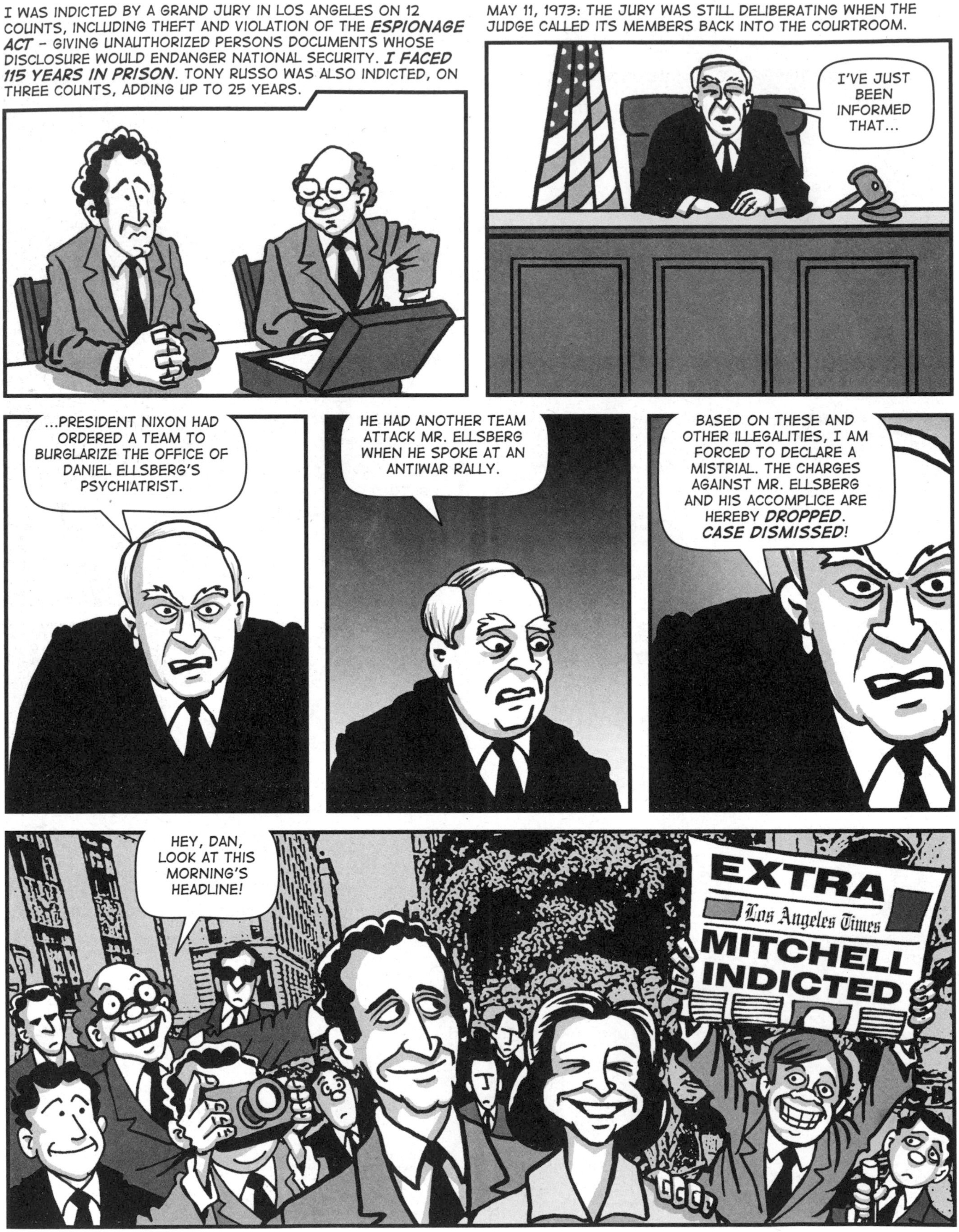
I WAS INDICTED BY A GRAND JURY IN LOS ANGELES ON 12 COUNTS, INCLUDING THEFT AND VIOLATION OF THE ***ESPIONAGE ACT*** – GIVING UNAUTHORIZED PERSONS DOCUMENTS WHOSE DISCLOSURE WOULD ENDANGER NATIONAL SECURITY. ***I FACED 115 YEARS IN PRISON***. TONY RUSSO WAS ALSO INDICTED, ON THREE COUNTS, ADDING UP TO 25 YEARS.
MAY 11, 1973: THE JURY WAS STILL DELIBERATING WHEN THE JUDGE CALLED ITS MEMBERS BACK INTO THE COURTROOM.
I'VE JUST BEEN INFORMED THAT...
...PRESIDENT NIXON HAD ORDERED A TEAM TO BURGLARIZE THE OFFICE OF DANIEL ELLSBERG'S PSYCHIATRIST.
HE HAD ANOTHER TEAM ATTACK MR. ELLSBERG WHEN HE SPOKE AT AN ANTIWAR RALLY.
BASED ON THESE AND OTHER ILLEGALITIES, I AM FORCED TO DECLARE A MISTRIAL. THE CHARGES AGAINST MR. ELLSBERG AND HIS ACCOMPLICE ARE HEREBY ***DROPPED***. ***CASE DISMISSED***!
HEY, DAN, LOOK AT THIS MORNING'S HEADLINE!
EXTRA
Los Angeles Times
MITCHELL INDICTED

Hostage to Imperialism

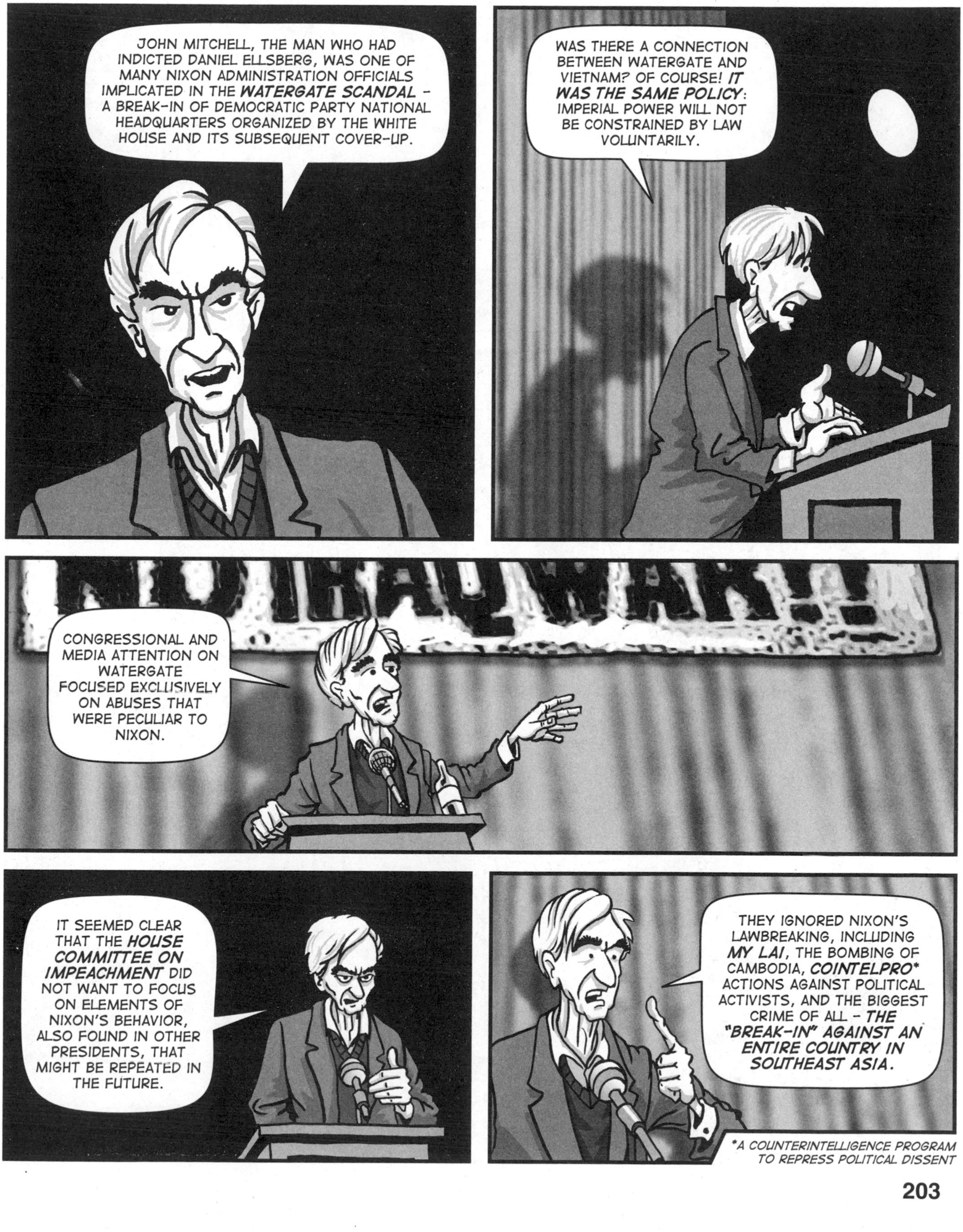

JOHN MITCHELL, THE MAN WHO HAD INDICTED DANIEL ELLSBERG, WAS ONE OF MANY NIXON ADMINISTRATION OFFICIALS IMPLICATED IN THE ***WATERGATE SCANDAL*** - A BREAK-IN OF DEMOCRATIC PARTY NATIONAL HEADQUARTERS ORGANIZED BY THE WHITE HOUSE AND ITS SUBSEQUENT COVER-UP.
WAS THERE A CONNECTION BETWEEN WATERGATE AND VIETNAM? OF COURSE! ***IT WAS THE SAME POLICY***: IMPERIAL POWER WILL NOT BE CONSTRAINED BY LAW VOLUNTARILY.
CONGRESSIONAL AND MEDIA ATTENTION ON WATERGATE FOCUSED EXCLUSIVELY ON ABUSES THAT WERE PECULIAR TO NIXON.
IT SEEMED CLEAR THAT THE ***HOUSE COMMITTEE ON IMPEACHMENT*** DID NOT WANT TO FOCUS ON ELEMENTS OF NIXON'S BEHAVIOR, ALSO FOUND IN OTHER PRESIDENTS, THAT MIGHT BE REPEATED IN THE FUTURE.
THEY IGNORED NIXON'S LAWBREAKING, INCLUDING ***MY LAI***, THE BOMBING OF CAMBODIA, ***COINTELPRO***** ACTIONS AGAINST POLITICAL ACTIVISTS, AND THE BIGGEST CRIME OF ALL - ***THE "BREAK-IN" AGAINST AN ENTIRE COUNTRY IN SOUTHEAST ASIA***.

**A COUNTERINTELLIGENCE PROGRAM TO REPRESS POLITICAL DISSENT*

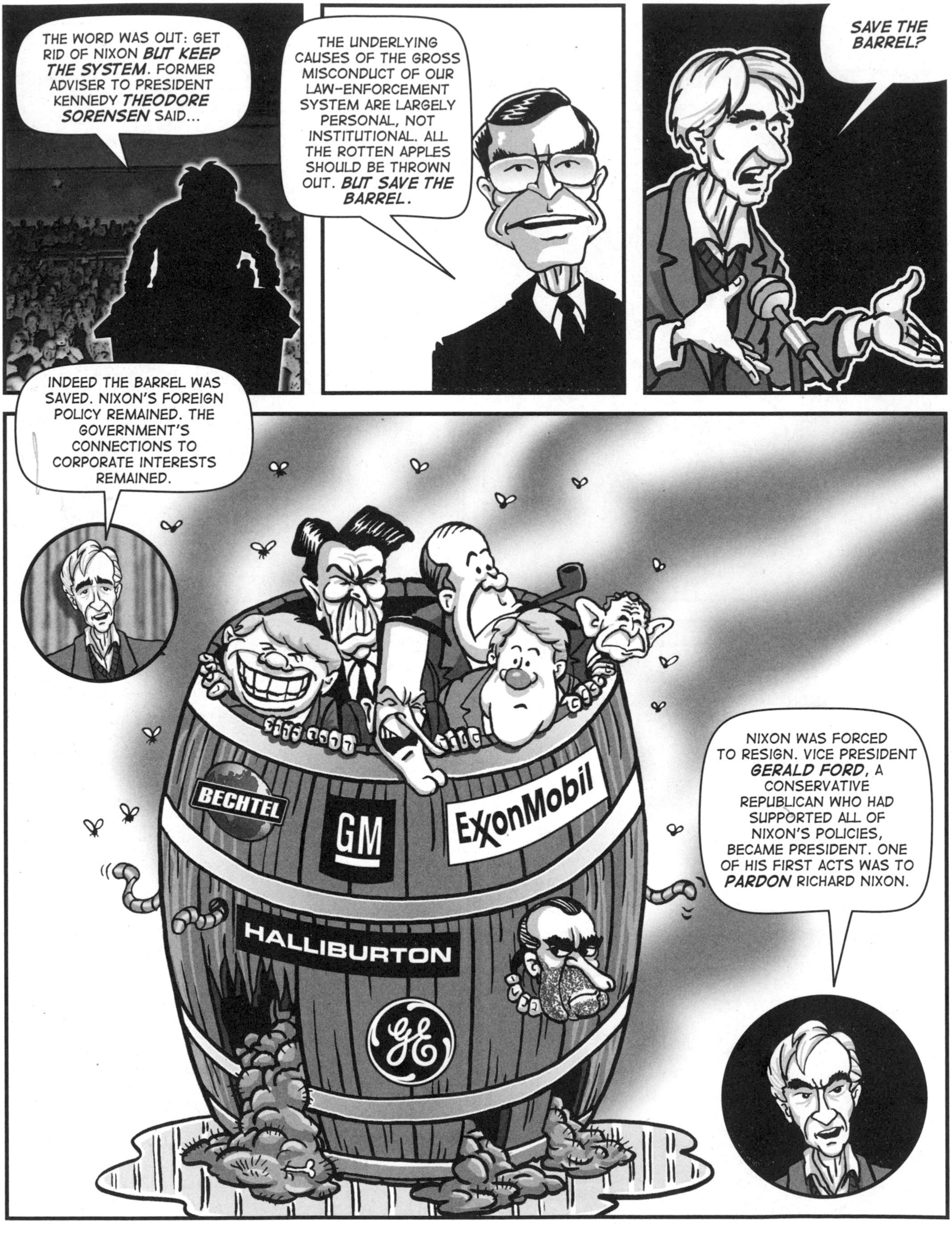
THE WORD WAS OUT: GET RID OF NIXON BUT KEEP THE SYSTEM. FORMER ADVISER TO PRESIDENT KENNEDY THEODORE SORENSEN SAID...
THE UNDERLYING CAUSES OF THE GROSS MISCONDUCT OF OUR LAW-ENFORCEMENT SYSTEM ARE LARGELY PERSONAL, NOT INSTITUTIONAL. ALL THE ROTTEN APPLES SHOULD BE THROWN OUT. BUT SAVE THE BARREL.
SAVE THE BARREL?
INDEED THE BARREL WAS SAVED. NIXON'S FOREIGN POLICY REMAINED. THE GOVERNMENT'S CONNECTIONS TO CORPORATE INTERESTS REMAINED.
BECHTEL
GM
ExxonMobil
HALLIBURTON
GE
NIXON WAS FORCED TO RESIGN. VICE PRESIDENT GERALD FORD, A CONSERVATIVE REPUBLICAN WHO HAD SUPPORTED ALL OF NIXON'S POLICIES, BECAME PRESIDENT. ONE OF HIS FIRST ACTS WAS TO PARDON RICHARD NIXON.

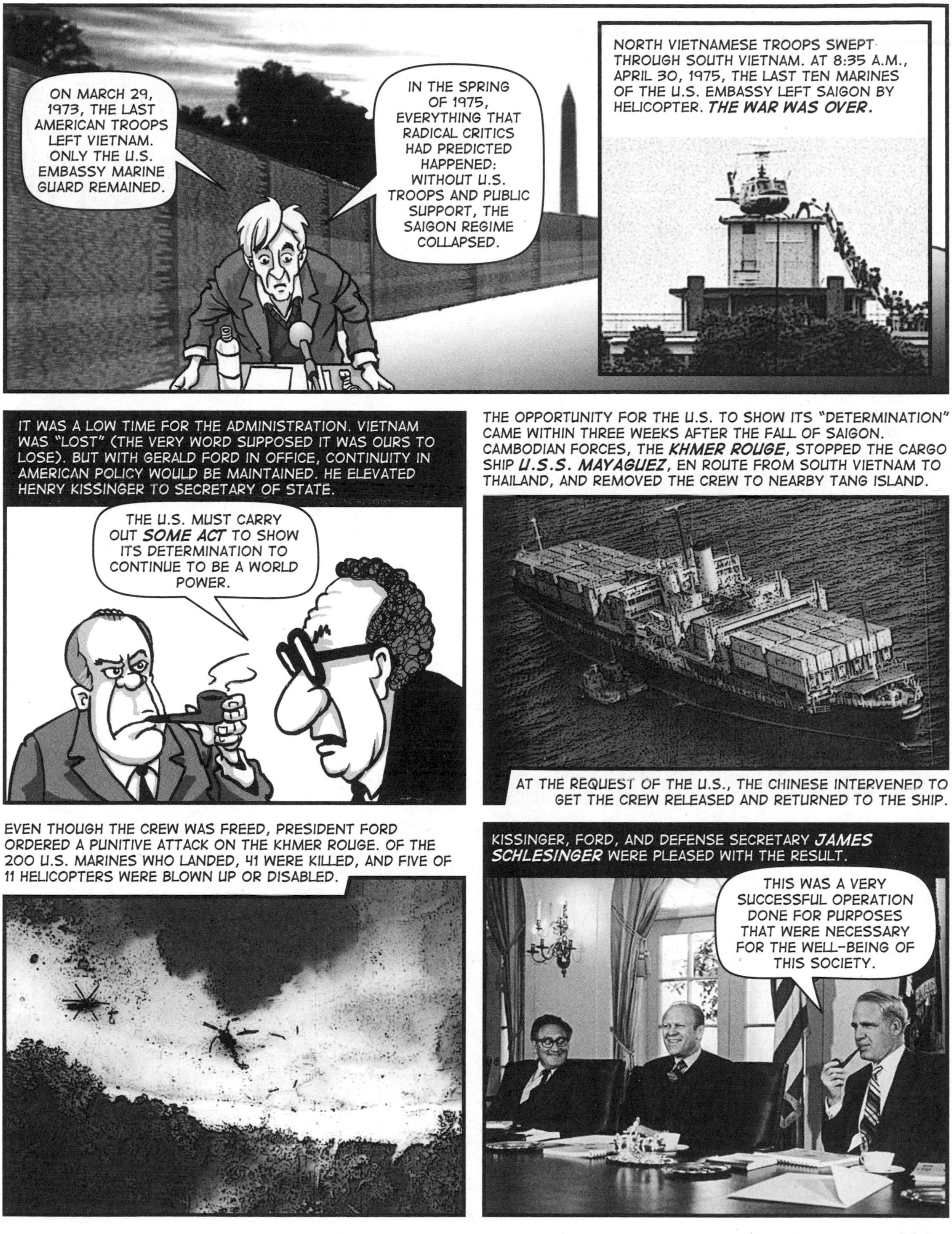
ON MARCH 29, 1973, THE LAST AMERICAN TROOPS LEFT VIETNAM. ONLY THE U.S. EMBASSY MARINE GUARD REMAINED.
IN THE SPRING OF 1975, EVERYTHING THAT RADICAL CRITICS HAD PREDICTED HAPPENED: WITHOUT U.S. TROOPS AND PUBLIC SUPPORT, THE SAIGON REGIME COLLAPSED.
NORTH VIETNAMESE TROOPS SWEPT THROUGH SOUTH VIETNAM. AT 8:35 A.M., APRIL 30, 1975, THE LAST TEN MARINES OF THE U.S. EMBASSY LEFT SAIGON BY HELICOPTER. ***THE WAR WAS OVER.***
IT WAS A LOW TIME FOR THE ADMINISTRATION. VIETNAM WAS "LOST" (THE VERY WORD SUPPOSED IT WAS OURS TO LOSE). BUT WITH GERALD FORD IN OFFICE, CONTINUITY IN AMERICAN POLICY WOULD BE MAINTAINED. HE ELEVATED HENRY KISSINGER TO SECRETARY OF STATE.
THE U.S. MUST CARRY OUT ***SOME ACT*** TO SHOW ITS DETERMINATION TO CONTINUE TO BE A WORLD POWER.
THE OPPORTUNITY FOR THE U.S. TO SHOW ITS "DETERMINATION" CAME WITHIN THREE WEEKS AFTER THE FALL OF SAIGON. CAMBODIAN FORCES, THE ***KHMER ROUGE***, STOPPED THE CARGO SHIP ***U.S.S. MAYAGUEZ***, EN ROUTE FROM SOUTH VIETNAM TO THAILAND, AND REMOVED THE CREW TO NEARBY TANG ISLAND.
AT THE REQUEST OF THE U.S., THE CHINESE INTERVENED TO GET THE CREW RELEASED AND RETURNED TO THE SHIP.
EVEN THOUGH THE CREW WAS FREED, PRESIDENT FORD ORDERED A PUNITIVE ATTACK ON THE KHMER ROUGE. OF THE 200 U.S. MARINES WHO LANDED, 41 WERE KILLED, AND FIVE OF 11 HELICOPTERS WERE BLOWN UP OR DISABLED.
KISSINGER, FORD, AND DEFENSE SECRETARY ***JAMES SCHLESINGER*** WERE PLEASED WITH THE RESULT.
THIS WAS A VERY SUCCESSFUL OPERATION DONE FOR PURPOSES THAT WERE NECESSARY FOR THE WELL-BEING OF THIS SOCIETY.

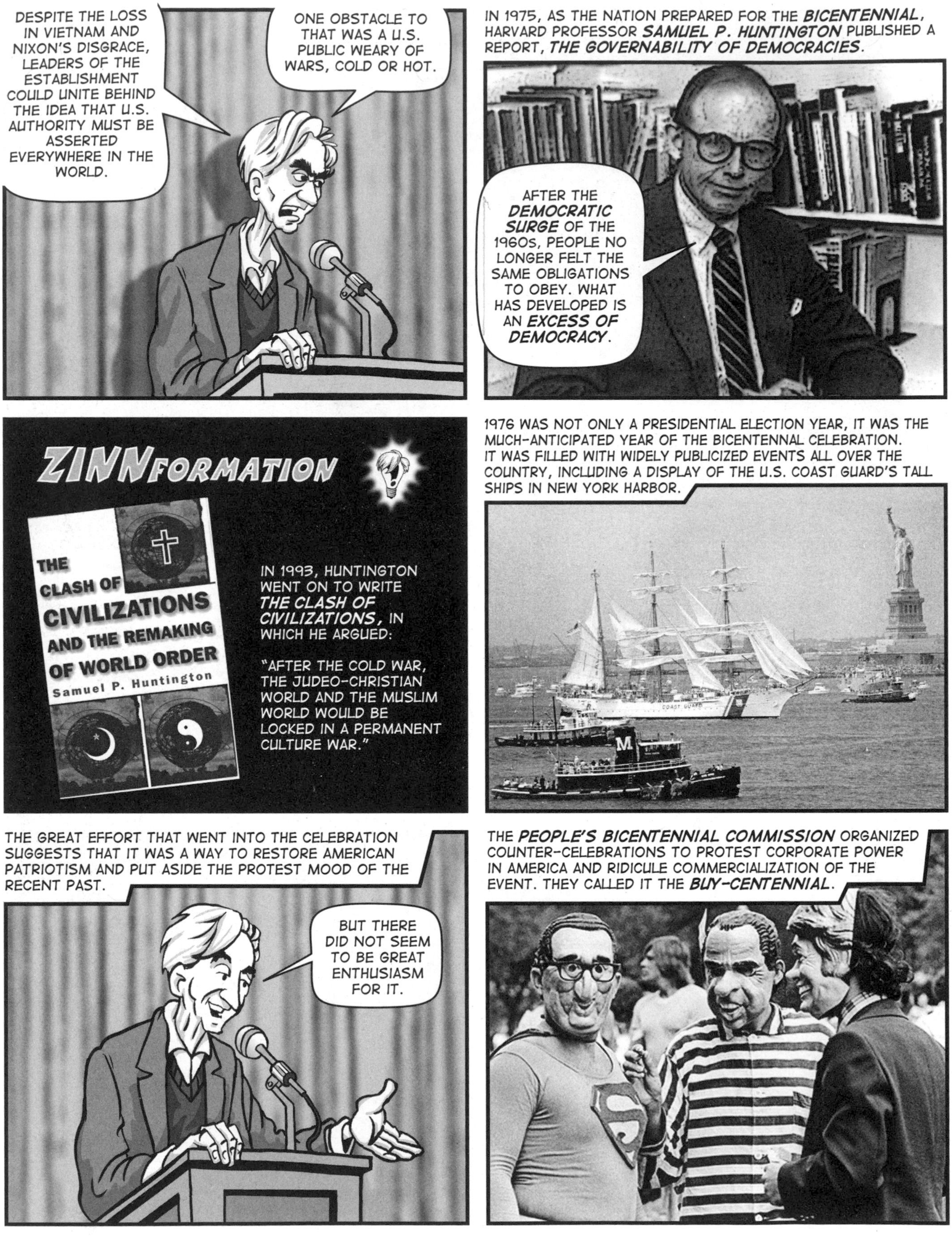
DESPITE THE LOSS IN VIETNAM AND NIXON'S DISGRACE, LEADERS OF THE ESTABLISHMENT COULD UNITE BEHIND THE IDEA THAT U.S. AUTHORITY MUST BE ASSERTED EVERYWHERE IN THE WORLD.
ONE OBSTACLE TO THAT WAS A U.S. PUBLIC WEARY OF WARS, COLD OR HOT.
IN 1975, AS THE NATION PREPARED FOR THE ***BICENTENNIAL***, HARVARD PROFESSOR ***SAMUEL P. HUNTINGTON*** PUBLISHED A REPORT, ***THE GOVERNABILITY OF DEMOCRACIES***.
AFTER THE ***DEMOCRATIC SURGE*** OF THE 1960S, PEOPLE NO LONGER FELT THE SAME OBLIGATIONS TO OBEY. WHAT HAS DEVELOPED IS AN ***EXCESS OF DEMOCRACY***.
ZINNFORMATION
THE CLASH OF CIVILIZATIONS AND THE REMAKING OF WORLD ORDER
Samuel P. Huntington
IN 1993, HUNTINGTON WENT ON TO WRITE ***THE CLASH OF CIVILIZATIONS***, IN WHICH HE ARGUED:
"AFTER THE COLD WAR, THE JUDEO-CHRISTIAN WORLD AND THE MUSLIM WORLD WOULD BE LOCKED IN A PERMANENT CULTURE WAR."
1976 WAS NOT ONLY A PRESIDENTIAL ELECTION YEAR, IT WAS THE MUCH-ANTICIPATED YEAR OF THE BICENTENNAL CELEBRATION. IT WAS FILLED WITH WIDELY PUBLICIZED EVENTS ALL OVER THE COUNTRY, INCLUDING A DISPLAY OF THE U.S. COAST GUARD'S TALL SHIPS IN NEW YORK HARBOR.
COAST GUARD
M
THE GREAT EFFORT THAT WENT INTO THE CELEBRATION SUGGESTS THAT IT WAS A WAY TO RESTORE AMERICAN PATRIOTISM AND PUT ASIDE THE PROTEST MOOD OF THE RECENT PAST.
BUT THERE DID NOT SEEM TO BE GREAT ENTHUSIASM FOR IT.
THE ***PEOPLE'S BICENTENNIAL COMMISSION*** ORGANIZED COUNTER-CELEBRATIONS TO PROTEST CORPORATE POWER IN AMERICA AND RIDICULE COMMERCIALIZATION OF THE EVENT. THEY CALLED IT THE ***BUY-CENTENNIAL***.
S

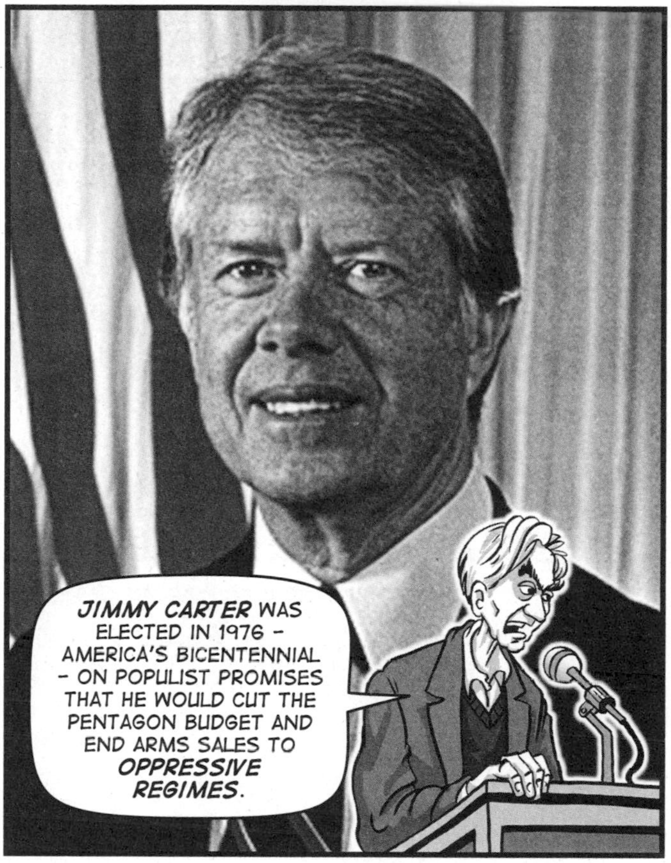
JIMMY CARTER WAS ELECTED IN 1976 - AMERICA'S BICENTENNIAL - ON POPULIST PROMISES THAT HE WOULD CUT THE PENTAGON BUDGET AND END ARMS SALES TO OPPRESSIVE REGIMES.

BUT CARTER'S FIRST BUDGET INCREASED THE PENTAGON BUDGET BY $10 BILLION, AND MOST OF THE ARMS SALES TO DICTATORS CONTINUED.

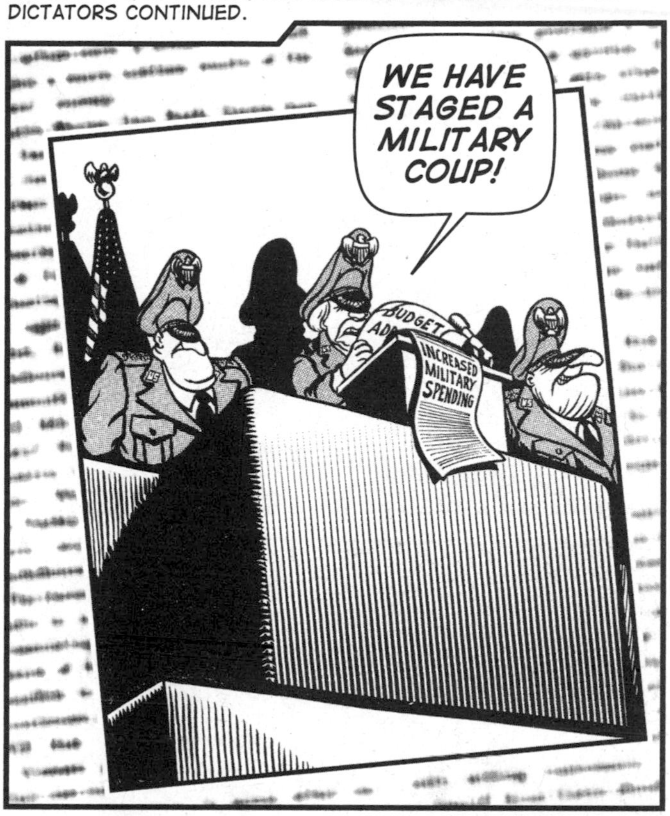
WE HAVE STAGED A MILITARY COUP!
BUDGET
INCREASED MILITARY SPENDING

CARTER'S ECONOMIC POLICIES WERE MEANT TO PLEASE ***WALL STREET*** AND REASSURE THE BUSINESS COMMUNITY. WORKING PEOPLE AND THE POOR SUFFERED HIGH UNEMPLOYMENT AND INFLATION.

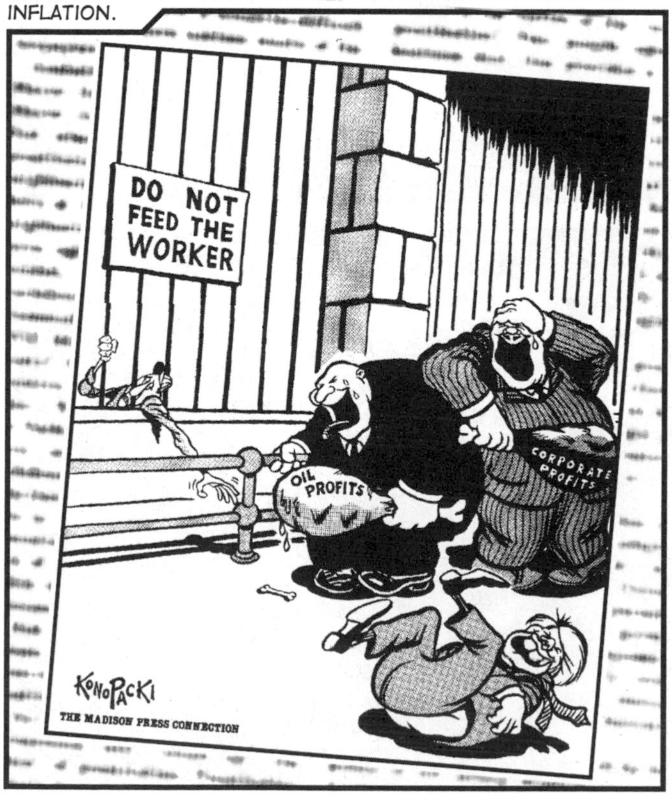
DO NOT FEED THE WORKER
OIL PROFITS
CORPORATE PROFITS
KONOPACKI
THE MADISON PRESS CONNECTION

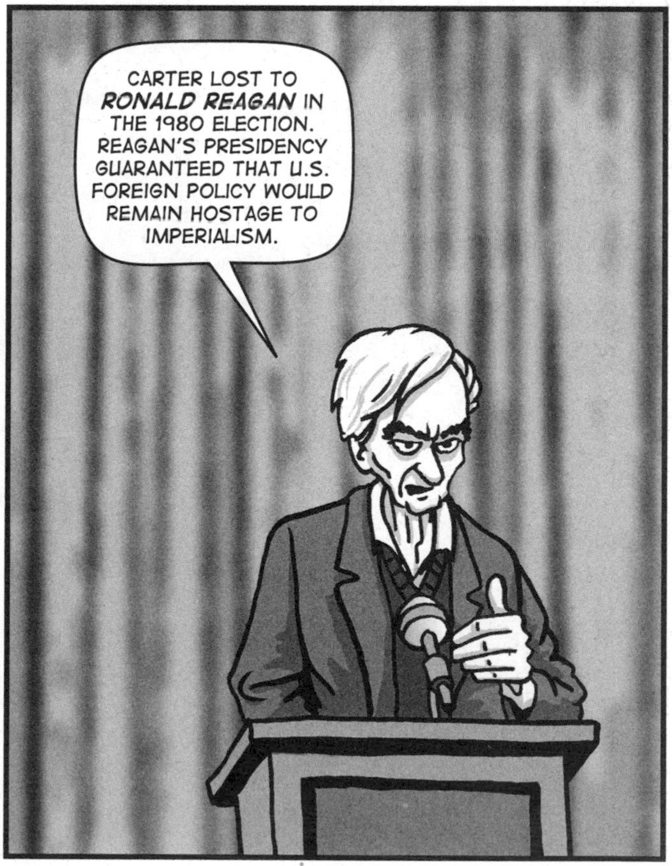
CARTER LOST TO RONALD REAGAN IN THE 1980 ELECTION. REAGAN'S PRESIDENCY GUARANTEED THAT U.S. FOREIGN POLICY WOULD REMAIN HOSTAGE TO IMPERIALISM.

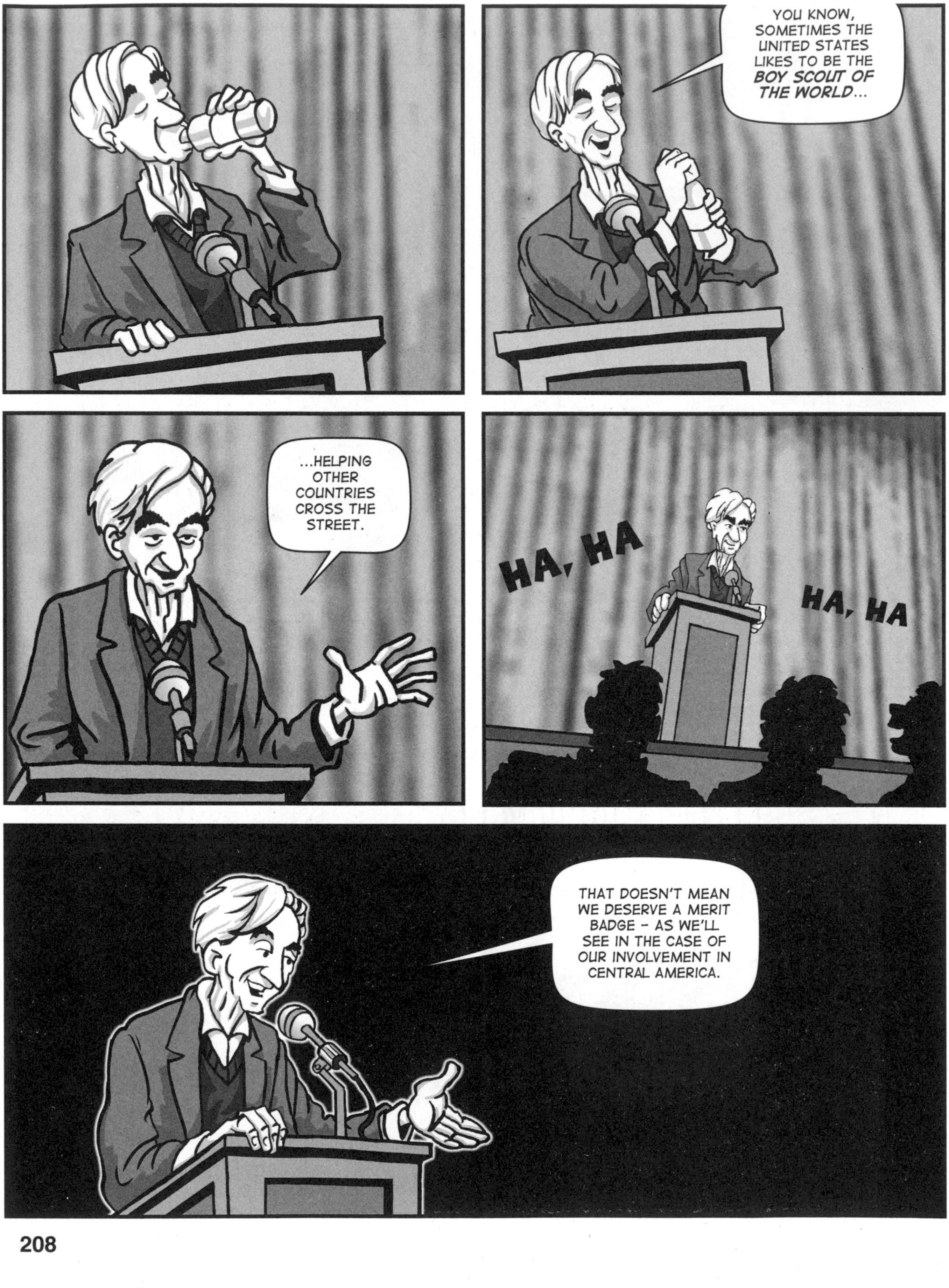
YOU KNOW, SOMETIMES THE UNITED STATES LIKES TO BE THE BOY SCOUT OF THE WORLD...
...HELPING OTHER COUNTRIES CROSS THE STREET.
HA, HA
HA, HA
THAT DOESN'T MEAN WE DESERVE A MERIT BADGE – AS WE'LL SEE IN THE CASE OF OUR INVOLVEMENT IN CENTRAL AMERICA.

Chapter XI

RESURGENCE OF EMPIRE

*"Wake up, Pancho Nicaragua, grab your machete
There's a lot of weeds to cut
grab your machete and guitar."*

*Father Ernesto Cardenal
Nicaraguan Minister of Culture 1979–87*

The Sandinista Revolution

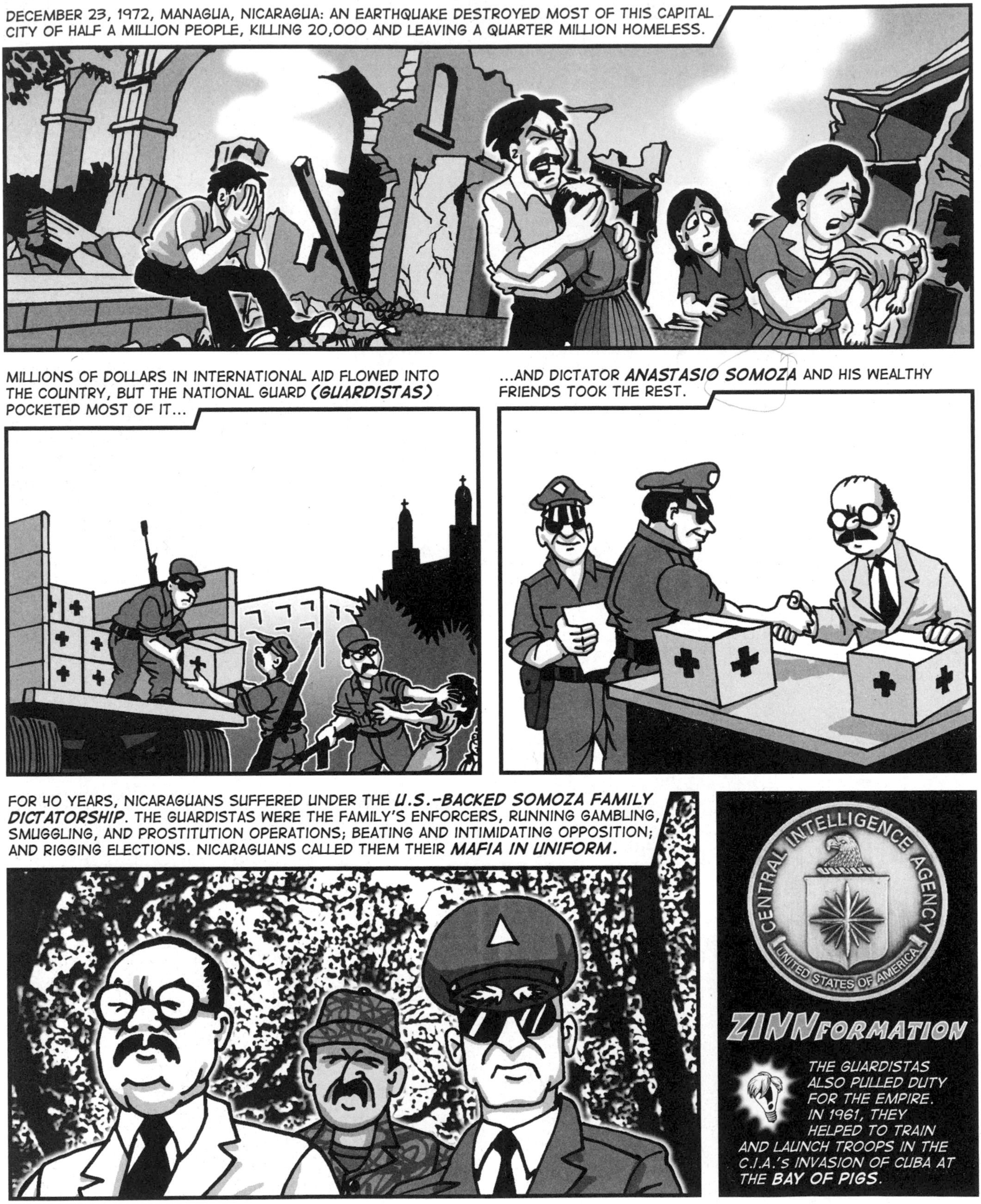
DECEMBER 23, 1972, MANAGUA, NICARAGUA: AN EARTHQUAKE DESTROYED MOST OF THIS CAPITAL CITY OF HALF A MILLION PEOPLE, KILLING 20,000 AND LEAVING A QUARTER MILLION HOMELESS.
MILLIONS OF DOLLARS IN INTERNATIONAL AID FLOWED INTO THE COUNTRY, BUT THE NATIONAL GUARD *(GUARDISTAS)* POCKETED MOST OF IT...
...AND DICTATOR ***ANASTASIO SOMOZA*** AND HIS WEALTHY FRIENDS TOOK THE REST.
FOR 40 YEARS, NICARAGUANS SUFFERED UNDER THE ***U.S.-BACKED SOMOZA FAMILY DICTATORSHIP***. THE GUARDISTAS WERE THE FAMILY'S ENFORCERS, RUNNING GAMBLING, SMUGGLING, AND PROSTITUTION OPERATIONS; BEATING AND INTIMIDATING OPPOSITION; AND RIGGING ELECTIONS. NICARAGUANS CALLED THEM THEIR ***MAFIA IN UNIFORM***.
CENTRAL INTELLIGENCE AGENCY
UNITED STATES OF AMERICA
ZINNFORMATION
THE GUARDISTAS ALSO PULLED DUTY FOR THE EMPIRE. IN 1961, THEY HELPED TO TRAIN AND LAUNCH TROOPS IN THE C.I.A.'s INVASION OF CUBA AT THE **BAY OF PIGS**.

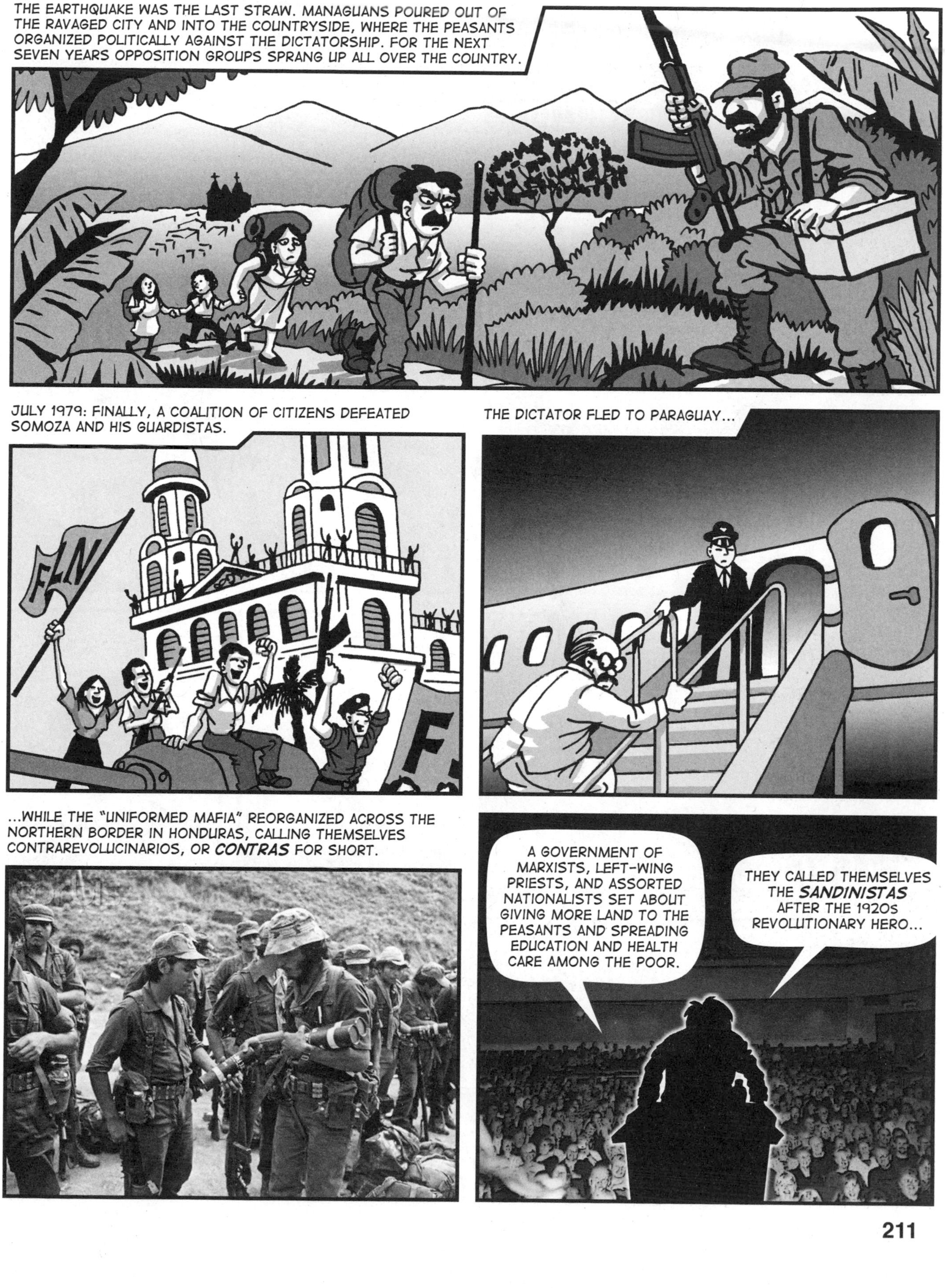
THE EARTHQUAKE WAS THE LAST STRAW. MANAGUANS POURED OUT OF THE RAVAGED CITY AND INTO THE COUNTRYSIDE, WHERE THE PEASANTS ORGANIZED POLITICALLY AGAINST THE DICTATORSHIP. FOR THE NEXT SEVEN YEARS OPPOSITION GROUPS SPRANG UP ALL OVER THE COUNTRY.
JULY 1979: FINALLY, A COALITION OF CITIZENS DEFEATED SOMOZA AND HIS GUARDISTAS.
FLN
THE DICTATOR FLED TO PARAGUAY...
...WHILE THE "UNIFORMED MAFIA" REORGANIZED ACROSS THE NORTHERN BORDER IN HONDURAS, CALLING THEMSELVES CONTRAREVOLUCINARIOS, OR ***CONTRAS*** FOR SHORT.
A GOVERNMENT OF MARXISTS, LEFT-WING PRIESTS, AND ASSORTED NATIONALISTS SET ABOUT GIVING MORE LAND TO THE PEASANTS AND SPREADING EDUCATION AND HEALTH CARE AMONG THE POOR.
THEY CALLED THEMSELVES THE ***SANDINISTAS*** AFTER THE 1920s REVOLUTIONARY HERO...

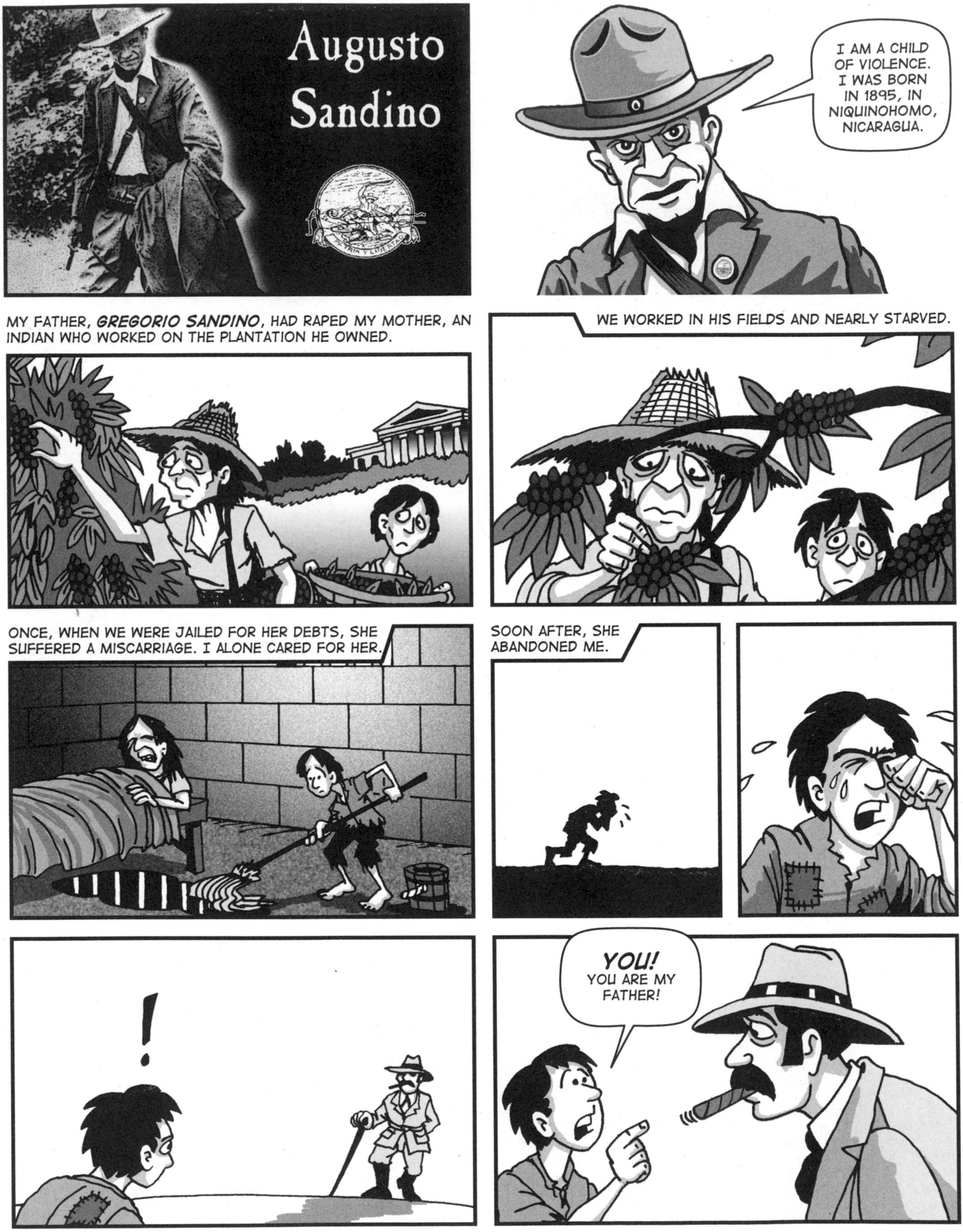
Augusto Sandino
I AM A CHILD OF VIOLENCE. I WAS BORN IN 1895, IN NIQUINOHOMO, NICARAGUA.
MY FATHER, GREGORIO SANDINO, HAD RAPED MY MOTHER, AN INDIAN WHO WORKED ON THE PLANTATION HE OWNED.
WE WORKED IN HIS FIELDS AND NEARLY STARVED.
ONCE, WHEN WE WERE JAILED FOR HER DEBTS, SHE SUFFERED A MISCARRIAGE. I ALONE CARED FOR HER.
SOON AFTER, SHE ABANDONED ME.
!
YOU! YOU ARE MY FATHER!

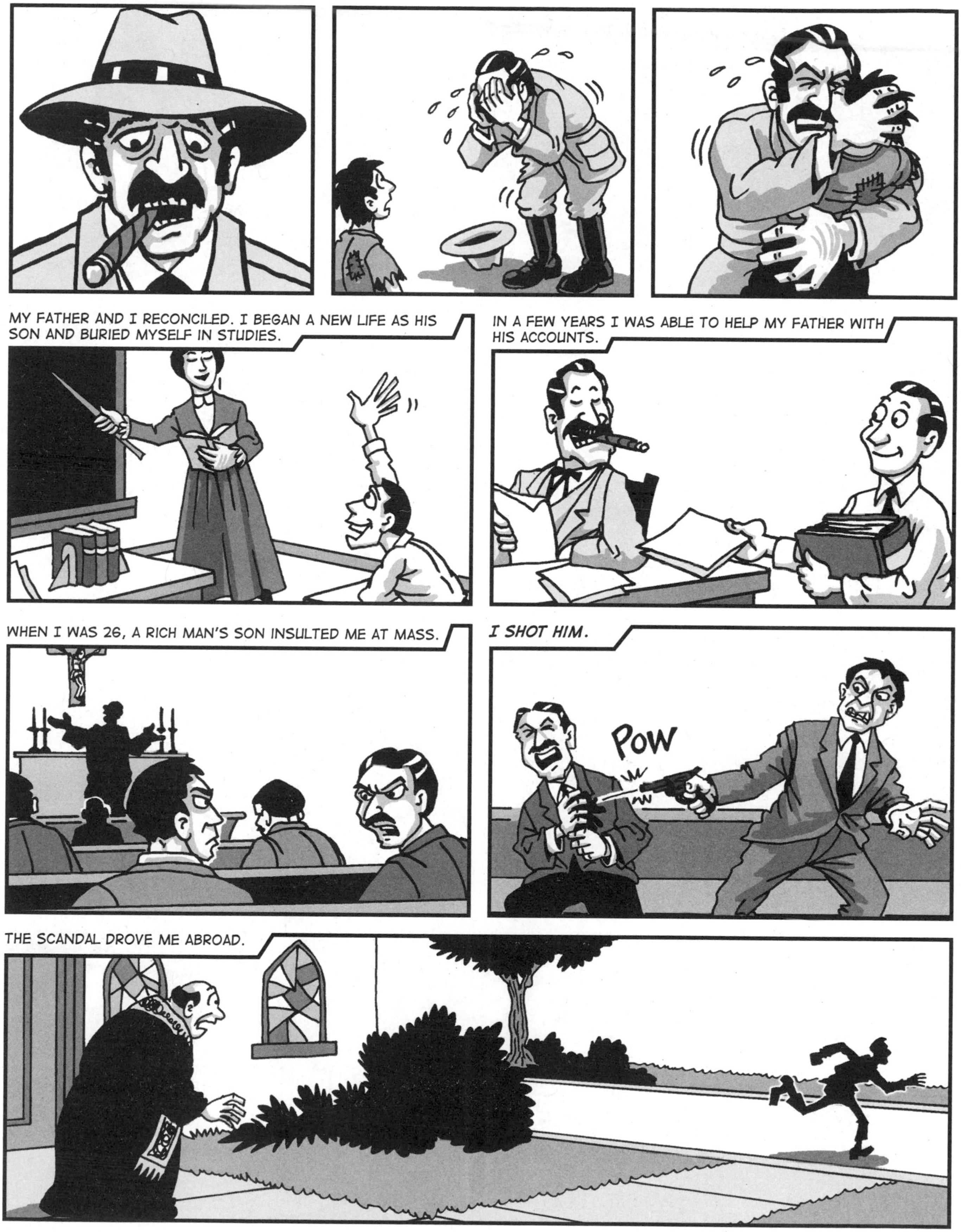
MY FATHER AND I RECONCILED. I BEGAN A NEW LIFE AS HIS SON AND BURIED MYSELF IN STUDIES.
IN A FEW YEARS I WAS ABLE TO HELP MY FATHER WITH HIS ACCOUNTS.
WHEN I WAS 26, A RICH MAN'S SON INSULTED ME AT MASS.
I SHOT HIM.
POW
THE SCANDAL DROVE ME ABROAD.

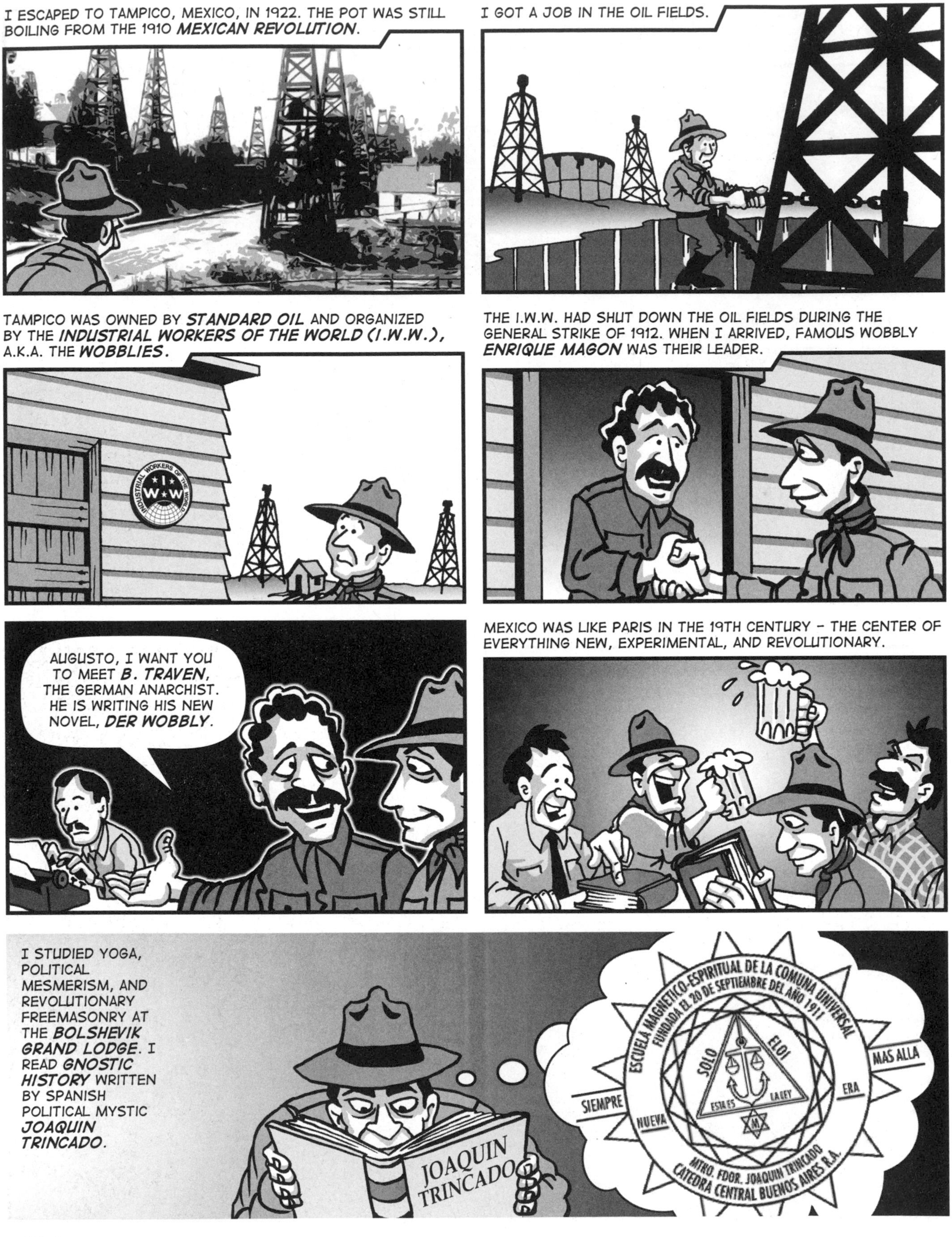
I ESCAPED TO TAMPICO, MEXICO, IN 1922. THE POT WAS STILL BOILING FROM THE 1910 ***MEXICAN REVOLUTION***.
I GOT A JOB IN THE OIL FIELDS.
TAMPICO WAS OWNED BY ***STANDARD OIL*** AND ORGANIZED BY THE ***INDUSTRIAL WORKERS OF THE WORLD (I.W.W.)***, A.K.A. THE ***WOBBLIES***.
INDUSTRIAL WORKERS OF THE WORLD
I W W
THE I.W.W. HAD SHUT DOWN THE OIL FIELDS DURING THE GENERAL STRIKE OF 1912. WHEN I ARRIVED, FAMOUS WOBBLY ***ENRIQUE MAGON*** WAS THEIR LEADER.
AUGUSTO, I WANT YOU TO MEET ***B. TRAVEN***, THE GERMAN ANARCHIST. HE IS WRITING HIS NEW NOVEL, ***DER WOBBLY***.
MEXICO WAS LIKE PARIS IN THE 19TH CENTURY - THE CENTER OF EVERYTHING NEW, EXPERIMENTAL, AND REVOLUTIONARY.
I STUDIED YOGA, POLITICAL MESMERISM, AND REVOLUTIONARY FREEMASONRY AT THE ***BOLSHEVIK GRAND LODGE***. I READ ***GNOSTIC HISTORY*** WRITTEN BY SPANISH POLITICAL MYSTIC ***JOAQUIN TRINCADO***.
JOAQUIN TRINCADO
ESCUELA MAGNETICO-ESPIRITUAL DE LA COMUNA UNIVERSAL
FUNDADA EL 20 DE SEPTIEMBRE DEL AÑO 1911
SOLO
ELOI
ESTA ES
LA LEY
MAS ALLA
ERA
SIEMPRE
NUEVA
MTRO. FDOR. JOAQUIN TRINCADO
CATEDRA CENTRAL BUENOS AIRES R.A.

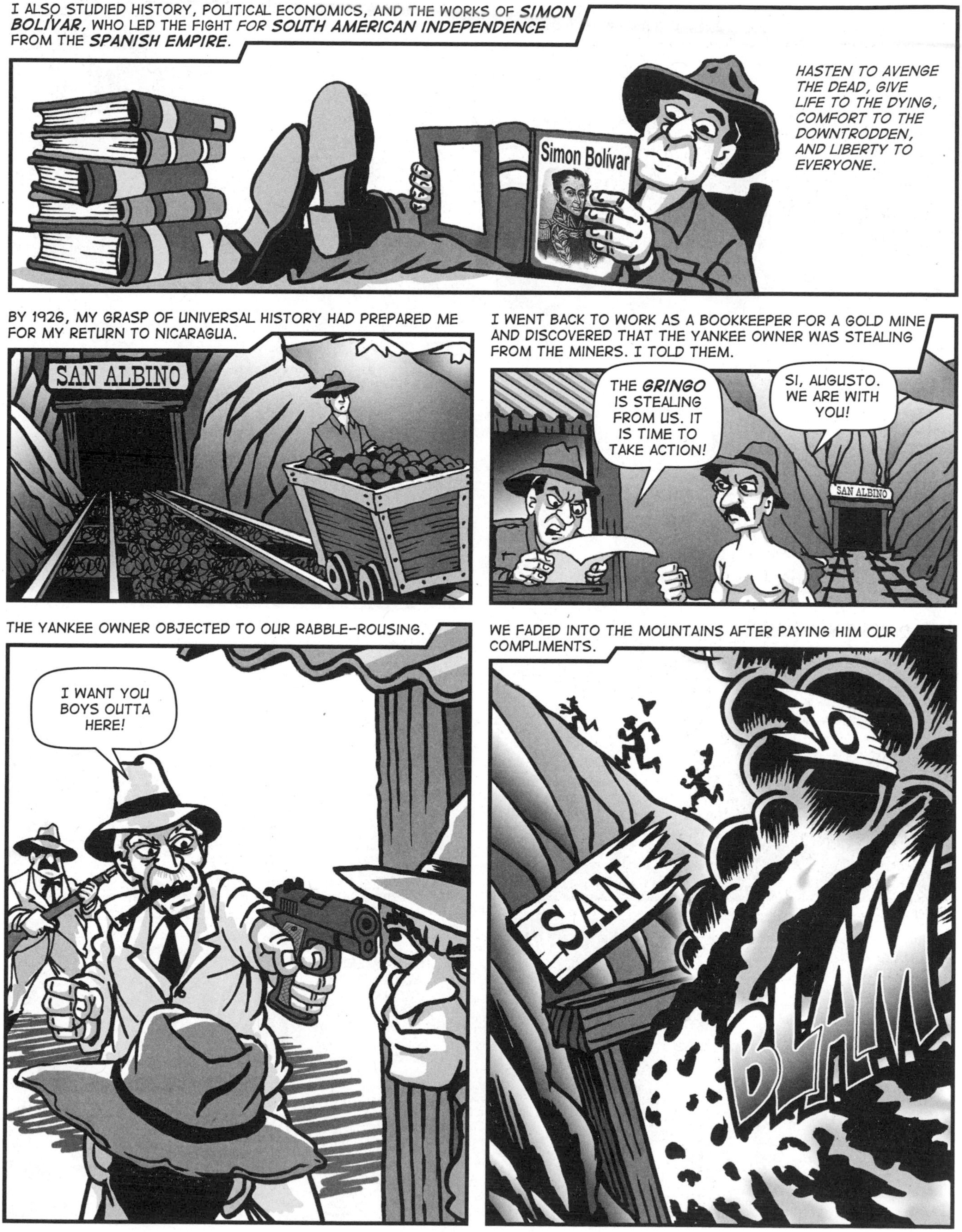
I ALSO STUDIED HISTORY, POLITICAL ECONOMICS, AND THE WORKS OF *SIMON BOLÍVAR,* WHO LED THE FIGHT FOR *SOUTH AMERICAN INDEPENDENCE* FROM THE *SPANISH EMPIRE*.
Simon Bolívar
HASTEN TO AVENGE THE DEAD, GIVE LIFE TO THE DYING, COMFORT TO THE DOWNTRODDEN, AND LIBERTY TO EVERYONE.
BY 1926, MY GRASP OF UNIVERSAL HISTORY HAD PREPARED ME FOR MY RETURN TO NICARAGUA.
SAN ALBINO
I WENT BACK TO WORK AS A BOOKKEEPER FOR A GOLD MINE AND DISCOVERED THAT THE YANKEE OWNER WAS STEALING FROM THE MINERS. I TOLD THEM.
THE *GRINGO* IS STEALING FROM US. IT IS TIME TO TAKE ACTION!
SI, AUGUSTO. WE ARE WITH YOU!
SAN ALBINO
THE YANKEE OWNER OBJECTED TO OUR RABBLE-ROUSING.
I WANT YOU BOYS OUTTA HERE!
WE FADED INTO THE MOUNTAINS AFTER PAYING HIM OUR COMPLIMENTS.
SAN
NO
BLAM

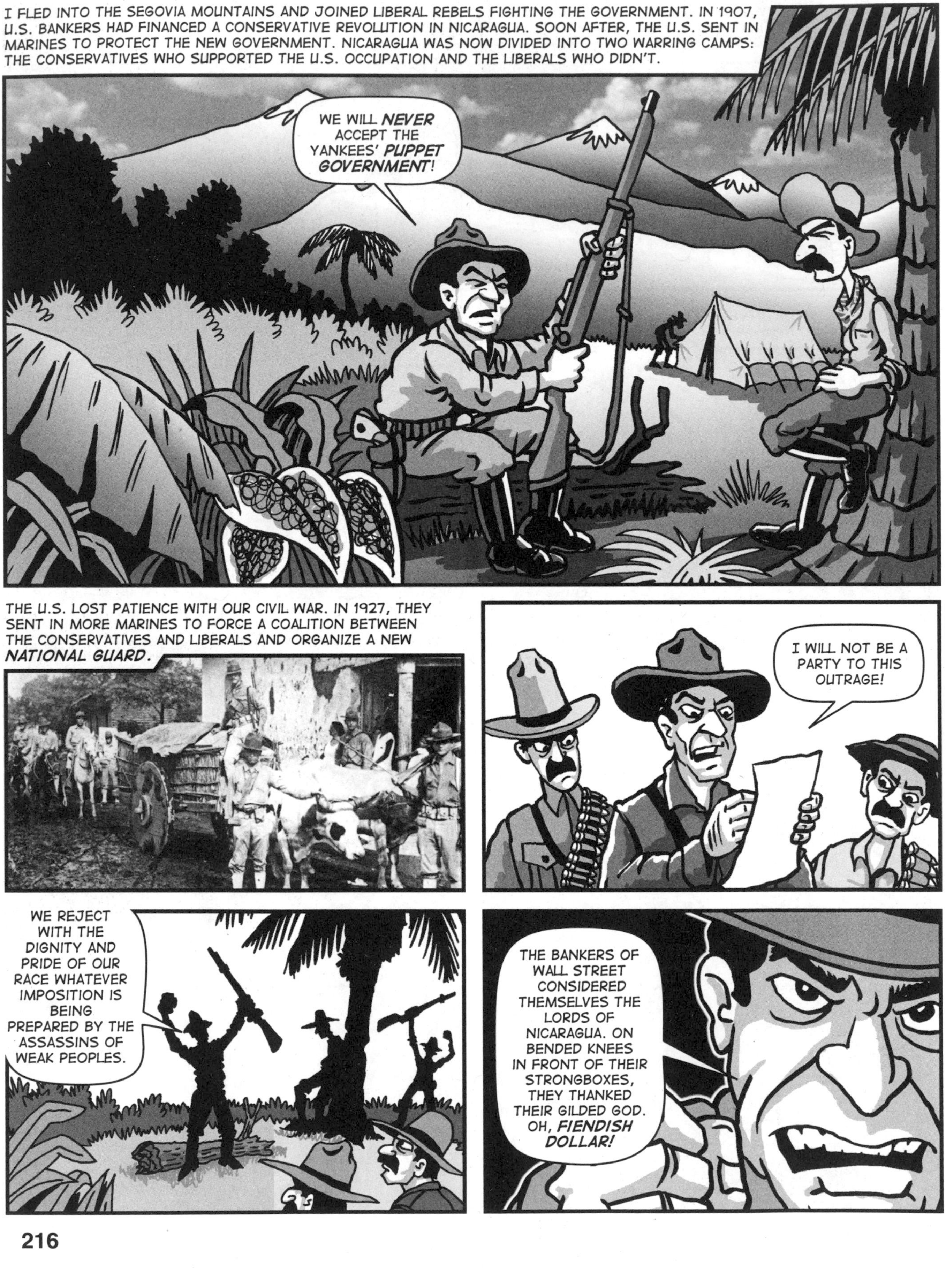
I FLED INTO THE SEGOVIA MOUNTAINS AND JOINED LIBERAL REBELS FIGHTING THE GOVERNMENT. IN 1907, U.S. BANKERS HAD FINANCED A CONSERVATIVE REVOLUTION IN NICARAGUA. SOON AFTER, THE U.S. SENT IN MARINES TO PROTECT THE NEW GOVERNMENT. NICARAGUA WAS NOW DIVIDED INTO TWO WARRING CAMPS: THE CONSERVATIVES WHO SUPPORTED THE U.S. OCCUPATION AND THE LIBERALS WHO DIDN'T.
WE WILL ***NEVER*** ACCEPT THE YANKEES' ***PUPPET GOVERNMENT***!
THE U.S. LOST PATIENCE WITH OUR CIVIL WAR. IN 1927, THEY SENT IN MORE MARINES TO FORCE A COALITION BETWEEN THE CONSERVATIVES AND LIBERALS AND ORGANIZE A NEW ***NATIONAL GUARD***.
I WILL NOT BE A PARTY TO THIS OUTRAGE!
WE REJECT WITH THE DIGNITY AND PRIDE OF OUR RACE WHATEVER IMPOSITION IS BEING PREPARED BY THE ASSASSINS OF WEAK PEOPLES.
THE BANKERS OF WALL STREET CONSIDERED THEMSELVES THE LORDS OF NICARAGUA. ON BENDED KNEES IN FRONT OF THEIR STRONGBOXES, THEY THANKED THEIR GILDED GOD. OH, ***FIENDISH DOLLAR!***

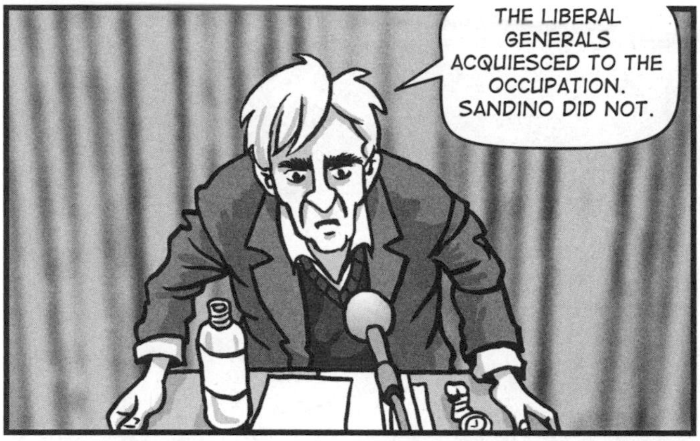
THE LIBERAL GENERALS ACQUIESCED TO THE OCCUPATION. SANDINO DID NOT.

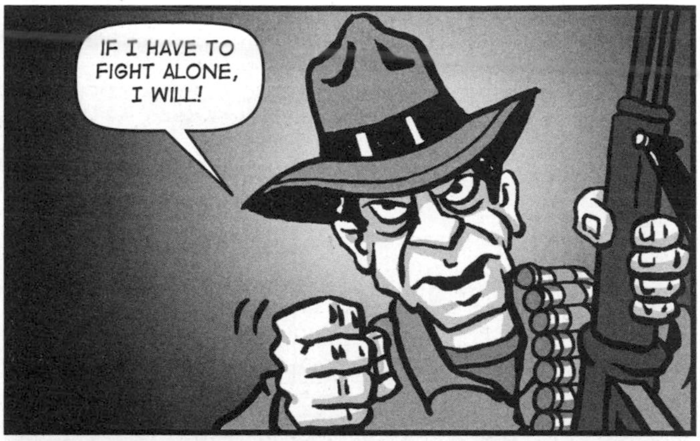
IF I HAVE TO FIGHT ALONE, I WILL!

SANDINO'S RESISTANCE MADE HIM THE ***HERO OF NICARAGUAN NATIONALISM***. THE YANKEE DEPRESSION AND A MASSIVE EARTHQUAKE IN MANAGUA IN 1931 PUSHED HIM INTO EVEN GREATER PROMINENCE.

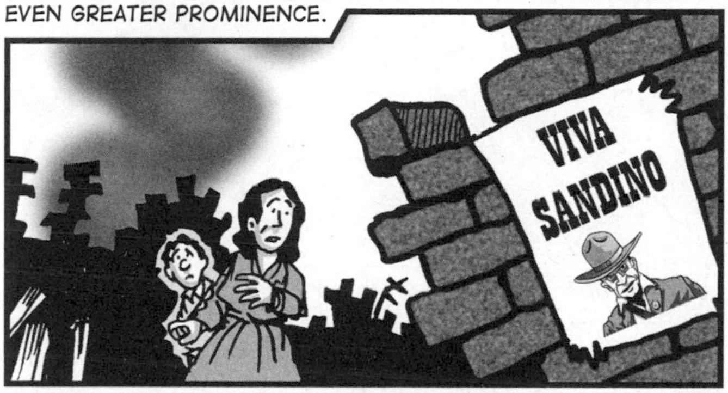
VIVA SANDINO

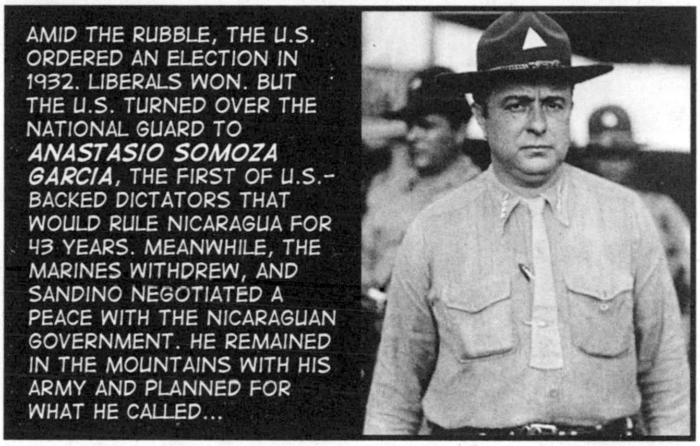
AMID THE RUBBLE, THE U.S. ORDERED AN ELECTION IN 1932. LIBERALS WON. BUT THE U.S. TURNED OVER THE NATIONAL GUARD TO ***ANASTASIO SOMOZA GARCIA,*** THE FIRST OF U.S.-BACKED DICTATORS THAT WOULD RULE NICARAGUA FOR 43 YEARS. MEANWHILE, THE MARINES WITHDREW, AND SANDINO NEGOTIATED A PEACE WITH THE NICARAGUAN GOVERNMENT. HE REMAINED IN THE MOUNTAINS WITH HIS ARMY AND PLANNED FOR WHAT HE CALLED...

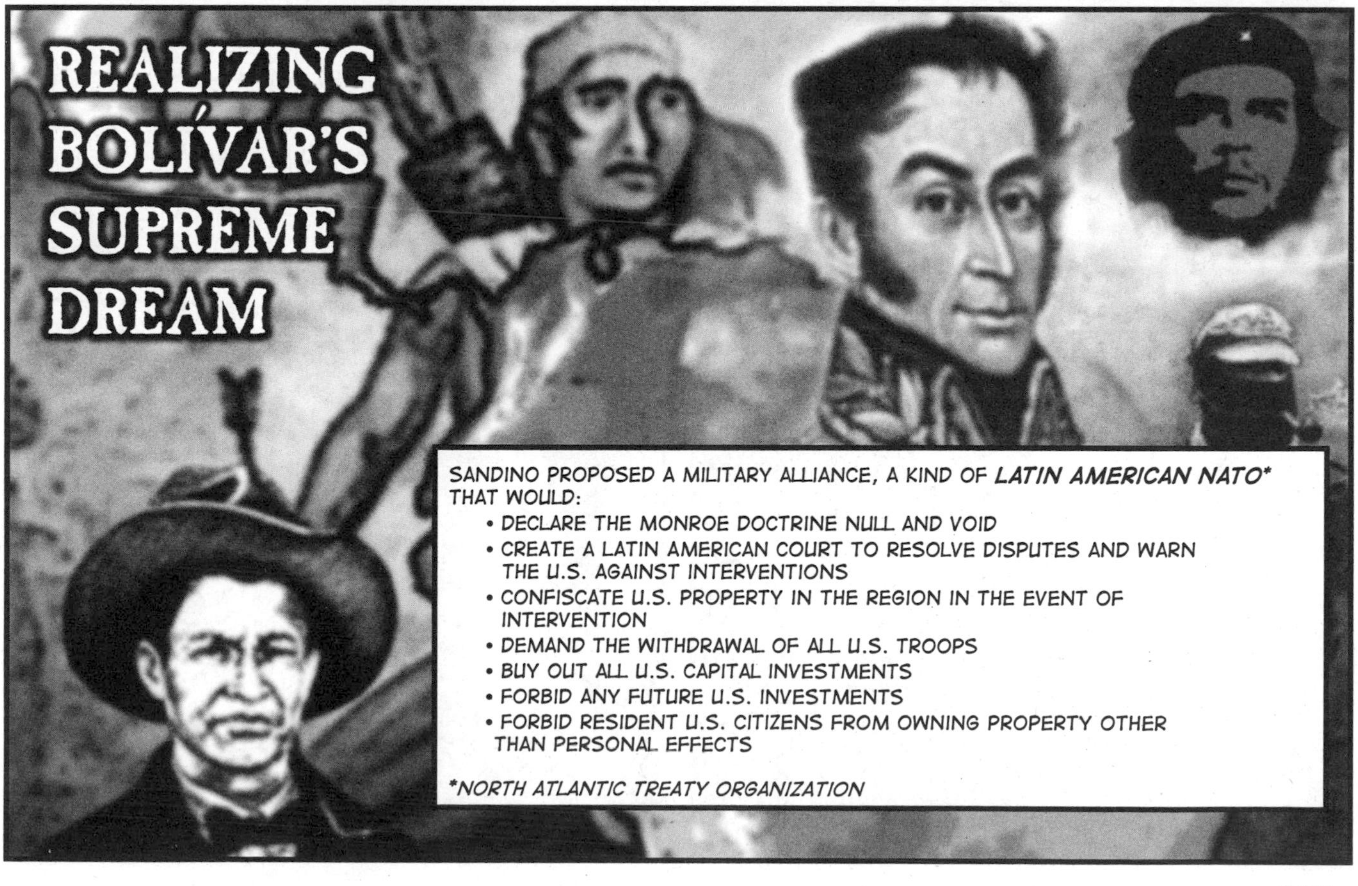
REALIZING BOLÍVAR'S SUPREME DREAM
SANDINO PROPOSED A MILITARY ALLIANCE, A KIND OF ***LATIN AMERICAN NATO**** THAT WOULD:
• DECLARE THE MONROE DOCTRINE NULL AND VOID
• CREATE A LATIN AMERICAN COURT TO RESOLVE DISPUTES AND WARN THE U.S. AGAINST INTERVENTIONS
• CONFISCATE U.S. PROPERTY IN THE REGION IN THE EVENT OF INTERVENTION
• DEMAND THE WITHDRAWAL OF ALL U.S. TROOPS
• BUY OUT ALL U.S. CAPITAL INVESTMENTS
• FORBID ANY FUTURE U.S. INVESTMENTS
• FORBID RESIDENT U.S. CITIZENS FROM OWNING PROPERTY OTHER THAN PERSONAL EFFECTS
*NORTH ATLANTIC TREATY ORGANIZATION

OF COURSE, IT WAS JUST A DREAM - A DANGEROUS DREAM. AT 10:00 P.M. ON FEBRUARY 21, 1934, SANDINO LEFT A CORDIAL LATE DINNER AT THE PRESIDENTIAL PALACE...

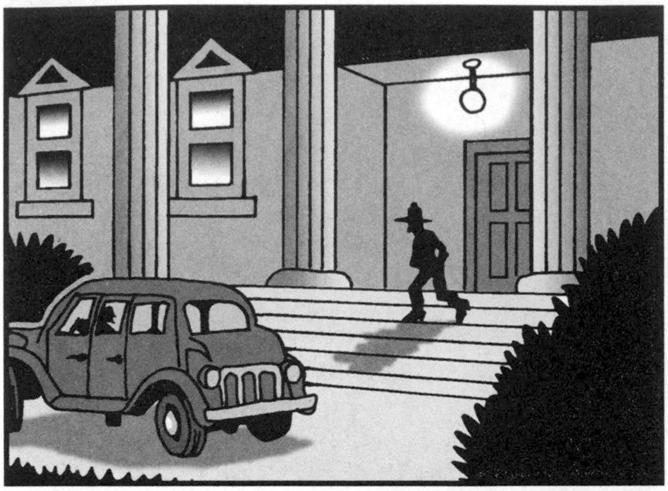

...UNAWARE OF THE PLOT AGAINST HIM.

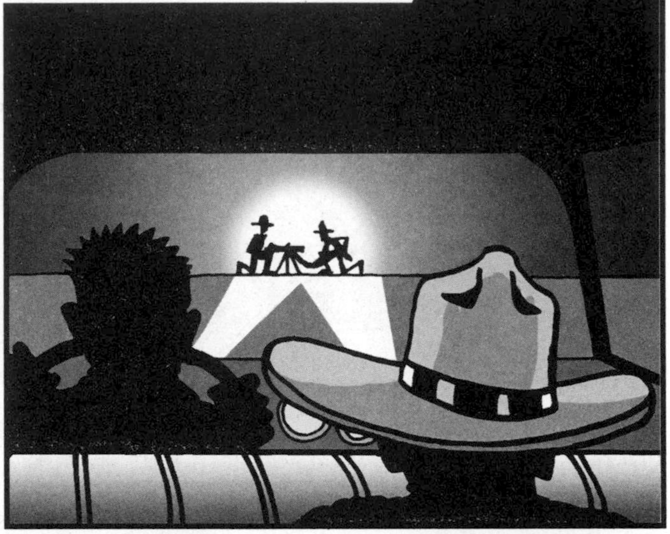

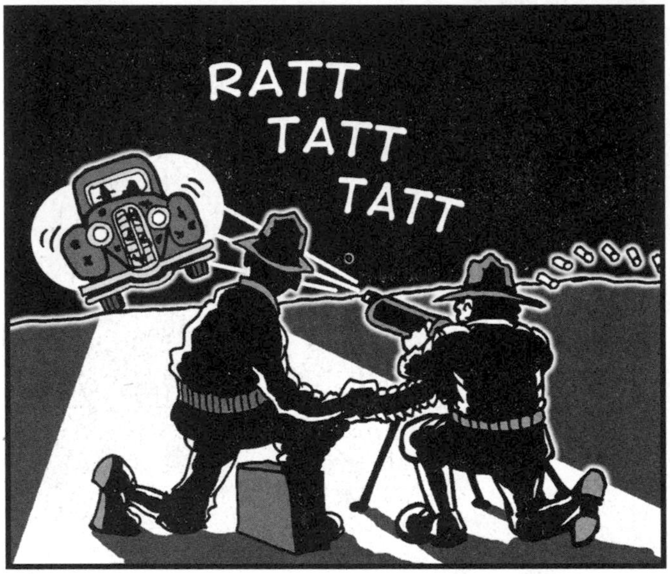
RATT
TATT
TATT

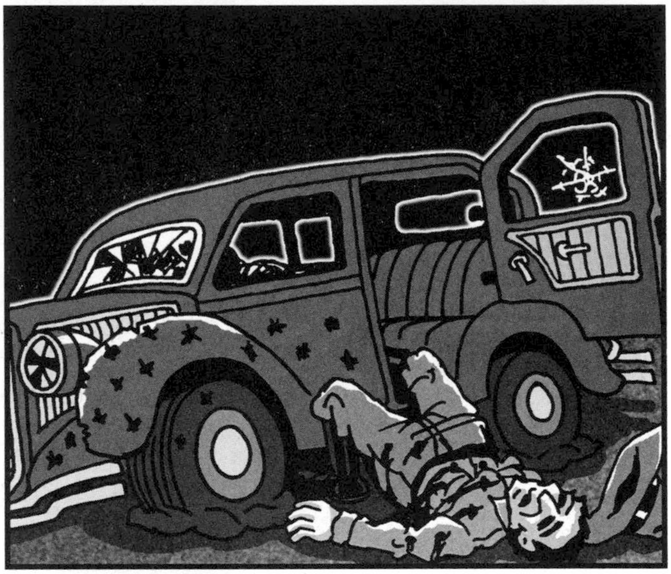

MEANWHILE, SANDINO'S FATHER WAS BEING HELD IN PRISON.

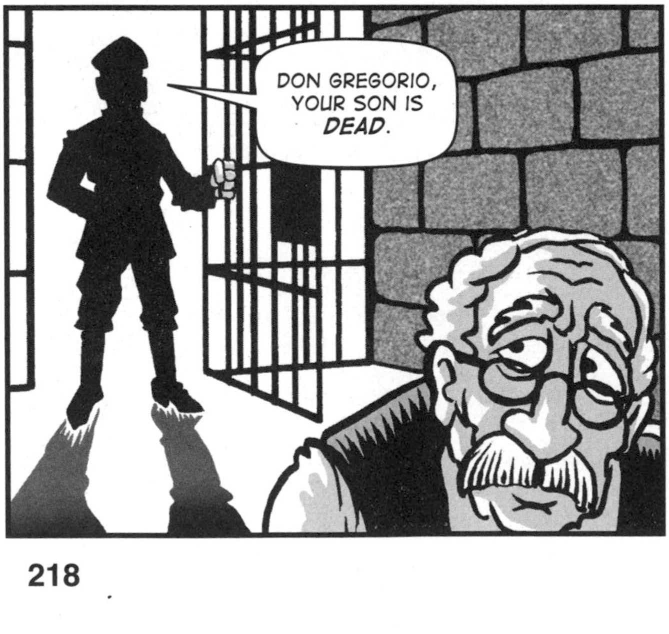
DON GREGORIO, YOUR SON IS *DEAD*.

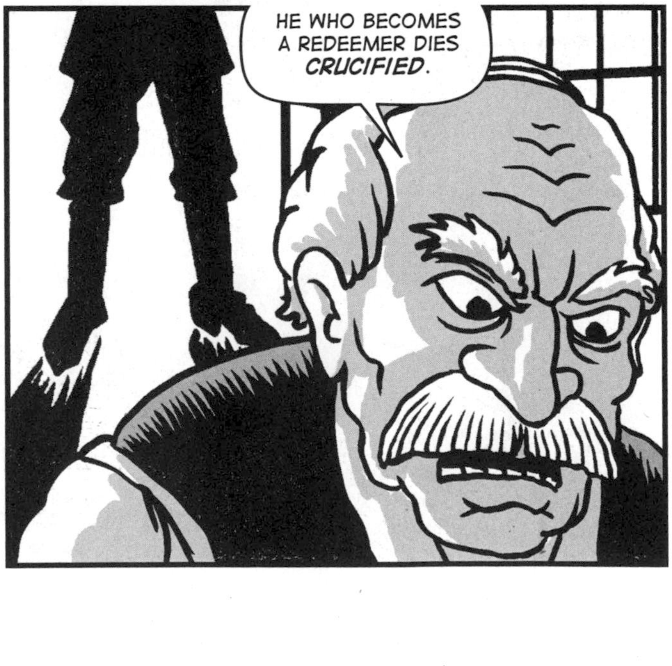
HE WHO BECOMES A REDEEMER DIES *CRUCIFIED*.

THE ASSASSINS BURIED SANDINO AT A REMOTE AIRSTRIP...

...AFTER STEALING HIS WATCH.

THIRTY-THREE YEARS LATER, CUBAN REVOLUTIONARY *CHE GUEVARA* WAS KILLED BY C.I.A. AGENTS, WHO TOOK HIS WATCH AS A TROPHY BEFORE THEY CUT OFF HIS HANDS...

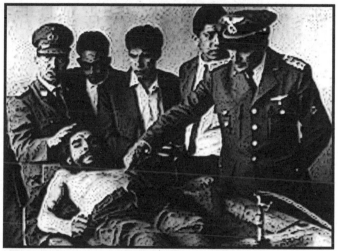

...AND BURIED HIM UNDER AN AIRSTRIP.

AUGUSTO SANDINO'S MYSTICISM INCLUDED THE BELIEF THAT REVOLUTIONARIES ARE REINCARNATED TO CONTINUE THE STRUGGLE.

PERHAPS THE REINCARNATION IS NOT OF THE REVOLUTIONARY BUT OF THE *REVOLUTION.*

The Covert War in Central America

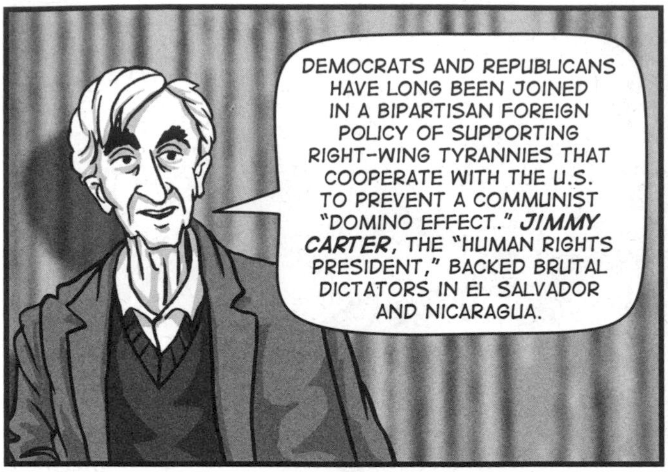
DEMOCRATS AND REPUBLICANS HAVE LONG BEEN JOINED IN A BIPARTISAN FOREIGN POLICY OF SUPPORTING RIGHT-WING TYRANNIES THAT COOPERATE WITH THE U.S. TO PREVENT A COMMUNIST "DOMINO EFFECT." JIMMY CARTER, THE "HUMAN RIGHTS PRESIDENT," BACKED BRUTAL DICTATORS IN EL SALVADOR AND NICARAGUA.

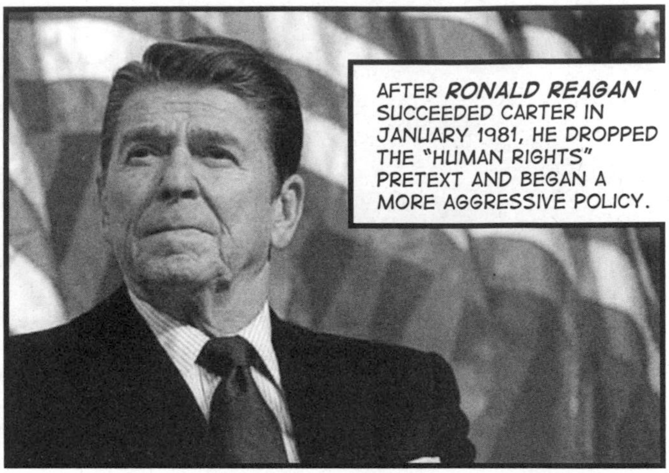
AFTER RONALD REAGAN SUCCEEDED CARTER IN JANUARY 1981, HE DROPPED THE "HUMAN RIGHTS" PRETEXT AND BEGAN A MORE AGGRESSIVE POLICY.

MILITARY JUNTAS HAD RULED EL SALVADOR FOR DECADES. BY THE LATE 1970s, MILITARY ***DEATH SQUADS*** HAD OBLITERATED THE URBAN LEFTIST OPPOSITION. IN 1980, REBEL GUERRILLA GROUPS FORMED THE ***FARABUNDO MARTI NATIONAL LIBERATION FRONT (F.M.L.N.).***

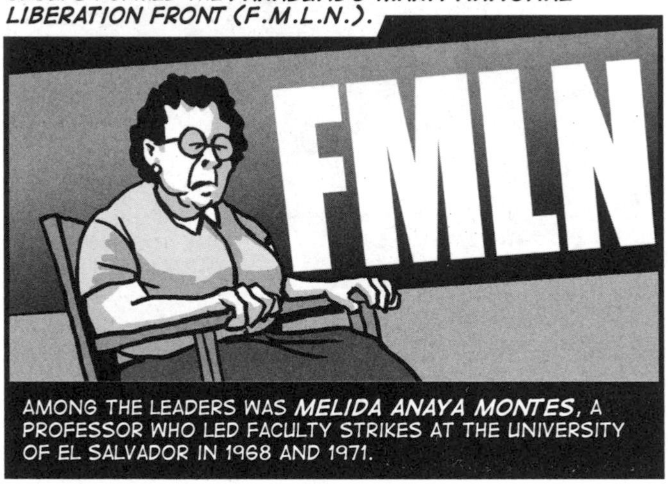
FMLN
AMONG THE LEADERS WAS MELIDA ANAYA MONTES, A PROFESSOR WHO LED FACULTY STRIKES AT THE UNIVERSITY OF EL SALVADOR IN 1968 AND 1971.

REAGAN CONSIDERED THE F.M.L.N. A COMMUNIST THREAT. IN MARCH 1981, HE DRAMATICALLY INCREASED MILITARY AID TO EL SALVADOR'S RIGHT-WING DICTATORSHIP. C.I.A. DIRECTOR ***WILLIAM CASEY*** BLAMED THE SALVADORAN REBELLION ON THE SANDINISTAS IN NICARAGUA.

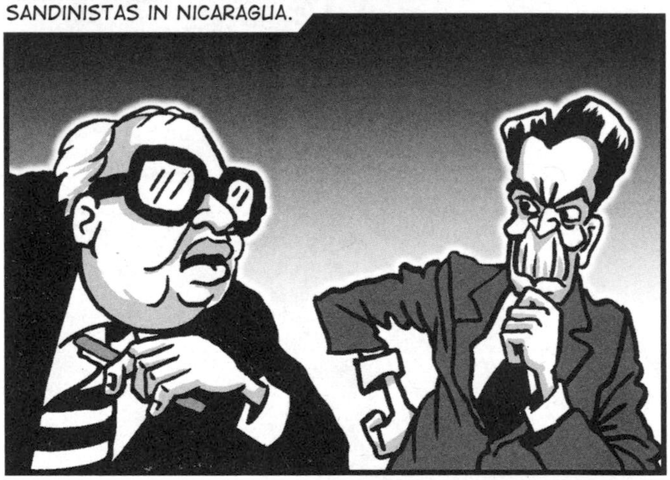

LATER IN 1981, REAGAN AUTHORIZED $19 MILLION FOR THE C.I.A. TO FORM AND FUND A COUNTERREVOLUTIONARY ARMY - THE CONTRAS - TO OVERTHROW THE LEFTIST SANDINISTA GOVERNMENT IN NICARAGUA. HIS MEDDLING IN BOTH COUNTRIES ACCOMPLISHED ITS OBJECTIVE: COVERT WAR IN CENTRAL AMERICA.

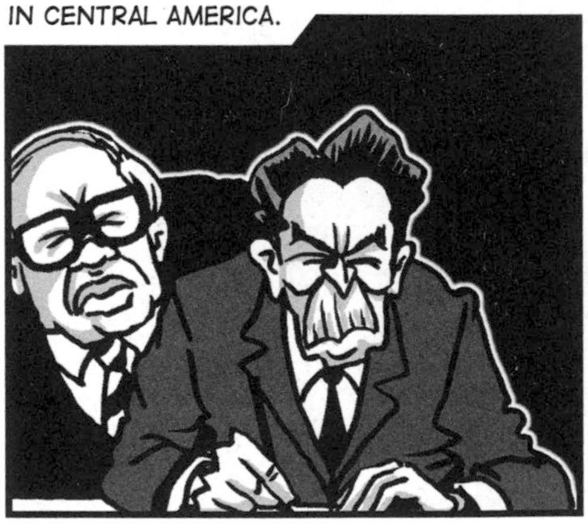

DECEMBER 10, 1981: UNITS OF THE ***ATLACATL BATTALION***, FUNDED AND TRAINED BY THE U.S., ARRIVED AT THE SALVADORAN VILLAGE OF EL MOZOTE SEARCHING FOR REBELS.

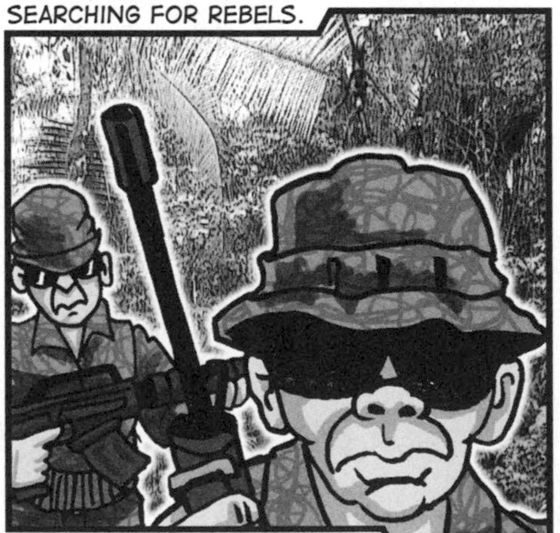

THEY FOUND ONLY REFUGEES.

ZINNFORMATION

THE U.S. ARMY TRAINED OFFICERS OF THE ATLACATL BATTALION AT THE INFAMOUS ***SCHOOL OF THE AMERICAS (S.O.A)***. MANY S.O.A. GRADUATES WENT ON TO COMMIT ATROCITIES THROUGHOUT LATIN AMERICA. BECAUSE OF CITIZEN PROTESTS, THE U.S. GOVERNMENT SHUT DOWN S.O.A. IN 2000 AND REOPENED IT IN JANUARY 2001 AS THE ***WESTERN HEMISPHERE INSTITUTE FOR SECURITY COOPERATION.***

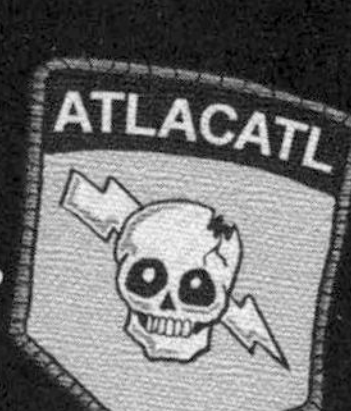
ATLACATL

Massacre at El Mozote (The Thistle)

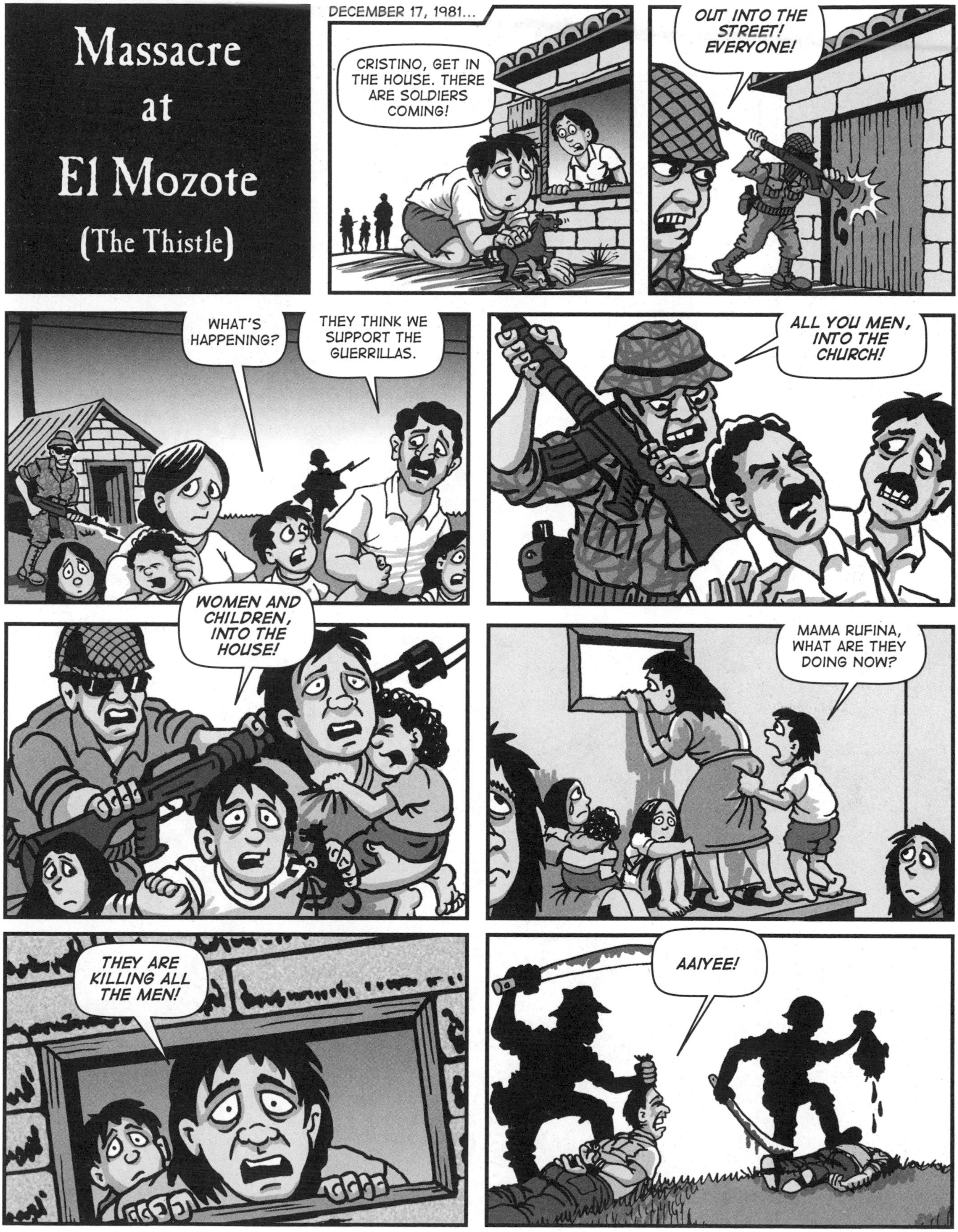

DECEMBER 17, 1981...
CRISTINO, GET IN THE HOUSE. THERE ARE SOLDIERS COMING!
OUT INTO THE STREET! EVERYONE!
WHAT'S HAPPENING?
THEY THINK WE SUPPORT THE GUERRILLAS.
ALL YOU MEN, INTO THE CHURCH!
WOMEN AND CHILDREN, INTO THE HOUSE!
MAMA RUFINA, WHAT ARE THEY DOING NOW?
THEY ARE KILLING ALL THE MEN!
AAIYEE!

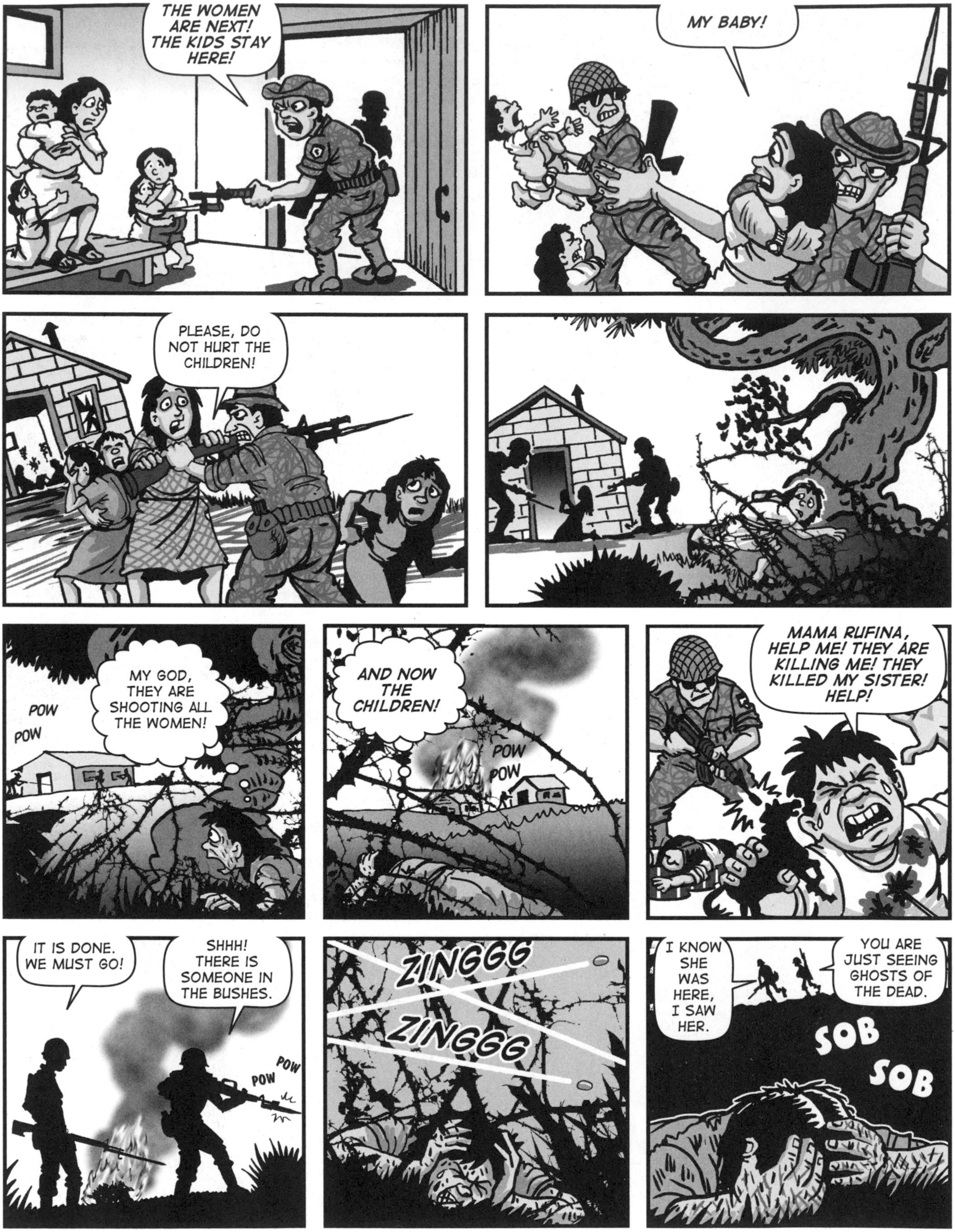
THE WOMEN ARE NEXT! THE KIDS STAY HERE!
MY BABY!
PLEASE, DO NOT HURT THE CHILDREN!
POW
POW
MY GOD, THEY ARE SHOOTING ALL THE WOMEN!
AND NOW THE CHILDREN!
POW
POW
MAMA RUFINA, HELP ME! THEY ARE KILLING ME! THEY KILLED MY SISTER! HELP!
IT IS DONE. WE MUST GO!
SHHH! THERE IS SOMEONE IN THE BUSHES.
POW
POW
ZINGGG
ZINGGG
I KNOW SHE WAS HERE, I SAW HER.
YOU ARE JUST SEEING GHOSTS OF THE DEAD.
SOB
SOB

DAYS LATER, THE F.M.L.N. DISCOVERED THE CARNAGE. ON DECEMBER 24, 1981, THEIR REBEL RADIO REPORTED THE MASSACRE.

THIS IS *RADIO VENCEREMOS!* SOLDIERS HAVE MASSACRED HUNDREDS AT EL MOZOTE!

THE F.M.L.N. CONTACTED *NEW YORK TIMES* REPORTER *RAYMOND BONNER* AND TOOK HIM AND PHOTOGRAPHER *SUSAN MEISELAS* TO THE SITE.

WE HAVE AN EYEWITNESS, IF YOU WANT TO INTERVIEW HER.

MY NAME IS *RUFINA AMAYA*. I HID IN THE THORNS UNTIL THE SOLDIERS LEFT. EVERYONE WAS DEAD, INCLUDING MY HUSBAND AND MY FOUR CHILDREN.

ON JANUARY 17, 1982, BONNER'S STORY APPEARED IN THE NEW YORK TIMES.

JANUARY 27, 1982.

MASSACRE OF HUNDREDS REPORTED IN SALVADOR VILLAGE

BY RAYMOND BONNER
Special to the New York Times

From interviews with people who live in the

TO KEEP AID FLOWING, CONGRESS REQUIRED PRESIDENT REAGAN TO CERTIFY THAT EL SALVADOR WAS IMPROVING ITS HUMAN RIGHTS RECORD. AFTER BONNER'S REPORT, HE DID.

THE SALVADORAN GOVERNMENT IS MAKING A CONCERTED AND SIGNIFICANT EFFORT TO COMPLY WITH INTERNATIONALLY RECOGNIZED HUMAN RIGHTS.

ASSISTANT SECRETARY OF STATE FOR HUMAN RIGHTS *ELLIOT ABRAMS* DENOUNCED REPORTS OF THE MASSACRE AT EL MOZOTE AS FICTION.

THIS IS NOTHING BUT COMMUNIST PROPAGANDA.

U.S. DEP... ...TATE

BOWING TO PRESSURE FROM THE WHITE HOUSE, THE TIMES PULLED BONNER OFF THE STORY.

THE CIVIL WAR IN EL SALVADOR ENDED IN 1992. A TRUTH COMMISSION SENT FORENSIC SCIENTISTS TO EL MOZOTE.

IT WAS ALL TRUE. IT WAS POLICY.

223

The Contra War

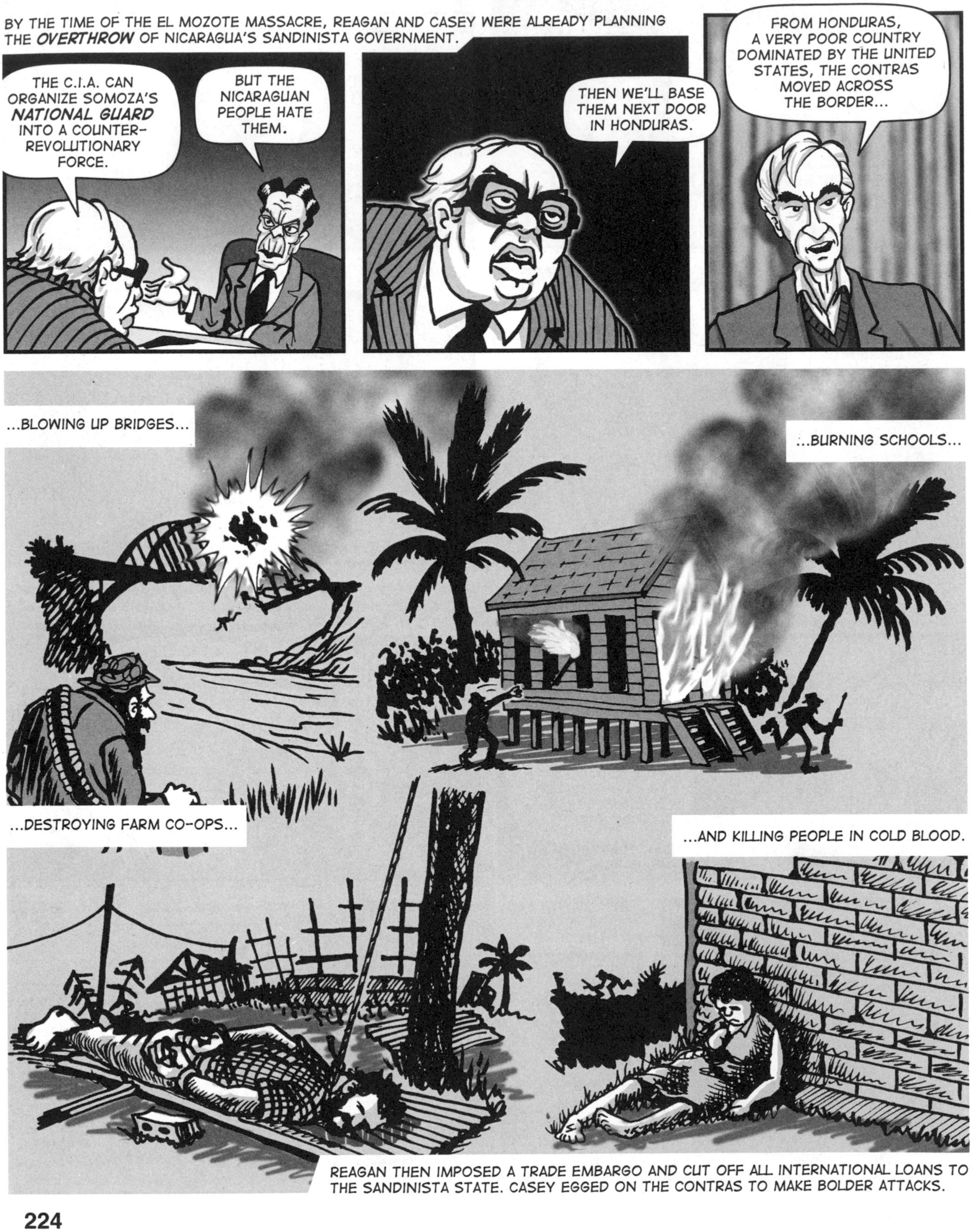
BY THE TIME OF THE EL MOZOTE MASSACRE, REAGAN AND CASEY WERE ALREADY PLANNING THE OVERTHROW OF NICARAGUA'S SANDINISTA GOVERNMENT.
THE C.I.A. CAN ORGANIZE SOMOZA'S NATIONAL GUARD INTO A COUNTER-REVOLUTIONARY FORCE.
BUT THE NICARAGUAN PEOPLE HATE THEM.
THEN WE'LL BASE THEM NEXT DOOR IN HONDURAS.
FROM HONDURAS, A VERY POOR COUNTRY DOMINATED BY THE UNITED STATES, THE CONTRAS MOVED ACROSS THE BORDER...
...BLOWING UP BRIDGES...
...BURNING SCHOOLS...
...DESTROYING FARM CO-OPS...
...AND KILLING PEOPLE IN COLD BLOOD.
REAGAN THEN IMPOSED A TRADE EMBARGO AND CUT OFF ALL INTERNATIONAL LOANS TO THE SANDINISTA STATE. CASEY EGGED ON THE CONTRAS TO MAKE BOLDER ATTACKS.

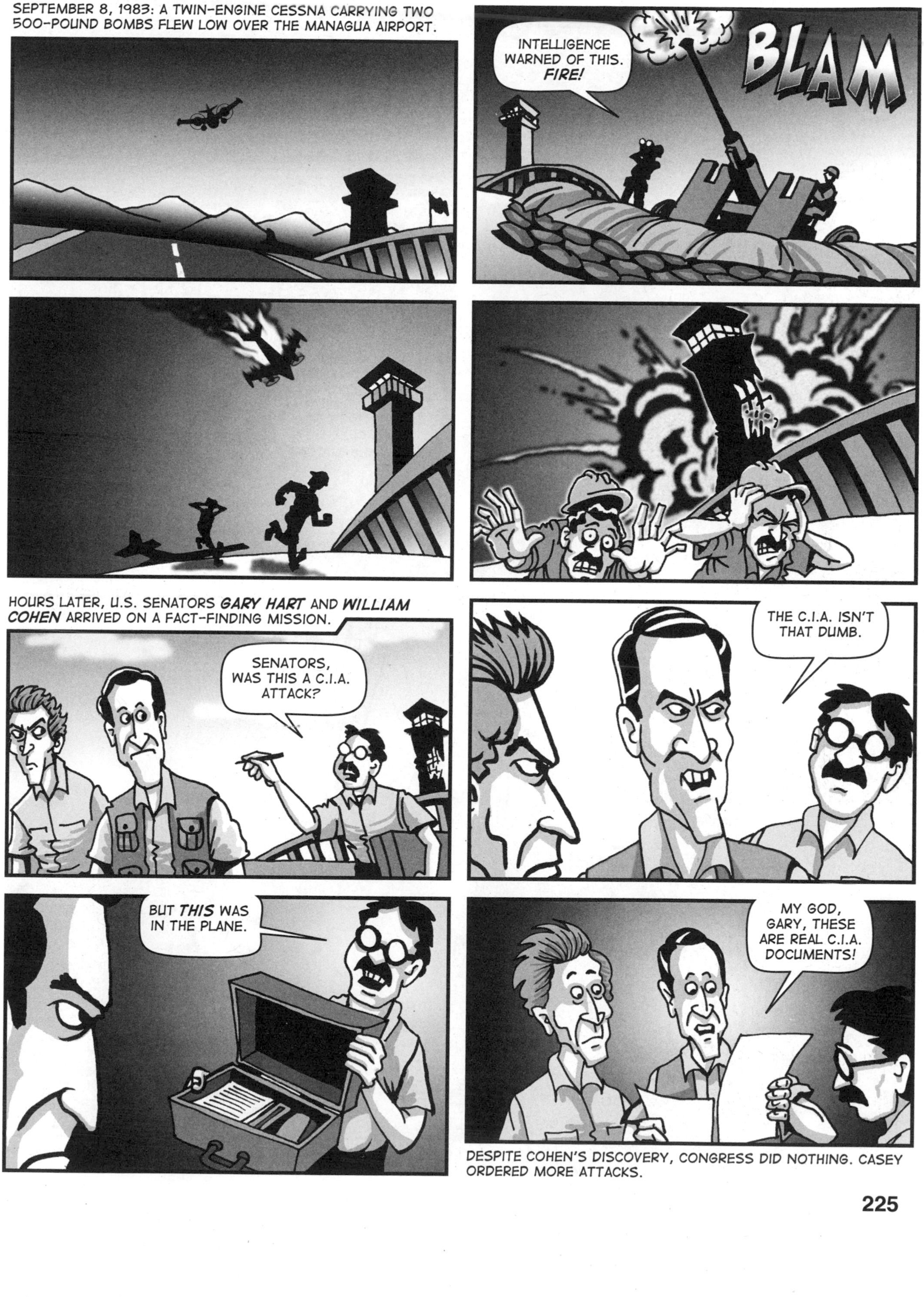

SEPTEMBER 8, 1983: A TWIN-ENGINE CESSNA CARRYING TWO 500-POUND BOMBS FLEW LOW OVER THE MANAGUA AIRPORT.
INTELLIGENCE WARNED OF THIS. FIRE!
BLAM
HOURS LATER, U.S. SENATORS GARY HART AND WILLIAM COHEN ARRIVED ON A FACT-FINDING MISSION.
SENATORS, WAS THIS A C.I.A. ATTACK?
THE C.I.A. ISN'T THAT DUMB.
BUT THIS WAS IN THE PLANE.
MY GOD, GARY, THESE ARE REAL C.I.A. DOCUMENTS!
DESPITE COHEN'S DISCOVERY, CONGRESS DID NOTHING. CASEY ORDERED MORE ATTACKS.

OCTOBER 11, 1983, BAY OF CORINTO, NICARAGUA: THE CONTRAS BLEW UP OIL STORAGE TANKS.

OCTOBER 14, 1983, PORT OF SANDINO: AN OIL PLATFORM WAS ATTACKED.

EXXON ANNOUNCED THAT IT WAS TOO DANGEROUS TO BRING IN MORE TANKERS. THE CONTRAS TOOK THE CREDIT.

TO TOP IT OFF, THE C.I.A. MINED THE HARBORS. WHEN A BRITISH SHIP STRUCK A MINE...

...CONGRESS FINALLY HAD ENOUGH AND REJECTED THE ADMINISTRATION'S REQUEST FOR AN ADDITIONAL $21 MILLION IN CONTRA AID.

The Iran-Contra Scandal

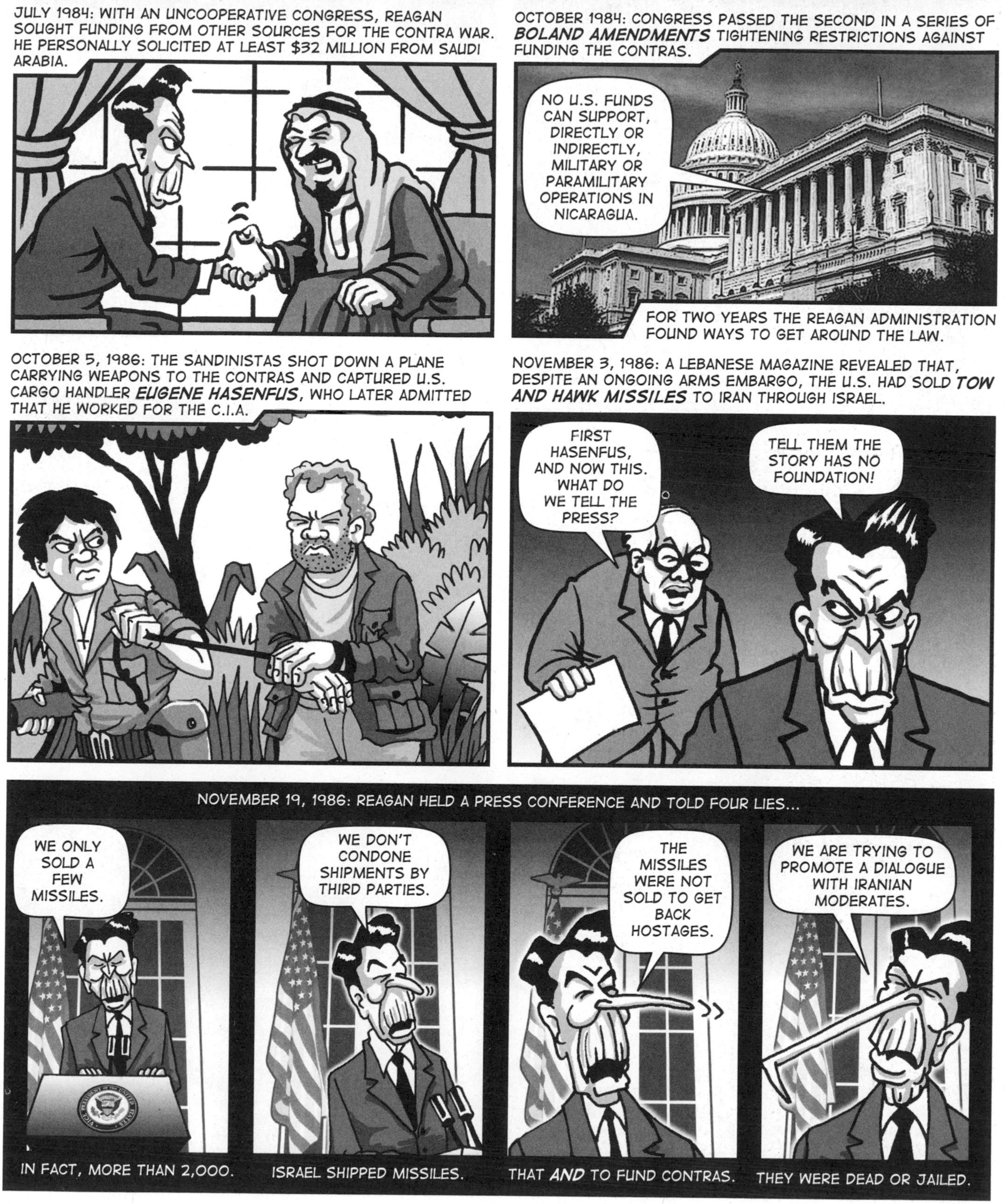
JULY 1984: WITH AN UNCOOPERATIVE CONGRESS, REAGAN SOUGHT FUNDING FROM OTHER SOURCES FOR THE CONTRA WAR. HE PERSONALLY SOLICITED AT LEAST $32 MILLION FROM SAUDI ARABIA.
OCTOBER 1984: CONGRESS PASSED THE SECOND IN A SERIES OF BOLAND AMENDMENTS TIGHTENING RESTRICTIONS AGAINST FUNDING THE CONTRAS.
NO U.S. FUNDS CAN SUPPORT, DIRECTLY OR INDIRECTLY, MILITARY OR PARAMILITARY OPERATIONS IN NICARAGUA.
FOR TWO YEARS THE REAGAN ADMINISTRATION FOUND WAYS TO GET AROUND THE LAW.
OCTOBER 5, 1986: THE SANDINISTAS SHOT DOWN A PLANE CARRYING WEAPONS TO THE CONTRAS AND CAPTURED U.S. CARGO HANDLER EUGENE HASENFUS, WHO LATER ADMITTED THAT HE WORKED FOR THE C.I.A.
NOVEMBER 3, 1986: A LEBANESE MAGAZINE REVEALED THAT, DESPITE AN ONGOING ARMS EMBARGO, THE U.S. HAD SOLD TOW AND HAWK MISSILES TO IRAN THROUGH ISRAEL.
FIRST HASENFUS, AND NOW THIS. WHAT DO WE TELL THE PRESS?
TELL THEM THE STORY HAS NO FOUNDATION!
NOVEMBER 19, 1986: REAGAN HELD A PRESS CONFERENCE AND TOLD FOUR LIES...
WE ONLY SOLD A FEW MISSILES.
IN FACT, MORE THAN 2,000.
WE DON'T CONDONE SHIPMENTS BY THIRD PARTIES.
ISRAEL SHIPPED MISSILES.
THE MISSILES WERE NOT SOLD TO GET BACK HOSTAGES.
THAT AND TO FUND CONTRAS.
WE ARE TRYING TO PROMOTE A DIALOGUE WITH IRANIAN MODERATES.
THEY WERE DEAD OR JAILED.

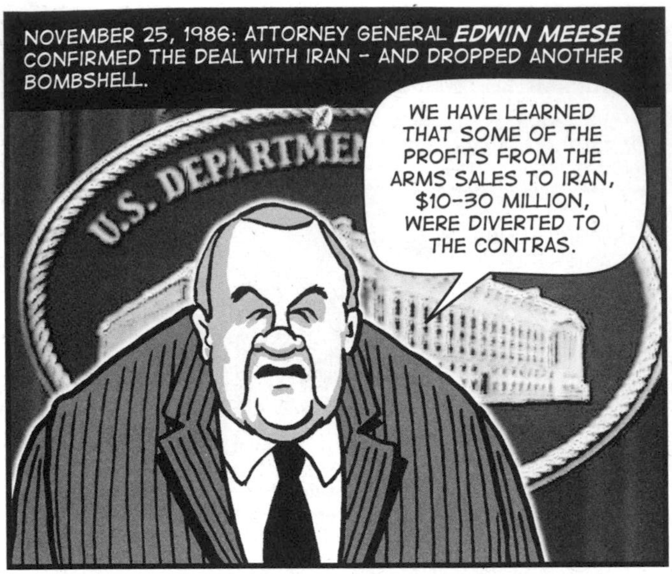
NOVEMBER 25, 1986: ATTORNEY GENERAL ***EDWIN MEESE*** CONFIRMED THE DEAL WITH IRAN – AND DROPPED ANOTHER BOMBSHELL.
WE HAVE LEARNED THAT SOME OF THE PROFITS FROM THE ARMS SALES TO IRAN, $10–30 MILLION, WERE DIVERTED TO THE CONTRAS.
U.S. DEPARTMEN

CONGRESS HELD HEARINGS. THOUGH MANY GOVERNMENT OFFICIALS ***LIED UNDER OATH***, THE HEARINGS REVEALED A COMPLEX WEB OF CLANDESTINE DEALINGS WITH NUMEROUS COUNTRIES TO AID THE CONTRAS.

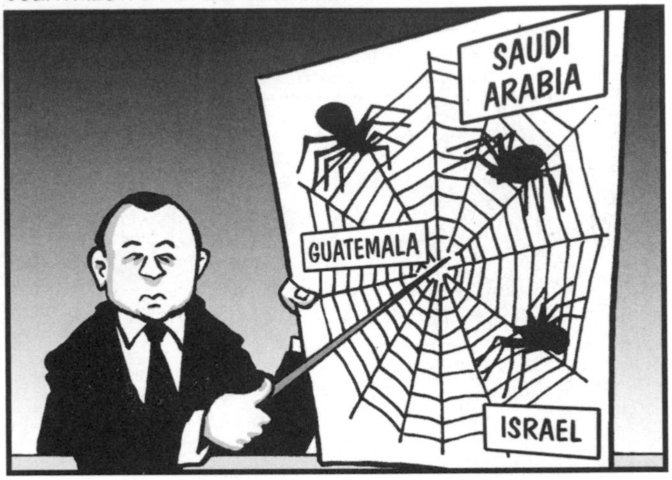
SAUDI ARABIA
GUATEMALA
ISRAEL

THOUGH PRESIDENT REAGAN AND VICE PRESIDENT ***GEORGE H. W. BUSH*** WERE INVOLVED, NEITHER WAS INDICTED. RATHER, THE CONGRESSIONAL COMMITTEE PUT LESSER CULPRITS, LIKE ***OLIVER NORTH*** AND ***JOHN POINDEXTER***, ON THE WITNESS STAND. SEVERAL OF THEM WERE INDICTED.

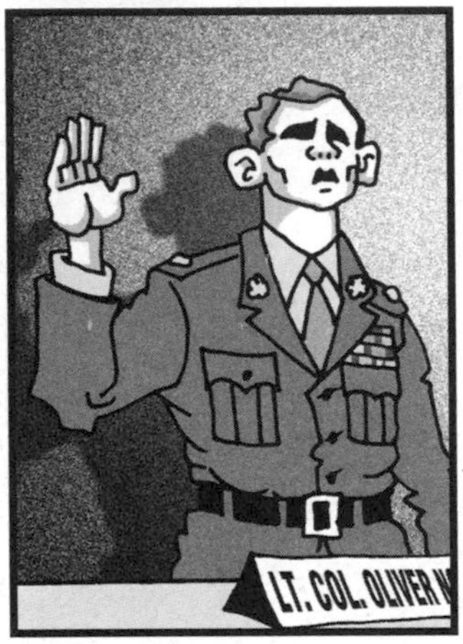
LT. COL. OLIVER

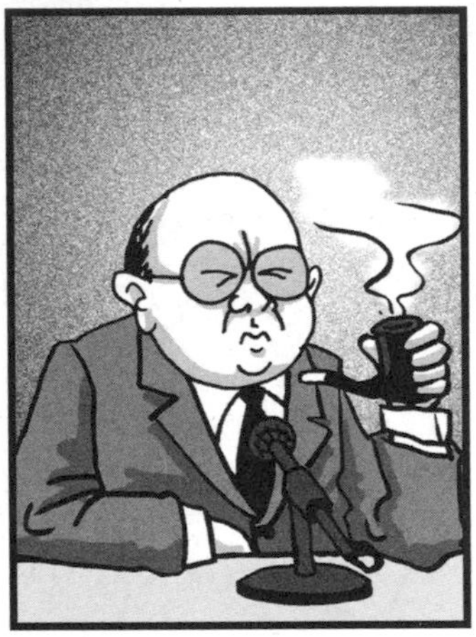

AS FOR THE MAJOR CULPRITS, REAGAN RETIRED IN PEACE, AND VICE PRESIDENT BUSH WAS ELECTED THE NEXT PRESIDENT OF THE UNITED STATES.

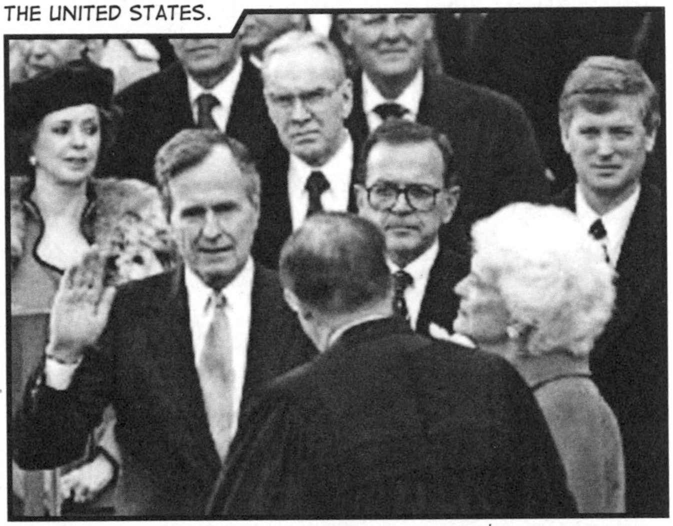

FROM 1986 TO 1989, CONGRESS INVESTIGATED LINKS BETWEEN DRUGS AND FOREIGN POLICY. IN THE SENATE, THE ***KERRY COMMITTEE*** FOUND:

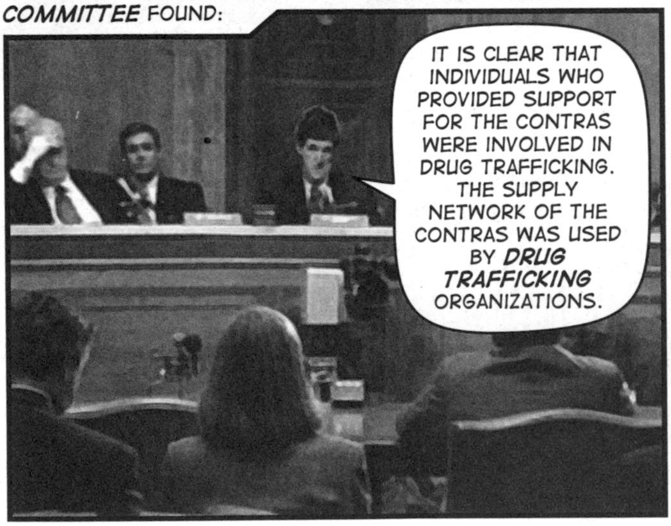
IT IS CLEAR THAT INDIVIDUALS WHO PROVIDED SUPPORT FOR THE CONTRAS WERE INVOLVED IN DRUG TRAFFICKING. THE SUPPLY NETWORK OF THE CONTRAS WAS USED BY ***DRUG TRAFFICKING*** ORGANIZATIONS.

ZINNFORMATION

IN 1996, CALIFORNIA REPORTER ***GARY WEBB*** WROTE A THREE-PART SERIES FOR THE ***SAN JOSE MERCURY NEWS*** CALLED ***DARK ALLIANCE***. THE SERIES DESCRIBED C.I.A. KNOWLEDGE OF CONTRA DRUG SMUGGLING.

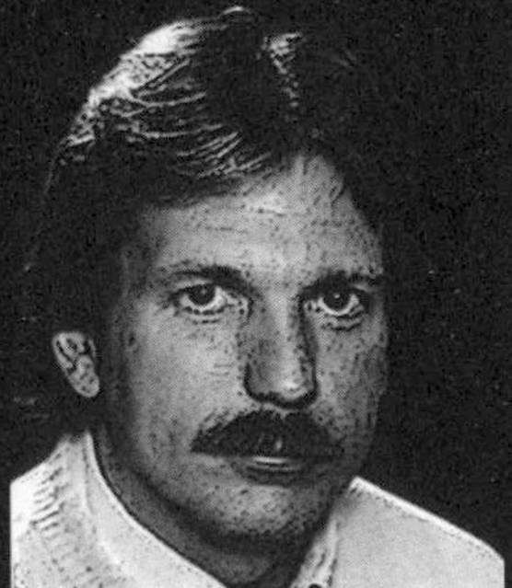

WHEN THE NEW YORK TIMES AND OTHER MAJOR NEWSPAPERS ATTACKED THE STORY, WHICH WAS NEVER DISPROVED, THE MERCURY NEWS FIRED WEBB, DESTROYING HIS CAREER. WEBB COMMITTED SUICIDE IN 2004.

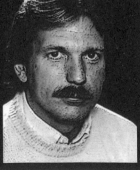

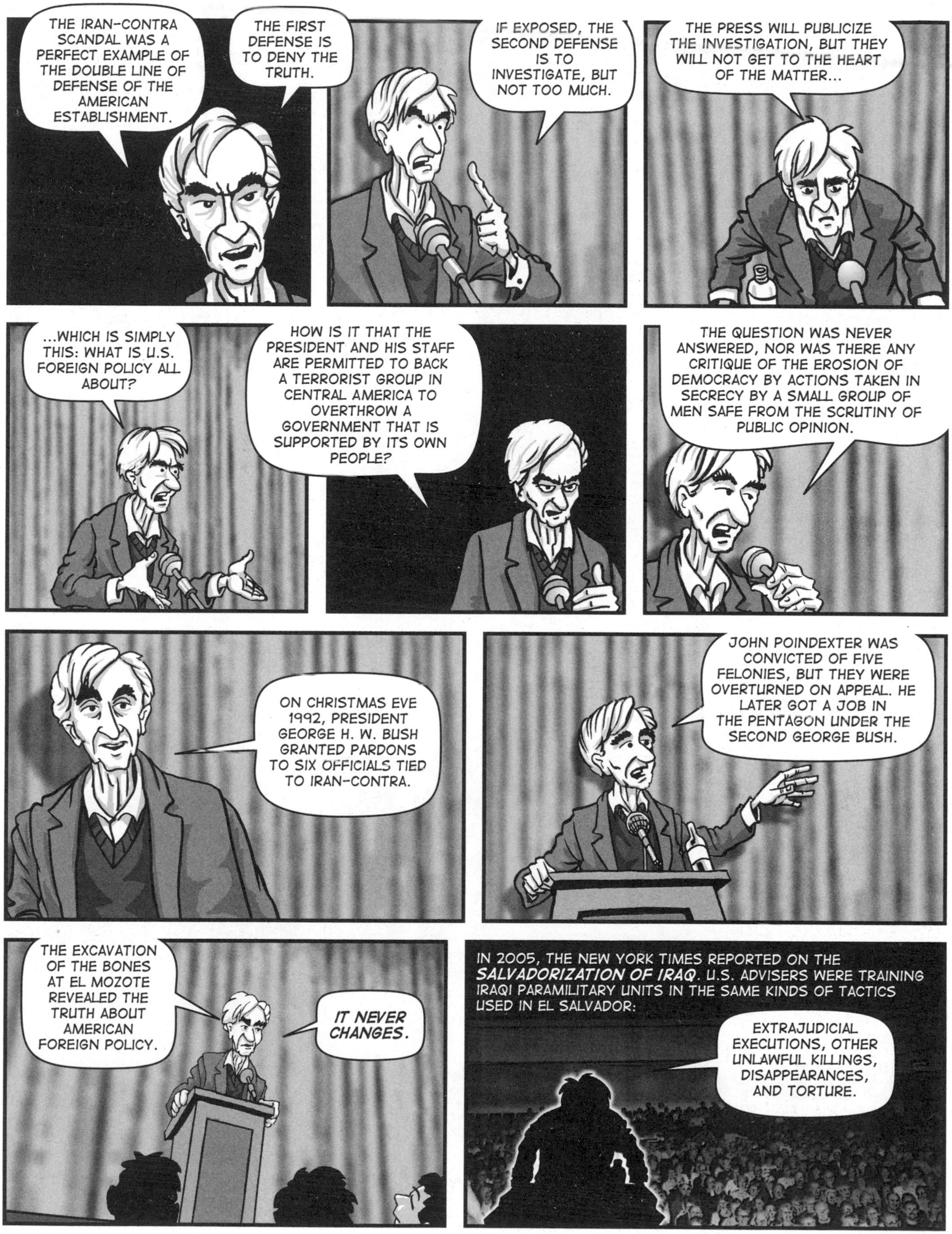

THE IRAN-CONTRA SCANDAL WAS A PERFECT EXAMPLE OF THE DOUBLE LINE OF DEFENSE OF THE AMERICAN ESTABLISHMENT.
THE FIRST DEFENSE IS TO DENY THE TRUTH.
IF EXPOSED, THE SECOND DEFENSE IS TO INVESTIGATE, BUT NOT TOO MUCH.
THE PRESS WILL PUBLICIZE THE INVESTIGATION, BUT THEY WILL NOT GET TO THE HEART OF THE MATTER...
...WHICH IS SIMPLY THIS: WHAT IS U.S. FOREIGN POLICY ALL ABOUT?
HOW IS IT THAT THE PRESIDENT AND HIS STAFF ARE PERMITTED TO BACK A TERRORIST GROUP IN CENTRAL AMERICA TO OVERTHROW A GOVERNMENT THAT IS SUPPORTED BY ITS OWN PEOPLE?
THE QUESTION WAS NEVER ANSWERED, NOR WAS THERE ANY CRITIQUE OF THE EROSION OF DEMOCRACY BY ACTIONS TAKEN IN SECRECY BY A SMALL GROUP OF MEN SAFE FROM THE SCRUTINY OF PUBLIC OPINION.
ON CHRISTMAS EVE 1992, PRESIDENT GEORGE H. W. BUSH GRANTED PARDONS TO SIX OFFICIALS TIED TO IRAN-CONTRA.
JOHN POINDEXTER WAS CONVICTED OF FIVE FELONIES, BUT THEY WERE OVERTURNED ON APPEAL. HE LATER GOT A JOB IN THE PENTAGON UNDER THE SECOND GEORGE BUSH.
THE EXCAVATION OF THE BONES AT EL MOZOTE REVEALED THE TRUTH ABOUT AMERICAN FOREIGN POLICY.
IT NEVER CHANGES.
IN 2005, THE NEW YORK TIMES REPORTED ON THE ***SALVADORIZATION OF IRAQ***. U.S. ADVISERS WERE TRAINING IRAQI PARAMILITARY UNITS IN THE SAME KINDS OF TACTICS USED IN EL SALVADOR:
EXTRAJUDICIAL EXECUTIONS, OTHER UNLAWFUL KILLINGS, DISAPPEARANCES, AND TORTURE.

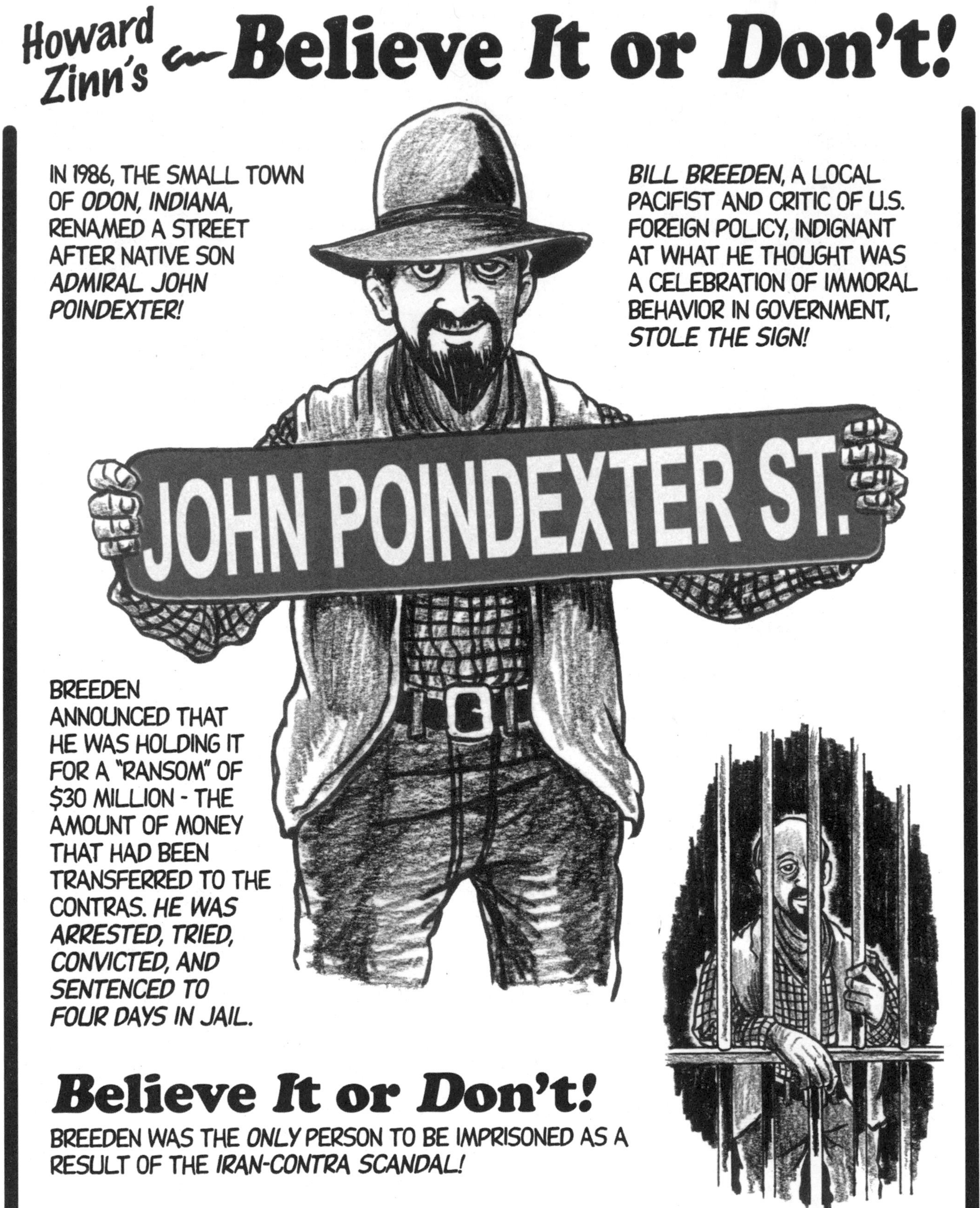
Howard Zinn's Believe It or Don't!
IN 1986, THE SMALL TOWN OF ODON, INDIANA, RENAMED A STREET AFTER NATIVE SON ADMIRAL JOHN POINDEXTER!
BILL BREEDEN, A LOCAL PACIFIST AND CRITIC OF U.S. FOREIGN POLICY, INDIGNANT AT WHAT HE THOUGHT WAS A CELEBRATION OF IMMORAL BEHAVIOR IN GOVERNMENT, STOLE THE SIGN!
JOHN POINDEXTER ST.
BREEDEN ANNOUNCED THAT HE WAS HOLDING IT FOR A "RANSOM" OF $30 MILLION - THE AMOUNT OF MONEY THAT HAD BEEN TRANSFERRED TO THE CONTRAS. HE WAS ARRESTED, TRIED, CONVICTED, AND SENTENCED TO FOUR DAYS IN JAIL.
Believe It or Don't!
BREEDEN WAS THE ONLY PERSON TO BE IMPRISONED AS A RESULT OF THE IRAN-CONTRA SCANDAL!

Chapter XII
COVERT ACTION AND REACTION

*"In the back of everybody's mind hung the suspicion that, with the admission of the shah to the United States, the countdown for another coup d'etat had begun. Such was our fate again, we were convinced, and it would be irreversible.
We now had to reverse the irreversible."*

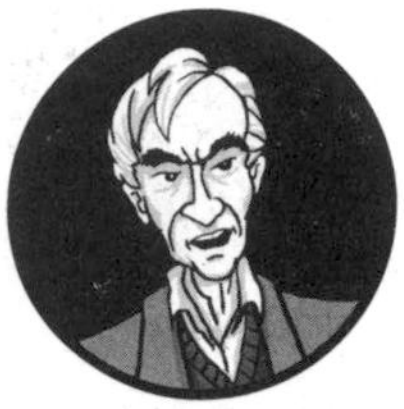

Iran: Overthrowing Democracy

ON NOVEMBER 4, 1979, ANGRY IRANIANS ***SEIZED THE U.S. EMBASSY*** IN THE CAPITAL CITY OF TEHRAN AND TOOK EVERYONE HOSTAGE. THEY DEMANDED THAT ***MOHAMMAD REZA PAHLEVI***, THE NOTORIOUS SHAH (KING) WHO HAD FLED WITH U.S. HELP WHEN REBELLION SWEPT THE COUNTRY, BE RETURNED TO FACE TRIAL. ***THE IRANIANS HELD THE EMBASSY AND 52 HOSTAGES FOR 444 DAYS.***

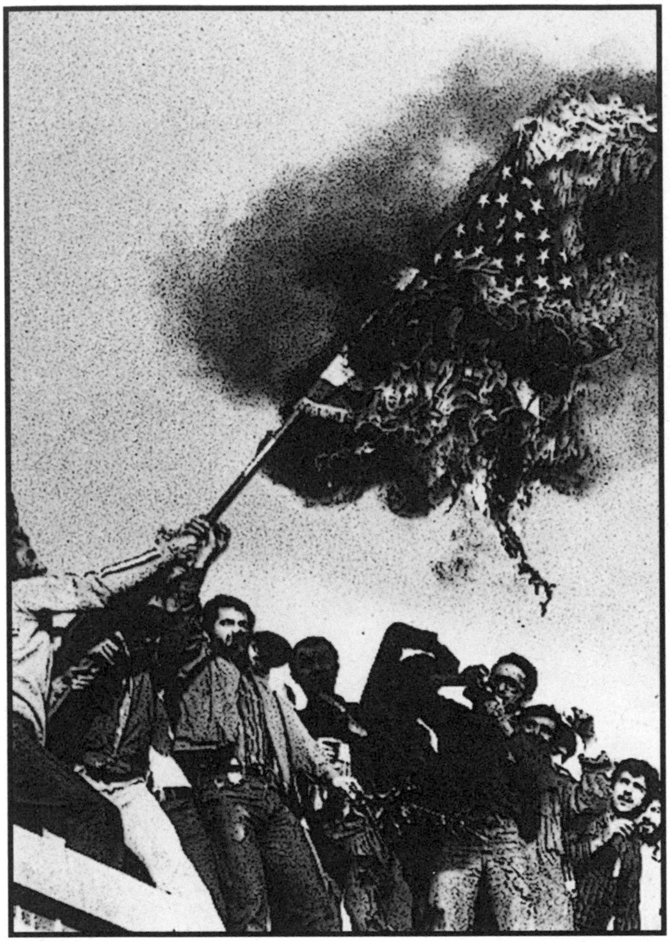

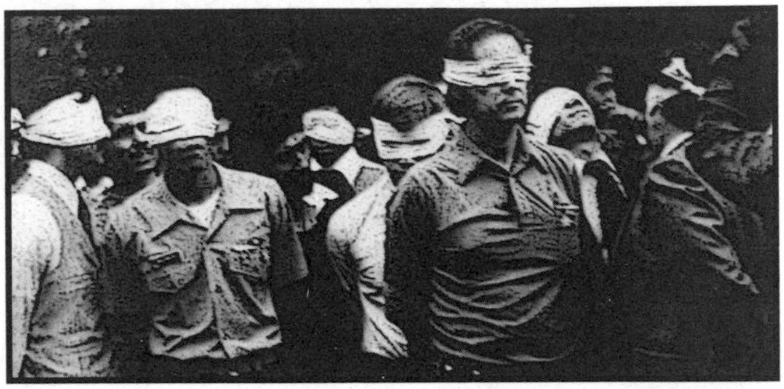

THE HOSTAGE TAKERS ALSO DEMANDED AN APOLOGY FROM THE U.S. FOR OVERTHROWING THE GOVERNMENT OF DR. ***MOHAMMAD MOSSADEGH*** IN 1953.

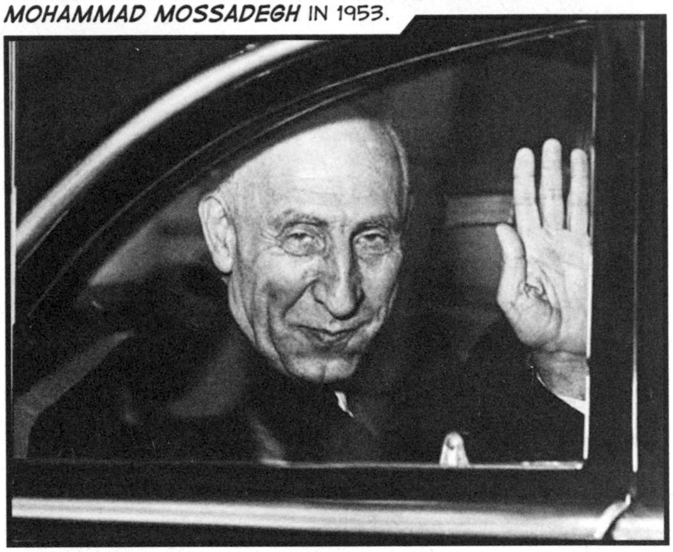

AT THE EMBASSY, HOSTAGE TAKERS DISCOVERED SHREDDED PAPERS DOCUMENTING U.S. INTELLIGENCE ACTIVITY IN THE MIDDLE EAST, SOUTH ASIA, AND SOVIET UNION.

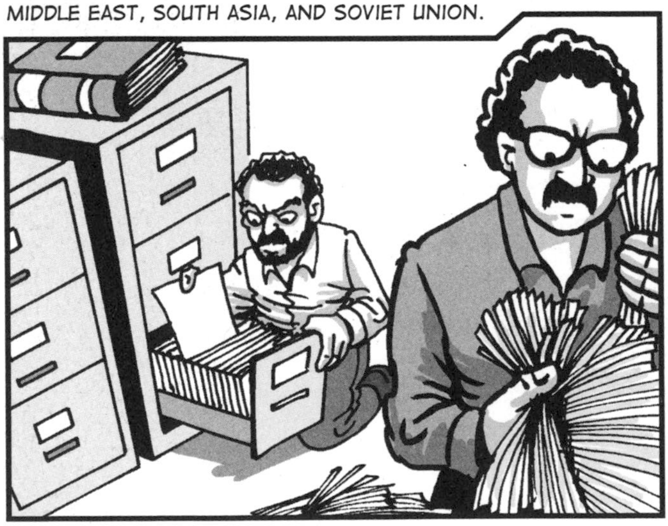

WOMEN EXPERIENCED IN WEAVING THE COMPLEX PATTERNS OF PERSIAN RUGS PIECED THE DOCUMENTS BACK TOGETHER.

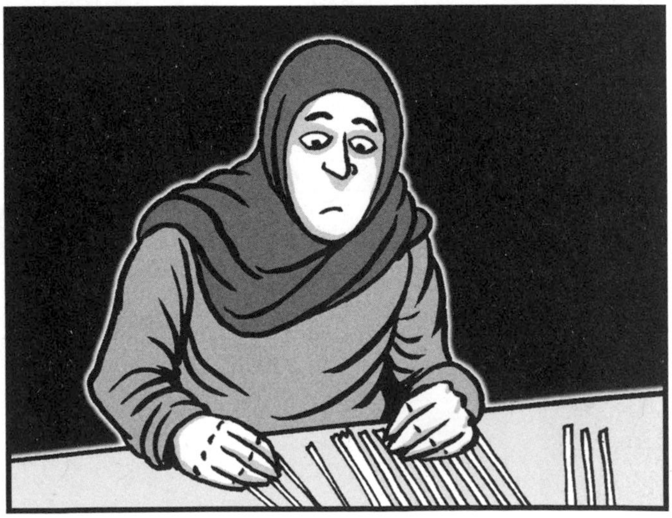

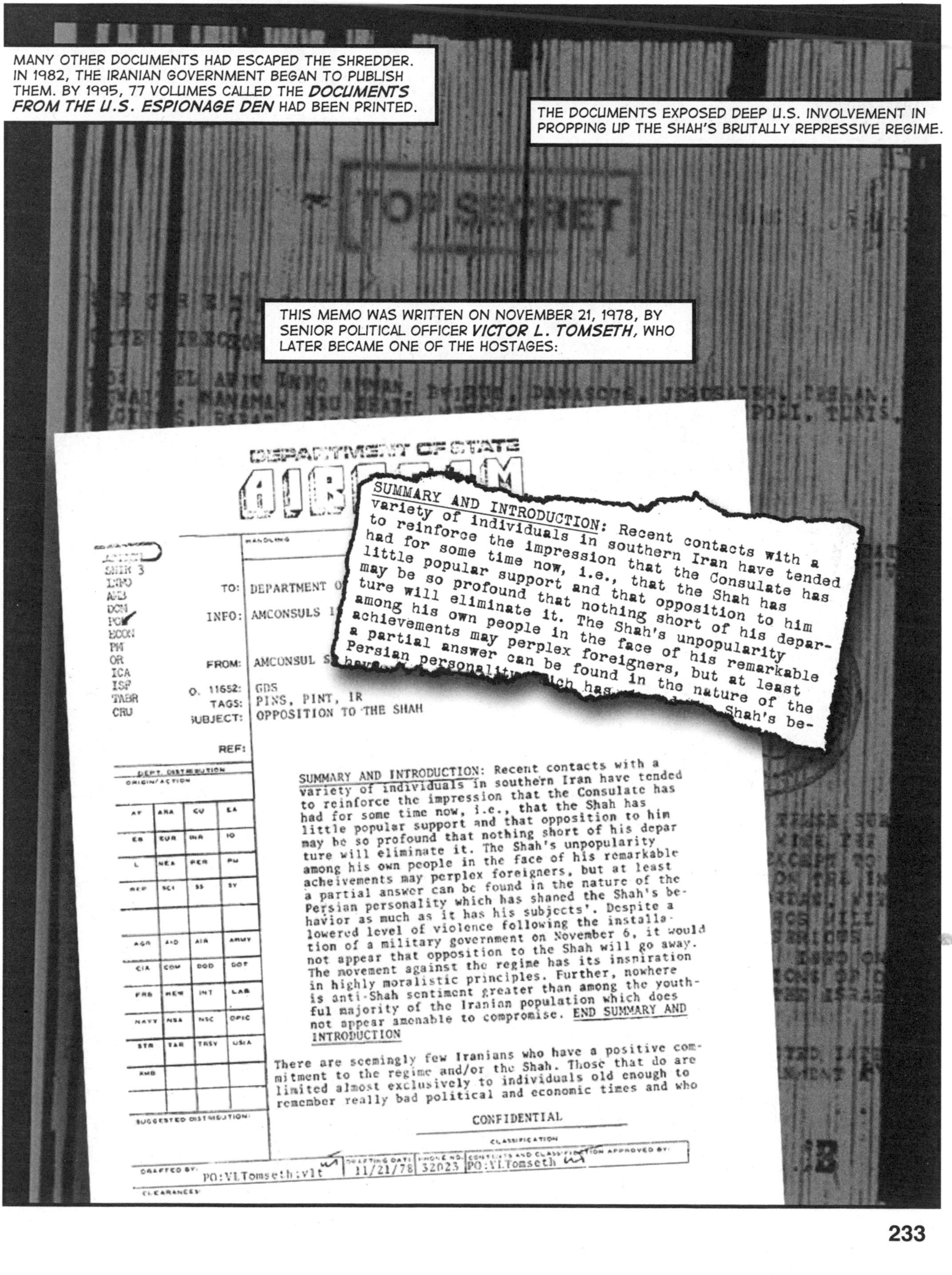
MANY OTHER DOCUMENTS HAD ESCAPED THE SHREDDER. IN 1982, THE IRANIAN GOVERNMENT BEGAN TO PUBLISH THEM. BY 1995, 77 VOLUMES CALLED THE *DOCUMENTS FROM THE U.S. ESPIONAGE DEN* HAD BEEN PRINTED.
THE DOCUMENTS EXPOSED DEEP U.S. INVOLVEMENT IN PROPPING UP THE SHAH'S BRUTALLY REPRESSIVE REGIME.
TOP SECRET
THIS MEMO WAS WRITTEN ON NOVEMBER 21, 1978, BY SENIOR POLITICAL OFFICER *VICTOR L. TOMSETH,* WHO LATER BECAME ONE OF THE HOSTAGES:
DEPARTMENT OF STATE
AIRGRAM
SUMMARY AND INTRODUCTION: Recent contacts with a variety of individuals in southern Iran have tended to reinforce the impression that the Consulate has had for some time now, i.e., that the Shah has little popular support and that opposition to him may be so profound that nothing short of his departure will eliminate it. The Shah's unpopularity among his own people in the face of his remarkable achievements may perplex foreigners, but at least a partial answer can be found in the nature of the Persian personality ... Shah's be-
TO: DEPARTMENT O
INFO: AMCONSULS I
FROM: AMCONSUL S
O. 11652: GDS
TAGS: PINS, PINT, IR
SUBJECT: OPPOSITION TO THE SHAH
REF:
SUMMARY AND INTRODUCTION: Recent contacts with a variety of individuals in southern Iran have tended to reinforce the impression that the Consulate has had for some time now, i.e., that the Shah has little popular support and that opposition to him may be so profound that nothing short of his departure will eliminate it. The Shah's unpopularity among his own people in the face of his remarkable acheivements may perplex foreigners, but at least a partial answer can be found in the nature of the Persian personality which has shaped the Shah's behavior as much as it has his subjects'. Despite a lowered level of violence following the installation of a military government on November 6, it would not appear that opposition to the Shah will go away. The movement against the regime has its inspiration in highly moralistic principles. Further, nowhere is anti-Shah sentiment greater than among the youthful majority of the Iranian population which does not appear amenable to compromise. END SUMMARY AND INTRODUCTION
There are seemingly few Iranians who have a positive commitment to the regime and/or the Shah. Those that do are limited almost exclusively to individuals old enough to remember really bad political and economic times and who
CONFIDENTIAL
CLASSIFICATION
DRAFTED BY: PO:VLTomseth:vlt
DRAFTING DATE: 11/21/78
PHONE NO. 32023
CONTENTS AND CLASSIFICATION APPROVED BY: PO:VLTomseth
CLEARANCES:

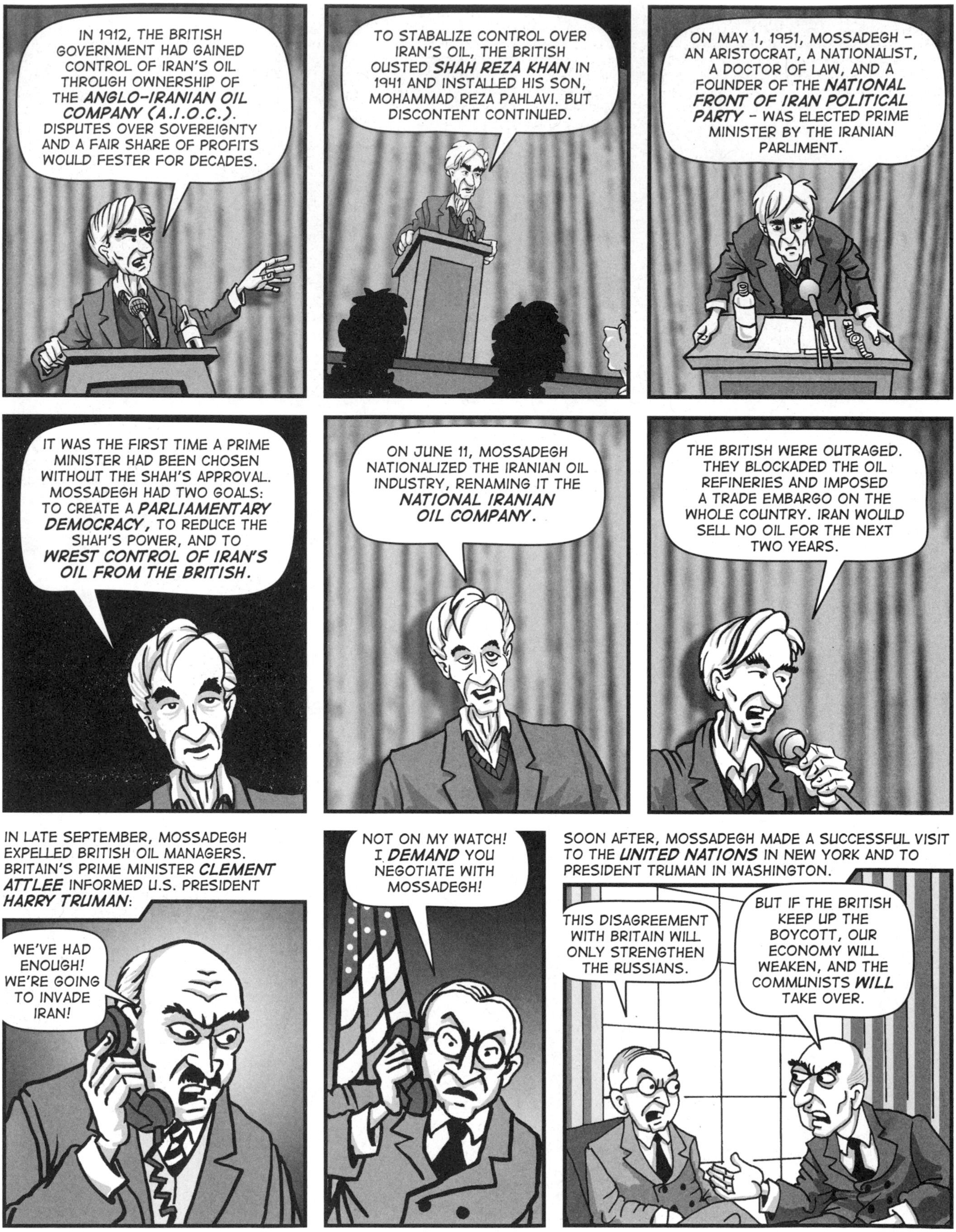
IN 1912, THE BRITISH GOVERNMENT HAD GAINED CONTROL OF IRAN'S OIL THROUGH OWNERSHIP OF THE ANGLO-IRANIAN OIL COMPANY (A.I.O.C.). DISPUTES OVER SOVEREIGNTY AND A FAIR SHARE OF PROFITS WOULD FESTER FOR DECADES.
TO STABALIZE CONTROL OVER IRAN'S OIL, THE BRITISH OUSTED SHAH REZA KHAN IN 1941 AND INSTALLED HIS SON, MOHAMMAD REZA PAHLAVI. BUT DISCONTENT CONTINUED.
ON MAY 1, 1951, MOSSADEGH – AN ARISTOCRAT, A NATIONALIST, A DOCTOR OF LAW, AND A FOUNDER OF THE NATIONAL FRONT OF IRAN POLITICAL PARTY – WAS ELECTED PRIME MINISTER BY THE IRANIAN PARLIMENT.
IT WAS THE FIRST TIME A PRIME MINISTER HAD BEEN CHOSEN WITHOUT THE SHAH'S APPROVAL. MOSSADEGH HAD TWO GOALS: TO CREATE A PARLIAMENTARY DEMOCRACY, TO REDUCE THE SHAH'S POWER, AND TO WREST CONTROL OF IRAN'S OIL FROM THE BRITISH.
ON JUNE 11, MOSSADEGH NATIONALIZED THE IRANIAN OIL INDUSTRY, RENAMING IT THE NATIONAL IRANIAN OIL COMPANY.
THE BRITISH WERE OUTRAGED. THEY BLOCKADED THE OIL REFINERIES AND IMPOSED A TRADE EMBARGO ON THE WHOLE COUNTRY. IRAN WOULD SELL NO OIL FOR THE NEXT TWO YEARS.
IN LATE SEPTEMBER, MOSSADEGH EXPELLED BRITISH OIL MANAGERS. BRITAIN'S PRIME MINISTER CLEMENT ATTLEE INFORMED U.S. PRESIDENT HARRY TRUMAN:
WE'VE HAD ENOUGH! WE'RE GOING TO INVADE IRAN!
NOT ON MY WATCH! I DEMAND YOU NEGOTIATE WITH MOSSADEGH!
SOON AFTER, MOSSADEGH MADE A SUCCESSFUL VISIT TO THE UNITED NATIONS IN NEW YORK AND TO PRESIDENT TRUMAN IN WASHINGTON.
THIS DISAGREEMENT WITH BRITAIN WILL ONLY STRENGTHEN THE RUSSIANS.
BUT IF THE BRITISH KEEP UP THE BOYCOTT, OUR ECONOMY WILL WEAKEN, AND THE COMMUNISTS WILL TAKE OVER.

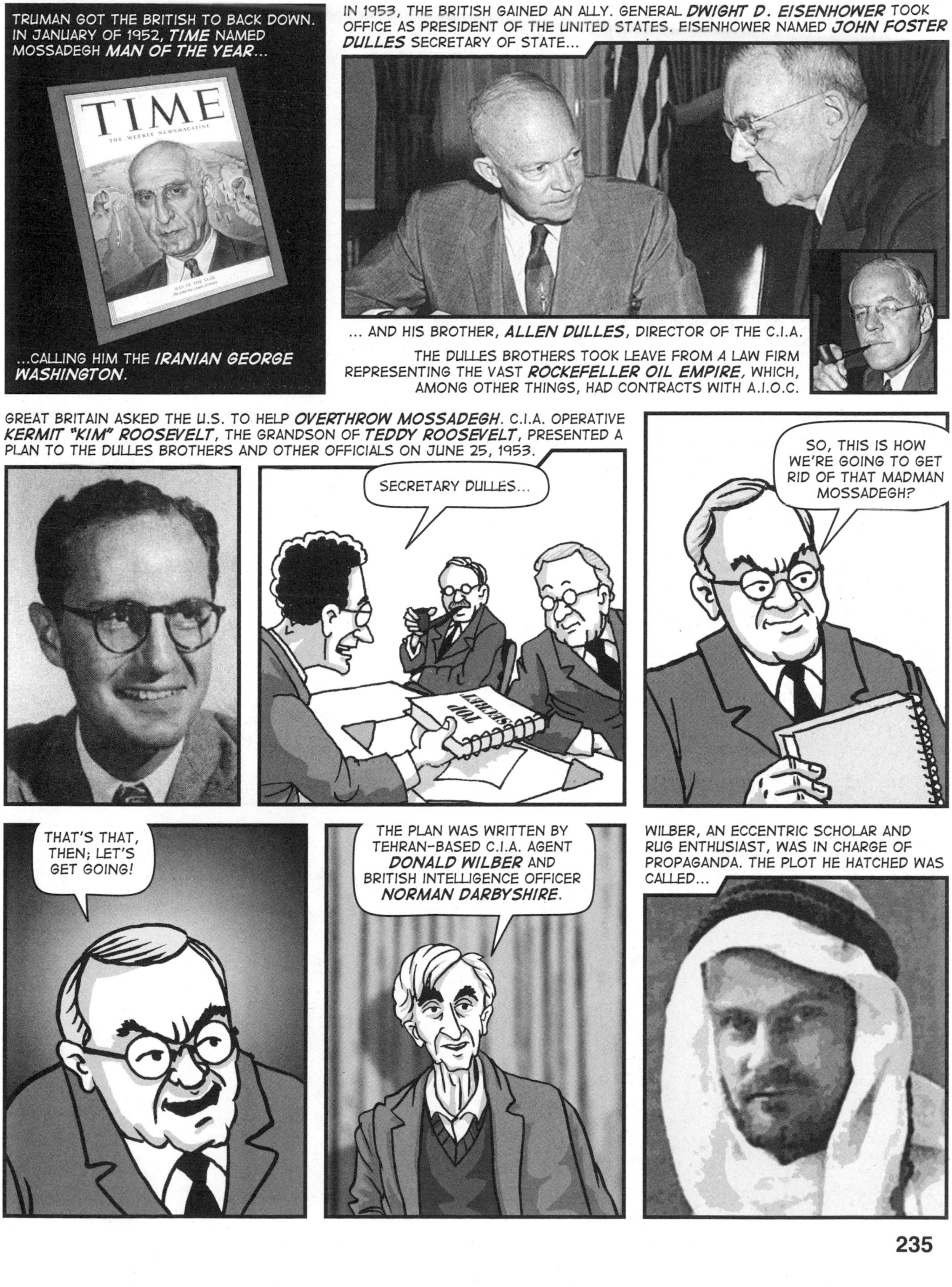
TRUMAN GOT THE BRITISH TO BACK DOWN. IN JANUARY OF 1952, TIME NAMED MOSSADEGH MAN OF THE YEAR...
TIME
THE WEEKLY NEWSMAGAZINE
...CALLING HIM THE IRANIAN GEORGE WASHINGTON.
IN 1953, THE BRITISH GAINED AN ALLY. GENERAL DWIGHT D. EISENHOWER TOOK OFFICE AS PRESIDENT OF THE UNITED STATES. EISENHOWER NAMED JOHN FOSTER DULLES SECRETARY OF STATE...
... AND HIS BROTHER, ALLEN DULLES, DIRECTOR OF THE C.I.A.
THE DULLES BROTHERS TOOK LEAVE FROM A LAW FIRM REPRESENTING THE VAST ROCKEFELLER OIL EMPIRE, WHICH, AMONG OTHER THINGS, HAD CONTRACTS WITH A.I.O.C.
GREAT BRITAIN ASKED THE U.S. TO HELP OVERTHROW MOSSADEGH. C.I.A. OPERATIVE KERMIT "KIM" ROOSEVELT, THE GRANDSON OF TEDDY ROOSEVELT, PRESENTED A PLAN TO THE DULLES BROTHERS AND OTHER OFFICIALS ON JUNE 25, 1953.
SECRETARY DULLES...
TOP SECRET
SO, THIS IS HOW WE'RE GOING TO GET RID OF THAT MADMAN MOSSADEGH?
THAT'S THAT, THEN; LET'S GET GOING!
THE PLAN WAS WRITTEN BY TEHRAN-BASED C.I.A. AGENT DONALD WILBER AND BRITISH INTELLIGENCE OFFICER NORMAN DARBYSHIRE.
WILBER, AN ECCENTRIC SCHOLAR AND RUG ENTHUSIAST, WAS IN CHARGE OF PROPAGANDA. THE PLOT HE HATCHED WAS CALLED...

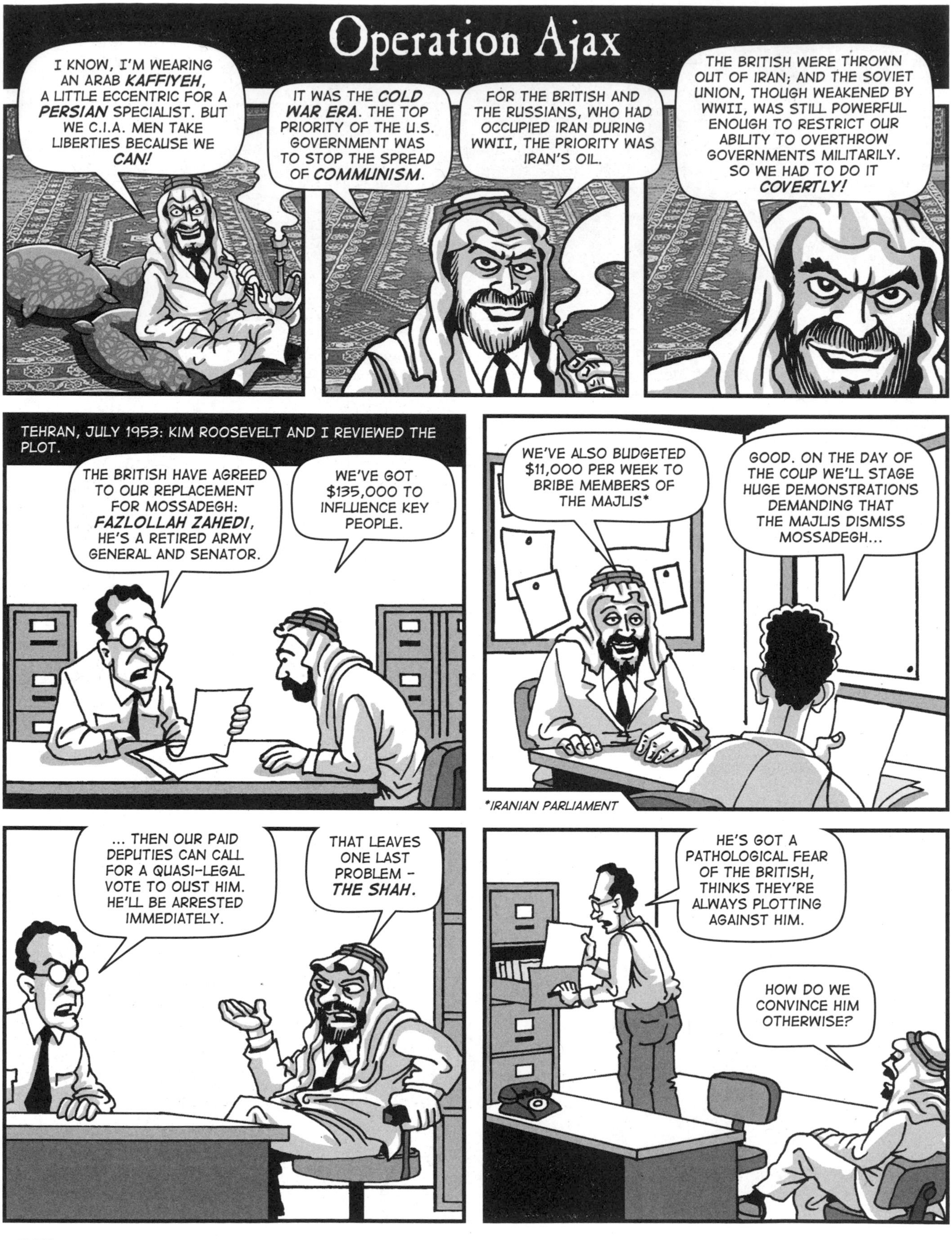
Operation Ajax
I KNOW, I'M WEARING AN ARAB KAFFIYEH, A LITTLE ECCENTRIC FOR A PERSIAN SPECIALIST. BUT WE C.I.A. MEN TAKE LIBERTIES BECAUSE WE CAN!
IT WAS THE COLD WAR ERA. THE TOP PRIORITY OF THE U.S. GOVERNMENT WAS TO STOP THE SPREAD OF COMMUNISM.
FOR THE BRITISH AND THE RUSSIANS, WHO HAD OCCUPIED IRAN DURING WWII, THE PRIORITY WAS IRAN'S OIL.
THE BRITISH WERE THROWN OUT OF IRAN; AND THE SOVIET UNION, THOUGH WEAKENED BY WWII, WAS STILL POWERFUL ENOUGH TO RESTRICT OUR ABILITY TO OVERTHROW GOVERNMENTS MILITARILY. SO WE HAD TO DO IT COVERTLY!
TEHRAN, JULY 1953: KIM ROOSEVELT AND I REVIEWED THE PLOT.
THE BRITISH HAVE AGREED TO OUR REPLACEMENT FOR MOSSADEGH: FAZLOLLAH ZAHEDI, HE'S A RETIRED ARMY GENERAL AND SENATOR.
WE'VE GOT $135,000 TO INFLUENCE KEY PEOPLE.
WE'VE ALSO BUDGETED $11,000 PER WEEK TO BRIBE MEMBERS OF THE MAJLIS*
GOOD. ON THE DAY OF THE COUP WE'LL STAGE HUGE DEMONSTRATIONS DEMANDING THAT THE MAJLIS DISMISS MOSSADEGH...
*IRANIAN PARLIAMENT
... THEN OUR PAID DEPUTIES CAN CALL FOR A QUASI-LEGAL VOTE TO OUST HIM. HE'LL BE ARRESTED IMMEDIATELY.
THAT LEAVES ONE LAST PROBLEM - THE SHAH.
HE'S GOT A PATHOLOGICAL FEAR OF THE BRITISH, THINKS THEY'RE ALWAYS PLOTTING AGAINST HIM.
HOW DO WE CONVINCE HIM OTHERWISE?

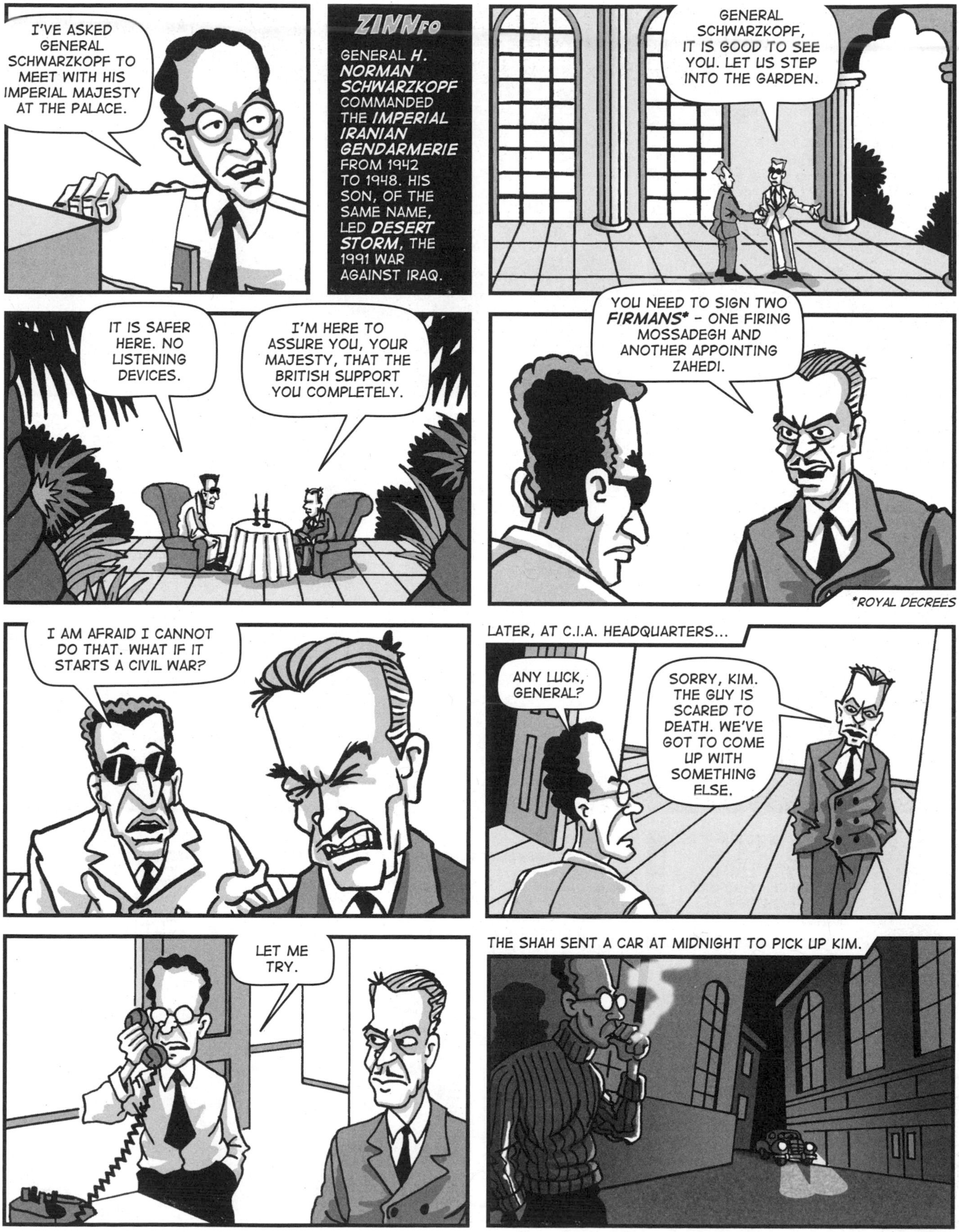
I'VE ASKED GENERAL SCHWARZKOPF TO MEET WITH HIS IMPERIAL MAJESTY AT THE PALACE.
ZINNFO
GENERAL H. NORMAN SCHWARZKOPF COMMANDED THE IMPERIAL IRANIAN GENDARMERIE FROM 1942 TO 1948. HIS SON, OF THE SAME NAME, LED DESERT STORM, THE 1991 WAR AGAINST IRAQ.
GENERAL SCHWARZKOPF, IT IS GOOD TO SEE YOU. LET US STEP INTO THE GARDEN.
IT IS SAFER HERE. NO LISTENING DEVICES.
I'M HERE TO ASSURE YOU, YOUR MAJESTY, THAT THE BRITISH SUPPORT YOU COMPLETELY.
YOU NEED TO SIGN TWO FIRMANS* - ONE FIRING MOSSADEGH AND ANOTHER APPOINTING ZAHEDI.
*ROYAL DECREES
I AM AFRAID I CANNOT DO THAT. WHAT IF IT STARTS A CIVIL WAR?
LATER, AT C.I.A. HEADQUARTERS...
ANY LUCK, GENERAL?
SORRY, KIM. THE GUY IS SCARED TO DEATH. WE'VE GOT TO COME UP WITH SOMETHING ELSE.
LET ME TRY.
THE SHAH SENT A CAR AT MIDNIGHT TO PICK UP KIM.

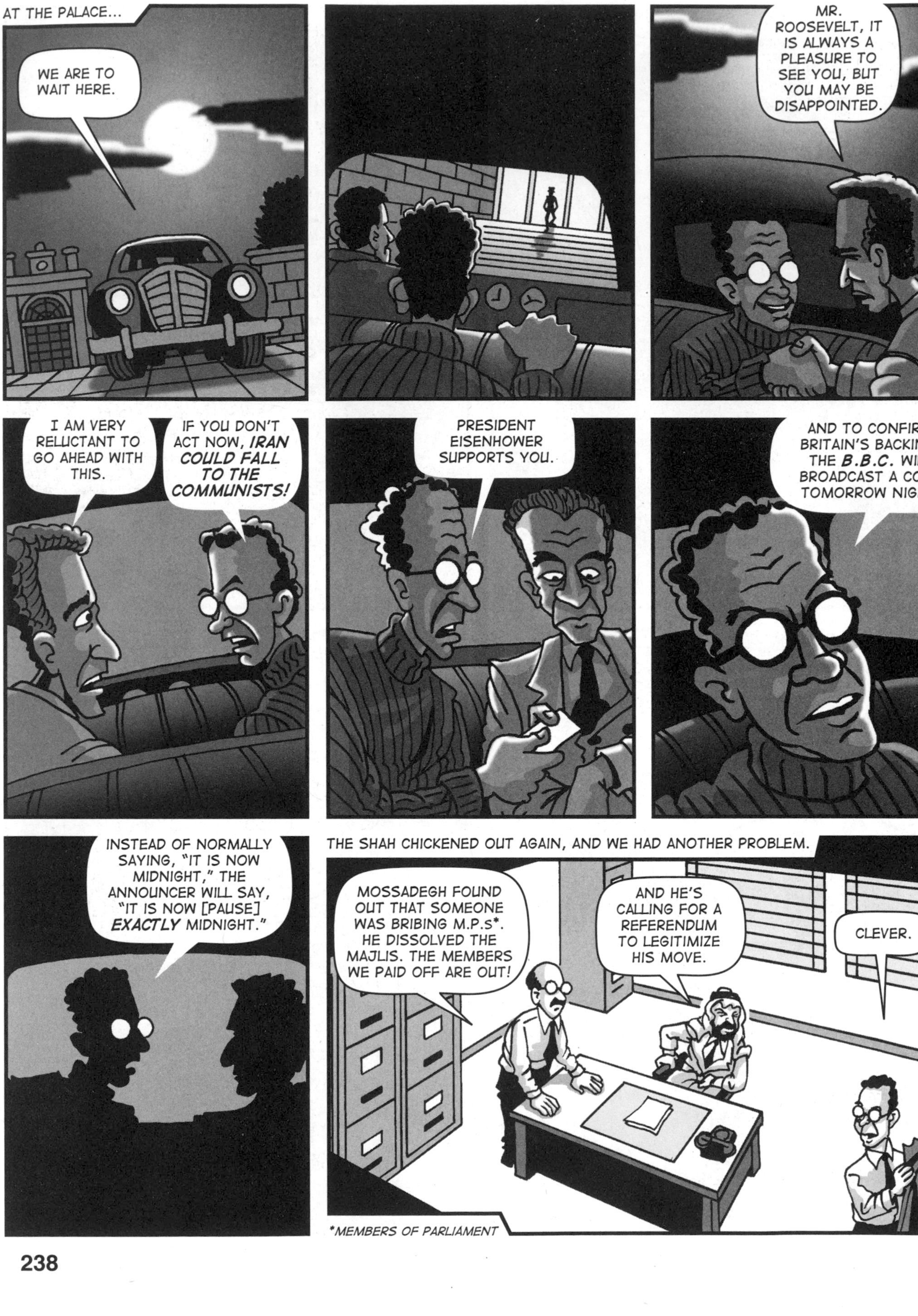
AT THE PALACE...
WE ARE TO WAIT HERE.
MR. ROOSEVELT, IT IS ALWAYS A PLEASURE TO SEE YOU, BUT YOU MAY BE DISAPPOINTED.
I AM VERY RELUCTANT TO GO AHEAD WITH THIS.
IF YOU DON'T ACT NOW, IRAN COULD FALL TO THE COMMUNISTS!
PRESIDENT EISENHOWER SUPPORTS YOU.
AND TO CONFIRM BRITAIN'S BACKING, THE B.B.C. WILL BROADCAST A CODE TOMORROW NIGHT.
INSTEAD OF NORMALLY SAYING, "IT IS NOW MIDNIGHT," THE ANNOUNCER WILL SAY, "IT IS NOW [PAUSE] EXACTLY MIDNIGHT."
THE SHAH CHICKENED OUT AGAIN, AND WE HAD ANOTHER PROBLEM.
MOSSADEGH FOUND OUT THAT SOMEONE WAS BRIBING M.P.s*. HE DISSOLVED THE MAJLIS. THE MEMBERS WE PAID OFF ARE OUT!
AND HE'S CALLING FOR A REFERENDUM TO LEGITIMIZE HIS MOVE.
CLEVER.
*MEMBERS OF PARLIAMENT

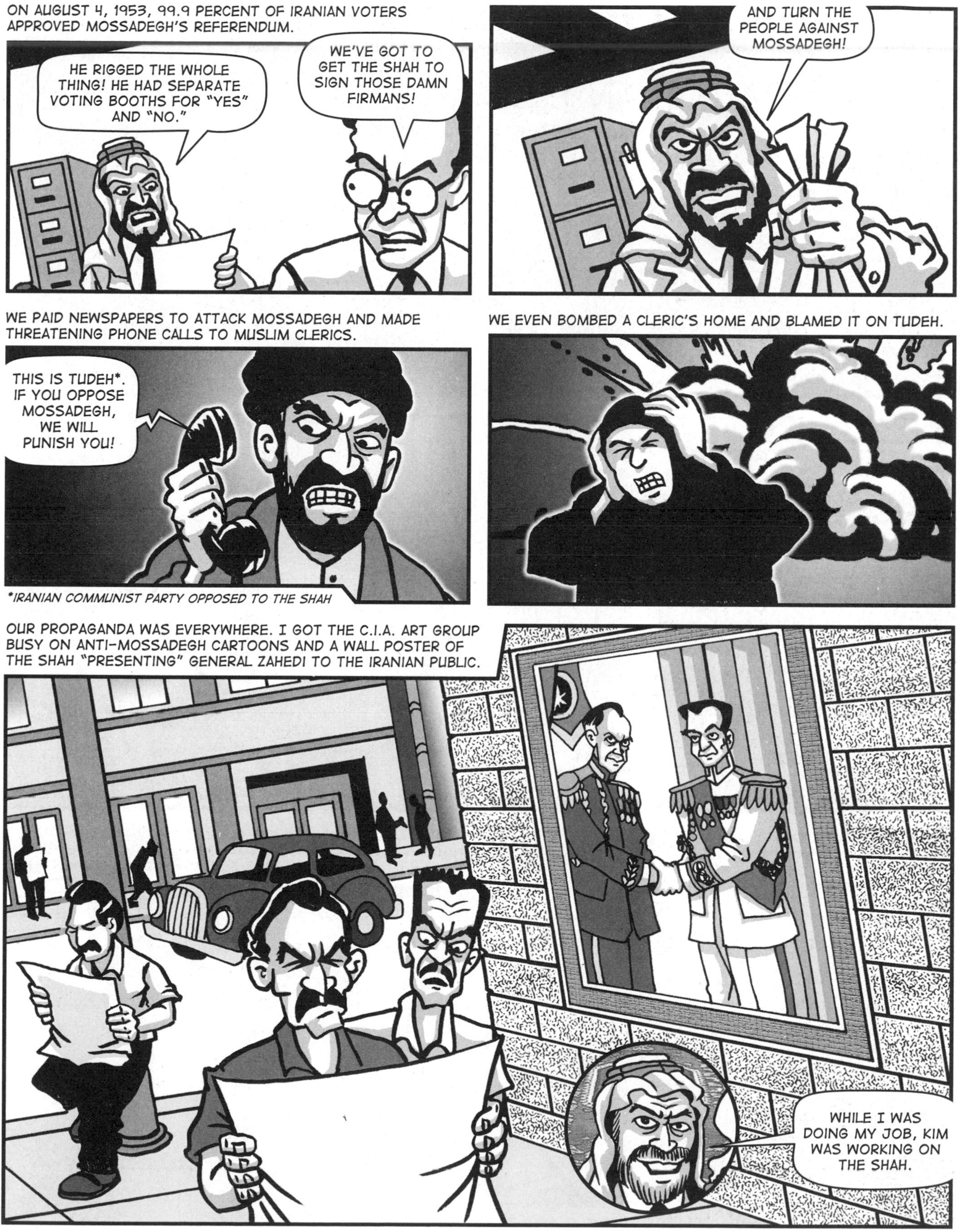
ON AUGUST 4, 1953, 99.9 PERCENT OF IRANIAN VOTERS APPROVED MOSSADEGH'S REFERENDUM.
HE RIGGED THE WHOLE THING! HE HAD SEPARATE VOTING BOOTHS FOR "YES" AND "NO."
WE'VE GOT TO GET THE SHAH TO SIGN THOSE DAMN FIRMANS!
AND TURN THE PEOPLE AGAINST MOSSADEGH!
WE PAID NEWSPAPERS TO ATTACK MOSSADEGH AND MADE THREATENING PHONE CALLS TO MUSLIM CLERICS.
THIS IS TUDEH*. IF YOU OPPOSE MOSSADEGH, WE WILL PUNISH YOU!
*IRANIAN COMMUNIST PARTY OPPOSED TO THE SHAH
WE EVEN BOMBED A CLERIC'S HOME AND BLAMED IT ON TUDEH.
OUR PROPAGANDA WAS EVERYWHERE. I GOT THE C.I.A. ART GROUP BUSY ON ANTI-MOSSADEGH CARTOONS AND A WALL POSTER OF THE SHAH "PRESENTING" GENERAL ZAHEDI TO THE IRANIAN PUBLIC.
WHILE I WAS DOING MY JOB, KIM WAS WORKING ON THE SHAH.

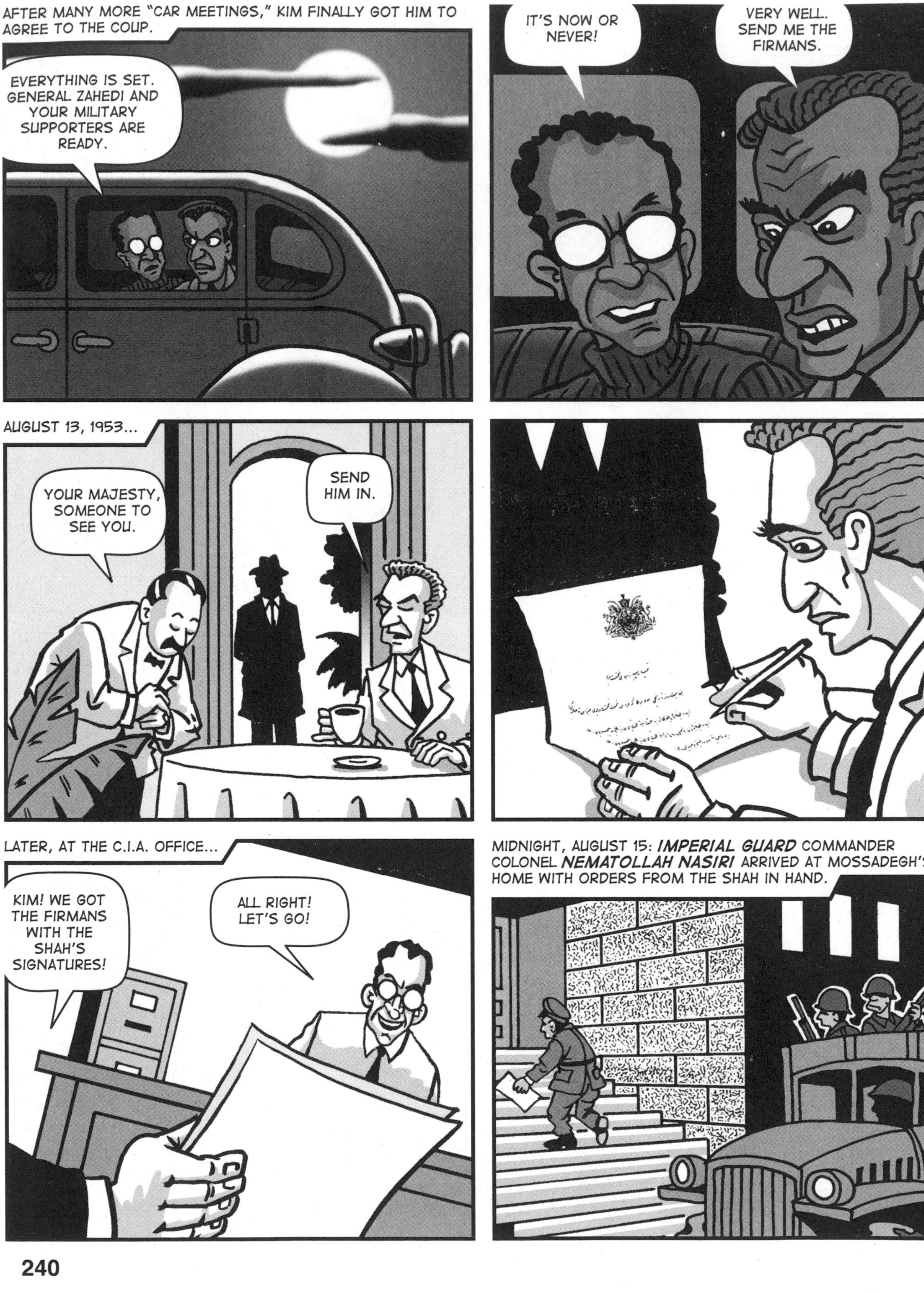
AFTER MANY MORE "CAR MEETINGS," KIM FINALLY GOT HIM TO AGREE TO THE COUP.
EVERYTHING IS SET. GENERAL ZAHEDI AND YOUR MILITARY SUPPORTERS ARE READY.
IT'S NOW OR NEVER!
VERY WELL. SEND ME THE FIRMANS.
AUGUST 13, 1953...
YOUR MAJESTY, SOMEONE TO SEE YOU.
SEND HIM IN.
LATER, AT THE C.I.A. OFFICE...
KIM! WE GOT THE FIRMANS WITH THE SHAH'S SIGNATURES!
ALL RIGHT! LET'S GO!
MIDNIGHT, AUGUST 15: IMPERIAL GUARD COMMANDER COLONEL NEMATOLLAH NASIRI ARRIVED AT MOSSADEGH'S HOME WITH ORDERS FROM THE SHAH IN HAND.

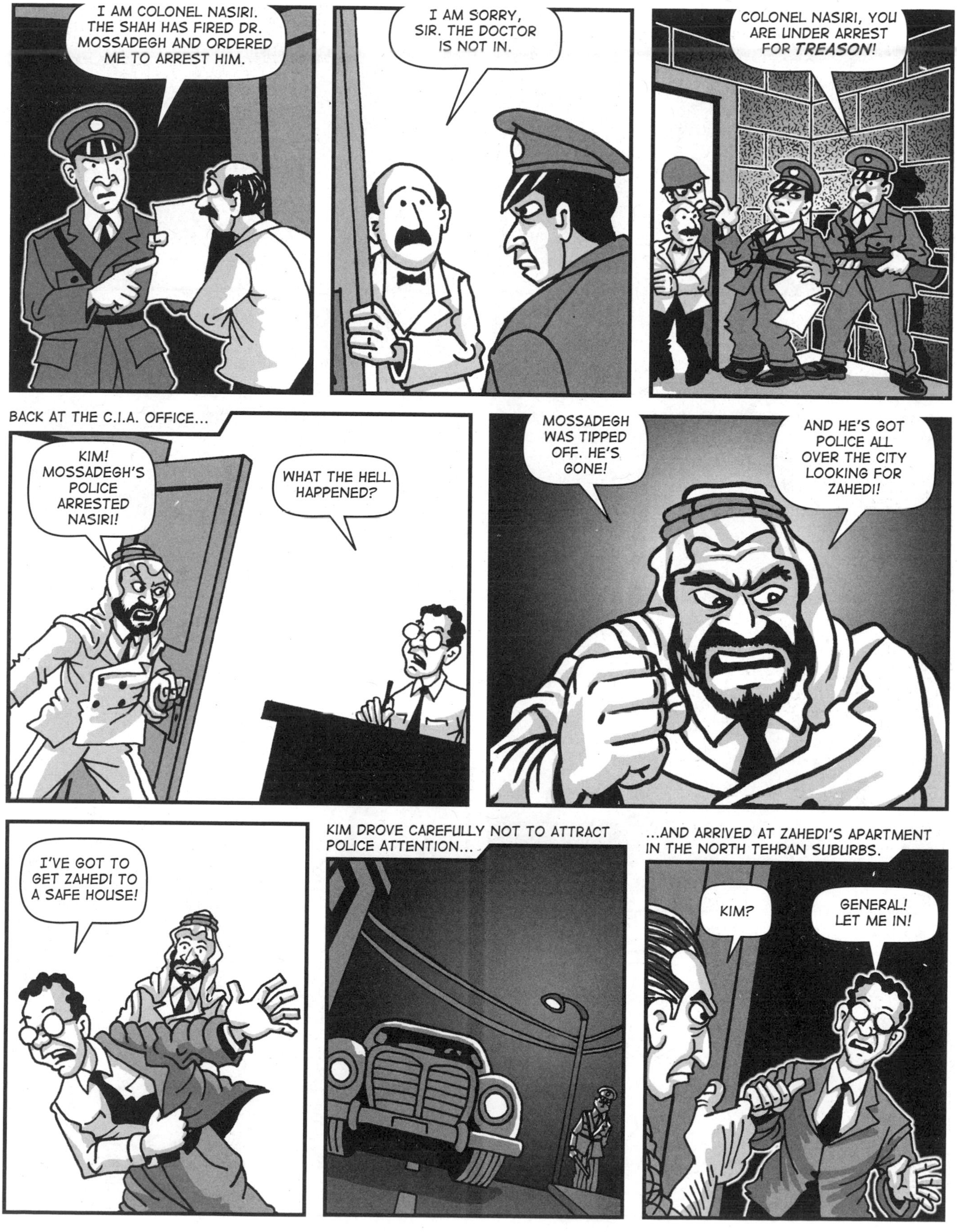
I AM COLONEL NASIRI. THE SHAH HAS FIRED DR. MOSSADEGH AND ORDERED ME TO ARREST HIM.
I AM SORRY, SIR. THE DOCTOR IS NOT IN.
COLONEL NASIRI, YOU ARE UNDER ARREST FOR *TREASON*!
BACK AT THE C.I.A. OFFICE...
KIM! MOSSADEGH'S POLICE ARRESTED NASIRI!
WHAT THE HELL HAPPENED?
MOSSADEGH WAS TIPPED OFF. HE'S GONE!
AND HE'S GOT POLICE ALL OVER THE CITY LOOKING FOR ZAHEDI!
I'VE GOT TO GET ZAHEDI TO A SAFE HOUSE!
KIM DROVE CAREFULLY NOT TO ATTRACT POLICE ATTENTION...
...AND ARRIVED AT ZAHEDI'S APARTMENT IN THE NORTH TEHRAN SUBURBS.
KIM?
GENERAL! LET ME IN!

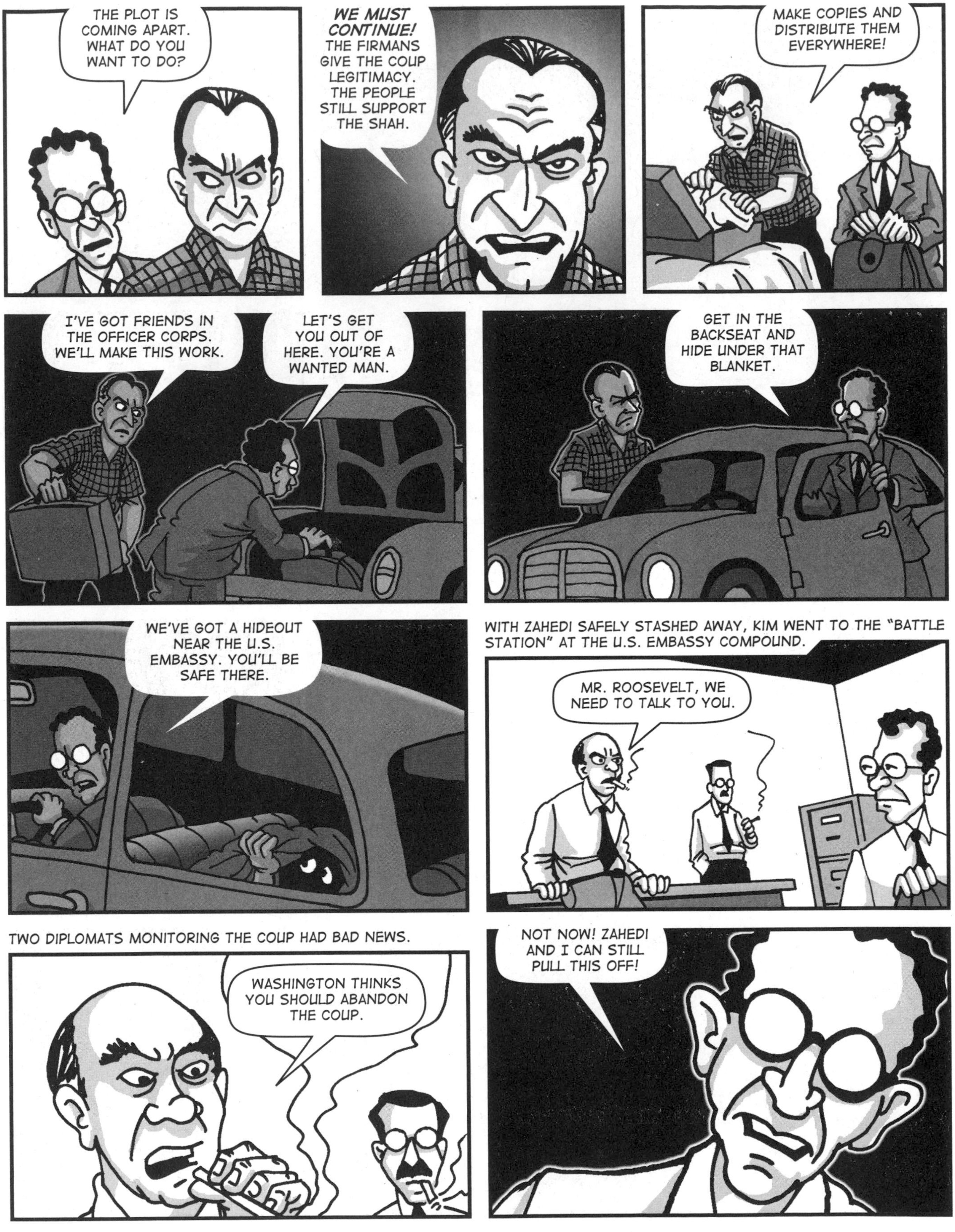
THE PLOT IS COMING APART. WHAT DO YOU WANT TO DO?
WE MUST CONTINUE! THE FIRMANS GIVE THE COUP LEGITIMACY. THE PEOPLE STILL SUPPORT THE SHAH.
MAKE COPIES AND DISTRIBUTE THEM EVERYWHERE!
I'VE GOT FRIENDS IN THE OFFICER CORPS. WE'LL MAKE THIS WORK.
LET'S GET YOU OUT OF HERE. YOU'RE A WANTED MAN.
GET IN THE BACKSEAT AND HIDE UNDER THAT BLANKET.
WE'VE GOT A HIDEOUT NEAR THE U.S. EMBASSY. YOU'LL BE SAFE THERE.
WITH ZAHEDI SAFELY STASHED AWAY, KIM WENT TO THE "BATTLE STATION" AT THE U.S. EMBASSY COMPOUND.
MR. ROOSEVELT, WE NEED TO TALK TO YOU.
TWO DIPLOMATS MONITORING THE COUP HAD BAD NEWS.
WASHINGTON THINKS YOU SHOULD ABANDON THE COUP.
NOT NOW! ZAHEDI AND I CAN STILL PULL THIS OFF!

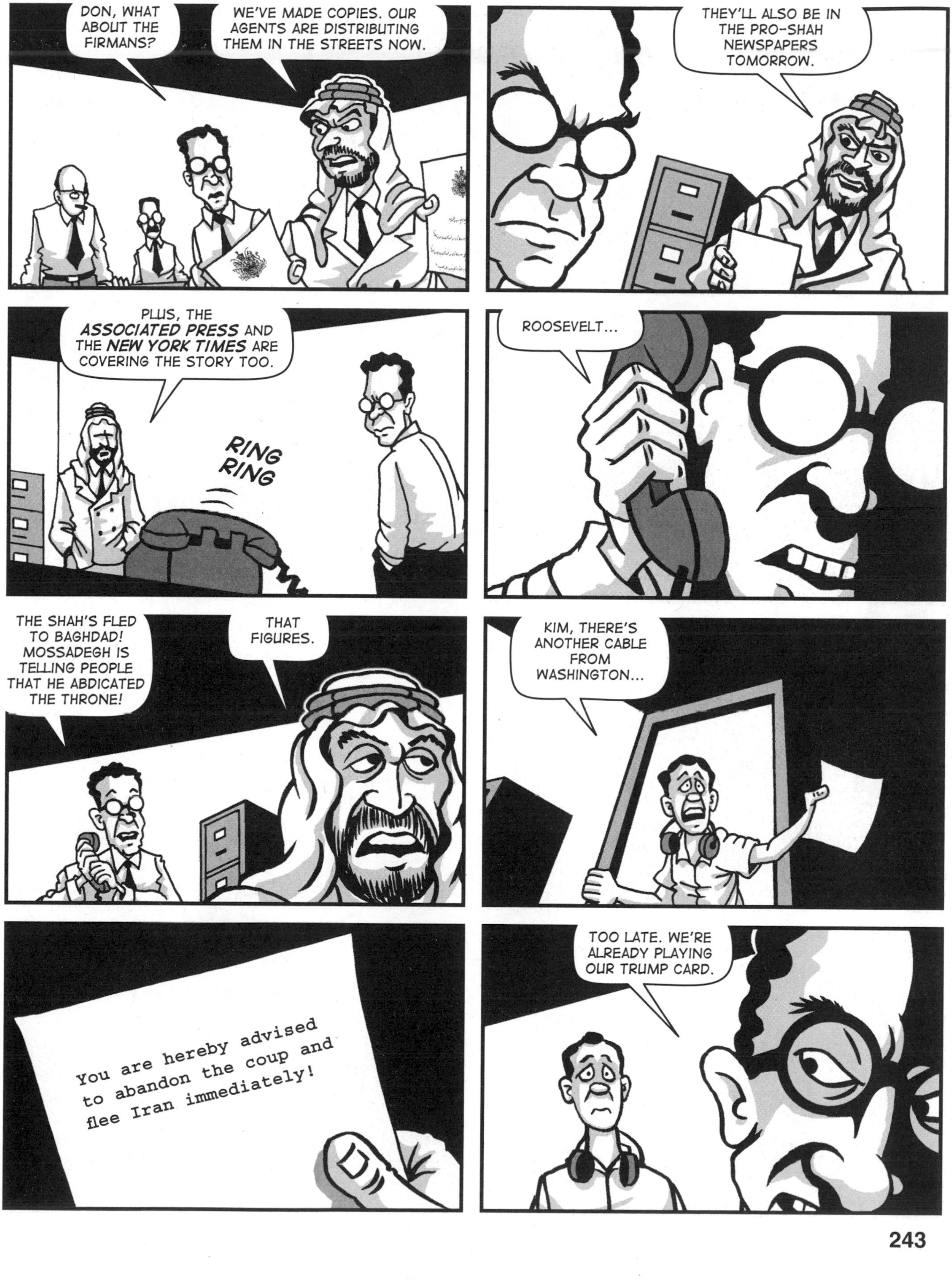
DON, WHAT ABOUT THE FIRMANS?
WE'VE MADE COPIES. OUR AGENTS ARE DISTRIBUTING THEM IN THE STREETS NOW.
THEY'LL ALSO BE IN THE PRO-SHAH NEWSPAPERS TOMORROW.
PLUS, THE ***ASSOCIATED PRESS*** AND THE ***NEW YORK TIMES*** ARE COVERING THE STORY TOO.
RING RING
ROOSEVELT...
THE SHAH'S FLED TO BAGHDAD! MOSSADEGH IS TELLING PEOPLE THAT HE ABDICATED THE THRONE!
THAT FIGURES.
KIM, THERE'S ANOTHER CABLE FROM WASHINGTON...
You are hereby advised to abandon the coup and flee Iran immediately!
TOO LATE. WE'RE ALREADY PLAYING OUR TRUMP CARD.

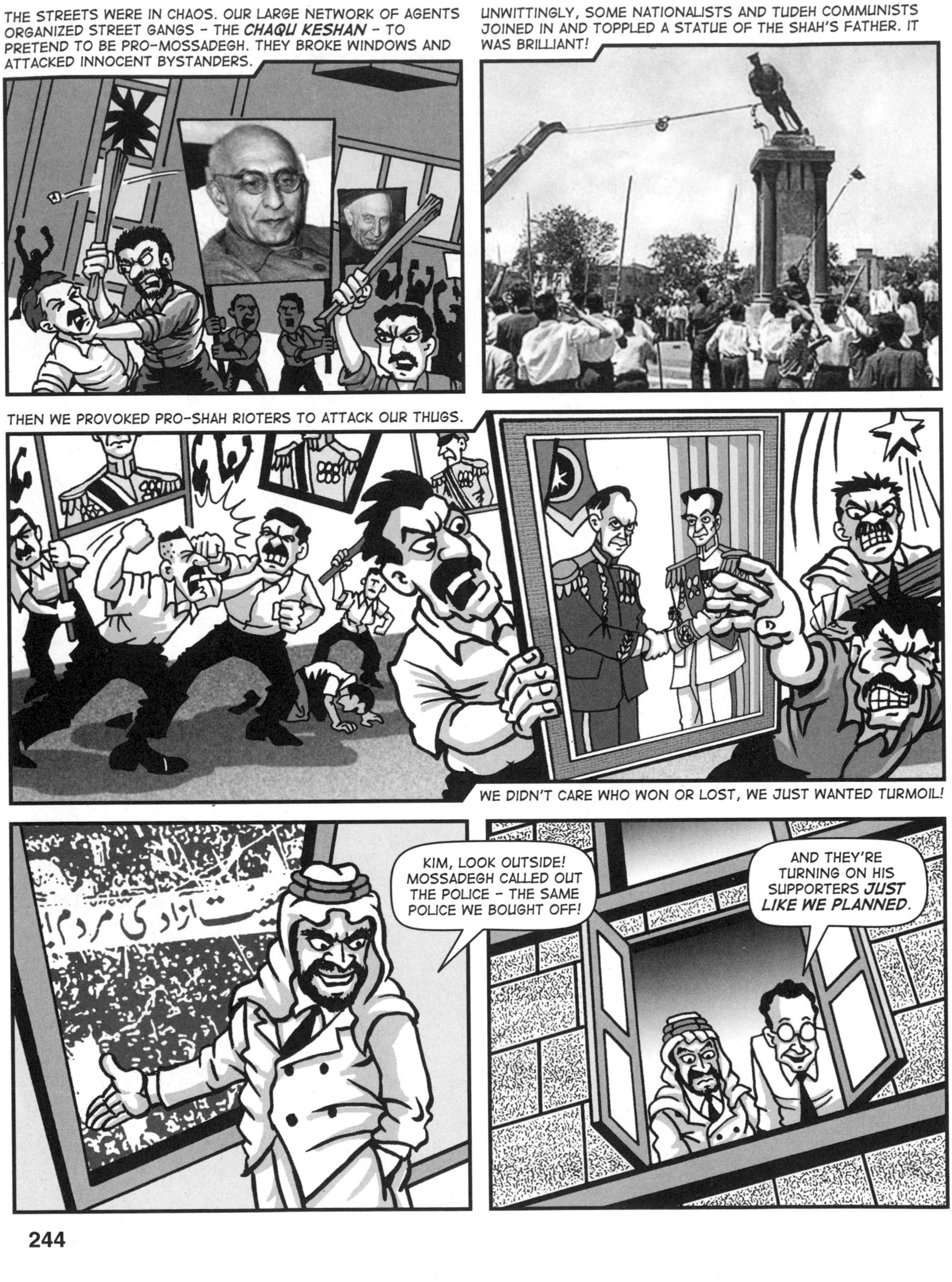
THE STREETS WERE IN CHAOS. OUR LARGE NETWORK OF AGENTS ORGANIZED STREET GANGS – THE ***CHAQU KESHAN*** – TO PRETEND TO BE PRO-MOSSADEGH. THEY BROKE WINDOWS AND ATTACKED INNOCENT BYSTANDERS.
UNWITTINGLY, SOME NATIONALISTS AND TUDEH COMMUNISTS JOINED IN AND TOPPLED A STATUE OF THE SHAH'S FATHER. IT WAS BRILLIANT!
THEN WE PROVOKED PRO-SHAH RIOTERS TO ATTACK OUR THUGS.
WE DIDN'T CARE WHO WON OR LOST, WE JUST WANTED TURMOIL!
KIM, LOOK OUTSIDE! MOSSADEGH CALLED OUT THE POLICE – THE SAME POLICE WE BOUGHT OFF!
AND THEY'RE TURNING ON HIS SUPPORTERS ***JUST LIKE WE PLANNED***.

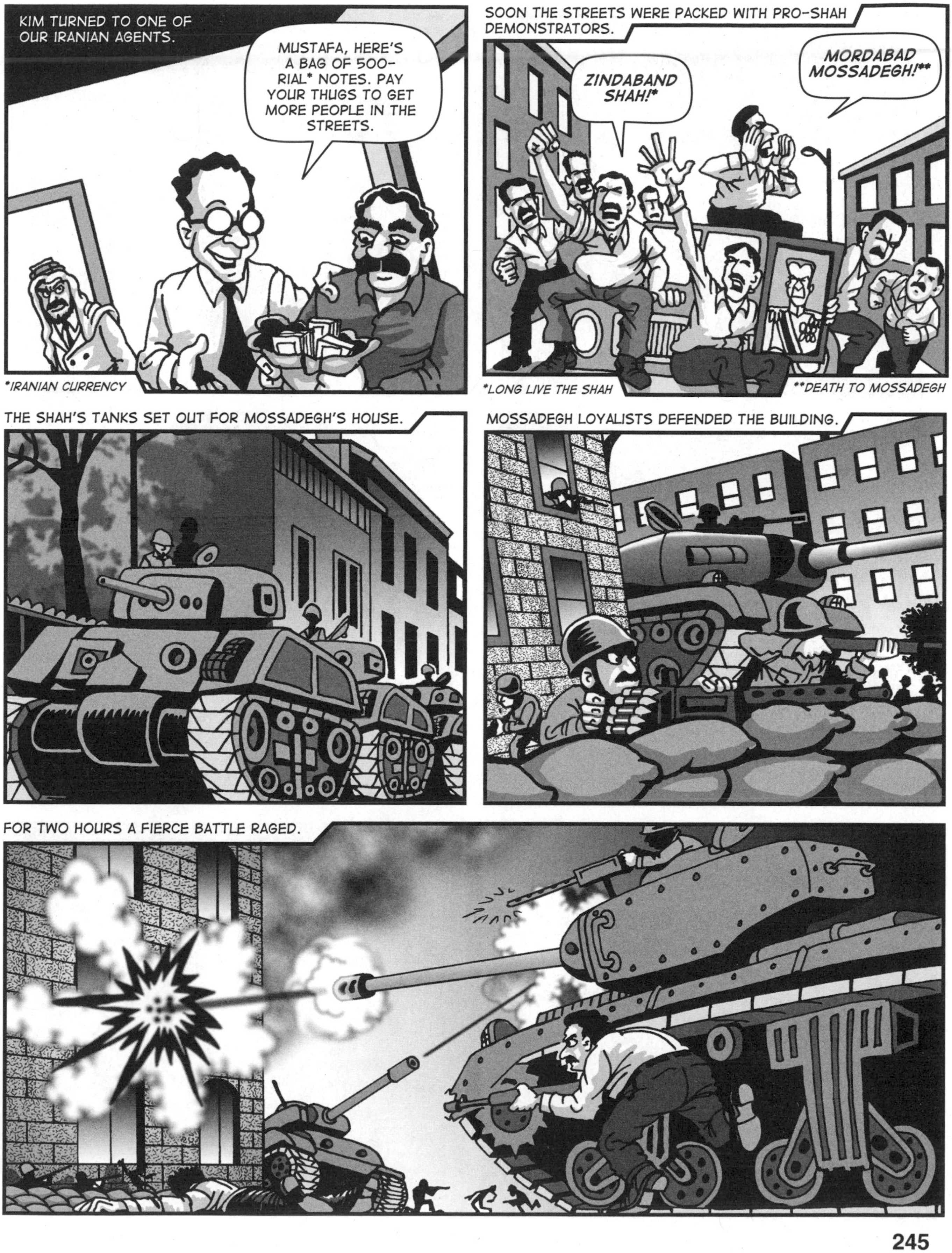
KIM TURNED TO ONE OF OUR IRANIAN AGENTS.
MUSTAFA, HERE'S A BAG OF 500-RIAL* NOTES. PAY YOUR THUGS TO GET MORE PEOPLE IN THE STREETS.
*IRANIAN CURRENCY
SOON THE STREETS WERE PACKED WITH PRO-SHAH DEMONSTRATORS.
ZINDABAND SHAH!*
MORDABAD MOSSADEGH!**
*LONG LIVE THE SHAH
**DEATH TO MOSSADEGH
THE SHAH'S TANKS SET OUT FOR MOSSADEGH'S HOUSE.
MOSSADEGH LOYALISTS DEFENDED THE BUILDING.
FOR TWO HOURS A FIERCE BATTLE RAGED.

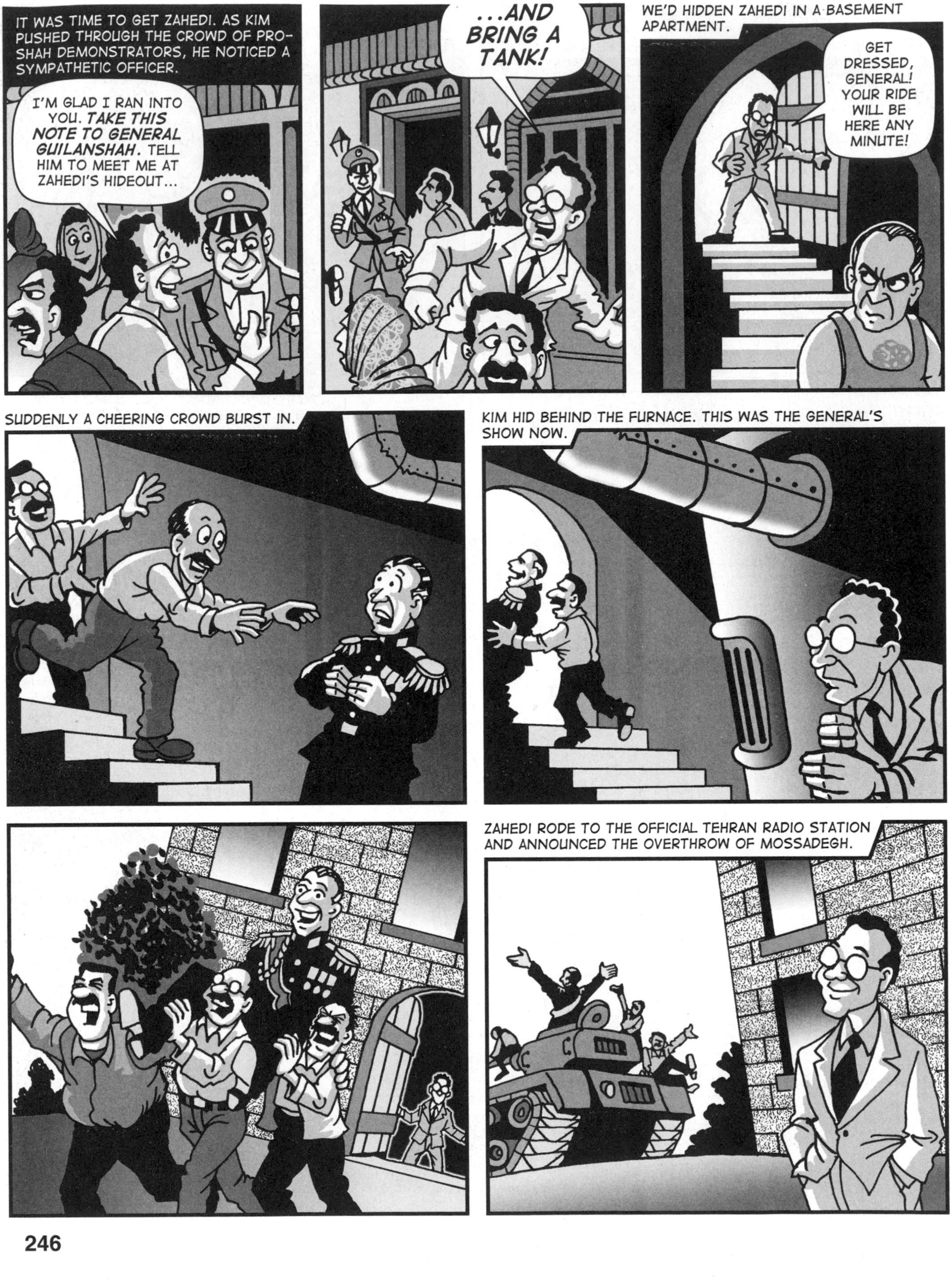
IT WAS TIME TO GET ZAHEDI. AS KIM PUSHED THROUGH THE CROWD OF PRO-SHAH DEMONSTRATORS, HE NOTICED A SYMPATHETIC OFFICER.
I'M GLAD I RAN INTO YOU. TAKE THIS NOTE TO GENERAL GUILANSHAH. TELL HIM TO MEET ME AT ZAHEDI'S HIDEOUT...
...AND BRING A TANK!
WE'D HIDDEN ZAHEDI IN A BASEMENT APARTMENT.
GET DRESSED, GENERAL! YOUR RIDE WILL BE HERE ANY MINUTE!
SUDDENLY A CHEERING CROWD BURST IN.
KIM HID BEHIND THE FURNACE. THIS WAS THE GENERAL'S SHOW NOW.
ZAHEDI RODE TO THE OFFICIAL TEHRAN RADIO STATION AND ANNOUNCED THE OVERTHROW OF MOSSADEGH.

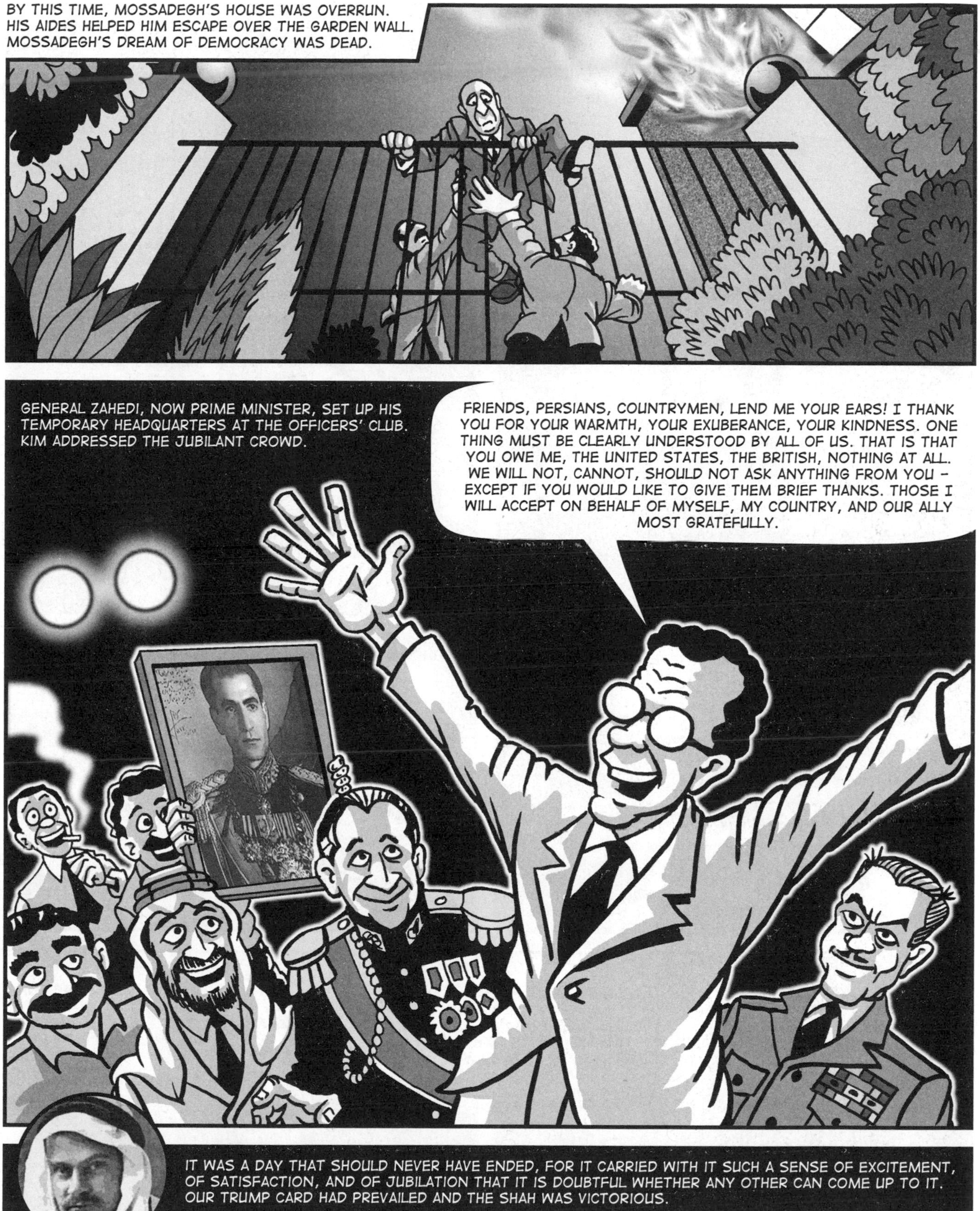
BY THIS TIME, MOSSADEGH'S HOUSE WAS OVERRUN.
HIS AIDES HELPED HIM ESCAPE OVER THE GARDEN WALL.
MOSSADEGH'S DREAM OF DEMOCRACY WAS DEAD.
GENERAL ZAHEDI, NOW PRIME MINISTER, SET UP HIS TEMPORARY HEADQUARTERS AT THE OFFICERS' CLUB. KIM ADDRESSED THE JUBILANT CROWD.
FRIENDS, PERSIANS, COUNTRYMEN, LEND ME YOUR EARS! I THANK YOU FOR YOUR WARMTH, YOUR EXUBERANCE, YOUR KINDNESS. ONE THING MUST BE CLEARLY UNDERSTOOD BY ALL OF US. THAT IS THAT YOU OWE ME, THE UNITED STATES, THE BRITISH, NOTHING AT ALL. WE WILL NOT, CANNOT, SHOULD NOT ASK ANYTHING FROM YOU - EXCEPT IF YOU WOULD LIKE TO GIVE THEM BRIEF THANKS. THOSE I WILL ACCEPT ON BEHALF OF MYSELF, MY COUNTRY, AND OUR ALLY MOST GRATEFULLY.
IT WAS A DAY THAT SHOULD NEVER HAVE ENDED, FOR IT CARRIED WITH IT SUCH A SENSE OF EXCITEMENT, OF SATISFACTION, AND OF JUBILATION THAT IT IS DOUBTFUL WHETHER ANY OTHER CAN COME UP TO IT. OUR TRUMP CARD HAD PREVAILED AND THE SHAH WAS VICTORIOUS.

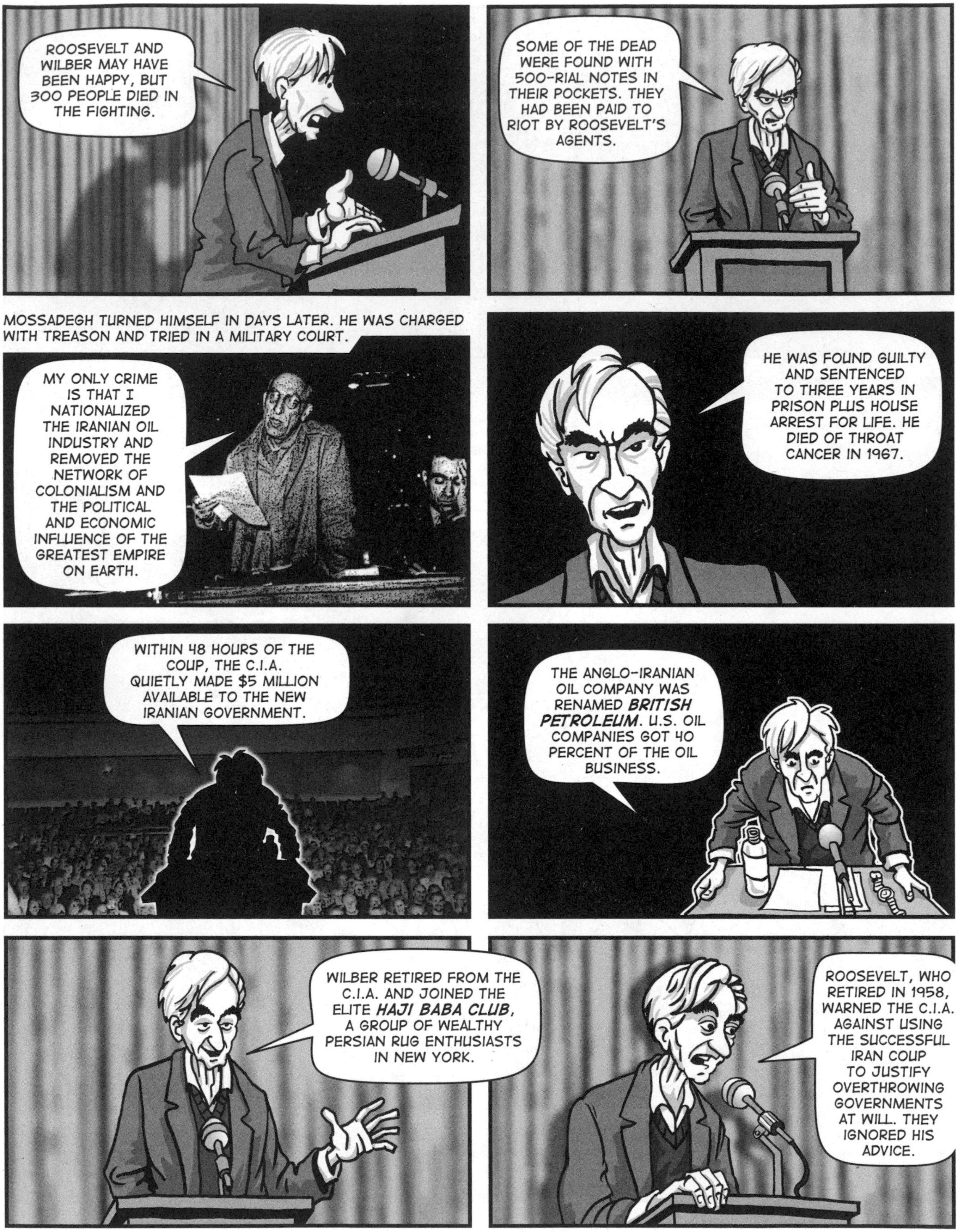
ROOSEVELT AND WILBER MAY HAVE BEEN HAPPY, BUT 300 PEOPLE DIED IN THE FIGHTING.
SOME OF THE DEAD WERE FOUND WITH 500-RIAL NOTES IN THEIR POCKETS. THEY HAD BEEN PAID TO RIOT BY ROOSEVELT'S AGENTS.
MOSSADEGH TURNED HIMSELF IN DAYS LATER. HE WAS CHARGED WITH TREASON AND TRIED IN A MILITARY COURT.
MY ONLY CRIME IS THAT I NATIONALIZED THE IRANIAN OIL INDUSTRY AND REMOVED THE NETWORK OF COLONIALISM AND THE POLITICAL AND ECONOMIC INFLUENCE OF THE GREATEST EMPIRE ON EARTH.
HE WAS FOUND GUILTY AND SENTENCED TO THREE YEARS IN PRISON PLUS HOUSE ARREST FOR LIFE. HE DIED OF THROAT CANCER IN 1967.
WITHIN 48 HOURS OF THE COUP, THE C.I.A. QUIETLY MADE $5 MILLION AVAILABLE TO THE NEW IRANIAN GOVERNMENT.
THE ANGLO-IRANIAN OIL COMPANY WAS RENAMED ***BRITISH PETROLEUM***. U.S. OIL COMPANIES GOT 40 PERCENT OF THE OIL BUSINESS.
WILBER RETIRED FROM THE C.I.A. AND JOINED THE ELITE ***HAJI BABA CLUB***, A GROUP OF WEALTHY PERSIAN RUG ENTHUSIASTS IN NEW YORK.
ROOSEVELT, WHO RETIRED IN 1958, WARNED THE C.I.A. AGAINST USING THE SUCCESSFUL IRAN COUP TO JUSTIFY OVERTHROWING GOVERNMENTS AT WILL. THEY IGNORED HIS ADVICE.

Rule and Ruin of the Shah

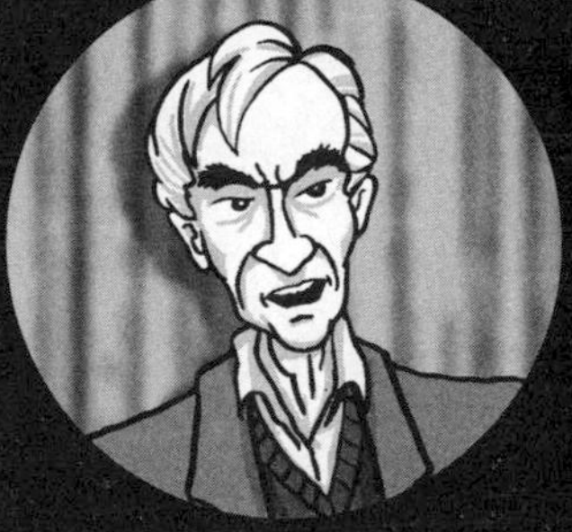

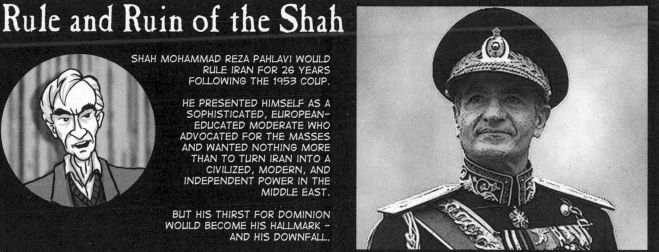

SHAH MOHAMMAD REZA PAHLAVI WOULD RULE IRAN FOR 26 YEARS FOLLOWING THE 1953 COUP.

HE PRESENTED HIMSELF AS A SOPHISTICATED, EUROPEAN-EDUCATED MODERATE WHO ADVOCATED FOR THE MASSES AND WANTED NOTHING MORE THAN TO TURN IRAN INTO A CIVILIZED, MODERN, AND INDEPENDENT POWER IN THE MIDDLE EAST.

BUT HIS THIRST FOR DOMINION WOULD BECOME HIS HALLMARK – AND HIS DOWNFALL.

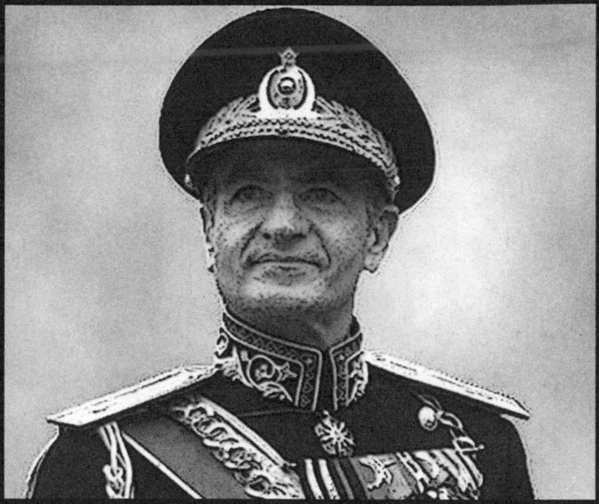

THE SHAH RETURNED TO IRAN WITH A VENGEANCE. HE OVERSAW THE ARREST OF 600 MILITARY OFFICERS LOYAL TO MOSSADEGH (60 WERE SHOT TO DEATH) AND THE EXECUTION OF SEVERAL STUDENT LEADERS. LEADING SUPPORTERS OF THE TUDEH AND NATIONAL PARTIES WERE IMPRISONED OR KILLED; BOTH PARTIES WERE BANNED.

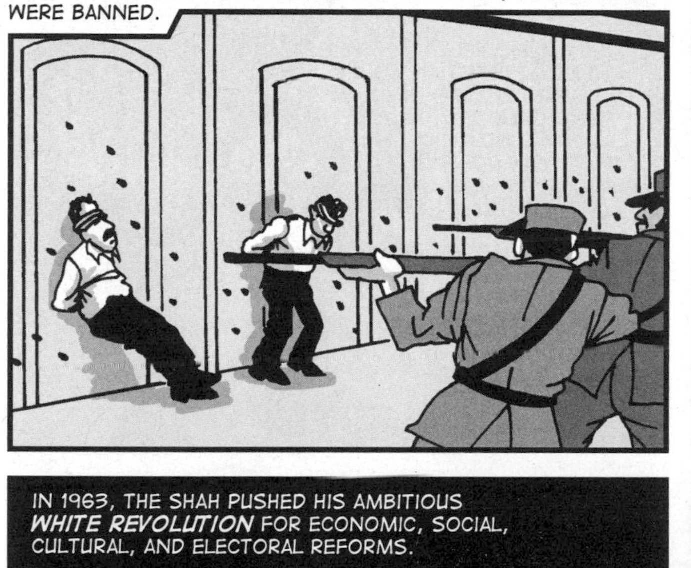

HE RAN THROUGH A STRING OF PRIME MINISTERS (GENERAL ZAHEDI LASTED ONLY TWO YEARS), INCREASING HIS OWN POWER IN THE PROCESS. THE MAJLIS TOOK NOTICE AND BECAME LITTLE MORE THAN A RUBBER STAMP FOR THE SHAH'S AGENDA.

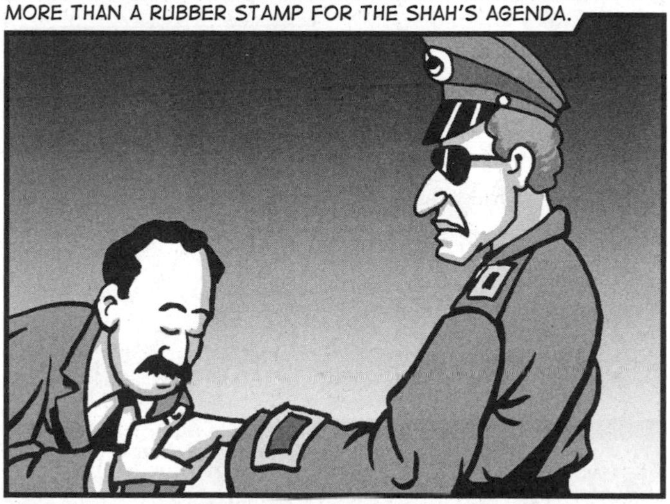

IN 1963, THE SHAH PUSHED HIS AMBITIOUS ***WHITE REVOLUTION*** FOR ECONOMIC, SOCIAL, CULTURAL, AND ELECTORAL REFORMS.

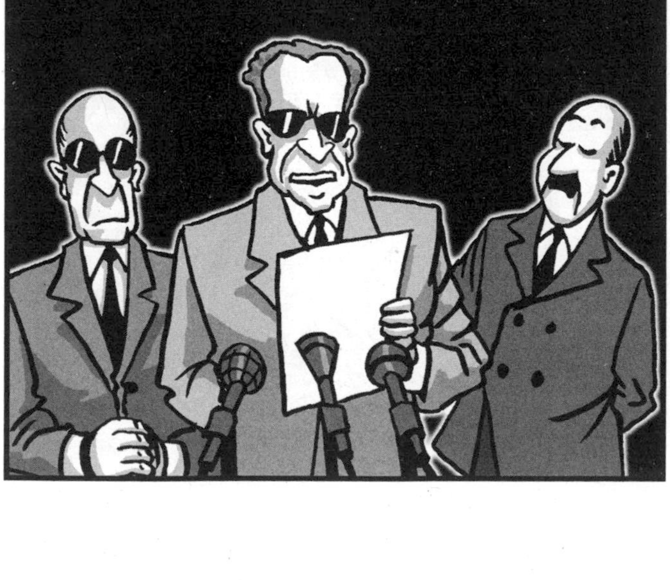

THE WHITE REVOLUTION INFURIATED ***MUSLIM CLERICS***.

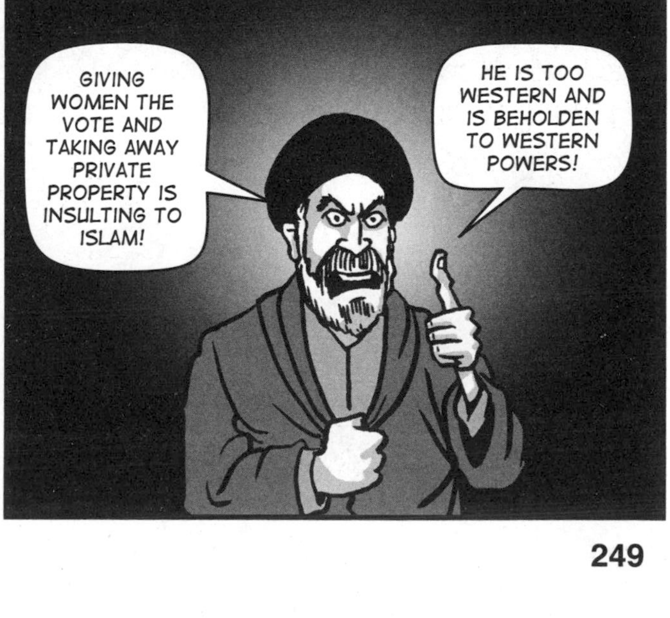
GIVING WOMEN THE VOTE AND TAKING AWAY PRIVATE PROPERTY IS INSULTING TO ISLAM!
HE IS TOO WESTERN AND IS BEHOLDEN TO WESTERN POWERS!

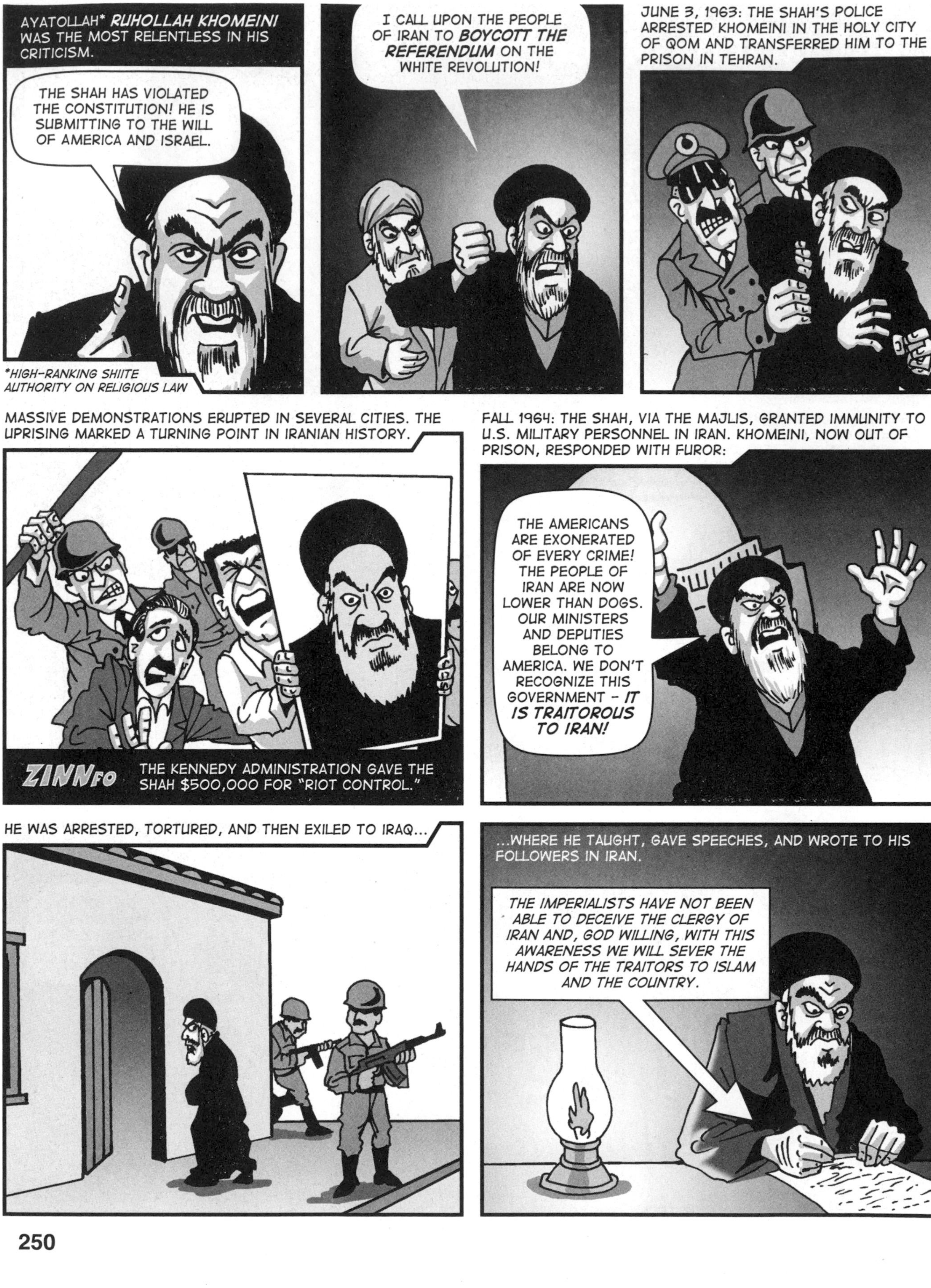
AYATOLLAH* RUHOLLAH KHOMEINI WAS THE MOST RELENTLESS IN HIS CRITICISM.
THE SHAH HAS VIOLATED THE CONSTITUTION! HE IS SUBMITTING TO THE WILL OF AMERICA AND ISRAEL.
*HIGH-RANKING SHIITE AUTHORITY ON RELIGIOUS LAW
I CALL UPON THE PEOPLE OF IRAN TO BOYCOTT THE REFERENDUM ON THE WHITE REVOLUTION!
JUNE 3, 1963: THE SHAH'S POLICE ARRESTED KHOMEINI IN THE HOLY CITY OF QOM AND TRANSFERRED HIM TO THE PRISON IN TEHRAN.
MASSIVE DEMONSTRATIONS ERUPTED IN SEVERAL CITIES. THE UPRISING MARKED A TURNING POINT IN IRANIAN HISTORY.
ZINNFO
THE KENNEDY ADMINISTRATION GAVE THE SHAH $500,000 FOR "RIOT CONTROL."
FALL 1964: THE SHAH, VIA THE MAJLIS, GRANTED IMMUNITY TO U.S. MILITARY PERSONNEL IN IRAN. KHOMEINI, NOW OUT OF PRISON, RESPONDED WITH FUROR:
THE AMERICANS ARE EXONERATED OF EVERY CRIME! THE PEOPLE OF IRAN ARE NOW LOWER THAN DOGS. OUR MINISTERS AND DEPUTIES BELONG TO AMERICA. WE DON'T RECOGNIZE THIS GOVERNMENT – IT IS TRAITOROUS TO IRAN!
HE WAS ARRESTED, TORTURED, AND THEN EXILED TO IRAQ...
...WHERE HE TAUGHT, GAVE SPEECHES, AND WROTE TO HIS FOLLOWERS IN IRAN.
THE IMPERIALISTS HAVE NOT BEEN ABLE TO DECEIVE THE CLERGY OF IRAN AND, GOD WILLING, WITH THIS AWARENESS WE WILL SEVER THE HANDS OF THE TRAITORS TO ISLAM AND THE COUNTRY.

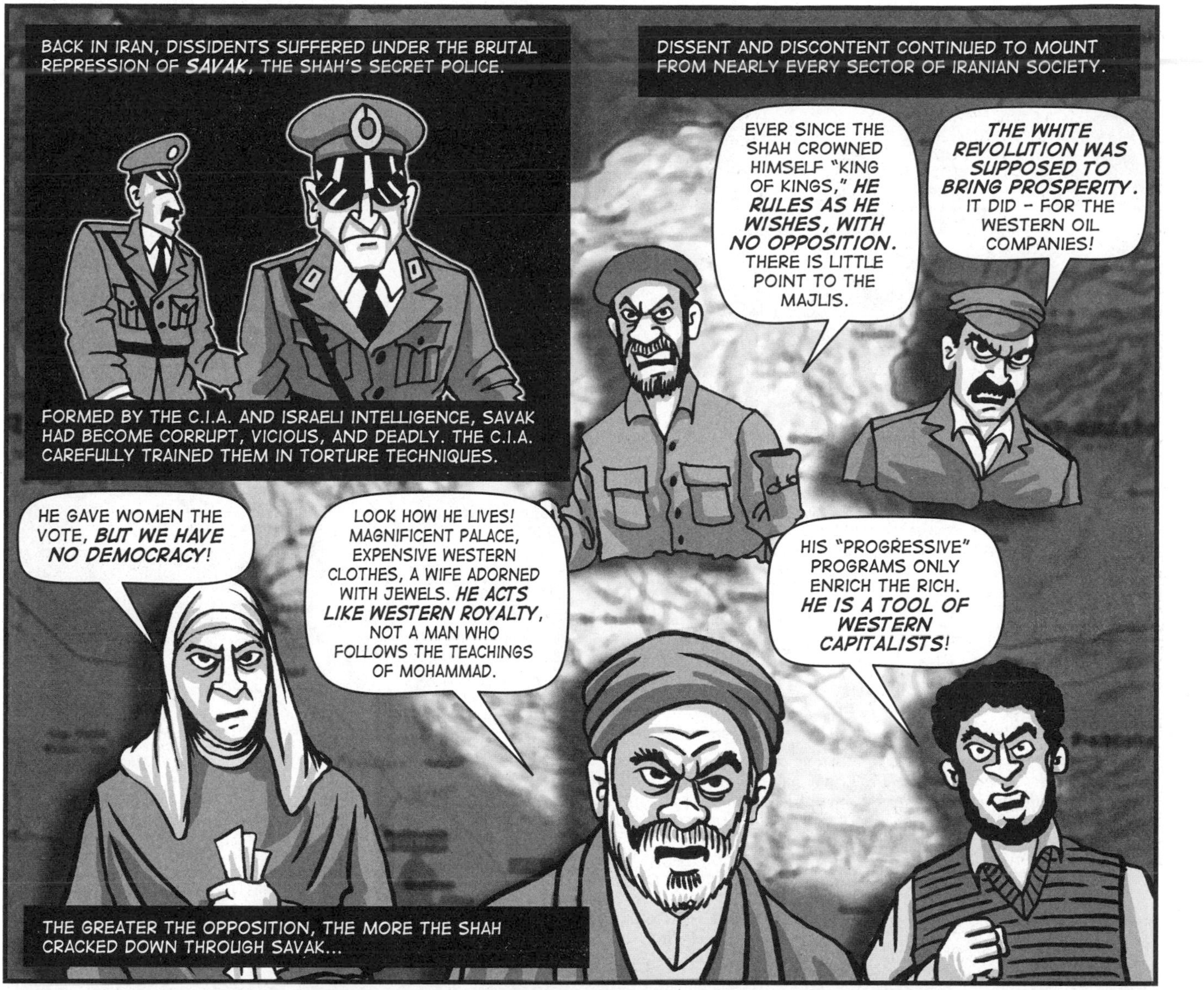

BACK IN IRAN, DISSIDENTS SUFFERED UNDER THE BRUTAL REPRESSION OF SAVAK, THE SHAH'S SECRET POLICE.
FORMED BY THE C.I.A. AND ISRAELI INTELLIGENCE, SAVAK HAD BECOME CORRUPT, VICIOUS, AND DEADLY. THE C.I.A. CAREFULLY TRAINED THEM IN TORTURE TECHNIQUES.
DISSENT AND DISCONTENT CONTINUED TO MOUNT FROM NEARLY EVERY SECTOR OF IRANIAN SOCIETY.
EVER SINCE THE SHAH CROWNED HIMSELF "KING OF KINGS," HE RULES AS HE WISHES, WITH NO OPPOSITION. THERE IS LITTLE POINT TO THE MAJLIS.
THE WHITE REVOLUTION WAS SUPPOSED TO BRING PROSPERITY. IT DID - FOR THE WESTERN OIL COMPANIES!
HE GAVE WOMEN THE VOTE, BUT WE HAVE NO DEMOCRACY!
LOOK HOW HE LIVES! MAGNIFICENT PALACE, EXPENSIVE WESTERN CLOTHES, A WIFE ADORNED WITH JEWELS. HE ACTS LIKE WESTERN ROYALTY, NOT A MAN WHO FOLLOWS THE TEACHINGS OF MOHAMMAD.
HIS "PROGRESSIVE" PROGRAMS ONLY ENRICH THE RICH. HE IS A TOOL OF WESTERN CAPITALISTS!
THE GREATER THE OPPOSITION, THE MORE THE SHAH CRACKED DOWN THROUGH SAVAK...

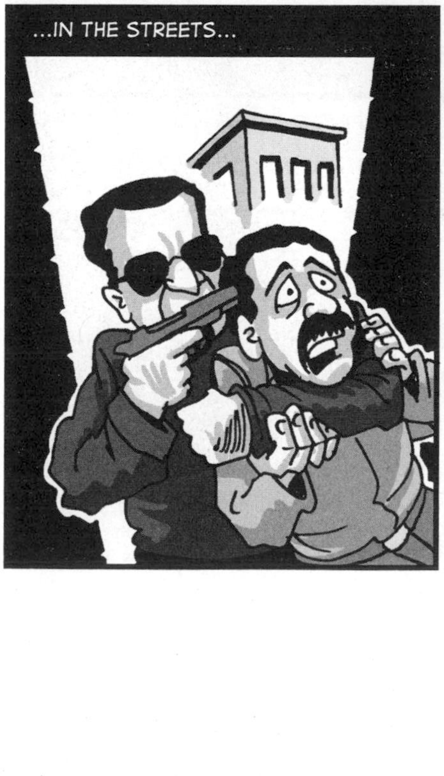

...IN THE STREETS...

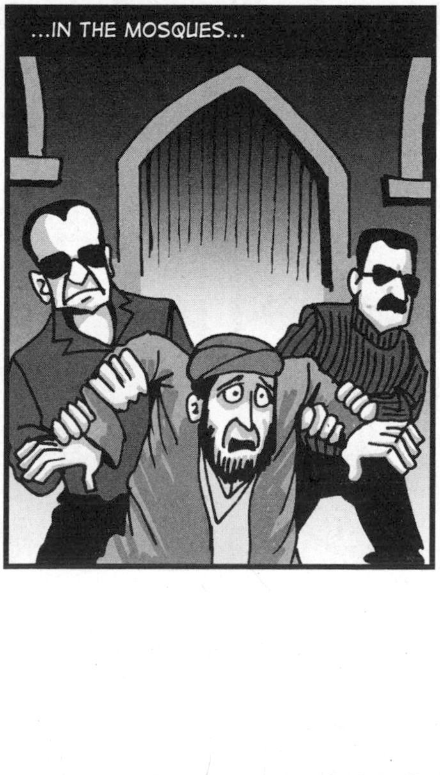

...IN THE MOSQUES...

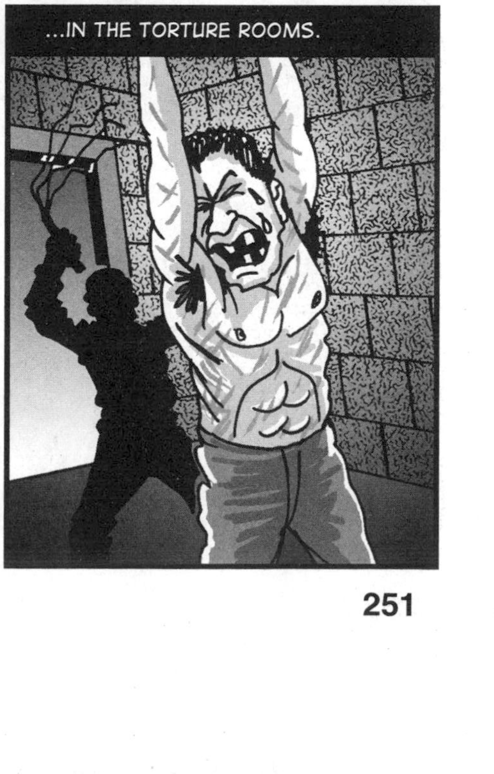

...IN THE TORTURE ROOMS.

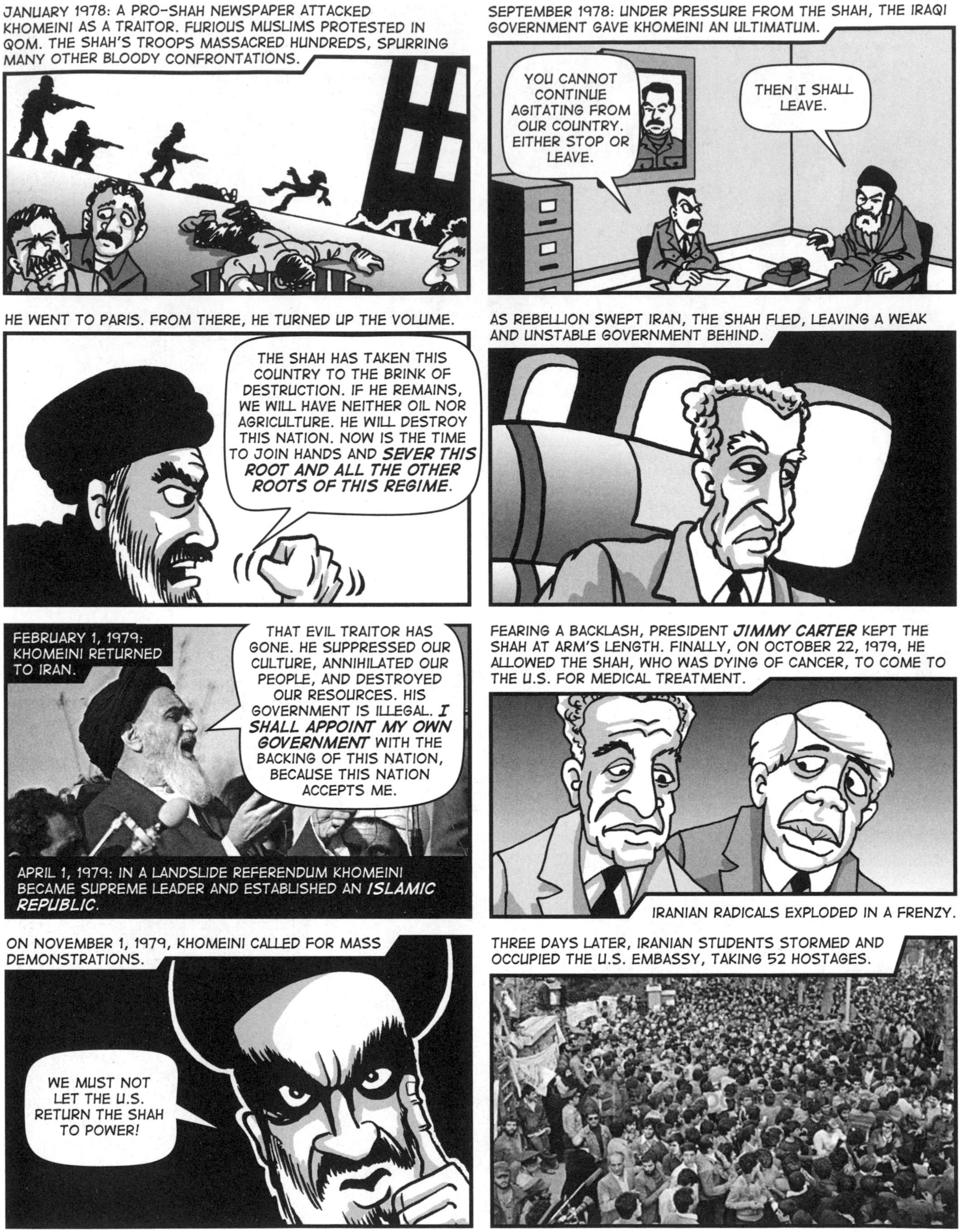
JANUARY 1978: A PRO-SHAH NEWSPAPER ATTACKED KHOMEINI AS A TRAITOR. FURIOUS MUSLIMS PROTESTED IN QOM. THE SHAH'S TROOPS MASSACRED HUNDREDS, SPURRING MANY OTHER BLOODY CONFRONTATIONS.
SEPTEMBER 1978: UNDER PRESSURE FROM THE SHAH, THE IRAQI GOVERNMENT GAVE KHOMEINI AN ULTIMATUM.
YOU CANNOT CONTINUE AGITATING FROM OUR COUNTRY. EITHER STOP OR LEAVE.
THEN I SHALL LEAVE.
HE WENT TO PARIS. FROM THERE, HE TURNED UP THE VOLUME.
THE SHAH HAS TAKEN THIS COUNTRY TO THE BRINK OF DESTRUCTION. IF HE REMAINS, WE WILL HAVE NEITHER OIL NOR AGRICULTURE. HE WILL DESTROY THIS NATION. NOW IS THE TIME TO JOIN HANDS AND *SEVER THIS ROOT AND ALL THE OTHER ROOTS OF THIS REGIME*.
AS REBELLION SWEPT IRAN, THE SHAH FLED, LEAVING A WEAK AND UNSTABLE GOVERNMENT BEHIND.
FEBRUARY 1, 1979: KHOMEINI RETURNED TO IRAN.
THAT EVIL TRAITOR HAS GONE. HE SUPPRESSED OUR CULTURE, ANNIHILATED OUR PEOPLE, AND DESTROYED OUR RESOURCES. HIS GOVERNMENT IS ILLEGAL. *I SHALL APPOINT MY OWN GOVERNMENT* WITH THE BACKING OF THIS NATION, BECAUSE THIS NATION ACCEPTS ME.
APRIL 1, 1979: IN A LANDSLIDE REFERENDUM KHOMEINI BECAME SUPREME LEADER AND ESTABLISHED AN *ISLAMIC REPUBLIC*.
FEARING A BACKLASH, PRESIDENT *JIMMY CARTER* KEPT THE SHAH AT ARM'S LENGTH. FINALLY, ON OCTOBER 22, 1979, HE ALLOWED THE SHAH, WHO WAS DYING OF CANCER, TO COME TO THE U.S. FOR MEDICAL TREATMENT.
IRANIAN RADICALS EXPLODED IN A FRENZY.
ON NOVEMBER 1, 1979, KHOMEINI CALLED FOR MASS DEMONSTRATIONS.
WE MUST NOT LET THE U.S. RETURN THE SHAH TO POWER!
THREE DAYS LATER, IRANIAN STUDENTS STORMED AND OCCUPIED THE U.S. EMBASSY, TAKING 52 HOSTAGES.

THE HOSTAGE TAKERS REMEMBERED THEIR HISTORY.

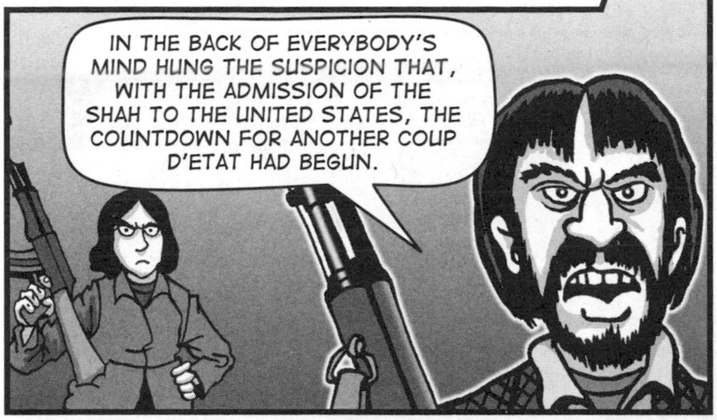
IN THE BACK OF EVERYBODY'S MIND HUNG THE SUSPICION THAT, WITH THE ADMISSION OF THE SHAH TO THE UNITED STATES, THE COUNTDOWN FOR ANOTHER COUP D'ETAT HAD BEGUN.

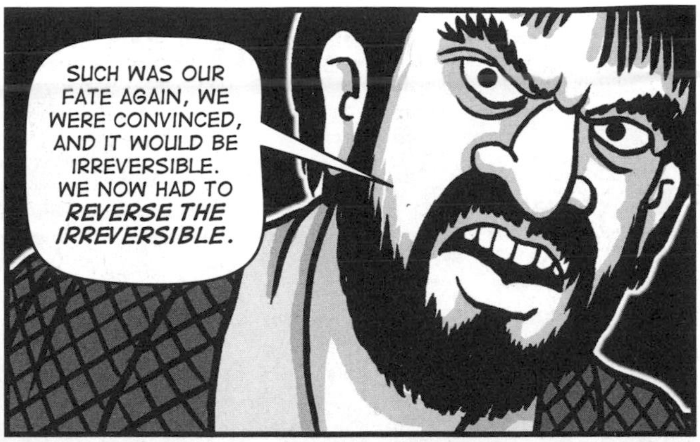
SUCH WAS OUR FATE AGAIN, WE WERE CONVINCED, AND IT WOULD BE IRREVERSIBLE. WE NOW HAD TO ***REVERSE THE IRREVERSIBLE***.

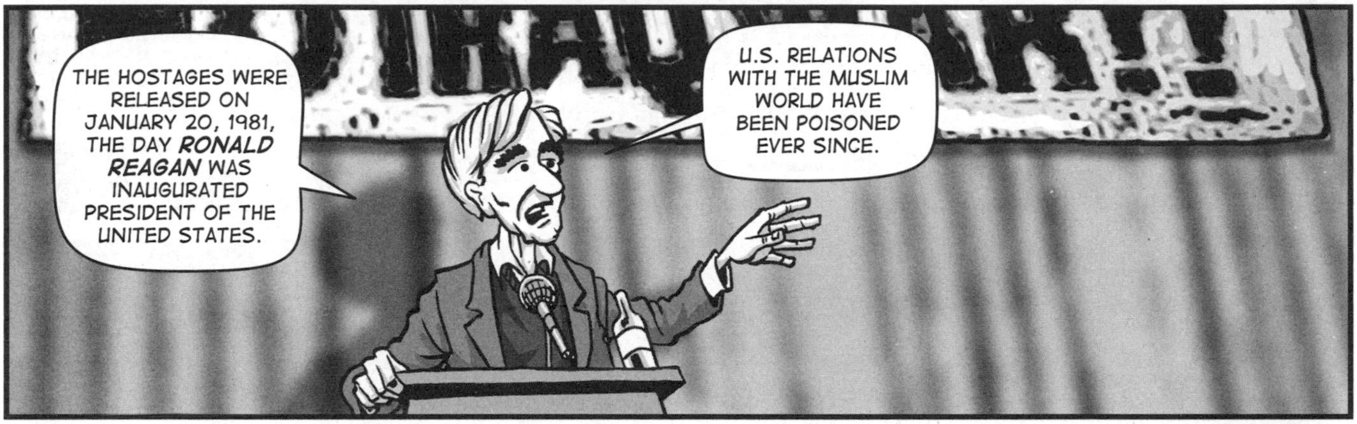
THE HOSTAGES WERE RELEASED ON JANUARY 20, 1981, THE DAY ***RONALD REAGAN*** WAS INAUGURATED PRESIDENT OF THE UNITED STATES.
U.S. RELATIONS WITH THE MUSLIM WORLD HAVE BEEN POISONED EVER SINCE.

ONE WONDERS: WHAT WOULD IRAN BE LIKE TODAY IF MOSSADEGH'S DREAM OF DEMOCRACY HAD COME TRUE?

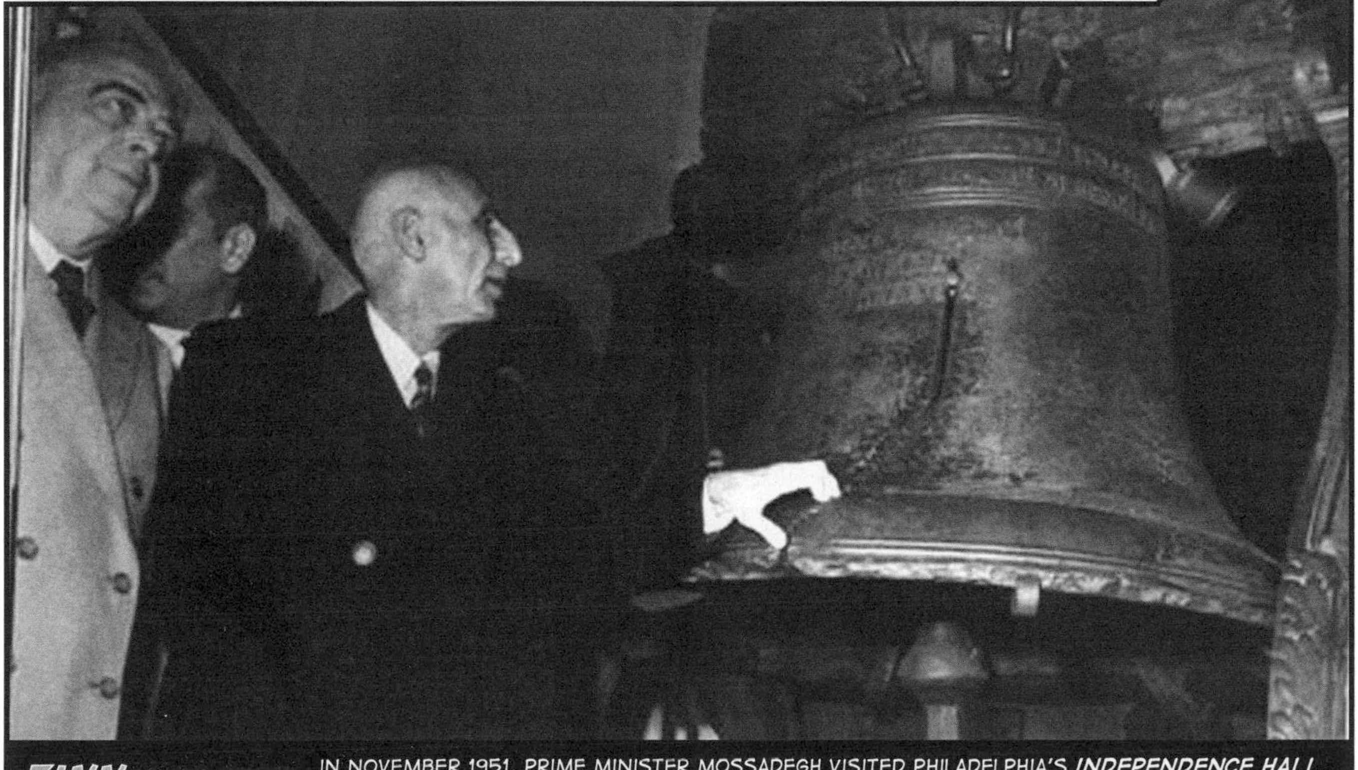

ZINNFORMATION IN NOVEMBER 1951, PRIME MINISTER MOSSADEGH VISITED PHILADELPHIA'S ***INDEPENDENCE HALL***. HERE HE IS SEEN EXAMINING THE ***LIBERTY BELL*** WITH MAYOR ***BERNARD SAMUEL***.

Permanent War: The Bipartisan Consensus

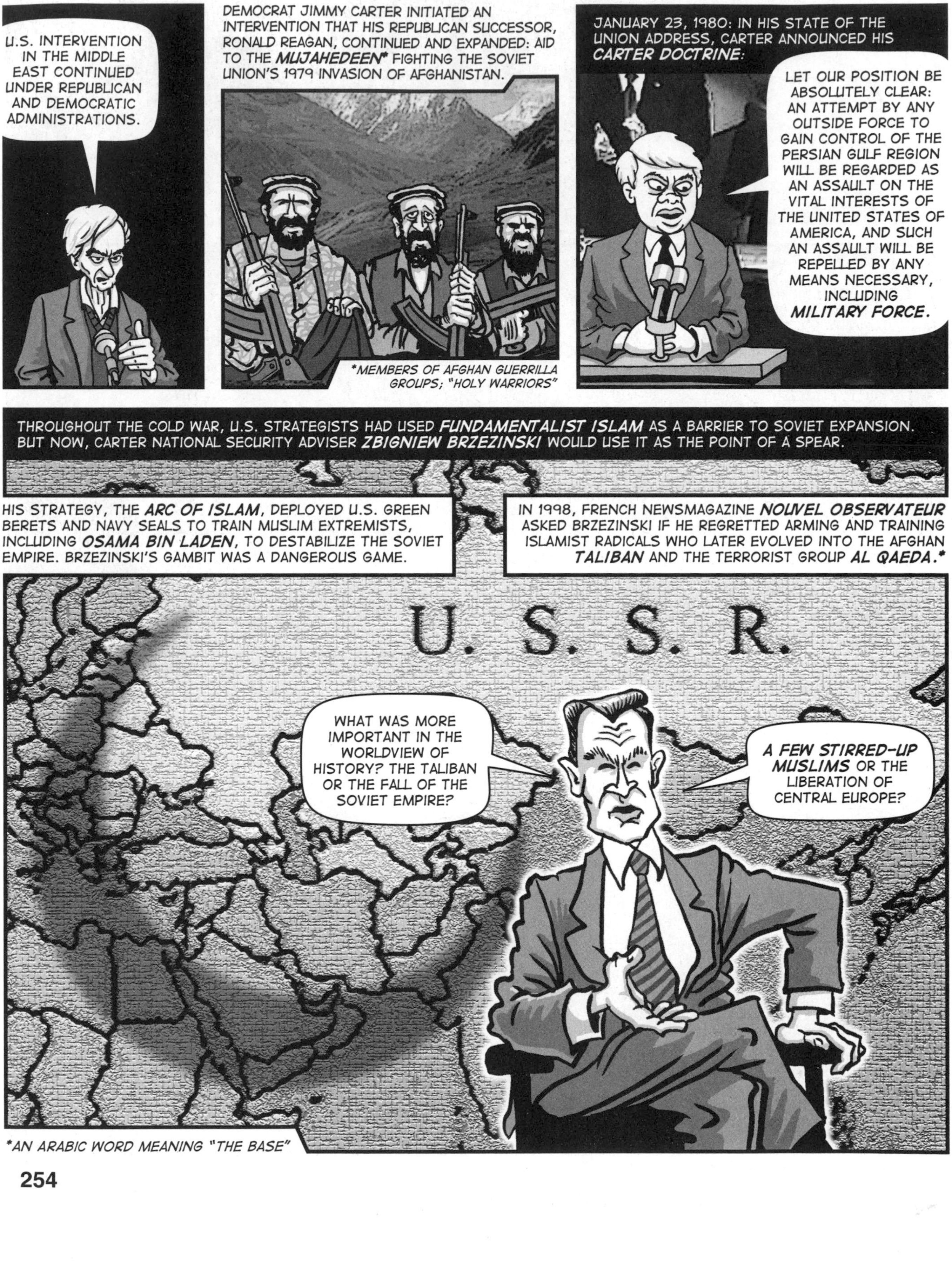
U.S. INTERVENTION IN THE MIDDLE EAST CONTINUED UNDER REPUBLICAN AND DEMOCRATIC ADMINISTRATIONS.
DEMOCRAT JIMMY CARTER INITIATED AN INTERVENTION THAT HIS REPUBLICAN SUCCESSOR, RONALD REAGAN, CONTINUED AND EXPANDED: AID TO THE MUJAHEDEEN* FIGHTING THE SOVIET UNION'S 1979 INVASION OF AFGHANISTAN.
*MEMBERS OF AFGHAN GUERRILLA GROUPS; "HOLY WARRIORS"
JANUARY 23, 1980: IN HIS STATE OF THE UNION ADDRESS, CARTER ANNOUNCED HIS CARTER DOCTRINE:
LET OUR POSITION BE ABSOLUTELY CLEAR: AN ATTEMPT BY ANY OUTSIDE FORCE TO GAIN CONTROL OF THE PERSIAN GULF REGION WILL BE REGARDED AS AN ASSAULT ON THE VITAL INTERESTS OF THE UNITED STATES OF AMERICA, AND SUCH AN ASSAULT WILL BE REPELLED BY ANY MEANS NECESSARY, INCLUDING MILITARY FORCE.
THROUGHOUT THE COLD WAR, U.S. STRATEGISTS HAD USED FUNDAMENTALIST ISLAM AS A BARRIER TO SOVIET EXPANSION. BUT NOW, CARTER NATIONAL SECURITY ADVISER ZBIGNIEW BRZEZINSKI WOULD USE IT AS THE POINT OF A SPEAR.
HIS STRATEGY, THE ARC OF ISLAM, DEPLOYED U.S. GREEN BERETS AND NAVY SEALS TO TRAIN MUSLIM EXTREMISTS, INCLUDING OSAMA BIN LADEN, TO DESTABILIZE THE SOVIET EMPIRE. BRZEZINSKI'S GAMBIT WAS A DANGEROUS GAME.
IN 1998, FRENCH NEWSMAGAZINE NOUVEL OBSERVATEUR ASKED BRZEZINSKI IF HE REGRETTED ARMING AND TRAINING ISLAMIST RADICALS WHO LATER EVOLVED INTO THE AFGHAN TALIBAN AND THE TERRORIST GROUP AL QAEDA.*
U. S. S. R.
WHAT WAS MORE IMPORTANT IN THE WORLDVIEW OF HISTORY? THE TALIBAN OR THE FALL OF THE SOVIET EMPIRE?
A FEW STIRRED-UP MUSLIMS OR THE LIBERATION OF CENTRAL EUROPE?
*AN ARABIC WORD MEANING "THE BASE"

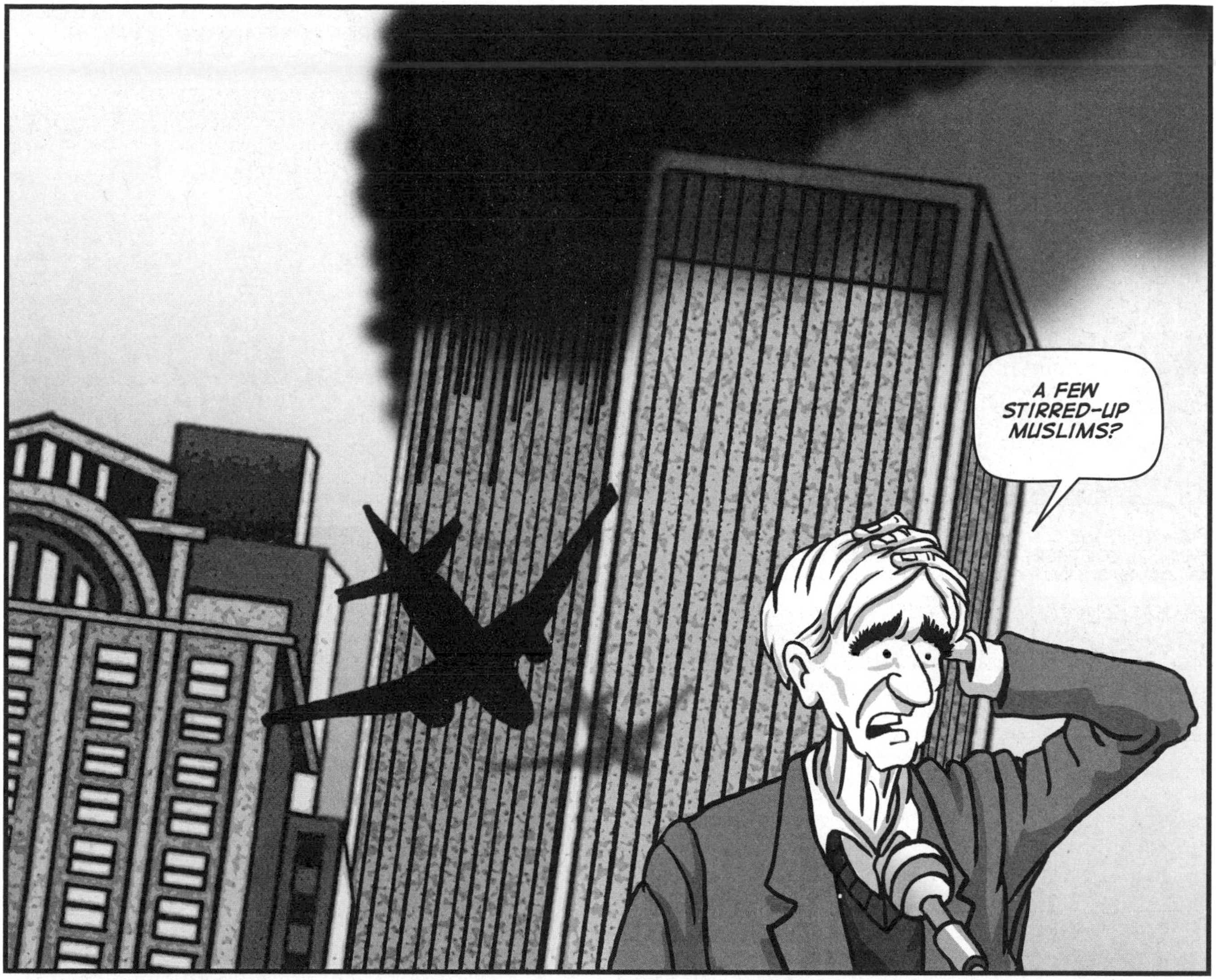
A FEW STIRRED-UP MUSLIMS?

WHEN REAGAN BECAME PRESIDENT, AMERICAN INTERVENTION IN THE MIDDLE EAST ESCALATED. DIRECTLY AND THROUGH PROXIES, THE U.S. PROVIDED WEAPONS TO BOTH COUNTRIES IN THE IRAN-IRAQ WAR.

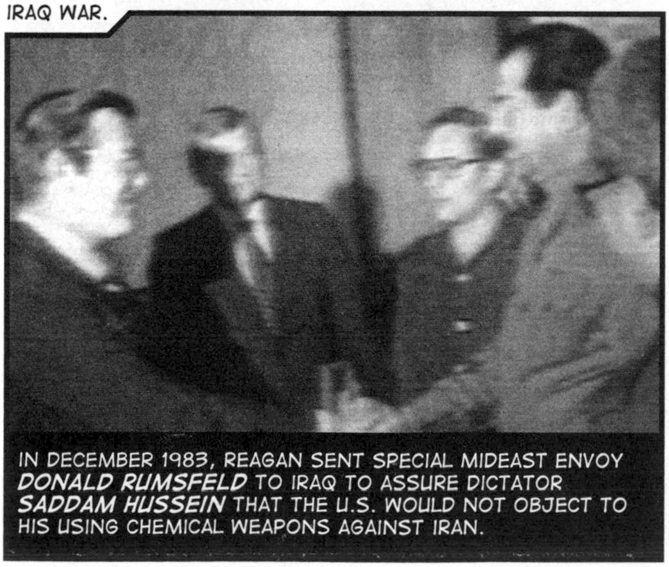
IN DECEMBER 1983, REAGAN SENT SPECIAL MIDEAST ENVOY ***DONALD RUMSFELD*** TO IRAQ TO ASSURE DICTATOR ***SADDAM HUSSEIN*** THAT THE U.S. WOULD NOT OBJECT TO HIS USING CHEMICAL WEAPONS AGAINST IRAN.

THE WAR ENDED IN 1988 WITH UP TO 1.5 MILLION DEAD.

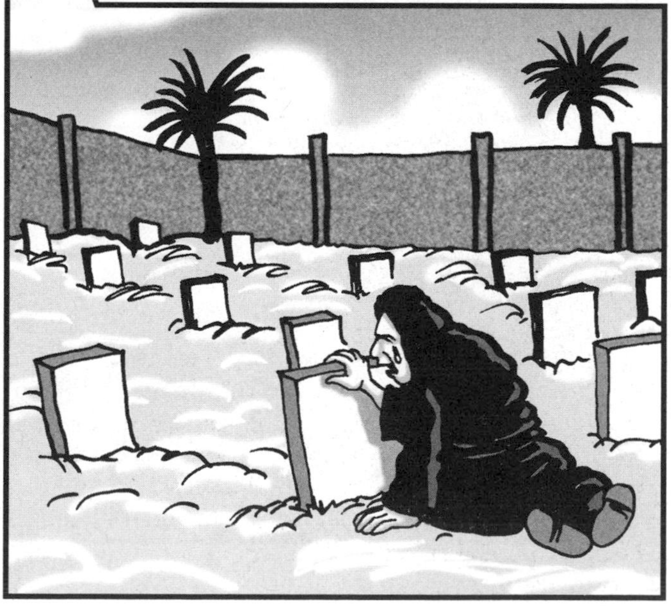

REAGAN ALSO BEEFED UP SUPPORT FOR THE MUJAHEDEEN IN AFGHANISTAN WITH MORE FUNDS - AND C.I.A. TRAINING.

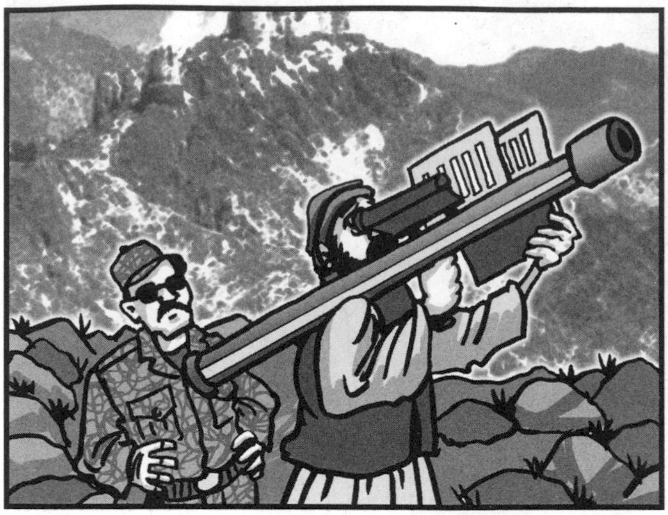

BETWEEN 1982 AND 1992, MORE THAN 35,000 MUSLIM RADICALS FROM 43 ISLAMIC COUNTRIES POURED INTO AFGHANISTAN.

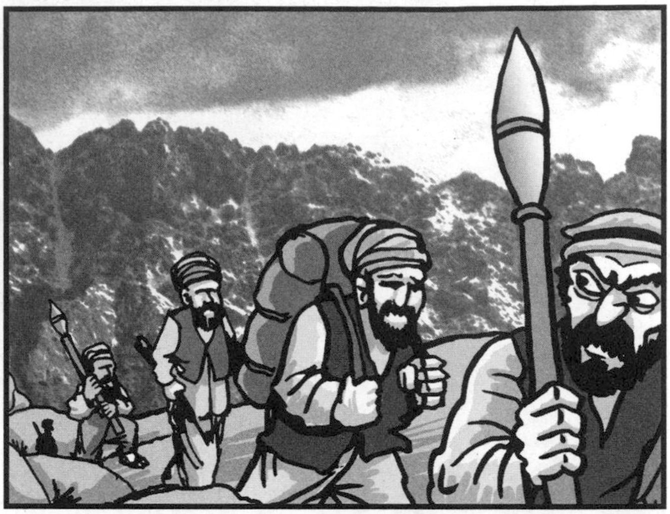

1989: THE LAST SOVIET SOLDIER LEFT AFGHANISTAN. SOME MUJAHEDEEN REGROUPED AS AL QAEDA, LED BY ITS FOUNDER AND BENEFACTOR, OSAMA BIN LADEN.

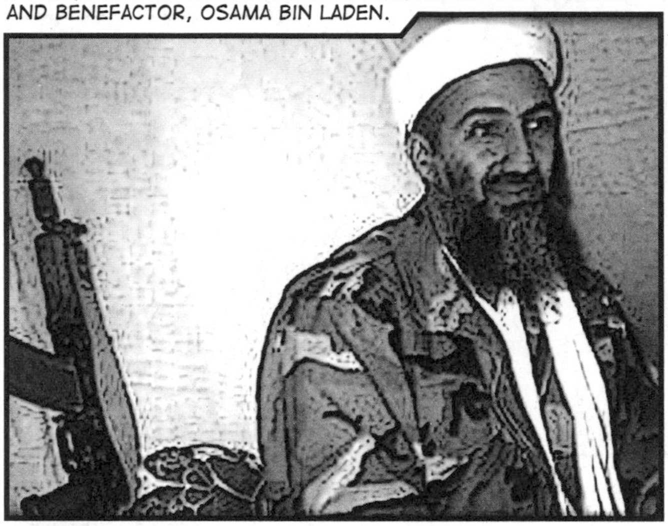

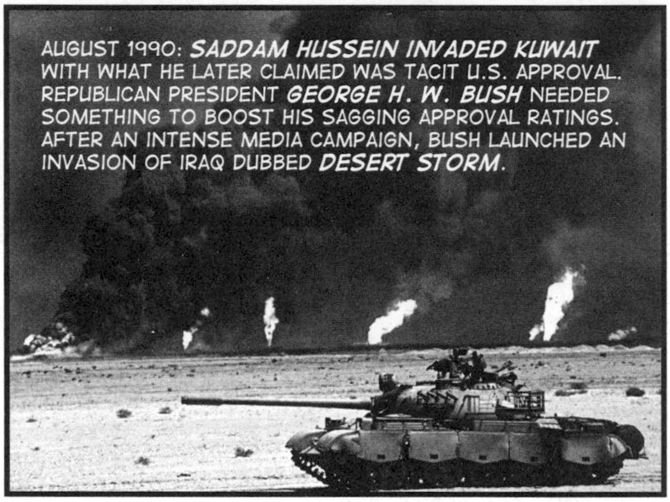
AUGUST 1990: SADDAM HUSSEIN INVADED KUWAIT WITH WHAT HE LATER CLAIMED WAS TACIT U.S. APPROVAL. REPUBLICAN PRESIDENT GEORGE H. W. BUSH NEEDED SOMETHING TO BOOST HIS SAGGING APPROVAL RATINGS. AFTER AN INTENSE MEDIA CAMPAIGN, BUSH LAUNCHED AN INVASION OF IRAQ DUBBED DESERT STORM.

THE EXERCISE OF MILITARY POWER WAS MEANT TO PURGE THE AMERICAN PEOPLE OF THE ***VIETNAM SYNDROME***, A DISTASTE FOR MILITARY INTERVENTIONISM.

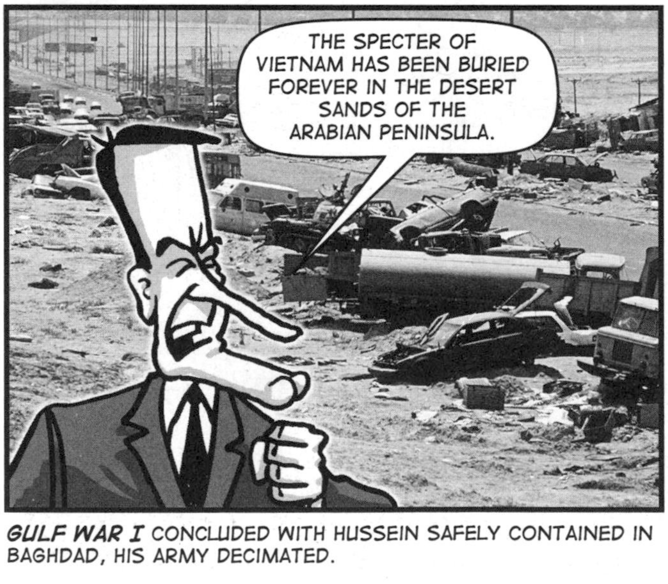
THE SPECTER OF VIETNAM HAS BEEN BURIED FOREVER IN THE DESERT SANDS OF THE ARABIAN PENINSULA.

GULF WAR I CONCLUDED WITH HUSSEIN SAFELY CONTAINED IN BAGHDAD, HIS ARMY DECIMATED.

OVER THE NEXT SEVERAL YEARS, IRAQ RAPIDLY DETERIORATED UNDER A STRICT, U.N.-IMPOSED EMBARGO THAT REPORTEDLY CAUSED THE DEATHS OF 1.25 MILLION PEOPLE, INCLUDING MORE THAN ***500,000 CHILDREN***.

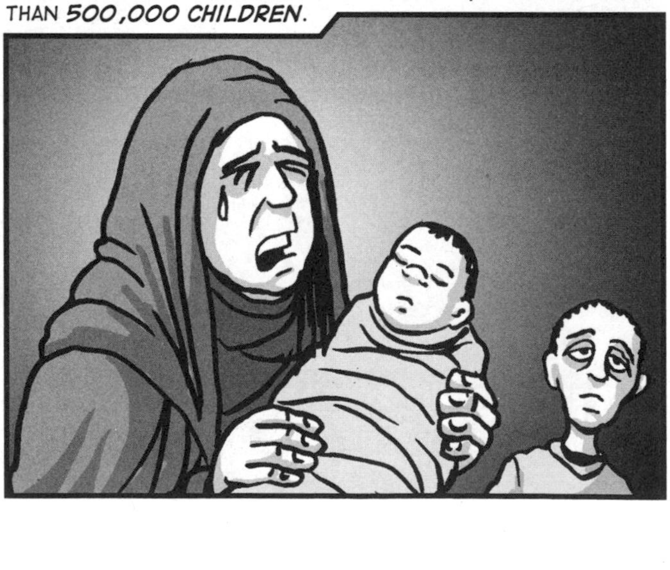

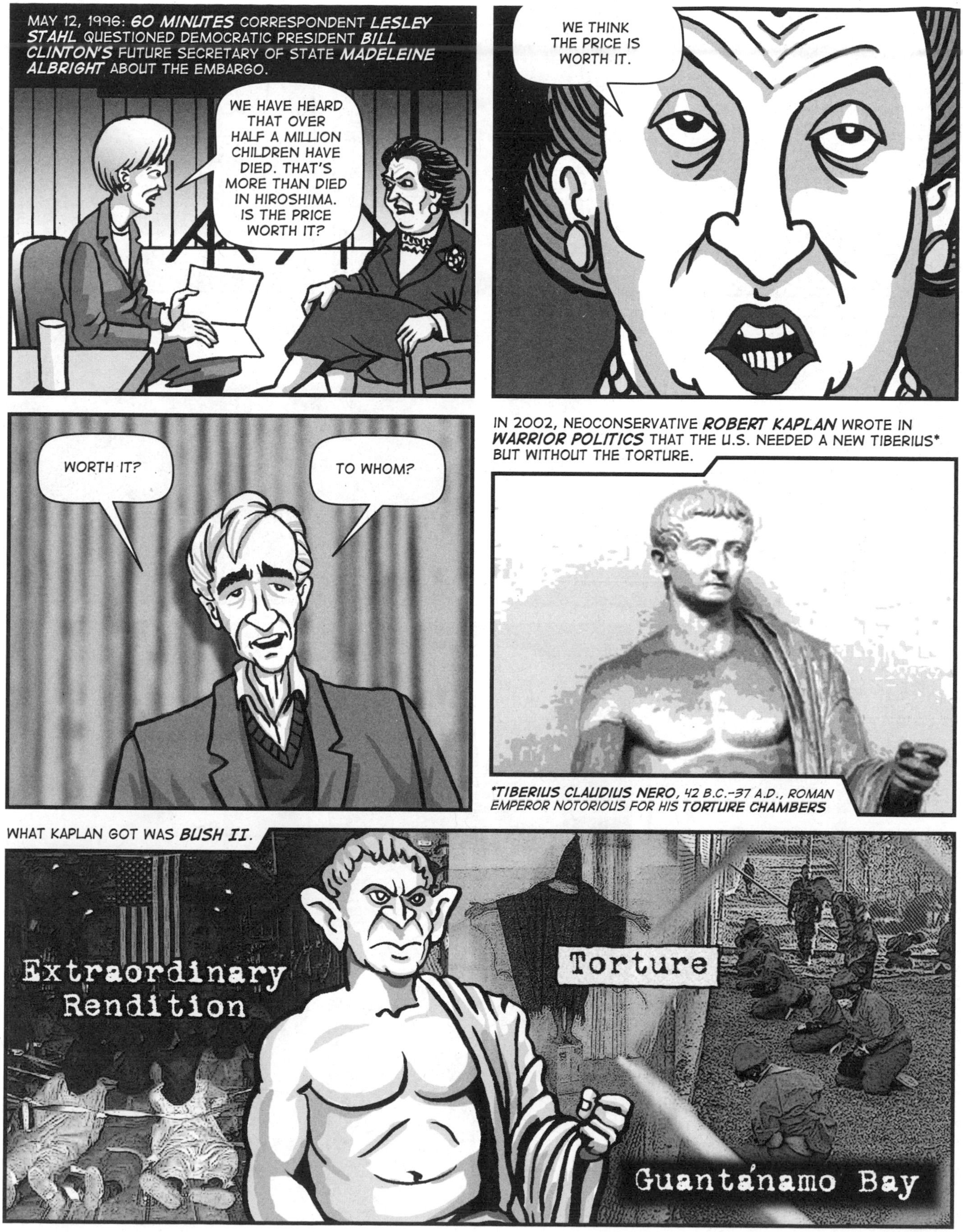
MAY 12, 1996: 60 MINUTES CORRESPONDENT LESLEY STAHL QUESTIONED DEMOCRATIC PRESIDENT BILL CLINTON'S FUTURE SECRETARY OF STATE MADELEINE ALBRIGHT ABOUT THE EMBARGO.
WE HAVE HEARD THAT OVER HALF A MILLION CHILDREN HAVE DIED. THAT'S MORE THAN DIED IN HIROSHIMA. IS THE PRICE WORTH IT?
WE THINK THE PRICE IS WORTH IT.
WORTH IT?
TO WHOM?
IN 2002, NEOCONSERVATIVE ROBERT KAPLAN WROTE IN WARRIOR POLITICS THAT THE U.S. NEEDED A NEW TIBERIUS* BUT WITHOUT THE TORTURE.
*TIBERIUS CLAUDIUS NERO, 42 B.C.-37 A.D., ROMAN EMPEROR NOTORIOUS FOR HIS TORTURE CHAMBERS
WHAT KAPLAN GOT WAS BUSH II.
Extraordinary Rendition
Torture
Guantánamo Bay

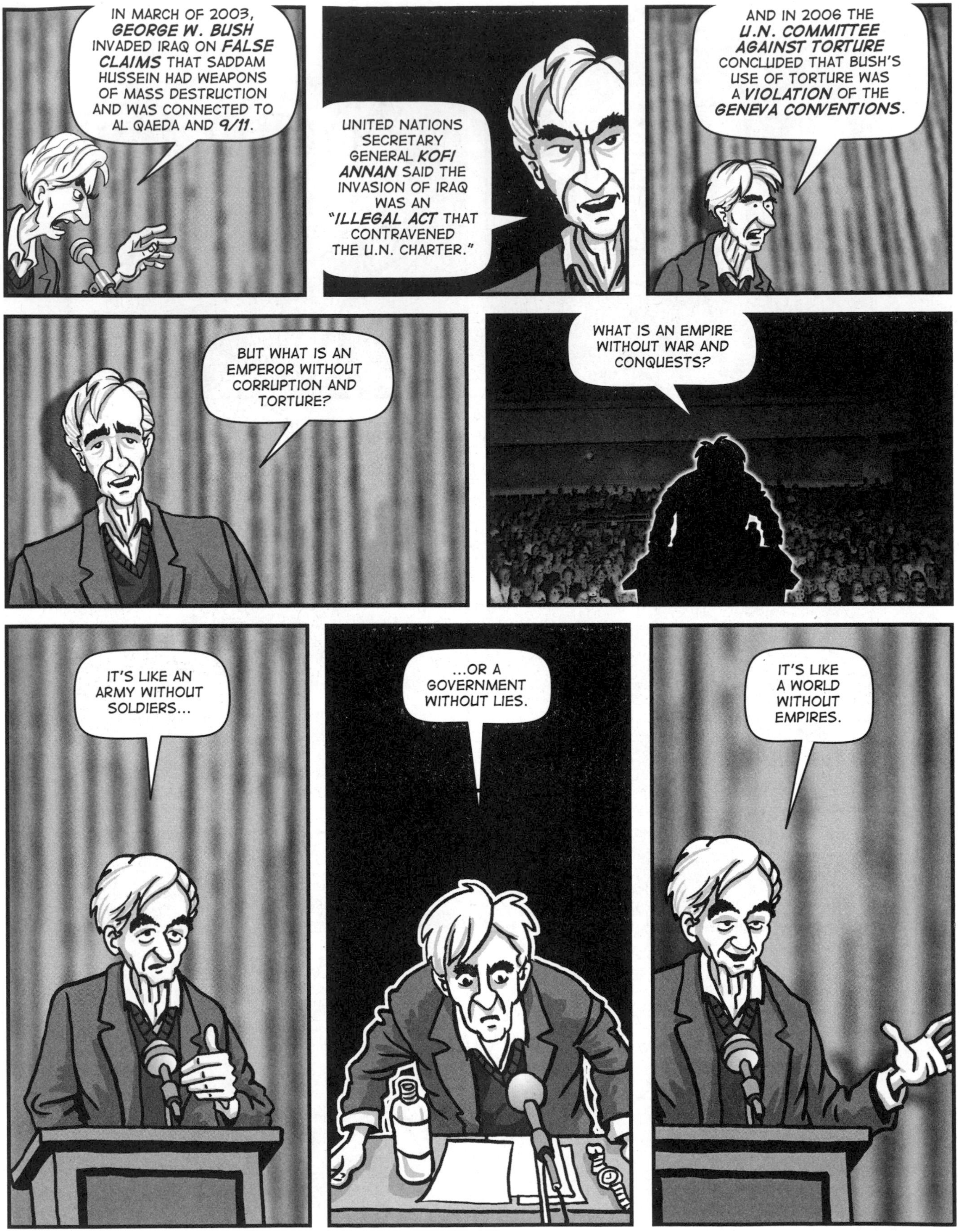
IN MARCH OF 2003, GEORGE W. BUSH INVADED IRAQ ON FALSE CLAIMS THAT SADDAM HUSSEIN HAD WEAPONS OF MASS DESTRUCTION AND WAS CONNECTED TO AL QAEDA AND 9/11.
UNITED NATIONS SECRETARY GENERAL KOFI ANNAN SAID THE INVASION OF IRAQ WAS AN "ILLEGAL ACT THAT CONTRAVENED THE U.N. CHARTER."
AND IN 2006 THE U.N. COMMITTEE AGAINST TORTURE CONCLUDED THAT BUSH'S USE OF TORTURE WAS A VIOLATION OF THE GENEVA CONVENTIONS.
BUT WHAT IS AN EMPEROR WITHOUT CORRUPTION AND TORTURE?
WHAT IS AN EMPIRE WITHOUT WAR AND CONQUESTS?
IT'S LIKE AN ARMY WITHOUT SOLDIERS...
...OR A GOVERNMENT WITHOUT LIES.
IT'S LIKE A WORLD WITHOUT EMPIRES.

Epilogue

THE POSSIBILITY OF HOPE

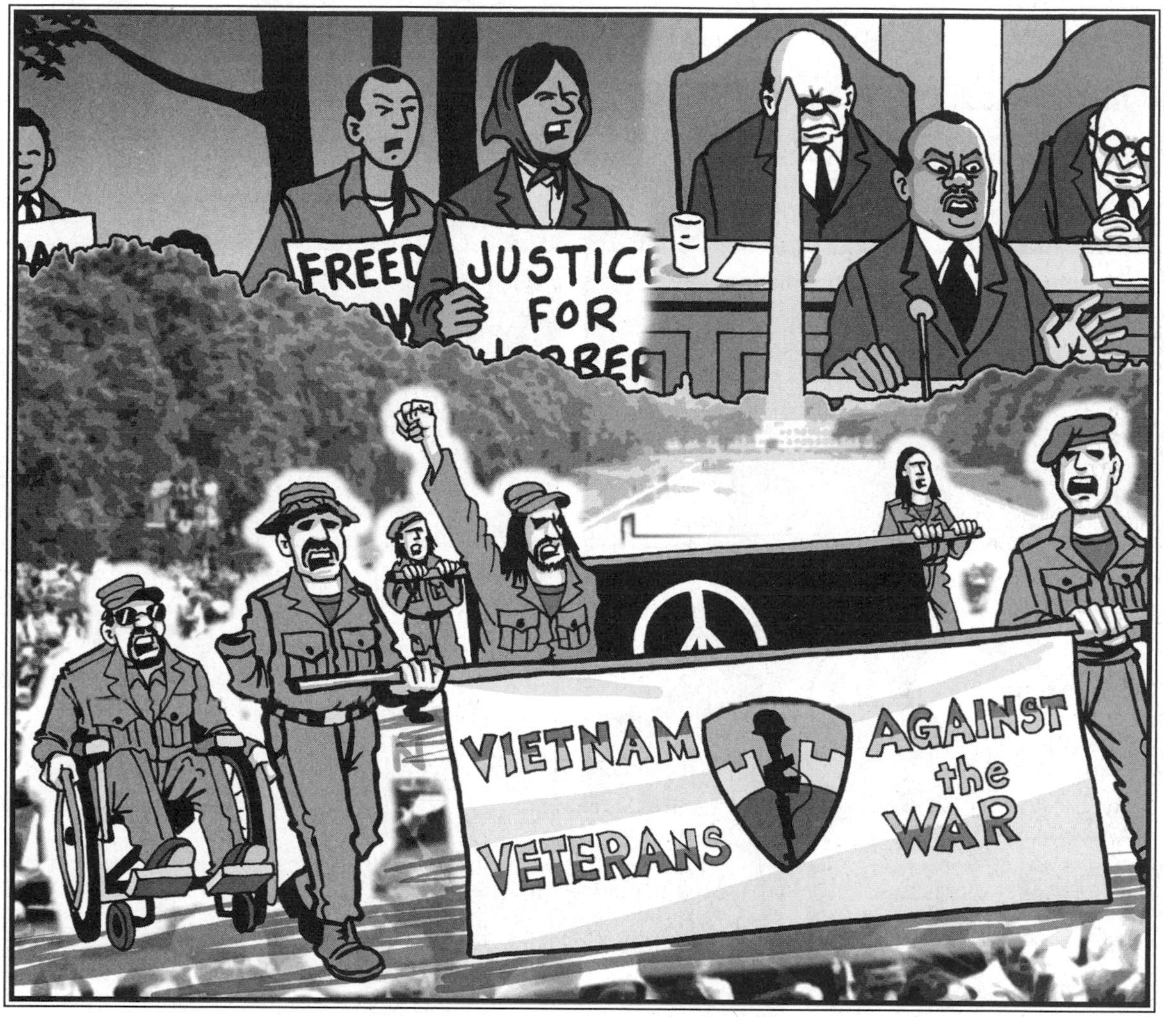
VIETNAM VETERANS
AGAINST the WAR

"To be hopeful in bad times is not just foolishly romantic. It is based on the fact that human history is a history not only of cruelty but also of compassion, sacrifice, courage, kindness."

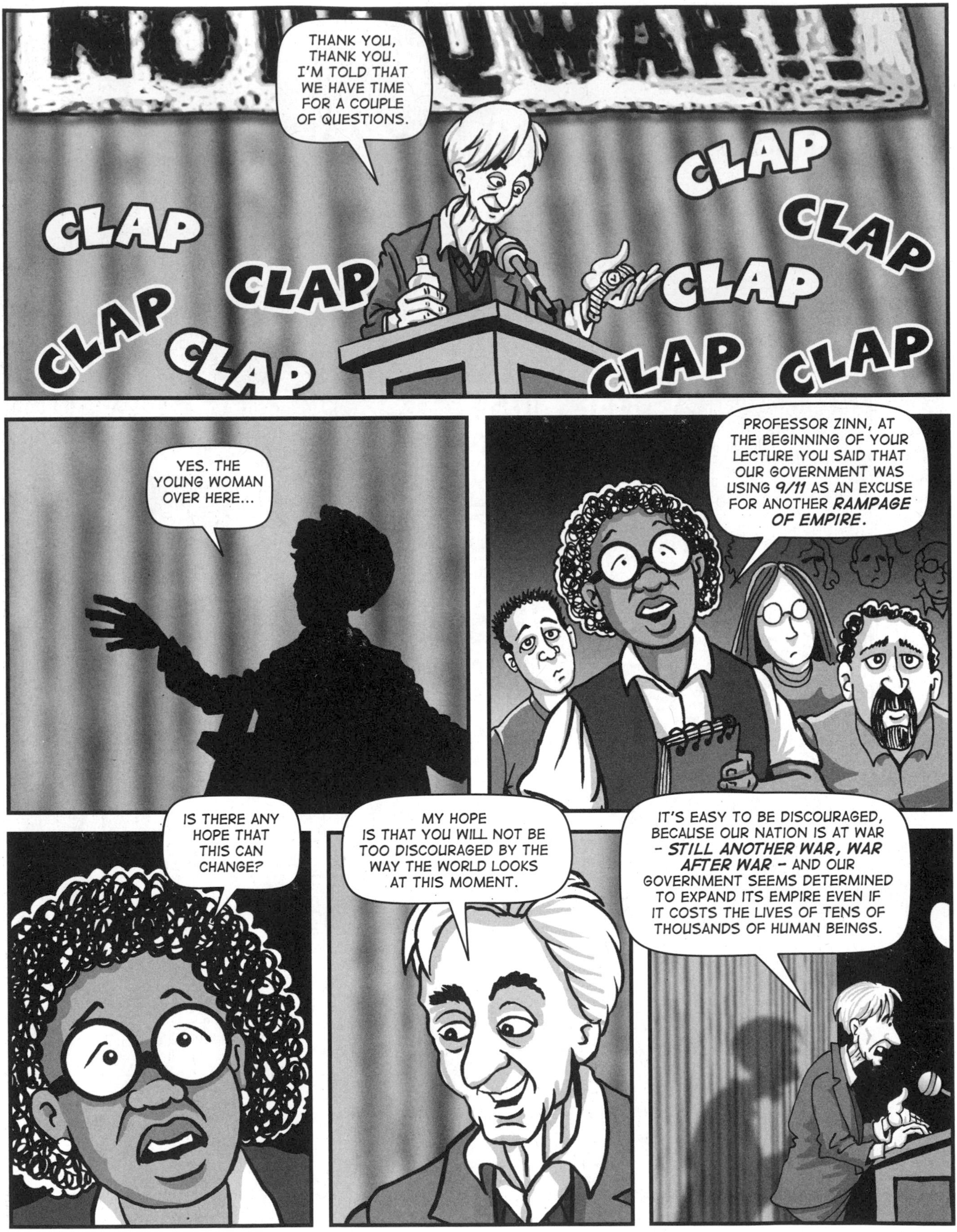

NO WAR!!
THANK YOU, THANK YOU. I'M TOLD THAT WE HAVE TIME FOR A COUPLE OF QUESTIONS.
CLAP CLAP CLAP CLAP CLAP CLAP CLAP CLAP CLAP
YES. THE YOUNG WOMAN OVER HERE...
PROFESSOR ZINN, AT THE BEGINNING OF YOUR LECTURE YOU SAID THAT OUR GOVERNMENT WAS USING 9/11 AS AN EXCUSE FOR ANOTHER RAMPAGE OF EMPIRE.
IS THERE ANY HOPE THAT THIS CAN CHANGE?
MY HOPE IS THAT YOU WILL NOT BE TOO DISCOURAGED BY THE WAY THE WORLD LOOKS AT THIS MOMENT.
IT'S EASY TO BE DISCOURAGED, BECAUSE OUR NATION IS AT WAR - STILL ANOTHER WAR, WAR AFTER WAR - AND OUR GOVERNMENT SEEMS DETERMINED TO EXPAND ITS EMPIRE EVEN IF IT COSTS THE LIVES OF TENS OF THOUSANDS OF HUMAN BEINGS.

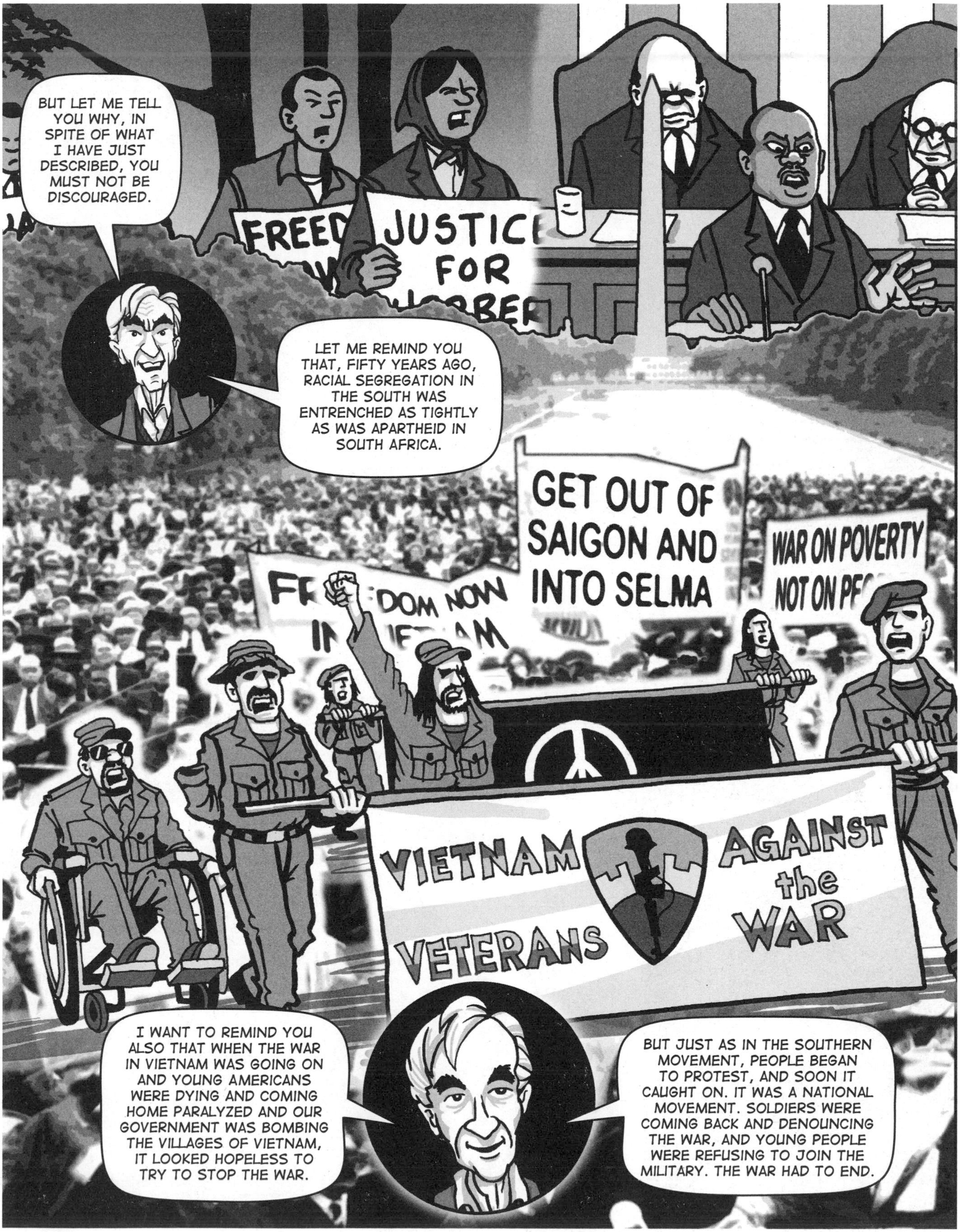
BUT LET ME TELL YOU WHY, IN SPITE OF WHAT I HAVE JUST DESCRIBED, YOU MUST NOT BE DISCOURAGED.
FREED
JUSTICE FOR
LET ME REMIND YOU THAT, FIFTY YEARS AGO, RACIAL SEGREGATION IN THE SOUTH WAS ENTRENCHED AS TIGHTLY AS WAS APARTHEID IN SOUTH AFRICA.
GET OUT OF SAIGON AND INTO SELMA
WAR ON POVERTY
VIETNAM VETERANS AGAINST the WAR
I WANT TO REMIND YOU ALSO THAT WHEN THE WAR IN VIETNAM WAS GOING ON AND YOUNG AMERICANS WERE DYING AND COMING HOME PARALYZED AND OUR GOVERNMENT WAS BOMBING THE VILLAGES OF VIETNAM, IT LOOKED HOPELESS TO TRY TO STOP THE WAR.
BUT JUST AS IN THE SOUTHERN MOVEMENT, PEOPLE BEGAN TO PROTEST, AND SOON IT CAUGHT ON. IT WAS A NATIONAL MOVEMENT. SOLDIERS WERE COMING BACK AND DENOUNCING THE WAR, AND YOUNG PEOPLE WERE REFUSING TO JOIN THE MILITARY. THE WAR HAD TO END.

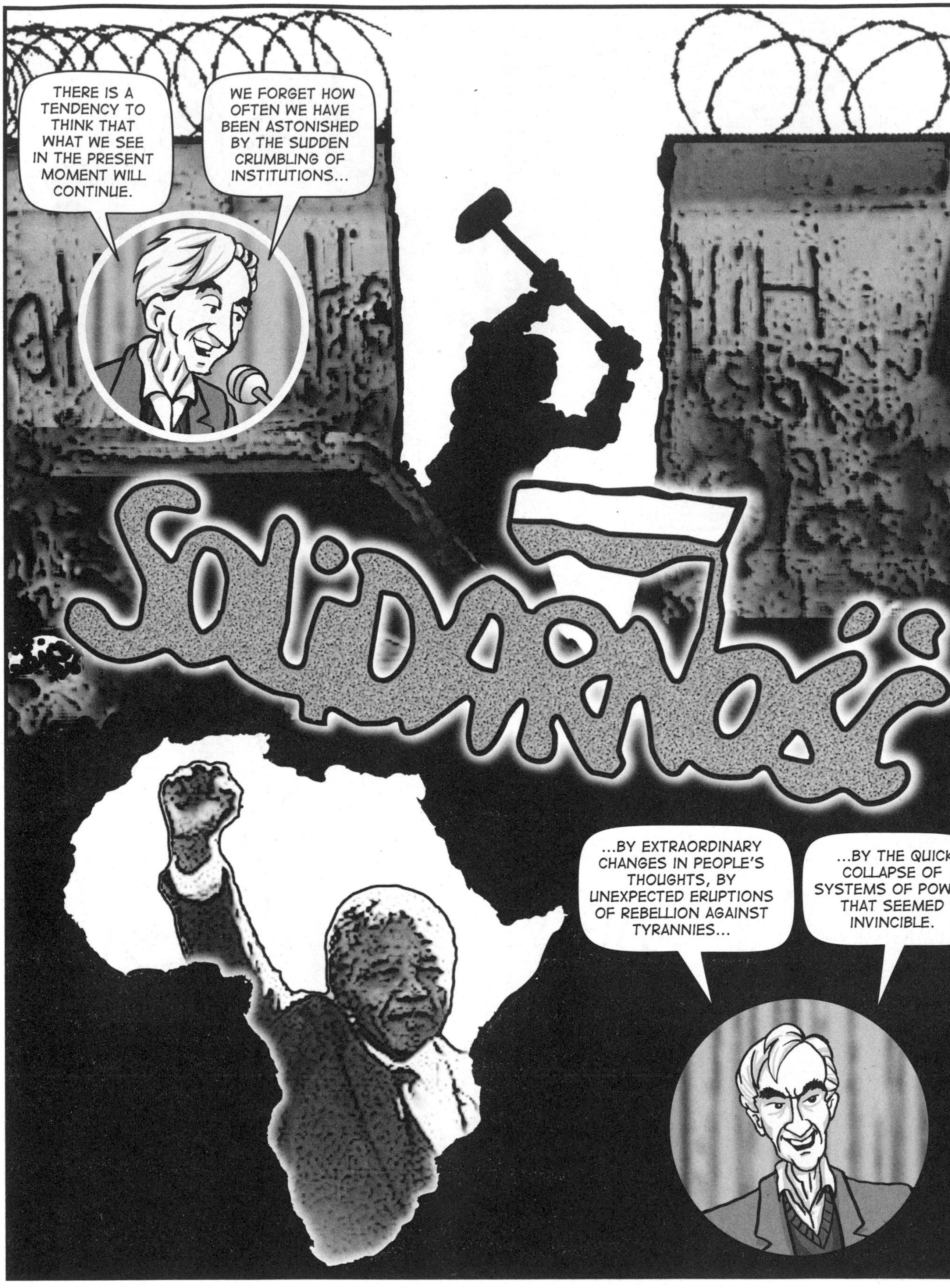
THERE IS A TENDENCY TO THINK THAT WHAT WE SEE IN THE PRESENT MOMENT WILL CONTINUE.
WE FORGET HOW OFTEN WE HAVE BEEN ASTONISHED BY THE SUDDEN CRUMBLING OF INSTITUTIONS...
...BY EXTRAORDINARY CHANGES IN PEOPLE'S THOUGHTS, BY UNEXPECTED ERUPTIONS OF REBELLION AGAINST TYRANNIES...
...BY THE QUICK COLLAPSE OF SYSTEMS OF POWER THAT SEEMED INVINCIBLE.

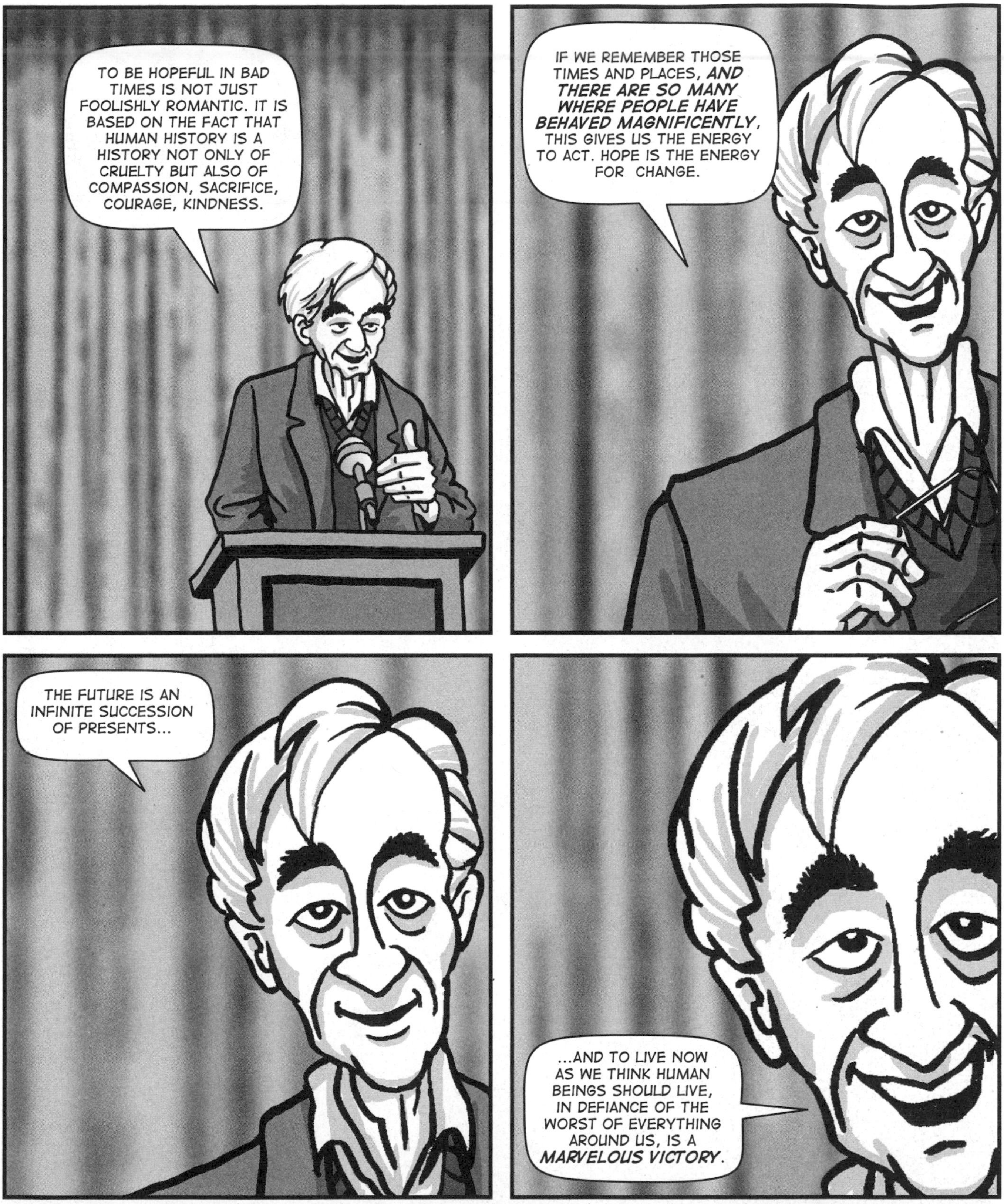
TO BE HOPEFUL IN BAD TIMES IS NOT JUST FOOLISHLY ROMANTIC. IT IS BASED ON THE FACT THAT HUMAN HISTORY IS A HISTORY NOT ONLY OF CRUELTY BUT ALSO OF COMPASSION, SACRIFICE, COURAGE, KINDNESS.
IF WE REMEMBER THOSE TIMES AND PLACES, ***AND THERE ARE SO MANY WHERE PEOPLE HAVE BEHAVED MAGNIFICENTLY***, THIS GIVES US THE ENERGY TO ACT. HOPE IS THE ENERGY FOR CHANGE.
THE FUTURE IS AN INFINITE SUCCESSION OF PRESENTS...
...AND TO LIVE NOW AS WE THINK HUMAN BEINGS SHOULD LIVE, IN DEFIANCE OF THE WORST OF EVERYTHING AROUND US, IS A ***MARVELOUS VICTORY***.

END

Bibliography

Howard Zinn's *A People's History of the United States*, now in its 7th edition, is the basic source of information for this volume, along with Zinn's memoir, *You Can't Be Neutral on a Moving Train*. A notably progressive U.S. history survey textbook by John Faragher et al., *Out of Many* (now in its 6th edition), has been the major supplementary source, and William Appleman Williams's *Empire as a Way of Life* (1982) has offered us an insightful overview of the U.S. empire in its various phases. Specific references, listed by chapter, are provided below to assist the reader of this book in learning more about the subjects discussed. Three recent nonfiction comic art volumes may also be of related interest: *WOBBLIES! A Graphic History of the Industrial Workers of the World* (2005); *A Dangerous Woman: The Graphic Biography of Emma Goldman* (2007); and *Students for a Democratic Society: A Graphic History* (2008).

PROLOGUE
Zinn, Howard. "The Old Way of Thinking." *Progressive*, November 2001.

CHAPTER I: THE INTERNAL EMPIRE
Kaplan, Amy, ed. *The Anarchy of Empire in the Making of U.S. Culture.* Cambridge: Harvard University Press, 2002.

Limerick, Patricia Nelson. *The Legacy of Conquest: The Unbroken Past of the American West.* New York: Norton, 1987.

Neihardt, John G., ed. *Black Elk Speaks: Being the Life Story of a Holy Man of the Oglala Sioux.* Lincoln: University of Nebraska Press, 1961.

Salvatore, Nick. *Eugene V. Debs.* Urbana: University of Illinois Press, 1982.

Stephanson, Anders. *Manifest Destiny: American Expansion and the Empire of Right.* New York: Norton, 1995.

CHAPTER II: THE SPANISH-AMERICAN WAR
Allen, Douglas. *Frederic Remington and the Spanish-American War.* New York: Crown, 1971.

Beale, Howard K. *Theodore Roosevelt and the Rise of America to World Power.* New York: Colliers Books, 1962.

Foner, Philip S. *Antonio Maceo: The Bronze Titan of Cuba's Struggle for Independence.* New York: Monthly Review Press, 1977.

Freidel, Frank. *The Splendid Little War.* Boston: Little, Brown, 1958.

Gatewood, William, Jr. *Black Americans and the White Man's Burden.* Urbana: University of Illinois, 1975.

Johnson, Edward A. *History of Negro Soldiers in the Spanish-American War.* Raleigh, NC: Capital Printing Co., 1899. Reprinted in 1970 by Johnson Reprint Co. as part of the Basic Afro-American Reprint Library.

Krause, Paul. *The Battle for Homestead, 1880–1892.* Pittsburgh: University of Pittsburgh Press, 1992.

LaFeber, Walter. *The New Empire: An Interpretation of American Expansion, 1860–1898.* Ithaca: Cornell University Press, 1963.

Rickover, Hyman George. *How the Battleship Maine Was Destroyed.* Annapolis: Naval Institute Press, 1994.

CHAPTER III: THE INVASION OF THE PHILIPPINES
Bain, David Howard. *Sitting in Darkness: Americans in the Philippines.* Boston: Houghton Mifflin, 1984.

Brands, H. W. *Bound to Empire: The United States and the Philippines.* New York: Oxford Univerisity Press, 1992.

Ignacio, Abe, Enrique de la Cruz, Jorge Emmanuel, and Helen Toribio, eds. *The Forbidden Book: The Philippine-American War in Political Cartoons.* San Francisco: T'Boli Publishing and Distribution, 2004.

Lane, Jack C. *Armed Progressive: General Leonard Wood.* San Rafael, CA: Presidio Press, 1978.

Miller, Stuart Creighton. *"Benevolent Assimilation": The American Conquest of the Philippines, 1899–1903.* New Haven: Yale University Press, 1982.

Zwick, Jim, ed. *Mark Twain's Weapons of Satire: Anti-Imperialist Writings on the Philippine-American War*. Syracuse: Syracuse University Press, 1992.

CHAPTER IV: WAR IS THE HEALTH OF THE STATE

Ambrosius, Lloyd E. *Woodrow Wilson and the American Diplomatic Tradition*. New York: Cambridge University Press, 1987.

Chambers, John W. *To Raise an Army: The Draft in Modern America*. New York: Free Press, 1987.

Early, Frances H. *A World Without War: How U.S. Feminists and Pacifists Resisted World War I*. Syracuse: Syracuse University Press, 1997.

Hannigan, Robert. *The New World Power: American Foreign Policy, 1898–1917*. Philadelphia: University of Pennsylvania Press, 2002.

Marshall, S. L. A. *The American Heritage History of World War I*. New York: American Heritage Press, 1964.

McGovern, George S., and Leonard F. Guttridge. *The Great Coalfield War*. Boston: Houghton Mifflin, 1972.

Montgomery, David. *The Fall of the House of Labor*. Cambridge, UK: Cambridge University Press, 1987.

Preston, William. *Aliens and Dissenters: Federal Suppression of Radicals, 1903–1933*. Cambridge: Harvard University Press, 1963.

Wexler, Alice. *Emma Goldman in America*. Boston: Beacon Books, 1982.

Williams, William Appleman. *The Shaping of American Diplomacy: Readings and Documents in American Foreign Relations*. Chicago: Rand McNally, 1956.

CHAPTER V: GROWING UP CLASS CONSCIOUS

Craig, Douglas B. *Fireside Politics: Radio and Political Culture in the United States, 1920–1940*. Baltimore: Johns Hopkins Press, 2000.

Terkel, Studs. *Hard Times*. New York: Pantheon, 1970.

Topp, Michael M. *The Sacco and Vanzetti Case*. Boston: Bedford-St. Martins, 2005.

Zinn, Howard. *You Can't Be Neutral on a Moving Train: A Personal History of Our Times*. Boston: Beacon Press, 1994.

———. *Emma: A Play in Two Acts About Emma Goldman, American Anarchist*. Cambridge: South End Press, 2002.

CHAPTER VI: WORLD WAR II: A PEOPLE'S WAR?

Colley, David P. *Blood for Dignity: The Story of the First Integrated Combat Unit in the U.S. Army*. New York: St. Martins Press, 2003.

Crane, Conrad C. *Bombs, Cities, and Civilians*. Lawrence: University of Kansas Press, 1993.

Gardner, Lloyd C. *Spheres of Influence: The Great Powers Partition Europe, from Munich to Yalta*. Chicago: Ivan Dee, 1993.

Iriye, Akira. *The Origins of the Second World War in Asia and the Pacific*. New York: Longmans, 1987.

Mandel, Ernest. *The Meaning of the Second World War*. New York: Verso, 1986.

Sherry, Michael S. *The Rise of American Air Power*. New Haven: Yale University Press, 1987.

CHAPTER VII: THE COOL WAR

Blum, William. *Rogue State: A Guide to the World's Only Superpower*. Monroe, ME: Common Courage Press, 2000.

Jones, Gerard. *Men of Tomorrow: Geeks, Gangsters and the Birth of the Comic Book*. New York: Basic Books, 2004.

Kelley, Robin D. G. *Race Rebels: Culture, Politics, and the Black Working Class*. New York: Macmillan, 1994.

Lipsitz, George. *Dangerous Crossroads*. New York: Verso, 1994.

———. *Footsteps in the Dark*. Minneapolis: University of Minnesota, 2007

———. *A Rainbow at Midnight: Labor and Culture in the 1940s*. New York: Praeger, 1980.

———. *Time Passages: Collective Memory and American Popular Culture*. Minneapolis: University of Minnesota Press, 1990.

Macias, Anthony. "Bringing Music to the People: Race, Urban Culture, and Municipal Politics in Postwar Los Angeles." *American Quarterly*, vol. 56, no. 3, September 2004, pp. 693–717.

May, Elaine. *Homeward Bound*. New York: Basic Books, 1988.

May, Lary, ed. *Recasting America: Culture and Politics in the Age of the Cold War*. Chicago: University of Chicago Press, 1989.

CHAPTER VIII: CHILDREN OF THE EMPIRE

Anderson, Terry H. *The Movement and the Sixties*. New York: Oxford University Press, 1995.

Cortright, David. *Soldiers in Revolt: GI Resistance*

During the Vietnam War. Chicago: Haymaket, 2006. Introduction by Howard Zinn.

Department of the Army 18th Military Police Brigade. "Report of Investigation Concerning USARV Installation Stockade," September 13, 1968. See http://www.sirnosir.com/archives_and_resources/library/investigations/lbj_investigation/cover.html.

Engelhardt, Tom. *The End of Victory Culture*. New York: Basic Books, 1995.

Hixson, Walter L., ed. *The Vietnam Antiwar Movement*. New York: Garland Publishers, 2000.

McMillian, John, and Paul Buhle, eds., *The New Left Revisited*. Philadelphia: Temple University Press, 2003.

Moser, Richard R. *The New Winter Soldiers: GI and Veteran Dissent During the Vietnam Era*. New Brunswick, NJ: Rutgers University Press, 1996.

Zinn, Howard. *SNCC: The New Abolitionists*. Boston: Beacon Press, 1965.

CHAPTER IX: LAND OF BURNING CHILDREN

Akwesasne Notes. *Voices from Wounded Knee, 1973, in the Words of the Participants*. Rooseveltown, NY: Mohawk Nation, via Rooseveltown, 1974.

Anderson, Terry H. *The Movement and the Sixties*.

Banks, Dennis. *Ojibwa Warrior: Dennis Banks and the Rise of the American Indian Movement*. Norman: University of Oklahoma Press, 2004.

Foley, Michael S. *Confronting the War Machine: Draft Resistance During the Vietnam War*. Chapel Hill: University of North Carolina Press, 2003.

Garrow, David. *The FBI and Martin Luther King, Jr.* New Haven: Yale University Press, 1983.

Zimmerman, Bill. *Airlift to Wounded Knee*. Chicago: Swallow Press, 1976.

CHAPTER X: THE SAME ROTTING BARREL

Ellsberg, Daniel. *Secrets: A Memoir of Vietnam and the Pentagon Papers*. New York: Penguin Books, 2003.

CHAPTER XI: RESURGENCE OF EMPIRE

Danner, Mark. *The Massacre at El Mozote: A Parable of the Cold War*. New York: Vintage Books, 1994.

"Drugs, Law Enforcement and Foreign Policy: A Report on the Subcommittee on Narcotics, Terrorism and International Operations," vol. 1, April 13, 1989, pp. 9, 399.

Grandin, Greg. *Empire's Workshop: Latin America, the United States and the Rise of the New Imperialism*. New York: Metropolitan Books, 2006.

Hodges, Donald Clark. *Sandino's Communism: Spiritual Politics for the Twenty-first Century*. Austin: University of Texas Press, 1992.

———. *Intellectual Foundations of the Nicaraguan Revolution*. Austin: University of Texas Press, 1986.

Morley, Morris H. *Washington, Somoza and the Sandinistas*. New York: Cambridge University Press, 1994.

Woodward, Bob. *Veil: The Secret Wars of the CIA, 1981–1987*. New York: Simon and Schuster, 1987.

CHAPTER XII: COVERT ACTION AND REACTION

Dreyfuss, Robert. *Devil's Game: How the United States Helped Unleash Fundamentalist Islam*. New York: Metropolitan Books, 2005.

Farmanfarmaian, Manucher and Roxanne Farmanfarmaian. *Blood and Oil: Memoirs of a Persian Prince*. New York: Random House, 1997.

Gasiorowski, Mark and Malcolm Byrne, eds. *Mohammad Mossadegh and the 1953 Coup in Iraq*. Syracuse: Syracuse University Press, 2004.

Kinzer, Stephen. *Overthrow: America's History of Regime Change from Hawaii to Iraq*. New York: Times Books, 2006.

———. *All The Shah's Men: An American Coup and the Roots of Middle East Terror*. Hoboken: John Wiley and Sons, 2003.

McCoy, Alfred W. *A Question of Torture: CIA Interrogation from the Cold War to the War on Terror*. New York: Metropolitan Books, 2006.

Rashid, Ahmed. *Taliban: Militant Islam, Oil and Fundamentalism in Central Asia*. New Haven: Yale University Press, 2000.

Ridgeway, James. *The March to War*. New York: Four Walls Eight Windows, 1991.

Roosevelt, Kermit. *Countercoup: The Struggle for the Control of Iran*. New York: McGraw-Hill, 1979.

Wilber, Donald N. "Clandestine Service History: Overthrow of Premier Mossadeq of Iran, November 1952–August 1953." [CIA] CS Historical Paper no. 208. March 1954.

EPILOGUE

Zinn, Howard. "The Optimism of Uncertainty." http://www.thenation.com/doc/20040920/zinn.

———. "Against Discouragement." http://www.tomdispatch.com/post/2728/graduation_day_with_howard_zinn.

Credits

Grateful acknowledgment is made to the following for use of the photographs and documents in this volume:

AP Images: 106 (Sacco and Vanzetti), 108 (Sacco and Vanzetti demonstration), 117 (Empire State Building), 130 (napalm bombing aftermath), 139 (Greek civil war), 178 (church bombing victims), 179 (newspapers), 180 (H. Rap Brown), 201 (Daniel Ellsberg), 231, 232 (flag burning), 235 (Allen Dulles), 244 (statue toppling), 252 (storming of U.S. embassy), 256 (Osama bin Laden); *The Atlanta Journal-Constitution*: 153 (newspaper article); Bettmann/CORBIS: 139 (Ferdinand Marcos), 183 (Dan Berrigan arrest), 202 (Daniel Ellsberg on street), 205 (U.S. embassy evacuation), 217 (Anastasio Somoza Garcia), 219 (Che Guevara), 232 (hostages), 248 (Mohammad Mossadegh trial), 257 (Tiberius statue); *Chicago Defender*: 123 (newspaper front page); Collection of James Allen and John Littlefield, © 2005: 68 (the lynching of Garfield Burley and Curtis Brown, October 8, 1902, Newbern, Tennessee), 122 (the lynching of Thomas Shipp and Abram Smith, August 7, 1930, Marion, Indiana), 158 (the lynching of George Meadows, January 15, 1889, Pratt Mines, Alabama); *The Commercial Appeal*: 122 (profiteer cartoon by Cal Alley); Congressional Quarterly/Getty Images: 228 (Gary Webb); Consolidated News Pictures/Getty Images: 205 (Henry Kissinger, Gerald Ford, and James Schlesinger); Denver Public Library, Western History Collection: 79 (Ludlow tent dwellers); John Paul Filo, ©1970: 184 (Kent State shooting); Franklin D. Roosevelt Library Digital Archives: 125 (Japanese internment sign), 127 (Roosevelt and Ibn Saud); George Bush Presidential Library: 228 (George Bush inauguration); Getty Images: 255 (Donald Rumsfeld with Saddam Hussein); Hulton-Deutsch Collection/CORBIS: 120 (invasion of Ethiopia); Imperial War Museum: 85 (enlistment poster); Indiana State University, Debs Collection, Cunningham Memorial Library: 22 (Eugene V. Debs), 90 (Debs rally); Alain Keler/Sygma/Corbis: 252 (Ayatollah Khomeini); Einar E. Kvaran: 81 (Ludlow monument); Library of Congress: 18 (John D. Rockefeller), 19 (1893 Depression), 31, 39 (William McKinley), 43 (USS *Maine* explosion), 45 (soldiers on dock), 49 (victory photo), 54 (William McKinley), 57 (Battle of Manila), 68 (W. E. B. DuBois), 69 (Elihu Root), 71 (Mark Twain; Leonard Wood), 83 (W. E. B. DuBois), 84 (Woodrow Wilson), 89 (Uncle Sam poster), 92 (Leonard Wood), 93 (poster of soldier with bayonet), 97 (National Women's Party picketing), 101 (Emma Goldman on trolley; Goldman mugshot), 119 (bombers), 121 (Mexico 1846; Cuba 1898), 122 (civilians hanged by German soldiers; John L. Lewis), 137 (Harry S. Truman), 178 (march on Washington), 192 (arrestees on bus); Lyndon Baines Johnson Library and Museum: 160 (signing of Voting Rights Act); Michigan State University Library, Special Collections Division: 108 (*Daily Worker* cartoon); Jonathan Moller: 139 (bones in Guatemala); National Archives and Records Administration: 10 (Ghost Dance), 11 (Oglala Sioux), 16 (Chief Big Foot), 29 (Teddy Roosevelt), 47–48 (Battle at El Viso), 50 (hospital tent; two wounded soldiers), 51 (flag-raising in Santiago), 68 (soldiers on benches), 127 (Yalta conference; Ibn Saud entourage), 137 (GIs with newspapers), 174 (Long Binh jail), 178 (John F. Kennedy meeting; Martin Luther King, Jr.), 179 (Vietnam War), 192 (Sioux treaty), 220 (Ronald Reagan), 232 (Mohammad Mossadegh in car), 235 (Dwight D. Eisenhower with John Foster Dulles; Donald Wilber), 244 (Mossadegh portraits), 247 (Donald Wilber), 253 (Mossadegh in Philadelphia); *The New York Times*, June 13, 1971 [© 1971 *The New York Times*. All rights reserved. Used by permission and protected by the Copyright Laws of the United States. The printing, copying, redistribution, or retransmission of the Material without express written consent is prohibited]: 200 (newspaper front page); Smithsonian Institution National Archives: 17 (Indian massacre burial pit); Time Life Pictures/Getty Images: 235 (*Time* magazine); University of North Carolina at Chapel Hill: 68 (Henry M. Turner); Claude Urraca/Sygma/Corbis: 211 (Contras); U.S. Army: 256 (tank in Operation Desert Storm); U.S. Coast Guard: 206 (bicentennial in New York Harbor); U.S. House of Representatives: 89 (Champ Clark); U.S. Naval Historical Center: 29 (troops on duty), 59 (warships firing; Fort San Antonio de Abad), 118 (bunks aboard the *Queen Mary*), 121 (Pearl Harbor); U.S. Postal Service: 124 (Charles Drew stamp); White House Historical Association: 207 (Jimmy Carter); Wisconsin State Historical Society: 25 (*Harper's Weekly* cover), 76 (Woodrow Wilson); Woodrow Wilson Presidential Library: 99 (women's rally); Woody Guthrie Publications, Inc., administered by Bug Music: 79–81 (lyrics from "The Ludlow Massacre"); Jim Zwick, ed., *Mark Twain's Weapons of Satire: Anti-Imperialist Writings on the Philippine-American War*: 53, 66, 73 (mass grave in the Philippines).

Acknowledgments

Thanks to Phil Ball for his generous support in acts large and small. Also to the Bread and Puppet Theater, to Giuliana Chamedes for her contributions to the script, to Ambre Ivol, Dan Schwarz, Brian Strassburg, and Grace Wagner.

Special thanks to Mike Cullinane, Ph.D., University of Wisconsin associate director for the Center for Southeast Asian Studies, for his help on the Philippines. Also to Enrique de la Cruz, Jorge Emmanuel, and Helen Toribio, authors of *The Forbidden Book: The Philippine-American War in Political Cartoons,* for their scholarship and inspiration, and to Jim Zwick for his help with the Moro Massacre story.

To Steve Fraser and Tom Engelhardt of the American Empire Project and to our literary agent, Rick Balkin.

And finally our most heartfelt gratitude to all the people at Metropolitan Books who were involved in the project, including Sara Bershtel, Lisa Fyfe, Grigory Tovbis, Meryl Levavi, researcher Laura Wyss, and especially to senior editor Riva Hocherman, who had the know-how to challenge us to produce a better book and the patience to let us do it.

Index

Note: Page numbers in bold face refer to illustrations.

272

The People Behind
A People's History of American Empire

HOWARD ZINN is the author of the classic *A People's History of the United States*. Zinn, professor emeritus at Boston University, has received the Lannan Foundation Literary Award for Nonfiction and the Eugene V. Debs award for his writing and political activism; in 2003 he was also awarded the Prix des Amis du Monde diplomatique. He has published numerous books, including *The Zinn Reader*, the autobiographical *You Can't Be Neutral on a Moving Train*, and the play *Marx in Soho*.

MIKE KONOPACKI, a cartoonist and illustrator from Madison, Wisconsin, created the pages and art in this volume and contributed to the script. Konopacki and fellow cartoonist Gary Huck formed Huck/Konopacki Labor Cartoons, which has been syndicated in the U.S. and Canada since 1983. His cartoons are on the Web at www.solidarity.com/hkcartoons.

PAUL BUHLE is a senior lecturer in the History and American Civilizations departments at Brown University and the author or editor of thirty-three books. He is the editor of this volume.

WITH

DAVE WAGNER, principal researcher and scriptwriter, is a former city editor of *The Phoenix Gazette* and political editor of *The Arizona Republic*. He has coauthored a number of books with Paul Buhle, including *Radical Hollywood* and *Hide in Plain Sight*.

KATHY WILKES, script doctor and editor, has also contributed her expertise on design, research, and content development. Wilkes, a longtime labor activist, is the former communications director of the International Longshore and Warehouse Union and editor of the union's award-winning newspaper, *The Dispatcher*.

The American Empire Project

In an era of unprecedented military strength, leaders of the United States, the global hyperpower, have increasingly embraced imperial ambitions. How did this significant shift in purpose and policy come about? And what lies down the road?

The American Empire Project is a response to the changes that have occurred in American's strategic thinking as well as in its military and economic posture. Empire, long considered an offense against America's democratic heritage, now threatens to define the relationship between our country and the rest of the world. The American Empire Project publishes books that question this development, examine the origins of U.S. imperial aspirations, analyze their ramifications at home and abroad, and discuss alternatives to this dangerous trend.

The project was conceived by Tom Engelhardt and Steve Fraser, editors who are themselves historians and writers. Published by Metropolitan Books, an imprint of Henry Holt and Company, its titles include *Hegemony or Survival, Failed States, Imperial Ambitions,* and *What We Say Goes* by Noam Chomsky, *Blowback, The Sorrows of Empire,* and *Nemesis* by Chalmers Johnson, *Crusade* by James Carroll, *How to Succeed at Globalization* by El Fisgón, *Blood and Oil* by Michael Klare, *Dilemmas of Domination* by Walden Bello, *War Powers* by Peter Irons, *Devil's Game* by Robert Dreyfuss, *Empire's Workshop* by Greg Grandin, *A Question of Torture* by Alfred McCoy, *Iraq: The Logic of Withdrawal* by Anthony Arnove, and *In the Name of Democracy,* edited by Jeremy Brecher, Jill Cutler, and Brendan Smith.

For more information about the American Empire Project and for a list of forthcoming titles, please visit www.americanempireproject.com.

OCT   2008